EGYPT
HANDBOOK

SECOND EDITION

EGYPT
HANDBOOK
SECOND EDITION

KATHY HANSEN

MOON
PUBLICATIONS, INC.

EGYPT HANDBOOK

Published by
Moon Publications, Inc.
P.O. Box 3040
Chico, California 95927-3040, USA

Printed by
Colorcraft Ltd.

Library of Congress Cataloging in Publication Data
Hansen, Kathy, 1943
   Egypt handbook / Kathy Hansen— 2nd ed.
      p.   cm.
   Includes bibliographical references and index.
   ISBN 0-918373-89-1
   1. Egypt—Guidebooks.   I. Title.
DT45.H36   1993.   92-33716
916.204'55——dc20   CIP

Editor: Elizabeth Rhudy
Copy Editor: Deana Corbitt
Production & Design: Carey Wilson
Cartographers: Bob Race, Brian Bardwell, Anne Hikido
Index: Mark Arends, David Burnett

Front cover photo: Egypt, Nile River, two falucca boats sailing down the river, *by Fridmar Damm*
Frontispiece: Jan Kirk

Printed in Hong Kong

Please send all comments,
corrections, additions,
amendments, and critiques to:

KATHY HANSEN
MOON PUBLICATIONS, INC.
P.O. Box 3040
CHICO, CA 95927, USA

Printing History
   1st edition—February 1990
   Reprinted
      October 1991
   2nd edition—June 1993

To Allan,
the wind beneath my wings.

ACKNOWLEDGEMENTS

Without the invaluable help of numerous people, *Egypt Handbook* would never have appeared. First I'd like to thank the late Dr. Ahmed Khadry, former Director of the Egyptian Antiquities Organization and his numerous staff throughout Egypt for their help. Everywhere I was met with courtesy by more Egyptians than I can name, but Dr. Muhammad Saleh, Director of the Antiquities Museum, Dr. Rifat Abdul Azim, curator of the Islamic Museum, and Ibrahim Soliman, inspector on the West Bank of Luxor, have spent inordinate amounts of time with me.

In addition, I must thank Dr. Lanny Bell and the staff at Chicago House in Luxor for their always-generous help. Many thanks to Ann and Ken Robinson who helped me gather information, to Bill and Ann-Marie Harrison who provided support services, and to Renz and Martha Mezzera who always had an extra bed available when I needed one. To Dr. William Murnane, Dr. Steve Goodman, Dr. E.C. Krupp, Dr. Gay Robbins, Dr. Christiane Zivie, Dr. Christian Lobben, Hanny Hamrush, and Terry Moore, who read and commented upon sections of the manuscript, my grateful appreciation. To Dr. C. Keller, Susan Weeks, Cassandra Vivian, Michael and Angela Jones, Joanne Zembel, Dick Vedery, Robert Betts, Amira, and all the staff at ARCE, my thanks for the copious amounts of information and help. To Dave Goodman, Allan Hansen, and Carolyn McHenry, thanks for use of photos; to Omar Zahr of Naggar Tours, Sue Mahfuz and Khalid Sour, Fathi Salib, Gamil Bakhir, Mahmud Kamel, and Abdel Rashad of the Egyptian Tourist Authority, and my drivers Izat and Yousif who not only drove but took care of me, I'm ever grateful for your support and help. And to Carolyn McHenry, who got me into this mess in the first place.

To the support staff at Moon, my thanks for your outstanding work. Thanks also to Dover Publications, Inc., for their help with my Arabic vocabulary appendix. And to my family, who not only contributed their talents to this project, but endured the writing for more months than they care to remember, my humble love.

IS THIS BOOK OUT OF DATE?

Egypt is facing exciting if trying times. Attempting to rebuild an aging and inadequate infrastructure, to expand its manufacturing, and cope with an ever-expanding population, the country is experiencing rapid and massive inflation. Therefore, it's impossible to quote realistic prices. Nevertheless, in order to give you an idea of the demands on your pocketbook, we've included some figures. By the time you get to Egypt, they will have gone up; use these quotes only as general guides.

Please help us keep *Egypt Handbook* up to date. If you find a hot new attraction, if we have neglected to include your favorite spot or an important bit of information, if you find an error (including one on a map or plan), or anything contrary to what we have told you, please let us know.

CONTENTS

MAPS AND PLANS

CHARTS

ABBREVIATIONS

a/c—air conditioned
C—centigrade
km—kilometer

Sh.—Sharia (street)
tel.—telephone number

MAP SYMBOLS

━━━	EXPRESSWAY	○	SMALL VILLAGES & TOWNS	━ ━	INTERNATIONAL BOUNDARY
───	MAIN HIGHWAY	○	LARGER TOWNS & CITIES	─ ·· ─	POLITICAL ADMINISTRATION BOUNDARY
───	SECONDARY ROAD	▲	MOUNTAIN	═══	BRIDGE
─ ─ ─	UNPAVED ROAD	■	POINT OF INTEREST	⬠	MIDAN
─ · ─ · ─	FOOT PATH	★	SPECIAL POINT OF INTEREST	─ ─ ─	FERRY
▭▭▭	RAILROAD	✕	AIRPORT	▨	WATER

PREFACE

For forty centuries, Egypt has drawn tourists and pilgrims. Land of arcane knowledge and fabulous architecture, it spawned and nourished its ideas and innovations and spread them to the Western world. Today, the country still serves as crossroads between East and West, between old and new. Its mixture of history and diverse cultures continues to entice visitors, just as it has through the millennia.

The Egyptians of the New Kingdom cruised down the Nile to the Great Pyramid, already 1,500 years old. They gazed in awe at these artificial mountains built by ancient god-kings; ladders to eternity that still dominate the plateau above the Nile River. The conquering Greeks, Romans, and Arabs tapped ancient knowledge and adopted elements of the native culture while stamping it with their own imprint. And like modern visitors, they too flocked to the monuments.

But Egypt offers more than just ancient temples and tombs; the ideas behind their creation give us a glimpse of our own origins. What often begins as a tour to gape at monuments built for ancient and strange gods can quickly become a pilgrimage to our own cultural and intellectual roots.

Although polytheism dominated Egypt's early religion, Jews settled and built temples to their single god. In early Christian times, ancient Egyptian images burned their way into Christianity; Jewish doctrine as well as ancient ideas of resurrection and everlasting life may well have shaped the new beliefs. When Muslims conquered the country, Egypt maintained a core of Coptic Christians, and today Egypt provides a meeting place for these two great religions.

In the Greek ages, Alexandria's eminent school and library developed and disseminated Egyptian technology and learning. During the Middle Ages, direct contact with the West was cut off by the Arab invasion, and Muslim scholars cherished the ancient learning and built on its foundations. Their work seeped into Europe during the Crusades and translations of classical and Islamic treatises fueled the Renaissance.

In addition, the ideas and lives of the ancient people touch us directly. The hieroglyphic writing on the walls of their tombs tells stories not dissimilar to our own: of individuals proud of their accomplishments, worried about the younger generation, and themselves prey to jealousy and ambition. Their literature is full of proverbial wisdom, swashbuckling adventures, and passionate love poems. Their art, which showed reality not as the eye saw it but as the mind knew it to exist, still touches the modern subconscious.

The countryside itself, unchanged for thousands of years, mirrors ancient life in early civilizations. Drawings of oxen plowing fields seeded and harvested by hand, bread baking in round, clay ovens, and the abundant birds being netted in the fertile Delta are reproduced daily in modern, living tableaux. Although Egypt's countryside is now changing with the modernization of agriculture, the connections with our collective past remain unmistakable.

BOB RACE

RED LAND, BLACK LAND

Egypt, land of contrasts, reflects brilliant light and deep shadow, holds verdant soil and sterile sand. The Egyptians themselves have always understood their country's desert/oasis duality, for they called it the Two Lands. To them the Red Land, the stark desert, was Chaos. Its god was Seth, lord of the bitter wind and howling dust storms. The Red Land's deep, rocky canyons housed the fierce nomads who struck without warning. The Black Land, in contrast,

was home. Watched over by Osiris, god of fertility and resurrection, the Egyptians peacefully irrigated their fields, which lay along the margins of the Nile, creating a way of life that has spanned 5,000 years. Yet neither land alone could have produced Egyptian civilization. It took, as the ancients understood, a precise balance between desert and loam, between Chaos and Order, a state of the world the Egyptians called Ma'at.

THE LAND AND CLIMATE

The Arab Republic of Egypt occupies the northeastern corner of Africa, lying within the great Sahara Desert, that arid swath of land that stretches across the top of the continent. It is bordered on the north by the Mediterranean Sea, on the south by the Republic of Sudan, on the west by Libya, and on the east by Israel, the Gulf of Aqaba, and the Red Sea. This geographical position made Egypt a hub of world trade. Commerce from the Near East crossed the top of Sinai and the Suez Strait, while goods

from Central Africa flowed down the Nile and via the Mediterranean to Europe. Caravans followed the western oases through the desert to the Libyan coast, and Asian wares came up the Red Sea. Today, worldwide shipping transits the locks of the Suez Canal.

With a million square kilometers of land, Egypt is twice the size of Texas. Barren deserts occupy more than 96% of the country's total area. The Nile separates the dune-filled waste of the Western Desert from the mountainous Eastern Desert.

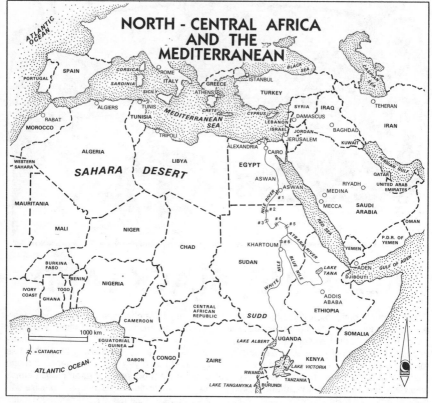

NORTH - CENTRAL AFRICA AND THE MEDITERRANEAN

These two deserts, the Nile Valley, and the Sinai Peninsula make up Egypt's four geographic areas.

BLACK LAND

Over the centuries, the Nile River created Egypt's Black Land. From the river's sources deep in Africa, it stretches 1,500 km northward to its delta, which blooms like a lotus flower. In the south, the river is hemmed in by mountains, and the desert sands blowing across their ridges frame its shores. As the river runs north, the mountains lower and the valley widens. Here the Black Land begins, its ancient, rich soils deposited by the floodwaters of the Nile. Beyond Cairo, the river branches, its triangular delta stretching 160 km,

widening to 250 km at the coast. Cairo and the delta make up Lower Egypt; the area between modern Cairo and roughly Abydos, Middle Egypt; and the southern Nile Valley, Upper Egypt. This ribbon of dark, fertile soil, a long narrow oasis slashing across the desert, encompasses only four percent of Egypt's territory, yet supports 99% of her population.

Until the harnessing of the Nile, which began late in the 19th century, the river rose and over-flowed its banks every summer. In May, the Egyptian soil would lie parched and cracked in the blistering sun. The ancient Egyptians would pray to Hapi, their fleshy god of the Nile with his female breasts of fecundity, for a perfect flood—not so high as to wash away their irrigation works or homes, but high enough to reach all the arable land, providing it with nourishment for their vegetables, vines, and grains. In early June, a green wave of humus-rich water initiated the annual miracle of inundation. By the middle of the month, floodwaters would reach Aswan and in another week, Cairo. Within another month, the green tide would shift to red, as the rain scoured the Ethiopian hillsides, sending silt-laden waters heavy with rich, red alluvium to submerge the thirsty land. The waters, filling canals and irrigation basins, would continue to rise until October.

At the flood's height, the Egyptians would build dikes, damming the water in basins. Once the water had dropped its silt and saturated the ground, they would drain the basins, and the damp alluvium was ready to plant. Today, because of the High Dam, irrigation canals run sedately full, supplying expanded farmlands year-round with the life-giving moisture of the Nile. Unfortunately, the silt settles out in Lake Nasser, forcing modern farmers to fertilize, a chore never faced by their ancestors.

The Nile

Egypt has been called the gift of the Nile, whose lifeblood flows from sources deep in the south. The ancient Egyptians believed the river's wellspring was near Aswan, where it gushed forth from subterranean caverns. More modern explorers have traced its headwaters deep into the African heartland. In these southern areas, rain is abundant, and its runoff forms three major tributaries; the White Nile, the Blue Nile, and the Atbara. These rivers join in Sudan and then flow north across the desert. The White Nile, from its source in Uganda, rolls through Lake Victoria and Lake Albert. Once the cascading river reaches the Sudanese plain, it slows to meander through the vast swamps and marshes called the Sudd (Arabic for "blockage" or "stoppage"). Choked with tall grasses and reeds, these shallow sloughs nearly engulf the river. Not until it reaches northern Sudan does the White Nile become a navigable waterway. At Khartoum, it joins the Blue Nile. Originating in the Ethiopian highlands, the Blue Nile, swollen by spring rains and melting snow, created the annual summer floods. The waters of this river, cold and silt-laden, mix only hesitantly with the main stream, and for nearly a mile below their

junction the Blue and the White Niles run side by side within their common banks.

At Khartoum, the Nile plunges into a sandstone and granite canyon where its waters roil through a series of cataracts (unnavigable rapids interspersed with stretches of calm water). The ancient Egyptians identified six such cataracts, and since they invaded Nubia (modern Sudan) from the north, they numbered the cataracts in the order they found them. Thus the Nile, flowing north, reaches the sixth cataract first. Between the sixth and the fifth cataract, the river is joined by its final major tributary, the Atbara. This river, like the Blue Nile, originates in the Ethiopian Plateau and contributed to the annual inundation in the north. From the mouth of the Atbara, the Nile slips northward through granite and sandstone cliffs and over three more cataracts. Today the second cataract and the narrow strip of farmland that lay between the river and its towering banks are submerged behind the Aswan High Dam. The rocks of the first cataract, just north of Aswan, lie exposed, tamed water from the dam swirling softly around them.

Upper Egypt

North of the dam, the Nile spills around the rocky islands of the first cataract. Flowing steadily north, the river passes the pharaonic temples at Luxor (ancient Thebes). At Qina, the river swings abruptly east and then loops back in a great curve; the Qina Bend. Not until the river swings north once more does the valley begin to widen. South of Aswan (near Isna), sandstone gives way to limestone where the river persistently hugs the cliffs of the Eastern Desert. Thus most of the cultivable land in Upper Egypt, with the exception of the horseshoe-shaped plain of Kom Ombo, lies along the western bank. This narrow fertile strip of the Nile was homeland to Egypt's militant pharaohs, who dominated the country during much of its early history.

Middle Egypt

The border was never exactly fixed, but Middle Egypt begins near Abydos, where the desert escarpments recede, the croplands widen, and the limestone cliffs that line the banks begin their gradual descent into Cairo. Just outside Cairo the Fayyum depression branches off from the main valley like a bud on the lotus blossom

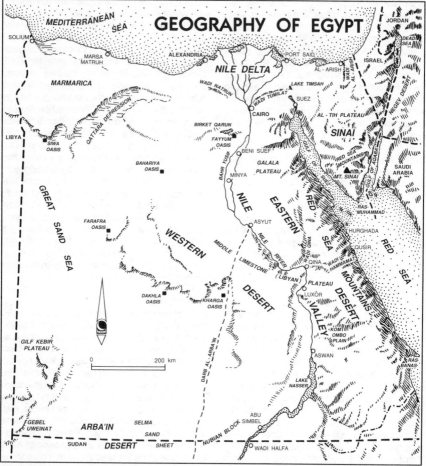

GEOGRAPHY OF EGYPT

© MOON PUBLICATIONS, INC.

of the Nile. The Bahr Yusif links the Fayyum to the main river, and its waters flow across the western ridge and into the depression through Lahun or Hawarah Gap, where, after irrigating about 200 square km, it collects in the brackish Birket (Lake) Qarun, which lies about 45 meters below sea level. Subject to the same flooding as the central valley, the Fayyum's green fields, lush vineyards, and prolific orchards testify to its fertility. Beyond Lahun, about 22 km south of Cairo, the pharaonic capital of Memphis

once stood. This city, perched at the tip of the delta, controlled not only the trade routes crossing from the desert, but all of Egypt. As the delta shifted northward, so did the capital, until it settled at present-day Cairo.

Lower Egypt

Just north of Cairo the Nile branches, spreading water and alluvium over the delta, which fans along the Mediterranean coast between Alexandria and Port Said. In ancient times, a half dozen branches of the river laced this triangular area, creating a nearly impassible swamp choked with papyrus and reeds. By modern times however, slow water flow and increased silting had reduced the river to two branches; the Rosetta and the Damietta. These forks feed a latticework of waterways that blends into the coastal marshes, filling irrigation canals and spilling into the lakes and lagoons festooning the Mediterranean shore. The delta, with twice as much arable land as Middle and Upper Egypt combined, includes some of Africa's most fertile soils.

RED LAND

Beyond the Nile's cliffs lie desolate sands and arid hills. Although the desert's popular image is one of vast, sweeping dunes, sand covers less than a seventh of Egypt's Red Land. Most of the area is either paved with small stones or encrusted with limestone, gypsum, or salt. Deep depressions, often ringed by steep bluffs and containing oases, are scattered throughout the western wastelands. Granite and limestone mountains thrust up, and pediments (eroded remnants of high plateaus) stand solitary guard. The weathering that produced this topography is as unique as the desert itself, and the omnipresent wind played a leading role.

Because the dearth of vegetation offers broad expanses of unprotected land where no grass binds the soil and no trees check their force, scouring winds are particularly destructive in the desert. Modern aerial and satellite photos clearly show massive grooves and troughs aligned with the curving paths of the prevailing northern winds. The winds, which can reach near hurricane speeds (125-160 km per hour), strip precious topsoil from fields, disperse weeds and insects, and whip up dust storms that block roads, clog ditches and canals, and bury crops. They sandblast pediments into forms resembling pyramids and sphinxes, and they create vast depressions throughout the desert. Wind also exposes the stones that cover the desert floor, forming vast expanses of stony wasteland, called the *reg*.

Where sand is plentiful, the wind piles it into gigantic dunes. Although their shapes vary, dunes invariably present a long, solid, gently sloping windward side and a shorter, steeper leeward side. This steep leeward slope, soft and absorbent, stores water from the desert's infrequent rains and offers easy digging for sand dwellers who excavate cool burrows to escape the desert sun. The long windward slope, as any Bedouin knows, is packed hard and makes easy walking for his horse or camel.

The size and shape of sand dunes depend upon the strength and directional consistency of the prevailing winds as well as the amount of sand available. A *barchan,* for example, is a crescent-shaped dune with its horns pointing downwind, formed when the winds are constant and the amount of sand is limited. If the winds shift, the sand forms the multiple arms of a star-shaped dune called a *rhourd.* Where sand abounds, the winds build a series of gigantic longitudinal dunes, some nearly 70 meters tall. These vast fields of rolling dunes, called *ergs,* stretch across the desert floor for kilometers. In the Western Desert, the Libyan Erg covers more than 880,600 square kilometers. While dunes can move nearly a meter per day, many of them are ancient and stable—fossil dunes immobile for centuries.

The Western (Libyan) Desert

From the Nile's western bluffs, sand- and gravel-strewn flatlands stretch west, covering more than two-thirds of Egypt's territory. Three plateaus make up this Western Desert. In the south, Nubian sandstones comprise the Arba'in Desert, named after the camel trail that bisects it. This area receives little rainfall and endures constant winds (4-18 km/h), but the sandstones of this plateau freely transmit water and in fact supply much of that found in the oases. The Gilf Kebir Plateau rises in the southwestern corner, while much of the rest of the area is paved with great, flat sand sheets that make a perfect surface for the cars and motorcycles of Pharaoh's Rally. Although traditionally these sheets were credited to the wind, increasing research points to their deposition by water. From just south of Siwa, along the western edges of the oases, to beyond the Sudanese border, these sheets are buried by long (300 km), narrow *seif* dunes a few km wide. Row upon row of these dunes, collectively known as the Great

Sand Sea, march across this vast expanse of desert. Driven by the northern winds, these shifting mountains of sand have throughout Egypt's history sheltered her western border. To the east, the basin of Kharga Oasis (Wadi Gadid or New Valley) stretches 220 km, and to the north, a series of uninhabited (in modern times) depressions runs along the plateau's edge, separating the sandstones from the limestones.

Bisected by the Nile, the Middle or Libyan Plateau is virtually a rock desert or *hamada*. Oases border its edges; Kharga and Dakhla to the south and east, Farafra and Bahariya to the northeast. Due north, it merges nearly imperceptibly with the second massive limestone plateau. In the center of this Northern Plateau (also called Marmarica and Qattara Plateau) lies the Qattara Depression, one of the deepest and largest undrained basins of the Sahara. Siwa Oasis, famous for its people and dates, lies to the west, and Wadi Natrun, home of the Christian monasteries, to the southeast. North of Qattara, the tableland slopes toward the Mediterranean Sea, its gravel surface folding into gentle undulations. Limestone deposits run across northern Africa from ancient Cyrenaica, framing the scalloped coastline.

The Western Desert has no external drainage systems; the runoff from its occasional rainstorms pours into central depressions, forming ephemeral lakes that, when dry, leave deposits of salts, such as the natron used by the ancient Egyptians for embalming. Water is limited to artesian wells located in a string of oases that run in a series of depressions across the plateaus. These oases (Kharga, Dakhla, Farafra, Bahariya, and Siwa) form a sweeping south-north arc that supported a caravan route, Egypt's only south-north passage other than the Nile. This route was never easy, however. In fact, the Persian king Cambyses lost an entire army between Kharga and Siwa; no traces of it have ever been found.

The Eastern (Arabian) Desert

In the south, the Eastern Desert rises 2,000 meters in steep hills and scarps to the Red Sea mountains. This backbone of volcanics, granites, sediments, and metamorphic rocks hugs the Red Sea coast; the little sand that accumulates lies mostly on their eastern side. To the west and north, the mountains give way to the plateaus intersected by ancient drainage beds, relics from Pleistocene times when heavy rains scoured their slopes. Similar gullies, called *wadis,* transsect the mountains as well. With the exception of Wadi Qina, which runs 200 km from north to south along the western foothills, they coalesce into major east-west arteries. Runoff from ancient storms deposited small alluvial fans at the mouths of these *wadis,* where early settlers of the Nile Valley built their villages. They used the *wadis* as highways, establishing major trading routes to the Near East, roads still used today. In the mountains, on the bare, arid, and isolated slopes, prehistoric man mined flint for knives, and pharaohs' workers quarried granite for their monuments. Between Qina and the Red Sea, three centuries of Roman emperors mined imperial porphyry; their fortresses, quarries, and dry wells remain scattered along their ancient roads, which lace the surrounding hills.

Today, during occasional storms, rainwater quickly percolates into the gravel and sand lining these *wadi* beds, creating underground reserves that can be tapped by shallow wells. This water also feeds natural springs scattered throughout the range.

Sinai

Sinai's 61,000 square km are separated from the rest of Egypt by the Red Sea and the chain of lakes and waterways forming the Suez Canal. To the south, the triangular thumb of land is bounded by the Gulf of Suez (west) and the Gulf of Aqaba (east). This subcontinent links Africa (at Suez) and Asia. Occupying six percent of Egypt's total land area, it is a geological extension of the Eastern Desert. The peaks on Sinai's southern tip, though now separated by the waters of the Red Sea, once formed part of the Red Sea mountains. From the southern tip at Ras Muhammad, rugged, granite mountains dominate the peninsula's lower third. Many of the peaks in this complex jumble of igneous and metamorphic rocks exceed 2,000 meters, higher than any of their counterparts on Egypt's African coast. Their steep-sided ravines, scoured by massive desert storms, have cut down to the desert floor. Gebel Musa (Mt. Sinai) rises to 2,280 meters and Gebel Katrina (Mt. St. Catherine) to 2,641 meters, making it Egypt's highest peak.

To the north, the limestone plateau of al-Tih slopes toward the Mediterranean. Like the mountains to the south, al-Tih's rocks match the sedimentary deposits found on corresponding plateaus of the Eastern Desert. This central plain is bounded by fault scarps: on the east by the crack that formed the Dead Sea and the Gulf of Aqaba; on the west by the one that created the Gulf of Suez. Dotted with mountains, it's still subject to faulting, and here too, storm runoff has widened and deepened the ravines. The largest, Wadi Arish, runs nearly two-thirds of the peninsula's length. Chains of *barchan* dunes rising 80-100 meters run parallel to the Mediterranean coastline. These dunes, with their ability to collect and absorb water from the coastal rains, provide an important water resource to be tapped by shallow wells.

GEOLOGY

Egypt's geological history lies like an opened book in her stark slopes and abraded cliff faces. Exposed by the incessant winds and biting rains, the land's layered pages, fractured and folded, eroded and etched by water and weather, tell the story of an area once an ocean, now a desert. The remains of tiny sea creatures and extinct monsters lie tucked in the striated rocks. Extruded lava dikes and flows dot the eastern mountains. On bleaching sands lie the bones of tropical animals now banished by the drying climate to the African interior. Yet the story is not as clear as geologists would like. The rain and wind have destroyed some layers completely, while ocean and river sediments have covered others. But by studying the earthen cores of wells bored for water or oil, geologists have been sorting out Egypt's geological history.

Early Egypt

Egypt, like the rest of the world, was formed by movements of the earth's crust. Fractured into plates, this crust fits together like pieces of a jigsaw puzzle. Some plates carry only ocean, while others have chains of volcanic islands or pieces of continent built on them; some have both. Currents in the earth's molten mantle shift these plates, and like ice cubes in a punchbowl, they drift, colliding and separating throughout

geological history. Rifts open in the crust, and magma from the earth's interior rises up, forcing the plates on either side apart; such rifts are today widening the Atlantic Ocean and forcing Sinai ever farther from the African part of Egypt. Since space on the earth is limited, the opposite edges of such moving plates crash. Oceanic plates, being less buoyant than continental ones, dive under the land. If two continents collide, they wrinkle each other's edges, throwing up great chains of mountains like the Himalayas.

In Egypt, the oldest section of land lies in the southwest corner (Gilf Kebir) near the junction of Egypt, Libya, and Sudan. While geologists are unsure of its original northern border, it fell short of the areas now occupied by the Mediterranean coastline, the delta, and the Eastern Desert. In late Proterozoic times, continental drift smashed a series of island arcs or small continents into the northern and eastern sides of the developing African continent, forcing up an early version of the Red Sea hills, mountains that eroded and covered the country with their sediment.

Following this pan-African collision, the land that is now Egypt lay at the mid-southern latitudes and was attached to Turkey on the north and Saudi Arabia on the east. The entire mass, driven by continental drift, moved south until Cairo reached a latitude of 70 degrees south, and then slowly moved north to its present location with Cairo about 30 degrees north. This movement shifted Egypt's climate, allowing extensive water and even glacial movements to shape her landscape.

For much of this geologic history, Egypt was submerged. Massive floods ebbed and returned, their precise causes unknown. Some geologists attribute the flooding to periodic lifts and drops of the landmasses, while others believe the ancient seas rose and fell with the advance and retreat of European glaciers. Sandstone, limestone, chalk, and marl, formed of sediments and the remains of algae, plankton, and coral, were deposited by the covering seas. In the south, where flooding was minimal, the earliest layers of Nubian sandstone lie exposed on the desert floor. To the north, the sea water deposited increasing layers of sediments and the depth of these formations increases in direct proportion to the time the land was flooded. Thus a wedge of sedimentary layers lies beneath the desert's flat surface; deepest near the Mediterranean coastline, where 1,500 meters of chalk, limestone, and shale overlay the Nubian sandstone and their basement layer of granite and schist.

In early Paleozoic times, the land would become the basins of the Kharga and Dakhla oases subsided and by the end of the era, volcanos associated with the continental collisions that formed the supercontinent Pangea began to build the Red Sea Hills. By Mesozoic times, Africa had rifted from Europe, the Atlantic was beginning to widen, and Turkey broke away from Egypt. Not until Neogine times did the Red Sea start to open, separating Sinai from Saudi Arabia.

The First Nile

Roughly six million years ago, shifting landmasses created a high shelf across the Strait of Gibraltar. Water evaporating from the drying Mediterranean fell as rain over the Red Sea mountains, feeding the headwaters of Egypt's first great river system. Roaring out of the eastern hills and boiling along a path sketched by a series of tectonic faults, it swept across Egypt's high plateau and cascaded 40 meters, in a series of spectacular waterfalls, into the vanishing Mediterranean. As sea level continued to fall, the river hewed out a chasm rivaling the Grand Canyon of the Colorado River in both size and depth. Then, five million years ago, in a spectacular display of hydraulics, the dam at Gibraltar broke. Sea water filled the gorge incised by the early Nile, creating a long, saline gulf stretching from the delta to Aswan. The Grand Canyon of the Nile became a fjord of the rising Mediterranean.

Ancient Nile Rivers

Following the reflooding of the Mediterranean, winter cloudbursts, more frequent then than now, fell over the western plateaus and the Red Sea mountains. These rains lowered the peaks and chiseled out *wadis*. The massive amounts of sediment they carried converted the gulf to an estuary and then into a river channel, filling the gorge, driving the sea water north, and building a massive wedge of sediments underlying the modern delta. This second of the five Niles that flowed and ebbed

through the valley had no connections with Africa, but arose only within Egypt.

By Pleistocene times, Egypt's climate was already beginning its shift to desert, but the trend was offset by interspersed wet periods (pluvials). The Nile ebbed and flowed with these shifts of climate, which may have been linked to the advance and retreat of European glaciers. With the drying climate, the second Nile withered and died. However, later periods of rain fed the third large river, its sediments testifying to its Egyptian sources. Only with the fourth river did the waters from Ethiopia cut across an elevated Nubian massif and carve out the cataracts. During a hyperarid period, however, this connection was severed. The waters of ephemeral rivers flowing through the valley arose within Egypt—the runoff from several pluvials.

Modern Nile

Only when the waters from Africa once more carved their way through the Nubian block of granite did the modern Nile begin to take shape. About 200,000 years ago, this block nearly severed the river's flow into Egypt. The Nile, a fifth of its previous size, cut its way across the elevated block, forming the cataracts. During this time, the fickle river nearly dried three times; geologists attribute these phases to shifts in climate linked to the fluctuating glaciers in Europe as well as tectonic movements that raised and lowered the Nubian block. Thus the Nile's African connection is new (in geologic time), with the Ethiopian (Blue Nile) link occuring in the middle Pleistocene. Until recent times the central African White Nile formed a series of interiorly drained lakes. Even today, if the slightest tipping of the southern Sudanese plateau occurred, the Nile, separated from its African and Ethiopian sources, would run dry.

CLIMATE

With the exception of the strip bordering the Nile and the Mediterranean Sea, Egypt is desert, and this desert can be as contradictory and capricious as it is deadly. In spite of the Sahara's notorious heat, it can be bone-chilling cold. In the center of dry wastelands it spawns flash floods.

CLIMATE CHART

Temperatures given in Celsius/Fahrenheit

Month	ALEXANDRIA High	Low	CAIRO High	Low	LUXOR High	Low	ASWAN High	Low
January	19/66	10/51	19/66	07/45	23/74	5/42	24/75	09/49
March	21/70	12/54	24/75	10/51	30/86	10/50	31/88	14/57
May	27/80	17/63	32/90	16/62	39/103	20/69	39/103	23/73
July	30/86	23/73	35/96	21/71	41/107	22/72	41/107	25/78
September	30/86	22/72	31/89	20/68	39/103	21/71	39/103	24/74
November	25/77	17/62	25/78	13/57	31/87	12/54	31/88	16/61

Temperature

Relative humidity averages 15% and can drop to as low as five percent in the arid interior. Therefore, unbuffered by moisture in the air, the land experiences violent temperature swings. As soon as the morning sun appears, sand and rock begin to heat, radiating their warmth into the dry air. Daytime temperatures may reach nearly 54° C (130° F) in the shade—if you can find any—and temperatures as high as 78° C (170° F) have been recorded. When the sun sets, the desert cools as rapidly as it warmed. The gravel wastelands, lacking plants and moisture to store the day's heat, loose their energy to the dry and cloudless night. Twenty-four-hour low temperatures can range from 16° C (60° F) to 2° C (36° F), and shifts over 37° C (100° F) have been recorded. In summer, the sun burns down incessantly from monotonous blue skies. But as the sun slides southward in the fall, the country cools. Upper Egypt generally remains dry, while in the north, clouds blow in from the Mediterranean, and Lower Egypt gets its seasonal winter rains, totaling 6-20 centimeters.

Rains

Rainstorms in the desert are as uncommon as they are unpredictable. Not tied to any major climatic patterns, they are atmospheric accidents, freak storms swept by chance over the desert. They may be decades apart: Kharga Oasis, for example, has gone 17 years between rains. When storms do strike, they are often violent, localized, and unexpected. A single storm may drop more precipitation than the area's total annual rainfall. Runoff from these storms carries massive loads of silt and debris. The sparse vegetation cannot check the water, and millions of gallons boil down the watersheds, washing away all in their path and flooding *wadis* hundreds of kilometers from the storm. In such torrential downpours, whole mud-brick villages have melted and washed away.

Although rain is normally sparse, it nevertheless shapes the desert. It seeps into rocks, and during winter nights freezes and expands, cracking rocks with a report as loud as a gunshot. Moisture also draws iron and manganese to the surface of desert rocks, where the sun oxidizes them into a hard, dark varnish. Rainwater collects in temporary pools; its capillary action leaches salts and minerals to the surface, and upon evaporation, forms vast salt pans and gypsum crusts which coat desert depressions.

Wind

In contrast to its rains, Egypt's winds are predictable. They sweep across the land from the north, bringing cooling breezes from the Mediterranean. These northerlies have made the Nile River an easy and dependable thoroughfare: sailboats can ride the current north, the wind south. Only the limestone cliffs (which rise nearly 2,000 meters) at the Qina Bend block the wind. In the desert, the winds can shift rivulets of sand or can swirl clouds of dust aloft, winnowing the yellow grains from gravel beds, heaping it even higher on the dunes. Yet, no matter how fierce the wind, it can only lift sand five to six feet from the ground, creating a shifting, billowing layer above the land. Such storms can sandblast through telephone poles, eat away the bases of rocks, and polish desert varnish to a high sheen. Dust, in contrast, rides the winds high; while a sandstorm will leave a camel rider's head above the sand, a dust storm can block out the sun, blanketing his world in darkness. In camps, such storms filter sand under tents, into sleeping bags, between toes, and into hair.

Spring winds, called khamsins for the 50 days they traditionally blow, come from the south. A khamsin is preceded by a subtle change in the atmosphere, causing animals to become restless and human tempers to flare. As the winds cross the desert, the temperature rises sharply. The dunes begin to "smoke," as the air currents ruffle the slopes, dislodging the dust that had been packed by the prevailing winds. Increasing

strength, the khamsins swirl more dust aloft, turning the sky rose-violet, then black. Huge, dark columns sweep across the desert, blanketing all in their path with fine dust. Each storm may blow for several days, but at the end of the khamsin season, summer comes to Egypt.

Egypt's Changing Climate

In modern times, the Egyptians have fought the capriciousness of the Nile floods by harnessing the river with a system of barrages and, ultimately, by building the Aswan High Dam. Traditionally, Egypt's hot, dry days were unleavened with clouds, but with the advent of this dam, massive evaporation from Lake Nasser has increased the humidity; overcast days are no longer an exception. The increased moisture has lessened the desert's swings of temperature along the Nile Valley, making Egypt's climate less extreme but more humid, and perhaps increasing the country's rainfall.

Yardangs, natural erosional formations, may give a clue to why the similarly shaped pyramids and even the Great Sphinx have survived so many centuries.

LOUISE FOOTE

FLORA AND FAUNA

At the end of the Pleistocene Epoch 50,000 years ago, the area of Egypt's Western Desert was acacia savanna. Cypress, olive trees, and oleander had worked their way south across the Mediterranean to Egypt's coast and river valley, and from southern Africa giraffes, gazelles, and ostriches moved north into the grasslands. Lions followed their prey, as did jackals, vultures, kites, and hawks. Migrating birds established flyways over the rich land, where they stopped to rest and feed. Marshes, thick with papyrus and floating lotus, provided nesting sites for waterfowl and gave homes to crocodiles and hippopotami. The seas, river, and lakes teemed with fish.

Over a million years ago, the savanna became desert. The encroaching sands pushed plants and animals alike toward the ever-shrinking waters, and the giraffes and lions retreated to Sub-Saharan Africa. Eventually only the river and the oases remained damp, isolating small pockets of flora and fauna. Today, large expanses of scrubland along the Mediterranean coast and delta marsh blend with open parklands, but the largest habitat is the desert and its semiarid borderlands.

DESERT PLANTS

Like animals, desert plants have developed defenses for survival; many grow thorns to discourage animals from browsing on them. Sparsely scattered, they inhabit basins where moisture from infrequent rain collects. They send down extensive root systems to claim water over large areas—often more of the plant lies under the ground than above. Plants also cling to ledges in rocky outcroppings where weathering stone has provided a toehold of soil. In the vast *ergs* they grow on the lee side of the dunes, where the loosely packed sand soaks up the occasional rain, storing it against evaporation. Annual plants survive in the desert by lying fallow between rains. Following a storm, the desert bursts into bloom; delicate green leaves and bright flowers carpet each rocky swale, nestling in hollows. The plants, having evolved compressed life cycles, grow, bloom, and go to seed within days, as if filmed in time-lapse photography. Their tough-coated, heat-resistant seeds scatter in the ever-present wind, or, if equipped with stickers, hitch a ride on animal fur or human clothes.

A predominant member of Egypt's desert flora is the acacia tree, and several species produced timber for ancient ships, lintels, and coffins. The tamarisk grows to large bushes or small trees. Mangrove occupies the southern tip of Sinai, the farthest north this shrub is known to live throughout the world. The dainty ice plant thrives throughout the northern deserts, blossoming in pale yellow a couple of weeks after a rainstorm. The prickly pear cactus was introduced from the north. The bitter melon, which grows throughout sandy areas, forms small, unpalatable fruits, while spiky stems of camel thorn cover the sands, providing grazing for camels and goats. In areas where water is available under the sand, coarse Halfa-grass grows in thick clumps.

Palms

Flourishing in the oases and along the Nile, palms sink their roots deep into the moisture-rich earth. They grow particularly well where the arid climate encourages the growth of their bright orange reproductive plumes. To produce fruit, date palms must be hand fertilized, so in winter, owners climb their trees to wrap flowering stalks with pollen. In summer, the branches burst from the wrappings and by fall, droop heavily with their load of fruit, which is hand harvested by the grove owners. Several types of dates are available in Egypt; those from Siwa being renowned for their delicate flavor. Egyptians use the gray, dead foliage to make windbreaks, roofs, and crates. The dom palm, depicted on pharaonic tomb walls, grows only south of Asyut; their branching trunks were a favorite nesting place of baboons, and the tree became associated with the god Thoth.

PLANTS OF THE BLACK LAND

Egypt's subtropical climate nourishes both temperate and tropical plants. The lush gardens and productive fields of the Nile Valley and Mediterranean coast testify to the land's fertility. This richness led the ancient Egyptians to reclaim as much area as possible, draining the marshes and expanding their irrigation systems to reach higher elevations.

Lotus

Three types of these water lilies grow in Egypt: the true lotus, introduced by the Romans from Asia; the wide-petaled, white water lily, still common in canals and ponds in the Fayyum and throughout the delta, and the blue variety with its narrow petals and sweet fragrance, a symbol of Upper Egypt. Ancient Egyptians wore this blue flower as decoration, slipped it into their wine for its narcotic effect, and used its buds and flowers as inspiration for columns and capitals. Today, this lily (which also has a white form) is rare; the best place to see it is in the pond in front of the Antiquities Museum in Cairo. Note: the roots of all species of lotus are poisonous if ingested.

Papyrus

Symbolic counterpart of the lotus, the papyrus was the heraldic plant of Lower Egypt, where it once grew in tall, thick clumps. From its stems, the Egyptians made writing material similar to paper by breaking open the stocks and placing narrow strips from the inner stems at right-angled layers and then pounding the sheet until the strips fused. Papyrus was produced until the 10th century A.D., when it was finally supplanted by paper. The plant's stalks and rhizomes also provided food, mats, and ropes. Very little wild papyrus is to be found in Egypt, but some can be seen in the Antiquities Museum gardens and on Jacob's Island, where a private company (Dr. Ragib) has planted fields of it. The closely related sedge is found in ditches and damp areas; symbol of Upper Egypt, it appeared along with the bee in one of the kings' royal names.

Trees

Trees such as the pomegranate and sycamore, which were known in ancient times, still grow in Egypt. Australian pine and eucalyptus have been introduced and planted for windbreaks. Most trees now, however, form extensive mixed orchards: citron, lemon, orange, lime, and tangerine. The mulberry, exclusive food of silkworms, was introduced when the secrets of silk production were smuggled from China in the 6th century. The banana tree probably entered Egypt in medieval times. Since then, a wide variety of ornamentals have been introduced: banyan, bombax, coral, flame, jacaranda, and rubber trees; Persian lilacs and oleander.

DESERT DWELLERS

The plants and animals that remained in the desert adapted to high temperatures and scarce water. To conserve water, these creatures have evolved specialized body structures, like the scarab beetle's protective coating. Others can slow their heart rates and breathing, reducing their metabolic rates—a desert form of hibernation. Animals shift their activities and life cycles as well; many are active only at night, seeking daytime shelter from the burning sun to conserve water and keep body temperatures from soaring. The mouse-like jerboa retires into his hole after an early morning hunt for seeds and insects. The fennec, a small desert fox, has adapted his own schedule to that of his rodent prey, hunting late in the evening or early morning; to escape the midday heat, he uses his well-developed forelegs to excavate a cool burrow. Like the large-eared fennec, many desert animals have oversized ears, not only to increase their ability to hear low-frequency sounds in the warm, dry air, but also to dissipate body heat. Often the soles of desert dwellers' feet are covered with hair, insulating them from the burning ground and preventing them from sinking into its soft, loose sand.

For desert reptiles, protection from the heat is even more important. Many insulate themselves by "swimming" into the cool sand. The tracks of the skink may suddenly vanish, but he will be found buried at the end of his trail, with just his eyes and the tip of his nose showing. The poisonous viper does likewise, wiggling below the desert's surface; only his eyes and horns mark his hiding spot.

Mammals

A number of the large herbivores that used to roam the desert have vanished, due in part to overhunting during the last two centuries. Gazelles, however, can still be found lying in the shade of an acacia tree, grazing in cool hours, or stealing into oases for a drink. Two species of wild goat, the Nubian ibex and the Barbary sheep, still occupy isolated mountainous areas.

Camels: Long associated with the desert, the camel's ability to store vast amounts of water in the fatty tissues of its hump has enabled man to travel the waterless land between oases. Since camels are not shown in pharaonic tombs, most historians once believed they were introduced by the Romans, but increasing evidence points to their presence in Egypt at least 500 years earlier. The Egyptian camel, a one-humped dromedary, may well have been the mount of ancient barbarians and for this reason was not included in tomb scenes.

Carnivores: The jackal is probably the best known of Egypt's canines. This large black and yellow animal is commonly assumed to have been worshipped by the ancient Egyptians as Anubis, god of the dead. However, modern zoologists think, due to Anubis's bushy tail, that the model was a fox. Two species of fox, the red or Nile fox and the lighter-colored sand fox, still inhabit the country, as does the closely related, buff-colored fennec. Wolves lived in ancient Egypt, and some zoologists suspect a few remain; they are definitely found in Sinai. Perhaps because of the disappearance of the ungulates, but certainly due to hunting pressure, Egypt's large cats like the leopard and cheetah are now seldom seen. Several types of weasel with striped backs inhabit sandy areas, and a

Large ears not only help these fennec pups to hear but also cool them.

solid-colored variety occupies houses in Cairo and Alexandria. The striped hyena still lives in rocky caves along the Nile Valley and sometimes enters villages during the night. Peasants believe that eating the hyena's heart will give them courage and that its whiskers and eyes protect them from the evil eye.

Rodents and Small Mammals: Egypt has one species of hare, yellowish to buff gray, which inhabits the desert. The hyrax is a small rodent-like animal that feeds on plants and occupies rock falls and crevices; white streaks of dung on the rocks are an indication that hyrax dens will be close by but perhaps uninhabited, for the rocks remain bleached for long periods. Gerbils, the closely related dipodils, and the mouse-like jirds can be found in all the desert areas, especially at the borders of the cultivated areas. Fat sand rats live in the saline soils and salt marshes of the desert; their natural curiosity makes them appear docile, but if handled they will bite viciously. Of all the small mammals of Egypt, however, the jerboa is the most novel. Adapted for bipedal locomotion, it looks and leaps like a small kangaroo. Jerboas are active at night and hide during the day in sand-plugged burrows dug under trees or shrubs.

Reptiles

Lizards abound in Egypt's deserts, and most resemble those found in other areas though some, like the fringed-toe lizard, are especially adapted for sand. The Egyptian skink digs into the sand with its flattened snout. Spiny-tailed lizards, named for the spiky rings around their tails, also inhabit the arid lands.

Snakes: Sand vipers are light yellowish or grayish, with a darker tail. The horned sand viper was known to the ancients and appears as the hieroglyph "F." These snakes, though poisonous, are not aggressive and only strike if handled or stepped on. On the other hand, the carpet viper, which often inhabits dry agricultural areas and ruins, is dangerous. Though nocturnal, its habitat brings it in closer contact with humans, and its aggression coupled with its highly toxic venom makes it Egypt's most dangerous snake. The carpet viper sometimes warns before striking by rubbing its scales together, but it often attacks indiscriminately, frequently leaping several feet from its coil. This sandy reddish or gray snake is distinguished by the light-colored "X" that appears on its head. Egypt is also home to two diminutive boas whose nasty tempers make up for their small size. Like most arid land snakes, they spend much of their time buried in rough sand or hiding in rodent holes, but if aggravated, they bite. The Theban sand boa is yellow-gray with dark spots and speckles, while the javelin boa is redder in color.

Invertebrates

Many creatures have adapted to the arid Egyptian deserts. Locusts, for example, invaded Egypt regularly, appearing without warning on the prevailing winds from their endemic areas in the Middle East and Asia. One of the traditional plagues Moses visited upon pharaoh's lands, great flocks measuring up to 50 square km stripped entire regions.

Scorpions: Of these eight-legged arachnids that grow from 8-20 centimeters, the smaller, paler type is the more poisonous. Scorpions typically inhabit dry, sandy areas, crawling into rocky crevices or burying themselves under the sand. However, they must drink and therefore often invade gardens, houses, and even plush hotels. Common in Upper Egypt, these nocturnal hunters lie in wait for their prey, but since they don't see well, they can attack a human hand or foot as well as a cricket or bettle. In ancient Egypt, the scorpion was sacred to the goddess Selket, who wore its body—minus stinger—as a crown.

Beetles: Of Egypt's many species of beetle, the most famous is the scarab, known to the ancient Egyptians as Khepri, symbol of the rising sun. On earth, the scarab collects a ball of dung rolling it along until it finds a place to bury both itself and the dung, where it can then eat in peace. The Egyptians thought the emerging beetle was reborn of itself and therefore gave it the role of shoving the life-giving sun over the horizon each morning. The scarab beetle tends to be nocturnal and consequently is not often seen during the day.

ANIMALS OF THE BLACK LAND

While the desert environment limits the animals and plants to those that can survive in arid conditions, the Nile Valley and Delta are more hospitable. Much of Egypt's flora and fauna originally came from Mediterranean areas, and Egypt's Black Land has served as a transition zone between Europe and Africa. In this temperate area, many plants and animals from around the world find a comfortable home.

Mammals

The large wild animals of the marsh and valley, like many of their desert counterparts, have disappeared. The once-common hippopotamus is now found only far to the south. The Egyptian mongoose, however, still inhabits the delta and northern Nile Valley. This strong swimmer was known to the ancients as "Pharaoh's cat." The delta is still home to two types of wild cats, which ancient Egyptians mummified and probably worshipped. The jungle cat or swamp cat, dark-coated with clear, pale stripes and spots, prowls the dense cover of sugarcane and wild reeds. The wild cat, in contrast, is buff with indistinct markings, and is similar to a modern house cat except for its more slender body and longer legs and tail. Either type could have been the ancestor of the domesticated cat.

Domestic Animals: Wild oxen undoubtedly inhabited Egypt in the late Pleistocene Epoch and became extremely important to early Egyptians: Hathor, goddess of the sky, was a cow; the bull was also pharaoh, symbolizing a merciless crusher of Egypt's enemies, and special Apis bulls were worshipped at Memphis. Early settlers hunted wild cattle, and by the pharaonic period they were assimilated into domestic herds. Today, cattle still draw plows and turn waterwheels as well as provide milk and meat. Water buffalos, a recent import, now augment the bovine population. Egyptians also raise goats and a special species of fat-tailed sheep; they consider their tails a delicacy. The donkey, a domesticate of wild ass forebears, is still Egypt's primary beast of burden.

Rodents: Like most damp areas, the Black Land accommodates its share of rodents. The black and yellow field rat, the brown house rat, and the introduced Norway rat live in cultivated fields, villages, and cities. The common house mouse inhabits much of the country, and the golden spiny mouse, at home in the south Sinai and the Eastern Desert, also invades human habitats.

Bats: Many of Egypt's bats live in ancient pyramids, temples, and tombs. You can find them clinging to ceilings and dark crevices, their guano and pungent urine proof of their residence. Most species fly to the river, where they feed on the abundant insect life; only the Egyptian fruit bat, with its short tail and fox-like face, is not insectivorous.

Reptiles

The terrestrial tortoise is represented by several species; many young individuals appear in pet shops—they are listed as a protected species, and you're not allowed to take them out of the country. Although the soft-shelled terrapin was common in ancient times, this dark brown turtle is increasingly rare. It inhabits the Nile, living off fish, amphibians, and small vertebrates, and can grow to a meter in length; if caught, it bites savagely. Another riverbank inhabitant, the keel-tailed water monitor, is also rare. The Nile crocodile is now only found in the southern part of Egypt, on Lake Nasser. One of the most common lizards, the gecko, invades houses to scramble around ceilings in pursuit of insects and spiders. Chameleons, with their spiky crests and prehensile tails, hunt insects throughout the Nile Delta and Valley.

Snakes: Most of Egypt's snakes are nonpoisonous. The diced water snake, its olive gray skin marked with dark spots in groups of five, lives wherever it finds suitably wet habitats. The reddish gray Clifford's snake is common in fields and around houses in the Nile Valley. Although nonpoisonous, it's aggressive and bites without provocation. The family of cat snakes are large-eyed nocturnal reptiles. While they have venomous teeth at the rear of their mouths, this fang position makes these slow-moving and nonaggressive snakes nearly harmless. The only cat snake that might be dangerous is the aggressive and unpredictable Montpelier. Large, active, and powerful, it is recognizable by its glossy black color and four paler stripes. The only similar-appearing snakes are the molias, lighter, less-aggressive animals that live in the desert and can raise a cobra-like hood.

Cobras: Of Egypt's snakes, the cobras are best known. Slender and small-headed, they can expand the ribs in their neck to form their well-known hood. A symbol of Lower Egypt, their destructive power was a gift of the sun-god Re and protected the pharaoh. Of the two species generally found, the more common is the Egyptian cobra, which inhabits all but the most arid areas of Egypt. This sandy olive snake is fearless and active, and its curiosity can turn into aggressiveness. The black-necked or spitting cobra is limited to Upper Egypt and is distinguished by a few reddish scales and a dark band on the underside of its hood. This snake aims at its victim's eyes and can fire its venom from its front teeth for distances up to three meters. Both snakes are nocturnal, escaping the daytime heat by hiding in rocky crevices, but they live near villages so be careful when poking around ruins.

Invertebrates

In summer, flies invade farm and city alike, especially in Upper Egypt where the traditional trade in fly whisks is as brisk as it is ancient. Fortunately, however, the most common housefly disappears at dusk. The ancients thought the fly had magical powers, and golden flies, symbols of courage and valor, were presented to eminent aristocracy. Mosquitoes, common in the north, include *Culex, Anopheles,* and *Aedes.* Not only can they make life uncomfortable, some can transmit malaria. Larger cities have a nightly spraying program to keep them in check.

Bees: The bees and wasps in Egypt usually keep to themselves unless provoked. Ancient Egyptians were consummate beekeepers, using the honey as a sweetener and the wax for making unguents. In addition to the honeybee, Egypt has large, black carpenter bees, which bore into dead tree trunks or lumber to make nests.

The only potentially dangerous spider is a relative of the black widow, but its toxicity is low. The nonpoisonous wind-spider, which races across the desert on long powerful legs, has large jaws, an aggressive personality, and an unhesitating sharp bite. Millipedes are harmless, but some of the centipedes can deliver a poisonous bite. In summer, both native and migrant dragonflies hover over the Nile. Cockroaches, harmless if annoying scavengers, invade human habitations throughout Egypt. Both body and head lice infect humans in Egypt, while mites, fleas, and bedbugs live in low-class hotels.

BIRDS

For eons, Egypt has served as a flyway for European and Asian birds migrating through Africa. The country's diverse habitats accommodate birds that live and breed, overwinter, or pass through as visitors. However, increased hunting, loss of habitat to farming and development, and misuse of pesticides have threatened many species, such as the black-shouldered kite and Egyptian plover.

Sea Birds
In spring and fall, Egyptian seas are invaded by migrant white pelicans. In the Red Sea, brown boobies breed in the warm waters of Jubal Island and the Gulf of Suez near Hurghada. Cormorants, dark brown birds distinguishable from the similar loon by their longer tails and hooked bills, visit these same cool waters.

Wading Birds
Of the herons and egrets in Egypt, the cattle egret is the most common. During the day, flocks scour fields for insects, and in evenings, they roost together, turning whole trees nearly white; for over 40 years, a colony has occupied the eucalyptus trees just outside the Giza Zoo. The little egret can be distinguished from the cattle egret by its black bill and legs and yellow feet. The western reef heron has both a black and white color phase; it breeds on islands and in mangrove swamps along the Red Sea coast. The gray heron and the darker, more reddish purple heron are winter visitors to lagoons and marshes.

White storks, with their black wing-margins, migrate across the Eastern Desert in considerable numbers from near Hurghada to Qina; although some flocks spend time in Egyptian fields, most continue to Sub-Saharan Africa. The greater flamingo breeds in several areas in Egypt. Migrating flocks of cranes, their elongated feathers curling over wings and tail, giving them a tufted appearance, often appear in Egyptian fields and marshes.

Water Birds
Grebes, frequent visitors to Egyptian lakes and lagoons, fly laboriously though they can dive

expertly for fish, crustaceans, tadpoles, and aquatic insects. In winter, ducks such as wigeons, teals, pintails, garganeys, and shovelers overwinter in the Fayyum and the delta. Of the geese found in the country, the native Egyptian goose, with its white wing patch, often feeds in pairs or small flocks along watercourses. Black- or gray-backed, white-breasted gulls and terns inhabit both the seashore and inland waters. The larger gulls are omnivorous, subsisting on aquatic animals at the water's surface or picking through refuse. Black-crowned terns, by contrast, fish by plunging headfirst into the water. Of the Red Sea terns, the large size, red bill, and black crown of the Caspian tern make it conspicuous.

Rails are compact marsh birds with secretive habits and unusual, often grunting voices. Both moorhens and coots are common in lakes and rivers, where they can be distinguished from ducks by their shorter bills and head-pumping habit while swimming. Plovers, often black masked, visit sandy beaches and mudflats, where they run in quick starts and stops while searching for insects and small marinelife. One of several species is the lapwing, whose crest and wide wings make it unmistakable in ancient temple and tomb carvings. Snipes and sand-

Many of the birds the ancient Egyptians knew still greet visitors.

LOUISE FOOTE

pipers are medium-sized waders, more slender than plovers, with longer legs and generally longer bills. These brown and black birds' markings appear more streaked or mottled; they usually inhabit shorelines along marshes and mudflats.

Desert Birds

Stone curlews or thick-knees are found in semidesert areas and dry fields. Not a standard curlew, the stone curlew has two white and black bars on its wing, while the Senegal thick-knee, found in orchards and gardens, is slightly smaller with a single wing stripe. The cream-colored courser is usually seen singly or in pairs; black wingtips and underwings, which are visible in flight, identify this desert breeder. Several species of larks are also common in the desert. The hoopoe lark, which eats land snails, is distinguished from the bar-tailed desert lark by the former's broad, white wing bars, black primary and secondary feathers, and musical song. The short-toed lark, smaller by comparison, is usually found in flocks, and has a sparrow-like bill. The crested lark is a resident breeding bird of fields and villages. Pairs of brown-necked ravens are common residents of the desert, as is the spotted sandgrouse, which is well adapted to arid conditions.

Game Birds

Like the sandgrouse, the sand partridge breeds in the desert, nesting on the stony *reg;* slightly larger than a quail, this brown bird is nearly invisible in the rocks where it makes its home. The quail, by contrast, is a common migrant especially in the fall when large numbers pass though Egypt on their way south.

Raptors

These birds breed both in the desert and in the Nile system; they appear near cultivated areas where they hunt for rodents, reptiles, or carrion. Black-shouldered kites, pale birds with black forewings, are usually found in agricultural areas; when hunting insects they hover before attacking. The black kite breeds near towns and villages and feeds on offal.

True falcons are streamlined birds of prey, their long, pointed wings built for speed rather than soaring. They hunt birds, rodents, and in-sects. The lanner and kestrel are common and served as the model for Horus, the falcon depicted in ancient carvings and paintings. The marsh harrier, a slim hawk with steeply angled wings, glides slowly and languidly as it searches for prey. In contrast, buzzard hawks are thick-set birds that soar in wide circles on broad wings looking for rodents, rabbits, or an occasional small bird or reptile. Eagles are larger, with longer wings and powerful bills nearly as long as their heads. The osprey is the only eagle-like bird that fishes, plunging feet-first into the water. The Egyptian vulture lives primarily in the desert, where it feeds on carrion. Sacred to the goddess Mut, the bird was the model for ancient Nekhbet, symbol of Upper Egypt. The nearly white barn owl lives in towns and villages, while the brown-spotted little owl prefers open farmland and semidesert. Both the long-eared and short-eared owls are migrants and winter visitors to the country.

Arboreal Birds

Of the doves, the turtle dove, marked by its rather long tail and black-and-white-striped area on the side of its neck, is common in gardens and farmlands. The palm or laughing dove, identified by its spotted neck and hysterical call, breeds in towns, villages, and desert oases. The rock dove, with its green and rose neck, mixes readily with its domestic descendant, the pigeon. Egyptians breed large numbers of domestic pigeons, building ornate cotes to house them; farmers raise the birds for food and for the guano, which they use as fertilizer. Although there are no parrots native to Egypt, a feral population of rose-ringed parakeets breed around the Cairo Zoo.

Songbirds

These birds comprise nearly half of Egypt's avian species. Though many produce beautiful calls, others such as the common gray-and-black hooded crow are poor songsters. The swallows are slim, streamlined birds about the size of sparrows but with long forked tails. The Egyptian subspecies has a red underside, while the European migrant is white or dusky; both build clay nests under eaves. The shorter-tailed sand martin excavates holes in sand banks, while the similar pale crag martin, which lacks distinctive markings, is found in the mountains. Though in the same order as songbirds, shrikes behave more like hawks, perching on conspicuous vantage points and waiting for small prey, which they often store by skewering on handy thorns or barbed wire. The red-backed, the great gray, and the masked shrikes, all with heavy hooked bills, are the most common in Egypt. Pipits are brown-streaked birds with thin bills and white outer tail feathers, while the wagtails are more slender and strongly patterned; both species wag their long tails incessantly.

A large group of songbirds with slender bills inhabits Egypt's fields and gardens. The bulbul has a dark head, brown wings, and a buff breast; by contrast, the rufous bush robin has a long red tail, bordered at either side of the tip with white. The bluethroat and redstart are winter visitors to gardens and shrubs, while the dark-headed, dark-backed stonechat prefers fields and semidesert. Several species of wheatear are distinguished by a black "T" on a white tail, the spotted-breasted song thrush is a winter visitor. Most of the musical warblers that visit Egypt tend to the duller shades of rust, brown, and buff. The graceful warbler with its exceptionally long tail with terminal black spots is easy to identify, as is the Sardinian warbler with its white breast, black head and red eye ring. The male Nile Valley sunbird is dark green on top with a brilliant yellow breast, but the female is drab brown and pale yellow. The male golden oriole is yellow except for a black eye patch and black wings. House sparrows are abundant in towns and villages; goldfinches and linnets visit the farmlands.

Other Birds
Egypt's aerial acrobats, swifts spend much of their lives on the wing, gliding between rapid spurts of flight on stiffly set wings. The common pallid swift can be told from the somewhat similarly shaped swallows by its slimmer, more scythe-like wings and high, shrieking call. Flocks of these birds scream around the cliffs at Deir al-Bahri. Kingfishers nest in holes dug along river banks. The brilliant blue, green, and red kingfisher plunges headlong into the water from a perch on a branch or stone, while the larger black-and-white pied kingfisher often hovers above the Nile or lakes before diving. Kingfishers were known to the ancients and often appear in marsh scenes.

Hoopoes: A distinctive bird, the hoopoe has black-and-white-striped wings and tail and a large crest it raises when excited. Arab folklore casts the hoopoe as the messenger between the prophet Sulayman and the Queen of Saba, and it was rewarded for its service with a feathered crown. Found in farmlands and gardens, the hoopoe is curious enough to appear nearly tame.

Bee Eaters: Brilliantly colored birds, bee eaters have tails with a pointed tip. The little green bee eater is the smallest of the three species occurring in Egypt and is named for its green throat. It hunts airborne insects, usually travels in small flocks, and nests in holes dug in sandy banks. The larger blue-cheeked bee eater has a chestnut throat, and the European bee eater has a yellow throat and brown back.

WATER ANIMALS

In pharaonic times, the Nile teemed with fish and most can still be found today: eel, mullet, chromis, carp, perch, and catfish. On the walls of temples, the triggerfish bares his great teeth, and the globefish puffs himself up with air to float belly up as if dead. In ancient times, fish were the staple of the peasants' diet, and even today Nile fish supply many of the fillets found on Egyptian tables. Swim in and photograph the

Noted for strangely shaped fins and a striped pattern, the lion fish inhabits coral reefs.

LOUISE FOOTE

species to travel north. The rare monk seal, though usually confined to the northern Mediterranean and the Black Sea, has been spotted along Egypt's northern coast.

Red Sea

The Red Sea lacks regular freshwater tributaries, and its evaporation exceeds its rainfall, a condition that has created a warm and salty (nearly five percent) sea. Extensive reefs border the coasts; outside their limits, the sea floor drops to over 600 meters. Submarine valleys sink to nearly 2,000 meters, but even at these depths, the waters are warm. Along the coasts, the fossilized coral bedrock is fringed by living reefs. The fish of the Red Sea are closely related to the tropical, Indo-Pacific species.

Reefs: Shallow coral shelves are inhabited by starfish, sea slugs, and anemone plus an occasional clown fish quietly basking in its protective grass-like tentacles. Clams, their jaws spotted with green or scarlet, nestle into the crevices. Schools of tiny damselfish glitter like clusters of emeralds and rubies; topaz and opal blennies shimmer against variegated corals. Butterfly fish in countless colors flit along the reefs; their eye-stripe and dark spot near their tail make predators guess which end is front. Pairs of angelfish, long dorsal fins narrowing into fine filaments, glide along the reefs, pause, and move on. Nudibranchs stream their gills behind them like delicate lace fluttering in the lazy, buoyant water; purple-plumed sea worms duck quickly into coral shelters; and sharp-clawed crabs scurry around clusters of prickly sea urchins living on the reefs. Sea horses and pipefish inhabit beds of sea grasses, while jellyfish, octopuses, and squid haunt the offshore currents.

Deeper Waters: Schools of green and yellow parrotfish as well as snappers, grunts, and puffers glide past the reefs, feeding on marine worms, tiny crabs, and other small prey. Triggerfish, filefish, and porcupine fish exhibit their scales of heavy armor. Dugongs, along with several species of marine turtle, are residents of the Red Sea, as are the common species of game fish.

Beware: The Red Sea contains a few dangerous species, but for the most part the waters are safe. Beware of scorpion fish, for their

JAN KIRK

Shells served as mankind's first jewelry; this golden specimen was a high-priced substitute from the Old Kingdom.

clear coastal waters and explore the color-splashed world of the reefs. The beaches of Ras Muhammad in Sinai are now nature preserves and offer some of the best scuba diving in the world. In Hurghada, an international fishing tournament sponsored by the Egyptian Angling Federation invites fishermen to try their luck for tuna, sailfish, barracuda, wahoo, jack trevally, dolphin, and bonito.

Mediterranean Sea

Most species of northern Atlantic fish also live in the cool waters of the Mediterranean, and wrasses are the most common fish along the northern coast. They live in rocks or reefs and feed on mollusks that they grind up with a second set of teeth located in their throats. The smaller gobies inhabit tidepools and mudflats, exploring the eel grass in shallows and inlets with their modified ventral fins, which form a sucking disk. Of little economic importance, they are the fish most often seen by visitors to the northern coast. In spite of the link between the Mediterranean and the Red Sea created by the Suez Canal, few fish have migrated, probably due to the brackish water of the Bitter Lakes and the differences in temperature and salinity of the two oceans. The blue-speckled parrotfish is one of the few bodies are covered with poisonous spines; a few, like the turkeyfish and dragonfish, are splashed with wild colors, but others, including the deadly stonefish, blend with their surroundings. The warm waters of the Red Sea do attract sharks: the large and fast mako, the tigershark (which loses its distinctive stripes as it matures), and the hammerhead are rare near the coasts, and with the exception of the hammerhead, they rarely attack if left undisturbed. Schools of long, slender barracuda cruise the waters but tend not to attack divers.

Occasionally moray eels lurk in the dark coral crevices and may bite if they feel threatened. Brightly colored surgeonfish can erect spines near their tails and cut an unwary diver, and near Nuweiba, a few groupers tantalized by divers feeding them have gotten aggressive, but a good bop on the head usually discourages them. Stingrays glide along the seafloors, their venomous spines jutting upward near the base of their whip-like tails. The round purple jellyfish are relatively harmless although they can give an irritating sting. Far more dangerous are the stinging spines of the purple anemone and the fire corals, which deliver venom through specialized cells.

Beaches: The gentle waters of the Red Sea wash up the twisted shells of whelks, oval limpets, as well as nautilus-shaped periwinkles. Tiny cerith shells look as if they came from the forehead of a miniature unicorn. The sea gives up clams and mussels—pairs of their ribbed or smooth shells still hinged. Pieces of sponge and fragments of coral—staghorn, mushroom, and brain—also appear as the waters recede.

Nile

The species of fish inhabiting the Nile come from the Mediterranean and, until the erection of the dams at Aswan, Sub-Saharan Africa. The numbers of Nile fish are decreasing due to pollution, fishing pressure, and in some cases (like the sardine schools in the delta estuaries), from a lack of nutrients caused by the High Dam. Nevertheless, fishing remains viable if diminished; many of the people in the delta and around Lake Nasser still make their living by it.

Although ancient priests regarded fish as religiously unclean, the fish of the Nile provided staple protein for the peasants. Paradoxically, these early dynastic people believed the Nile perch sacred to Neith, and they mummified large numbers. Modern specimens can reach two meters, weigh 80 kilograms, and fight fiercely when hooked. The African mormyridae, with long, down-curving tubular mouths and weak electric organs near their tails, have several Nile representatives; the oxyrhynchus or elephant-snout fish was associated with the goddess Hathor, and a blunt-snout relative lives in the delta region. The Nile is also home to large numbers of catfish, a popular food; the smaller qarmut make up most of the fisherman's haul. Natives avoid the electric catfish, which can deliver a 350-volt shock. Although mullet are considered a marinefish, the gray mullet inhabits the Nile and contributes to the fisherman's catch. The northern lungfish lives in the southern waters of the river and as the waters recede, hibernates in the dried mud of the banks. When threatened the inedible Nile puffer, like its marine cousins, inflates itself and floats as if dead.

BOB RACE

ANCIENT EGYPT

As the sun rises in the east, its light strikes the great pyramids at Giza. The stone, gray and dead, absorbs the light of the dawning sun, warms, and shimmers to life. The gigantic pyramids, once encased with limestone, would have reflected a blazing white light to the ancients, signaling the miraculous, daily rebirth of the world.

THE EGYPTIANS

The ancient Egyptians were a pragmatic people, their technical achievements grounded in their desire to solve simple, basic problems. They developed enough math, for example, to survey fields after the flood, but not enough to support theoretical astronomy. Their medical texts arose from their need to treat their sick and wounded, and these writings formed the basis for classical medicine—learning that ultimately found its way west. Yet despite their pragmatism

their literature was rich with feeling: fast-paced adventure stories and sophisticated love poems. Egypt's writing, technology, and religion, transmitted through the Greeks, Romans, and Arabs, consolidated and built the foundations of Western civilization.

God-king
Religion was central to ancient Egyptian civilization, shaping the culture and dominating daily life. The early Egyptians lived under a powerful king who they considered a god. This god-king was responsible for the well-being of his people; he alone could intercede with the gods to ensure that the Nile would rise to optimum flood and that the sun would appear each morning. His rule was absolute; only his responsibility to his people, personified by Ma'at, goddess of order, truth, and justice, constrained his divine right. Upon earth, he was all-powerful, and upon death, he joined the gods in a world of eternity. During the Old Kingdom, residence in the abode

of the dead was restricted to the king and those who had served him, for this father-like pharaoh, responsible for his people in life, could also take them with him into life after death. In later eras, although the king remained "divine," he ruled more by political and military power, while the privilege of everlasting life in the netherworld filtered down to the nobles and, eventually, to much of the remaining population.

Kings' Names

Early kings wrote their names in a rectangular frame called a *serekh*. In this format, the name appeared atop a palace facade and was in turn surmounted by a hawk; the enclosed name was the king's Horus (hawk) name. By the end of the 1st Dynasty, kings were using a second, throne name introduced by the hieroglyphs of the bee and sedge (see Figure 1, "Kings of Upper and Lower Egypt") and/or a vulture and cobra (see Figure 2, "The Two Ladies," i.e., patron goddesses of Upper and Lower Egypt). Beginning with the Old Kingdom, kings used several names, including the Horus, the Two Ladies, the prenomen (Figure 1), and the nomen (Figure 3, "Son of Re"), the goose and sun. Some pharaohs, when the throne was in dispute, substituted the flag and

HEIROGLYPHICS

1. *Kings of Upper and Lower Egypt*

2. *The Two Ladies*

3. *Son of Re*

4. *The Good God*

nefer of Figure 4 ("The Good God") for Figure 1. Kings surrounded their names (both their throne name and birth name) with a cartouche, an oval enclosed by a knotted rope which symbolized "that which the sun disk encircles."

PHARAONIC HISTORY

With the exception of the king lists discovered at Saqqara, Abydos, and Karnak, the ancient Egyptians left few official historical records. In fact, Egypt's first historian was a Greek, Manetho, a 3rd-century-B.C. priest from the delta. At the request of his Greek rulers, the Ptolemies, he compiled a history of Egypt. Basing his work on ancient records and religious traditions, Manetho grouped families of rulers into 30 dynasties, beginning with Menes' unification and ending with the reign of Nectanebo II. Although his scholarship was remarkable, his sources, some already 3,000 years old, were garbled and mixed with myths and legends. Moreover, like many other ancient historians, Manetho had a shaky grasp of chronology and therefore listed the dynasties governing a divided Egypt as following one another rather than as ruling contemporaneously. Neverthe-

less, modern archaeological discoveries have shown that his material is essentially accurate.

Manetho's account has since been augmented by the discovery of ancient trade dockets, legal briefs, inventories, tax records, and diplomatic correspondence. However, these sources are often damaged and ancient scribes' penmanship is difficult to decipher, making the texts vague and confusing. Thus modern scholars must weave together threads of information from temple inscriptions, stelae, and papyrus fragments. Even so, these records are gradually fleshing out Egypt's extensive history.

Modern historians have noted recurring cycles during the 30 centuries of pharaonic rule in which periods of prosperity alternated with times of stress and civil disorder. They divided the pinnacles into four groups: the Old, Middle, and New kingdoms and the Late Period. These kingdoms are separated by Intermediate Periods when, under weaker rulers, Middle and Upper Egypt were quick to secede, fragmenting the central government and breaking the administrative backbone of the country. Although the exact reasons for the breakdown of central rule are not understood, deterioration in the climate, internal political and economic pressure from ambitious provincial rulers, and the accumulated economic drain by temple, cult, and private foundations all contributed. During the Intermediate Periods, the lack of centralized government reduced foreign trade and border security; food and resource distribution failed, and prosperity declined throughout Egypt. During these times (nearly half the pharaonic period), independent feudal princes ruled Egypt, but ultimately a strong local ruler would take advantage of the national power vacuum and reunite the land, which, after all, shared language, culture, and religion.

PREHISTORIC EGYPT

Though Egypt's prehistoric times are shrouded in a fog of uncertainty, modern paleontologists have been able to trace the glitter of the pharaonic period deep into its prehistoric past, finding the roots of Egyptian civilization. Stone tools uncovered near Abu Simbel are only slightly younger than those discovered by the Leakeys at Olduvai; by 70,000 B.C., Paleolithic people had built primitive dwellings and stone hearths throughout Egypt. These toolmakers tamed fire, tanned leather, buried their dead, and perhaps practiced magic and recited rituals. Extensive game and plant life, coupled with access to gold and copper deposits, enabled early Egyptians to forge a complex society, which spread north, eventually establishing ties with the Middle East and Europe. By the end of the period, Egypt had established her threefold identity as Garden of Eden, cradle of civilization, and crossroads of the world.

Mesolithic Culture
After 30,000 B.C., the climate turned drier, and the inhabitants retreated to fertile pockets along the Nile Valley and the oases. The growing isolation created by the developing wastelands

hampered their movements and sequestered their cultures, allowing separate and distinct traditions to develop. A few tribes, in response to dwindling game, plunged headlong into new technologies. Developing flint arrowheads and sickles for wild-grain harvesting, they created the earliest microlithic (small blade) cultures in the world. But most early Egyptians continued to live by hunting, fishing, and gathering until the introduction of farming from the Near East created the Neolithic revolution.

Neolithic Period
Around 7000 B.C., domesticated sheep and goats and cultivated cereals filtered across the Sinai along Mideast trade routes. The hunter-gatherer communities converted to agriculture, and the region's growing population stratified in an increasingly advanced culture. When the rains of the Neolithic subpluvials (7300 and 4000 B.C.) reversed Egypt's slide toward desert, the land bloomed. Sub-Saharan animals returned to the vast plateaus, followed by the more adventurous Nile people who would become nomadic herders. Those who remained behind became farmers, laying the foundations for the agricultural predynastic civilizations that would dominate the Nile Valley. But these isolated groups lying along the riverbank failed to unify, and the differences between Upper and Lower Egypt grew.

Lower Egyptians
Some of the earliest settlements were uncovered in Fayyum, where bone harpoons and stone points show the inhabitants were fishermen and hunters. However, they also stored emmer wheat and barley, crops known from western Asia, in underground silos lined with well-woven basketwork, indications of nascent farming. They wove flax, perhaps cultivated, into linen and wore personal ornaments of seashells from the Mediterranean and beads from the middle of the Sahara, indications of early trade.

The people of the delta lived in scattered villages where they raised sheep, goats, and probably cattle and pigs on lowland meadows. They made pottery from coarse, straw-tempered clay, raised emmer wheat and barley, which they stored in large communal vessels, and lived in sparsely scattered groups of pole shelters that evolved into villages of semi-subterranean adobe huts. Late in the Neolithic period, when Asiatics and Libyans filtered through the delta's porous borders, northern ports began importing Aegean and Levantine goods and ideas. At the trading center of Ma'adi, just south of modern Cairo, archaeologists discovered underground storage pits still containing traces of grain and oils—Neolithic investment capital. Here, too, villagers set aside an area for smelting copper ores, perhaps Egypt's first factory. Nevertheless, cultural and political traditions from the south also gave rise to classical Egyptian civilization.

Upper Egyptians

The earliest Neolithic farming community uncovered by archaeologists belonged to the Badarians. These people grew grain and flax, hunted, and mined mineral deposits in the surrounding desert. They traded for shells from the Red Sea, turquoise from Sinai, and pine, cedar, and other woods from Syria. They dressed in linen or skins stitched with bone needles (kilts and shirts) and painted their bodies with green malachite, powdered and mixed to a paste. Their jewelry included belts of blue-glazed steatite beads strung with occasional turquoise ones, bracelets of ivory, bone, and horn, and combs carved in the shapes of animals or birds. The Badarians buried their dead in cemeteries, segregating the graves of the wealthy elite. They wrapped their deceased rulers in leather or reed mats and surrounded them with costly grave goods: flint knives, slate palettes, cosmetics,

JAN KIRK

The earliest of Egypt's cultures made beautiful pottery, embellishing it with textures, drawings, and even molded animals like this crocodile.

glazed beads, amulets, and masses of their distinctive black-topped red pottery filled with food for the hereafter.

Naqada: About 4000 B.C., the Naqada I (Amratian) culture succeeded the Badarian. Settlements became larger, and in a direct continuation of the Badarian traditions, the Naqada I people improved stoneworking and carving techniques. With the advent of the Naqada II (Gerzean) culture, Upper Egypt changed rapidly. Expanded contacts with southwest Asia, perhaps through trade for the gold in the Eastern Desert, fostered increasingly complex social and economic institutions. Wider markets led to craft specialization, and by this period, these early Egyptians may have mass-produced their pottery on the slow wheel. Steadily increasing commerce enabled the growth of towns that controlled the trade routes, and their rulers became wealthy and powerful. Demand for ivory and ebony expanded trade with Nubia, which assimilated much of the Upper Egyptian culture. Burial goods by then included copper tools and weapons (both hammered and cast) , as well as gold and silver ornaments, and jewelry—the standard provisions for eternity. By the end of the period, such treasures were buried in painted tombs. Thus Egypt's predynastic populations established the rituals, developed customs, and implemented technologies that led to historical pharaonic civilization.

ARCHAIC/EARLY DYNASTIC PERIOD

By 3300 B.C., predynastic Upper Egyptians had developed extensive irrigation systems and well-established trade routes across the Eastern Desert to the Red Sea, importing ideas, technology, and goods from the Near East. Secure within their borders, Egyptians never built elaborate, fortified city-states like their Middle Eastern neighbors, preferring instead to remain in smaller, rural villages. Egyptians did, however, create political connections that eventually unified into regional divisions the Greeks called *nomes*. By the dawn of historical times, a single ruler had conquered the narrow strip of cultivated land along the Nile that made up the southern *nomes* and ruled it from Hieraconpolis. By contrast, the scattered and heterogeneous settlements of the delta formed loosely knit confederations of independent districts. But by 3100 B.C., Menes, the legendary king of Upper Egypt, had conquered the delta, uniting Upper and Lower Egypt.

Shadowy Menes

The identity of Menes is not certain. He has been linked with Aha as well as with Narmer. Whatever his identity, it's clear that by Menes' reign, Egypt was governed by one god-king. District *nomes* were ruled by the king's governors, and they collected the state's taxes, housed the army, employed scribes to keep state records, and maintained thousands of craftsmen to produce ornamental goods for king, palace, temple, and tomb. Under governmental auspices, art and learning flourished, and as artists and scholars reworked Near Eastern ideas in the Egyptian idiom, Mesopotamian motifs vanished. In short, by 3100 B.C. Egyptian kings had established a national identity forming the basis of later empires.

JAN KIRK

The Narmer Palette shows the unification of the Two Lands, some of the earliest hieroglyphic writing, and the foundations of Egyptian art.

Menes moved his capital north to Memphis, for its location at the apex of the delta gave the king control of both Upper and Lower Egypt. Royal graves got richer, writing became more articulate, and art and architecture began their climb toward greatness. But not all was well in this Eden. Although the kings of the 1st Dynasty maintained their rule over both Upper and Lower Egypt, those in the 2nd Dynasty were embroiled in an enigmatic dispute that may have given rise to the legend of the Contendings of Horus and Seth. (See p. 40.)

THE OLD KINGDOM (CIRCA 2686-2040 B.C.)

Strong rulers of the 3rd Dynasty, however, buried the squabble, and Egypt entered its first great era. This Pyramid Age continued the directions established in the Archaic Period. In the Old Kingdom, architects started building with stone, and sculptors learned to handle it as easily as they did clay. Literature and medicine advanced, and the priests, attempting to reconcile the chaotic collection of gods and goddesses, codified Egypt's theologies. At Heliopolis and Memphis, two great religious centers developed; the former, still active when the Greeks arrived in 332 B.C., tutored Plato. Although Egypt's kings ruled through the strong, well-organized civil service inherited from their archaic predecessors, their own magical rituals summoned the Nile to rise on schedule. They ensured that the universe was in rhythm, the cosmic order balanced. Ma'at reigned.

Third Dynasty

Kings of this dynasty secured Sinai, guaranteeing access to the area's turquoise mines. Priesthoods at both Memphis and Heliopolis continued to gain power under royal patronage. Society stratified into titleholders—literary men who wielded authority derived from the king; their subordinates, who included craftsmen, quarrymen, and soldiers; and the illiterate peasants who supported the entire kingdom with their agriculture. The arts, bound to the growing mortuary cults, flourished. When King Djoser commissioned his eternal mortuary complex at Saqqara, his multitalented chan-

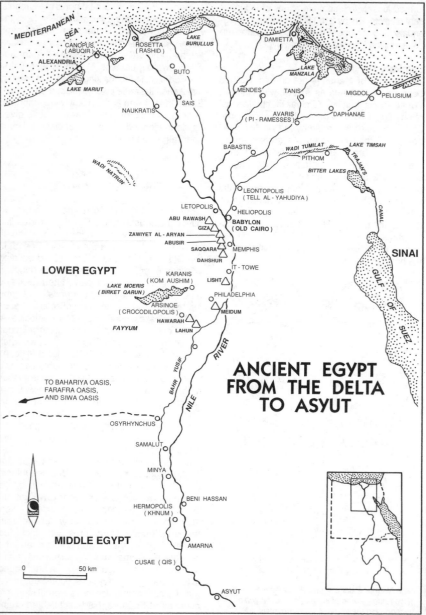

ANCIENT EGYPT
FROM THE DELTA
TO ASYUT

© MOON PUBLICATIONS, INC. / 2

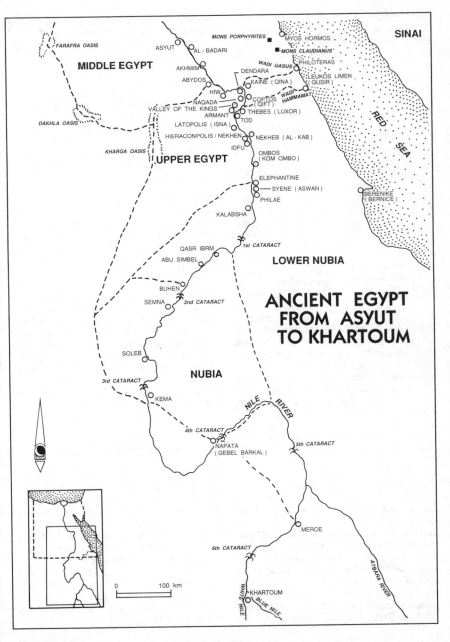

MIDDLE EGYPT

FARAFRA OASIS
ASYUT
AL - BADARI
AKHMIM
ABYDOS
DENDARA
HIW
KAINE (QINA)
NAQADA
VALLEY OF THE KINGS
COPTOS (GIFT)
ARMANT
THEBES (LUXOR)
LATOPOLIS (ISNA)
TOD
HIERACONPOLIS / NEKHEN
IDFU
NEKHEB (AL - KAB)
OMBOS (KOM OMBO)
DAKHLA OASIS
KHARGA OASIS
UPPER EGYPT
ELEPHANTINE
SYENE (ASWAN)
PHILAE
KALABSHA

MONS PORPHYRITES
MYOS HORMOS
SINAI
MONS CLAUDIANUS
PHILOTERAS
WADI GASUS
LEUKOS LIMEN (QUSIR)
WADI HAMMAMAT
RED SEA
BERENIKE (BERNICE)

QASR IBRM
ABU SIMBEL
1st CATARACT
LOWER NUBIA

BUHEN
SEMNA
2nd CATARACT

ANCIENT EGYPT
FROM ASYUT
TO KHARTOUM

SOLEB
3rd CATARACT
KEMA
NUBIA
4th CATARACT
NAPATA (GEBEL BARKAL)
5th CATARACT

NILE RIVER

MEROE

ATBARA RIVER

6th CATARACT

WHITE NILE
BLUE NILE
KHARTOUM

NORTH

0   100 km

cellor Imhotep used dressed stone rather than mud brick, revolutionizing Egyptian architecture. This innovation later inspired the gigantic 4th Dynasty pyramids, which still dominate the Giza Plateau.

Fourth Dynasty
Expanding the lavishness of the preceding dynasty, these kings perfected the art of pyramid

SUSAN MARSHALL

King Menkaure and his queen show the confidence that was the hallmark of the Old Kingdom

building, epitomized by the Great Pyramid complex at Giza. Here, burials have yielded treasures of ancient artwork: massive yet refined portraits in granite, exquisite painted reliefs, delicate jewelry, and gold-encrusted furniture. Snefru, the first king of the dynasty, conquered Nubia and pushed Egypt's borders south to the second cataract, where he founded the fortress at

Buhen. He also strengthened ties with Sinai and developed the copper and turquoise mines there. His son Khufu moved the royal cemetery north to Giza, where his son Khafre and grandson Menkaure added their own smaller pyramids to the plateau. Royal authority peaked during this era, and the king's power was virtually unchecked. The kings established vast estates to finance their mortuary cult and lavished gifts of tombs, funerary furnishings, and estates on their families and courtiers.

Fifth And Sixth Dynasties
Persistent royal family difficulties ultimately ended the 4th Dynasty. Userkaf married Khenthawes, sister and perhaps widow of Shepseskaf, last of the 4th Dynasty pharaohs. He and his two successors, according to Middle Kingdom literature, called themselves Sons of Re. Alongside their personal monuments, they erected vast temples dedicated to his solar cult. Like their forebears, they sent campaigns to Libya, Syria, and Palestine, imported wood from Byblos, and mounted expeditions into Sinai, Punt, and Nubia. Throughout

the 6th Dynasty, the priests continued to consolidate their power and wealth, but financing cult endowments strained both the royal treasury and private resources, and eventually impoverished the country. During this time, leaders of important families in the *nomes* assumed title to local governorships by right of heredity, thus loosening the kings' grip on the provinces. In spite of royal marriages into powerful provincial families, the kings continued to lose control of the country, and with the end of Pepi II's 90-year reign, central control disintegrated, the country fragmented, and Egypt slid toward anarchy.

First Intermediate Period
The pharaoh's loss of political control was aggravated by the end of the Neolithic wet phase. Because the rains on the Abyssinian plateau failed, the Nile Valley was plagued by a series of inadequate floods. Dry winds denuded the fields and famine followed. Such events damaged the status of the kings who had failed, in the eyes of their subjects, to safeguard Ma'at. Egypt's political, social, and religious systems were weakened, and real power came to be held by petty kinglets—local rulers who husbanded their crops, their herds, and their people. Although the monarchs of Memphis remained titular heads of the country, they now found their power only equal to that of local rulers. In the face of this power vacuum, local Bedouin and Asiatics from the east slipped into the delta.

MIDDLE KINGDOM (CIRCA 2040-1570 B.C.)

Squabbles among Egypt's feudal barons eventually sorted out the most powerful, and by about 2100 B.C. kings of Herakleopolis (near modern Beni Suef) had swept the Asiatics and Bedouins from Lower Egypt and controlled the delta. In the south, Theban princes ruled from Elephantine to Abydos, and border skirmishes between the two powers became increasingly violent. Ultimately, the Theban king Mentuhotep, supported by a small but desert-hardened army, marched north, crushed the Herakleopolian forces, captured the capital by siege, and became the "Ruler of the Two Lands."

Eleventh Dynasty

Mentuhotep and his descendants wasted little time in reestablishing Mediterranean trade routes and moving once more into Nubia. They also reopened mining operations in the Eastern Desert and Sinai, and sent ships to Byblos and Punt. These rulers had become aware of the fragility of the state and its need to accommodate the hopes of the ordinary man. During this time, however, the local rulers (*nomarchs*) maintained much of their power, and the king continued to face sporadic uprisings. Although still considered a god, the pharaoh now ruled more by personal talent than by divine right; only a series of strong and naturally gifted rulers, backed by a loyal core of nobles and a large royal bodyguard, brought stability to the Middle Kingdom.

Twelfth Dynasty

In 1991 B.C., Amenemhet, former vizier and army officer from Aswan, seized the throne. Realizing the difficulty of ruling the empire from Thebes, he moved the capital north to Itch-towy (near modern al-Lisht), where his royal court revived Old Kingdom art, architecture, and literature. But despite this artistic facade, the serene self-confidence of the Old Kingdom, which had been based on an immutable order of the universe, gave way to an uneasy realism grounded in materialism, individualism, and military power. To ensure peaceful transitions of the crown, kings appointed their chosen successors as co-regents.

Senwosret: Although political stability increased, the nobles remained fractious for another 150 years and were only subdued in the middle 1800s by Senwosret (Sesostris) III. Middle Kingdom pharaohs subjugated Nubia, building a string of forts as far south as the third cataract to protect overland and river trade. They also increased protection of their trading and mining rights in Palestine, Syria, and Sinai, bringing wealth and power to the land they ruled.

Amenemhet: When the Middle Kingdom pharaoh Amenemhet III ascended the throne, Egypt appeared to be at the peak of her power. The government was both balanced and fair, and large numbers of individuals shared technological advances and benefited from extensive

The kings of the Middle Kingdom, like Amenemhet, appeared more human, their faces showing their individuality and the heavy responsibility that lay on their shoulders.

public works. In the Fayyum, engineers diverted water into a massive lake (Birket Qarun), controlled flooding, and opened new lands to cultivation. As consumer demand increased, trade routes protected by a strong, competent army brought Egypt the raw materials demanded by the people's rising materialism and their mortuary cults. Art and literature, fed by the luxury and stability of the royal court, flourished until the end of the 18th century B.C. To keep pace with Egypt's rising population, her farmers brought marginal land into production, but the diminishing returns from such land, as well as the demands of the temples and mortuary cults, eventually strained the economy. Ultimately, these stresses, coupled with disastrous high floods, corroded the supports of the Middle Kingdom, which folded inward and slowly died.

Second Intermediate Period

Although Methano's king lists imply 60 to 90 rulers for the 13th Dynasty, the country remained remarkably stable. Perhaps Senwosret, by removing power from the monarchs and concentrating it in the hands of his court officials (a move that may well have resulted in the overthrow of his own family), gave power to a family of viziers who exercised real control. The inordinate number of kings can be divided into several groups: an early group, which ruled both Upper and (for the most part) Lower Egypt; a succeeding dynasty that ruled Upper Egypt; a group of "foreign kings" who ruled Lower Egypt, and a number of petty, self-appointed kinglets. Of these groups, the foreign kings or Huksos eventually controlled most of Egypt.

Throughout the Middle Kingdom, Asiatics filtered into Egypt and became assimilated. As the Middle Kingdom died, these Hyksos rose to power in the delta, assuming pharaonic titles and power. Although Egyptian writers depicted the period as one of strife and hardship introduced by cruel, destructive barbarians, archaeological excavations suggest that Egypt under the Hyksos suffered less than the ancient literature implies. Like their predecessors, these "foreign kings" kept both the Mediterranean and Nubian trade routes open. They also introduced technical innovations such as the horse-drawn chariot, the composite bow, the *shaduf* for raising irrigation waters, and the vertical loom. The ruling class adopted pharaonic trappings and built tombs, but continued to worship their Semitic god, whom the Egyptians quickly identified with Seth. The historian Manetho grouped the six foreign princes who ruled from the delta into the 15th Dynasty, and the Egyptians apparently considered them legitimate rulers. Nonetheless, Egyptian pride never forgot the chafing of the foreign yoke, and after that time the country kept a wary eye on the powerful Asiatic neighbors to her east.

Egypt Fragmented

When the Hyksos set up their northern kingdom, Nubia broke away from the empire, and the powerful southern Kushite tribe established a parallel kingdom. These people, exposed to pharaonic civilization throughout the Middle Kingdom, had adopted Egyptian customs. Now they kept their African gold, timber, and slaves at home. However, toward the end of the Second Intermediate Period the Theban princes were once more gathering strength. The Hyksos, from their delta capital at Avaris, could maintain only limited control of Middle Egypt; as their grasp weakened, they formed an uneasy alliance with the Kushites in an attempt to forestall Theban power. The Hyksos, now unable to sail south on the Nile, had to depend on the desert route through the western oases to maintain contact with their Nubian allies. Despite having enemies on both sides, the Thebans continued to expand their power base; this growth created the shifting alliances and sporadic wars that marked the late 17th century B.C. In 1570, Ahmose I expelled the Hyksos, reunited the Two Lands, and inaugurated the New Kingdom.

NEW KINGDOM (CIRCA 1570-664 B.C.)

The 16th century marked a period of international conquest, with the Egyptians, the Near Eastern powers, and, at times, the Nubian kingdom of Kush, all striving to increase their domains. Egypt, under the leadership of a series of warrior pharaohs, established military posts along the upper Nile and far into Nubia. Her armies, now staffed by professional officers and increasing numbers of mercenaries, marched eastward, expanding her frontiers into Syria. At this point, Egypt, no longer content to control trade by setting up merchant colonies, opted for overt military rule, creating vassal states either ruled by Egyptian viceroys or loyal Asiatic princes. This conquest of the Middle East ended

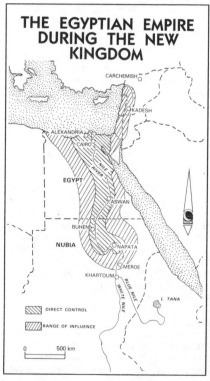

THE EGYPTIAN EMPIRE DURING THE NEW KINGDOM

CARCHEMISH

KADESH

ALEXANDRIA
CAIRO

EGYPT

NILE RIVER

ASWAN

BUHEN

NUBIA

NAPATA

MEROE

KHARTOUM

BLUE NILE

WHITE NILE

L. TANA

▨ DIRECT CONTROL

▨ RANGE OF INFLUENCE

0   500 km

© MOON PUBLICATIONS, INC.

Egypt's political isolation. Bureaucrats turned to diplomacy, and immigrants from throughout the empire swelled Egypt's population, introducing new customs, fashions, and languages. New ideas and new deities invaded the country. Art, literature, and architecture, as well as the minor crafts, reached a peak of international sophistication. Foreign booty, tribute, and trade enabled rulers to build vast temples for their patron gods and to finance their own mortuary cults. The 18th Dynasty included the first warrior kings (the Thutmosides), two heretical rulers, and the boy-king Tutankhamun, who left the treasure-filled tomb discovered by Howard Carter.

Warrior Kings

After vanquishing the Hyksos, Ahmose I and his successors reunited Egypt, founding the 18th Dynasty, and established an administration that lasted nearly unchanged for 500 years. Under the auspices of their Theban god Amun, they invaded Nubia. Reaching the fifth cataract, they repaired Middle Kingdom fortresses and built a string of new ones to control the trade routes. As a result, Nubia became even more Egyptianized, once again supplying Egypt with gold, ivory, ebony, resins, carnelian, amethyst, leopard skins, ostrich plumes, and slaves.

The pharaohs, their pride still stinging from foreign domination, invaded the East and conquered the loose confederations of city-states in Syria and Palestine, pushing Egyptian political control nearly to Carchemish. The pharaohs appointed local Asiatic governors, taking their sons to Egypt—"for education." Such measures ensured loyalty from the rulers as well as preparing a pool of pro-Egyptian aristocracy to govern in the future. In addition, Egypt exacted annual tribute from her colonies, by force when necessary. Thebes, "City of a Thousand Gates," became the capital of the ancient world, where the local god Amun received uncounted riches from victorious pharaohs thankful for their triumphs.

With the rise of the empire, the pharaoh became a national hero, the incarnation of the warrior-god Montu. Surrounded by his professional officers, he was the active head of a military caste and personally led his armies into the field. This military power, coupled with strong

domestic policies, gave the government the resilience to survive nearly unscathed the internal power struggles and religious heresies to come.

Queen Hatshepsut

With the death of Thutmose II, his widow, Queen Hatshepsut, assumed co-regency with his young son, Thutmose III. But she became disenchanted with her behind-the-scenes role, and usurped the throne. With the empire well established by her warrior forebears, she turned her royal gaze inward, embarking on a massive building program to restore temples neglected during the Hyksos domination and subsequent wars. Her ships sailed to Punt, the fabled land lying somewhere to the east along the African coast, returning with untold wealth—gold, myrrh, spices, and exotic monkeys which the court demanded as pets. With her trusted advisor, Senenmut, she built her mortuary temple on the west bank of Thebes. Today known as Deir al-Bahri, it is a building so well designed and so well integrated with its surroundings that it remains an international architectural showpiece.

Thutmosides

Upon Hatshepsut's death, the young Thutmose III regained full control of his throne. The queen had not actively pursued the military statesmanship of the empire, and the Asiatic kingdoms were again threatening Egypt's control of the Middle East. Thutmose, rather than idly kicking his heels at court, marched east, forced the Asiatics into submission, and over the next 20 years pushed Egypt's empire to the Euphrates River. Thutmose's successors kept an equally firm hand on the empire and cemented relationships by marrying Mitannian princesses. Pharaohs, thankful for Amun's support, gave him a

Thutmose III was the greatest of Egypt's warrior kings, extending the empire's boundaries to the Orantes in Syria and deep into Nubia.

healthy cut of the expanding empire's spoils, building him vast temples and granting him estates throughout Egypt. So rich and powerful did Amun's priesthood become, that by the end of Amenhotep III's reign in 1349, it rivaled the pharaoh in wealth and influence. Upon his death, his son Amenhotep IV had to cope with a threatening political schism due to the wealth and power of Amun's priests.

Amenhotep IV/Akhenaten

Amenhotep IV was an enigmatic figure who, in an unprecedented move, threw the weight of his office behind a new religious cult: Aton —the round disk of the sun at its zenith. Amenhotep

changed his name to Akhenaten in honor of his new god and ordered the royal court to convert. He closed all Amun's temples, disbanded the priesthood, confiscated the god's estates, and moved the empire's capital to al-Amarna in Middle Egypt, where he laid out a new city on virgin desert. But Akhenaten's religion, which verged on an austere monotheism, never appealed to the conservative Egyptians, and after his death his heresy was buried even as the desert winds swept sand over his short-lived city; his name was erased from monuments, and his body vanished. Today Egyptologists can only speculate on the reasons for his uncharacteristic theological rebellion. Some claim he was a religious visionary who wished to introduce an abstract god, one without specific Egyptian qualities, who might be accepted by both native and foreign populations of the New Kingdom. Others suggest that his tactics were political moves designed to break the ever-increasing power of the Theban priests. Still others point out that by setting up a god for which he alone was the intermediary, Akhenaten hoped to return the kingship to the absolute divine power of the Old Kingdom.

During Akhenaten's reign, the Hittites of

Egypt's heretic king, Akhenaten, attempted to revolutionize politics, religion, and art.

Anatolia moved into the Middle East. They captured the Mitanni capital in northern Mesopotamia, and one by one subdued the remaining city-states of the Levant. Seeing them crumple under Hittite power, Egypt's Syrian allies begged the pharaoh for support, but Akhenaten sent little help. After his death, the border states and Syria fell to the expanding Hittite empire; at home, Akhenaten's successors were trying to stabilize Egypt's domestic turmoil. Following a confused transition period, Akhenaten's aged adviser and priest Ay bundled up the new young pharaoh Tutankhaton, changed his name to Tutankhamun to distance him from his predecessor's revolt, took him off to Thebes, and restored Amun to his temples. At Tut's death, Ay mounted the throne only to be followed in four years by Akhenaten's former general, Horemheb. But even he could neither win the war nor establish lasting peace with the Hittites.

Nineteenth Dynasty

Horemheb passed the throne to his aging general, Ramesses, and though this pharaoh ruled only briefly, his family held Egypt's crown for over a century. The 19th Dynasty, which he founded, produced several warrior kings who embarked on an ambitious program to return Egypt's prestige to the pinnacle on which it had stood under Thutmose III. Seti I marched his armies into Palestine and by the end of his reign had forced several border states to once more declare allegiance to Egypt.

Ramesses II: Seti's policy was continued by his son Ramesses II, who moved the political capital north to Piramesse in the eastern delta where he could keep a closer watch on the Asiatics, leaving Thebes as Egypt's cultural, religious, and ceremonial center. From the delta, Ramesses continued the reconquest of Asia. His confrontation with the Hittites at the Battle of Kadesh was indecisive, although Ramesses' personal bravery averted military disaster; in Egypt the battle was represented as a great victory in spite of the fact that the Egyptians achieved none of their objectives. Fifteen years later, the two empires ratified a treaty, and copies of this pact (the oldest known) written in Akkadian (the *lingua franca* of the age) have been found in both Egypt and the Hittite capital in Turkey.

But the negotiated peace did not last long, for throughout the ancient world whole cultures were on the move. Ramesses II had had to deal with invasions of northern "Peoples of the Sea" in the opening years of his reign, and his son Merneptah repulsed a massive joint attack of these people and Libyans. These threats, coupled with royal family squabbles at home, made the closing years of the 19th Dynasty turbulent.

Twentieth Dynasty

In 1185 B.C., Sethnakht (apparently a distant relative of the reigning house) took control of Egypt, but it was his son Ramesses III who firmly established the 20th Dynasty. Like previous rulers, he had to repel continuing invasions, and by the end of his reign, economic difficulties, which were to continue throughout the era, surfaced. The royal treasury was overextended, in part because of the wars, in part due to bad harvests and maladministration. At Thebes, artists staged strikes (for their wages of grain), and tomb robbing reached epidemic proportions. Although investigated, the robberies were not stopped, and reading between the hieroglyphs of court documents, historians have concluded that bribery and kickbacks were common. (In an attempt to save at least the royal mummies, Theban priests bundled them up and stashed most in two separate tombs, where they remained hidden and forgotten until the 20th century.) These scandals rocked the administration and underscored the deepening economic depression, while roving bands of Libyans made the country unsafe. Finally, Panehsy, viceroy of Nubia, seized the area around Thebes (the Thebaid) and restored order. A few years later, the king's general Herihor retook Thebes and appointed himself High

SUSAN MARSHALL

Perhaps Egypt's best-known pharoah, Ramesses II followed in Thutmose III's footsteps (regaining much of the country's empire) and built countless temples, including the one at Abu Simbel.

Priest of Amun, and by the end of the dynasty was governing Egypt as king. Although loyal to the pharaoh, Herihor ruled independently, thus splitting Egypt both militarily and politically. Concurrently, at the northern capital, the government official (and possible son-in-law of the king) Smendes was governing for an ineffectual Ramesses XI, at whose death the New Kingdom came to an end.

Third Intermediate Period

Throughout the 400 years of this era, Egypt lay in political fragments. Even when the country was united in name, dissenting factions secured varying degrees of autonomy. The pharaohs kept their capital in the north, but the high priests who were governors of Thebes remained a perpetual thorn in the rulers' sides, and north and south drifted further apart. Many of the dynasties attempted to control the fragmenting political system by delegating combined civil, religious, and military powers to royal relatives, thus scrapping the traditional balance of powers. Intermarriages failed to mitigate tensions between royal families, and throughout the era multiple dynasties ruled simultaneously from different parts of the country. Immigrants not only introduced new religions but also rose to political power. In fact, Egypt spent much of the Third Intermediate Period under foreign pharaohs, and fragmentation was exacerbated by external threats from Kushites, Libyans, and Asiatics.

Tanites

Kings who resided in Tanis maintained nominal control of the Egyptian government, but by now the dual crown was an empty symbol. These kings, preferring burial near Tanis, abandoned the Theban tombs although they continued the temple-building programs. With this shift in royal attention, the south became effectively independent. Centralized power continued to fade, international prestige vanished, and by the end of the dynasty, true political power lay in the hands of Libyan army commanders who had settled in the delta several centuries before.

Libyans

Labeled Bubastite, after their delta capital at Bubastis, this 22nd Dynasty was, despite its origins, thoroughly Egyptianized. In fact, the dynasty traced its roots well back into the New Kingdom when their military forebears had settled near Heliopolis. Thus, the pomp and tradition that had accompanied former royal houses continued for another 100 years under these rulers. Infused with a new vigor, the dynasty reunited the delta princes and even brought Thebes back under its sway. Its first pharaoh, Shoshenq I, (the biblical Shishak) invaded Palestine about 925 B.C. and plundered Solomon's temple. He also renewed trading contacts with Byblos and may have raided south into Nubia. The booty enabled him to revive building projects, adding among other items the first court to Amun's temple at Karnak, with its Bubastite Portal.

Although the Libyans tried to pursue aggressive foreign policies, trouble at home continued to plague them. They attempted to control Thebes by appointing a Libyan princess as divine consort of Amun. In her, they created a powerful leader through whom they could circumvent the priesthood, enforce their policies, and yet allow the restless area a degree of de facto independence. Like a vestal virgin of Rome, this princess never married (and thus could not found a competitive royal line), but with the oracle of Amun ruled the southern capital. A junior branch of the royal family, supported by Theban officials, installed a co-dynasty (the 23rd) at Leontopolis, thereby formally splitting Egypt, a move that only exacerbated dynastic squabbles.

Kushites

As the Libyan dynasties disintegrated in the middle of the 8th century B.C., Piankhy left his Nubian homeland and entered Thebes, where he was deliriously welcomed as restorer of order and orthodoxy. He forced the Libyan votaress, Amun's divine consort, to adopt a Kushite princess as her successor. This Afro-Egyptian civilization, taking its inspiration from classic ancient models, briefly revitalized Egypt's culture. Energetic Kushite pharaohs undertook extensive restoration and building projects, especially at Karnak, where one of Taharqa's columns still dominates the first courtyard.

Although the Kushites brought long-needed stability to Egyptian politics, they, along with in-

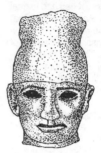

Taharqa was typical of the Nubian (Kushite) kings who attempted to reintroduce classical pharaonic civilization into Egypt during the Late Period.

SUSAN MARSHALL

dependent princedoms in the delta, mistakenly meddled in the Middle East. Assyria had become the new superpower, and Egyptian agents fomented revolt against the growing empire. To rid themselves of the Egyptians' troublesome influence, the Assyrians marched on the delta, where the petty princedoms, faced with the most powerful army of their world, immediately capitulated. The Kushites prudently withdrew to the south and the Assyrians, secure in their victory, returned to their conquest of the Middle East.

Meanwhile, the Kushites under Shabaka wasted little time conquering the delta and regaining Egypt. Ignoring their earlier rout, they again stirred up trouble for the eastern empire. Exasperated, the Assyrians sacked Memphis, then Thebes. The Kushites, their lesson learned at last, retreated to their own domains, where they became progressively more African.

With the retreat of the Kushites, the Assyrian general Assurbanipal—who by now should have known better—withdrew from Egypt, leaving the delta in charge of Psamtik, prince of Sais, who swore loyalty to the foreigner. However, once the sun no longer glinted off the iron armor of Assyrian troops, the Egyptian prince declared himself pharaoh, founding the 26th (Saite) Dynasty.

LATE PERIOD (664-30 B.C.)

The Late Period marks the final years that Egypt functioned as an independent political entity. Under pressure from the major civilizations of the eastern Mediterranean and the Near East, the Egyptians adapted their institutions and technology to face the recurrent challenges to their cultural identity. To keep pace militarily, the Saite kings introduced the ramming war-galley, relied on foreign mercenaries, and joined foreign alliances. Religion too evolved, with animal worship, the cult of Isis, and ancestor-cults becoming popular. By the end of the period, Egyptians realized that kings were not always righteous allies of the gods, but that they often acted in ways that violated Ma'at. This conviction struck a deadly blow at the ideological power base of the god-king, the keystone of Egyptian civilization.

Saites

Kings of the 26th Dynasty created the last great age of pharaonic civilization. Psamtik I came to the throne of the small kingdom of Sais, and while the Assyrians were busy with the Persians, he subdued rival delta princes with his army of Greek, Lydian, and Carian mercenaries. To control Upper Egypt he gained the loyalty of the Theban mayor, Mentuemhat, appointed loyalists to key positions, and demanded that the divine votaress of Amun adopt his daughter. By the time of his death in 610 B.C., Psamtik had consolidated the kingdom and Egypt rose once more as a great nation of the Middle East. The Saites embarked on commercial ventures and even, according to their records, dispatched an expedition to circumnavigate Africa. Corn and wool exports made Egypt the breadbasket of the ancient world and opened the country to the Mediterranean. Large numbers of Greeks and Jews began settling in Egypt, bringing yet more trade. The Saites gave the Greeks a site in the delta where they built their own city, Naucratis, and the Jews developed a similar colony, complete with a synagogue, at Elephantine. These concessions to foreigners angered the native Egyptians, who felt they were becoming second-class citizens. By the end of the period, this last indigenous dynasty seemed as oppressive as those preceding it.

The Persians

In 525 B.C., the Persians invaded Egypt, quickly overrunning the delta. Cambyses and his successor Darius (having learned from Assyria's mistakes) kept a tight rein on the country. These Persian kings adopted pharaonic regalia and engaged in building programs: Darius erected a temple to Amun at Kharga Oasis and completed the canal that connected the Nile to the Red Sea. But the Persians' repressive rule was never popular, and Egyptian rebellion continued, culminating in a brief period of native rule when Amyratacus of Sais liberated the country in 404.

The Warring Kings: Once they had driven out the Persians, these kings found their power shaky, with home rule marred by internal squabbles and sporadic Persian attempts to reannex the country. These pharaohs allied themselves with the Greeks and some rebellious Persian vassals or satraps. Persia, busy with problems at home, couldn't mount a serious campaign to bring the Egyptian satraps back into line. During the half century of uneasy peace snatched from the Persians, Egyptian kings undertook building and trading projects, but their reigns, as Aldred notes in *The Egyptians,* were "the last twitch of dying pharaonic Egypt, and it was only the embalmed corpse that then passed in turn to the Persian kings, the Greek Ptolemies, and the Roman emperors."

In 343 B.C., the Persians returned, the reigning pharaoh Nectanebo II fled to Nubia, and Egypt once more fell under Persian rule. But this second Persian period was as turbulent as it was brief, ending in 332, when Alexander the Great crushed Darius' forces at Issus and added the Persian Empire to his conquests.

PTOLEMAIC PERIOD

Alexander the Great stayed in Egypt only long enough to consult the oracle at Siwa Oasis, hear himself proclaimed son of Amun and pharaoh of Egypt, and design the city of Alexandria on the Mediterranean coast. With his death in 323 B.C., Alexander's generals divided his empire. Ptolemy took Egypt and in 306 declared himself pharaoh, establishing Egypt's last dynasty, the Ptolemaic.

Greek Ptolemies

Under these rulers, Alexandria became the cultural and intellectual center of the ancient world. The Ptolemies improved irrigation and drainage to reclaim cultivable land, introduced cotton and better wine-producing grapes, and increased foreign trade, making more luxury goods available. These kings, like the foreign rulers before them, adopted Egyptian royal trappings. They added Egypt's religion to their own, worshipping the gods of eternity, building temples, and being mummified and buried in hieroglyph-encrusted coffins. Retired Greek soldiers were granted land as reward for past services, and many took Egyptian wives.

In the main, though, the elite of this new Egypt looked to the west for their models rather than to the ancient, native past. Nevertheless, the pervasive Egyptian ideals and beliefs permeated the foreign communities in Egypt and from there spread throughout the Western world. For the masses of Egypt's *fallahin,* however, little changed, for they remained under-privileged and over-taxed. Privileges be-

SUSAN MARSHALL

Alexander the Great added Egypt to his conquests in 332 B.C., laying the foundation for Greek rule under his Macedonian general Ptolemy and his family.

longed to those who adopted Greek language and culture. The native population continued to be restless, and between 206 and 186, Upper Egypt openly rebelled. The drain on the treasury to suppress the revolts as well as reckless foreign policy and exhaustive family quarrels brought Egypt increasingly under the influence of Rome. With the last Ptolemy, Cleopatra VII, pharaonic Egypt was nearing her end.

Cleopatra

During the reign of this most famous of Egypt's queens, Rome was flexing her military muscle; by using shrewd politics and even shrewder feminism, Cleopatra kept Egypt out of Roman hands for nearly 20 years. Her fatal error was aligning herself with Mark Antony in his power struggle against Octavius. After their combined forces lost to Octavius at Actium, and knowing that Octavius intended to drag her through the streets of Rome behind his chariot, Cleopatra, so legend tells us, held an asp to her breast, and ended over three thousand years of pharaonic rule.

PHARAONIC RELIGION

Egyptian theology intertwined with politics and economics to create Egypt's civilization, and religious precepts were woven into the very fabric of Egyptians' lives. Although they believed in an ideal world unchanged from the time of creation, their religious practices underwent subtle changes over the centuries—shifts in emphasis, a waxing and waning of popular gods rather than upheavals in the underlying metaphysical and theological base.

THEOLOGY

Egyptian religion was grounded in Ma'at, a concept of universal order and balance. Originally the word may have meant "that which is straight," i.e., a rule or measure. The Egyptians, however, used the word in both a physical and moral sense to mean right, true, real, genuine, righteous, just, and steadfast. For example, *khesbet ma'at* was real lapis lazuli, not the imitation blue paste called faience. A man who was *ma'at* was upright and honest. Because of Ma'at the sun rose each morning in the east, traversed the sky, and set in the west. The goddess Ma'at was the personification of physical balance and moral law, a concept that formed the backbone of pharaonic philosophy. But more than that, belief in Ma'at pervaded every class of ancient Egypt and became a moral duty, a code of behavior befitting an Egyptian.

Religious Roots

The intense regionalism of protodynastic Egypt created strong ties to local gods—a plethora of fetishes, idols, and deified animals. Cult centers grew up within Neolithic villages and each had its own god/goddess and unique mythology. When conquered, these villages assimilated the deities and the rituals of their masters, and when the Two Lands became united, the country inherited a host of gods and diverse legends, customs, and rituals. Although Egyptians occasionally added new gods (such as the Greek Serapis) they discarded none. To the foreigners who encountered the Egyptian religion, it was an incomprehensible, contradictory, and many-faceted mystery—one that remained deeply rooted in the folk-experience of the people.

To simplify the chaos, Old Kingdom priests from several religious centers attempted to construct a more systematic dogma. To reduce the number of gods, they blended their identities. Horus, the hawk-god, was linked to the sun-god Re and at the same time became Horus, son of Osiris; because Horus was the gods' designated ruler of earth, he became inseparable from the divine yet human pharaoh. Hathor, cow to the sacred bull, became entangled with Nut (the sky), Sekhmet (the lioness), Isis (wife of Osiris and mother of Horus), and in the New Kingdom, Mut

BRUCE HANSEN

Ma'at, goddess of truth and judgment, symbolized the balance underlying the philosophical ideals of ancient Egypt.

(wife of Amun). These hybrid gods also maintained their own distinct identities. The Thebans, for example, worshipped their local Amun as god of the wind, but also paid him homage as the sun-god Amun-Re and as the god of fertility Amun-Min. Worship of national gods was the duty of the pharaoh and a series of priests to whom he delegated his powers. Meanwhile, commoners continued to pray to their personal ancestral gods, asking Bastet, the cat-goddess, for happiness or Taweret, the hippopotamus-deity, for protection in childbirth.

Imagery

Though often paradoxical to the Western mind, this shifting pantheon offered no conflict to the Egyptians, who believed that their gods could inhabit various cult statues and assume multiple names at whim. A god could also appear as several different animals, each a pictorial metaphor of a separate attribute. For instance, Thoth, royal recorder, god of the scribes, and personification of the moon, is identified with both the ibis and the baboon. Horus the hawk often carries the solar disk, surrounded by the uraeus snake, upon his beaked head, and later paintings show him as a hawk-headed man. Such fantastic combinations are symbolic expressions to be read as visual metaphors: thus Horus, who rules mankind, possesses the nurturing power of the sun, which sails daily across

BRUCE HANSEN

Horus the hawk-god assimilated many older gods as ancient Egyptian religion developed.

the sky on its hawk-like wings. Ancient Egyptians accepted such religious metaphors, whether painted or written, on their own terms, embracing their gestaltic entirety.

RITUAL

Egyptian rites have come down to us through hymns, prayers, or magical formulae, but many of these hieroglyphic texts are obscure, incomplete, or both. Since the ancient Egyptians left us no concise treatise on their religious beliefs or practices, Egyptologists must interpret these texts in light of the evidence uncovered by archaeology, a job akin to explaining Luther's Reformation by standing inside Chartres Cathedral and studying the liturgy of Catholic Mass.

The Priests

In ancient Egypt, the pharaoh provided food, shelter, and riches for the gods, who in return took up residence in cult images and showered the king—and through him humanity—with a safe land, abundant harvest, and eternal life. The pharaoh himself was the high priest of Egypt, required to perform the daily rituals in the hidden, holy sanctuaries of the temples where the statues of the gods stood. In practice, however, the king appointed proxies who through ritual became pharaoh and carried out the rites. These high priests (as emissaries of the king) would make sacrifices to the gods each morning and evening, offerings from lands the crown had given them for the support of their temples. The subordinate *web* priests handled the god's statue, ritual instruments, and cult objects, while lector priests, experts in sacred texts, ensured that the rites were carried out according to dogma. To maintain their ritual purity, priests were circumcised, shaved their bodies every other day, wore only linen garments and papyrus sandals, washed twice a day and twice a night, and could not eat fish or beans. State officials often held priestly rank or administered temple estates, and military men, on retirement, frequently became clergy. Local individuals rotated through temples, serving for several months as lay priests; wives of local dignitaries were chantresses in the temple choir, and priestesses sang and danced to entertain their god.

Daily Rites

Each morning, the high priest would break the seal on the sanctuary door, after which the clergy would remove the god's statue, the earthly abode of his spirit, wash and anoint it with fine oil, and dress the figure in clean vestments. While temple musicians gladdened their god's heart with song, the priests laid before him offerings selected from the lists on temple walls. When the principal god had absorbed what he wished from the offering, the priests gave the sacrifice to the lesser gods who inhabited the same temple, and afterward divided it among themselves.

Gods In Public

Normally the gods were only accessible to the priests, but on special occasions they appeared to their worshippers. Enthroned in portable shrines—scaled-down models of royal barges or barques—the gods were borne on the shoulders of their priests. During a public festival, the god would offer his blessing to his people, hear their petitions, and render judgments in litigation. The Egyptians believed that the god, by making his bearers move forward or backward, answered their questions yes or no. Perhaps these oracles allowed authorities to deliver fair verdicts where normal channels had failed.

Festivals

Gods also visited each other, traveling between their river temples via festival barques, accompanied by joyous merrymakers. Amun of Karnak, for example, called upon his counterpart Amun of Luxor during the festival of Opet. He also traveled once a year across the Nile to the mortuary temple of the reigning king during the Feast of the Valley. Horus of Idfu received Hathor of Dendera in the third month of summer during the Feast of the Beautiful Meeting. At the Festival of the New Year, priests carried cult statues to the temple roof so that the gods could drink in the first rays of the sun on New Year's Day. In addition, festivals of Osiris were popular throughout the country; the largest, similar to a medieval passion play, was held yearly at Abydos. These feasts, coupled with monthly or seasonal celebrations for regional gods or in honor of some great event (e.g., Ramesses III's victory over the Libyans in 1172 B.C.), provided Egyptians with welcome relief from their otherwise tedious labor.

MYTHOLOGY

Egyptian mythology has come down to us primarily through New Kingdom papyri. The tales, though sophisticated, articulate, and complex artistic creations, undoubtedly originated in the spoken folklore of the ancients. Like the Greek tales that followed them, Egyptian myths gave gods and goddesses human traits and passions, and in so doing made these deities not only appealing to ancient Egyptians but also to modern readers.

Creation

Central to Egyptian theology were the creation myths, and though each religious center had a slightly different version, all had much in common. At the First Time, there existed only a vast, dark, watery chaos—Nun. From this primordial ocean, a hillock arose, much as land appeared within the receding floodwaters of the Nile. The creative force was either Nun himself or an unseen, self-created god. This god then brought into being the air, the sky, the earth, and all the inhabitants thereof. The creative force was identified by each religious center as their own god: Atum of Heliopolis, Ptah of Memphis, Thoth of Hermopolis, and Amun of Thebes. Underlying this apparent simplicity, however, are continuous paradoxes. For example, Atum is said to be self-created, yet in other passages, he is the son of Nun. By the 5th Dynasty, Atum had been assimilated to Re, and the sun was worshipped as Atum-Re. But Re, the midday sun, had been born of Nut, who was the granddaughter of Atum. Even the high priests of Heliopolis couldn't make such circular mythology run in straight lines; mere laymen didn't even try.

The Ogdoad: One of the oldest versions of the creation myth appears in the doctrines of Hermopolis and centers upon four pairs of gods and goddesses: Nun/Naunet (water), Huh/Hauhet (eternity), Kuk/Kauket (darkness), and Kerh/Kerhet or alternatively, Amun/Amaunet (the unseen, the air/wind). These eight brought forth a Cosmic Egg from which the sun Re hatched and in turn fashioned the rest of the world.

The Great Cackler: In another version of the myth a celestial goose (the Great Cackler) laid the Cosmic Egg on the primordial mound, which rose from the waters of Chaos (the Sea of Two Knives). When the cult of Thoth invaded the area, the creation story accommodated him as the ibis that had laid the Cosmic Egg.

Other variations told of a lotus flower that rose from the Sea of the Two Knives and opened, bearing the divine child Re or, alternatively, the scarab beetle. In yet another explanation, Nut-Hathor, cow to Geb's bull, bore Re, "Bull of the Sun," and humans by extension were the "cattle of Re." At Elephantine, Egyptians believed the ram-potter Khnum formed mankind from the clay of the Nile, throwing both the individual and his spiritual double (*ka*) on his potter's wheel.

Atum of Heliopolis: The priests of Heliopolis attributed the creative force to their own god, Atum ("He Who Created Himself"), who emerged as a hillock from Nun. Alone, he united with his shadow or inseminated himself to bring forth his son Shu, god of air and embodiment of the life principle, and a daughter, Tefnut, goddess of moisture. This pair became the parents of Geb, the earth, and his sister/wife Nut, the sky. In turn, these grandchildren of Atum bore four offspring: Isis, Osiris, Nephthys, and Seth. Horus, the archetype of the pharaohs, was the son of Isis and Osiris. Though these last five gods may have originated at other religious centers, they were incorporated into the Heliopolian cosmology, and all nine gods formed the Greater Ennead.

Khnum fashioned an individual and his soul (ka) on his potter's wheel.

LOUISE FOOTE

Ptah of Memphis: The priests of Memphis, perhaps sensing political conflict with the sun cult just to the north at Heliopolis, claimed that Ptah, Patron of the Crafts, the Creator, the Great Artificer, was the original god of creation, the unseen, all-powerful Father who begot Atum by pronouncing his name. The latter then created the rest of the universe, as suggested by their northern neighbors. Thus Ptah's priests, in a theologically slick move, slipped Ptah to the head of the religious line.

The God-kings

Egyptians believed that Atum-Re ruled over the world he had created until he became old. The rule passed first to his son Shu, then to Geb. When Geb became too old to rule, Egypt was divided between Re's two great-grandsons, Osiris and Seth. Seth, unhappy with only half a kingdom, murdered his brother, hid the body, and usurped the crown. Isis, sister/widow of Osiris, searched the world until she found his body, at which time Seth again appeared, hacked his brother's body into pieces and scattered the remains. When Isis found the pieces, she bandaged him back together, creating the first mummy. With the magical help of Thoth, Anubis, and her sister Nephthys, Isis resurrected Osiris. He stayed on earth just long enough for Isis to conceive a son, then traveled to the netherworld, where he ruled as king and judge of the dead. Isis spent the next several years hiding herself and her child, Horus, from Seth.

The Contendings of Horus and Seth: Horus, when grown, learned of his father's death at the hands of his uncle and set out to avenge the murder. He first appeared before a court of gods to claim his throne. Seth was incensed and challenged Horus to justify his claim in combat. Seth, older and more cunning, nearly won but he lacked Horus's ally, his mother Isis, who used all her magic to ensure her son's succession to the throne. In spite of this help, however, Horus never gained a clear victory, and the gods decided to appeal to Osiris himself, who informed them in no uncertain terms that his son was the rightful heir. Seth protested, but Osiris ended the argument by pointing out that he, lord of the underworld, was the ultimate judge. Horus claimed his father's throne, and Seth had to be content to rule the deserts and mountains.

The Soul

The Egyptians had no equivalent to the modern concept of a soul but broke the personality into several components. The *ka,* for example, was the cosmic double born with a person, and when that person died, the *ka* lived on, residing in the tomb, where it inhabited the mummy, or lacking that, a statue of the deceased. Identified by its symbol of two upraised arms, the *ka,* the Egyptians believed, required food and drink for subsistence, and so they made elaborate provisions and offerings to it. The deceased's shadow was similar to our ghost, while his *ab,* the heart, represented the seat of intellect and conscience. The *ren,* or the deceased's name, was perhaps the most important of all the components, for without it inscribed in his tomb, an individual's entire spiritual being vanished forever.

BOB RACE

A man's ka was his double but it wore the raised hands to distinguish it from the corporeal body.

The *ba,* shown as a human-headed bird, symbolized the individual's general vitality, his dynamic spirit that could emerge to wander the earth and invade the realms of the living. The deceased's relatives would address letters and prayers to his *ba,* asking for help or imploring it to quit messing with mortal lives. The *bas,* the Egyptians believed, carried lanterns and these innumerable lights created the stars of the night sky.

The Judgment

Unlike the soul of the king, whose union with Osiris seemed assured, those of ordinary mortals had to be judged. The deceased first declared his innocence of wrongdoing to 72 gods of the underworld: "I have not killed; I have not added to the weight of the balance; I have not caused pain; I have not caused tears; I have not deprived cattle of their pasture; I have not held back water in its season. . . ." Then, led by Horus into the Hall of Truth, he watched the weighing of his heart (seat of his soul) against the feather of Ma'at. The scales, attended by Anubis, had to just balance or the soul would be devoured by Ammut, a monster who was part crocodile, part lion. The royal scribe Thoth recorded the results, and then Horus led the pure of heart to Osiris, who granted him eternal life.

The Netherworld

Egyptian literature identifies the kingdom of Osiris as Duat and speaks of it as lying beyond earth in a valley bisected by a river, the celestial Nile. Its dark confines, inhabited by the spirits of the dead, were lighted only when the sun-god passed through it on his barque during his nightly journey from his setting in the west to his rising in the east. Another picture of the netherworld shows the Fields of Yaru (reeds), where Egyptians expected to live a perfected form of their daily lives, sowing and harvesting barley and spelt that would grow to supernatural heights, hunting and fishing among the delta's marshes, and feasting at rich banquets.

Cult Of Osiris

With the social collapse of the First Intermediate Period, the landed gentry usurped the magic rituals and prayers previously reserved for pharaohs. By direct appeal to Osiris, they now made their own way to the bountiful Fields of Yaru. During the New Kingdom, Osirian beliefs flooded society, eventually reaching all but the lowest social orders. Any man if rich enough could support a mortuary cult, that included food for the *ka*, the proper burial rites, and magical prayer texts, crib sheets he would use to protect his soul on its hazardous journey to Duat.

LAND OF THE DEAD

To ensure eternal life, the deceased's relatives had to follow the ritual precedent set by Isis for Osiris; the same rituals were used for the funerals of both men and women. The body, attended by priests in the guise of Anubis and Thoth and guarded by priestesses of Isis and Nephthys, was put aboard a funeral barque and taken across the Nile to the western land of the dead. Once there, the priests mummified the body, patterning the ritual after Isis's original wrapping of Osiris. Then the coffin was transferred by sledge to the entrance of the tomb where priests, the deceased's son, or in the case of kings, his successor, placed a ceremonial adz to the mummy's lips and with ritual prayers, "opened his mouth," thereby ensuring the rebirth of his soul. The mummy was purified by anointing it with water, and at the next sunrise, the multifaceted soul was reborn.

Egyptians believed not only in their survival in Duat, but also in magical texts and incantations that could convert models, statues, and pictures into real objects. This belief, coupled with the need for a spiritual house for the *ka*, led the Egyptians to try to preserve the body, entomb it in a "house of eternity," and equip it with models and pictures that magically provided the deceased's every wish.

From predynastic times, burials became more complex and grave goods increased in number and variety, often including items the deceased had used in life: clothes, chairs, beds, jewelry, weapons, and tools. Egyptians also made items especially for tombs; models of serving dishes or tiny sides of beef would, by magic incantations, become corporeal. Small servant figures, often of wood, made the deceased's bread or beer and cared for his possessions, while doll-like concubines accompanied men to their graves. With time, statuettes were grouped into miniature scenes of cattle counting, fishing, spinning and weaving flax, etc.; some tombs even contained diminutive armies. Such magical substitutes were intended to serve the deceased in Duat.

Shabti Figures

A special class of statuette, the *shabti* figure was originally intended to provide a substitute residence for the *ka*. The earliest of these mummiform figures were made of wax or wood and often had their own small coffins. By New Kingdom times, however, the concept of a substitute body had been expanded to include the idea of a substitute laborer. The figures were now often carved of stone and in addition to the deceased's name, they had directions written on them: if the deceased was called to manual labor such as cutting canals, rebuilding dykes, or cultivating fields, the *shabti* was to answer, "Here

JAN KIRK

The deceased's heart was weighed on the scales of justice by Anubis against the feather of Ma'at. Ibis-headed Thoth recorded the verdict: if the heart failed the test, it was fed to the lion-monster.

am I." In order to do this work, the figures carried tools: hoes, baskets, and mattocks. Glazed figures appeared in the 18th Dynasty and by the end of the New Kingdom were common. Over time, increasing numbers of *shabtis* accompanied burials—ultimately a figure for each day of the year. Of course, such large crews needed supervisors, and these too were provided—one for every ten workers. Called *ushabtis* during the Late Period, these mummiform figures continued to be included in burials until the end of the dynastic period.

Magical Walls

More secure than models, however, were the scenes carved on the walls of the tomb, for the workers and objects painted there were nonportable and enduring. Carvings included games, tools, weights, measures, looms, furniture, and toilet objects—replacements for original equipment that might decay or be stolen. Scenes not only depict rows of offering bearers, but also the actual harvesting of the goods. Pairs of paintings show the deceased hunting wild birds in the marsh with a throwing stick as well as one that shows him fishing with a spear from a papyrus skiff. Additional panels depict estate workers fishing with nets and trapping birds with a clapnet. Tableaux involving the estate often included the manor house with its owner ensconced in his office conducting daily business. Outside the manor, carpenters and jewelers ply their trades while field hands plow Nile loam and reap its harvest. Cows mate, calve, and are slaughtered in an endless cycle of production for the deceased.

Canopic Jars

Erroneously named by the Greeks after the delta town of Canopus, these sets of four jars held the liver, lungs, stomach, and intestines of the deceased. Although occasionally the jars were mummiform (Tut's), the most common had stoppers decorated with the heads of the four sons of Horus: Imsety, Hapi, Duamutef, and Qebsennuef. These four deities guarded the internal organs removed from the body during mummification. Man-headed Imsety held the liver; ape-headed Hapi, the lungs; jackal-headed Duamutef, the stomach; and the falcon-headed Qebsennuef, the intestines. As

guardians of the four cardinal directions, these figures also appear on bricks inserted into the corners of the tomb, or in paintings (either with human or animal heads) standing on a lotus blossom.

Amulets

Amulets, small figures of gods or animals, protected both the living and the dead. Of mummy amulets, the most important was the heart scarab, placed on the breast where it exhorted the heart to not act as a hostile witness against the deceased during his judgment. The Eye of Horus, the *wedjat*, symbol of Re's power, protected from the evil eye; a pair included on the sarcophagus let the deceased see into eternity. The *djed*-pillar was a prehistoric fetish not yet well explained, but whatever its exact symbolism, it was closely linked with regeneration of life. The *ankh* symbolized divine, eternal existence, and as such the gods often held it to the king's nostrils, giving him "breath of life." Because of its cruciform shape, the Copts adopted it as their *crux ansata*. A similar amulet, the *tet* or knot of Isis, brought the wearer, alive or dead, the magical protection of the goddess. The *sa* was also a symbol of protection, representing a herdsman's rolled-up shelter of papyrus. The *was*-scepter, placed in the tomb to ensure divine prosperity, contained the life-giving power of its canine protective spirit.

Coffins

Early Egyptians buried their dead wrapped in skins or reed mats, but by late predynastic times they began using wicker baskets. In the Archaic Period, they interred bodies in reed coffins, which, in the Old Kingdom, evolved into simple rectangular chests. Made from large planks of imported wood, the coffins carried painted decoration: a pair of *wedjat* eyes and designs in imitation of the decorative reed matting early Egyptians had hung on their walls. To protect the bodies, these simple boxes were sealed inside large stone sarcophagi. During the First Intermediate Period, coffins became more elaborate and decoration included magical texts and spells the deceased would need in Duat.

By the 12th Dynasty, embalmers were making masks of linen and gesso to reproduce the features of the deceased, and these masks, lengthened with decorated breastplates, evolved into anthropoid coffins resembling the mummy. The outsides of these coffins were painted to imitate the jewels and finery the dead wore to meet Osiris. Not content with the increasing ornamentation, Egyptians ultimately enclosed the body in several such coffins, like a nested set of dolls. As designs became more elaborate, many of the coffins were covered with feathered textures representing the protective wings of Isis. Molded plaster and linen gave way to wood, and in the case of Tutankhamun, gold inlaid with carnelian and lapis lazuli. These coffins were set within stone sarcophagi, and in the Late Period, these sarcophagi themselves became mummiform.

Mummification

In predynastic burials, the body, protected only by skins or a reed mat, was directly interred in a shallow pit. The hot, dry sand desiccated the corpse, preserving the skin and hair. Such well-preserved corpses, if accidentally uncovered, may have led to the idea of mummification. However, as the tombs of royalty became deeper and more elaborate and the bodies were cut off from the drying sand, they quickly decomposed. In an attempt to preserve them, early priests dried the bodies in natron, a naturally occurring sodium compound. During the Archaic Period, embalmers swathed the body with close-fitting bandages, recreating its contours. They wrapped the limbs individually and protected the nails with gold covers; they molded breasts, genitalia, and facial features in gum-impregnated bandages, and highlighted the details with paint. In an attempt to improve preservation, Old Kingdom embalmers removed the viscera from the body through a slit in the left side, preserved them separately, and then wrapped the corpse in resin-soaked linen.

New Kingdom: By the New Kingdom, the embalmers' art had reached its pinnacle, and Egyptian undertakers offered three classes of mummification. In the lower-priced procedures, the internal organs were either dissolved with anal injections of oils and spices or the body was merely washed and anointed before being returned to the family. By contrast, in the most expensive process embalmers removed the brain as well as the viscera and packed the corpse in natron for about 40 days. When the body had dried, embalmers washed it with palm wine and crushed incense, packed the skull with resin-soaked linen, and reproduced the lifelike contours of the body by subcutaneous packing of sawdust, butter, linen, and/or mud, mixed with myrrh, cassia, and other spices. Finally, they inserted artificial eyes into the empty sockets, augmented the deceased's natural hair with fake tresses, and painted the face (or often the entire body) in ocher—red for men and yellow for women. The body was again washed and then wrapped in fine, gum-coated linen, and the organs were placed in four separate canopic jars.

Late Mummies: Following the New Kingdom, craftsmanship in general declined, and the art of mummification was no exception. Beginning with the 22nd Dynasty, priests paid more attention to the external appearance of the mummy than to internal preservation. To retard decomposition, they poured molten resin into the skull and body cavity, often embalming maggots and beetles feeding off the corpse. The hot resin also turned the skin of the mummies of this period black, a condition that, during the Victorian period, led to their being ground up and sold throughout the world as magical potions.

Tutankhamun's gold mask marks the care and wealth lavished on the king's funerary equipment.

By the Ptolemaic age, mummification had become a commercial enterprise, many of its religious connections lost. Outer bandages, often elaborately pleated in geometrical patterns, were interspersed with gilded studs. Three separate pieces of painted cartonnage made from glue and waste-paper shrouded the head and shoulders, chest, and feet. In Roman times, wooden portraits painted during the deceased's lifetime and hung in his house were cut to size and incorporated into the wrappings. The practice of mummification continued even into the Christian era, but since religious beliefs no longer required the likeness of the deceased to be preserved, the treatment of the body was superficial. With the Muslim invasion of Egypt, mummification ceased.

AMULET SIGNS

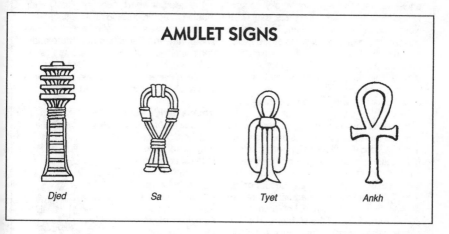

Djed   *Sa*   *Tyet*   *Ankh*

GODS AND GODDESSES

Egypt's gods fell into two types: those who rose to national prominence, and local gods to which the *fallahin* addressed their prayers and petitions. The national gods were generally cosmic deities—often anthropomorphic—representing wind, earth, sky, or sun. Linked to multiple religious centers, they were worshipped by the pharaoh and his court. In contrast, the local gods, perhaps descendants of early tribal totems, were often depicted as animals. By the New Kingdom they had evolved into human-bodied, animal-headed creatures, although such beasts may have simply been drawings of priests masked to represent the god or goddess in ritual.

Some of the more popular gods were grouped into triads (a god, his goddess, and their child) and worshipped at regional centers. Most deities can be identified by their associated totems, but in some cases a single animal is associated with several gods. For example, the jackal/dog, in addition to representing Anubis, is the symbol of Duamutef (a son of Horus) and of the warrior god of Lycopolis, Wepwawet. Worshippers could identify human gods and goddesses by their headdresses until the Late Period, when religious iconography became increasingly confused.

Amun (a-MOON)
"The Unseen One," Amun was an obscure deity of Thebes until the Middle Kingdom, when the political power of the Theban pharaohs elevated him to national status. In the New Kingdom, he was identified with the goose (the Great Cackler) and Min (Amun-Min), a god of fertility. He also usurped the position of Montu, god of war, and became assimilated with the great sun-god as Amun-Re. In his ram-headed form (Auf-Re) he sailed through the Duat, giving renewed life to the souls of the dead. In short (according to Theban theology), Amun created all things, ordered time and the seasons, sailed over the heavens controlling the winds and the clouds, and sustained all life. He also appears as the shrouded, ithyphallic figure of Min, or more commonly as a human wearing ram's horns or a dual-feathered *atef* crown.

Anubis (a-NOO-bis)
This jackal or fox, the deity of embalming, was lord of the hallowed land; from either side of the tomb's entrance, he guarded the mummy from evil. Though he helped Isis restore Osiris to life, he was also harbinger of death. It

was he who weighed the dead souls against Ma'at's feather of truth. Anubis was depicted as a recumbent black canine, his large ears pricked alertly forward. Alternatively, he appeared in human form with a canine head.

Anukis
Goddess of the first cataract area, Anukis was wife of Khnum and mother of Satis and therefore a member of the Elephantine triad. A human goddess, she wore a high crown of feathers and held a tall papyrus scepter.

Apis
The sacred bull of Ptah, Apis resided at Memphis, where his godly spirit inhabited a black bull marked with a white triangle on its forehead and a crescent on its flank. When the Apis bull died, it was mummified and buried at

LOUISE FOOTE

the Serapeum at Saqqara, and priests searched for a new calf with sacred markings.

Apophis

A symbol of chaos, Apophis was the serpent demon threatening the sun during its journey

through Duat. Defeated by the powers of order, he was chained and transfixed with knives. The blood that gushed from his wounds dyed the evening and morning skies red.

Aton

The sun at its zenith, Aton sent strong, bright rays streaming down from his red disk to nourish the land, his life-giving beams ending in human hands. Aton was

embodied in the concept of Re until singled out from the other sun-gods by Akhenaten. Following the Amarna heresy, Aton retired once more into obscurity.

Atum (a-TOOM)

This sun-deity was the early god of Heliopolis. In the bud of a lotus flower, he rose from the chaos of Nun and created the gods. As Lord of the Two Lands he wore the double crown of Upper and Lower Egypt. After Re emerged as the embodiment of the creative powers of the sun, Atum became the setting sun and was often shown as an old man tottering toward the western horizon.

Wedjat: The single eye of Atum, the *wedjat* was symbol of the burning power of the sun. Mankind sprang from tears which fell from it. Used as an amulet, it offered protection from the evil eye and conferred upon the wearer vision and thus spiritual understanding. A pair of such eyes on coffins let the dead see into the spiritual world.

Bastet

This early dynastic cat-goddess of the delta was worshipped for her virility, strength, and agility. At first associated with the more violent Sekhmet, she slew the serpent Apophis nightly. Later, after her destructive powers had been assumed by the lion-headed Sekhmet, she became goddess of joy. The Libyans of the 22nd Dynasty adopted her when they made their capital in her home city of Bubastis. Here votive offerings of mummified cats were interred at a vast cemetery, and in the Late Period, her cult festivals were celebrated with processions of barges and orgiastic ceremonies.

Bes

Originally a lion-god, Bes is always shown full face and as a dwarf with round ears, his mane stylized into a decorative collar. At first protector of the royal family, he eventually ex-

tended his care to all Egyptians. He attended women in childbirth and watched over the newborn. His squat form appeared on marriage beds, mirror handles, perfume jars, and eventually on the pillows of mummies. He often played musical instruments and along with his role as protector, he was a god of good humor who entertained the other gods. In the Late Period, he was popularized by the Romans in his fighter (Aha) aspect as a god of war.

Buto (BOO-to)

Identified with Wadjet, the cobra-goddess Buto of the delta became the national goddess of Lower Egypt. Known as the papyrus-

BRUCE HANSEN

LOUISE FOOTE

BOB RACE

colored (green) one, she, along with Nekhbet (the vulture) of Upper Egypt, decorated the king's crown. Personification of the sun's burning heat, she was both the eye of the sun and the force of its terrible heat.

Geb
Son of Shu and god of the earth, Geb was married to his sister Nut, the sky. Re, displeased with their close embrace, ordered Shu (the air) to separate them. All three are usually shown together. Geb's green recumbent form, a symbol of vegetation, embodies the hills and valleys of the earth. Following the reign of his father, Geb ruled the world, establishing order and prosperity. When he was tired, he abdicated in favor of both Osiris and Seth, thereby triggering a prolonged feud between the brothers.

Hapi
God of the Nile and its flood, Hapi watered the meadows and the desert oases and brought the dew.

He lived in an island cavern near the first cataract of the Nile, below which the river arose from the netherworld in two great whirlpools. He is often shown as a pair of gods—one wearing the sedge of Lower Egypt, the other the lotus of Upper Egypt—unifying the country by tying the flowers stems together with the symbol of immortality. Shown with a green-blue body and a female breast indicating his fertility, this god is not to be confused with Hapi, the ape-headed son of Horus, deity of the canopic jars.

Hathor (HAT-hor)
Goddess of love and joy, Hathor was the universal-mother goddess. She gave birth to the sun-god and suckled Horus and his human representative, the reigning pharaoh. Daughter of Re and Nut, she was portrayed as a cow, and the sun disk flanked with horns formed her headdress. She is also often shown with a human face, her bovine ears framed by two large curls of human hair. This full-faced image of Hathor gave form to the musical

sistrum and later to the capitals of the columns found in her temples.

Horus
This falcon or hawk was the sky-god of the early Nile Valley dwellers. His eyes were the sun and the moon, and as lord of the sun and sky, his hawk head was surmounted by a sun disk encircled by a uraeus. Since Horus was also son of Osiris, he soon became confused with the sky-god and Horus therefore appears in both solar and Osirian myths.

Imhotep
The high priest of Heliopolis during the 3rd Dynasty, Imhotep was the keeper of knowledge.

Designer of Djoser's step pyramid, he was also a scholar, philosopher, author, and doctor. By New Kingdom times, he was being worshipped as a scribe and healer; the Greeks identified him with their own Asclepius.

Isis

Best known as the sister/wife of Osiris, she

became identified not only as the mother of the king, but also as the great mother-goddess. She helped Osiris civilize the world, instituted marriage, and taught women the domestic arts. In her character as enchantress, she restored Osiris to life and defended

Horus with her spells. Her magic could protect mortal children as well. In early times, she is shown with a throne on her headdress. She and her sister Nephthys were also often depicted as kites lamenting the deceased. After the New Kingdom she was often confused with Hathor and therefore appears frequently wearing cow's horns and the sun disk. Her cult, identified with mysterious rites in Ptolemaic times, eventually spread throughout the Roman world.

Khepri

The young, rising sun, Khepri came into existence *de novo,* a trait that caused Egyptians to liken him to the scarab beetle. A manifestation of Atum, he eventually became equated with Re. He rose each morning from the eastern hills, between the Lions of East and West, born from the womb of the sky-goddess Nut. Because of his daily rebirth, he also was linked to Osiris as a symbol of resurrection.

Khnum (kh-NOOM)

From ancient times, the ram-headed Khnum dwelt at the first cataract. On his potter's wheel, he threw both men and gods, each with their own *ka.* Although once a creator god, the ascendence of Amun-Re demoted Khnum to working under his orders. He appears with the horizontal, twisted horns of a sheep species that became extinct during the Middle Kingdom.

Khonsu

The "traveler," Khonsu crossed the night sky as the moon-god. Lord of truth, he gave oracles and cast spells over evil spirits. As the son of Amun and Mut, he became, like them, a source of fertility and growth, a giver of life, and he often accompanied Thoth as timekeeper. This third member of the Theban triad is often shown either as a young boy with his hair in the side-lock of youth or—as an echo of the Isis, Osiris, Horus triad—with the head of a hawk. The crescent moon surmounted by the disk of the full moon became his crown.

Ma'at

The goddess of truth and balance, Ma'at was brought into the world by Re to shed light in place of the darkness of chaos, bringing peace to the land. As the wife of Thoth, she was also crew member of the solar barque; her priests were

judges. Against her or her feather, the heart of the dead must balance.

BRUCE HANSEN

Mertseger
Mistress of the west, beloved of Him Who Makes Silence, this cobra-goddess ruled from the pyramid-shaped Peak of the West across the Nile from Thebes. Described as the lion of the summit, she pursued the sinful, punishing with illness and death those who failed to pay her respect.

Min
A god of fertility, Min was worshipped as a giver of sexual prowess. From his home in Coptos, he also protected the Eastern Desert (Wadi Hammamat) and the caravan routes to the Red Sea. He became increasingly popular in the New Kingdom and, identified with Amun-Re, presided over the orgiastic harvest festivals. An ithyphallic, bearded figure, he is enveloped in a mummy cloth and wears a double-feather crown with streamers down its back.

BRUCE HANSEN

Montu
This ancient southern god rose to national prominence during the 11th Dynasty when his local princes became kings. Originally a war god, this falcon-headed deity also became the soul of Re. With the rise of the New Kingdom, he was replaced at Thebes by Amun but retained his role as warrior god of the imperial pharaohs.

Mut (MOOT)
A predynastic vulture-goddess of Thebes, Mut became Divine Mother and during the New Kingdom was linked with Nekhbet as protectress of Upper Egypt. When Amun came to power in the 18th Dynasty, she was married to him, assimilating his earlier wife, Amaunet. Mother of Khonsu, this Mistress of Heaven wore a vulture headdress and a uraeus surmounted by the double crown of Upper and Lower Egypt.

Neith
Ancient huntress of the delta, or a warrior goddess, Neith was also known as the Great Goddess, mother of the gods. Although often called daughter of Re, she was also said to have borne him. Later, Egyptians identified her variously as the mother of Sobek, Isis, Horus, and Osiris, and during the 26th Dynasty, supported by hometown pharaohs, she gained national recognition as the goddess of weaving and protectress of canopic jars. She usually wore the red crown of Lower Egypt and carried a shield crossed with arrows, a symbol she could also wear as a crown.

Nekhbet
Vulture-goddess of al-Kab, Nekhbet early on came to represent Upper Egypt and along with Buto, decorated the pharaoh's crown. She usually appeared as a vulture or a woman with a vulture headdress.

Nephthys
Sister of Isis and wife of Seth (god of aridity), Nephthys had conceived no children. To become pregnant, she deceived Osiris, either by getting him drunk or by magically disguising herself as Isis; the result of their union was Anubis. Afraid of Seth, she fled to her sister; when Seth murdered his brother, she helped Isis find and revitalize his corpse.

Thus with protective wings hovering, she stands at the head of the deceased's coffin while Isis guards the foot. She appears much like her sister, but wears her own hieroglyph symbol upon her head.

Nun (NOON)

In his role as Chaos, the primordial waters that filled the original universe, Nun created the first god, who then created the world and all that inhabited it. His snake demons plagued the souls of the netherworld, and his great serpent of chaos, Apophis, barred Re's path through Duat and had to be slain each night so that the golden disk could rise between the Mountains of Dawn.

Nut (NOOT)

Sister/wife of Geb and goddess of the sky, Nut often was shown as a cow (opposite to Geb's bull) or as a woman who spanned the sky supporting herself on her fingers and toes. She is often held in this position by Shu, who stands above Geb. Each evening, Nut swallowed the setting sun, which traveled through her star-studded body to emerge from her womb at sunrise. Considered a symbol of resurrection, she often appeared in sarcophagi—the heaven from which the dead would arise.

Osiris

An ancient corn deity, Osiris—with Isis—civilized mankind by teaching agriculture. His fertility cult, based first in the delta, soon spread throughout the rest of the country. As a fertility god, his inevitable tie to death and rebirth linked him with burial rites and by the 5th Dynasty he had absorbed the funerary gods of Abydos. At first only pharaohs identified with him, but eventually his cult attracted all Egyptians. He is shown in mummy bandages, holding the royal crook and flail and wearing the *atef* crown.

Ptah

The creator-god of Memphis, Ptah originated in late predynastic times as the Great Craftsman. In his role of Divine Artificer, he was a skilled engineer, stonemason, metalworker, and artist. With the rise of the religious center at Memphis, he became the Great Creator who, with a word, brought the universe into being. However, this intellectual concept never appealed to mainstream Egyptian theology, and his cult was limited. Like most creator gods, he soon became linked with death and is shown with shaven head and cap, dressed in the close shroud of a mummy and carrying the *was*-scepter.

Re

The sun itself and the god of that sun, Re manifested himself in multiple forms: the beetle Khepri (the rising sun), the hawk-headed Re-Herakhty ("Horus of the Horizon"), the disk Aton (the midday sun), and Atum (the setting sun). In his royal barque, he rose each morning in the east, traversed the sky, and in the evening disappeared into the western Land of the Dead, where during the night he sailed the celestial Nile through Duat, overcoming Chaos to emerge once more in triumphant sunrise. This westward journey soon linked Re to the netherworld and Osiris. He was also assimilated to Sobek (Sobek-Re) and Amun (Amun-Re). As Father of Man, he was the first pharaoh, establishing the Egyptian way of life. At Heliopolis, his Ben-Ben stone (a triangle atop a pedestal) became the object of cult worship, and the priests claimed that their temple, the House of the Ben-Ben, was built on the primordial hill that had arisen from Nun. Depending upon his aspect, Re assumed different forms: the beetle, the disk, or most commonly, a hawk (or hawk-headed man) surmounted by the sun disk encircled by an uraeus.

Sekhmet

The lioness, violent counterpart to Bastet, Sekhmet enforced the order of the world. As Re's eye, she could bring disease and death to mankind; as a fiery uraeus, she defended the king. The desert winds were her hot breath, and she not only controlled the henchmen of Seth but also chained the serpent Apophis. Although identified with Mut during the New Kingdom at Thebes, she was better known as Ptah's consort at Memphis.

Selket

Honored by the predynastic King Scorpion, this goddess of fertility was one of four protectresses of the sources of the Nile. She helped Isis perform the funerary rites for Osiris and protect the infant Horus. She eventually entered the netherworld, where she guarded the bound Apophis. Selket, the lady of the scorpion, was goddess of the west, and like Isis Nephthys, she often protected the dead with outstretched, winged arms.

BOB RACE

Serapis

Introduced by Ptolemy I, Serapis was a composite god created with attributes of Osiris and the Apis bull of Memphis. The Greeks also saw in this bull-god characteristics of their own gods Zeus, Dionysus, and Hades. Though his cult center was in Alexandria, his worship, like that of Isis, spread throughout the ancient world.

Seshat

Goddess of writing, Seshat recorded the regnal years allotted to the king, and as lady of the builders laid out the ground plans for new temples. She dressed in a panther skin, carried a palm leaf upon which she wrote, and wore a seven-pointed star surmounted by a bow.

Seth

Brother of Osiris, Seth was the Upper Egyptian counterpart to Horus of Lower Egypt, and together they were known as the Lords of the Two Lands. As one half of the Egyptians' dualistic worldview, this god of wind and storms was by no means comparable with the western Satan. To the Egyptians, good and evil were not similar to the Asian concepts of yin and yang; Ma'at was balance and chaos must therefore exist to complement order. Worship of Seth, without the connotations of modern devil-worship, continued throughout the entire pharaonic period. During the New Kingdom, he stood at the prow of Re's night boat to slay the monster snake. Considered chief god of the Hyksos, he was also patron of the warrior Ramesside kings (hence the name Seti). In the Late Period, he became lord of non-Egyptian lands and only then became a national enemy. Seth appears as a dog-like animal with a peculiar, down-curving snout, square ears, and a tail in the form of an arrow. He also is portrayed as a man with a Seth-animal head.

Shu (SHOO)

Son of Re and father of Geb and Nut, Shu was the air, or more esoterically, emptiness. Succeeding his father Re, he ruled earth until his son Geb succeeded him. Although occasionally shown with the head of a lion, he normally appeared as a human with a feather on his head. Most often he is shown lifting his daughter Nut from the recumbent Geb.

Sobek

This crocodile-deity was worshipped in the Fayyum, especially by Middle Kingdom rulers.

As national god, he became identified with Re as Sobek-Re, and with the hawk, Horus. Thus he was occasionally pictured as a hawk-headed crocodile; more commonly he was entirely reptilian, often with Amun's crown of ram's horns and feathers. Sobek remained a fearsome if beneficent deity, and into the Late Period a sacred crocodile, ears and feet decorated with precious stones and gold, lived and was worshipped at the lake in the Fayyum.

Taweret

This hippopotamus-deity of childbirth was also called Taurt, Apet, or Opet. She attended queens in royal labor and assisted at the daily rebirth of the sun. Bes often accompanied her, and amulets to both appear frequently on mummies as talismans to ensure rebirth. A pregnant hippo with pendant human breasts, she stands upright on lion paws, her crocodile tail hanging straight down her back. She leans on the magical *sa* knot of protection, often carries the ankh, and may wear Hathor's horns and solar disk.

Tefnut (tef-NOOT)

Wife/sister of Shu, she bore Geb and Nut. She was often equated with the moon, but eventually became more closely connected with Re and the uraeus.

Thoth

An ancient and complex deity, Thoth probably originated in the delta. To the Middle Egyptians at Hermopolis he was the demiurge who created the world, the Great Cackler who laid the Cosmic Egg. The Master of Words, and thus of magic, he was worshipped by scribes,

who claimed he invented mathematics, astronomy, and engineering. A searcher after truth, he defended Osiris, represented Horus before the tribunal of gods, and in later times, recorded the weighing of the deceased's heart in the Hall of Truth. He was Re's second eye, the white disk of the moon, which sailed across the night sky with the souls of the dead. He became reckoner of time and author of the sacred laws of Egypt. He appears as an ibis (or an ibis-headed man) or as a dog-headed baboon, wearing the moon crescent and disk.

LOUISE FOOTE

LOUISE FOOTE

BRUCE HANSEN

EGYPTIAN ART

In ancient Egypt, art was not created for beauty (though the Egyptians undoubtedly enjoyed this aspect) but in celebration of religion, for artists felt part of the same magical process that both formed the Egyptian universe and daily maintained it. In spite of these religious links, the arts produced secular spin-offs—paintings and fine furniture for palaces and wealthy homes. Once Egyptian artists had worked out formulas that satisfied them, they made only minor innovations, never escaping the reality of their art's function: the support of national religious beliefs. To that end, these arts followed rigid canons that dictated both the form and the style of Egyptian art. Nevertheless, its design and execution speak with an inner vision of reality.

Craftsmen

In ancient Egypt, painters and sculptors worked in communal studios with metalsmiths, joiners, and jewelers. Disciples of Ptah, they created their pieces under the guidance of a master craftsman, a mentor who was often familiar with several crafts under his direction. Schools of artisans worked with infinite patience and care, their incredible skill born of long years of rigorous apprenticeship. For larger pieces, tasks were divided; on reliefs, for instance, the outlining, carving, and painting were each done by separate craftsmen. On stone colossi, teams of workers spread out over the entire figure, individuals carving their own portion of the piece; so closely attuned to each other were these craftsmen that the final sculpture looked as if it were molded by a single hand.

Much of Egypt's art, although created by committee and according to a rulebook, transcends such limitations. In spite of primitive tools and techniques, ancient Egyptian craftsmen created jewelry, furniture, leather goods, and stoneware to discriminating standards set by their wealthy clientele. Although provincial work rarely attained royal standards, and royal work itself declined during periods of unrest, the artisans of Egypt's cultural heights created a vast and outstanding collection of art.

Conventions

Egyptian motifs and formulae already appear in the designs of archaic mace heads and cosmetic pallets: the field divided into horizontal registers, the general use of space and the inclusion of hieroglyphs within the composition, differences in rank shown by differences in size, and the combined full-face and profile view of the human body. Old Kingdom artists divided their human figures into three roughly equal sections—the knee, the waist, and the hairline (preferred because crowns both varied in height and concealed the top of the head). With these guides, the craftsmen could produce different-sized drawings in correct proportions, and by the Middle Kingdom, the guidelines had evolved into true grids. Artists used these grids to both lay out and copy scenes, techniques still used by modern artists. During the Amarna period, the canon shifted, producing taller figures, and when artists at the end of the period reverted to the classical proportions, a transition period (apparent in Tut's tomb) produced short figures with larger than normal heads.

In sculpture, men sitting on a throne were shown with their hands flat on their thighs; if standing they advanced the left foot, while women stood with both feet together. Wives or consorts appeared to the left of their mates, and scribes sat cross-legged with papyri rolls spread on their laps. In block statues the sitter drew up his legs, crossed his arms on top of his knees, and enveloped himself in his cloak. However, such conventions were not stringently applied to depictions of the lower classes.

Most figures were drawn facing right, and in the case of nobles, this orientation enabled artists to aesthetically frame the figure with the staff and baton. However, drawing a mirror image was difficult because the staff and baton must be held in ritually correct hands, thereby creating awkward compositions. Ancient artists solved the problem by placing the staff, for example, in the ritually correct left hand, which was then mounted on a right arm.

Conventions Extended to Animals: Lizards were drawn from above while crocodiles appeared in profile, a distinction perhaps rooted in size. No such claim can be made for bees (drawn in profile) and flies (from above); here the difference was pure convention. Food piled upon tables is shown stacked vertically above the surface, which itself might be tipped so the viewer can see the entire top. Contents of boxes were drawn above the sides, often appearing to hang from the lid, but in some cases, boxes and pots appear transparent in order to show their contents. All these conventions attempted to depict an object in its most recognizable form and thus to capture its essence.

Perspective

Like all artists, the Egyptians wrestled with the difficulty of rendering three-dimensional forms in two planes. Classical Western artists developed perspective—a series of tricks to fool the eye and make the viewer believe an object exists in three-dimensional space. The Egyptians, on the other hand, chose to show the object not as it appeared to the eye, but as they knew it to be. For their formal royal and religious art, Egyptian artists chose to draw the body in profile while rendering the crown, eye, shoulders, breast, and occasionally the waist and tunic, in front view and then superimposing them on the profile figure. Feet always appeared in profile, big toe toward the observer and exhibiting its full length. Such composites created easily recognizable, unmistakable forms. The most remarkable aspect of Egyptian drawing is that these pasted-together figures work artistically.

Painting

Most paintings were created directly on stone or, when the stone was unsuitable, on a thick coating of straw and mud plastered with gypsum. Master artists, working first on gesso-coated boards or pottery shards, sketched their designs and overlaid them with grids. To transfer the design, craftsmen stretched strings coated in wet paint across the wall and by snapping them, created a large base grid. They then blocked in the scenes and decorations as they appeared on the original sketch, the master correcting the shapes. In figures on royal tombs and in temples, the most important figures (king and gods) were drawn by the master draftsman himself in sweeping, sure strokes. Painters filled the outlines with broad masses of color, then once more the master refined the figures, adding detail and sharpening the contours. Only in the post-Amarna period did artists experiment with shading, although artists of all periods delighted in delicate texture, creating life-like fur, feathers, wood grain, veined stone, and polychrome glass.

Pigments

Egyptian artists created their colors from naturally occurring irons, ochers, azurites, malachite, and carbon. These materials gave them a limited palette of red, yellow, blue, green, and black, which they mixed with white (gypsum or lime) to lighten colors as well as make them more opaque. Blue, in ancient times as today, tended to shift color and fade, but Egyptians developed a pigment that held its color well; called Egyptian blue, it was prized by artists throughout the ancient world. Less successful was the green they made from copper salts, which often faded to a rusty color. Artists also tried plumbago for black, but this pigment tended to separate from its carrier and fall off the walls, leaving figures with pale straw-colored hair or wigs rather than the traditional black. Painters dissolved their pigments in a water-soluble gum and applied them with reed brushes. These pigments were applied to dry, not wet, walls; thus ancient Egyptian painting, though often mis-labeled fresco, was simple tempera. With skillful juxtaposition of flat colors from a limited palette, they created vibrant visual designs.

Relief

Egyptian artists carved two types of relief: raised bas-relief and sunk relief *en creux*. In bas-relief, craftsmen cut away the entire background, leaving the figures and inscriptions raised against the field. In the second method, they incised the figures' outlines into the background and then modeled the subject within these contours. In a third, bastard-type relief, they cut figures away from their background as in the bas-relief, but as the carver moved away from the figure, he decreased the depth, grading the cut into the original level of the stone and giving the appearance of true bas-relief. Artists either painted the reliefs directly on fine quality limestone or, in the case of softer stone, first coated it with gesso to give a smooth, white surface for the pigments.

Sculpture

By early dynastic periods, sculpture in the round was well developed. With flint adzes and chisels, sculptors carved bone, ivory, and wood into votive forms that already had an Egyptian feel. By the 3rd Dynasty, artists were working in hard stone with copper tools, ground emery, and stone hammers. Their figures faced forward, and even if the left foot was advanced, the sculpture's balance remained aligned with a severe, vertical bisecting line. The bodies neither leaned nor twisted; their rigidity proclaimed that their artists had hewn them from stone blocks rather than from softer materials. Nevertheless, the masters of Egyptian sculpture were able to coax remarkable plasticity from this recalcitrant medium.

To create statues, the sculptor first snapped tightened strings dipped in paint on at least three sides of the block, creating a grid. He then drew in the figure's left, right, and front views. With stone hammers and drills fed with an emery slurry, the craftsmen began pounding and drilling away the extraneous rock. As the guidelines were chipped away, the artist redrew them again and again, gradually integrating the three views. To save labor, much of the roughing out was done at the quarry; the lighter block was then shipped to its eventual site to be finished. The softer stones (limestone, sandstone, steatite, and serpentine) would yield to the woodworkers' tools—copper chisels, bow-drills, saws, and adzes. But hard stones were hell on copper and had to be worked with equally hard stone; only with the introduction of bronze could sculptors use metal tools.

Woodworking

Wood and ivory (elephant or hippo) statues appear in the oldest graves, but fine work became possible only after the introduction of copper tools in the early dynastic period. Egyptian craftsmen, in spite of the scarcity of native material, became premier woodworkers. Using only the small pieces of wood available, they became masters of joinery; in many of their larger statues, they carved limbs separately and doweled them into the body, hiding the joint with clothing or gesso.

Furniture design was elegant, and individually carved legs and bosses became miniature works of art. Inlay, including both wood and ivory, although known from the early dynastic periods onward, was perfected by New Kingdom artists. Perhaps the apex of the carpenter's technical skills was demonstrated in the chariots he built with small pieces of different types of wood bound together to give strength and flexibility— a concept lost until the development of the American buggy late in the 19th century.

Metalworking

Ore-smelting techniques were introduced into Egypt before the dynastic period, but only small quantities of metal cast were available. Nevertheless, metalworkers made needles and borers, hammered native copper into weapons, and drilled gold and iron beads to string as jewelry. Although copper figures (sheets hammered over wooden cores) appeared in the Old Kingdom, only in the Middle Kingdom did craftsmen develop skill in casting metal. Using the lost-wax method, they molded figurines in solid gold, silver, and bronze, and by the New Kingdom sculptors were casting large statues in bronze around a clay core that remained within the piece.

Jewelry

Jewelry-making began with the Stone Age Egyptians, who strung decorative shells and stones into necklaces, bracelets, and girdles. Naqada cultures added gold, silver, and beads of meteoric iron as well as beads of beaten copper, carved ivory, bone, mollusk, and tortoise shell. For the first time, glaze is applied to a composition base rather than a stone core to create faience. Other beads are drilled from such hard stones as chalcedony, agate, turquoise, carnelian, haematite, and obsidian. These early cultures imported lapis lazuli from Afghanistan, and by predynastic times ruling families were creating jeweled badges. During the Old Kingdom, the rich wore anklets, bracelets, and necklaces made with multiple strings of tiny beads of differing shapes, often separated by gold spacers. To prevent slippage, the heavy collars were balanced by weighted counterpoises that hung down the wearer's back. In short, Old Kingdom jewelry, like much of its art, was massive, serving as costly status symbols for royalty.

With the rise of the Middle Kingdom, jewelry-making reached its peak. Ornaments became lighter, more delicate and refined. Blessed with an effective sense of design, Middle Kingdom jewelers coupled impeccable taste and a complete mastery of technique to successfully combine precious metals and semiprecious stones. Working for temple estates, kings, and the powerful middle class, Egyptian jewelers created hair ornaments and crowns, colorful necklaces, bracelets, and girdles. Often they mixed stones with balls, shells, or large decorative beads, all cast of gold. For the poorer patron or for the dead, they often substituted cheaper materials, but their craft never faltered.

Ceramics

The predynastic pottery made from Nile mud was simple yet elegant, delicately thin and well balanced. The original black-topped, polished red ware gave way to decorated pots and these designs, transferred to other media, occupied Egyptian artists throughout the pharaonic period. By the 1st Dynasty, however, imported pottery supplanted the native ware for elegant tables. The only exception to the utilitarian bent for pottery was during the middle of the 18th Dynasty, when potters painted buff-colored clay in blue designs, picking out details in red and black.

Although Egyptians used clay extensively for both bricks and pottery, they made few terra-cotta figures—most commonly, the crude predynastic female models with upraised arms. The only other statues, apart from animals,

were figurines of women or bound captives that may have been used in magical fertility rituals or to control enemies. However, Egyptians did make statuettes of faience (finely ground quartz or rock crystal dampened with a weak solution of natron or salt and heated, which produced a coherent if friable mass amenable to being worked with the fingers or cast in a mold). These figures were then glazed with a copper-alkaline glaze to give them their typical blue color. Similar to ancient glass, Egyptian glazes also covered early pottery, decorative tiles, faience plates and cups, and in the Late Period, large numbers of molded *shabtis*.

Glass

Possibly because of its intractable nature and fragility, glass was not used extensively until the 18th Dynasty. Workers melted quartz sand, natron, and a coloring agent (often copper or malachite—clear glass was not made by the ancients) in a clay crucible. They designed a core in the shape of the vessel on the end of a rod and dipped it into the molten glass. A few swirls in the mixture yielded an irregular, bubble-filled vessel. For decoration, the glassmaker could pinch out a spout or add a handle. Multicolored designs were created by winding thin glass rods of different colors around the still-warm vessel. By drawing a sharp instrument across this semiviscous surface, the craftsman created bands, loops, or chevrons. Glassblowing was not introduced until Ptolemaic times.

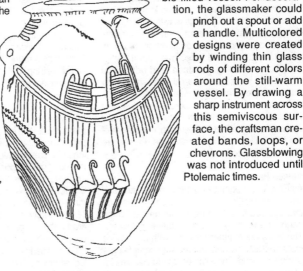

JAN KIRK

Motifs, like this boat with banks of oars and shelters on the deck from a predynastic pot, soon spread to the walls of temples and tombs.

EGYPTIAN ARCHITECTURE

Architects built massive vaults, safe houses for the deceased's *ka,* and raised glorious temples as homes for the gods. These eternal buildings were decorated with carvings, paintings of scenes, and texts designed to magically supply goods for the afterlife, as well as prayers and charms to ensure safe passage to Duat, or sacrifices and rituals to appease the gods.

Early Buildings

Egypt's benign climate required only protection from the sun, and her early peoples built crude shelters of whatever was handy: loose frameworks of branches covered with skins or mats woven from rushes or grass. Neolithic settlers lived in houses of Nile mud. For this wattle-and-daub construction, they plastered mud against vertical reeds braced by bundles of rushes lashed horizontally across the wall. Flat roofs provided extra living space, their palm log rafters supported by tree trunks and covered with woven mats topped with mud. To keep soft, pithy palm columns from splitting under their load, builders wrapped the tops of the trunks with cording, and the splayed fronds created a primitive capital. They also bound tall, sturdy papyrus into similar columns. Early in the dynastic period, Egyptians began making sun-dried mud bricks and used them as main structural elements. They framed windows and doors with wooden sashes and screened them with decorative mats, which housewives rolled up like shades. Such materials were eminently suited for the warm, dry climate of the Nile Valley, and modern village houses are often similarly constructed.

Palace Facade

As Egyptians began using brick, they buttressed the exterior walls of royal palaces with bastions that evolved into a series of dummy entrance panels flanked by square, projecting towers. The walls were either covered with decorative mats or plastered and painted with complex geometric designs. This style of facade became increasingly popular and was applied to tomb walls, stone sarcophagi, wooden coffins, funerary stelae, and the panels of "false doors."

Stonework

Since early Egyptians had perfected techniques for hollowing out and sculpting vases, plates, and statues, they were soon able to substitute stone for the less durable mud brick and lumber. They used stone for tombs, mortuary complexes, and temples because these buildings were to last for eternity. The architecture of these structures, however, remained grounded in designs suitable for mud-brick, wood, woven matting, and papyrus-stem columns, and these original materials dictated both form and decorative details. For example, to prevent their mud walls from toppling outward, early Egyptians allowed mud and wet plaster to slide toward the bottom of the wall, creating an inward slope or batter, a feature retained long after stone construction had made such precaution unnecessary. Walls built of plant stalks often had their tops tied together and these bundles were stylized into the *kheker* frieze, which regularly adorned the tops of interior walls. These bundled reeds also gave rise to the cavetto (concave) cornice, which gracefully bridges the area between the top of the supporting wall and the roof of classical pharaonic buildings. The walls themselves were framed by a round torus molding, the remnants of reed stringers lashed together with a crisscrossed lacing.

Columns

Likewise, early columns clearly imitated their plant models. The stonemasons who carved palm-tree columns reproduced the rope bindings and created tall, slender capitals of curving fronds. They also imitated lotus and papyrus, adopting both the flowers and buds as capitals. Gradually, both columns and capitals lost their three-dimensional modeling, and by late in the 18th Dynasty, the stylized surfaces were covered with inscriptions. By Ptolemaic times, composite capitals resembled bouquets of papyrus, lotus, and sedge with sprays of wheat and grapes tucked among the leaves, creating an artistic, if artificial, design. Hathor or sistrum capitals consisted of four full-faced portraits of Hathor, her coiled curls tucked behind her bovine ears. The

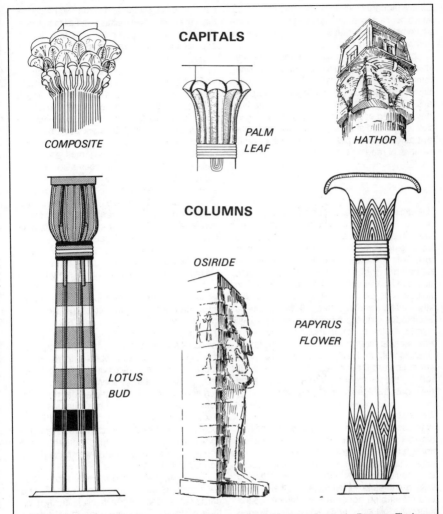

CAPITALS

COMPOSITE

PALM LEAF

HATHOR

COLUMNS

OSIRIDE

LOTUS BUD

PAPYRUS FLOWER

Egyptian architects used two types of columns: the rounded plant type, in which the capitals could be either buds or full flowers, and the square type, which normally had either a Hathor capital or an integral Osiride statue. From top left, clockwise: Elegant **composite** *capitals marked the Greco-Roman period.* **Palm leaf:** *The fronds of the tree formed the distinctive capital.* **Hathor** *capitals are square, the head of the goddess with cow ears surmounted by a sistrum in the shape of a temple.* **Papyrus:** *The base of this column swells outward and is ringed with leaf-sheaths; the blossom of the papyrus is distinguished by the stout outer leaves of the umbel.* **Osiride** *columns contain mummiform figures of the kings as Osiris, usually standing in front of the column rather than bearing weight.* **Lotus:** *These columns had straight shafts and both the bud and flower bear petal and calyx leaves of the same length.*

abacus (square block to support the architrave) above her head was shaped like a miniature temple complete with uraeus, a design also used in Hathor's musical rattle, the sistrum.

Egyptian builders also used square pillars, often incorporating a colossal statue of the king, commonly depicted as Osiris. In some cases, architects shaved off the corners of square pillars, creating eight- and 16-sided forms that they grooved or fluted to add texture and give play to light and shadow. Yet another style, the tent pole, imitated poles that once supported awnings of reed matting or hide.

TOMBS

The earliest Egyptians buried their dead in shallow graves scooped out of the loose desert soil. Later, in an attempt to protect the bodies from scavenging animals, they deepened the graves and piled sand and stones over the top, creating a mound symbolic of the hillock that had emerged from Nun at the First Time. By late in the predynastic period, they sunk grave shafts, either brick-lined or revetted with wood, several feet into the ground and painted the walls with murals. As the covering mounds grew taller, they became more rectangular, and mud-brick retaining walls both defined the mound's shape and supported the increasing height of its fill. Today, these mounded tombs are called mastabas, the Arabic word for bench.

Mastabas

By the beginning of the 1st Dynasty, tombs had evolved into elaborate structures with multiple storage rooms (for grave goods) set into the superstructure, and increasingly complex subterranean burial chambers. Mud-brick retaining walls rose three to eight meters, and their arched tops resembled house roofs. Palace facade outer walls, plastered and painted, distinguished royal tombs. Smaller mastabas of nobles surrounded these tombs, and the entire complex was enclosed by a protecting wall.

Throughout the pyramid period, courtiers and wealthy families continued to be buried in mastabas. During the Old Kingdom, stone replaced the outer mud-brick shell of the tomb, and a chapel for the celebration of the funerary

cult appeared. By the end of the Old Kingdom, mastaba design had matured and all tombs contained a subterranean burial chamber, a rectangular superstructure, and a chapel.

Stelae

The inhabitants of early tombs were identified by round-topped stone slabs called stelae, which stood at the southeastern corner of the mastaba. Here descendants or their priests left offerings for the deceased at tables enclosed by small chapels. These chapels soon appeared as niches set into the corners of the tombs, and eventually evolved into large cult rooms built into the superstructures. The stela was also moved inside and boasted a portrait of the deceased seated before a table piled high with offerings of bread and beer. Lists of offerings and grave goods assured the dead an eternal supply of incense, oils, linen, cattle, and fowl.

False Doors

Mastabas were equipped with dummy portals through which the ba could reach the outside world. These doors, often topped by a rolled-up screen, were surrounded by ornate moldings designed as palace facade. Soon the offering-table scene was moved from the stela to the panel above this narrow door, and frequently a statue of the deceased appeared in front of the door as if he were striding out of the tomb. Gradually the size of the cult room expanded, incorporating the false doors of other family members buried in adjacent shafts. Statues could also inhabit a sealed chamber next to the cult room called the serdab, which was connected to it via a slit or window; through the serdab, the statue of the deceased could watch the rituals performed in his honor.

As the superstructure became more complex, builders used more interior stone, and artists carved decorations in relief directly upon their surfaces. The false door, still the focal point of the chapel, became increasingly elaborate, as inscriptions and designs filled the lintel and jambs, spilling outward to cover the walls and pillars of the entire chapel. As the tombs continued to grow, the courtyard expanded, and additional storage rooms were added, as were supplementary complexes for wives, daughters, and sons.

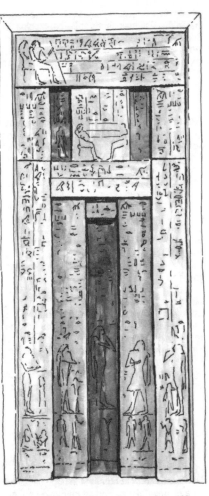

BOB RACE

False doors let the deceased communicate with the outside world.

Cliff Tombs

With the decentralization of the First Intermediate Period, nobles commonly excavated tombs in the cliff faces near their local homes. At first these tombs were similar to the mastabas, but gradually they imitated homes. In their quest to recreate their present abode in the afterlife, builders of the Middle Kingdom tombs at Beni Hassan (Middle Egypt) shipped out non-supporting lotus columns and false roof beams. They cut an exterior court and the entrance facade from the cliff itself. The living could reach these tombs via a steep causeway or a flight of stairs. Burial was in a single shaft set into the floor of the central room.

New Kingdom Tombs

By New Kingdom times, most tombs contained a court and entrance, a transverse entrance hall with scenes from the deceased's career and daily life, and a passage with funerary scenes leading to the chapel, which often had a recess for a statue or stela. The burial chamber was below, reached by a pit or tunnel from the chapel or, less frequently, the hall or court.

PYRAMIDS

Built over a period of nearly 1,000 years, pyramids line the west side of the Nile for 60 miles from Cairo to Middle Egypt. Although New Kingdom pharoahs abandoned building such structures, adopting a natural pyramid near Thebes, later Nubian dynasties revived the Old Kingdom traditions and architecture.

Beginning in the 3rd Dynasty with Djoser's complex at Saqqara, the architecture of royal burials and private tombs diverged. Imhotep built the step pyramid by stacking ever-smaller mastabas atop each other. At Meidum, King Huni built the first true pyramid, but now, its casing shed in jumbled masses at its foot, it shows only its rectangular core. The climax of pyramid building, however, occurred at Giza, where the kings of the 4th Dynasty erected three large stone structures, symbols of the primeval mound of creation.

Structure

Early pyramid builders cut burial chambers beneath the pyramid into the underlying bedrock. They hid the entrance to the access tunnel in the ground beyond the north face; only later did they locate both tunnels and burial chamber inside the structure. With futile hopes of foiling grave robbers, they blocked these tunnels with huge blocks of Aswan granite floated downriver.

Archaeologists are still unsure exactly how

the Giza pyramids were laid out and built, but some propose that the massive blocks were moved up earthen ramps that wound around the growing structures. Once this limestone core was built, the outside was sheathed in yet finer limestone from across the river, just south of modern Cairo. Workers would have then started from the top and worked back down, dismantling the ramp as they moved.

Mortuary Complex

The pyramid served as the central focus of a complex dedicated to the mortuary cult of the king. In keeping with earlier traditions, he built nearby mastabas for his nobles and often smaller subsidiary pyramids on the east or south side of his own tomb for his mother, wives, sisters, or daughters. A mortuary temple built against the pyramid's east face served as the focus of the king's mortuary cult. A covered causeway linked it to a valley temple that stood at the edge of the cultivation; the floodwaters came to the doors of this temple, enabling it to receive supplies. The king's priests and their retinue lived near the complex, often not far from the valley temple.

Later Pyramids

The tradition of burying the king under a pyramid continued throughout the Old Kingdom. However, by the 5th Dynasty, pyramids were no longer solid stone, but rubble-filled cores cased in limestone sheathing. This construction worked well until the Romans stripped the casing to burn for lime and the exposed rubble sloughed away, leaving only eroded hills.

The Middle Kingdom pyramids were built of mud brick, and though superficially like early earthen-filled pyramids, they were in fact built on limestone foundations, an engineering feat far more complex than designing the Old Kingdom stone models. These too have been stripped of their limestone casings, but much of the mud brick still remains, showing the skill with which they were constructed. Burial chambers increased in complexity, and entrances, apparently in an attempt to foil robbers, were relocated in the south side. New Kingdom kings, realizing the old pyramids were vulnerable, chose to hide their tombs under the pyramid-shaped mountain on the west bank across the Nile from Thebes. New Kingdom artists adopted the form for their

private graves, building small versions to guard the entrance to their tombs at Deir al-Medina. In Sudan, where Nubians prolonged Egyptian customs, native rulers constructed full-scale pyramids patterned after those of the Old Kingdom.

TEMPLES

Like tombs, the gods' temples were designed for eternity. Undoubtedly the first temples were houses like those predynastic people built for themselves but perhaps constructed by the best workers, with temple furnishings contributed by the most skillful carpenters and decorated with prized objects. The simplest form was rectangular with a single pitched roof. Closed-bud capitals on flower-stem columns supported a flaring cornice, a design endlessly reproduced in kiosks and small shrines. The god's house was distinguished from others by the banners flying in front of it, signifying that the god was at home.

Classical Temples

Later temples were designed as a paradigm to lead the visitor from the secular world into the dark, hidden mysteries of the gods, a trip backward in time to the primeval mound of creation. To do this, architects gradually lowered the ceilings, raised the floors, and decreased the light as rooms progressed toward the *naos,* the most sacred spot in the building. Access to the temple was guarded by a pair of gigantic pylons, their massive walls notched for flagpoles tipped in gold, that flew bright banners high above the pylon tops. This gateway opened into a courtyard surrounded on three sides by a colonnaded ambulatory, an area where, on festival days, the masses could congregate in hope of catching a glimpse of their god as he moved on the shoulders of his priests.

Beyond the courtyard lay the hypostyle ("upon columns") hall with its great pillars, lit by clerestory windows. The hypostyle hall represented the dense, primordial papyrus forests of the gods, and only Egypt's social elite could penetrate its semidarkness. At the end of the hall lay the chamber of the barque where the god, after he had been washed, anointed, and dressed, spent the day in the company of priests and high state

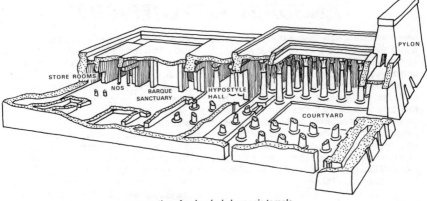

cross section of a classical pharaonic temple

officials. These rooms were only dimly lighted, although occasionally high windows were placed so that a shaft of light would strike the god. In the evening he retired even deeper into the temple, to the dark chapel complex, where only the pharaoh or the high priest could approach him. This secluded area was the god's home. Often two smaller chapels flanked the central niche of the main god (a manifestation of the Egyptians' preoccupation with triads), and behind this chapel complex stood storage chambers, which held treasure, archives, and grain, all part of the god's estates.

Ptolemaic Temples
In general, Ptolemaic temples followed the outlines of previous buildings. The only major change the Greeks made was moving rooftop rooms devoted to Osirian rituals of rebirth to a separate building called a *mamissi*, where the walls depicted not only Osiris' rebirth, but also that of the king. Like the temples before them, Ptolemaic buildings stood within walls and often had a sacred pool where the priests ritually bathed themselves. (Modern peasant women who are unable to conceive often sneak into old temple complexes at night to bathe in the holy water and pray to Isis for a child.) Outside the walls, great ceremonial ways lined with sphinxes led to the river and the holy quay. Often a chapel at the bank provided the god's shoulder-borne barque a resting place before he departed on the river in a real barge.

LANGUAGE AND LITERATURE

Like the visual arts, writing and literature supported religion and, as such, were tools of magic. Ptah created the world by uttering a word, and a person lived as long as his name existed; if it were erased, he vanished. So strong was the belief that written forms were imbued with life that in many tombs hieroglyphs in the shape of dangerous animals were either drawn incompletely or pierced by knives, thus rendering them harmless. Using their pictorial script, the Egyptians quickly moved their writing beyond primitive lists and labels and created elegant prayers, hymns, poems, and stories.

WRITING

Writing was not an Egyptian invention; the idea came from the earlier scripts of the Sumerians. Though the Egyptians took the concept of drawing pictures to represent objects or ideas, they quickly molded it to their own outlook, creating a formal script of carefully drawn animals and objects called hieroglyphs.

Hieroglyphs

These signs were of two types: ideograms and phonograms. Ideograms convey the meaning of a word by drawing its picture: a circle with a central dot, for example, means the sun. A phonogram takes the sound of one word (a part or the whole) and applies it to another, unrelated object; "sun" also becomes "son." The Egyptians also used hieroglyphs as a phonetic alphabet, not only as a single letter but also combinations of two letters and three letters: a quail chick hieroglyph was w, a pot represented nw, and a circle with a cross nwt. However, individual signs could be ambiguous, especially since Egyptians, like Arabs and Hebrews, wrote only the consonants. (Modern scholars conventionally add a short e to enable them to pronounce Egyptian words.) Therefore, the Egyptians added determinatives to their words, ideograms that made the meaning clear. To continue the idea in English, sn could mean "son," "sun," "sin," or "soon." Add a round circle and dot, the

word would be "sun," while the same letters followed with a human figure would mean "son." Not only did these signs stand for concrete objects, they could also stand for ideas: the sun could also mean day, shine, light, time, or to raise.

Hieratic

Hieroglyphs could be written left to right or right to left, vertically or horizontally. Readers began at the top and read into the faces of the animals or people. By the 3rd Dynasty, scribes using reed brushes softened and rounded hieroglyphs, creating a more fluid style, which, by the 11th Dynasty, became a distinctive cursive script called hieratic. Once written in vertical columns, it soon became predominantly horizontal (right to left), allowing the scribes to develop a true cursive hand. This script was used for both religious and secular purposes, but by the New Kingdom two distinct forms emerged; a formal, well-formed script for literary purposes and a more cursive type for business.

Writing Equipment

Stone carvers chiseled out formal hieroglyphs on tomb and temple walls, but scribes used reed brushes for most writing. They would cut rushes 15-25 cm long, trim the tip on a slant, and then chew the ends to break up the fibers. Reed pens, cut to a point and split at the top, only appeared with the Greeks in the 3rd century B.C. Scribes made inks by grinding carbon (black) and ocher (red), mixing each with a water-soluble gum, and letting them harden into cakes they could later dissolve with water on a brush, much like modern watercolor paints.

Papyrus

Although scribes wrote on linen, leather, vellum, limestone flakes, and pottery shards (the latter two called ostraca), the most famous writing material was papyrus. To make a writing surface, workers peeled the inner strips of the stalks from the plants, laid them in alternate layers at right angles and then pounded them until the juice from the fibers bonded the layers. The

HIEROGLYPHIC SIGNS

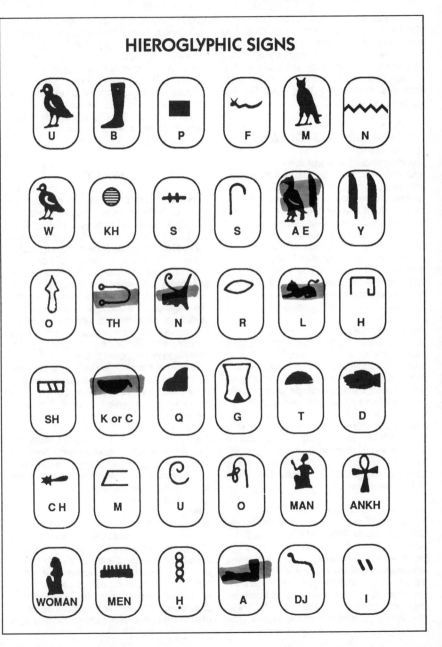

papyrus was then polished with a smooth stone, and it was ready to be inked. The scribes used the horizontal side (recto) first, then wrote on the side with the vertical strips (verso). If they needed more than the single sheet (about 40 by 50 cm), they glued multiple sheets together, forming a long roll; the Great Harris Papyrus measures 41 meters.

DECODING HIEROGLYPHS

Like most languages, Egyptian changed through time, and in addition to the classical hieroglyphs and hieratic, yet another script, demotic, emerged in the Late Period. Scribes used it for casual letters and business—contracts, lawsuits, and tax receipts—and for stories filled with vitality and color. Hieroglyphs, however, after a history of 3,500 years, died out in the 4th century A.D.; the Coptic Christians, though they continued to speak a late form of Egyptian, adapted the Greek alphabet. The knowledge of reading and writing in hieroglyphs was lost until early in the 19th century.

The Rosetta Stone

In 1799, while French soldiers were digging foundations for an addition to a fort at Rashid (Rosetta) near Alexandria, they uncovered a stone with inscriptions in Greek, hieroglyphs, and demotic, the only example of hieroglyphs coupled with a translation in a known language. The stone was conceded to the British in 1801 under the Treaty of Alexandria and shipped to the British Museum in 1802. For the next 20 years, attempts to decipher it made no headway although Thomas Young rightly deduced that the hieroglyphs within the rings (cartouches) were kings' names.

Jean Francois Champollion

To the young Frenchman Jean Francois Champollion, the decipherment of the Rosetta Stone became an obsession. As a linguist, he was well prepared for the task, being fluent in the classical languages as well as Hebrew and Coptic. Building on Young's work, he was able to decipher the name Ptolemy from the stone. He then used the four common letters, P,O,L, and T, to read Cleopatra's name in a cartouche on an obelisk

from Philae (now in London), thus confirming the alphabetic nature of the hieroglyphs. He continued to work with the symbols, using Coptic derivations whenever he could, to build up his vocabulary of signs and words. By 1823 he had published *Précis du Système Hièroglyphique*, which included not only royal names but lists of words, phrases, and even complete sentences. During his trip to Egypt (1822-24) he was able to read some of the inscriptions he was copying—the first man to do so in 1,400 years.

LITERATURE

Over the 3,000 years of pharaonic culture, three forms of the Egyptian language emerged: Old (c. 3100-2160 B.C.), Middle (c. 2160-1380 B.C.) and Late (c. 1380-715 B.C.). The Egyptians considered Middle Egyptian their classical language, but when Akhenaten moved Egypt's capital to al-Amarna, he decreed that business records and correspondence be written in Late Egyptian. During the New Kingdom, however, the vernacular language continued to change, and by Saite times it was called demotic. Nevertheless, Middle Egyptian remained the language for formal compositions and inscriptions, and scribes from the New Kingdom composed their literature (with the exception of the demotic tales of the Late and Greco-Roman periods) in a language as far removed from their vernacular as Old English is from ours. Using these languages, Egyptians created three types of literature: poetry, narrative prose, and an intermediate style with symmetrically structured sentences resembling the biblical proverbs. For excellent translations that capture much of the feel of Egypt's ancient writing, see Miriam Lichtheim's three volumes of *Ancient Egyptian Literature*.

Poetry

Egyptians wrote hymnic, lyric, didactic, and narrative poetry. To arouse the reader's emotions, Egyptian poets used parallel meanings and constructions, alliteration, and wordplay. Individual lines, whether a complete sentence or a part, contained a single unit of meaning. Although unrhymed, Egyptian poetry exploited the compact expressions and short sentences typical of all forms of Egyptian. Modern translators, to roughly approximate the original poems' verbal shape and rhythmic beat, strip sentences to the bone and make each line express a single idea.

Prayers And Hymns

One of Egypt's oldest literary forms, early prayers were simply a list of offerings for the *ka*. They later included requests for a good reception in the west, and during the New Kingdom, expectations for a blessed afterlife. The closely related hymns are nearly as old, the earliest addressing gods on behalf of the king. Soon they developed into elaborate and artful poems close in feel to the Bible's Book of Psalms. Cultic hymns, such as the cycle of Hathor, the hymns to Khnum, and the "Lamentations of Isis and Nephthys" were inscribed on temple walls. The most famous hymns, however, are those to the sun-god, Amun-Re, and his manifestation as Aton, the all-embracing creator-god. Although several hymns to him preceded the Amarna period, the most famous is Akhenaten's "Great Hymn to Aton," which has been extensively compared to the 24th Psalm. As the Egyptian religion became more democratic, hymns addressed gods who had become more personal. Introspection and humility crept into both prayers and hymns, and by the Late Period, a timelessness and quietude permeated the pagan beliefs that sustained the Egyptians throughout the upheavals of wars and foreign domination.

Songs

From earliest times, Egyptians sang. Tomb inscriptions above laborers give snatches of their working songs, similar to those sung by Egyptians today. Musicians using more sophisticated music entertained guests at formal dinners. The largest body of songs, however, comes from the cults. With harp accompaniment, the earliest songs praised death and the glorious world of the eternal. Later versions also lamented the passing of life, urging people to enjoy today: "Make holiday, / Do not weary of it! / Lo, none is allowed to take his goods with him, / Lo, none who departs comes back again!"

Epic narrative poetry appeared in the New Kingdom as part of larger histories, the *Battle of Kadesh* being the classic example. No longer just a brief song of triumph, the Kadesh poem sums up the story of the battle and itself is a new narrative form—the first epic poem.

Love Poems

Rich in elaborate wordplay and metaphors, love poems were a creation of the New Kingdom. Not the spontaneous outpourings of young lovers, they were crafted with deliberate, literary skill, giving them a freshness, immediacy, and universality. Sophisticated, but never sentimental or cloying, their sober strength displays the conceptual simplicity and terseness of language that were the hallmarks of ancient Egyptian literature.

Professional musicians, often blind, accompanied the singing at fancy parties and festivals.

JAN KIRK

Autobiography

As old as prayers, autobiographies grew from a simple list of titles—self-portraits that evolved into epitaphs. As an affirmation of moral worth, they blended the real with the ideal, stripping away the faulty and ephemeral. By the middle of the Old Kingdom, the terse and hesitant style gave way to a new loquacity and ability to capture formless experiences and ideas in words. The autobiographies of this period became works embodying narration, the catalogue of virtues, and elaborate prayers, including hymns to the gods and the king. These works often contained extensive historical information and continued to be written well into the Late Period.

Royal Inscriptions

In contrast to the autobiographies, kings' inscriptions centered on historical events. By the end of the Old Kingdom, they included brief notes of a single event, the yearly record of important events, and the king's decrees. By the New Kingdom, such monumental inscriptions blossomed into full and ornate expression, reinforcing the king's divinity and his role as leader in both war and the service of the gods.

Mortuary Texts

Despite developing skepticism during the Middle and New kingdoms, Egyptians still believed that their king's successful battle with the forces of darkness ensured their own spiritual existence, and they continued to decorate royal tombs with magic rituals for the pharaoh's journey through Duat. Originally such guides appeared in the Old Kingdom as the Pyramid Texts: a series of magic spells, prayers, and instructions engraved inside the pyramids of 5th Dynasty rulers. Ancient scribal priests blended these theological speculations, mythological allusions, and formulae for ritual performances into incantations that often reached a heightened intensity akin to poetry. During the Middle Kingdom, nobility usurped these guidelines and wrote them inside their coffins—thus creating the Coffin Texts.

Book Of The Dead

During the New Kingdom, Egyptians collected material from the Pyramid and Coffin texts, arranged it into chapters, and added vignettes, thereby creating the anthology of spells and prayers which collectively became known as the Book of the Dead. However, this "book" never emerged as a codified unit, but versions were compiled by the individuals who ordered them. The length and the quality of the copy varied in relation to the deceased's wealth and standing. While important chapters such as the judgment appeared in all editions, other less-popular segments only appear in isolated cases. Most versions were written on papyrus and contained drawings in colored ink. These rolls were buried with the deceased, either in his coffin or in a special container.

Book of What is in the Duat: The most famous of these texts, commonly referred to as the Book of the Dead, was known to the Egyptians as *What is in the Duat (Amduat)*. Also called *The Coming Forth by Day,* it decorated the walls of New Kingdom pharaohs' burial chambers. In the earliest versions, these texts spread across the walls as if they were gigantic, unrolled papyrus. Later, however, the work became more artistic, resembling other tomb decorations.

This book is one of several that describe the voyage of the sun-god on his solar barque along the celestial river of night, a trip which paralleled the deceased's spiritual journey through the netherworld. The text, split into three registers (the central one showing the celestial Nile) follows Re's journey through the 12 hours of the night. These writings, although translated, are not well understood, and the precise meanings of the depictions remain unknown. But in spite of its bizarre imagery, the *Book of What is in the Duat* teaches of the transformation of flesh into spirit—of Horus into Osiris, and links the transformation to the successful journey of the sun through the dark chaos of the night to emerge triumphant at the dawn.

Book of the Gates (Portals): A later text than the one above, this book is more fragmentary and even less understood. It too traces the journey of Re through the netherworld to rise in the morning as Khepri, but here the stress is on the barriers—the doors—between the hours, which are guarded by serpents.

Book of Caverns: This book, the newest of the funerary texts, presents yet a third view of Re's voyage. The writings, which surround the oval cocoons or "caves," deal with reward and punishment, and the fate of the enemies of Osiris.

In the sixth and final division, after victory over the forces of evil and the night, Khepri pushes the solar disk from between the two Mountains of the East and West toward the new day.

Book of Day and Book of Night: Popular ceiling decorations in royal tombs, these texts cover the roof of Ramesses VI's tomb in the Valley of the Kings at Luxor. The scenes depict the two goddesses of the sky; Nut of the Day and Nut of the Night, lying back to back. Nut of the Day occupies the front half of the ceiling, her body filled with solar disks (marking the 12 hours), with the dawning sun, supported by Khepri, emerging from her womb. The book ends at the twelfth hour, with the solar disk about to be swallowed by Nut and begin its nightly journey inside her body. The body of Nut of the Night is filled with the 36 *decan* stars used by the ancient Egyptians to tell time.

The Litany of Re: Often adorning the entrance to the tomb, the book lists the 74 ways the deceased can address Re. These multiple names, shown as mummiform outlines with diverse headdresses, gave the dead king magical power over the sun-god.

Book of the Divine Cow: The only tomb text with a mythical and magical context, it tells the story of the cow-goddess sent by Re to subdue mankind's rebellion. Taking the form of the lion-goddess Sekhmet, she smashed the revolt, but having tasted the blood of mankind, she could no longer be appeased. Re got the uncontrollable goddess drunk on beer (colored with red berries to imitate blood), and she reverted to her nurturing, joyful ways. Re then flung her into the sky where she became Nut, and drawings show this Divine Cow with her belly studded with stars; Shu stands beneath her, arms upraised, while the solar barque sails between her forelegs.

Narrative

Ancient Egyptians held a man well-versed in rhetoric in high regard, for eloquence, they believed, came from straight thinking. In a display of verbal wits, the *fallahin* in *Tale of the Elo-*

quent Peasant, receives justice, but only after his social betters enjoy his facility with words.

Many Egyptian stories tell of the gods' exploits, but along with such myths the Egyptians also wrote tales with human heroes like the "Shipwrecked Sailor," who encountered a fantastic dragon on a magic island. Over time, scribes introduced new themes and motifs while increasing the tales' complexity, but they steadfastly kept their direct style and the ability to sketch a situation with a few strokes. Their extraordinary vividness conveys the mood and feelings of the hero—a stylistic richness that still moves modern readers.

Instructions

Beginning with the Old Kingdom, the Instructions in Wisdom vividly displayed the Egyptians' pragmatic thought, tracing their religious feelings and speculations and forming their moral convictions. Written as proverbs, these sayings were strung together by a narrative in which father instructs son. The texts, a combination of useful and enlightening entertainment, lent themselves to emulation and variation, and each age filled them with new content, creating a repository of the nation's distilled wisdom. Their repeated editions testify to the Egyptians' optimistic belief that they could both teach and perfect mankind.

The New Kingdom Instructions mirror a society whose members lived in harmony with themselves and with nature. They met the cares of life with confidence; their gods ruled the world firmly and justly; life was both good and hard. But during the Late Period, the Egyptians recognized the problematic nature of human life and realized that all was not well on earth. Sages lamented about the evil condition of their country, and the Instructions now counseled endurance and self-control. This acceptance of fate and fortune as arbitrators of life invoked a Hellenistic universalism and pessimism that undermined the polytheistic culture of the entire Mediterranean, paving the way for the new Gospel of the kingdom of heaven.

THE COPTIC TRANSITION

Egypt's Greek and Roman rulers attempted to maintain pharaonic civilization, but their efforts only postponed its inevitable demise. During this period, native Egyptians, increasingly alienated from what had become the empty shell of their ancient culture, forged a unique civilization that bridged the period between Alexander's conquest in 332 B.C. and the Muslim invasion of A.D. 642. Known as Copts (from the Greek name for Egypt), these descendants of pharaonic Egyptians continued to hold many offices under the foreign rulers, positions that granted them a certain amount of power and wealth.

Exposed to new ideas generated in Alexandria and the rest of the Mediterranean world, the Copts, disenchanted with their own dying paganism, embraced Christianity early in the 2nd century A.D. With the conversion of Constantine, the Roman Empire became Christian, and Egypt was torn by interdenominational conflicts largely rooted in political and social differences. The bishops of the Holy Roman Empire declared the Copts heretics and excluded them from the mainstream of Christianity, but the Copts stood firm in what they considered their pure and original form of Christianity. They adapted their lives and their art to serve as expressions of their new faith, a faith which continues to nourish a large number of Egyptian Christians who have never converted to Islam.

HISTORY

During the Roman and Byzantine periods (30 B.C.-A.D. 642), Egypt was linked, through the port of Alexandria, with the Mediterranean world, and her history to a great extent became that of the Greeks and Romans who settled there. After its defeat at the battle at Actium in 30 B.C., Egypt became a province of the Roman Empire. The first two centuries of Roman rule brought the native Egyptians security, peace, and an ordered government, which created a measure of prosperity. Improvements like the saqiya (an ox-drawn waterwheel) and the norag (a wheeled sledge used as a thresher) increased Egypt's agricultural output, and Egyptian wheat fed much of Rome's empire. They expanded irrigation systems in the oases and reopened and expanded the mines in Sinai and the Red Sea hills. They established numerous ports along the Red Sea coast, and wells still line their ancient roads. Glass, metalware, textiles, pottery, faience, and perfumes manufactured by Egyptian craftsmen flowed into the empire's cities. Egyptian papyri preserved many classical Greek works, both literary and secular. Although features of Hellenistic culture were introduced into Egypt, extensive documents and traditional literature written in demotic testify that Egyptians still worshipped at their temples, mummified their dead, and believed that Anubis would help them through the judgment to live forever with Osiris. The Greeks and Romans adopted these same ideas, and their mummified bodies were encased in coffins with traditional Egyptian prayers and spells.

Roman Rule

Nevertheless the period brought increasing tensions. The emperors, who ruled from Rome, attempted to assume the pharaonic titles as had the Greeks before them. Although they rebuilt temples according to traditional architecture, the move ultimately failed, for Egyptians refused to honor these absentee rulers who no longer practiced the ceremonial functions of divine kingship. Roman garrisons stationed at Alexandria, Babylon (Old Cairo), and Syene (Aswan) secured the trade routes, but as imperial Rome became increasingly dependent upon Egypt to supply grain and treasure, the administrators overtaxed the country. Trajan drafted peasant farmers for the Roman army, and Hadrian exempted Greek citizens from taxation while increasing the liabilities of the *fallahin*. These heavily taxed peasants often revolted but were quickly defeated by the Roman army. Many abandoned their land and fled to the desert, where they lived in seclusion, presaging the development of Christian monasticism.

Roman Persecutions

During Roman rule, the Egyptians became increasingly alienated from the elite society that governed them. Their own religion, turning more and more to magic and adopted by increasing numbers of foreigners, no longer appealed to them. Thus the Egyptians welcomed the underground movement of Christianity with its already familiar message of resurrection. As the Christians' political strength increased, they soon came into conflict with the Romans. In A.D. 251, Decius ordered the Egyptians to worship at pagan altars, and any who couldn't show certificates of sacrifice were tortured. In 284, when Diocletian reorganized the empire, he introduced Latin as the official language, excluding from public service Egyptians who refused to learn it. The Egyptians, who had had enough, rebelled. Diocletian, equally fed up with the troublesome natives, confiscated property and leveled their houses, searched out and burned Christian literature, and killed thousands of Egyptians.

Unity And Division

When Emperor Constantine came to power, he converted to Christianity, and in A.D. 313 gave the church doctrine imperial sanction. As a result, large numbers of Greeks and Romans converted to the new faith. In Egypt, these conversions created a second type of Christian—the Melkite or emperor's man—and political tensions erupted into increasingly acrimonious religious conflicts over seemingly minor points of theology.

Nicene Council: In an attempt to solve the disputes, the emperor convened the first of a series of ecumenical councils at Nicea in A.D. 325. The conference was dominated by two Egyptians, Arius and Athanasius, who argued the merits of Christ's divine nature. Athanasius swayed the convention which approved the Nicene Creed affirming Christ's pure divinity. Constantine's successor, Constantius, intensified religious unrest by forcibly deposing Athanasius, and the turmoil continued until Theodosius I (375-395) reversed his action. The Christians continued to quarrel among themselves, and the split became more violent as the factions aligned themselves strongly along both political and social lines; the native Copts (Monophysites) pitted against Greek and Roman Orthodoxy (Melkites).

Council of Chalcedon: In a final attempt to unify the religion, the Chalcedon council was convened in A.D. 451. The bishops rewrote the Nicene Creed, but the Copts could no longer agree to this version. Declared heretics by the Eastern Orthodox Church, they were ejected from mainstream Christianity. In spite of this action, however, or perhaps because of it, the Coptic Church continued to grow, and by the reign of Justinian (525-565), they far outnumbered the Melkites. Although the emperor tried to enforce their obedience with jail and torture, he was unsuccessful. The Copts formally seceded and appointed their own patriarch of Alexandria; the split between the Coptic and the Orthodox churches was complete.

Byzantine Empire

In A.D. 326 Constantine transferred his capital to the ancient Greek town of Byzantium, which he renamed Constantinople. As the leading Christian city, Constantinople became a center of art and science, a home for both religious and secular learning. As such, it began to undermine Alexandria's reputation for knowledge, held since Ptolemaic times, and Egypt slipped even further away from the center of Mediterranean world.

The Muslim Invasion

Orthodox persecution of the Copts continued until the Arab invasion in A.D. 641. At this time, the native population saw the conquerers as saviors; the earliest Muslim rulers lived up to this ideal by declaring the Christians "People of the Book" and allowing them, with the payment of a special tax, to continue practicing their religion.

CHRISTIANITY

Tradition says that St. Mark brought the new religion to Egypt, preaching both at Alexandria and Old Cairo. The early roots of Christianity are difficult to trace, in part because of the secrecy maintained by the sect, which was intermittently persecuted. Although the religion must have been popular by the end of the 1st century, it only emerged in A.D. 180 when the Christian scholar Pantanaeus formed the Catechetical School of

Alexandria. Patterned after Greek models, the school taught science, mathematics, and humanities in addition to religion, and its leading figures, steeped in Hellenistic thought and scholarship, taught in Greek. Clement, a converted pagan, succeeded Pantanaeus and was in turn followed by Origen, the greatest of the Christian apologists. But Rome mistakenly dismissed the school as just another minor mystic sect.

Coptic Roots

As paganism declined, Christianity offered Egyptians a personal deity who promised resurrection. An updated version of their pharaonic beliefs, it gave Egyptians holy buildings (often within the precincts of ancient temples), altars, a priesthood, and purification (baptism) by holy water. Many concepts of the new religion fit old myths and images—the conflict of two brothers, man made from clay (whether by the rampotter Khnum or the Christian God), and God, who (like Anubis) weighed the hearts of the penitent. Egyptians were familiar with confessions from their Declaration of Innocence, and the Psalms sounded much like 18th Dynasty hymns dedicated to Amun or Aton.

Conversely, Egyptian ritual shaped Christianity, for the long-established practice of asceticism led Christians to escape from political persecution and moral temptation by retreating to the desert. Pilgrimages, such as the visits to Osiris's holy places, continued but shifted from pagan to Christian shrines. The Copts' belief that a deceased's soul is released from the body 40 days after death is perhaps rooted in the folk memory of the time taken for mummification, and the custom of both Copts and Muslims of taking food and flowers to cemeteries may well have its origins in pharaonic sacrifices for the *ka*.

Monasticism

During Roman times, many Christians withdrew to the desert. These hermits, reminiscent of the pre-Christian anchorites, at first lived solitary lives. Anthony, who settled in the Red Sea Mountains near the eastern coast, is the traditional founder of monasticism, and as his fame spread throughout Egypt, he gathered a following of disciples. Each monk maintained his own cell, congregating only to celebrate the Eucharist; and the groups of ascetics who settled at Wadi Natrun adopted a similar system. European monasticism, however, followed the rule of Pachom, who at his monastery in Middle Egypt relaxed the solitude, allowing monks to share work and eat together in a common refectory. From such Egyptian monasteries, monasticism spread throughout the world; St. Basil, who had visited Egypt about A.D. 357, brought it to the East, and St. Benedict did the same for the West.

Coptic Bible

When members of the sizable population of Jews who had lived in Egypt from at least New Kingdom times converted to Christianity, they translated their Hebrew Bible (the *Septuagint,* upon which all modern translations are based) into Greek. The earliest surviving Coptic Bibles date from the first half of the 4th century. Of similar age are the *Nag Hammadi Codices,* translations into Coptic of lost Greek originals of Gnostic and early Christian writings—many considered heretical by the modern church.

Liturgy

During the Greek period, the Egyptians adopted the Greek alphabet, using it to write their language (the last form of Egyptian) and adding

The Archangel Michael protects Shadrach, Meshach, and Abednego in this 10th century Coptic painting.

LOUISE FOOTE

a few hieroglyphs to depict sounds not found in Greek. Known as Coptic, it remained in use as a liturgical language until early in the 20th century (thereby providing Champollion with the key to the Rosetta Stone). Today, Arabic has replaced Coptic, and the old language now survives only as some of the Coptic months such as Tut (Thoth) and Hatur (Hathor). Coptic hymns, according to historians, were taken from ancient popular songs, but no trace of their musical notation remains. Greek sources, however, claim that the Copts chanted the seven Greek vowels; labeled the sounds of the seven stars, these tones remain the backbone of Coptic harmony.

Sacraments

Although the Copts withdrew from mainstream Christianity, their rituals remain remarkably similar to other branches of the church. They observe the seven sacraments of baptism, confirmation, eucharist, penance, matrimony, and unction for the ill as well as maintaining a tradition of apostolic succession dating back to the time of Christ. Children only a few weeks old are baptized by whole immersion in consecrated water, an act that simultaneously confirms them. Divorce is infrequent, granted only in cases of adultery or if a husband converts to Islam and takes a second wife.

Eucharist: Weekly services are long, nearly three hours, and men and women segregate themselves on either side of the church (men to the left, women to the right). The consecration of bread and wine occurs beyond a screen that divides the altar area from the congregation. Priests administer the Eucharist by dipping the bread in the wine and serving both on a spoon. Throughout the service, small boys swinging metal censers spread incense.

Fasts and Feasts: Although the Copts are forbidden to worship saints, many ask their favorites—the Virgin, St. Michael, or St. George—for intercession. They celebrate feast days of the saints throughout the year, but the most important days of the Coptic religious calendar are those of Lent and Easter. Unlike most other Christians, the Copts observe a two-week fast a month before Lent, as well as the 40-day fast of Lent proper, when the religious eat no meat, eggs, or fish, and drink neither wine nor coffee for

the entire period, and eat or drink nothing between sunrise and sunset. The fast ends Palm Sunday at a midnight Mass. The following day, the people take palm fronds blessed by the bishop or priest and weave crosses or baskets; in the afternoon, they visit the cemeteries.

The Copts celebrate their Christmas feast on 7 January, which follows Laila Kabir ("Big Night"), or Epiphany—the time the wise men were said to have reached Bethlehem; a midnight Mass ends 15 days of fasting. Recently, the Egyptians have started observing Western Christmas but as a secular holiday much like our New Year's Eve. Thus with only a few exceptions, the Copts worship in the same way, keep the same sacraments holy, and adhere to a ritual calendar similar to churches in the West.

Holy Family

Egyptians hold Mary, Joseph, and Jesus especially holy, and numerous places claim to have offered the trio rest and refreshment during their flight into Egypt. Joseph, tradition claims, worked as a carpenter at the Roman fortress of Babylon (Old Cairo), and the family began their flight up the Nile from a spot near modern Ma'adi, where a Coptic church now stands. Since Muslims accept Christ as a prophet, Egyptians of both religions share the pilgrimage to Gebel al-Tair, the mountain in Middle Egypt where the baby Jesus stayed a rock from falling with his hand, the print of which still remains. The tiny church at the top receives petitioners, and has a reputation for healing.

COPTIC ART

In spite of foreign domination, the Copts produced artwork stamped with their own indelible seal. As their work evolved, both their art and architecture became an expression of their faith. Master Coptic craftsmen, already well trained in weaving, glassblowing, and carving, found their skills in demand by their Roman, Byzantine, and Muslim masters. Coptic artists selected and transformed multiple themes, expressing them in techniques they developed as their own. Like their pharaonic forebears, the Copts chose to ignore representational art, electing instead to strip images to their archetypal skeletons.

Mediterranean Foundations

Unlike Christianity, Coptic art grew from its Greek and Roman antecedents. Greek artists who immigrated spread both classical themes and techniques throughout Egypt. Under their influence, pharaonic artists, who had lost the deft touch of previous generations, created designs that no longer flowed with linear poise; masses of figures filled any available space, distorting once delicately balanced scenes. The figures, too, changed; the sinuous grace of pharaohs, gods, and goddesses, for example, gave way to a more naturalistic molding—an unfortunate modification, yielding figures that one historian has called "all lumps and bumps." Classical naturalism pointed up the anatomical impossibilities of mounting a jackal or hawk head on a human body. Although the technically superb sculpture is startling, its firm grounding in realism prevents it from haunting the subconscious like the older pharaonic statues and reliefs.

Following the Roman victory in 30 B.C., Egyptian art continued to draw inspiration from the Mediterranean world. Increasingly the pharaonic and Hellenistic styles mixed, producing strange combinations, such as a Roman matron at Tuna al-Gebel who stands in three-quarters view, while Horus and Seth, both in typical pharaonic profile, pour libations over her. But around Alexandria and in the large Roman colonies in the Fayyum, artists continued to develop naturalistic styles, creating mosaics and paintings that bordered on impressionism. Especially well known are the funeral portraits; the so-called Fayyumic heads, which were inserted (instead of the cartonnage masks) in mummy wrappings. Many of these portraits were executed in encaustic—pigment dissolved in hot wax. The technique produced brilliant and long-lasting colors, making it a favored medium for much Byzantine work, especially religious icons.

Early Coptic Work

During this period, the work of the native Copts followed similar lines, at first dealing with pagan themes—both pharaonic and Mediterranean—copying the naturalistic Greek and Roman treatments. Soon, however, the artists began to distort their figures, sacrificing harmony for emphasis. Coptic figures have long waists and small, triangular heads that set off large, expressive eyes. Early figures were often carved so deeply in relief that they were nearly freestanding. Gradually, however, images became flatter until the reliefs lost all modeling, existing in two layers—a flat surface on which the subject had essentially been drawn, and a deep but equally flat background.

Christian Period

Following the Edict of Milan in A.D. 313, which freed the Christians to openly practice their religion, Coptic artists frankly embraced the symbols of the new faith, converting pagan images to Christian: Isis suckling Horus, for example, became the Virgin with Christ. Horus, encased up to his hawk head in Roman mail, sits astride his horse spearing the crocodile of Seth: a primal St. George slaying the dragon. Some scenes were Christianized by the addition of a specifically Christian symbol: in a stone panel St. Thecla, for example, menaced by flames and wild beasts, stands stripped to the waist like a Greek Venus while she raises a cross toward heaven.

Architecture

The Copts produced little in the way of monumental buildings, but the design of their churches and monasteries reflected their Egypto-Greco-Roman heritage. The Copts built basilicas; rectangular, three-aisled churches with raised central naves not unlike the clerestories of pharaonic temples. The central aisle lined with columns served to focus attention on the

A Coptic Horus dressed in Roman mail slays the crocodile/dragon of Seth.

Derived from Greek prototypes, Coptic capitals exhibited the same flat but deep relief of other Coptic stonework.

altar, which stood in an apse often enclosed with a half dome. The Copts spanned their roofs with trusses, a development the Romans had perfected, and capped them with barrel vaults. Whenever possible, they aligned their churches along an east-west axis, so that the congregation faced the rising sun. Many of the apses were three-fold, creating a tri-lobed sanctuary or *haykal*. These sanctuaries were screened from the congregation by ornate wooden *haykal* screens, often inlaid with beautiful icons. The screens cloaked the altar much as the ancient gods' barque stands must have been hidden in the ancient temples' *naos*. A raised pulpit reached by a staircase dominated the center of the nave, and in the sanctuary, a free-standing altar was covered by a wooden baldachin, its painted dome supported on four columns. At the entrance, the Copts added a narthex, a transverse entryway that created a baffled entrance, much like the sheltered gates of Roman temples, such as those at Kalabsha.

Decoration

The glory of the Coptic churches are their wooden screens, often made of small beads fitted together like a puzzle, their joints allowing for expansion of the wood. Coptic builders also carved elaborate stone pillars, decorating them with several bands of textures. To top these columns, they created a series of capitals developed from the Greek Corinthian design. The earliest forms, shaped like baskets, are alive with long naturalistic acanthus leaves. But like all Coptic art, the capitals soon grew stylized into nearly flat leaves covering the deep-set background with rhythmic patterns, their interlacing stems forming rondels, which at first held clusters of grapes and later crosses.

Decorative friezes followed a similar development; the naturalistic leaves and branches evolved into regular, sinuous patterns of coiling shapes. The grapes and leaves flattened into shapes that curved and bent to encircle crosses or animals. Identical patterns decorated the "broken pediments," which often sheltered a figure at their apex.

Painting

Coptic painters melded Roman naturalism with Byzantine formalism, but painting soon gave way to the same impulses as sculpture, and artists used simplified forms to create impact. Draperies no longer fell in soft folds but hung stiffly around figures that appear too small for their heads. Although perhaps appearing crude by some definitions, the expressive faces of Coptic figures dominate the compositions, both creating and focusing emotion.

Textiles

In pharaonic times, Egyptians excelled in weaving, and their Coptic descendants continued the tradition. Egyptian linen was world famous, and the Copts developed a variety of weaves. With loop piles and tapestry weaves they blended fibers into pictures more delicate than paintings, woven portraits with more nuances of shading than Roman encaustics. Coptic weavers could create such realistically swimming fish, their shadows reflecting off the shallow bottom of a pool, that one could nearly pluck them from the water. Subject to the same impulses as other artists, however, weavers soon reduced forms to simple mass and silhouette, employing the flying shuttle to sketch single-lined outlines much as Greek potters had delineated Attic black-figure ware. Copts adorned their tunics with woven bands designed along the same lines as the friezes, their decorative rondels inhabited with animals and human figures. Especially popular was the hunter, often mounted, a recurring theme throughout the Mediterranean world.

Muslim Influences

The Muslim conquest of Egypt, as throughout the Middle East, did little damage to the culture, and Coptic society and technology remained unaffected. However, the new connections with Syria, Palestine, and Persia, which had been forged through the empire, led Coptic craftsmen to travel abroad and return with new ideas and themes. They skillfully interwove these into their existing repertoire, transforming them into their own style. Under the new masters, Coptic art flourished until the end of the Fatimid period, by which time the separate Coptic and Muslim threads had become so interwoven that it is impossible to tease them apart. What emerged however, was an exceedingly high level of art that flourished and developed during Egypt's conversion to Islam in the following decades.

ISLAMIC EGYPT

In A.D. 610, a young Arab from Mecca began having visions of the Archangel Gabriel, who instructed him to reveal God's word to the world. Muhammad, in obedience, began preaching a new religion, Islam, to pagan traders and nomads. A nucleus of believers swelled into a passionate army, and at the end of the 7th century, Muslim armies mounted on swift war mares and brandishing swords of Damascus steel suddenly burst into the rich and cultured empires of Persia and Byzantium. Weakened by long-standing border wars, both fell easily, and by A.D. 750 the Muslims held lands from Spain to India. Conquering swiftly, the Muslims brought their language and religion to the countries they occupied, and though they took over the reins of government, they left the civilizations of their new subjects nearly intact.

Funded by trade in silk and spices, Arab governors adopted the ostentatious displays of their conquered courts, absorbing art, archi-tecture, literature, and music, melding Persian, Byzantine, and Egyptian motifs and techniques into Islamic art. Entranced with Greek philosophy and science, Muslim rulers employed armies of translators to render the works of Plato, Aristotle, and Galen in Arabic, thereby preserving them for European scholars of the Renaissance.

But perhaps the Arabs' greatest gift to the Middle East was unification under a common language and religion. Although subjugated peoples were not required to convert to Islam or become bilingual, selective taxation and sporadic decrees gradually converted the majority. Over the centuries, a central administration secured the trade routes, ensured a stable economy, and built an extensive communications network. The unifying force of common religion fostered the exchange of culture and technology, eventually evolving into the widespread, loosely knit culture recognized as Islamic.

EGYPT'S ISLAMIC HISTORY

When newly converted Muslims swept out of Arabia in the middle of the 7th century, Egypt quickly fell to their swords. Thereafter, the country's history became tightly interwoven with that of the rest of the Middle East. From the time of Amr Ibn al-As's conquest in 642 until Nasser's revolt in 1952, Egypt was ruled by a succession of foreign governors, khalifs, and sultans. Nevertheless, throughout its Islamic history, the country has played a major role in the power politics engulfing the rest of the Arab world, becoming a base for independent governors, a haven for ousted khalifs, a Muslim world leader, and a repository for Arabic art, culture, and learning.

EARLY MUSLIMS

With Muhammad's death in 632, Abu-Bakr, Muhammad's father-in-law, became his successor. The ruling tribal members declared their loyalty to him as khalif (successor) and obedience to the Prophet and thus to Allah. Abu-Bakr immediately conquered the Arabian peninsula

The Islamic Empire was founded by mounted warriors, and such armies continued to change the shape of the Middle East until the introduction of modern weapons.

and then sent his armies north into Persia, Palestine, and Syria. They defeated the Byzantine army in 636 and by 651 had conquered Persia.

Egyptian Conquest
With the halfhearted support of the second khalif, Umar, General Amr Ibn al-As (with an army of 4,000 men) crossed the Syrian-Egyptian border and laid siege to the Roman garrison at Babylon. As Christians ("People of the Book"), the Egyptians were given the usual opportunity to surrender and to either pay tribute or convert to Islam. Those who chose resistance would be put to the sword. Cyrus, the Byzantine governor and orthodox patriarch, spurned the offer and after a disastrous battle on the plains of Heliopolis, lost the fortress in 641. Amr then marched on Alexandria, taking the city late in the following year. He then established his capital, al-Fustat, outside the Roman fort south of modern Cairo.

The Shi'i Fracture
But because Muhammad had not established how succeeding leaders were to be chosen, all was not well in the Muslim camp. The first three khalifs were unanimously picked by the elders at al-Medina. However, the fourth khalif, Ali, a son of Muhammad's daughter Fatimia, claimed the khalifate by right of kinship. Dissension fractured the Muslim ranks, with members divided between Ali's supporters (the Shi'i) and others (the Sunni) who maintained that the office was elective, to be filled by a member of the Quraysh tribe. Ali's assassination, followed by that of his two sons, ruptured the Islamic world. Although this split was political rather than doctrinal, the isolated sects soon developed irreconcilable religious theologies as well.

The Umayyads (658-720)
Following the Shi'i split, the Sunni transferred the capital to Damascus and changed the once-elected khalifate to hereditary rule. Amr became governor of Egypt, and the empire allowed large numbers of Arabs to immigrate to Egypt and

MARK MORRIS

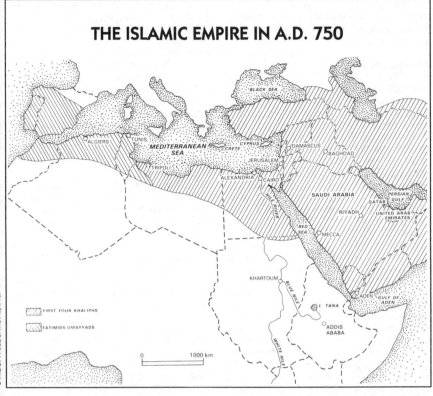

THE ISLAMIC EMPIRE IN A.D. 750

FIRST FOUR KHALIPHS

FATIMIDS UMAYYADS

0   1000 km

settle, intermarrying with the natives. By early in the 8th century, the official language of Egypt became Arabic, and Coptic administrators who wanted to keep their positions had to become bilingual. Islamic coins were minted and a postage system increasingly tied Egypt to the Middle East. The Copts, in response to increasing taxation, periodically revolted, only to be quashed. After each uprising, a few more Copts converted.

In the east, the Umayyads initiated a new wave of conquests that extended Muslim sway from the far edges of India and China, across North Africa, through the Strait of Gibraltar to Spain—an empire larger than that held by Alexander the Great. Millions of non-Arab converts brought their own cultures to the empire, and some, such as the Persians, although they

adopted the Arabic script, retained their own language. Such diversity caused later Umayyad rulers problems. Newly converted Persians, for example, found that in spite of Muhammad's high-sounding rhetoric, they were taxed at levels unequal to Arab Muslims. This policy created domestic unrest. In addition, the Shi'i faction, always unhappy with the Sunni regime, became increasingly restless, and even pious Sunnis, troubled by the conspicuous consumption of the Umayyad rulers, started agitating. The Umayyads, trying to defend their empire, failed to follow the shifting ideal of Islam, and many Muslims felt the empire had to return to "true" Islamic principles. Abu al-Abbas, a descendant of Muhammad's uncle, united the disparate Sunni factions, and by 750 his Abbasid army had routed the Umayyads. Although Abd al-

Rahman escaped to Spain where he founded the Umayyad Khaliphate of Cordoba, Marwan II, the last eastern Umayyad khalif, fled to Egypt, where he was captured and decapitated.

The Abbasids (750-1258)

The Abbasid revolt, for the first time, brought non-Arabs (primarily Persians and Turks) into the ruling class. The new khalifs moved the capital to Baghdad, strengthened the government, and supported the arts. Literature and music flourished, and Greek, Roman, Iranian, and Hindu works of philosophy, medicine, mathematics, astronomy, and other sciences, translated into Arabic, diffused into the Islamic culture. Muslim scholars preserved ancient learning, expanded upon its bases, and ultimately transferred it to the West, fueling the rebirth of learning that led to the Renaissance.

The rule of the fifth khalif, Harun al-Rashid (the original beguiled audience of *Tales for a 1001 Nights*), marked the golden age of the Islamic Empire. But the empire was too far-flung to be easily governed. In addition to the Umayyad outpost in Spain, a Shi'i had conquered North Africa. Both these rulers, one orthodox, the other dissident, declared themselves khalifs. These two, coupled with the Abbasid rule in Baghdad, gave the Islamic Empire three widely separated khalifs. Meanwhile, Turkish generals and Persian bureaucrats carved out their own little dynasties. Ultimately they wielded enough power to make the khalif little more than a figurehead, and the empire continued to fragment.

The Tulunids (868-905)

Under the Abbasids, Egypt was loosely governed by the khalif's appointees, many of whom ruled *in absentia*. The administration in Egypt disintegrated; taxes became intolerable and prices rose. In the middle of the 9th century, the khalif sent a Turkish governor, Ahmad Ibn Tulun, to control the protectorate. Working from al-Fustat, Tulun consolidated the government, steadied the economy, and imposed order. Seeing better uses for Egypt's treasury at home, he sent less and less of the tax revenues to Baghdad and built a second city, al-Qatai (the Quarters), north of al-Fustat. In 868 he declared Egypt independent, but he was careful to retain ties with the Abbasid khalifate. He be-

queathed the government to his sons but passed on little of his statesmanship.

In 905, Abbasid forces, responding to the corruption, famine, and plague that had swept Egypt, invaded, and for the next 30 years the country remained under Baghdad's control. However, Muslim provincial governors once again proved ineffectual, and in 969 a series of low Niles, famine, and chaotic administration tempted the Shi'i Fatimids (descendants of Muhammad's daughter Fatima) to invade.

The Fatimids (969-1171)

By the beginning of the 10th century, the Fatimids had become well established, and from their stronghold in North Africa the self-declared Khalif al-Muizz sent his general Gawhar into Egypt. He met with little resistance. After taking Fustat, Gawhar built his rulers a new administrative city, al-Qahira, the medieval center of modern Cairo. Al-Muizz, wanting to be closer to Mecca, uprooted his officers and moved, bag, baggage, and ancestors' bodies, to the new city. From there, the Fatimids amassed an empire covering North Africa, Sicily, and Syria.

Able administrators, the early Fatimids reduced taxes, expanded foreign trade to both Europe and India, and created economic stability. Soon the holy cities of Mecca and Medina and most of Syria came under the sway of the Fatimid khalif, and once more Egypt was the center of an empire. The Fatimids undertook large building programs, raising fortified walls and gates around Cairo and founding the prestigious University at al-Azhar. Literature, bookmaking, carving, textiles, and architecture flourished.

With the third khalif, "crazy" al-Hakim, Fatimid rule began to deteriorate. From a Christian family, he nevertheless embraced Islam with fervor, and persecuted Christians and Jews. He demanded al-Qahira be closed by day; by night, the city was alive with thousands of lanterns. He forbade women on the streets, and required Christians to wear heavy crosses if they went to a public bath. One of his followers, Muhammad Ibn Ismail al-Durzi, claimed Hakim was the incarnation of Allah, an assertion that so shocked the populace they stormed the palace demanding the blasphemer's head, but Durzi fled to Lebanon, where he founded the Druze sect.

One February night in 1021, Hakim rode off into the Moqattam Hills—only his favorite white donkey was ever found.

After Hakim, Egypt was ruled by a succession of ineffectual khalifs until Christian crusaders in 1168 invaded Egypt's northern shore. The Abbasid khalif in Baghdad sent an expedition to repel them, and its Sunni leader, Salah al-Din (Saladin), stopped the Christians and seized control of the government. In 1171 as the last Fatimid khalif lay dying, Salah al-Din ordered Friday prayers to be said in the name of the orthodox Abbasid khalif of Baghdad. The rule of the Shi'i had ended. Although independent, Egypt was once more under the religious sway of the Sunni Abassids.

MEDIEVAL EGYPT

Salah al-Din Yusif al-Ayyubi laid out plans to build a fortress (the Citadel) on Cairo's most easily defended hill and began expansion of the Fatimid walls to enclose the city. He had the pharaonic canal that fed the oasis at Fayyum re-dug, and built *madrasas* (colleges), making Cairo a great center for Islamic scholarship—a position it still retains. Salah al-Din didn't remain in Egypt long, for as soon as the country was secure, he turned it over to his brother al-Adil and his vizier al-Fadil and left to drive the Christian infidels from the Holy Land. The epitome of Muslim chivalry, he won the respect of the European knights against whom he fought, and they incorporated many of his ideals into their own codes. He charmed the Westerners with his knowledge and culture and became a primary character in Sir Walter Scott's novel *The Talisman*. From Salah al-Din's forces, Christian knights learned firsthand about Islamic improvements in fortifications and arms as well as medical knowledge.

The Ayyubids (1171-1250)
Salah al-Din gave his family name to the Egyptian dynasty that followed him, and his successors were able rulers. They expanded irrigation systems and secured travel and trading routes; the spice trade flourished, and in spite of a bout with famine caused by several low Niles, plague, and earthquakes, Egypt prospered. Waves of crusading Christians, however, continued to attack, and to strengthen her armies Egypt imported Turkish slaves and converted them to Islam. Called Mamluks, they formed a crack cavalry that easily repelled the Crusaders under Louis IX, capturing the French king. During this battle, the last of the Ayyubids line died in his tent. His death was concealed by his Mamluk wife, Shagarit al-Durr, who assumed control in his name and was proclaimed sultana.

Shagarit al-Durr
Shagarit al-Durr ruled for nearly a year before the Abbasid khalif told the Mamluks that if they couldn't find a man among them to rule the country, he'd send one. Under this pressure, Shagarit al-Durr forced the Mamluk Aybak to divorce his wife and marry her, and the Mamluk amirs elected him sultan. The pair ruled jointly for seven years until Shagarit became disenchanted with her husband and had him murdered. Enraged, the amirs imprisoned her in the Citadel, where she vented her fury by grinding up her jewels with a mortar and pestle so that no other woman would ever wear them. Three days later, the women of the harem, instigated by Aybak's former wife, beat Shagarit to death with their wooden bath clogs and threw her body over the citadel walls to the dogs. Eventually, her remains were gathered and buried in her mausoleum at Cairo.

The Mamluks (1250-1517)
The white slaves imported by Egyptian governors now ruled Egypt. As youngsters, they were converted to Islam, educated, and given military training. Many worked their way up through the army ranks, and when they reached a high enough rank, were freed by their masters, to whom they pledged their loyalty. Many were appointed to high governmental posts; advancement was by individual ability and open only to those who had been indentured. To supply their private armies, the Mamluks continued to import slaves, creating multiple power groups that dragged the native Egyptians into their fierce and frequent power struggles.

In general, since Mamluk culture was based on slavery, neither wives nor sons had any claim on a Mamluk's political or military power. Mamluk sons, denied both hereditary claims and the slavery that would grant them entry into politics, filtered into the Egyptian population. Although Mamluks controlled the court and the army, Egyptians continued to staff civil offices, financial agencies, the judiciary, and the professions.

The Bahri (River) Mamluks (1250-1382)

Named for their barracks on Rhoda Island, the Bahri Mamluks defended the Islamic empire from the Mongols, who in 1258 swept through Persia and captured Baghdad, massacring the khalif and nearly all his family. In 1260, they took Aleppo and Damascus and were launching attacks into the rest of Syria. At the end of that year, the Egyptian Mamluk General Baybars halted the horde at Ayn Jalut (Goliath's Spring), handing the Asians their first defeat. When their Syrian possessions rebelled, the Mongols retreated to Anatolia.

Baybars: Returning to Cairo, the victorious Mamluk general had the current sultan murdered and himself elected. Using both belligerence and diplomacy, he controlled the crusading Christians along the north coast of the Mediterranean. He installed the Abbasid Prince al-Mustansir as khalif at Cairo, thereby moving the Sunni religious center to Egypt and gaining control of the Hajaz and Mecca. The khalif remained a figurehead while the Mamluk sultans continued to rule the remnants of the Islamic Empire. After Baybars's death, his sons were quickly deposed and one of Baybars's generals, Qalawun elected sultan.

Qalawun: Qalawun, who founded a dynasty that lasted a hundred years, continued Baybars's policies. He kept both the Mongols and Christians at bay and made treaties with Emperor Rudolph of Hapsburg as well as other European princes. He continued the building program initiated by Baybars, contributing a hospital as well as a mosque and mausoleum that still stand in Cairo, monuments to the pinnacle of Mamluk architecture. Qalawun bought Circassian rather than Turkish Mamluks and housed them in the great circular keep in the Citadel. Qalawun was followed by his son Khalil (1290), who captured the Christian port of Acre, razed the Crusaders' castles and drove them to Cyprus.

Muhammad al-Nasir: Muhammad al-Nasir succeeded his brother Khalil, but owing to his age (nine) and internal dissension, the Amir Lagin ruled Egypt in his name. Nasir regained control in 1298, only to flee in 1309 before the power of Baybars II. When Nasir returned in 1310, he had Baybars put to death.

Externally, his reign was marked by security and prosperity. He made treaties with the Mongols and strengthened ties with Europe; trade flourished, and Egypt's borders remained unchallenged. Toward his amirs, however, he was distrustful and capricious, either loading them with rich gifts or ordering their execution. Turmoil continued under his sons and relatives, who were in general ineffectual or incompetent. Lacking strong sultans to control them, the Bahri (River) and Burgi (Tower) Mamluks were continually at loggerheads, using their local wars as excuses to plunder the civilian populations. In 1382 a Circassian slave took the throne, and control of Egypt shifted to the Burgi Mamluks.

The Burgi (Tower) Mamluks (1382-1517)

From the Citadel tower, the Burgi Mamluks ruled Egypt for the next 140 years, but their reign proved even more bloody and unstable than that of the Bahris. To help defend Syria from a new Mongol incursion under Timur-i Lang (Tamerlane), they assessed oppressive taxes. By 1403, famine and plague had combined to undermine the economy. The Christians and Jews were heavily taxed. Christians were required to wear a five-pound wooden cross around their necks; the Jews, a black ball. The amirs expanded state monopolies, but production dropped and the cost of living soared. From 1468-89, under the able Sultan Qaytbey, Egypt experienced a brief revival but the country was headed for crises. When the Portuguese discovered the Indian Ocean, Europe no longer had to transship its spices and silk through Egypt; the monopoly on trading income that had supported Egypt for centuries collapsed. Meanwhile, the Ottoman Turks, who were squabbling with Persia over Syria, took Constantinople in 1453, then Syria and Cairo.

Ottoman Turks (1517-1805)

In 1517, the Turkish sultan Selim hung the last Mamluk sultan from Cairo's southern gate, took the Abbasid khalif to his capital in Istanbul (Constantinople), and declared Egypt a Turkish possession. The pashas assigned to Cairo imposed heavy taxes, and although Cairo remained a religious center, the culture declined, trade decreased, and the economy plummeted.

Although the Turks had nominal control, Mamluk amirs did not fold their tents and steal away. Instead, they continued to import slaves from the Caucasus, and the army grew and split into several factions. To maintain control, the early pashas pitted rival Mamluk groups against each other, but Mamluk power continued to expand, and by the mid-17th century, the Mamluk beys, having appropriated much of Egypt's financial base, were running the country. Their power made Egypt nearly autonomous, and the country was once again treated to Mamluk squabbles while trade declined and ruinous taxes, famine, and disease impoverished the country.

MODERN HISTORY

By 1798, with the weakening of the Portuguese Empire, the French, eyeing lucrative and strategic land routes to the East, sent the young general Napoleon Bonaparte to invade Egypt. Under the pretext of protecting European merchants and regaining control for the Ottoman sultan, he easily defeated the Mamluk army in a battle outside Cairo, forcing open the door to Muslim Egypt.

The French Occupation
Although Bonaparte's seasoned army, equipped with modern guns and cannon, quickly dominated Lower Egypt, the Mamluks, holing up in Upper Egypt, controlled the precious grain supplies and harassed the French troops at will. Meanwhile, the English fleet under Admiral Nelson sank Napoleon's ships in a battle at Abuqir. Bonaparte, unsupported from home, after an unsuccessful attempt to conquer the Levant secretly retired to France, leaving Egypt in the charge of General Kleber.

French Savants
Napoleon had brought a company of fifty scientists and savants to record Egypt—its geography, history and culture. Staffed with mathematicians, astronomers, engineers, physicians, chemists, zoologists, a linguist, a composer, an architect, and artists, the company included some of the finest French minds of the time. The mathematician Fourier (Fourier Transformations) accompanied the groups as did Conté who, although famous for his pencils, proved to be a general inventor of exceptional quality.

The artist Denon joined the army, which was attempting to control Upper Egypt, and he, with the later help of many of his colleagues from the institute's headquarters in Cairo, risked their lives to draw the temples and survey the country. Squinting through eyes swollen nearly shut by infection, they melted down bullets for the lead when supplies of Conté's pencils couldn't keep up with their demand. In three years, the savants covered Egypt, studying the hydraulics, the flora and fauna, the people, and the historical monuments; many lost their health and not a few their lives. But their work, published serially from 1801, appeared as the 20-volume *Description de l'Égypte;* up till then the most complete study of a country ever conducted. Its publication aroused interest in Egypt's ancient past and in Islam, fueling the growing European fascination with the Middle East.

French Legacy
Meanwhile, Bonaparte's successor, Kleber, made peace with the Mamluks and convinced them to supply grain to his hungry army. But his successor was defeated by joint Anglo-Ottoman forces, and in 1801 the French army evacuated Egypt. In spite of their short stay (1798-1801), the French left a strong cultural impact. Although the people never accepted Bonaparte's protestations of Islam, they were aroused by French learning and science; French ultimately became the second language of Egypt's educated elite, and it was to France that the Muslim leaders sent Egyptians to learn science, art, and technology.

Muhammad Ali
A young Turkish officer who had arrived with the Ottoman forces, Muhammad Ali quickly worked his way through the army ranks until he commanded a unit of Albanian troops. He courted favor with the Egyptian religious leaders and merchants, and in the chaotic period following French withdrawal, the Egyptians forced the Ottomans to appoint him pasha. He founded a

dynasty that ruled Egypt until 1952, laying the foundations that both modernized and Westernized Egypt.

At Home: Upon assuming control of Egypt, Muhammad Ali had to neutralize the fractious Mamluk beys. In 1811 he invited them to a feast; as they left, he trapped them within the gates of the Citadel and slaughtered them. Muhammad Ali then turned his attention to establishing Egypt on a firm economic footing, enthusiastically importing Western technology and culture. He sent numbers of young Egyptians to study in Europe, and at home he fostered training in engineering and medicine by importing instructors from Europe.

To generate working capital, he confiscated grain held by the Mamluks in Upper Egypt and sold it to the hard-pressed English forces in Spain. He then nationalized the land and set up state monopolies, moves that enabled him to build canals, improve irrigation and transportation, and promote scientific agriculture. He introduced long-staple cotton into the delta, and the produce later filled the international void caused by the American Civil War. With a vision uniquely his, he transformed Egypt from a medieval culture to a modern civilization.

International Affairs: Once Muhammad Ali controlled Egypt, he turned his attention to the rest of the Middle East. At the request of the Ottomans, he took the Arabian peninsula in 1818 and in 1820 invaded the Sudan. Late in that decade, he joined the Ottoman forces against Greeks but lost his navy at Navarino. Angered at the Turks' refusal to grant him Syria and the Peloponnesus for his effort in the war, he moved against them. When his forces neared Istanbul, the Western powers (France, Britain, Austria, Russia, and Prussia), fearing for their lines of communication to India and Asia, forced him to withdraw. In compromise, the European nations pressured the Turks to grant him control of Sudan and to make the office of pasha hereditary for his family.

The Rise Of Nationalism

Muhammad Ali installed Egyptians in all but the highest governmental positions, and under the urging of his son Ibrahim Pasha, he also promoted Egyptians as army officers. By increasing educational opportunities, he created an intellectual elite and in the process rekindled in all Egyptians a new sense of pride in Egyptian accomplishments, a nationalism that would eventually topple his family from power.

British Intervention

His successors, however, were not as talented as he. His shortsighted grandson Abbas stripped the country for personal profit, contributing only the railroad linking Cairo and Alexandria to Suez. When he was assassinated by some of his companions, his uncle Said succeeded him. Said, in 1856, granted the French promoter Ferdinand de Lesseps a concession to build the Suez Canal; to finance it, Said had to borrow heavily. His successor, Ismail, was even more irresponsible, and his lavish personal spending and irresponsible fiscal policies brought Egypt to bankruptcy, forcing him to accept joint French-British control. By that time, Britain had acquired enough shares in the Suez Canal Company to give her power over it, and the French held the rest. In 1879, the two powers forced Ismail to abdicate in favor of his son Tawfiq.

National Unrest

Egyptian businessmen objected to the special concessions the British gave foreign businesses; native army officers opposed the control of promotions by the Circassians and Turks; Muslims chafed at Christian control; and all Egyptians deplored foreign rule in general. In 1879, fed by rising nationalism, a group of army officers led by Lieutenant Colonel Ahmad Urabi forced Tawfiq to form a new, liberalized government and appoint Urabi as minister of war. When Tawfiq requested British assistance to maintain his power, the army under Urabi revolted, Tawfiq fled, and the British navy bombarded Alexandria, and France and Italy both declined Britain's invitation to help stamp out the revolt, thereby relinquishing future control in Egyptian affairs. Under the guise of reestablishing Khedive Tawfiq, the English landed an expeditionary force at Ismailia, and after a battle in the delta, forced Urabi to surrender. As a result of the revolt, Urabi was banished, not to return to Egypt until 1899, a nearly forgotten figure.

British Control

Soon after Urabi's defeat, the British sent Lord Dufferin to Egypt to sort out the political mess.

1. Young girls learn homemaking tasks early. A wife wears her dowry in gold around her neck (D. Goodman); 2. a mud-brick home in Luxor (K. Hansen); 3. calishe drivers (K. Hansen)

An astute diplomat, Dufferin quickly realized that the British must come to terms with the new nationalistic movement, and recommended the creation of an elected government. The ruling khedive remained nominally in control, but decisions came from the British consuls.

Fiscal and governmental reform occupied the British, who wanted to accommodate as much as possible Egyptian political self-expression. The British balanced Egypt's budget, reformed the administration, and expanded economic and agricultural services. The improvements enabled the British to set up Egypt as supplier of raw goods to English industry; Egypt in turn became a market for English manufactured goods.

Increased profitability of cotton led to the building of the first Aswan Dam in 1902. But the dam raised subsoil water, which damaged crops and created economic hardship. In addition, cash crops like cotton required large capital for seeds, fertilizer and water. When prices declined, the *fallahin,* who had taken out loans, lost their land to a growing class of large landowners. The displaced and frustrated peasants took to violence, and the unrest culminated in the small delta town of Dinshwai, where villagers, incensed at a group of English army officers who were shooting their pigeons, rioted. During the confrontation, an officer was killed, and at a hastily convened court four peasants were sentenced to hang; others were flogged and given stiff jail terms. Although the event galvanized Egyptian resentment against the British occupation, the rising nationalism was halted by the outbreak of the First World War.

World War I

When Turkey joined the Central Powers, England, fearing for the Suez Canal and its communications with the East, declared Egypt a British protectorate, thereby ending nominal rule of the Ottoman Empire. Although British martial law quashed political wrangling, the Egyptians suffered from severe inflation and had to serve as manual laborers for the British army in Palestine. At the end of the conflict, Egyptians, hearing Woodrow Wilson's affirmation of national self-determination, demanded independence. The Wafd, a broadly based nationalist political party under the leadership of Sa'ad Zaghlul, took up the cause, and the party dominated Egyptian politics for the next 30 years.

The Constitution

In response to Egyptian agitation, the British sent a mission under Lord Milner, who suggested rescinding the protectorate, declaring Egypt independent, and forming an alliance between the two countries. In 1922, Khedive Fuad became Egypt's king, and Egypt gained nominal independence. The Wafd won landslide elections and under the leadership of Zaghlul set up a modicum of parliamentary government. Unfortunately, the constitution had given the king sweeping powers, and he gutted the parliament and ministerial posts. Fuad died in 1936, and his minor son Faruq inherited the throne. Although the British sponsored Egypt's entry into the League of Nations and agreed to remove troops except at the Suez Canal, the outbreak of war brought a halt to Egypt's movement toward true independence.

World War II

The Germans under Rommel invaded Egypt from the west, and by July 1942 they camped within 70 miles of Alexandria, but Montgomery's victory at al-Alamein kept Egypt under English rule. To counter anti-British/pro-German sentiments, British tanks surrounded Abdin Palace and forced King Faruq to appoint a pro-British government, drawing leaders from the Wafd. The Egyptians saw this capitulation as a betrayal of the cause for independence. As a result, the party lost much of its popularity, but with the backing of both the king and the British, stayed in power through the end of the war.

Postwar Politics

Early in 1945, Egypt, along with Iraq, Lebanon, Syria, Saudi Arabia, Transjordan, and (eventually) Yemen, signed a pact establishing the League of Arab States (Arab League). Headquartered in Cairo, it was designed to settle political questions in the Middle East. By the end of the year, Egypt had also joined the United Nations and, unable to come to terms with the British over Egyptian rights, submitted the problem of independence to the UN, which was unable to resolve it. But Egypt's attention was diverted by the creation of Israel in May 1948. The Arab League immediately invaded to suppress "terrorist Zionist gangs," but Israel handed them a sound defeat.

Domestic Discontent

At home, the government proved to be ineffective and unstable. In spite of new agreements with the British over Suez Canal revenues and the closing of the old consular courts, unrest continued. The king and his opulent court drew increasing criticism, and in January 1952, mobs torched European Cairo. Neither the British, the king, nor the government could control the people, and disorder continued. A group of Egyptian army officers seized the government on 22-23 July, and on 25 July, forced King Faruq to abdicate. The Free Officers had returned control of Egypt to Egyptians for the first time in two thousand years.

The Revolutionary Command Council

The group of officers, united by the desire to free Egypt and establish a more equitable government, formed the Revolutionary Command Council (RCC). However, as they had few concrete plans to implement their goals, they hoped that the political parties would come together to form a constitutional government. Such hopes quickly proved unfounded, and under the leadership of Lieutenant Colonel Gamal Abdul Nasser, the RCC took direct control. Nearly all the officers resigned their commissions and became ministers and bureaucrats. The RCC harshly suppressed workers' strikes, abolished political parties, arrested dissenters, and suspended the constitution. Although Muhammad Naguib had assumed the titles of president and prime minister, by the middle of 1954 Nasser had displaced him, winning complete control of the country.

Nasser

Nasser continued the directions which the RCC had begun. Under new laws, the government confiscated landholdings above 200 *feddans* (slightly over 200 acres) and increased the number of landholding peasants. Nevertheless, much of the property and wealth accumulated in the hands of village leaders, who even today wield considerable control. Labor legislation raised minimum wages, reduced working hours, and created more jobs in an attempt to reduce unemployment. Authorities also established rent controls and attempted to build housing for the masses of people flooding into Egyptian cities in search of work. Government spending increased to provide all citizens with an education and in a related move authorities pledged jobs to all university graduates, a policy that swelled the bureaucracy and disrupted its ability to function smoothly (if bureaucracies can ever be said to do so).

International Relations

In 1953, the British gave Sudan the option of self-government or administration under the Egyptians; the country ultimately chose to remove itself from Egyptian domination. Around the same time Nasser negotiated the Anglo-Egyptian Agreement, which required the British to withdraw from the Suez Canal by June 1956. Having thrown off colonialism, Nasser embraced a policy of neutrality that brought him (especially after the U.S. and the World Bank had refused to finance the Aswan High Dam) into close relations with the Soviet Union. The U.S.S.R. supplied capital and technical assistance for the dam as well as military supplies and expertise. In July 1956, Nasser decided to nationalize the Suez Canal, a move that upset the Western powers, who depended on the canal for the transport of Middle Eastern oil. The English, French, and Israelis formed an alliance and attacked in October 1956, quickly overrunning Sinai. The U.S. and the UN both worked toward the withdrawal of Israeli troops, and by March 1957 the United Nations Emergency Force occupied Sinai. Although Egypt had lost the war, Nasser had thrown off the foreign yoke and become a hero.

The Israeli Problem

Nevertheless, the problem of unsettled Palestinians remained. Arab governments, increasingly uneasy about guerrilla activities, wanted an organization to control them. In 1964 the Arab League, in an attempt to both give the Palestinians a government and control guerrillas, formed the Palestine Liberation Organization (PLO). The movement was loosely controlled by Egypt until 1969 when Yasir Arafat took over.

War Of 1967

Unrest in Palestine continued, and the Israeli leaders threatened to invade Syria if it didn't stop sponsoring guerrilla raids. Coming to Syria's aid, Egypt massed troops on Israel's border and closed the Gulf of Aqaba, cutting off Israeli access to Red Sea shipping. On 5 June, the Israelis invaded Egypt, Jordan, Syria, and Iraq, eliminated Egypt's air force while the planes were still on the ground, and overran Sinai. By 11 June, the Israelis held Sinai, the Gaza Strip, Jordan's West Bank, and Syria's Golan Heights.

Nasser, in the face of his military's shortcomings against Israel, restructured the army. Moving away from the Soviet arms and technicians, he demanded and received aid from Kuwait, Libya, and Saudi Arabia. He also reformed the government (replacing pro-Soviet ministers), overhauled Egypt's only political party—the Arab Socialist Union (ASU), and wrote a permanent constitution. Internationally, however, the Middle East remained tense: Israeli-Arab skirmishes continued, and rebellion broke out in Jordan when King Hussein suppressed the terrorist branches of the PLO. Fueling this civil war, Syria sent forces to support the guerrillas. Concerned as always with Arab unity, Nasser mediated a cease-fire between Hussein and Arafat on 27 September 1970. The following day he died of a heart attack. The Egyptians once more took to the streets, but this time to mourn their beloved leader, who, by renewing Egypt's interest in the Arab world, had given his people a sense of importance. He had also made education available throughout the country, and even rural Egyptians could obtain a college degree. Although Egypt's growing population taxed the gains from his economic reforms and the mineral-rich Sinai was under Israeli control, the Egyptians forgave their Nasser.

Sadat

Vice President Anwar al-Sadat was elected president in October. Although Sadat at first followed Nasser's policies, he soon moved frankly toward the West, severing his country's ties with the Soviet Union, and in July 1972 expelled Soviet advisors. To fulfill his myriad promises to his people, he joined with Syria in launching an assault against Israel. On 6 October 1973, the Egyptian army successfully stormed the Israelis' "invincible" defenses, the Bar-Lev Line. Although the Israelis quickly recovered, the incident gave the Egyptians a moral victory, and Sadat too became a hero to his country. A temporary cease-fire led to partial Israeli withdrawal from Sinai, and Egypt reopened the Suez Canal.

At home, Sadat restructured the government and allowed competitive elections. In July 1974 he formed the National Democratic Party (NDP), composed of his loyalists; other parties, although not outlawed, found it difficult to compete. He also allowed relative freedom for the Muslim Brotherhood, which he hoped could counteract the growing leftist influence. Sadat committed his government to fostering Arab unity and continuing the struggle with Israel for a Palestinian homeland. To strengthen Egypt's economy, he moved toward the West in a policy called *infitah* (opening). Encouraging private investment of both foreign and domestic capital, it gave individuals the freedom to develop their own wealth and property, encouraging small shops as well as giant international corporations.

Camp David

In 1977, realizing his country needed a reprieve from the wars with Israel, Sadat, in a dramatic move, flew to Jerusalem to negotiate a treaty with Prime Minister Menachem Begin. Although his people, tired of the war, generally supported his move, other Arab countries were shocked. Negotiations remained stalemated for over a year until President Carter invited the two leaders to Camp David, where they finally compromised. On 26 March 1979 they signed the Camp David Accords, which returned Sinai to Egypt and called for peace between Egypt and Israel. Sadat, hailed as a hero by the Western world as well as Egypt, was condemned by the Arab states which, with the exceptions of Oman and Sudan, voted to expel Egypt from the Arab League; they withdrew economic aid and severed relations.

Mubarak

On 6 October 1981, Sadat was slain by religious extremists, and his handpicked successor, Husni Mubarak, was overwhelmingly elected to Sadat's post. He consolidated his political power and, with the peace fostered by the Camp David

Accords, turned his attention to domestic affairs. He rooted out corrupt government officials and set about rebuilding the country's still-weak military forces. He also instituted policies that supported industrial growth, improved the country's infrastructure, and addressed social issues such as birth control. With the collapse of oil prices in 1986 and the uncertainty of the tourist market, Egypt's economy shriveled, and foreign loans to pay for these programs shrunk with it. Faced with a continuing population explosion and skyrocketing demands for goods and services, Mubarak now threads his way carefully between the conflicting demands of domestic programs and foreign creditors. So far, he's succeeded, and Egyptians seem encouraged at the future of their country.

On the international level, Mubarak has followed the same careful diplomacy. Through it, he has returned Egypt to a central position in the Middle East, for after the Camp David Accords, the Arab world had cut off relations with Egypt, ejecting her from OPEC (Organization of Petroleum Exporting Countries) and the Arab League. In 1984 Mubarak reestablished relations with Jordan; in 1987 the Arab League voted to allow their members, at their own discretion, to restore ties with Egypt; on 22 May, 1989, the league welcomed Egypt, after a 10-year absence, back into its fold.

Over the last few years, Egypt has taken an active role in dealing with terrorism, negotiating with the hijackers of the *Achille Lauro*, storming the EgyptAir airliner that had been hijacked, and lobbying Libya to release the terrorists accused of the Lockerbie bombing. In an attempt to find an "Arab solution" to the Persian Gulf crisis, Mubarak called a meeting of the Arab League in Cairo. When Iraq attempted to control Kuwait's seat at the meeting and refused to make concessions, 12 of 21 league members voted to send troops to Saudi Arabia. These nations—Egypt, Syria, Saudi Arabia, and the Gulf Arabs—created a moderate block with the potential to dominate Arab politics. Within that block, Egypt is best equipped, with her long-term relations with Israel, continued cooperation and interaction with the West, and new acceptance by her Islamic neighbors, to move back into her historical position as crossroads of East and West. As Yasir Arafat has said, "There is no war without Egypt, and there is no peace without Egypt."

President Husni Mubarak

ISLAM

In Arabic, Islam means submission, and those who practice the religion (Muslims) submit themselves to the will of Allah. Yet not all Muslims are the same. Islam has been imposed on indigenous races and cultures from India and Asia to the western coast of Africa. The people who inhabit these areas no more fit homogeneously into a mold than do Christians: they differ anthropologically, ideologically, and theologically. The differences in some cases appear irreconcilable and as in all religions, some sects are intolerant of others. Nevertheless, Islamic ideals and precepts have woven a cohesive if informal alliance in the Islamic world. Not only a religion, Islam is a way of life that lays the foundations for government and unifies the Arabic culture. Three areas of Islam—the religion, the state, and the culture—overlap and interact, often blending imperceptibly.

ISLAM'S FOUNDATIONS

By the beginning of the 6th century, the Bedouin of the Arabic Qurayshite tribe had settled around the brackish well and its pagan shrine (al-Kabah) at Mecca. They tapped into the lucrative Indian trade by demanding protection money and then took up trading themselves. Exchanging their herding society for capitalistic riches and urbanism, they created a trading capital at Mecca, which ultimately became the home of Islam.

Muhammad

An impoverished orphan of the Qurayshite family, Muhammad married an older, wealthy widow of the same tribe and took charge of her extensive trading caravans. In the course of his trading activities, he apparently mixed with Christian Arabs and Arab-Jews and was drawn to these monotheistic peoples with their holy books. As he grew older, he mourned the loss of his city's traditional values, rejecting its materialism and hypocrisy. Torn by doubts and aspirations, Muhammad sought solace in a hillside cave near Mecca, where the Archangel Gabriel appeared to him in the first of a series of visions that would span 22 years.

Although basing his new religion on these revelations, he included much Jewish ritual and theology; Abraham (through Hagar and Ishmael) was father of the Arabs, and his religion the mother of Islam. Muhammad included Jesus (Isa), by reason of his supernatural birth and miracle-working, as a distinguished prophet, considering him one of the line of prophets that began with Moses, included Samuel, Ezekiel, Zechariah, Abraham, John the Baptist, Mary, and ended with Muhammad.

The Early Years

Armed with his message, Muhammad the teacher was greeted with silence or verbal attacks. He was accused of being a soothsayer, a magician, and one possessed by a *jinn* (evil spirit). Yet, buoyed by his few converts—his wife and several close family members—he continued preaching and at last came to the attention of the powerful ruling aristocracy of Mecca. Allah was not new to the Meccans, for he was the principal deity enshrined in their pagan temple, al-Kabah. But like Akhenaten and Jesus before him, Muhammad wanted other gods suppressed, and his countrymen resisted.

The ruling clan of the Quraysh tribe, the Umayyads, feared that Muhammad's preaching would decrease the pilgrimages to their shrines, cutting into their pocketbooks. He also introduced the reprehensible idea that beggars and the destitute deserved a share of the wealth. Not only that, but Muhammad's teaching undermined many of the traditional values of the desert: family, clan, and tribe. Substituting faith for kinship, he claimed that common beliefs, not blood ties, made a brotherhood. Shrewd merchants that they were, the Umayyads saw nothing in Muhammad's offerings they wished to buy. In fact, the tribesmen realized that his religious success could generate political power that could rival their own, ultimately threatening Mecca's prestige, civil order, and economy.

The *Hegira*

The Umayyads made life so difficult for the Muslims, by then numbering several hundred, that they slipped out of Mecca and moved north to the village of Yathrib; where his camel stopped, Muhammad built a simple hut and Yathrib became "the City (of the Prophet)," Medina. "The journey" (often wrongly translated as "flight"), marks the end of the pre-Islamic period. The Muslim calendar begins with the year of 622, and its years are distinguished with "H" or "AH" (Anno Hegira—making A.D. 622 year 1 AH. In Medina, Muhammad continued to preach, gathering increasing numbers of followers.

People Of The Book
Because both Jews and Christians believed in one God, Muhammad considered them brothers in the fight against paganism. As such, Muhammad expected his Jewish neighbors in Medina to contribute to his war chest; he was soon disillusioned. By tradition, the Jews neither left Judaism nor accepted outsiders. His neighbors made it plain that they considered only themselves the seed of Abraham, God's chosen. In addition, they tactlessly pointed out to Muhammad that the expected Messiah could rise only from their own tribe. In response, Muhammad denounced the Jews and the cold war quickly heated up. A Jewish merchant's trick on a Muslim customer ignited conflict, and those Jews who survived sought refuge in Syria.

Disenchanted, Muhammad changed the direction of ritual prayer from Jerusalem to Mecca, declared Friday the day of congregational prayer, and established Ramadan, a pre-Islamic holy time, as a month of fasting. He sanctioned pilgrimage to al-Kabah and the kissing of the heavenly black stone (a prehistoric meteorite). By legitimizing the pilgrimage, Islam plunged deep into the rich heritage offered by polytheistic Arabia.

Return To Mecca
In 630, backed by a thousand armed followers, Muhammad marched to Mecca. When the Umayyads yielded, he made his way to al-Kabah, where he smashed the pagan idols. Many of the tribe converted, establishing Islam at the trading center. In the spring of 632, the prophet once more returned to Mecca, leading a group of believers in the first of the annual pilgrimages, and delivered one of the most noble sermons of his career, declaring, "Know ye that every Muslim is a brother unto every other Muslim and that ye are now one brotherhood." Three months later, Muhammad fell ill at his home in Medina and died.

THE RELIGION

Islam is the world's third major monotheistic religion. Its 800 million members make it the second-largest religion after Christianity. Its adherents, called Muslims ("Those who have submitted"), believe their teachings contain God's (Allah's) *final* revelations to the world—divine doctrine based on preceding Hebrew and Christian beliefs but as proclaimed by Muhammad, the last prophet. Islam's creed is simple: There is no other God but Allah, and Muhammad is his prophet. Paradise awaits those who obey Allah's commands; a tormenting hell receives those who don't.

The Koran
Islam is based on the Muslims' holy book, the Koran, a collection of Muhammad's revelations. Originally committed to memory and recited, the material was collected by the khalif Umar and finally codified in writing by the third khalif, Uthman, in 651. Unchanged since then, the Koran is divided into 114 chapters called *surah,* each of which is divided into a number of verses or *ayah.* The language of the Koran sprang from a well-developed Arabic tradition of oral poetry. According to Muslims, Allah chose classical written Arabic for his messages. Hailed for its beauty, the language, they say, is of the heavens, a concept often greeted with skepticism by its students. In order to learn the holy words for themselves, converts must learn to read Arabic, a requirement that fostered a literate society. The Koran itself is the source of community prayers and festivals, and like all religious directives, it dictates the Muslim's beliefs, rituals, and laws of conduct. Considered the work of God, it is divine, eternal, and immutable.

Islamic Doctrine
While Muhammad lived, he revealed Allah's will, including divine legislation. His death, however, closed the heavenly door. His followers turned to the Koran, and if the situation wasn't covered there, to the prophet's sayings and his actions—the *Hadith-Sunnah.* The *Hadith* is a collection of

Muhammad's sayings, the *Sunnah,* his attitudes and actions toward others. After his death, Islamic scholars sifted oral testimonies and reports, verified them, and by the Abbasid era had compiled the teachings into the Six Books. This written collection, coupled with the Koran, now serves as the basis for both personal conduct and sectarian legislation.

When faced with an issue not addressed by either the Koran or the *Hadith-Sunnah,* Muslim scholars study the problem. If three agree, the solution enters doctrine as consensus. In addition, scholars and jurists may solve modern questions with inference by analogy. This fourth source of Islamic doctrine, similar to Anglo-Saxon legal precedents, is based on solutions gleaned from the Koran, the *Hadith-Sunnah,* and consensus.

Islamic Law

As Islam grew, it confronted myriad legal problems that hadn't arisen during the prophet's lifetime. Since Islamic law developed concurrently throughout the empire, jurists with different legal backgrounds and traditions created their own interpretations, interweaving historical practice into their canons. These differing cultural foundations as well as extensive analogical reasoning led to slightly different interpretations of Islamic law that emerged within the orthodox Sunni framework. Each spawned its own school: the Malaki, the Hanafi, the Shafi'i, and the Hanbali.

All four schools are orthodox, and Sunni Muslims, although they can transfer their allegiance between the schools, must submit themselves to one. Many Northern Egyptians embrace the Persian-based Hanafi School. With its emphasis on reason and flexibility, it is the most liberal and adaptable. A few southern Egyptians, along with most North Africans, follow the oldest school, the Malaki. The Shafi'i, an attempt to reconcile the above two schools, attracts the majority of Egyptians. The fourth and most conservative is followed in Saudi Arabia, but has few adherents in Egypt. Nevertheless, the Islamic university at al-Azhar in Cairo offers classes in all four schools, as well as in the doctrines of the dissident Shi'i.

Shi'i

Early Shi'i believed they were ruled by a series of infallible leaders, imams, who were all descendants of Fatima and Ali. However, as a result of persecution, the 12th imam went into hiding and now the Shi'i community awaits the return of this concealed imam—a savior who will bring justice and peace. Until the imam's return, the sect is governed in his name by religious leaders and teachers. These men, who must be descendants of Ali, rule with the despotism of the original imams. While these leaders serve as models of behavior for their communities, they can also rule their devoted followers capriciously. The combination of individual power, a wronged and exiled leader, and a general feeling of persecution have combined to create impassioned believers like those who seized power in Iran.

The Five Pillars Of Islam

The Five Pillars form Islam's backbone. First, devout Muslims must declare their beliefs publicly: "I bear witness that there is no God but Allah and Muhammad is His Messenger." Second, they must face Mecca five times daily and pray: at daybreak, noon, afternoon, sunset, and night. Third, they must tithe; originally, this payment was voluntary, but in modern times, it has become a form of levied tax in some Islamic countries. Fourth, Muslims must fast throughout the daylight hours during the month of Ramadan. The Islamic religious calendar is lunar, so this period of fasting advances through the solar calendar about 10 days a year. Fasting is especially difficult during the long daylight hours when Ramadan falls in the summer. At nightfall entire cities surge to life as feasting and rejoicing break the daily fast.

Fifth; if possible, every Muslim must make at least one pilgrimage (al-Hajj) to Mecca during the month of Dhu al-Hijjah. Rigid rites govern both the trip itself and its religious climax. At the shrine, the devout must circle the Kabah seven times, run between two hills near the ancient springs seven times, and spend the ninth of the month on the plains of Mt. Arafat. The 10th day of Dhu al-Hijjah is the Id al-Adha, celebrated throughout the Islamic world with sacrifice, prayer, and feasting in memory of the prophet Ibrahim. Al-Hajj is the greatest proclamation of faith a Muslim can make, and those who undertake the journey often have the event painted on the walls of their homes.

Dogma

Islamic theology derives primarily from the Koran. Muslims believe in one true eternal and omnipotent creator, Allah, knower of all things, essence of all attributes. In description, Allah differs little from what the Western world calls God. He is attended by angelic spirits who at Allah's direction guard mankind. Muslims embrace the Scriptures (Kutub Allah), which incorporate parts of the three books preceding the Koran—the Torah, the Psalms, and the Gospels. But the Koran is definitive, and any sections of the first three texts that disagree with it are considered human corruptions of the will of Allah. Muslims adopted Jewish and Christian prophets, believing that each prophet spoke to his own people; Jesus, for example, rescued the Israelites. Muhammad was the last of the line, marking the end of prophetic revolutions. No other prophet can follow.

Muslims also believe that ultimately each man must face God's judgment, a day of resurrection, when the souls of the dead must give an accounting of their lives. Until that day, known only to Allah, an individual's life is predetermined by divine will. Man cannot, either by wisdom or foresight, avoid his predestined fate. He can however, choose to accept or reject Islam. Accepting it, the believer lives within the natural harmony of God's will; rejecting it leads to confusion and chaos.

Sufism

In reaction to the strict and rational approach taken by the orthodox believers, some Muslims turned to mysticism. Prohibited by mainstream Islam from practicing monasticism or mystical rites, the Sufi rejects the orthodox and rationalistic Allah. Thirsting for spiritual nourishment and union with the divine, he renounces property and pleasure. Instead he embraces asceticism, with its self-discipline, contemplation, and quietness. By losing self the ascetic finds the universal self and with it, a personal, warm, and loving Allah who dwells in the hearts of men. Like pagan and Christian mystics before him, the Sufi believes that spiritual knowledge must be gained by direct personal experience. In his quest, he seeks mystical union with Allah through ritual (the dances of the whirling dervishes), magic, hypnosis, and drugs.

In spite of persecution, the Sufi brotherhoods grew, achieving their height of influence under the Ottomans, when nearly every mosque in Cairo served as headquarters for a brotherhood. In modern times, as a reaction to the Muslims' perception of an increasingly immoral world, these brotherhoods are once more rebuilding. Nevertheless, the Sufi's withdrawal from the Muslim community and single-minded quest for Allah is not wholly approved by fellow Muslims: the dervishes, they say, pray as if everything depends upon Allah, but don't work as if everything depends upon themselves. However, in all fairness to the Sufis, the doctrine of divine will tends to create the same blind trust in more orthodox believers—those who ignore Muhammad's injunction to a bedouin whose camel wandered off during a visit to the Prophet: "Tie your camel's leg, then trust in Allah."

ISLAMIC DECORATIVE ARTS

Conquering lands between Spain and China, Muslims engulfed Persian and Byzantine art. Blending these styles with influences contributed by the Chinese in the east, the Scythian nomads in the north, and the Copts in Egypt, the Islamic Empire formulated its own distinctive artwork. By facilitating the exchange of artisans and ideas, the empire fostered the spread of both motifs and techniques. Islamic art is distinguished by its use of calligraphy as an integral part of design, by its strongly stylized and silhouetted figures often isolated in rondels, and by its *horror vacui*, which forced the artists to cover the entire surface of an object with intricate patterns.

Motifs

The Koran prohibits making idols, carefully separating the creation of life (which is Allah's prerogative) from the creations of man. Decorations for mosques and mausoleums are restricted to nonfigurative motifs, but even when figures are included in secular art, they tend to be stylistic rather than naturalistic. Since the strength of the prohibition on human figures varied throughout the empire and shifted with time, Fatimid and Persian art included numerous figures, both animal and human, in many of their sumptuous designs.

Early Islamic art in Egypt followed Roman and Coptic designs: increasingly abstract, convoluted vines surrounded individual figures or symbols, while Muslim horsemen continued the Roman, Persian, and Coptic traditions of equestrian figures. From the east came hunting motifs, the valor, courage, skill, and stamina of the hunter symbolizing leadership. The figures themselves were drawn in Near Eastern conventions: almond eyes, large nose, small mouth, and the hair drawn in a solid line across the forehead. Like the Coptic work, minimal shading and linear style stressed line rather than form.

From Central Asia came depictions of clean-shaven, moon-faced princes seated cross-legged, with cup (representing power) and flower (a symbol of paradise) in hand, surrounded by courtiers or listening to musicians. Birds, palmettes, sphinxes, deer, and hares all found their way into Islamic art. The lion or the hawk symbolized the power of kingship—motifs dating back to the pharaohs. Stylized animals reminiscent of the Scythians' fight their way across woodcarvings and textiles. Fish brought good wishes and blessings for eternal life. Flowers and gardens signified paradise, and the abstract twining tree of life reflected the sacred Persea tree of ancient Egypt. Several waves of Chinese art brought a new realism in the lively postures of animals and renderings of plants, introducing the idea of landscapes and such images as flying clouds, peonies, and dragons.

Arabesque

Brought to perfection by Muslim artists, the arabesque arranged interlaced lines and convoluted curves into geometrical patterns. The artists of ancient Egypt had already experimented with the form on tomb ceilings, while Greek, Roman, and Coptic artists continued to develop geometric-based designs, incorporating people and animals. The Muslims, however, raised this type of decoration from border or ceiling designs to one of central focus. These twisting, sinuous forms grew increasingly complex and abstract, their intricate designs and unending repetition inviting contemplation of the divine and the boundless unity of the universe.

THE ARTS OF THE BOOK

Since recreating or copying the words of Allah as revealed by Muhammad was holy work, scribes strove to make the beauty of their penmanship match the magnificence of the ideas, raising calligraphy to a fine art. To increase the beauty of their work, they decorated chapter headings and designed rosettes to mark the end of each verse.

Calligraphy

Kufic, the earliest form of the Arabic script, was angular, its thick letters yielding pronounced horizontal strokes that contrasted with its short verticals. As the script evolved, it became taller, its vertical strokes dominating the design. To enhance the words themselves, scribes developed a flowery variation of the script, ending each stroke with a trefoil, leaf, or flower. *Kufic* script was ideal for architectural decorations and is found carved in wood, stucco, and stone throughout Islamic monuments .

Naskhi, originally a common commercial script, was rounder and taller than *kufic* and gradually supplanted it, especially in books. (The easiest to read of the Arabic scripts, it forms the basis for modern printing.) Mamluk calligraphers adopted this writing, tuning it to their calligraphic skills and adding arabesque decorations that appeared as chapter headings and intricate rondels on opening pages.

By the 15th century, however, a third style, the elegantly cursive *nastaliq* script, had superseded others for literary texts. The artistic culmination of Islamic calligraphy, its forms appeared written in ink, painted in color, and as cutouts glued onto contrasting backgrounds (*decoupé*). In spite of complexities and derivations, the elegant script lost little of its clarity.

The major types of Islamic script include simple kufic, foliated *kufic,* floriated *kufic, naskhi, and* nastaliq.

Books

As showcases for the rich calligraphy of the Muslim masters, books also blossomed into works of art. Muslim scribes continued to use papyrus, but the more durable vellum or parchment held the words of the Koran. Paper, invented soon after the time of Christ by the Chinese, first appeared in the Islamic Empire when captured papermakers were taken to Samarkand, Baghdad, and Damascus. Used sparingly in the 8th century, paper only supplanted vellum several centuries later. The books themselves were bound either in leather or lacquer and included a triangular flap that covered the edges of the pages opposite the spine. The earliest leathers were stamped or tooled with geometric designs, but in the 15th century, overall patterns gave way to cut-leather central medallions and corners. The Muslims adopted colored-paper filigree and marbleized paper for their doublures (insides of the bindings). Lacquer bindings, made on a base of papier-mâché and gesso, were painted with watercolors, a technique soon found on pen cases, mirror covers, and similar small objects.

Painting

Kept alive by Christian artists, painting probably entered the Islamic world via the illustrations of classical scientific and medical texts. Like the pharaonic and Coptic painters before them, Islamic artists flattened perspective and rendered figures as well as foliage in stylized form. Scenes typically had a high horizon—often encompassing an entire hill—and portrayed the action from several vantage points. Figures' actions were stylized as well; like the gazelles in the jaws of the pharaohs' hunting dogs, the deer that are victims of archers' arrows or lions' jowls die passively, serenely.

After the Mongolian conquest in the 14th century, Persian painting adopted many Asian characteristics: convoluted flying clouds as well as graceful and delicately shaded rocks, trees, and flowers. The idea of incorporating illustrations into religious works may also come from the Chinese influence. These illustrations (suggested by some scholars as designed to instruct the Persian kings who couldn't read Arabic) evolved until they appeared as the central focus and ultimately the only design on the page.

Such paintings quickly led to entire albums of miniatures and by the end of the 16th century, these books testified to the acceptance of miniatures in their own right and not just as a supplement to Islamic literature.

CERAMICS

Entranced by the delicate Chinese tableware, Islamic potters first copied the effect (rather than the fabric) of precious T'ang porcelain and polychrome stoneware. Soon, however, they incorporated Islamic motifs and created their own techniques, producing large amounts of striking tableware and decorated tiles. Because of the mobility within the Islamic Empire, ceramic styles and techniques quickly spread, and Egypt played a major role in their production. Not since the simple but elegant pottery of the prehistoric societies had Egypt produced more than utilitarian ceramics.

Islamic potters employed both alkaline and lead glazes with clear, tinted, or colored opaque colors. They also perfected slip techniques, including both molded and colored solutions of fine clay applied to the pot before glazing. Typical of such underglaze painting were the austere black slip silhouettes under a clear or turquoise glaze popular in the second half of the 12th century.

Lusterware

The most notable product of Islamic studios, lusterware involves a complex underpainting technique, including several firings, that produces a range of iridescent colors. Islamic potters adapted the technique, which had first been used on glass early in the 9th century. They created shades of ruby red, brown, and yellow, though later the palette tended toward monochromatic browns. Lusterware remained popular under the Fatimids as the luxurious china of the court, and late in this period potters introduced a blue ground glaze (in addition to the traditional white) and occasionally reversed the silhouetted decoration, painting white figures on dark grounds. Gradually replaced by more trendy styles, lusterware reappeared in the second half of the 17th century as a coppery luster often with a turquoise glaze.

Carved, Cut, And Molded Ware

During the 10th century, the heavily incised lines of sgraffito ware were filled with contrasting colors, often green, under a yellow lead glaze. In response to Chinese porcelain, Muslim potters developed a white pierced ware; their best pieces were translucent, the glaze filling the pierced designs. Uncolored and unglazed, barbotine ware was built up with molded decorations applied (like icing on a cake) to the wet clay before the bisque firing.

Painted Polychrome Ware

Islamic enamelware, often gilded, embraced a seven-color palette: black, chestnut, red, white,

This Isnik polychrome vase from the early 17th century includes a harpy, the human-headed bird oddly reminiscent of the pharaonic human-headed ba bird.

pale blue, deep blue, and occasionally lilac. Around the second half of the 13th century, cobalt or turquoise grounds became popular, decorated in white, red, black, and gold leaf, a style strongly influenced by Chinese taste. A similar ware, Kubachi, emerged from northwest Persia in the mid-16th century, its black outlines colored with deep blue, turquoise, dull green, thick yellow ocher, and brown-red. The most beautiful ceramics, however, came from Turkey from about the same time. These delicate Isnik pieces decorated in brilliant black, deep cobalt, copper-green, turquoise, and red reflected late Chinese influence in its tendency toward naturalistic foliage. So beautiful was this ware that it was shipped to Venice and from there to Germany and the rest of Europe.

OTHER ARTS

The Muslims delighted in furniture and tools decorated with intricate arabesque designs. Superb craftsmen repeated the favored motifs in wood, bone, stucco, and metal, creating a collection of items of unsurpassed technical mastery and detailing.

Metalwork

Although many of the metalworking techniques used by Islamic artists date back to pharaonic times, they also reflect traditions well established in ancient Persia during the Sassian (A.D. 224-642) period. Under the Muslims, this tradition spread, creating both stylistic and iconographic uniformity throughout the Islamic Empire and influencing European metalsmiths. Working in gold, silver, bronze, brass, and steel, Muslim artisans shaped and decorated metal through casting, engraving, inlay, filigree, chasing, repoussé, openwork, and niello.

In Egypt, large amounts of Fatimid gold and silver were worked into ornate tools and decorations but little remains. More common are bronze and brass pieces produced during the Mamluk period—a time of rising prosperity. After the Mongols sacked Mosul, the royal artists fled to Cairo, where they established an outstanding metallurgy center, and for the warlike Mamluks they created arms and armor of unprecedented beauty. In *The Talisman,* Sir Walter Scott describes how Sal-

adin's sword parted a veil of finest silk when it settled over the blade. Made of legendary Damascus steel, (a process guarded for centuries by the Muslims); the hallmark of faint, wavy lines marked some of the sharpest and toughest blades ever forged. Although the raw steel was eventually traded to the West, Europeans were never able to duplicate the strong, sharp blades. Recent investigations have rediscovered the methods used to create Damascus steel, (the trick is forging it at low temperatures), and today, research is assessing its value in modern industry.

Carving

Working alongside Coptic artisans, Islamic artists shaped wood, stucco, and ivory, continuing traditional styles and motifs. The early Islamic work was deeply carved, its lines juxtaposing intense shadow against glaring highlight to establish crisp texture. Vines, leaves, and acanthus scrolls maintained much of their natural form, but like

KAREN WHITE

This 11th century door panel is typical of Fatimid work, which interlaced flowered arabesques and animal figures.

the later Coptic art—or perhaps because of it—Islamic carving soon drifted toward the abstract, its incised surface more tightly filled. Eventually the motifs, losing their semblance of reality, fell into an undulating linear style.

These forms gradually gave way to the concentric circles and interlocking arches popular during the reign of the Abbasids, which in turn were supplanted by slanting bevel lines typical of the Tulunids' stylized animals and birds. During the Fatimid period, secular woodcarving once more became realistic. By the 12th century compositions that had once sprawled freely over entire surfaces were confined to smaller units: hexagons, stars, and squares, each containing its own design. Decorative figures lost their realism, becoming silhouettes, a trend that continued into the Ayyubid period, when arabesques blended smoothly into abstract decorations of line and shape.

Concurrently, woodworkers developed *mashribiyya*, latticework of intricately turned wooden beads. Panels of *mashribiyya* screened townhouse windows and harem quarters from the direct sun while allowing cooling breezes to enter, giving privacy yet allowing the inhabitants to see and hear. Often called harem screens, they also veiled sanctuaries in churches and coffins in mausoleums.

Glass

The glassmaking traditions inherited from the Romans continued, the factories producing blown, molded, and cut glass of great beauty. From the 13th century glass was decorated with enamel and adorned with gold, like the exquisite mosque lamps of the Mamluk period. In Egypt, heraldic motifs like a cup or an eagle set in medallions often enhanced calligraphic designs. Beads of colored glass embedded in stucco created window screens of scintillating beauty called moon-glass after the rounded insets. In Egypt, Islamic artists also continued carving rock crystal, mostly in the form of ewers, some of which found their way into Europe.

TEXTILES

Famous throughout the world, Islamic textiles continued pharaonic and Coptic traditions. With the Muslim conquest, the new rulers simply employed the Copts, who continued to weave the traditional tunics with tapestry bands that ran over the shoulders and along the sleeves. The Arabs adopted this dress, adding narrow, horizontal bands just below the neck and the tops of the sleeves. The best-known product of these early weavers was the fine work called *tiraz*. Originally the Persian term applied only to the strips of calligraphy embroidered with silk on linen; later the name was applied to any cloth with an inscription, either embroidered or woven, and by extension, to the shops that produced the fabric. Fatimid period textile factories experimented with wax-resist dyeing known today as batik, and in later times, Muslims produced fabrics with gold and silver threads wrapped around silken cores.

As in previous periods, fine and decorated textiles were reserved for nobles and royalty, and Muslim rulers often presented such robes as gifts to European notables. By Mamluk times, weaving workshops throughout the empire produced volumes of silk, velvet, and brocade, which flooded domestic markets and supplied Europe with fabrics as refined as they were sumptuous.

Designs

As with other Islamic arts, textiles tended toward all-over design with an emphasis on geometric, arabesque, and floral motifs; the sharp, angular patterns were often printed on the fabric with wooden blocks. The vibrant colors and strong lines of Coptic designs softened into delicate weaving comparable to the miniature paintings. Ancient designs also reappeared, such as the Tree of Life, shown as a single, often potted, undulating vine. In later times, decoration included motifs adopted from paintings, metalwork, tiles, and carvings. Persian and Turkish textiles were basically floral, but the Turkish designs, more limited in colors, stood out boldly. They depended upon the intricate details of leaves and blossoms to soften their impact and never contained animal or human figures. From the Chinese, Muslim weavers adopted the interlocking foliage, a design dating from the Han Dynasty (202 B.C. to A.D. 220). Textile patterns with their broad repeats required skilled designers who could plan the compositions so as to hide the joins. Decoration shows infinite variety, and whatever its motif, artistic symmetry rather than naturalism rules Islamic design.

Carpets

Some of the earliest knotted carpets come from Turkey, and though not as finely worked as later rugs, they were already famous in the 13th century. Marco Polo called them the "best and loveliest in the world," and the Spanish Arab Ibn As'id testified to their worldwide distribution. Patterns of central geometric decoration were surrounded by borders containing *kufic* inscriptions, designs probably derived from felt carpets and tent hangings. In the 15th century, carpets specifically for European export contained similar designs; fragments found in Fustat show the geometric figures and *kufic* characters in red, blue, green, and brown against a gray background. At the same time "Turkish" designs with octagons set into diamonds appeared on a blue ground. The later "Ottoman" carpets (often depicted in Italian and Dutch paintings) were, in spite of their name, made in Egypt. Mongolian contacts introduced Chinese motifs such as dragons and clouds, which become interwoven with traditional Islamic designs. These carpets knotted of fine wool and silk soon found their way into Europe. Incredibly beautiful even when faded, their jewel-tone colors remind one of the age-worn glass in Gothic cathedrals.

ISLAMIC ARCHITECTURE

Early Muslims brought little of their own architecture to the countries they conquered, preferring to adapt what they found, recombining features in novel, functional, and beautiful ways. Although much of the impetus for such innovations came from the Middle East, Egyptian architects incorporated the achievements of earlier civilizations into their buildings. Grappling with challenges ranging from setting round domes on square bases to building impregnable fortifications, Muslim architects followed no fixed rules, deeming lightness and elegance their fundamental principles.

RELIGIOUS ARCHITECTURE

The Mosque

Over the last 1,200 years Muslim architects have created a stunning collection of buildings dedicated to Muhammad's message. Although there are three main types of mosques—courtyard, cruciform, and domed or Ottoman—all have common features. In their mosques, Muslims face Mecca and its Kabah, the sacred black stone, to pray. This direction, no matter what its coordinates, is called *qiblah* and the wall of the mosque in this direction is the *qiblah* wall. Mosques lack an altar, but the *mihrab*, a niche set into the *qiblah* wall, points like an arrow to Mecca and focuses the direction of prayers. Backing against the *qiblah* wall, the *minbar* (patterned on the Coptic pulpit) stands to its right, its odd-numbered steps closed by an ornate gate. Toward the center of the larger mosques, a high, fenced platform *(dikkah)* contains a stand for the Koran and provides a place for its reader. The floor of the mosque is covered with carpets, and the faithful remove their shoes and put them in a rack provided or carry them in their left hand. In the courtyard or *sahn* of nearly all mosques stands a fountain for ritual washing before prayers.

Courtyard Mosque: Of the three main types of mosques, the courtyard style is the earliest. Its roofless central court is surrounded on all sides by a high wall and covered, pillared ambulatories, the *riwaq*. Tradition claims it was modeled on Muhammad's home, but its design also echoes the courtyard that preceded the hypostyle hall in ancient temples. In Egypt, the

In a mosque, the wall that faces Mecca, the qiblah *wall, contains a niche, the* mihrab, *which marks the direction of prayer, and the* minbar, *or throne, from which the sermons are given.*

DAVID KEIFER

similarity is heightened because the Muslims recycled parts of pharaonic, Greek, and Coptic buildings. Christian churches undoubtedly also played an important role in the developing architecture, and some historians aver that the courtyard mosque developed from the basilica.

Cruciform Mosque: This type of mosque also contains a courtyard, but four large, arched wings called *liwans* face the court and form the large cross from which the building gets its name. In later forms, builders sealed off the original arcades with solid walls. This type of mosque often serves as a theological college or *madrasa,* and its four wings accommodate the four schools of Sunni law.

The Egyptian minaret, perhaps designed from the Pharos lighthouse at Alexandria, is square at the base, octagonal in the midsection, and round at the top.

KAREN WHITE

Ottoman Mosque: Developed from the Christian cathedrals such as Hagga Sofia and perfected by Turkish architects, the domed Ottoman mosque was imported into Egypt by the Turks but never became popular. If this type of mosque has a courtyard, it serves only as an annex. The large domed roof encloses the central part of the building, the weight of the massive main dome supported by smaller half-dome buttresses. In spite of the form's lack of popularity, the domes and slender minarets of Muhammad Ali's mosque dominate Cairo's skyline and have become a symbol of the city.

Minarets

Muhammad replaced the trumpet of the Jews and the bell of the Christians with the human voice to call the faithful to daily prayers. The earliest muezzins called from battlements or Christian bell towers. From this high point the crier's voice carried over the villages, and during Ramadan it held the lantern that, upon extinction, marked the beginning of the day-long fast. Most early mosques had only one minaret, but royally endowed buildings often had more. Minarets in Egypt tend to be layered: a square base, an octagonal midsection, and a circular top.

Decoration

Muslim architects attempted to break up the massive lines of their buildings, striving for the illusion of infinite space. Playing horizontal against vertical, ornate against plain, and mass against void, they created interest and tension. In the early mosques, stucco decoration, wooden friezes, inlaid patterns of marble, and arabesque screens all attempted to fool the eye. To create transitions between architectural levels, the artists designed stalactite decorations—the only true Arabic invention in architectural design. Created to play sun against shadow, these icicle-shaped hangings were carved in stone (exterior decoration) and wood (interior). Wooden ceilings were coffered and inlaid with geometric designs of interlocking stars and diamonds. Architects first raised timid domes on heavy squinches. Gradually they experimented with larger domes and eventually introduced pendentives. Ultimately their domes soared majestically toward Allah's heaven supported only by pillars—pillars the architects eased back toward the supporting walls, where they receded unnoticed into the arabesque designs. *Mashribiyya* screens fitted into large windows filtered the sunlight, breaking it up into dancing streams, and lusterware tiles dissolved supporting columns into patterns of light and shadow. Thus huge domes seem to float, weightless and formless, over filtered light.

Mausoleums

Other than those of a few Ottoman-style mosques, the domes that decorate Egypt's Islamic skylines cover the tombs of leaders and saints. Connected with a mosque endowed by the deceased, these square wings are invariably topped with a dome decorated with ribs, chevrons, or arabesques. Under these arching roofs lie the bodies of revered men and often their families. The decorations in the mausoleums match those of the mosque to which they are attached, and the tombs lie in the center of the room surrounded by a *mashribiyya* screen. These tombs, either a cenotaph or the actual grave of a local saint, have become centers where people pray, asking the holy man or woman to speak to Allah on their behalf.

Muslim architects bridged the transition zone between the square base and the dome in one of two ways: squinch or pendentive. Squinch construction imposes an octagonal ring between the dome and its square base. Often visible from the outside of the building, this octagonal drum lies across each corner of the square, and the dome weight falls evenly along the walls. The simplest squinches are rectangular bars, but in more decorative systems they are cut out either in stalactite decoration or as pseudo-arches. Most of Egypt's domes are of the squinch design, and can be identified by the supporting structure that spans each of the corners. Pendentive supports, instead of freeing the corners, concentrate the entire weight of the dome on them. Adopted from Byzantine construction (Hagga Sophia), this system supports the dome's load with lofty arches that meet at the corners. Creating a triangular transition, the pendentive flairs upward into the dome. Pendentive construction allowed Muslim architects to raise high domes on slender supports, but such pillars need buttressing, a requirement met by smaller half domes that created the typical bubbled look of the Ottoman-style Mosque.

MILITARY ARCHITECTURE

Under pressure from waves of crusading Christians, Muslim architects (picking up where the Romans had left off) transformed fortifications, and many of their innovations subsequently appeared in European castles. Machicolations,

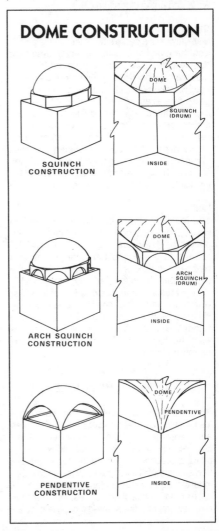

DOME CONSTRUCTION

SQUINCH CONSTRUCTION

DOME

SQUINCH (DRUM)

INSIDE

ARCH SQUINCH CONSTRUCTION

DOME

ARCH SQUINCH (DRUM)

INSIDE

PENDENTIVE CONSTRUCTION

DOME

PENDENTIVE

INSIDE

holes cut in the floors of galleries or parapets, let defenders pour scalding water or oil onto attackers. Loopholes for archers were originally narrow, vertical slots until Muslim architects beveled the sills, giving the archers a wide-angle view of the battlefield and enabling them to shoot nearly straight down at attackers. The most sweeping changes, however, were made in the walls and gates of fortified cities.

Gates

Gateways are a castle's most vulnerable points, and the creative Muslims strengthened their double gates by introducing a bend between the heavy portcullises, giving more space for machicolations, which appeared between the gates as well as over them. The bent gate also exposed the attackers to a line of archers installed above the extensive machicolations. In yet another refinement that appeared late in the medieval period, builders designed approaches to run exclusively along the left wall of the fortifications, thus exposing the attackers' unshielded right sides to extensive fire from within.

Walls

The Muslims also improved their defending walls. Single-walled Fatimid battlements exposed the defenders once the attackers had successfully stormed the fortifications and reached the interior of the compound. By the time Salah al-Din constructed the Citadel in Cairo, Muslims had designed double walls, which had individual sections that could be closed off with fortified doors. Thus to take the Citadel, attackers had to not only breach the walls, but take their hall-like interiors section by harrowing section.

CIVIC ARCHITECTURE

Private and secular Islamic buildings have fared less well than the religious or military structures and fewer remain. From the earliest times the Muslims who conquered Egypt endowed hospitals and schools, often connected to the patron's mosques. Historians know of these buildings through medieval literature, but little remains of their physical structures. Early palaces have also mostly disappeared though later build-

ings have been preserved. Most private homes have suffered similar fates, but the trading inns (caravansaries) have fared better.

Caravansaries

Located throughout the Islamic Empire, these buildings gave traders a secure place to spend a night. Built around a large courtyard that accommodated the pack animals, caravansaries provided merchants with lodgings and small, secure rooms for their goods. They dotted the trade routes and often became market centers themselves.

Private Homes

As was customary in most Mediterranean countries, Egyptian homes were constructed around open courtyards. Rarely taller than two stories, they were divided into public rooms where the men entertained guests, and the women's apartments. Entryways off the street led into a corridor (often with a bench for the *bowab* or doorman), which opened into the courtyard. The court contained a sitting area and nearly always a fountain. The major room of the house, the *qa'a,* served the owner as his general reception room, opening off the court. Totally separated from the *salamlik* (the men's rooms), the women's *haramlik* was reached by a stair from the courtyard. This wing, usually upstairs, contained private living apartments that looked onto the living areas below through *mashribiyya* screens. Windows onto the street were also screened, letting in the light northern breezes and enabling the women to keep an eye on the activities outside.

Built of insulating mud brick, Egyptian houses stayed relatively cool during the day, and the arid climate facilitated evaporative cooling by fountains. Like prehistoric Egyptians, the Copts and Muslims also took advantage of the prevailing north winds to cool their houses, building wind catchers that funneled breezes into the house. Even today, modern apartment buildings are designed around a central core that, as the hot air rises, circulates the air in the surrounding flats. Although modern cities like Cairo and Alexandria have a spate of Western-style air-conditioned buildings, architects, who have been studying the effectiveness of the old designs, are starting to incorporate these principles into their modern construction.

ISLAMIC LEARNING

With the stabilization of the Islamic Empire during the Abbasid period, the royal courts embraced ancient learning with fervor. Translations of Persian, Greek, and Roman texts stimulated intellectual debates and prolific writing. Arab scholars, attempting to reconcile Plato and Aristotle with the Koran, honed both their logic and language. The scope of their studies, the product of widely ranging curiosity, produced work on far-reaching topics; these philosophers brought their trained intellects to bear on mathematics, astronomy, optics, medicine, agriculture, and engineering, not only preserving the information passed on from classical learning, but actively building on its foundation. As this legacy of Islam's Golden Age spread west, Spanish translators converted both classical Greek works and those of Muslim scholars into Latin, providing the pool of knowledge that fueled the Renaissance. But perhaps the Muslims' most important endowment to the West was the questing fire of their drive for answers.

SCIENCE AND TECHNOLOGY

Islamic science, along with the general culture, flourished between the 9th and 13th centuries. During the later part of this era, just as the West was beginning to emerge from the Middle Ages, Latin translations of Arabic writings appeared in Europe where Western scholars often quoted them. In these texts, Muslim scholars not only preserved and transmitted ancient knowledge, but added their own original data and ideas. Thus they not only summed up classical works and documented additional Arab developments, they also provided the core and impetus for modern Western learning.

Muslim scientists drew on Greek texts as well as many from Persia and India, and their translations produced a collection of scientific learning surpassing even the library at Alexandria. Muslim scholars, in the process of codifying this knowledge, adapted their Arabic language to science, a move that, in turn, accelerated their scientific thought and ideas.

Mathematics

Arabic scholars introduced irrational numbers, adopted the zero (sifr), delineated the numerals we know as Arabic, and explored decimal fractions. They implemented the Babylonian arithmetical system of the astronomers and ultimately transmitted its 60 based degrees and minutes to the West. They wrote Arabic texts on algebra and solved quadratic equations, and their thinking on Euclid's ideas contributed to the eventual 19th century discovery of non-Euclidean geometry.

Astronomy

Although containing Indian and Persian elements, medieval Arabic astronomy remained primarily Greek; the Muslims concentrated on honing Ptolemy's sophisticated and powerful methods, making them even more accurate, efficient, and elegant. They also realized as early as the 11th century that his planetary theory had some holes, and by the 14th century, Arab astronomers had formulated their own planetary models, ideas that anticipated those of Copernicus. They also refined instruments used both for computing and observing the skies: quadrants, armillaries, and astrolabes. By the 13th century, their instruments equaled those used by Tycho Brahe in the 16th. To expand their astronomical calculations, they took the few known Indian trigonometric functions and developed the rest, and in the 13th century, Arab mathematicians split trigonometry from spherical astronomy, making it an Arab invention.

Life Sciences

Under the Islamic Empire the Muslims established life sciences on a level of sophistication previously unknown, developing its modern foundations. Interested in the healing arts, Muslims not only tapped folk wisdom, they also translated Syriac, Persian, Sanskrit, and Greek sources, including Hippocrates, Dioscorides, Galen, and Galen's commentators, as well as the works of Byzantine physicians.

Medicine: Ar-Razi (865-925) developed ideas and practices in psychiatric and internal medicine, diagnosis, chemotherapy and treatments that still remain valid. Ibn Butlan (died 1068) preached balance of clean air, moderate diet and drink, rest and work, wakefulness and slumber, and emotional reactions and involvement for general health. In addition, he recommended fine music to lift the morale of patients and help speed recovery, an idea currently under reinvestigation by modern physicians. Ibn al-Jazzar (died about 984) wrote a book on child care (from conception to adolescence) and Ibn Sa'id composed one on gynecology, embryology, and pediatrics. Ibn Maymun (1134-1204), under the Ayyubids, lectured and wrote on internal medicine, therapeutics, *materia medica,* and health and environment. Working in Egypt, he attracted budding scholars from around the Islamic Empire.

This interest in medicine, fueled at least in part by the Crusades, led to hospitals. The staff of these institutions, operated by private owners or government institutions, treated and cured disease, taught medicine, and conducted medical research. In short, they were the prototypes of modern hospitals. These hospitals served both men and women, and eventually expanded to offer care to rural areas, prisons, and "inner cities," programs only recently adopted in the West. Arab physicians developed eye surgery and treatments, methods unsurpassed until the 17th century. They studied anatomy and created surgical techniques and instruments that continue, with some modifications, to be used today.

Pharmacology: Medicine led to the study of drugs. Arab pharmacists made and commercially distributed ointments, conserves, troches, pills, elixirs, confections, tinctures, suppositories, and inhalations. Formulas for these skillfully prepared medications appeared in Arabic texts and eventually made their way into European pharmacopoeia from whence they continue to influence modern pharmacology.

Zoology: Scientific curiosity spilled over as well into zoology and veterinary medicine. Al-Jahiz (died about 869) wrote a comprehensive zoological study of Middle Eastern animals, including the kinds, characteristics, behavior, diseases and treatment. The zoological text of al-Damiri (died 1405), like many such works, not only contained basic descriptions of the animals, but also rudimentary concepts of evolutionary theory, including survival of the fittest. During the 9th century several Arab writers produced tracts on horsemanship and farriery, and additional books dealt with other animals, many including notes on the use of animal organs in disease treatments, a tradition that dated back to Aristotle.

Mechanics And Engineering

The quest for knowledge that pervaded the Islamic civilization also fueled mechanical inventions. Such technology, unfettered by ideologies, diffused readily; its osmosis and cross-fertilization transcended political and geographical boundaries. Like the other arts, mechanical developments of the 9th-13th centuries formed part of a continuous Middle Eastern tradition. Building on Egyptian, Greek, Roman, and Byzantine legacies, the Arabs designed and perfected such practical inventions as mills, pumps, and war machines. In addition, they built automata, fanciful devices including water clocks, moving figures, and fountains to entertain and delight the nobles of Islamic courts.

Although some authors have dismissed such devices as trivial, they nevertheless led to developing the delicate mechanisms and scientific instrumentation that ultimately laid the foundations for modern technology. The immediate ancestors of the elaborate European water clocks and great astronomical cathedral clocks, the automata were comparable to mechanical banks, vending machines, and calculating machines. But perhaps most important, the tradition of building automata that started with the Greeks ultimately led, at least in part, to a rationalistic, mechanistic explanation of the universe, a vital philosophy for the development of modern science.

Although Arab engineers did not understand (nor did they care to) the underlying theories of such mechanisms, they drew on a broad corpus of empirical data. Such knowledge enabled al-Jazari, in a 1206 book, to describe water-raising devices, which included the first description of segmental gears, cranks that were incorporated into a machine, and a reciprocating, two-cylinder pump.

Although al-Jazari and other Arab authors recorded some of the developments, many were simply passed on by word of mouth. The precise modes of diffusion are vague, but the large number of Arab ideas and terms that found their way into European engineering argue convincingly for an extensive heritage, directly or indirectly, from the Islamic world. Undoubtedly much of this information traveled with Islamic traders.

Trade And Commerce

The Arabs, already controlling trade routes in the Indian Ocean and the Arabian and Red seas by the time of Muhammad, extended their sway into the Mediterranean world. They developed and organized caravan routes and merchant fleets, and by the end of the 8th century, Muslim traders, working from their Middle Eastern hub, bartered their wares as far away as the east coast of China and (along the Caspian Sea, Volga River, and Baltic area) the southern reaches of Scandinavia. With the conquest of North Africa and Spain, their trade routes expanded, bringing Islamic scholarship, organizational skills, and technology with them.

Such commercial activity not only led to technological developments such as the compass and lateen sail (which let Arab ships sail into the wind), but spurred the development of municipal administration and control of commerce. In addition, merchant traders advanced the concept of the bill of exchange (a *sakk* or check), venture capital, joint stock companies, and partnerships, freeing investment capital.

But most importantly, the Islamic Empire, functioning much like a free-trade area, exported a multifaceted and cultural lifestyle. Through commercial trade routes and long years of Muslim rule in Spain and Sicily, Islamic science, literature, philosophy, art, architecture, and gracious living filtered into Europe. Not the military confrontations of the Crusades, but rather exotic goods, unique processes, advanced technology, and new concepts were introduced to a less-developed Europe. That this contribution has been largely forgotten in the West testifies to the total assimilation of Islamic influence and knowledge.

LITERATURE

The history of Arabic literature is tied closely to the language, which, in turn, gives it a unique quality. Arabic, the youngest member of the Semitic family, is based on roots of two or three consonants. From these bi- or tri-consonantal roots, Arabs form parts of speech by adding prefixes, suffixes, and infixes. The classic example is *ktb* (writing), which changes to *kataba* (to write), *kitab* (book), *kutubi* (bookseller), *kuttab* (school), *kitabah* (script), *maktab* (office), *maktabah* (bookstore), and *mukatabah* (correspondence). This pattern of variations on the idea conveyed by the basic root, when applied to large groups of consonantal roots, creates a regular rhythm and rhyme that are, especially in poetry, impossible to translate.

Pre-Islamic Poetry

Since these harmonious patterns invite rich elaboration of rhyme and rhythm, Arabs had developed a wealthy tradition of oral poetry. The poet was responsible for singing the praises of his tribe and the exploits of its members. Traditional poems had three distinct parts: the love prelude, in which the poet searched in vain for his departed love; the journey, in which the poet sang either praises to his horse or camel who shares the burden of the exhausting trip or beautiful and vividly realistic descriptions of the desert; and the main theme, which was devoted to the poet's own valor, that of his tribe, or the deprecation of his enemies. These lyrical epics recorded the tribal values of the early Arabs, glorifying honor, loyalty, generosity, courage, justice, hospitality, and tribal solidarity—traits still praised by the desert Bedouin.

The Golden Age

In the face of Muhammad's prohibition of pagan poetry, the poets, abandoning their position of official spokesmen for the tribes, switched their allegiance to the princes and their courts. In this setting, the old love prelude became valued for its own sake, and sensuous, urbane love poetry found its way West to influence such writers as the Frenchman Louis Aragon. The stilted, classical language of the Koran gave way to the simpler narrative developed by the scribes, and Muslim scholars developed not only literature and philosophy, but also science, medicine, and technology.

Inspired by the customs and literature of the earlier Persian Sassanids, Ibn al-Muqaffa translated Pahlavi's *Kalila and Dimna* (available in English translation by Ramsay Wood and Margaret Kilrenny, Paladin Books), the story of two jackals who meddle in a world of anthropomorphic animals, offering moral as well as practical advice to any who will listen. Ultimately derived from the Sanskrit *Fables of Bidpai*, the stories inspired works like La Fontaine's *Fables*. Prose of the period, however, reached its height with Abu Uthman Amr Ibn Bahr al-Jahiz (776-869), who wrote over 200 works on history, natural science, and human psychology, using his wit not only to entertain but to teach.

Poetry: In the face of new forms, poets split into two groups. The modernists rejected the classical forms, turning from the rigid, archaic style to the simple, spontaneous language in current use. Preoccupied with individual expression of their own attitudes and experiences, they produced sensuous love lyrics, religious poetry, and joyous if cynical wine songs. In reaction, the neoclassical poets revived the ancient forms, reinforcing them with artistic ornamentation that at its best combined tradition with innovation. Best loved by Westerners, Abu al-Ala' al-Ma'arri (died 1057), who, though he reflected the skepticism inherent in the anarchy of his era, also wrote of love, death, and immortality. His humor, irony, and love transcended both time and culture: "To humankind, O brother, consecrate / Thy heart, and shun the hundred Sects that prate / about the things they little know about— / Let all receive thy pity, none thy hate . . . / For my religion's love, and love alone."

The Silver Age

While the Mamluks were eroding Abbasid power, a rich tradition of prose works continued to develop and circulate widely. The best known in the West is *The Thousand and One Nights*. The 15th century original contained Persian tales from five centuries earlier, stories written slightly later in Baghdad, and yet others composed in Egypt during the 13th and 14th centuries. The tales are woven into a unity by the narrator Shaharazad, who saves her life by telling the king an endless series of tales. First translated by Antonine Galland into elegant French, the entertaining tales of Shaharazad influenced European taste and fed the continent's obsession with the exotic Middle East. Although Chaucer used the pattern in his *Canterbury Tales,* the stories also provided inspi-

ration for such poets as Byron and Wordsworth. But the tales were never popular at home, and were considered semiliterate; even in modern Arabic versions, the vernacular has been upgraded to a more classical style.

Popular in Egypt were tales like that of Baybars I, who ruled Egypt in the 13th century. Portraying him as a hero defending the commoners against roguish officials and oppressive soldiers, these stories show the street life in medieval Cairo and a cynical view of the court. *Sirat Baybars* sets romantic history against a rich tapestry of magic and superstition, and such tales, still entertaining, are sung in local coffee shops and at village celebrations.

Modern Literature

From the middle of the 13th century, Arabic literature declined, and not until exposure to Western culture in the Victorian era did it recover. An emerging educated class within Egypt read voraciously in French, English, and German, while increased printing capabilities revived the Arabic classics. At the same time, demand for easily read news spurred development of a more colloquial Arabic used by journalists. In addition, Arabic literature embraced Western forms, particularly the short story and the novel. At first only translated, the works were soon adapted by writers who substituted Arabic characters, settings, and circumstances.

In another short step, Muslim authors drew on Arab situations and sources for subjects, addressing Arab problems. M.H. Haykal's *Zaynab,* perhaps the first novel in Arabic, is the romantic story of an Egyptian girl in her changing world. In the short stories of Nagib Mahfuz, meticulously drawn characters face the changes and challenges of 20th century Egypt; in fact, Mahfuz's work, recognized by a Nobel Prize, has been pivotal for emerging modern Arabic literature.

Poetry has equally benefited from the changes in language and outlook. Free verse, rejecting the lifeless diction of the traditional language and forms, gives expression through imaginative images, symbols, metaphors, and dramatic monologues, encompassing subjects from specific cultural situations to universal conditions of human life. Egyptian writers, like all good and creative artists, continue to stretch their readers' minds and touch their souls.

BOB RACE

MODERN EGYPT

During the time of Muhammad, Egypt returned to its role as common ground between East and West, and since the 1952 revolution the country has emerged as the Middle East's cultural center. Cairo's symphony, ballet, and opera companies now stage their productions in a new opera house. *Al-Ahram,* the world's largest Arabic-language newspaper, transmits daily copy to international capitals, while radio, television, and movie companies based in Cairo produce works that entertain the entire Arab world. Publishers print magazines and books in the Cairene version of Arabic and market them equally widely. Egyptian physicians and architects study in Western universities and hospitals and return home to apply their skills.

Yet for all the Western influence, modern Egyptians have retained their cultural and intellectual identity. Architects returning to their Egyptian roots now design energy-efficient domed buildings with traditional central courts and fountains. While novelists write of the sociological and psychological problems of a society in transition, businessmen tussle with floating investment capital in the face of usury prohibitions in the Koran.

Government officials tailor family planning with one eye on the Koran and the other on the role of family in Arabic society. Farmers must reconcile tractors with small plots of land and perennial irrigation with fields that floodwaters once renewed. Perhaps the most difficult problems that modern Egyptians face, however, are with their own bureaucracy (swollen with poorly paid staff) and inflation—fueled by attempts to make the country internationally competitive. Like the generations before them, however, modern Egyptians face the frustrations in their lives with typical humor and creative solutions.

At the turn of the century, much of Egypt's wealth lay in the hands of large land-owning families, and the only other route open to social advancement lay with education. After the revolution, Egyptians flocked to the cities to pursue schooling and the security of a government job that would assure a boost up the social and economic ladder. Today, increasing numbers of practicing professionals make up a growing upper-middle class, and many Egyptians have opened small businesses ranging from buying their own taxi to running grocery stores or shops.

PEOPLE OF EGYPT

For centuries, Asiatic, Middle Eastern, European, and African people invaded Egypt, and many stayed. As a result, especially in northern Egypt, the people represent a cross section of international types. In spite of the general tendency toward intermarriage, however, four cultural groups remain: the Copts, the Bedouin, the Nubians and the Egyptian peasants or *fallahin*.

THE COPTS

Descendants of Egypt's pharaonic population, modern Copts are those who still cling to Christianity. Most live in Cairo as well as Middle and Upper Egypt, where they speak Arabic and, except in religious matters, blend in with their Muslim counterparts. Traditionally the bureaucratic class, the Copts throughout Egypt's history occupied positions of power, although they rarely commanded top positions. Economically, some Copts are still well off and many with educations have worked as professionals in Egypt and abroad. However, others are desperately poor—they gather the trash in Cairo and work marginal lands in Upper Egypt. In response to cultural and economic pressures imposed by the Muslims over the centuries, the number of Copts has steadily declined. Although the government maintains that few Copts remain in Egypt, others working with these people estimate the population at about 10% (some claim as high as 25%) of Egypt's total population. Copts are friendly to visitors and, pleased with any attention from fellow Christians, go out of their way to help.

THE *FALLAHIN*

The rural peasants provided the pharaohs with both the manpower to build their majestic monuments and the food to support the workers. Even today, the *fallahin* wrest two or three crops from their tiny fields in a futile attempt to feed Egypt's ever-expanding population. These farmers live in small villages, often settled by their pharaonic ancestors, scattered along the Nile.

Egyptian Villages

Most of the inhabitants live in mud-brick homes, their thick walls insulating against the afternoon heat. Flat roofs, exposed to the northern evening breezes, serve as cool sleeping quarters as well as storage areas. Villagers plaster the outer walls and often trim them in blue, a color they believe wards off the evil eye. As a man becomes richer, he can add a second story to his house perhaps for his married son. Those villagers who have made the journey to Mecca paint the story of their trip on the outer walls of their homes. Such *hajj* houses, along with the mosques, are the most distinguished buildings in a village.

Some villagers build ornate pigeon cotes close to their homes, using the birds as food and their droppings to fertilize crops. Many houses still have dirt floors and lack electricity or running water; women with jars balanced on their heads make the trek to the community well, and children with donkeys haul the precious liquid in jerry cans.

Family Life

Egyptians dote on their children, who as they grow up quickly take on adult duties. The younger ones start by herding sheep and goats. When the boys reach nine or 10, they begin leaning how to farm the land that will eventually be theirs. Young girls feed chickens, milk goats and water buffalo *(gamoosa),* make the dung patties used for fuel, and fetch water. At an early age, they learn to carry loads on their heads; starting with lightweight items such as bread loaves, they graduate to laundry, and then to large clay water jars. Their work gives them a grace of carriage that remains with them throughout their lives.

In Egyptian extended families, grandparents, aunts, uncles, and cousins all feel clan obligations, and these ties unite them in good times and bad. If an individual's crops fail, all relatives contribute from their own supplies. If an animal is fatally injured, the *fallahin* will slaughter it and each family within the clan will buy a portion, thus sharing the meat and contributing to the cost of replacing the animal. The clan elders arbitrate disagreements, even those between husbands and wives, and give opinions that range from farming techniques to religious obligations.

Dress

Outside her home, a married woman traditionally wears a black outer dress over her brightly colored housedress and covers her hair with a long veil, which often sweeps the ground behind her. She wears her dowry of gold necklaces and silver bracelets and anklets, insurance against poverty if her husband divorces her or she becomes widowed. Her husband dresses in a long robe *(galabayya),* cotton in summer and wool in winter. He often covers his head with a scarf wound like a turban and in the winter adds a wool jacket. The robes of both sexes cover the entire body, but their looseness allows a cooling circulation of air and serves as insulation. Although the black garments of the women heat up slightly quicker than the paler *galabayyas,* both, contrary to popular belief, maintain about the same temperature.

Food

At the end of the working day, rural Egyptians return to their villages, the *fallahin* leading his water buffalo or riding his donkey. A peaceful quiet settles over the mud-brick houses as families gather for their evening meal. Village women spend much of their lives cooking. They bake their *aysh* (bread) in clay ovens of ancient pattern, making both an unleavened type and *aysh shams* (sun bread), which they set in the sun to rise. The main meal consists of rice, *ful* beans, and vegetables. For special occasions (if meat is available), they will fix *fattah,* a dish with layers of bread, rice, and meat seasoned with vinegar and garlic and garnished with yogurt and nuts. The *fallahin* eat with bread rather than knives and forks, tearing the round loaf into finger-sized portions and dipping them into the serving dishes.

Feasts

On festival days, a village is anything but quiet. To celebrate the *mulid* (saint's day) of the village, the entire population turns out; the children sample the carnival rides and the adults visit, watch horse races, and take part in the rituals. During weddings, the village women decorate the bride with designs of henna, and after the wedding, whole villages accompany the bride and groom to their new home. The village women work together to prepare the ornate meals that accompany these celebrations. Isolation is inconceivable in an Egyptian village.

BEDOUIN

Wandering throughout Egypt's deserts, Bedouin nomads continually search for fresh grazing for their camels and goats and water for their families. They don't wander aimlessly, but return annually to various locations in their territory where the land and water can sustain them for the season. Little in the desert escapes the Bedouin's eye. He knows where and when he can find water and whether it's just brackish or toxic; shrubs tell him when it last rained and how much. Signs left in the sand proclaim who has been there before him, when, the directions from which they came and departed, the size of their flocks, and perhaps even the ages of their camels. Bedouin navigate by the stars, familiar landmarks, and stone markers left on a previous trek. They travel light, leaving caches hanging in trees. Other travelers, if in need, are

Egyptian women, dressed in conservative black outside their homes, do much of the work both in the home and fields.

KAREN WHITE

welcome to the food and water but are bound not to touch the remaining articles.

Clothes

The Bedouin dresses for the desert, his layered and flowing robes absorbing the sun's hot rays while allowing cooling breezes to circulate. He winds a cloth around his head and neck to retard moisture loss that can lead to heat stroke and to shield his face against the harsh, dry sand. Women wear black dresses and head covers embroidered in tiny cross-stitch designs: blue for unmarried women, red for married. They cover their faces with a veil highlighted in the same stitches and often decorated with shells and coins.

Homes

Bedouin live in tents of goat and camel hair panels that the women have woven on their narrow ground looms and stitched together. When the tribe moves, the Bedouin wife is in charge of dismantling the tent, packing it on the camels, and reassembling it at the new site. She can roll up the sides so that the cool breeze enters, or stake them down, making it secure in a sand storm. In case of divorce, the tent belongs to the woman; the man takes his domestic animals and leaves.

Nomadic Life

The Bedouin band into small, tightly knit tribes, and their leaders, picked for their wisdom and judgment, retain their positions by finesse and largesse, for their proud Bedouin brethren would find direct commands insulting. To the Bedouin, hospitality is mandatory, and guests are welcomed to a tent for three days and three nights. The teapot or coffee pot is always on for either kinsman or stranger. In exchange, the host expects conversation, for the Bedouin thus keeps abreast of the news.

If water is far away, the men and boys make the trip with camels, bringing it back in goatskins. They also go into the nearest town to exchange news and barter, trading rugs, cheese, milk, goats, and camels for cloth, jewelry, rifles, flour, rice, tea, sugar, and coffee. However, the modern inroads into the desert are changing the Bedouin's life. Many families have settled, building houses, and the handmade tents are disappearing. Trucks bring water in 100-gallon barrels and move goats to pasture. The Bedouin is investing in land and businesses, and sending his sons to school in Cairo. Although he still keeps himself apart from the sedentary Egyptian, his ancient desert lifestyle is vanishing; the Toyota pickup is steadily replacing the camel.

THE NUBIANS

Dark-skinned Nubians inhabit the narrow valley south of Aswan. Although modern studies have been unable to establish the ancestry of the Nubian people or trace changes in the race through history, they carry predominantly Caucasian genes and appear unrelated to other Africans. These people once farmed the narrow margins of the river, planting palm groves along its edge. Hoisting triangular lateen sails above their boats, they hauled rock, transported villagers, and fished the clear, cold Nile.

A distinct group for centuries, the Nubians (called Medjy) served the pharaohs as traders and elite military forces. (Middle Kingdom models show them marching in precise rows bearing shields and bows or spears.) During the Late Period Nubians traveled north, invading Luxor to reestablish classical pharaonic culture.

For centuries, the Nubians have taken great pride in their unique culture, refusing to intermarry, and in spite of centuries of inbreeding, the population shows little ill effect—weak traits must have been eliminated generations ago. In modern times, their pride has led to valiant attempts to maintain their village life even when nearly all of the men worked and lived hundreds of kilometers to the north. Today, transplanted from the lands inundated by the waters of Lake Nasser, these hard-working people are attempting to revive their culture in the face of economic and social pressures.

Village Life

Originally Nubian villages were closely knit, celebrating births and marriages with village-wide festivals, rituals that always included the river. The newborn child was washed in its life-giving flow, and at circumcision his foreskin was tossed as offering into the river. A bride and groom bathed separately in the fertile waters on the eve of their marriage, then again at dawn, together. After a death, at the end of mourning, the women came to the waters to wash from their faces the mud and blue dye that had been their badge of sorrow, and to offer henna and perfume to the spirits of the river. Although the Nubians converted first to Christianity and then to Islam, beliefs in the water angels persist, and the people continue to petition these spirits for favors and blessings.

Dislocations

The Nubian lifestyle suddenly changed when the British built the first Aswan dam in 1902. Its rising forebay drowned their *durra* plants, choked their date palms, and swallowed their mosques and homes, forcing the people to rebuild their villages higher up the barren slopes. They attempted to cultivate the new banks of the river, but the sandy soil lacked fertile silt and production levels fell. Many of the men left their families to seek work in the towns, traveling as far as Cairo.

The dam was raised three times within 75 years, ultimately sending over 85% of the Nubian men north to find work. The women and children left behind attempted to maintain the village customs, but with husbands and fathers returning only a couple times a year, traditional rites and festivals were often abandoned. In smaller ways, too, their lifestyle continued to change: tin pots, aluminum pans, and plastic plates replaced woven baskets, for the date palms that had supplied the fronds were now under the lake. The flat roofs, once supported by palm trunks, gave way to vaulted domes, and even dates themselves, a staple of the Nubian diet, had to be imported.

Although some villagers had earlier moved to Aswan, the High Dam forced a final exodus of the Nubians. When 50,000 trekked north, they could at last claim fertile land. Although living in an alien culture, they were no longer solely dependent on wages sent from the cities; families could bring their men home again. Thanks to government programs, the Nubians who have now settled around Aswan and Kom Ombo face a more promising future. Although many Nubian men still work in the cities, the demand for domestic help (jobs Nubians frequently filled) has nearly vanished, and they now can be found running some of the small shops ubiquitous in Egypt, driving cabs, or sailing faluccas. Others have opted for an education, and Nubians with college degrees make up part of Egypt's educated elite.

CITY LIVING

The bottoming-out of the cotton market coupled with a population explosion caused rural peasants to join the Nubians and flood the cities in search of jobs. These immigrants often settled together wherever they could find room, re-creating the culture of their village life in a city setting. However, jobs for the untrained are scarce, and these poor masses crowd the cities. Many live on rooftops (along with their goats and chickens) or inhabit the ornate tombs of the sultans on the east side of Cairo, for housing is a perpetual problem.

Cairo's acute housing shortage means all its inhabitants, from baker and cab driver to Harvard-educated lawyers, have trouble finding homes. Young men who want to marry must provide a house for their new wife, and many wait for years to get a flat. Often families double up, squeezing parents, grandparents, and children into four rooms. In spite of extensive building, the construction rate remains far below need, especially for moderately priced housing.

The growing population has also stressed the city's infrastructure, much of which dates from the British occupation at the turn of the century. Only recently, for example, with the opening of the subway in Cairo, has any real dent been made in chronic transportation problems. Mubarak's government, however, is upgrading the bus system and work continues on the water, sewage, and telephone systems.

City smog, traffic, noise, and crowding drive many families who can afford it to maintain homes in the country or in Alexandra, where they escape city pressures. Others join local sporting clubs, where they play tennis, golf, or ride horses. Those Egyptians who cannot afford these amenities relax with families and friends at public parks or along the river's banks.

GOVERNMENT

Unlike Western governments, those in the Middle East grew up with Islam. This religion (in contrast with Christianity, which often operated undergound) molded governments, and shaped them into that interdependence coupled with a persistent tradition of centralized authority based on strong, personal leadership (first exercised by the pharaohs and later by foreign rulers) carried over in the power vested in Egypt's president. In addition, Egypt's position in the Middle East requires its leaders to invest much of their time in foreign affairs, and close ties exist between foreign and domestic policy. Nevertheless, Egypt's recent trend toward private enterprise is diluting these once-tight relationships. But perhaps the overriding factor in government formation has been the modern Egyptians' intense rejection of foreign rulers. In exchange for their freedom, the Egyptians accept, and perhaps expect, strong central leadership.

The Presidency

After the revolution, Nasser, relying on his personal charisma, became a father figure to his people, assuming both the responsibility and the powers of a near-dictator. Sadat continued this trend, and Egypt's presidency is far more powerful than similar offices in the U.S., France, or Britain. Today, President Mubarek functions through a plethora of ministers who oversee everything from local governments, banking, and tourism to the Suez Canal, national defense, and political affairs.

The Legislature

The president must, however, look to the Egyptian People's Assembly for laws enabling him to implement his programs. An elected Parliament was founded in 1922, when England granted the country conditional independence. The Egyptian statesman Sa'ad Zaghlul, who educated British officials on the need for such independence, founded Egypt's first political party (the Wafd), which swept the parliamentary elections held in 1924. But the Parliament, hamstrung by legal controls imposed by both the king and the British, could make few decisions.

This legacy of ineffectiveness carries on in its modern-day counterpart, the People's Assembly.

People's Assembly: The original body had 360 members, including 10 presidential appointees from the Coptic community. In 1979, the Assembly was expanded to 392 delegates, of whom 30 must be women, and 10 are the appointed Copts. The People's Assembly meets for seven months each year (unless dissolved by the president, in which case new elections must follow within 60 days), and most sessions are open to the public. The Assembly makes laws by referring proposed legislation (by the president, his ministers, or Assembly members) to special committees for study. The measure is then brought to the floor by the consent of the Permanent Committee (the Assembly speaker and the several committee chairmen) to be considered by at least a majority of the house. If passed (ties are defeated), the bill becomes law on the date of its publication in the official Assembly journal, *Al Jarida al Rasmiya.*

Legislative Control: The president must outline his programs to the house at the beginning of its yearly session, and members have the right to question his ideas. Although the Budget Committee takes an active rule in allocating funds, the rest of the Assembly meddles little with the president's plans; following the lead of Sadat when he was speaker under Nasser, the legislature rarely exercises its constitutional powers to control or expel cabinet members.

Local Government

Egypt is broken down into 26 governorates: four made up of the cities of Cairo, Alexandria, Port Said, and Suez, nine provinces in the delta, eight in Upper Egypt, and five along the borders of the country. Each is headed by a provincial governor appointed by the president. Local government is three-tiered: *muhafazah* (governorate), *markaz* (center), and *qaryah* (village). Two governing bodies function at each level: the People's Councils elected by the populace, and the Executive Councils, appointed by Cairo. The first groups plan actions at the local levels, the second supervises and contributes technical information. In reality, the People's Councils, cut off from federal funding, have lost considerable power, and local governments are now run by governmental appointees.

JUDICIAL SYSTEM

A combination of the Islamic laws, the Napoleonic Code, and capitulations granted Westerners, Egyptian law was built from three separate but simultaneous systems: Islamic law, civil and criminal law, and extraterritorial law for foreign residents. The capitulations were phased out during the 1930s and '40s, and after the revolution the government abolished religious courts, transferring their duties to the secular system.

This system is supervised by a national Supreme Constitutional Court, which rules on disputed cases.

Lawyers
A public prosecutor's office is headed by the attorney general, an appointee of the minister of justice, who is supervised by the People's Assembly. This office, staffed by a number of prosecutors, reaches all levels of the justice system and is responsible for enforcement of criminal law judgments. The modern judicial system, like much in Egypt, has its roots in pharaonic law and as a result is slow and complex. However, in spite of its apparent lethargy, the department has served to counter some excesses by the president and state agencies.

ECONOMY

Egypt's economy is based on three main sectors: agriculture, industry and manufacturing, and services, including the revenues generated by the Suez Canal and the massive tourist industry. In addition, Egyptian workers abroad send home significant amounts of foreign currency, which helps Egypt's balance of trade.

AGRICULTURE

Since pharaonic times, Egypt's legendary fertile lands have supported first her own people and then a succession of foreign empires. To increase productivity, Muhammad Ali in the 1890s introduced long-staple cotton as a cash crop and began a long-term upgrade of Egypt's irrigation system. Building small dams and an extensive network of canals, coupled with the dams at Aswan, enabled farmers to grow two crops per year. Under this care, Egypt's *fallahin* continued to feed a population growing twice as fast as production until the 1970s, when for the first time in Egypt's history, the country had to import food.

Land

Long an agricultural country, Egypt's limited cultivable land (about three percent of the total area) formed the basis for her wealth and status. By the time of the 1952 revolution, however, Egypt's land was held by landlords, reducing many of the working villagers to poverty. In an attempt to redistribute this wealth, the new government undertook a series of reforms that effectively broke up large estates. But to maintain the efficiency associated with large acreages, the government forced the small landholders to form cooperatives, pooling equipment, supplies, and knowledge. The government also dictated which crops farmers could plant and maintained price controls over most items, especially export crops like cotton and basic foodstuffs like wheat.

Crops

In spite of the introduction of cash crops like cotton and sugarcane, cereal grains occupy over half of Egypt's agricultural acreage. Of the various field crops, barley is one of the oldest and was used in ancient times to make bread and beer, as was the more primitive emmer; bread wheat was introduced late in the dynastic period. Rice, now the most important food crop, appeared after the Muslim conquest, joining corn, wheat, barley, and millet.

In the countryside, farmers also grow fields of chick peas (*ful*) and lentils, both of which were known in dynastic times. The Egyptian lupine produces a bean sold as an appetizer from little carts in the street, and peanuts called sudanies are also sold this way or served in bars with beer. Farmers plant several types of vegetables, primarily tomatoes, potatoes, onions, and garlic. Egypt also grows a large variety of fruits; citrus orchards occupy over half the acreage devoted to fruits, and dates and grapes dominate the remainder. Ancient Egyptians treasured their fine wines, and pictures of vineyards and winemaking appeared on tombs throughout the pharaonic period. Wine belonged to the pharaoh and jars of fine vintages were sealed with his stamp, the premium years reserved for his table. Today, grape vines are trained over horizontal poles mounted on square brick pillars, and from their produce, Egyptian vintners can create good, inexpensive wines.

JAN KIRK

In both pharaonic times and today, cereals provide Egyptians with much of their food.

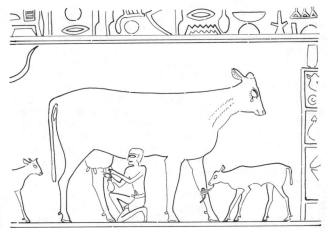

IAN KIRK

Cattle, which once formed the backbone of the Egyptian livestock industry, still wander the fields around villages.

The Arabs brought sugarcane when they colonized Egypt, and today it is widely grown in Upper Egypt, where small trains carry the sweet stalks to market. Berseem, an Egyptian alfalfa grown since pharaonic times, is still cut by hand to provide fodder for an increasing livestock industry. The dark green plant with yellow flowers, by fixing nitrogen, also renews the productivity of the soil. Great quantities of flax were grown in dynastic times; the ancients made linen from its stems and oil from its seeds, but it was replaced by cotton brought during the Muslim conquest.

Cotton: A superior long-staple cotton was introduced early in the 19th century from Africa, and in 1850 it was crossed with North American species; the hybrid was better than either of the parents, and quickly grew to dominate agricultural production. Cotton enabled Egypt to successfully enter international markets, and in response to worldwide demand, especially during the American Civil War, Egypt invested heavily in the cash crop. But at the end of the Civil War cotton prices fell, knocking the bottom out of Egypt's economy. This shrinking market coupled with the crop's demands on the soil and declining prices have decreased the numbers of *feddans* planted. Nevertheless, Egypt still produces nearly 40% of the world's cotton (over half the crop supplies domestic mills), and it remains one of Egypt's largest cash crops.

Livestock

Integrated with crop farming, animal husbandry currently produces additional protein often scarce in Egyptian diets. For much of the year, however, lack of land for pasturage and stored fodder hampers the industry, and animals are fed crop residues such as stalks, husks, and bran; only when these sources are exhausted do farmers cut their precious berseem. Cattle and water buffalo, raised primarily as draft animals, also produce milk, meat, and skins; farmers utilize their manure as fertilizer and fuel. Goats, scavenging much of their food, are inexpensive sources of milk, meat, and hides. Sheep, kept both by farm families and nomads, produce wool and meat; small amounts of pork are consumed only by the Copts and foreigners.

Poultry: Native chickens produce over 90% of Egypt's eggs, and though they're resistant to local diseases, they're poor producers of meat. To increase production, the government-owned General Poultry Company has developed modern methods and in cooperation with 2,700 private commercial farms produces nearly five million broilers every seven weeks.

Fishing

Although a rich source of protein, Egypt's fisheries have yet to fully develop. In addition to commercial fishing on the Nile, fishing along the Mediterranean coast at the mouth of the Nile once took in about 100,000 tons, primarily of sardines, but the completion of the Aswan High Dam cut off the nutrients that flowed down the river, and the catch fell drastically. The fishing industry on Lake Nasser is developing.

INDUSTRY AND MANUFACTURING

Muhammad Ali pushed Egypt's economy toward manufacturing, but British tariff regulations discouraged local production. Until World War I, a few cotton mills, beer distilleries, and sugar refineries made up Egyptian industry. Following the war, Egyptian industry grew and diversified, and by the revolution the country was producing cement, petroleum and chemical products, paper, and modern textiles. The government then nationalized industry, but bureaucrats, unable to run large businesses requiring modern management techniques, foundered in governmental regulations. They faced forced overstaffing, high turnover rates of skilled labor, capricious investments, and fluctuating capital.

During the Nasser period, only consumer goods were produced by private industry, but Sadat, realizing the difficulties faced by the nationalized companies, began integrating them with the private sector. Coupled with his "open door" policy, this quiet move toward privatization brought Egypt joint ventures with Western companies, which contributed both technology and capital. Today, joint ventures and plants that manufacture or assemble products under licenses contribute a major share of Egypt's domestic wealth, and Mubarak intends to continue reducing government constraints, which bodes well for Egypt's manufacturers.

Labor
Perhaps Egypt's most valuable resource is her people. With limited land available, much of Egypt's rural population has migrated to the cities in search of work. Although initially untrained, many have conquered technical skills, but because of low pay, have taken jobs abroad; Egyptian industry misses their skills but gratefully acknowledges the wages they send home as a large contribution to the country's balance of trade.

Energy
Domestic oil and gas account for nearly three-fourths of Egypt's energy consumption, the other major source being hydroelectricity. Since the Nile River's fall is limited, the completion of the Aswan High Dam (with its 2,100-megawatt generation station) has nearly exhausted the river's hydroelectric generating capacity. To increase production, Egypt will have to rely on thermal generation, oil products, and increasingly, natural gas. As electrification pushes even deeper into rural Egypt, additional sources will be needed, and government officials are already discussing nuclear power plants to meet electricity needs late in this century, and experimental windmill fields dot the landscape along the Red Sea coast.

Petroleum
Although the Romans noticed oil seepage near the mouth of the Gulf of Suez, and Egypt's first well was drilled in 1886, commercial production only began in 1913. Compared to the rest of the Middle East, Egypt produces little oil; the majority comes from three fields in Sinai and offshore in the Gulf of Suez. Nevertheless, Egypt's oil revenues contribute nearly a seventh of Egypt's gross domestic product.

SERVICES

Suez Canal
The majority of the fees Egypt receives from Suez Canal traffic are generated by tankers hauling Middle Eastern oil to markets around the world. The canal, closed by the October 1973 war, was reopened in June 1975, but it could no longer accommodate the larger ships then transporting oil. A widening and deepening project was completed in 1980, and yet another is currently in progress. As a result, the canal has regained much of her trade and is the second largest contributor to Egypt's foreign exchange earnings. Also shipping oil, Suez-Mediterranean (SUMED) maintains dual 42-inch pipelines that connect the Gulf of Suez to Alexandria and channel some 80 million tons of crude to the Mediterranean port.

Tourism
After oil revenues and wages sent home by Egyptians working abroad, tourism is Egypt's third largest revenue source. Antiquities have

1. Ships of the desert are ubiquitous in Egypt. (K. Hansen); **2.** Tourists at Giza can get around the site by horse-drawn gig. (K. Hansen); **3.** Although 18-wheelers are invading Egypt's highways, the four-footed variety still covers most of the local short-hauls. (A. Hansen); **4.** old wooden *saqiya* with pottery jars (D. Goodman)

1. Philae (A. Hansen); **2.** In Upper Egypt, the desert moves right to the Nile's edge, pitting its golden knife-edges against the sapphire flow. (A. Hansen)

drawn tourists since Greek and Roman times, and foreigners still flock to the temples and tombs of the ancient pharaohs. But Egypt also offers Europeans a sunny playland where they can escape the winter chill and scuba or snorkel in some of the world's most beautiful waters. Fellow Arabs visit Egypt's Islamic monuments, attend the renowned university at al-Azhar, sample the culture, or observe Cairo's "wicked" nightlife. Although hotel space has traditionally been tight, especially in the winter season, new construction by major hotel chains has both eased the crunch and brought European standards to Egypt's resorts.

LANGUAGE

Arabic is a complex language based on roots of two or three consonants. The forms this root can take are complex, and are preserved primarily in classical literature and the Koran. In the hundreds of years Arabic has been spoken, people have shortened and simplified the words used. While each country speaks a slightly different dialect, that of Cairo, because of its prominence in communications (radio, television, movies, and journalism) has become standard throughout the Middle East. Luckily, the Cairene dialect has not only shortened the forms of the words themselves, but simplified their pronunciation.

Learning Arabic

While Arabic, due to the single roots of its various parts of speech, in theory should be simple, in practice the variations on the roots follow complex rules. Therefore, the easiest way to learn Arabic is to speak it, and Egyptians are most encouraging and helpful if you make any attempt. Start at home with a set of tapes; the best is Barron's *Getting by in Arabic*, which includes a book and two cassettes in Egyptian Arabic. For those who really want to learn the language, Audio-Forum puts out an excellent set of 12 tapes and a text in Egyptian Arabic. Either program will help you with pronunciation and give you a feel for the language.

To use your Arabic while traveling, pick up a copy of Dover's *Say it in Arabic*, a small, well-designed phrasebook that includes conjugations of common verbs; it's available in most Cairo bookstores. Egyptians are always happy to tell you the names of things in Arabic, but since plurals seem to follow few rules, ask for the plural form as well, and memorize the two together.

Reading And Writing

Learning to read and write in Arabic is a challenge, for the alphabet is complex. The Arabic alphabet, written from right to left, appears to the uninitiated like shorthand (a form, in fact, derived from Arabic). Arabs do not use capital letters, but each letter has its own forms that change depending upon its place in a word—initial, medial, and end, as well as a free-standing form. Vowels are not included in most writing, so you already have to know the word to read it. Nevertheless, if learning to read and write in Arabic interests you, see the "Booklist."

Numbers

Do, however, make an effort to learn the numbers, so that you can read addresses, bus numbers, and phone numbers. Unlike the alphabet, which is written right to left, numbers run left to right, like Western numerals. Several systems of transliteration exist, and they are not necessarily compatible, so once you have chosen a book to learn from, don't plan on changing systems.

Speaking Arabic

The Arabic alphabet consists of 26 consonants and three vowels, each with a long and short form. Most of the consonants are the same as those in English, but several consonants appear in two forms in Arabic—the first is like the English version, the second we translate with hard or harsh derivations: h (hah), s (sahd), d (dahd), t (tah), and z (thah). Variously written in transliteration with capital letters, dots, or bars, they are pronounced like their unstressed counterparts but with the tongue and lips relaxed.

More difficult however, are the sounds for which English has no equivalents. The *ayn* is most notorious; often written as an apostrophe ('), this glottal stop is formed by a quick closing in the back of the throat—like the *tt* a Cockney uses to say *better,* or the New Yorker's *bottle.*

The *rayn* (or *ghayn*) most closely resembles the French *r,* like gargling deep in the back of the throat (regular *r* is always pronounced with a trill, like Spanish or Italian). *Kh (khah)* is a hard guttural sound, like clearing the throat, similar to the *ch* in German or in the Scottish lo*ch*.

Be aware of the few letters which Cairenes pronounce differently from the classical or the Upper Egyptian dialect:. *Th (theh)* sounds like an *s* in Cairene; *j (jeem)* appears as *g,* a form of

z (thal) is pronounced like a *d,* and the *q (qahf)* becomes a guttural stop similar to the *ayn.*

Although Arabic only contains three written vowels (long and short forms, giving a total of six), the consonants surrounding them shift their pronunciations to a wide range of vowel sounds. To keep things simple, however, start with this set of six: short *a* as in hat or cat, long *a* as in father or far; short *i* as in ill, long as in ice; short *u* as in luck, long like the double *oo* in noon or *ow* in how.

0	1	2	3	4	5	6	7	8	9
٠	١	٢	٣	٤	٥	٦	٧	٨	٩
·	١	٢	٣	٤	٥	٦	٧	٨	٩

BOB KACE

TRAVEL IN EGYPT

Egypt, though modernizing rapidly, is still a third world country. Many of its people are desperately poor, living without running water, electricity, or sanitation in mud houses. As a result, the country is cheap to visit, but unless you're used to traveling in primitive conditions, stick to the tourist facilities. On the other hand, if you like to travel on your own,

don't mind innumerable complications, and can put up with a considerable amount of discomfort, by all means tackle the public transportation systems and stay in some of the smaller hotels. The Egyptians are friendly, and with the exception of those who prey on the tourist trade, will go out of their way to make your stay in their country pleasant.

GETTING READY

DOCUMENTS

Passports

Visitors to Egypt must hold passports valid for at least three months beyond the proposed date of entry. Before you leave, make several photocopies of the page showing the passport number as well as the date and place it was issued (British subjects need all four introduction pages showing date and place of issue). Keep at least one copy separate from your passport in case of loss; as for the others, you'll be amazed how

often you will use them for checking into hotels and for general identification. Always carry your passport with you while in Egypt; you'll need it to change money, to register, and for identification, especially at some police checkpoints.

The U.S. Embassy in Cairo suggests that Americans register their passports upon arrival; that way, in case of loss or theft, the embassy will not have to telex the States for proof of citizenship. If your passport is lost, immediately file a report with the local police. Take a copy of this report, along with a couple of photos, to the consular section of the embassy or the local

WHAT TO TAKE

Luggage

If you'll be traveling on your own in Egypt, take only one main bag or backpack that you can easily handle; stored luggage rooms are infrequent, although hotels may let you leave gear. For extra goodies you pick up in Egypt, you can pack a folding suitcase or extra duffel, or buy cheap suitcases there: Cairo natives get them in the shopping area east of Midan Opera. Wheeled suitcases, while nice in slick hotel lobbies, do not work nearly as well on rough sidewalks or dirt; for those with wheels for their carry-on luggage, note that the arrival at Cairo Airport has a long flight of stairs. Backpacks with internal frames that convert to soft suitcases give you versatility without inviting the prejudice sometimes shown to backpackers. Mountain Equipment, Inc., (MEI), 4776 East Jensen Ave., Fresno, CA 93725-1704, tel. (800) MEI-PACK/(209) 486-8211, makes a series of rugged packs with bendable frames that move the load off your back—a considerable advantage in Egypt's heat.

Consider taking a daypack for your water, food, camera, film, and writing supplies. Many companies like MEI piggyback daypacks onto their larger packs, an ideal solution. Small fannypacks or ski-packs can replace a purse or vulnerable pocket.

Clothes

Take warm clothes (even long underwear) in winter. Spring and fall can be both chilly and warm; sweaters, sweatshirts, and a light windbreaker will let you layer clothes. Older homes and hotels can be cold, so take a warm bathrobe, especially if you rent rooms without private baths. In summer, wear cotton, including underwear. Loose, long sleeves and pants will not only protect you from the burning sun, they also keep you cool. A hat or scarf in winter will keep your ears warm; a summer hat protects your face, neck, and ears. If you like to go clambering about ruins, bring a light pair of hiking boots. Otherwise sturdy walking shoes are okay. Do not wear open-toed sandals.

Toiletries

Most personal items are available in large cities and in deluxe hotel shops, but they can be expensive. The brands you like may appear only sporadically, so bring your favorites. A good supply of sunscreen, 10 SPF or higher, is vital, as is sunblock for your nose and lubrication for your lips. Equally important is a heavy-duty skin cream, as non-oily as possible. A compact kit with Band-Aids, antiseptic cream, aspirin, safety pins, a small sewing kit, premoistened towelettes, and toilet paper makes a good traveling companion. You might also want to bring contraceptives and tampons. For details on medicines available in Egypt, see "Health."

Supplies

Although AA batteries are available in Egypt, they are often old, and some have even leaked; C and D batteries (especially heavy-duty) are nearly impossible to find; bring your own. Also bring a heavy-duty mosquito repellent, like Deep Woods Off or Muskoil. If you have a favorite brand of instant coffee, bring it. Artificial sweetener is hard to find in Egypt. Nuts are scarce and good chocolate is expensive; both make good gifts. Photographers should bring film (twice as much as you think you'll need) and lens paper. Anyone allergic to dust might consider a package of disposable facemasks for the tombs.

Gear To Take

Flashlight
Flyswatter
Compass
Signaling mirror
Pocketknife
Water purifier
Water bottles or canteen
Sleepsack (hostel sheets)
Daypack
Converter/adapter plugs
Scotch tape
Glue
String
Plastic "Zip Lock" bags
Soap (skin and laundry)
Coffee kit (heating element and cups)
Sunglasses
Washcloth and towel
Travel clock
Tweezers
Waterproof matches

consulate, where you can get a new one. Finally, you'll have to trot along to the Government Center with your new passport and the police report for more paperwork. The process takes three days, so take care of your passport.

Visas

To enter Egypt, you must have a visa stamped into your passport. Although you can get a visa on arrival at the Cairo airport or in Alexandria, it's easier and quicker to apply ahead. You cannot get visas at Taba, Rafiah, Aswan, or Suez, so if you are coming in from Israel, Sudan, or Jordan you must apply before you leave. Visas are available from any Egyptian Consulate, but the cost can vary. In the U.S., you can get a visa at the nearest Egyptian Consulate either in person or by mail. Request an application form, then return it with your passport, a passport-size photo, the date of your departure, the length of your stay (tell them a month—the maximum time on a single visa—to give yourself leeway), a self-addressed, stamped envelope (for return of your passport), and US$12 (although the price can vary between consulates). Send a money order or certified check. They will stamp your visa in the passport and return it. You may also apply for relatives and friends; include all documents and fees as above. Allow 10 days. Tourist visas permit you to stay in Egypt for only *one* month. (So-called three- or six-month visas mean you must *enter* Egypt within three or six months of its date of issue.) Past a two-week grace period, or a total of six weeks from the time you enter the country, you must renew your visa or pay heavy fines when you try to leave. No matter what your visa says, *all entry visas are good for only one month and one entry.* If you will be leaving Egypt and then returning, you must have a reentry visa, which you can get at the Mugama'a in Cairo.

Renewing Visas

To extend your visa, you must first change US$180 into Egyptian currency, thereby proving you have the means to support yourself for another month. For longer extensions, change enough money to cover the entire time (at $180/month), and you'll only have to go through the paperwork once. If you're renewing individual visas for several family members, be sure to get separate exchange receipts for each member of the family. The government will keep these receipts, so you will be unable to use them as proof of legal exchange when buying plane tickets or paying for fancy hotel accommodations.

Take your receipts and your passport to the Mugama'a, the tall, gray, curved building at the south end of Midan Tahrir. Visa windows are up the right stairway; at the top, take a sharp left and walk to the end of the corridor. At window number one, you pay a small fee and pick up your renewal forms. Once you've completed this paperwork, take it to one of windows 23 through 27 (labeled Non-Arab: Europe, North and South America, Australia) and the clerk will issue you a new visa. (I once had a visa stamp refuse to stick to my passport and had to buy a new one—so take some glue or tape.)

Special Visas

Do not plan on going to Egypt and getting a job; the government is stingy with its work visas. If you will be working for a company in Egypt, they will get your business visa; otherwise, you must enter on a tourist visa. Student visas are granted in October for one year. Contact the Egyptian Consulate in Washington D.C. The Egyptian government will issue group visas to tours, but all members of the group must stay together. If you want time on your own, get an individual visa. If you are entering Egypt from Israel at Taba, you can get either a regular visa or a week-long, Sinai-only visa. (See "The Sinai Peninsula," p. 472.)

Egypt is among the few Arab countries that will let you visit with an Israeli visa or entry stamp in your passport, but remember, Egyptian border stamps issued at Rafiah or Taba are sure evidence that you've been to Israel, and other Arab countries may well refuse to admit you. To complicate matters, some Egyptian immigration officials at these borders resist issuing separate border stamps, a common practice in Israel. Israeli officials will frequently put the border stamp on a separate paper so that you can remove it from your passport. Although you can apply for a new or second passport, you're better off arranging your schedule so that you do not cross these Israeli-Egypt borders and then try to enter other Arab countries.

EMBASSIES AND CONSULATES IN EGYPT

NAME	ADDRESS	DISTRICT	CITY	TEL.
Australia	Cairo Plaza, Cornishe al-Nil	Bulaq	Cairo	777-900/777-994
Canada	6 Muhammad Fahmi al Sayed	Garden City	Cairo	354-3110/354-3119
Great Britain	7 Ahmed Ragheb	Garden City	Cairo	354-0850-9
	3 Mena Kafr Abdu	Roushdy	Alexandria	546-7001
Greece	18 Aisha al-Taymuria	Garden City	Cairo	355-1074/355-0443
Israel	6 Ibn Malak	Giza	Cairo	729-329/728-264
Sudan	3 Ibrahim	Garden City	Cairo	354-5034/354-9661
U.S.	5 Latin America	Garden City	Cairo	355-7371/354-8211
	10 Hurriya		Alexandria	482-1911

EGYPTIAN EMBASSIES AND CONSULATES

NAME	ADDRESS	TEL.
Australia	125 Monaro Crescent, Red Hill, Canberra ACT 2603	(062) 950-394
Canada	454 Laurier Ave., E. Ottawa, Ontario K1N 6R3	(613) 234-4931
	3754 Cote des Neiges, Montreal, Quebec H3H 7V6	(514) 936-7781
France	56 Avenue D'iena, Paris 16	(01) 47-20-9770
Great Britain	26 South London W1	(4471) 499-2401/2567
Israel	54 Basel, Tel Aviv	(03) 22-4152
	34 Dror, Eukat	(059) 76-115
Italy	00199 Roma Villa, Savoia	(06) 855-5361/
	via Salaria 267 Roma C.P. 7133	854-9980
Jordan	Jebel Amman, Amman	62-9526
Spain	Velazquez, 69 Madrid 28006	(01) 411-6445
Sudan	Sh. al-Gama, al-Morgan, Khartoum	72-836
U.S.	2310 Decatur Pl., Washington, D.C. 20008	(202) 232-5400/234-3903
	1110 Second Ave., New York, NY 10022	(212) 759-7120
	3001 Pacific Ave., San Francisco, CA 94115	(415) 346-9700
	30 S. Michigan 7th Floor, Chicago, IL 60603	(312) 443-1190
	2000 West Loop South, Houston, TX 77027	(713) 961-4915

Registering

Once in Egypt, you must register with the local police within seven days. Hotels routinely give your passport to the proper authorities to stamp. If, however, you are staying in a private home or an apartment, the owner must register you. You (or your host) must register at the passport office in major cities: Cairo, Alexandria, Marsa Matruh, Sharm al-Sheikh, Aswan, or Luxor. Once the original stamp is in your passport, you can often use a copy to register, which eliminates the risk of handing your passport over to an unknown landlord. Any time you change residence, you must re-register, which is why each hotel you visit will take your passport. Although others register you, ultimately you are responsible, so check your passport for the triangular registration stamp. Even if a hotel has taken your passport, double check; hotels occasionally collect passports and forget to register them. Immigration officials will check on your way out, so if you discover you are unregistered and the week time limit has already passed, contact your embassy. Officials there can write a letter of apology, and you can then often register without penalty.

Inoculations

Egypt does not require vaccinations for North American and European visitors. However, if you come from (or have traveled through) an area infected with cholera or yellow fever you must be inoculated against these diseases. Cholera vaccinations are valid for six months, beginning six days from the date of the injection; yellow fever is good for 10 years, beginning 10 days from the shot. Be sure that your vaccination information is contained on an **International Vaccination Certificate**, and carry it with your passport. Egypt is a member of the World Health Organization, so if you arrive without records of needed shots, you'll find yourself quarantined. If you plan to travel in Sudan, check if meningitis or cholera vaccinations are recommended or required. (For additional suggested inoculations, see "Immunizations" in the "Health" section.) Egypt currently does not require tourists to show proof of a negative **AIDS** test, but if you'll be working there you may have to take a test *in Egypt;* inquire of your employer.

Other Documents

If you want to drive (God forbid) in Egypt, you'll need an **International Driver's License.** If you hold a valid national license, and are over 18, your national auto club will issue an international one (in the U.S., about $10). You will need to carry your domestic and international licenses when driving. You will also need an International Insurance Certificate (green card). Most rental agencies include coverage in their contracts, but you may want to investigate buying one before you leave. Check with your national auto club. An **International Student Identity Card (ISIC)** gives you up to 50% discounts on train and plane fares as well as museum and antiquities fees. (See "Student Tips" under "Miscellaneous Information" below.) Non-students under 26 years old can buy a **Federation of International Youth Travel Organization (FIYTO)** card; although not as widely accepted as the ISIC, it provides some discounts. Student body cards are normally not accepted in Egypt, although you can always try. **Youth hostels** provide cheap beds in many major cities, so you may want to join. (See "Hostels" under "Accomodations.") **Business cards** also make good identification. Take plenty, or you can have

nice ones inexpensively made at nearly any printer in Cairo; printed in Arabic on the back, they're not only conversation pieces at home, but they are helpful in Egypt, for many Egyptians who are fluent in spoken English cannot read or write it. Although **travel permits** are no longer required to visit Siwa Oasis, some areas are still restricted to foreigners. For current information, check with the main Tourist Office in Cairo (Sh. Adly).

If you're planning on visiting out-of-the-way places that need special permissions, be sure to take plenty of **passport-size photos** with you— a dozen is not unreasonable. If you prefer, you can get poor-quality copies made in Cairo (in front of the Mugama'a building) and in most large cities, but bringing enough from home eliminates one more time-consuming detail. Consider black-and-white prints; they're legal, and for large numbers are often cheaper than color. Although the rumor persists that students who can produce some type of affiliation with archaeology programs can get an **antiquities pass,** the Egyptian Antiquities Organization has really tightened up on the requirements; don't waste your time.

CUSTOMS

Entering Egypt

You can bring in 200 cigarettes or 50 cigars, three liters of liquor, and a small quantity of perfume. Personal effects you will take with you upon leaving are exempt from duty. However, you may have to declare radios, tape decks, electric typewriters or computers, extensive camera equipment, and perhaps pay a deposit against possible duty if you should sell them within the country. Although some visitors have had trouble getting video cameras into Egypt, most customs officials now allow them. If yours is impounded, be sure to get a receipt and then contact your embassy.

Egypt practices censorship; that means customs officials can confiscate books, magazines, photos, and videotapes essentially at their discretion. Smuggling in *Playboy,* although lucrative, is risky. Technically you are permitted to bring in and leave with any amount of foreign currency, provided you declare it on a Customs

Currency Declaration Form (form D) and have it stamped as you enter the country. Airlines are supposed to have these forms, but they rarely do; getting them from Egyptian customs is even more difficult. If they stop you on the way out, not having the form is your responsibility and legally they can confiscate your money. Although such confiscation seems rare, forestall any hassles by not carrying large amounts of cash; use traveler's checks or letters of credit instead; *always* get and keep exchange receipts, hotel bills, and other expenses; and convert only as many Egyptian pounds as you'll need.

Drugs are off-limits. Do not buy nor attempt to transport them across any borders—including the border at the duty-free area at Port Said. Customs agents target casually dressed students for searches—dress like a business executive and they probably won't touch you. Since Mubarak took office, the government has been cracking down; mood-altering substances are illegal, and the penalty for possession is stiff. If you're lucky, you'll get booted out of the country; otherwise, you can watch the sun set over the pyramids through bars. Although alcohol is permitted in Egypt, Jordan, and Israel, it may be confiscated at the borders of less progressive Middle Eastern countries. Avoid being an unsuspecting courier: don't carry or deliver packages or letters for strangers. **Remember:** if you end up in jail, your consulate or embassy officers can only visit you, provide a list of attorneys, and inform family or friends as to your whereabouts. They cannot bend the country's laws for you.

You cannot import **firearms;** they will be taken by customs and returned to you upon departure from Egypt. For transporting **animals,** you need a veterinary certificate of good health and a current rabies inoculation certificate. The government levies a small tax on dogs and requires you to attach an official identification tag to the collar. (For information on importing cars, see "Getting Around.")

Leaving Egypt

You may take out gifts and souvenirs made in Egypt, but exporting antiquities is illegal, and the authorities can get nasty about it. You may take up to LE70 out of the country without declaring it. You can also mail goods through shops or agents, provided the items are not for commercial use. If you wish to mail a package yourself, you must get an export permit or use a shipping company. (See "Mail" under "General Information.")

American Customs

Americans who have been out of the states at least 48 hours may bring back US$400 worth of personal or household goods duty-free. Actual purchase price determines the goods' value, so keep receipts or a running list of what you buy and how much it cost. Families may pool their exemptions, but items totaling above the limit are assessed 10% on the next US$1000. However, you cannot import more than 100 cigars, 200 cigarettes (one carton), and one liter of wine or liquor. Unless you're over 21 you may not bring alcoholic beverages into the U.S., and you must carry all declared goods with you. Bringing nonprescription drugs into the U.S. is illegal, so keep copies of prescriptions or a doctor's note of need, and leave medicines in their original bottles.

Since Egypt is named in the Generalized System of Preferences (GSP), goods made in Egypt are exempt from duty and therefore do not count as part of the US$400 allowance. If you take foreign-made goods bought in the U.S. abroad, especially new watches, cameras, and tape decks, you may have to produce receipts proving you bought them in the States. If in doubt, take the items to the nearest customs office before you leave and have the agent register them; there is no fee for this service. Otherwise, you may have to pay duty on them. Obviously old items cause no such problem. With the exception of liquor, tobacco, or perfume, you can mail up to US$50 worth of items home. Mark the nature of the gift and its accurate price on the outside of the package. If the box is worth more than US$50, the post office will collect customs due and add a small surcharge. You can also mail home excess baggage; mark it "American goods returned." Remember, however, you need an export license to mail goods out of Egypt, so it's best to have a shop or a shipping company send them for you. Be aware that Egyptian customs agents will go through your shipment with a fine-toothed comb and probably steal anything they consider valuable. If you must ship, insure it and don't mail anything that's not expendable.

MONEY

In Egypt, money and currency regulations cause more headaches than nearly any other subject.

Pounds And Piasters

Legal tender is the Egyptian pound (LE) or *ginih.* This decimal-based pound is broken up into 100 piasters (PT) or *irsh,* and piasters were once further divided into 100 *millims,* but few of these old coins remain in circulation. Older paper money was issued in graded sizes: the larger the bill, the more it was worth. However, newer currency has a standard size; only the colors and the numerals differentiate the denominations: LE100, LE50, LE20, green; LE10, red; LE5, blue; LE1, brown. The bills are marked in Arabic numbers on one side and Western numbers on the other, and most pose no problems. Be careful, though, with the 10 and the one; the similarity in background colors coupled with the Arabic 10, which is written with a one and an inconspicuous dot, can lead to confusion. Counterfeit LE50 notes made an appearance, so be wary of them; LE100s seem fine.

Piaster bills are still sized according to their value and color-coded: 50PT, light brown; 25PT, light green; 10PT, black; and 5PT, purple. Coins, which are all under a pound, are marked only in Arabic, so learn the numbers listed in the "Language" section, p. 118. To complicate matters, the coins, even within a single denomination, vary in both size and design. Also, a few of the old half-piaster and *millim* coins still circulate; they're legal tender, but some merchants will not take them. Neither will they easily accept worn or torn bills; if you spot old coins or torn bills in your change, you might be wise to play Egyptian and refuse them. You will find Egyptians reluctant to part with change, so hoard yours; you'll need it for purchases in bazaars, cab fares, and tips.

Exchange Rates

Although it was once tied to the British pound sterling, the value of the Egyptian pound is now set by the government at LE0.82 per American dollar. The government has effectively floated the pound by instituting a tourist rate, which has been hovering about LE3.30 per U.S. dollar.

Since the Egyptian pound is not traded on international money markets, it's valueless outside Egypt.

Currency Regulations

In an attempt to dampen the once-thriving black market, the Egyptian government has produced a tangled web of currency regulations, one of which often requires visitors to produce official bank receipts for money changed from foreign currency into pounds. For example, to buy international boat and airline tickets with pounds, you must show such a receipt. (Within Egypt, however, you may freely use pounds for travel.) And when using pounds to pay three-, four-, and five-star hotel bills, you must present proof of legal exchange. Lacking receipts, you may generally use a recognized credit card; your dollar amounts are exchanged at the current tourist rate.

You will have to change money to extend your visa if you stay longer than six weeks. When changing money officially, the bank will give you two forms; one says you sold dollars, the other that you bought pounds. The officials at the Mugama'a building will keep the one that says you bought pounds, which puts you in the interesting position of not having proof that you legally changed money. Although some hotels will accept the receipt that you sold dollars, travel agents and airline companies emphatically will not. You will either have to use other currency or credit cards, or exchange additional money.

Changing Money

Major hotels throughout Egypt maintain banks; check with them for business hours. In general,

EXCHANGE RATES
(December 1992)

U.S. dollar	=	LE 3.30
Pound sterling	=	LE 2.15
French franc	=	LE 0.60
Deutchemark	=	LE 2.10
Australian dollar	=	LE 2.30
Canadian dollar	=	LE 2.60
New Zealand dollar	=	LE 1.70

Egyptian banks are open Mon.-Thurs. and Sat. 0830-1300; Sun. 1000-1200. Most foreign banks are open Sun.-Thurs. 0830-1330. The tourist exchange rate fluctuates and most banks have the rate posted—often outside their doors. In addition to commercial banks, agencies such as American Express and Cook's maintain banks; if you want dollars, pounds sterling, or deutsche marks from your traveler's checks, you may need to go directly to one of these banks. Hotels also maintain banks where you can change money; those in five-star hotels are often open 24 hours. For arriving visitors, the bank at the Cairo Airport is open 24 hours daily, and the banks at the ports open whenever a ship docks. All trade at the current tourist rate. However, if you change money through hotels, restaurants, or shops, confirm the rate and check the commission; they sometimes charge more than established banks.

You can reconvert pounds at most banks and at the airport in the main hall *before* you enter the departure lounge. However, to change pounds, you must deduct at least LE30/day from your legally changed money receipts, a hassle that makes reconverting them hardly worthwhile. An easier and quicker policy is to not get more Egyptian pounds than you can spend.

Checks And Credit Cards

Traveler's checks are honored at most tourist shops, hotels, and restaurants. If your checks are lost or stolen, refunds are easiest to get from American Express, Barclay's, Cook's, and Visa. To expedite the process be sure to keep your receipts in a safe place *separate from your checks,* and keep a record of the ones you cash. As an additional safeguard, leave a list of your checks with someone at home, and carry a separate supply of cash or checks. The above checks are accepted throughout Egypt, although you can usually cash some lesser-known checks in large cities. It's nearly impossible to buy foreign currency traveler's checks in Egypt with pounds unless you have declared currency on Form D; then the bank will subtract LE30/day and issue checks only on the amount remaining. **Credit cards,** especially American Express, Diners Club, Carte Blanche, MasterCard (Eurocard), and Visa, are accepted at deluxe hotels and restaurants as well as air-

line companies. You can also get cash advances on Visa and MasterCard at Bank of America up to your cash-advance limit; the privilege will cost you two percent and pays only in Egyptian pounds: You can cash a **personal check** at most American Express banks if you have an American Express card; they'll give you dollars if available, or pounds. Green card holders can get up to $1000 per 21 days, the first $200 in cash and the rest in traveler's checks; gold card holders can get $5000/21 days, the first $500 in cash, the rest in traveler's checks. However, at most offices you can turn right around and cash your traveler's checks. They will have to telex the States first (at least an hour's delay). You will need your passport to cash checks or change money.

Sending Money

Avoid sending money if you can; carry a separate stash of credit cards, traveler's checks, or cash. Although most banks can wire money to their corresponding banks in Egypt, the transactions are expensive. American Express guarantees money to arrive within 72 hours; the first $200 in local cash, the rest in U.S. dollars in traveler's checks; to send $1000 costs about $70. Money sent by mail is nearly always stolen, and the American Embassy is too busy to routinely help stranded tourists. In short, plan ahead and have enough money available.

MISCELLANEOUS INFORMATION

Disabled Travelers

Although Egypt is not the ideal place for wheelchair-bound travelers, the country is beginning to respond to their needs. For most, the friendliness of the natives and their willingness to help strangers make up for the awkwardness of the facilities. Disabled people on a tour should have no difficulties, but those who travel alone and/or on a budget will have to get advance information on availability of facilities. Do not depend on tourist authorities, as their information is often dated. Instead, contact one of the following agencies: **Mobility International USA,** Box 3551, Eugene, OR 97403, tel. (503) 343-1284 (voice or TDD); in the U.K., 228 Borough St., London SE1 1JX, tel. (01) 403-5688. This organization provides information not only on travel programs and destinations, but also on work programs; **Travel Information Center,** Moss Rehabilitation Hospital, 1200 W. Tabor Rd., Philadelphia, PA 19141, tel. (215) 329-5715, helps plan your trip for a small fee; or contact the **Travel Agency for the Disabled,** Dr. Sami Bishara, ETAMS, 13 Qasr al-Nil, #8, Cairo, Egypt, tel. 752-462/754-721, fax 741-491; he organizes tours to Cairo and Luxor for mobility-impaired visitors. **Facts on File,** 460 Park Ave. S, New York, NY 10016, tel. (800) 322-8755, publishes *Access to the World: A Travel Guide for the Handicapped,* which lists information on tours and organizations; **Twin Peaks Press,** P.O. Box 129, Vancouver, WA 98666, tel. (800) 637-2256 or (206) 694-2462, puts out *Directory of Travel Agencies for the Disabled, Travel Guide for the Disabled,* and *Wheelchair Vagabond.* **Whole Persons Tours** publishes the magazine *The Itinerary* for disabled travelers. In the U.K. you can contact **The Royal Association for Disability and Rehabilitation (RADAR),** 25 Mortimer St., London, W1N 8AB, tel. (071) 637-5400 for books for the disabled. Blind people who depend on a guide dog should take a sighted companion at least until the dog becomes accustomed to the sounds, sights, and traffic of Egypt. And whatever your disability, check with individual hotels, railway stations, airports, and other services about accommodating your specific needs before you go.

Student Tips
International Student Identity Cards (ISIC) entitle you to discounts (up to 50%) on railways, airlines (including EgyptAir), ferries, and at antiquities. Student discounts are often not posted, so ask. You can now get student identification cards at the University of Cairo's Faculty of Medicine building near Manyal Palace. You will need about LE7, a photo, and proof of student status (this need not be a student body card, but anything that you must have been a student to get). Or you can get them from the **Council on International Educational Exchange (CIEE),** 205 E. 42nd St., New York, NY 10017, tel. (212) 661-1414; in San Francisco, 312 Sutter St., San Francisco 94108, tel. (415) 421-3473 or (800) GET-AN-ID. You will need to send proof of student status (a photo-

copy of your transcript or a letter from the school stating you're a full-time student), a passport-size photo with your name printed on the back, your birthdate, nationality, home phone, and US$10. Allow at least a month for processing; cards are good to the end of the calendar year in which they're bought. If you're not a student but are under 26 years old, consider getting a **Federation of International Youth Travel Organization (FIYTO)** card. Although not as widely accepted in Egypt as the ISIC, it will occasionally get you discounts; it's available from CIEE offices.

Senior Travelers
The **Elderhostel,** 75 Federal St., Boston, MA, 02110, tel. (617) 462-7788, offers short-term (two to four weeks) programs in Egypt. You must be 60 or over (companions must be over 50). Programs cover a variety of subjects, but you need no formal education; scholarships are available. The **National Council On Senior Citizens,** 1331 F St. NW, Washington, D.C. 20004, tel. (202) 347-8800, offers information and discounts to its members as well as supplemental Medicare insurance to those over 65. The **Bureau of Consular Affairs** puts out *Travel Tips for Senior Citizens,* available through the Government Printing Office, Washington, D.C. 20401, tel. (202) 783-3238; $1; allow about a month for delivery.

Study In Egypt
The **American University in Cairo (AUC)** offers the most thorough and extensive programs: regular degrees, a year-abroad program, a year-long course of intensive Arabic-language classes, and summer sessions with courses on Middle Eastern history, society, and culture. The campus occupies the south end of Midan Tahrir, at 113 Sh. Qasr al-Aini, Box 2511, tel. 354-2964. Licensed and chartered in the U.S., AUC is affiliated with many American schools, and credits are normally transferable. Guaranteed Student Loans can be applied to tuition. For information write: American University in Cairo, Office of Admissions (LG), 866 United Nations Plaza, New York, NY 10017, tel. (212) 421-6320, or contact the cultural counselor at the **Egyptian Education Bureau,** 2200 Kalorama Rd. NW, Washington, D.C. 20008, tel. (202) 265-6400.

They also have information on the Egyptian Universities, including the ones in Cairo, Alexandria, and al-Azhar.

Language Institutes: Several private organizations offer short-term programs in colloquial and classical Arabic. See "Language Studies" in "Cairo," p. 252.

Working In Egypt

The best way to get work in Egypt is through a foreign firm. Several engineering companies, medical houses, and archaeological projects hire foreigners to work in Egypt. Most sign on people in their home countries, so going to Egypt and getting work once you're there is difficult; if you don't have special skills it's impossible. If you want to try, contact the **American Chamber of Commerce in Egypt,** Marriott Hotel, tel. 340-8888, ext. 1541, for the directory of member companies. *They do not provide referrals.* Your library will have reference books on working abroad, such as the *Prentice Hall Global Action Plan: Looking for Employment in Foreign Countries,* by World Trade Press, and *The Overseas List.* If you're interested in teaching, contact the **Institute of International Education (IIE),** 809 United Nations Plaza, New York, NY 10017, tel. (212) 888-8200, or the **Teachers of English as a Second Language,** Rt. 6 Box 174, New Orleans, LA 70129.

Archaeology: Individuals can explore opportunities for archaeological work by writing for the **Archaeological Institutes of America's** *Archaeological Fieldwork Opportunities Bulletin,* 627 Commonwealth Ave., Boston, MA, 02215, (617) 353-9361. **Volunteers for Peace,** 43 Tiffany Rd., Belmont, VT 05730, tel. (802) 259-2759, sponsors workcamps in Egypt. Join the **American Research Center in Egypt,** Kevorkian Center, New York University, Washington Square South, New York, NY 10003, tel. (212) 998-8890 and read their newsletter to keep abreast of work in Egypt. Unless you have a knowledge of archaeology or specialized technical skills, chances of joining an expedition as paid staff are slim, but many projects will take inexperienced people provided they pay their own way.

Other Jobs: For most jobs, you must have marketable skills, and while a knowledge of Arabic is not required, it's helpful. The **International Association for the Exchange of Students for Technical Experience (IAESTE)** and the **Association for International Practical Training, (AIPT),** Parkview Bldg., 10480 Little Patuxent Parkway, Columbia, MD 21044, tel. (301) 997-2200, sponsors exchange traineeships in Egypt for full-time undergraduates and graduates; applicants work in technical fields for businesses in Egypt. A sister organization, the **Association Internationale des Etudiants en Sciences Economiques et Commerciales (AIESEC),** caters to business students; applications are through local college chapters. For information and a list of chapters, contact AIESEC at 481 Broadway, Suite 608, New York, NY 10003, tel. (212) 979-7400.

GETTING THERE

There are two general ways to visit Egypt: by organized tour or on your own. If you've had no experience traveling in third world countries, you may want to take a tour. Tour organizers confirm your hotel reservations, hire private buses, plan itineraries to outstanding sites, and provide knowledgeable guides. But tours can shut out the sense, the feel, the textures of Egypt and her people. For those visitors in good physical condition who have plenty of time, are used to delays, and can cope with poverty, individual travel in Egypt is easy and rewarding.

Travel Agents

Whether you decide to travel alone or in a group, a knowledgeable travel agent is a treasure. Shop around until you find one who is willing to plan the kind of trip you want. In the U.S., most agencies make their profits from commissions paid them by airlines, tour companies, and hotels on each booking, but like American Express some Egyptian agencies will charge you for confirmed bookings and often increase the cost of the rooms, tickets, etc. Always ask if there is a service or cover charge.

Package Tours

Package tours usually include airfare, transportation within the country, hotels, sightseeing, and most meals. Multiple-country packages allot only a few days or a week in Egypt, which is not enough to see the country. However, several companies provide tours of Egypt only, and many allow you to extend your stay on your own—a nice compromise. The cost of such a tour will vary with the time of year and current airfares; many of these packages include a Nile cruise and a couple of weeks of first-class living for little more than the standard airfare to Egypt. Some tour agencies like **Abercrombie & Kent International,** 1520 Kensington Rd., Oak Brook, IL 60521, (708) 954-2944, (800) 323-7308; **Travel Plans International,** 1200 Harger Rd., Box 3875, Oak Brook, IL 60521, (708) 573-1400, (800) 323-7600; and **Travcoa World Tours,** Box 2630, Newport Beach, CA 92658, (714) 476-2800, (800) 992-2003, (800) 992-2004 (CA), routinely offer trips accompanied by an Egyptologist or archaeologist. **Swan Helenic Cruises Ltd.,** 77 New Oxford St., London WC1A 1PP, tel. (071) 831-1515/1234, or their American representatives, **Esplanade Tours,** 591 Boylston St. Boston, MA 02116, tel. (617) 266-7465, (800) 426-5492, arrange tours to special archaeological sites that focus on art treasures, and ornithological cruises with tour leaders from the Royal Society for the Protection of Birds.

Specialized Visits

Organized diving, fishing, trekking, and special studies programs are open to all comers. Diving vacations along the Red Sea are organized by South Sinai Travel and other tour companies that supply gear and instruction as part of their vacation package. For short (weekend) excursions, contact the Cairo Divers' Club or attend one of their meetings on the first Monday of each month at the Nile Hilton. For more information, send for the Egyptian Tourist Authority's free brochure, *Dive the Red Sea.* Fishing enthusiasts can contact Safi Sahrawi, Executive Director of the Egyptian Angling Federation in Cairo, tel. (02) 574-3612 or 772-386. Hiking, camping, and camel trekking information is available through most travel agents, or contact South Sinai Travel. Through them you can also arrange camping trips to Middle and Upper Egypt as well as several days of falucca sailing up or down the Nile. For cultural trips, check current issues of magazines like *Archaeology, Smithsonian,* or *Natural History,* which contain ads for specialized tours. In addition large universities offer travel/study plans; some carry college credit. Yet another option is to form your own specialized tour, convincing friends interested in Egypt to join you. For culturally oriented study-programs contact Elderhostel (see p. 127); you must be at least 60 years of age (or accompanied by someone who is) to be eligible for this program.

If you're traveling on your own, design a personal research project. Ancient Egyptian history and technology encompass nearly every interest, so use your trip to examine the roots of your favorite pastime. If possible, try to enroll in a nearby college and lay out your project as part of an individual study program. Enrollment will enable your director to write a letter of introduction to the Egyptian Antiquities Department or to specific museums where you might want to work. Lacking educational support doesn't exclude you from such a project, however. Join the American Research Center in Egypt (see p. 128) and then write the Chairman of the Antiquities Department, Abbassia Fakhryabd-Elnoor #4, Cairo, Egypt. Outline—in specific terms—what you wish to do. When your research is complete, be sure to write up your project and send them a copy.

TRAVEL BY AIR

Airplanes are the quickest and least expensive way to cross the Atlantic, and once in Europe, your choices of travel expand to include trains, buses, and ferries as well. If you'll only be visiting Egypt, consider traveling the entire way by plane. If you don't want to make the entire flight at one stretch, spend a night in London or Paris; such a stop gives you a breather, especially if you're traveling from the West Coast of the U.S. or similar distances. Beware, however, that spending a night or otherwise breaking your trip in England or Europe will limit your luggage to 20 kilos (44 pounds). Standard airfares to Egypt are prohibitive, but most airlines discount fares outside the peak season of 15 May (occasionally 1 June) to 15 September. First-class fares push $5000, with business class at $3000. Economy class shifts along the $2000-3000 line, with APEX fares (up to 60 days) hovering between $1000-1500 and 14-90 days running 1500-1700. Youth (12-26) are about $700 and students (18-31 years—must be able to prove student status), about $900. EgyptAir offers a standby ticket for available space out and confirmed seat home: $600-700 for adults, $450-500 children. Or take advantage of the discounts generated by deregulation—if you can figure out what they are. The cheapest fares from New York are offered by Pakistani Air, which provides good food and timely service. EgyptAir and El Al, the national airlines of Egypt and Israel, sometimes offer special fares to their countries. If you fly to Tel Aviv, you can continue on to Cairo or opt for less expensive overland travel.

If you have plenty of time, you might want to expand your trip by flying to England or Europe before continuing south. Where you go depends upon how you decide to cross the Mediterranean: by boat or plane. There are flights out of most Italian airports to Cairo. If you're planning to fly from Athens, check with the U.S. State Department's travel advisory hotline, tel. (202) 647-5225.

Nearly all major airlines fly into Cairo, and many serve Luxor and Sharm al-Sheik (Sinai) directly. In addition to EgyptAir, **Zas**, originally a private cargo and charter line, now flies scheduled runs within Egypt and to Europe and the rest of the Middle East. The demand for airline seats can be high (especially between Cairo and Middle Eastern destinations), so book early, reconfirm your reservations, and get to the airport well ahead of your flight. Occasionally you can find bargain fares such as those in London's bucket shops, which sell surplus tickets for airlines, but in general to fly to Egypt from Great Britain or Northern Europe is expensive, with standard fares running about US$500 one way. You should buy return tickets outside Egypt, as the government now taxes international tickets 10%, including those charged to credit cards.

Advance-purchase Excursion (APEX) Fares

APEX fares consistently offer the best deal, with confirmed reservations but limited flexibility in changing the dates you plan to fly. In addition, APEX tickets permit arrival and departure from different cities and in some cases, even on different airlines. Unfortunately, you must conform to time limits, paying more than 14 days before you leave and spending no more than 60 or 90 days at your destination. The APEX option is well known, so if you plan on traveling in the summer, be sure to book early.

Discounted Fares

Although economical, charter flights have been plagued by cancellations, delays, and on occasion, extra charges. In addition, tickets are restrictive and nonrefundable. Although still popular during the summer, the number of charter companies is decreasing due to competition with consolidators who book large blocks of tickets on standard airlines at discounted rates. These tickets, less restrictive than charters, are available through travel agents. Many of these discounted fares are cheap to Europe, and then you can travel from there to Egypt by several routes. If you want to fly directly to Egypt and have joined the American Research Center (see p. 128), check with their office for member discounts.

Other Options

If you travel light, consider serving as a courier for companies who need someone to shepherd baggage on a flight. Check with a courier service such as **Now Voyager,** 74 Varick St. #307, New York, NY 10013, tel. (212) 431-1616; **World Courier,** tel. (800) 221-6600, or check your yellow pages under Air Courier Services.

EGYPT BY LAND AND SEA

Overland

Heading south from Europe by **train** is cheaper than flying and often more fun. Those under 26 can use B.I.J. (formally B.I.G.E.) tickets, available from Eurotrain, represented in the U.S. by CIEE. Otherwise, consider Eurailpasses, which are especially economical if you're traveling with

ADRIATICA REPRESENTATIVES

LOCATION	NAME	ADDRESS	TEL.	TELEX
Alexandria	Menatours	28 Sh. al-Ghorfa al Tigariya	809-676	54097
Cairo	Adriatica	12 Sh. Talaat Harb	743-213/743-144	
Iraklion	Creta Travel Bureau	20/22 Epimenidou St.	227-002	262138
Piraeus	Gilnavi Agencies	97 Akti Misouli at Favierou	418-1901	212458
Venice	Adriatica di Mar	Zattere 1412	781-866	410045

a friend in the off-season. Although these passes cover certain ferry connections, sleeping accommodations on ferries and night trains cost extra. **Bus** companies such as Magic Bus, 67 New Bond St., London, tel. (01) 32-3747 and 20 Filellinon 20, Athens; or Miracle Bus, 408 The Strand, London WC2; tel. (01) 379-6066 offer another option. Their routes connect most major European cities; check wherever you land for their offices.

By Boat

Two types of boat services connect Egypt with the European continent: luxury liners and seagoing ferries. Among the Mediterranean cruise lines that call at Alexandria or Port Said are Cunard, Epirotiki, Paquet, Royal Viking Line, Sea Goddess Cruises, and Sun Line Cruises.

Ferries: Run by Adriatic Lines, car ferries link Venice and Bari, Italy; Piraeus (Athens), Greece; and Iraklion, Crete, to Alexandria. The boats run several times a month, and the trip takes three days from Venice, one from Athens or Crete. Fares from Venice run US$560-950 in winter; summer US$280-475; from Piraeus rates are US$195-340 in winter and from Iraklion, US$130-220. Single supplements are 50%; students (to age 30) and youths (to age 26) are offered discounts of 12-18%; families get a discount, as do Eurailpass holders (30%). Schedules are available from any representative and listed in Cook's timetables. Due to rough seas in winter, the ferries do not take passengers.

To the Middle East: The Egyptian Navigation Company, 26 Sherif, Cairo, tel. (02) 393-8278, or 1 El-Hurriya Ave., Alexandria, tel. (03) 472-0824,

runs regular ferries from Suez and Nuwebia to Jeddah and Aqaba. Misr Edco Shipping Co. (book through Mina Tours, 14 Talaat Harb, tel. 02-776-951) serves Suez, Aqaba, and Jeddah. North African Tourist Shipping, 171 Muhammad Farid, tel. (02) 391-3081/391-4682, sails between Port Said, Cyprus, and Haifa.

EGYPT FROM HER NEIGHBORS

Egypt From Israel

By Air: The quickest way to get from Israel to Egypt is by air, which also eliminates border hassles and a border crossing stamp at Rafiah. Both Air Sinai (Wed., Thurs., Fri., and Sun.) and El Al (daily except Fri. and Sat.) connect Tel Aviv to Cairo; the flight takes 1 1/2 hours. Space can be tight, so book reservations early. EgyptAir handles reservations for Air Sinai, and El Al maintains offices in Cairo at 5 Sh. al-Makrsi, Zamalek, tel. (02) 341-1620.

By Land: Tour agents in Tel Aviv and Jerusalem offer package deals to Egypt, and if their package includes hotel reservations in Cairo you many not have to change US$150 upon entering Egypt. Alternatively, you can take a bus to the Israeli border at Rafiah or Taba; United Tours, Travcoa, and Holy Land Tours run buses from Tel Aviv or Jerusalem to Cairo. In Cairo, **Travco Egypt** (3 Ishaak Yacoub, Zamalek; tel. (02) 340-0235, telex 92926) buses depart Sun.-Fri. from the Cairo Sheraton at 0500 for Tel Aviv and Jerusalem. **East Delta** lines (see "Getting Around" below), and American Express (15 Qasr al-Nil St., tel. 750-444) buses depart from the front of the Antiquities Museum Sun.-Fri. at 0630. Tickets run about $25-30 OW; you may need official exchange receipts to use LE. You can also take local buses, service taxis, or private taxis. If you opt for one of these, at the borders you'll have to leave your vehicle, walk across, then get additional transportation to Cairo. If you're coming by bus to Rafiah and the daily Cairo bus has already left, you can get a shared taxi to al-Arish and another cab from there into Cairo. From Rafiah to Cairo figure about six hours. If you miss the bus from Taba, you'll have to spend the night. If you're going on to Cairo, you may also have to spend the night in Sharm al-Sheikh. Whichever route you choose, be sure to stock up on food

and drink before you leave Israel, for little is available along the way.

Egypt From Africa

The border between Egypt and Libya is now open, and buses (Golden Jet) ply the route from Alexandria and Marsa Matruh west. Americans, however, are prohibited from entering Libya; intrepid sorts have nevertheless made the journey. Other nationalities should check with their embassies. Much of the western part of the Libyan Desert remains under military control and off-limits to civilians. From Sudan, Sudan Airways and EgyptAir offer once-a-week flights from Khartoum to Aswan and more frequent service to Cairo. A

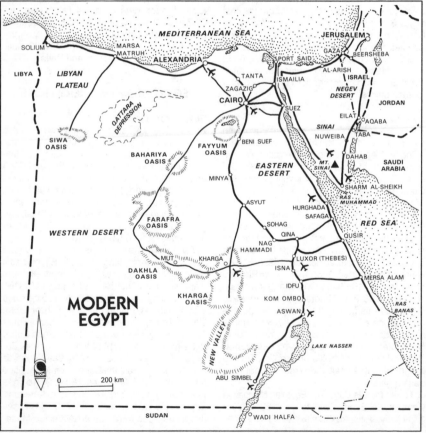

MODERN EGYPT

0   200 km

© MOON PUBLICATIONS, INC.

slower, less dependable, and more uncomfortable option is the train from Khartoum to Wadi Halfa and then across Lake Nasser by what has been euphemistically called "rustic steamer." The boat trip (scheduled Mon., Thurs., and occasionally Sat.) takes about 30 hours—once it starts; you'll need your own food, drink, and bedding. The ferry schedule does not coordinate well with the train, so you may find yourself stuck in Wadi Halfa for a few days. If you choose to visit Sudan from Egypt, you will have to get a visa in Cairo—you will not be allowed to leave Aswan without one. They are available in most countries and in Cairo, where a Sudanese visa takes three to four weeks minimum (Sudan Embassy, 3 Sh. Ibrahimi, Garden City, tel. (02) 354-9661/354-5658). You will need a letter from your consulate and your passport must not have an Israeli stamp. For travel information via the steamer, contact the Nile Navigation Company, 8 Sh. Qasr al-Nil, Cairo, or the General Nile Company for River Transport, 7 Atlas Building, Aswan, tel. (097) 323-348.

GETTING AROUND

Once inside Egypt you have several options for seeing the country. The easiest though most expensive is to join organized sightseeing tours run by travel agents. These may be booked through an independent agent (Cook's, Misr Travel, etc.), your hotel, or the local Tourist Office. Slightly less expensive are organized camping trips into Middle Egypt and Sinai booked through South Sinai Travel. (See "Cairo—Practicalities," p. 253.) **Salauco Tours,** 47 Sh. al-Falaki, tel. (02) 355-0906, fax 344-4796, arranges low-cost tours for independent travelers by coordinating transportation not only in Cairo but throughout the country. You can often find Dr. Hossam Abu Shady and his wife Anny in the first class ticket area of Ramesses Station in Cairo; the company, while unusual, gets good reviews.

Public transportation inside Egypt ranges from the deluxe intracity buses to the backs of overcrowded, speeding pickups. Comfort, travel time, and safety are directly related to price. If you opt for local buses and trains, you will inevitably find yourself embroiled in disagreements, the victim of fouled-up schedules, or the target of the occasional huckster. Remember, Egyptians live with this type of interference and treat it with a grain of humor and a healthy pinch of patience; to keep your sanity, follow their lead. Outside the main cities, you'll have to stretch your limited Arabic vocabulary to its breaking point. Nevertheless, traveling among the Egyptians is worth the effort, for outside Cairo and the tourist areas, people want to make you, their guest, feel at home and will go out of their way to help solve your problems.

Travel Limitations
Foreigners must stay on Egypt's main roads, and though this and other restrictions are gradually being relaxed, if you violate them, the police may seize your passport and hold you for questioning; usually a sincere apology solves any problems. The coasts, the secondary roads in the delta and the Western Desert, and all areas of the Sinai except the main tourist areas and their connecting roads are off-limits.

Leftover land mines from World War II and the Israeli wars are one of the reasons for closing the coasts along the Mediterranean and Red seas. (Two British children have been killed by a mine at Ras Banas.) If you travel in these areas, keep to recognized beaches or go with a guide. All the southern oases have been removed from the prohibited list, including Siwa.

If you wish to travel in restricted areas, take three passport photos and your passport to the Travel Permits Department of the Ministry of the Interior. In Cairo, apply at the corner of Shs. Sheikh Rihan and Nubar; in Alexandria, at Sh. Ferrana, just off Sh. al-Hurriya. If you tell them were you want to go, when, and why, they will usually grant permission; the process takes at least a week.

PUBLIC TRANSPORT

By Air
EgyptAir flies daily between Cairo and Luxor/Aswan, Abu Simbel, Hurghada, and Alexandria as well as twice a week to New Valley (Kharga); the airline maintains offices

throughout Egypt. **Air Sinai** connects Cairo with Hurghada, Sharm al-Sheikh, St. Catherine's Monastery, al-Arish, Elat, and Tel Aviv. Air Sinai's main office is in the Nile Hilton; in other locations, EgyptAir handles Air Sinai information. The domestic airline **Zas** covers Luxor, Aswan, Abu Simbel, Hurghada, and Sharm al-Sheikh from Cairo. The company maintains offices at the airports in Cairo, Hurghada, and Sharm al-Sheikh as well as working through Spring Tours and South Sinai Travel agents.

Although you can only pay for international tickets with Egyptian pounds when they are accompanied by a currency-exchange receipt, you can freely use pounds for domestic travel. Domestic tickets are available overseas, but they are cheaper in Egypt. Always reconfirm your reservations, no matter what flight. Flights to Upper Egypt are often crowded, so get your tickets early. These flights also tend to be overbooked and seats are not reserved, so get to the airport an hour or two before flight time. In Cairo, allow at least 30 minutes for the trip to the airport, an hour in rush times. If you must travel and the flight is already booked, go to the airport on a standby basis; frequently there are no-shows.

By Train

Cities and villages of Egypt are linked by a frequent if aging train service, and along its miles of track the countryside of Egypt unfolds, revealing its ageless rhythm of rural life. Trains come in four classes. First class *(daraga oola)*, with reserved seating in reclining armchairs, boasts air-conditioning, waiter service, and no passengers standing in the aisles. Second-class superior *(daraga tania mumtaaza)* resembles first except that passengers crowd the aisles, and the fare runs about half that of first class. Standard second class *(daraga tania aadia)*, offers padded bench seating and open windows instead of air-conditioning. Third class *(daraga talta)* has wooden benches and open doors for ventilation. Most cars are dirty, even many of the first-class ones, and are showing their age and lack of upkeep. Unless you're traveling to a major city, all stations are marked in Arabic, so you'll have to ask where to get off. Most foreigners who live in Egypt travel only first class, definitely no lower than second, for below that the trains are unbelievably crowded, noisy, and unreli-

able. The big exception to this generalization are the sleeper trains run by the French Wagon-Lits Company. These trains, while not plush, are a comfortable way to get to Luxor or Aswan, saving a night's room cost, although fares have skyrocketed and they are no longer the bargain they used to be. Tickets for the independent traveler are increasingly hard to get; surly agents at the Cairo station who once condescended to sell berths a week ahead now only ungraciously take your money three days ahead. Several new passenger runs are making day trains more feasible. Between Cairo and Alexandria, the Turbini hits the tracks three times daily each way, making the trip in just two hours. The "Gray Ghost" flits along the roadbed between Cairo to Luxor with just a single stop in Asyut. Since the tracks are in poor shape, the trains all rock a good deal; if you're sensitive to motion, consider another mode of transportation.

Rail Tickets: Railway tickets may be either colored slips of paper, first class (blue) or second class (pink), or cardboard rectangles. Both types include the number of the train, the car number, the seat number(s) the date (day/month) and the departure time, ususally in that order; it may or may not include the platform number. Cars are marked with the number on their sides. If you want to explore Egypt by train, investigate the Egyptian Railway pass, the equivalent of the Eurailpass. Dubbed a "kilometre," they are available at the train stations in Alexandria and Cairo. Cost depends upon the distance and time you want to travel (For details, see p. 257). Otherwise, buy regular tickets; they're usually available no more than a week ahead of the time you want to leave. Students with ISIC cards get half off ticket purchases except for sleeper trains.

If you'll be traveling during the last week of Ramadan, over Easter Week, or in summer when the more popular trains quickly fill up, book early. You cannot purchase roundtrip tickets, so if you know when you'll be returning, book the return on your arrival. Most travel agents will buy first-class tickets for you for a small fee, often worth the time it would take to stand in line yourself. However, if you're riding second or third class and you don't mind standing, you can board sold-out trains and buy a ticket from the conductor for fare plus a small penalty fee (a pound or so). For a small fee, you can either return or change tickets by returning them to the stationmaster at the depot from where you would have departed *before* that train leaves. See "Cairo—Practicalities" for train schedules, or pick up a copy of the *Egyptian Railways Timetable* available in English for LE1 at Ramesses Station in Cairo. (Occasionally they're available at Alexandria.)

By Bus

Local intercity buses are a cheap but decidedly uncomfortable way to get around in Egypt. They are old, dirty, and break down with incredible regularity. However, if you have the time and don't mind the hassles, they do connect places that are otherwise inaccessible. The major mode of travel for most Egyptians, they run frequently, usually between 0500 or 0600 and mid to late afternoon. On some routes (like Cairo to Sinai) buses leave at night; these almost always have videos that boisterous Egyptians turn up full volume—take heavy-duty earplugs. Many of the routes are adding better quality buses, often with a/c (when it works); tickets run a few pounds more. For some buses, you simply board, find a seat, and pay the driver or conductor. For others, you'll need to buy tickets ahead, either several hours or a couple of days; these buses have reserved seats.

Super Jet and **East Delta** run plush buses; clean, air-conditioned, with video (usually played at a more civilized volume), and on-board catering along the desert road between Cairo and Alexandria; Golden Arrow serves Luxor, Aswan, and Hurghada, and ones nearly as good serve Sinai and the Red Sea coast. Bus stations open 0500 or 0600 and remain open until most of the buses have left. They also open an hour or so before night runs. In larger cities, buses of different companies, or from the same company but for different destinations, may leave from different terminals.

By Boat

For centuries, the Nile has provided Egypt with a major aquatic highway. The north-running current and the prevailing north winds still drive yachts and heavily loaded barges upstream and down, but in the last 10 to 20 years the river has become dominated by motorized cruise ships catering to tourists. Over 200 of them ply the river between Aswan and Abydos, and at the beginning and end of the winter season make the trip from Luxor to Cairo. Most offer three- to five-night cruises between Luxor and Aswan; some include Abydos and Dendera—a worthwhile addition, as these are two of the most interesting and beautiful temples in Egypt. Some are now routinely offering 10- to 11-night excursions that take in Middle Egypt—the outstanding Middle Kingdom tombs at Beni Hassan, and at Akhenaten's capital of al-Amarna—then on to Cairo. One of the nicest ways to see Egypt, the riverboats dock at major sites and conduct guided tours to the antiquities. Although they are expensive, their trouble-free comfort gives one a truly enjoyable vacation—air-conditioned luxury in the midst of Egypt's desert heat. Good cruises are run by most major hotels as well as private companies like Naggar and Club Med, but be aware that some boats fall considerably below the five-star class. Before you buy tickets from anyone but a well-known operator, try to see the boat. High season (Oct. 1-April 30) prices run $130-200 pp per night (five-star) and $75-140 (four-star); shoulder season (May and Sept.) run about 15% less; low season (June 1-Aug. 30) sees reductions of up to 50%. Some companies offer student rates. Prices usually include all meals, service, taxes, and sightseeing with a trained guide or Egyptologist. Most tours are booked from abroad or through the main offices in Cairo. If you don't mind taking a chance, try to book passage in Luxor or Aswan on a space available basis; sometimes you can bargain, and you'll get a chance to see the boat. Space can be tight in the high season; it's more available in summer.

A cheaper and often more fun option is to hire a falucca and sail the Nile. Most trips run from Aswan to Luxor (four to five days) or Luxor to Aswan (an additional day); it's best to sail with the current (south to north) in case the wind dies and leaves you becalmed. Deal with the boatman and see if he'll supply food (most do) and sleeping gear (most do not). A large falucca will sleep eight, and the cost can be split accordingly. The only drawback to a falucca is that its low decks coupled with the Nile's high banks will hide some of the shore from view. On the bank at night, watch your gear; robberies do occur.

By Taxi

Of all of Egypt's transportation systems, the taxis are perhaps the best value. In the large cities, they relieve you of the problems inherent in driving in Egypt as well as finding a place to park. By international standards, their fares are cheap: for a few dollars, drivers will fight the traffic within sprawling Cairo. With the exception of limousines, cabs in Egypt are not radio-dispatched but operate out of large stands scattered throughout the area and off the streets. In Cairo, they're black (or dark blue) and white; in Alexandria, orange and black; in the rest of the country, they come in a variety of colors. Although many cabbies off the normal tourist routes charge less, they probably speak little or no English; few drivers read English, so have addresses written out in Arabic.

The large number of cabs on the streets may lull you into the falsely secure impression of always being able to hail one, but they can be impossible to find during rush-hour traffic. If you go into native or isolated areas, consider having the cab wait for you, and don't pay the driver until you return. Many cabbies tend to "adopt" their passengers, so if you're unsure of the area and you trust your driver, ask him to accompany you. If he agrees, be sure to tip him for the extra effort. Cabs are all numbered, so if by the off chance you run into a problem, take the cab's number and report the problem to the police or tourist authority.

Service Taxis: In Egypt, there are two general types of taxis: private and service (or shared). The latter run from a central stand, leave when they are crammed full, and like small minibuses, run along given routes for a fixed pp fee. These monochrome Peugeots usually take seven passengers, but in Egypt, there's "always room for two more"; if you want extra room, buy an extra seat (fares run LE5-25 or so, depending on the distance). Your luggage will go on the top rack along with the Egyptians' and will arrive, *in sha'allah* with you. Shared taxis run both between and within cities. They're cheap if uncomfortable, and it takes a little digging to find their stands, routes, and fares. The drivers of intercity taxis are often reckless, and riding with one may bring you face to face with at least another taxi, if not your maker. In contrast, however, most city drivers are relatively careful.

ALAN HANSEN

service taxi: room for one more?

In some areas, local transportation is by pickup; the rates are fixed. The government is discouraging foreigners from using these covered minitrucks, but it's not yet uniformly enforced.

Private Taxis: Although more expensive, private taxis (taxi special) take you exactly (*in sha'allah*) where you want to go. In Egypt, cabs are supposed to be metered and the rates set by the government, but the fares are so low that they don't even cover gas. As a result, the meters in most cabs are "broken." To find out the going fares, ask at your hotel or the local Tourist Office. If you know how much you should pay, just hand the driver the exact amount as you get out of the cab. He may try to get more, but ignore his protests and walk off. If you can't find out the fare, bargain with the driver before you get into the cab.

In a few places, primarily in Cairo, cab drivers have banded together and set prices for certain routes. You can recognize them because they will tell you the fare before you get into the cab, or before they start off. These cabs can cost a little more than those picked randomly off the street, but the drivers usually speak English, drive well, know the city, and do not pick up additional passengers. These advantages plus the lack of hassles are often worth the few extra pounds. All fees include tips, unless the service has been especially good. Always have the exact change for cab fares, as most drivers will not willingly make change. Sometimes drivers will take a long way around and then try to get more than the agreed amount—don't give in; stick to the original deal.

Often a cab driver will stop to pick up another passenger; this is common practice, especially in rush hours, but most drivers will ask your permission. Since cabs, especially in Cairo, are in such short supply, most passengers agree. However, you will not split the fee with the additional passenger; you each pay as private fares. On the other hand, don't hesitate to hail a cab on the street that already has a passenger. If the driver is looking for extra passengers, he will slow down; as he does, yell out your general destination; if it is on his route, he'll stop.

Taxis by the Day: For less than the cost of renting a car, you can often hire a cab and driver for the day. Figure about LE15-20/hour. You can ask your hotel to recommend someone, or if you've ridden with a driver you like, ask him if he's free to take you for the day. Some cabs belong to a company, and others are owned by their driver, so specific arrangements may vary. For example, if you like the driver but the cab is owned by the company, you may want to pay him both a fare and a tip; if he owns his own cab, just give him the lump sum. If you hire a driver for a long trip, the cost will be more; be sure he understands he's not to let anyone else drive the car. Most Tourist Offices maintain a list of suggested prices for specific trips; often the drivers feel they're low, so you still may have to bargain.

Limousines

Several companies run radio-dispatched limo services in the larger cities, and Misr Limousine keeps a fleet of Mercedeses at Cairo Airport. They cost slightly more than cabs, but you can call and have them dispatched into areas not usually covered by taxis. You can also rent one of these Mercedes and a driver by the day.

PRIVATE CARS

A car gives you the freedom to see Egypt at your own pace. International companies rent cars, with or without drivers, by the day, week, or month. A few even rent campers, and since gas is inexpensive, it is a good way for a group to visit some of the more remote regions. To drive in Egypt, you'll need an International Driver's License, but don't blithely plan on renting a car and driving yourself, even if you're experienced in handling cars in foreign lands; driving in Egypt is an experience rarely equaled and never to be forgotten. The Automobile Club of Egypt, 10 Sh. Qasr al-Nil, Cairo, tel. (02) 743-355, can supply information on driving in Egypt. By the way, the club maintains a plush restaurant for members, and the Touring Club of Egypt is affiliated with it. (The AAA international card is accepted by the Automobile Club of Egypt.)

Driving Yourself

Although Egyptians drive on the right, no other common rule seems to apply, and Cairo, with its millions of cars, is especially challenging. In Egypt, the car that leads, even by millimeters, has the right of way. A big exception is buses, which always have (take) the right of way. Egypt's roads are not well maintained, and when traffic unsnarls, many Egyptians drive recklessly. Traffic lanes are meaningless, and vehicles flow like eddying currents, sweeping around obstacles from donkey carts to open and unmarked manholes. The trick to driving in Egypt is to always look ahead; you're responsible for those in front of you. Communicate via your horn like the Egyptians: two soft beeps for "I'm here beside you and coming by" and one long, sustained beep for "I can't (won't) stop, and I'm coming through." The driver who extends his hand, fingers upward, tips together, is signaling "Caution, don't pass now." Conversely, if all's clear, drivers will extend their fingers outward and flip them forward, indicating you can pass.

On rural roads, trucks and cars routinely pass in the face of oncoming traffic; the vehicles simply convert a two-lane road into three, the two outside cars pulling onto the shoulders of the road if necessary. Usually, but not always, the passing car will flash his lights, and oncoming traffic is expected to yield. Pay attention to road conditions because holes (deep ones) will not necessarily be marked; in fact, some of the manholes even when covered sit six to 10 inches above or below the pavement.

Don't drive at night if you can possibly avoid it; Egyptians drive with no lights (so they won't blind the oncoming car). When they see another car approaching, they will flash their lights on (usually high beam) so you'll know they're there, then off again, on again. Roads in Egypt are paved, but are in varying degrees of repair; some of the better ones are toll roads, costing a pound or so. Main trunk routes link the oases; part of the international Cairo to Cape Town Highway connects Cairo and Upper Egypt. The main roads in Sinai are good and have little traffic. A network of smaller roads criss-cross the delta, but be sure you have governmental permission to wander off the main thoroughfares.

Avoid the main delta road to Alexandria if you can; although widened to four lanes in most places, it still carries speeding traffic (including heavy trucks) and is laced with donkeys, horses, camels, bicycles, and motorscooters. Use the desert toll road, which is nearly a freeway and much safer.

Desert Driving

If you rent a car or camper to drive to outlying areas, check with someone who has just traveled your route to get accurate information. Some of the desert roads are not paved, so be sure to stay on the track to avoid getting stuck in the desert sand; if possible, take two vehicles. Desert climates are tough on engines, and cars break down at the most inopportune times and places. Carry water for both overheated radiators and humans. Take tools, spare parts, and plenty of gas; service stations and mechanics, depending on your route, can be scarce. Most important, know where you're going. If you're in doubt, be sure to hire a guide to the more remote regions, and let someone know where you're going and when you should be back. Remember, the desert can be deadly; the Persian King Cambyses lost an entire army between Cairo and Siwa, the remains of which have yet to be found.

Renting Cars

Hertz, Avis, Budget, Max, and other international companies rent cars in Cairo, Alexandria, Hurghada, and Sinai. See the "Transportation" sections in those chapters for more details. You must be at least 25 years old and have an International Driver's License, which is valid for a year. Take your credit card, for many companies require a healthy deposit (LE500). The campers sleep six and permit you to cook your own food, so it's not as expensive as it might seem.

Most agencies require insurance if you drive yourself; in case of an accident, be sure to get an immediate written report (it will be in Arabic) from the investigating police as well as a statement from the doctor who first treats any injuries, otherwise your insurance may not cover the costs. In the cities, consider hiring a driver with the car; traffic is hectic and parking nearly nonexistent.

Importing Cars

Visitors in Egypt can bring cars into the country for 90 days without paying customs duty, provided they have a triptych or *carnet de passage en douane* from a recognized auto club such as AAA; otherwise you'll have to pay a deposit against duty (nearly the cost of the car). You can extend this period by another three months through the Egyptian Automobile Association; apply at least a month in advance. You must also have an International Driver's License valid for the 90 days and the car must have an international motor vehicle license. You can also import motor bikes, scooters, motorcycles, boats, and caravan trailers under a triptych. Be sure you get the paperwork *before* you leave for Egypt. After customs agents verify that the owner has no fixed residence in Egypt they issue a 90-day tax exemption label; you must display it on your front window. If the vehicle remains in Egypt past the 90-day limit, you'll have to pay LE20/day until you ship the car out of the county. You must, by law, carry third-party personal liability insurance obtained in Egypt; rates are reasonable and depend upon engine size and power and the value of the car. Spare parts are not always available, and when they are, they're expensive; bring your own. Many international car makers maintain their own repair agencies, so check with your dealer.

Service Stations

In Cairo and Alexandria, gas (called petrol or benzene) is plentiful, but outside these areas service stations can be scarce. Especially when traveling in the desert, plan on carrying extra gas. It's sold by the liter, and is low in octane, so use super unless your car has been specially adjusted. Plan on cleaning your fuel filter often, as impurities in the gas as well as the ever-present dust clog up the workings of any engine.

Hitchhiking

Although it's not a common practice in Egypt, most drivers are more than willing to give you a lift, but you'll need to help with the gas. As in all countries hitchhiking, especially for women alone, can be dangerous.

ACCOMMODATIONS

At the turn of the century, when Egypt became the watering hole for rich Victorians, savvy foreigners began building accommodations to suit the wealthy visitors. Of these plush hotels, several, like the Winter Palace in Luxor and the Old Cataract in Aswan, still cater to guests. These hotels have been renovated and once more offer good accommodations with pleasant service. New building has added large numbers of modern and expensive chain hotels. Good alternatives are the smaller, private hotels, which offer nearly the same services as the giants. Their smaller staff gets to know you and goes out of its way to make you comfortable. Although such hotels don't appear in most tourist lists, with a little scouting you can find them throughout Egypt. A few pensions are better than their ratings would suggest, and visitors with tight budgets can use hostels or campgrounds.

HOTELS

The quantity and quality of hotels in Egypt vary directly with the area's fame and tourist count. In Cairo, Alexandria, Luxor, Aswan, and Hurghada, glittering high rises dominate the landscape. By contrast, most offerings in Middle Egypt are humble; running hot water and a flushing toilet count as luxuries.

Classes And Standards

The Egyptian government rates hotels: five-star (deluxe), four-star (first class), three-star (standard), two-star (tourist), and one-star (pension). The ratings tend to run about a star or two low, although the government is reinspecting most hotels, attempting to bring them into line. Ratings dictate prices, which are quoted in U.S. currency for three- to five-star hotels, and in pounds for the others: five-star, $80-150; four-star, $40-80; three-star, $30-50; and two- and one-stars, LE25-40 and LE15-25, respectively. In three-star and above hotels, if you pay with pounds, you must present a currency exchange receipt; otherwise, you'll have to use internationally accepted currency, traveler's checks, or credit cards.

Many hotels include compulsory breakfast, a charge often not included in posted room rates, and some hotels require half-board—breakfast and either lunch or dinner. If you eat it or not, you'll be billed for the meal. Although some of these breakfasts are more substantial than continental-style rolls and coffee, most are not; a delightful exception is breakfast at some of the smaller hotels, especially those in outlying areas, which dish up an Egyptian-style breakfast of eggs, beans (*ful*), cheese, fruit, toast, and coffee. Local taxes can up basic room rates by 14-24%, so ask if meals and taxes are included in quoted room prices. Inflation is rampant in Egypt, and hotels are constantly applying to the government to raise their rates; thus what is a good deal at press time can soon be marginal. Where prices are quoted, they are *in no way guaranteed,* but are included only as a guide. Always check with the hotels for current rates. During the high season (winter) you should make reservations and take your confirmation with you when you check in.

Five-star Hotels

Today a plethora of modern high rises built by such international hotel companies as Hilton, Sheraton, Inter-Continental, Ramada, Oberoi,

the Winter Palace Hotel
in Luxor

KATHY HANSEN

Movenpick, and Club Mediteranee dominate the hotel industry. Except for a few palaces converted into deluxe hotels, most five-star hotels resemble their modern counterparts throughout the world; air-conditioning, heat, color TV, and private baths highlight their plush rooms. Most offer restaurants, bars, 24-hour coffee shops, swimming pools, health clubs, banks, airline and limousine reservations, car rentals, and small shops. Although their facilities and service stand out in Egypt, they fall slightly below their Western counterparts. However, their rates are slightly lower as well. Staying in such a high rise is comfortable but expensive and except for decorative motifs, quite un-Egyptian. However, many, such as the Nile Hilton in Cairo, are handy centers in which to eat, conduct business, or steal an occasional night of pure luxury.

Four-star Hotels
This heterogeneous group includes both older hotels and many new, privately owned smaller establishments. All are air-conditioned and most have private baths, televisions and phones in the rooms, and often refrigerators, and offer the same services as their more expensive counterparts listed above. However, their facilities are less luxurious than five-star hotels.

Three-star Hotels
In general, these hotels are clean and well kept, if ordinary. Some of the older ones are being rebuilt, while the newer ones often lie outside the cities' main areas. These small establishments are trying to provide outstanding service and clean facilities with plumbing that works. In Egypt, this role is not easy to fulfill, but newly trained managers and staff in many of the establishments are trying their best, and it shows. Many offer TVs, phones, or suites that can accommodate families. Most have air-conditioning, private baths, and hot water.

Two- And One-star Hotels
Similar to three-star hotels except for price, these establishments are frequently in the heart of town, enabling you to make use of the least-expensive forms of transportation. Often they occupy the upper floors of office buildings. They're seldom listed in tourist information, but with a little effort, you'll be able to dig up clean, cheap, and sometimes homey places throughout Egypt. The facilities are generally limited to a restaurant, which may only serve one entree a night. However, the food is usually native and often good, and the staff friendly. Air-conditioning or fans may or may not be available and often cost extra. Not all staff members will speak English, so drag out your phrase book and learn a little more Arabic; staying in these hotels gives you a sense of living in Egypt.

Choosing Accommodations

When deciding where to stay in Egypt, the first step is to *accurately* assess your lifestyle. People visiting third world countries tend to select accommodations that fall below their expectations and standards. How long can you *really* go without a hot shower in a hot, dusty environment? If you make a mistake, admit it and move up a class in hotels. Do not judge all facilities by inexpensive ones you may have chosen; in Egypt you tend to get what you pay for. Rooms vary within a hotel, especially the older ones, so always look at your specific room before you take it. If you're not satisfied with the first offering, ask to see another; you won't insult the manager. Many smaller hotels do not have private baths, but often the public ones are close to your room. Have the management demonstrate their hot water by running it out of *your* sink or shower.

Hotel Reservations

Although modern building projects have expanded the numbers of beds available, most are luxury accommodations. If you plan on spending time in the smaller hotels, especially during their tourist season, you'd best write ahead. Don't arrive in Cairo without hotel reservations, for in spite of recent building activity, finding a suitable place at the last minute, especially when you're tired, is an unneeded trauma.

In the U.S. you can book reservations at any of the large chains through their toll-free 800 numbers; most three- to five-star hotels will confirm reservations by telex or fax, but some smaller hotels don't always reply. However, if they've received your letter, they will save you a room. Remember, however, that mail in Egypt is erratic, so the management may never get your letter. The best compromise is to book a more expensive hotel for the first night; the next day, when you are refreshed, change your accommodations if you want. When you book your own rooms at one of the smaller hotels by phone, be sure to get the name of the clerk you speak to, and if you've written, take a copy of your letter. If you've booked through a travel agent, he should supply you with written confirmation.

OTHER ACCOMMODATIONS

Hostels

Accommodations offered by the 15 youth hostels scattered throughout Egypt vary in quality, but all are cheap; a few pounds per day. Usually you needn't make reservations, but it's a good idea to arrive early to be sure you get a bed. Although Egyptian hostels require an International Youth Hostel Federation (IYHF) card, individual hostels don't always enforce the rule. All hostels have kitchen facilities, and most have curfews. If you stay in a hostel, you'll have to watch your valuables; take your passport and money to bed with you. For more information, contact the Egyptian Youth Hostel Association, 7 Sh. Abdul Hamid-Said, Cairo, tel. (02) 758-099.

Camping

In several tourist areas formal campgrounds have sprung up. Populated with large tents, many complete with floors, these campgrounds offer few amenities, and none have hookups for trailers or campers. Most private-property owners will let you camp if you ask permission. Camping on public grounds is usually permitted, except on certain beaches in the Red Sea area, but always check before you spread your bedroll. Women should not camp alone.

Flats

Renting apartments for longer-term stays is an option, especially for a family planning to spend a lot of time in a major city. Although most flats are expensive (LE400 per month and up), you can find an occasional bargain. Drawbacks include having to deal with uncooperative plumbing and erratic electricity. If the flat doesn't already have a phone, it will be practically impossible to get one installed. If it does have one, make sure it works; many don't.

Some real estate agencies handle rentals, although you may have better luck checking with foreign businesses or walking the streets in a neighborhood you like and asking the *bowabs* (doormen) if they know of any vacancies. If you rent, your *bowab* is supposed to take care of most minor problems, but for major failures (like the death of a hot water heater) you'll have to deal with the owner. It helps if he lives close by and is available. Also, be sure any potential problems, such as a faulty stove or refrigerator, are cleared up before you sign a rental agreement and fork over your money.

Dealing With Problems

Staying in Egypt can be fraught with problems most of us don't ever consider. For example, a lack of hot water may not be a hotel problem but a failure of the city water system. Such failures are a way of life for most Egyptians, and you cannot change the system by berating hotel employees. Be patient; water will soon return. Electricity is also intermittent, causing lights to go out and elevators to stop between floors. The same solution applies: be patient. Carry a flashlight wherever you go as well as reading material or other projects; then you can just sit on the floor and read until the power comes back on.

In Egypt, even getting to your hotel can be a problem. Trading on the Egyptians' reputation for helpfulness, con men abound, steering many an unsuspecting tourist into rundown and dirty hotels. Although some cab drivers are paid by hotels to deliver unsuspecting guests to their doors, most con men loiter outside the airport terminal. They are slick, going to extremes to set themselves up as helpful friends, pointing out where to find buses, trams, or trains. Their ruses even involve stories of fictional riots and curfews. To combat con men, beware of any stories regarding your hotel and/or reservations; go and check on such information yourself.

BOB RACE

FOOD AND DRINK

In Egypt, dining out can range from stand-up sandwich bars to luxurious five-course meals. Although most of the best and expensive restaurants are in large hotels, you can also find small, inexpensive establishments that serve good Egyptian food for only a few pounds. If you're in a hurry, try the local snack bars. While the cubbyholes off the street (which probably have running water) are generally safe, avoid the street vendors unless the food is peelable or hot; Western stomachs often revolt at this less-than-sanitary fare. The larger cities even have Western-style fast-food chains like Wimpy's and Kentucky Fried Chicken, but they're relatively expensive. In cities both food and water are safe although the change in your diet may produce short-term gastrointestinal upsets.

EGYPTIAN MEALS

Although Egyptian eating habits may seem erratic, most natives begin the day with a light breakfast of beans (or bean cakes), eggs, and/or pickles, cheeses, and jams. Most families eat their large, starchy lunch around 1400-1700 and follow it with a siesta. They may take a British-style tea at 1700 or 1800 and eat a light supper (often leftovers from lunch) late in the evening. Dinner parties, however, are scheduled late, often no earlier than 2100, with the meal served an hour or two later. In restaurants lunch is normally 1300-1600, dinner 2000-2400.

Restaurants

In Egypt, as in the rest of the world, restaurants are only as good as the cooks they employ, and cooks seem to be continually changing. For current information on the best restaurants, the expatriate community is unbeatable, and the magazine *Cairo Today* includes monthly tips listing places to try, and publishes an annual dining-guide. Most establishments use native ingredients and will offer fruits and vegetables in season. Menus are in both Arabic and English except in Alexandria, where they are in Arabic and French. In large restaurants, the maitre d'hotel will speak English, French, and possibly German, Italian, or Greek. These establishments serve a mixture of international cuisine but often include Egyptian or Middle Eastern fare as well. Most hotels also maintain 24-hour coffee shops. Breakfasts range LE15-25; lunches and dinners, LE25-75. (There is little difference in the cost of lunch and dinner.)

Many of the smaller, Egyptian-style restaurants specialize in basic meat and fava-bean dishes. They are simple and inexpensive (LE5-15), but only for the tourist who is adventurous. Waiters speak little English, so use your phrase book. No matter what class of restaurant you patronize, you'll undoubtedly have trouble getting the bill: *"Al-hi-SAAB min FAD-luk"* usually does the trick. Although a 12-15% service charge is added to the bill, the waiter may never see it; if you like the service, tip him directly.

Snack Bars

Throughout Egypt, little stand-up shops dispense the Egyptian version of fast food. Most of these shops in major cities are clean and offer quick, inexpensive, and nutritious meals if your insides have adapted to local food. Ordering in these shops can be an adventure: watch the natives and see if they first pay and then order or vice versa—the practice varies. Most shops have helpful staff, but during their busy times you may have to push your way into the pack of Egyptians to get waited on. You can buy roasted chickens that the shop will season for you; usually they're available after about 1800. You can also get *shawirma,* lamb cooked on a vertical spit, available most of the day. Unfortunately some of these small establishments have picked up the idea that foreigners are rich and may try to inflate the price; confirm the cost before you order.

Egyptian Home Cooking

If you're lucky, you may be invited to dine in an Egyptian home. There are no set times for dinner; often the hours will depend upon your host's profession. Although invitations may be issued for as late as 0100, generally if no time is set, guests are expected between 2100-2200 hours. If you wish, you may bring flowers, chocolates, or a bottle of wine (if your hosts drink—many Muslims do not). You will be introduced to other guests and perhaps the host's entire family, many of whom will not stay to eat; in the villages, you may find yourself eating with only the patriarch of the family, other members remaining in the background until you finish your meal.

Dining customs vary throughout the country, so try to follow examples set by your host and any fellow guests. Depending upon the family's own customs and the size of the party, men and women may split up for cocktails (nonalcoholic drinks in strict Muslim homes) and then rejoin at the dinner table, where seating is usually random. All the food is set in the middle of the table at the beginning of the meal. If no silverware is provided, use your bread as a combination fork and spoon. Muslim traditions dictate that the right hand be used for eating, but strict adherence to this custom varies. Guests are not expected to clear their plates, and you'll need to refuse more than once to convince your host that you really can't eat anymore. Complimenting the hostess on her cooking skills as well as (for women) asking her for recipes are in good taste and appreciated. After dinner, guests remove from the dining room to drink mint tea or coffee. Wait at least a half-hour from the end of the meal before you take your leave; compliment the cook again, and extend your thanks *(alf shokren)*.

NATIVE FOODS

Egyptian food reflects the country's melting-pot history; native cooks using local ingredients have modified Greek, Turkish, Lebanese, Palestinian, and Syrian traditions to suit Egyptian budgets, customs, and tastes. The dishes are simple; made with naturally ripened fruits and vegetables and seasoned with fresh spices, they're good and hearty. Food in the south, closely linked to North African cuisine, is more zesty than that found in the north, but neither is especially hot. The best cooking is often found in the smaller towns. Although Egyptian cooking can be bland and oily when poorly done, most of the cuisine is delicious. Enjoy!

Bread

The mainstay of Egyptian diets, *aysh* (bread) comes in several forms. The most common is a pita type made either with refined white flour called *aysh shami,* or with coarse, whole wheat, *aysh baladi.* Stuffed with any of several fillings, it becomes the Egyptian sandwich. *Aysh shams* is bread made from leavened dough allowed to rise in the sun, while plain *aysh* comes in long, skinny, French-style loaves. If you find yourself faced with hard, dry *aysh,* do like the Egyptians: soften it in water, and if you have a fire available, warm it over the open flame.

aysh *dough ready for baking; lizard not included*

DAVID GOODMAN

Beans

Along with *aysh,* the native *ful* bean supplies most of Egypt's people with their daily rations. *Ful* can be cooked several ways: in *ful midamess,* the whole beans are boiled, with vegetables if desired, and then mashed with onions, tomatoes, and spices. This mixture is often served with an egg for breakfast, without the egg for other meals. A similar sauce, cooked down into a paste and stuffed into *aysh baladi,* is the filling for the sandwiches sold on the street. Alternatively, *ful* beans are soaked, minced, mixed with spices, formed into patties (called *ta'miyya* in Cairo and *falaafil* in Alexandria), and deep-fried. These patties, garnished with tomato, lettuce, and *tihina* sauce, are stuffed into *aysh* and sold on the street.

Molokhiyya

A leafy, green, summer vegetable, *molokhiyya* is distinctively Egyptian, and locals will proudly serve you their traditional thick soup made from it. The chopped leaves are generally stewed in chicken stock, and served with or without pieces of chicken, rabbit, or lamb. This soup can also be served with crushed bread or over rice. If you're served it straight, it's polite to dunk your *aysh.*

Mezze

These small dishes of various forms are usually served with drinks. Those resembling dips are made with *tihina,* an oil paste of sesame seeds. *Tihina* mixed with oil and seasoned with garlic or chili and lemon can be served alone, but when combined with mashed eggplant and served as a dip or sauce for salads, its called *baba-ghanoug.* In Alexandria, chickpeas are added to the *tihina* to make *hummus bi tihina.* *Tihina* also forms the base for many general-purpose sauces served with fish and meats and replaces mayonnaise on Egyptian sandwiches. *Turshi* includes a variety of vegetables soaked in spicy brine—it's always good with beer.

Soups And Salads

In addition to *molokhiyya,* the Egyptians make a variety of meat *(lahma),* vegetable *(khudaar),* and fish *(samak)* soups known collectively as *shurbit,* and all are delicious. Salads *(salata)* can be made of greens, tomatoes, potatoes, or eggs, as well as with beans and yogurt. Western-type salad bars have come into vogue in the larger cities, and here, for a few pounds, you can make a whole meal of the fresh produce. Yogurt *(laban zabadi)* is fresh and unflavored; you can sweeten it if you wish with honey, jams, preserves, or mint. It rests easy on an upset stomach.

Main Courses

Rice and bread form the bulk of Egyptian main courses, which may be served either as lunch or dinner. For most Egyptians, meat is a luxury used in small amounts, cooked with vegetables, and served with or over rice, but meat dishes comprise most restaurant fare.

Torly, a mixed-vegetable casserole or stew, is usually made with lamb, or occasionally with beef, onions, potatoes, beans, and peas. To make Egyptian-style kebab, cooks season chunks of lamb in onion, marjoram, and lemon juice and then roast them on a spit over an open fire. *Kufta* is ground lamb flavored with spices and onions which is rolled into long narrow "meatballs" and roasted like kebab, with which it's often served. Pork is considered unclean by Muslims and is available only in Christian areas. "Beef" is often *gamoosa* (water buffalo), and though meat from Western-type cattle is available, this beef is not aged, the animals are often old and gamey-tasting, and their meat is best avoided in most places.

Although native chickens *(firaakh)* are often scrawny and tough, imported fowl are plump, tender, and tasty. You can order grilled chicken *(firaakh mashwi)* in a restaurant or buy one already cooked at the street-side rotisseries and fix your own meal. *Hamaam* (pigeons) are raised throughout Egypt, and when stuffed with seasoned rice and grilled, constitute a national delicacy. They are small, so you will need to order several; the best are usually served in small, local restaurants where you may even have to give the cook a day's notice (a good sign), but beware—*hamaam* are occasionally served with their heads buried in the stuffing.

Egyptians serve both freshwater and seagoing fish under the general term of *samak.* The best fish seem to be near the coasts (ocean variety) or in Aswan, where they are caught from Lake Nasser. As well as the common bass and sole, try *gambari* (shrimp), calamari (squid), *gandofli* (scallops), and *ti'baan* (eel). The latter, a white meat with a delicate salmon flavoring, can be bought on the street already deep-fried.

Vegetables

Ruzz (rice) is often varied by cooking it with nuts, onions, vegetables, or small amounts of meat. *Bataatis* (potatoes) are usually fried but can also be boiled or stuffed. Egyptians stuff green vegetables with mixtures of rice; *wara'anub,* for example, is made from boiled grape leaves filled with small amounts of spiced rice with or without ground meat. Westerners often know them by the Greek name of *dolmadas* or *dolmas,* but beware ordering them by that name; in Egypt, *dolma* refers to a mixture of stuffed vegetables.

Cheese

Native cheese (*gibna*) comes in two varieties: *gibna beida,* similar to feta, and *gibna rumy,* a sharp, hard, pale yellow cheese. These are the ones normally used in salads and sandwiches, but gouda, cheddar, bleu, and other Western types are becoming available. *Mish* is a spiced, dry cheese made into a paste and served as an hors d'oeuvre.

Fruits

In Egypt a multitude of fresh fruits are available year-round, but since all are tree- or vine-ripened, only those in season appear in *suqs* (markets) or on vendors' stands. In the winter, *mohz* (bananas), *beleh* (dates), and *burtu'aan* (any of several varieties of oranges) appear. Special treats are *burtu'aan bedummoh* (pink oranges), whose skin looks like most oranges, but their pulp is red and sweet. The Egyptian summer is blessed with *battiikh* (melon), *khukh* (peach), *berku* (plum) and *'anub* (grapes). *Tin shawki* is a cactus fruit that appears in August or September. Buying fruits on the street is safe as long as you can peel them, but beware of watermelons; they may have been injected with water (which can be contaminated) to increase their weight.

Nuts

Goz (nuts) and *mohammasat* (dried seeds) are popular snack foods in Egypt, and vendors can be found selling them nearly anywhere. All are tasty; try *bundo* (hazelnuts), *loz* (almonds), or *fuzdo* (pistachios). If you like peanuts, the *ful sudani* are especially tasty in Aswan.

Desserts

Egyptian desserts of pastry or puddings are usually drenched in honey syrup. Baklava (filo dough, honey, and nuts) is one of the less sweet; *fatir* are pancakes stuffed with everything from eggs to apricots; and *basbousa,* quite sweet, is made of semolina pastry soaked in honey and topped with hazelnuts. *Umm ali,* a delight named for a Mamluk queen, is raisin

Alexandria fruit stand

cake soaked in milk and served hot. *Kanafa* is a dish of batter "strings" fried on a hot grill and stuffed with nuts, meats, or sweets. Egyptian rice pudding is called *mahallabiyya* and is served topped with pistachios. French-style pastries are called *gatoh*, but are usually heavy and tough. Good chocolate candies are likewise difficult to find, though Western-style candy bars are beginning to make their appearance. The Egyptian ice cream runs closer to ice milk or sherbet than cream; Dolce brand is a little thicker. Most restaurants and many homes serve fresh fruit for desserts, and it makes a perfect, light conclusion to most meals.

Shopping For Food

The easiest way to stretch your food budget is to patronize the local stands and *suqs,* buying fresh fruit and vegetables you can eat raw. The prices are normally posted in Arabic and are fixed. Since there is no bargaining involved, you can just point to what you want, indicate how many or how much, and hold out your money; most vendors and small storekeepers are scrupulously honest. Small, local grocery stores occupy nearly every street corner and sell canned goods, preserves, bread, cheese, and soda pop as well as staples at government-fixed prices. If the local grocery doesn't stock beer, there is probably a store nearby that does; ask. Here or at the brewery you can buy Stella by the case. Bakeries supply various types of bread and pastries at fixed prices.

DRINKS

Coffee

Developed and popularized in the Middle East, the drinking of *ahwa* (coffee) remains a national tradition, and local coffeehouses still cater to men who come to drink coffee, discuss politics, play *tawla* (backgammon), listen to "Oriental" (Egyptian) music, and smoke the *hukah* or *shiisha* (water pipe or hubbly-bubbly). Although the traditional poetry and high-powered politics have migrated to fancy homes and offices, the coffee remains. You will also be offered the thick, strong, but tasty brew in homes, offices, and bazaar shops. This Turkish coffee is made from finely powdered beans brewed

in a small pot. As the water just begins to boil, the grounds float to the surface in a dark foam; the *ahwa* is brought to you still in the pot and is poured into a demitasse. The heavier grounds sink to the bottom of the cup and the lighter ones form a foam on the top, the mark of a perfectly brewed cup. Sip carefully to avoid the grounds in the bottom of the cup. (If you don't like the foam, you can blow it aside under the guise of cooling your drink.)

Although Turkish coffee has a reputation for being tart, its actual flavor depends on the mix of beans used in the grind; the larger the percentage of Arabica, the sweeter and more chocolate the flavor. *Ahwa* comes in several versions: *ahwa sada* is black, *ahwa ariha* is lightly sweetened with sugar, *ahwa mazboot* is moderately sweetened, and *ahwa ziyada* is very sweet. You must specify the amount of sugar at the time you order, for it's sweetened in the pot. Most people order *mazboot,* which cuts the tartness; *ahwa* is never served with cream. Most hotel and restaurant breakfasts include strong French coffee usually called Nescafe; you may have to specially order it with sugar *(bil sukkar)* or milk *(bil laban).*

Tea And Other Hot Drinks

Egyptians adopted the custom of formal afternoon tea from their English occupiers, and it's served similarly, with milk, lemon, and sugar on the side. The domestic or Bedouin version of *shay* is boiled rather than steeped and is often saturated with sugar; this strong tea is served in glasses. A refreshing change from after-dinner coffee is *shay bil na'na'* or mint tea; dried mint is mixed with tea leaves and the mixture is brewed like regular tea. *Kakoow bil laban* (hot chocolate) is available during the winter, as is *mahlab,* a thick liquid that tastes like a cross between Ovaltine and oatmeal. *Karkaday,* a clear, bright red, native drink especially popular in the south, is made by steeping dried hibiscus flowers, sweetened to taste, and served either hot or cold; the locals claim this delicious drink calms the nerves.

Cold Drinks

Bottled water *(mayya ma'daniyya)* is available in all areas frequented by tourists; both large and small bottles are sold on the street and from ice buckets at most of the antiquities sites. Be sure the cap is sealed. *Mayya shurb* or *mayya ahday* (drinking water) is safe in most metropolitan areas.

A delectable treat in Egypt are the fresh fruit juices (*asiir*) available at small stalls throughout Egypt. The shopkeepers blend the whole fruit and small amounts of ice and sugar water and then strain this mash into your glass—the resulting drinks have been described as ambrosia. Juices, which are made from fruits in season, include *farawla* (strawberry), *manga* (mango), *mohz,* (banana) and *burtu'aan* (orange) and are especially welcome in hot weather. In addition to pure fruit juices, you can also get them made of vegetables such as *khiyar* (cucumber), *tamaatim* (tomato), and *gazar* (carrot). For a new experience, experiment with some of their combination drinks: *nuss wa nuss* (carrot and orange), an unexpectedly delightful concoction, or *mohz bi-laban,* a blend of bananas and milk; an Egyptian milkshake. *Asiir lamoon,* common throughout Egypt, is a strong, sweet version of lemonade. In the past few years canned and packaged juices have become common, but their flavor cannot compare with the freshly made varieties.

Western soft drinks are ubiquitous in Egypt, but most are domestically bottled. You can find Schwepps, Fanta, Seven-Up, Coke, and Pepsi; club soda is also available, but Collins mix is nearly nonexistent. If you buy from street-side vendors, you're expected to drink the soda right there and return the bottle; if you want to take a bottle with you, you'll have to pay for it.

Alcoholic Drinks

Although devout Muslims refrain from drinking alcohol, beer, wine, and hard liquor are available in bars, restaurants, and some grocery shops. Imported beer and wine are the most expensive, but the local *biira* called Stella is a light lager that is quite good, provided it has not sat in the sun too long. It comes in large (about 20 oz.) bottles and runs about LE4-5. Stella Export, available in bars and restaurants, is more expensive (LE4), comes in smaller bottles, and is stronger—closer in alcohol content to most Western beers. Marzen, a dark, bock beer, appears briefly during the spring; Aswali is the dark beer made in Aswan.

Although Egypt was once noted for her wines, the quality has slipped markedly, especially in the last 30 years. Although you can still happen upon a good bottle here and there, most is just passable; Gianaclis is about the best white, Omar Khayyam and Pharaoh are popular reds, and Rubis d'Egypte a passable rosé. Egyptian brandy is drinkable only when diluted, and the local rum is not much better. However, *zibib,* the Egyptian version of Greek ouzo or Mexican anasato, is good either on the rocks or diluted with water (which turns it milky) as a before-dinner cocktail. Other hard liquors are imported and therefore are limited (the ports at Suez and Alexandria seem to have the widest variety) and expensive. If you drink regularly, plan on stocking up at a duty-free store before you enter Egypt.

HEALTH

Although Egypt is still a developing country, the government has improved public health in most metropolitan areas; in general, visitors risk few problems, and exposure to health hazards depends on the areas you visit. In fact, the most dangerous aspect of a trip to Egypt is crossing the street in Cairo traffic. For most visitors, only climate and changes in diet create health problems. Eat regularly and well; drink plenty of water, for Egypt's insidious heat not only dehydrates the unwary but makes visitors impatient and irritable. Food and water are usually safe in most developed areas, but if you're off the beaten path, take the few simple precautions discussed below.

GENERAL HEALTH

Egypt's dry air and unending dust make daily showers nearly mandatory, shriveling skin and frazzling hair. Both men and women should take a good supply of heavy-duty skin cream and hair conditioner. For women, powder over a cream foundation limits the dust that sticks to your face. Take prompt care of any cuts, grazes, or skin irritations, for dust and flies can quickly spread infections. Especially watch eye irritations; trachoma is a contagious infection that can result in blindness if not quickly treated. Be

1. An ever-present sense of humor has carried Egyptians through centuries of oppression. (K. Hansen); **2.** *fallahin* (D. Goodman); **3.** Washing dishes is a child's chore no matter which country she calls home. (D. Goodman); **4.** carrying water from the public well (K. Hansen)

1. the courtyard of Ibn Tulun's mosque (A. Hansen);
2. Colossal figures of Ramesses and his wife Nefertari stride out from the façade
of her Hathor Temple at Abu Simbel. (K. Hansen)

careful around animals, even domesticated ones: camels can bite, horses kick, and an oxen's foot can smash a toe. In short, be aware and use the same common sense precautions you employ at home.

Preventive Medicine
Before you leave home, get routine checkups, both medical and dental. Allow at least a month to get suggested vaccinations (p. 154), for not all inoculations can be given at the same time. Your local public health department gives most shots or can suggest special clinics; be sure the shots are entered on your International Vaccination Certificate (yellow card). If you wear glasses, get a spare set, and if you use contacts, consider taking a pair of glasses, because Egypt's perennial desert dust may irritate your eyes. Although medicines are easily available in Egypt, getting a specific brand may be difficult, so fill personal prescriptions before you go. To avoid hassles in the unlikely event of an incoming customs inspection, leave all medicines in their original bottles, and if you need to carry drug paraphernalia like syringes, get a note from your doctor.

If you are allergic to medications such as penicillin or have a disease not easily recognized like diabetes, epilepsy, or a heart condition, consider getting and *wearing* a **Medic Alert** tag. Internationally recognized, the tag lists your problem as well as the Medic Alert 24-hour hot line, through which hospital personnel can get your medical history. Membership is $35; write to Medic Alert Foundation International, P.O. Box 1009, Turlock, CA 95381-1009 or call (800) ID-ALERT [432-5378] or (209) 668-3333. Allow seven to eight weeks to process your application.

Insurance
Also check with your insurance carrier to be sure your health coverage extends to foreign countries. Most Blue Cross and student health plans do, but Medicare, with certain exceptions, does not. If you are not covered, get some medical insurance. ISIC carries accident and sickness insurance, and CIEE has a low-cost plan as does the American Automobile Association (AAA). Other policies, often including baggage and life insurance, are available through travel or insurance agents. Since many are geared to the tour market, their costs and coverage vary; read through several and select the one best suited to the kind of traveling you will be doing. If you get medical treatment in Egypt, you will probably have to pay the bill yourself, then on your return submit documentation (request detailed receipts in English) to whichever insurance covers you.

Another option is **International Association for Medical Assistance to Travelers (IAMAT).** Their fees range from $25-30 a visit, and membership is free, although a donation is requested. Contact IAMAT at 417 Center St., Lewiston, NY 14092, tel. (716) 754-4883; or 40 Regal Rd., Guelph, Ontario, N1K 1B5, Canada, tel. (519) 836-0102; or 1287 St. Clair Ave. W, Toronto, Ontario M6E 1B8, Canada, tel. (416) 652-0137. You can request their pamphlets, *How to Avoid Traveler's Diarrhea* and *How to Adjust to the Heat.*

Water
Tradition says that a drink from the Nile ensures your return to Egypt, but in fact it's more likely to give you a case of schistosomiasis. Historically, Egypt's drinking water, plentifully supplied by her immortal river, was laden with diseases. Today, thanks to the government's concerted efforts to improve sanitation, tap water in major cities like Cairo, Alexandria, Luxor, and Aswan is in general palatable and safe. Nevertheless, many visitors still prefer inexpensive and readily available bottled spring water, which is both tastier and easier on sensitive intestines. When buying bottles, be sure the cap is sealed; enterprising natives have been known to refill and market used containers.

Treating Water: If you'll be spending time away from civilization, plan on sterilizing the water in some places. You can boil it, treat it with chemicals, or filter it; the method you use depends upon the condition of the water, available equipment, and the amount you need. Boiling water for 20 minutes kills all common infectious organisms, including the hepatitis virus. Alternatively, water can be chemically purified by adding either chlorine or iodine. Although Halazone, a common source of chlorine, is widely used, it doesn't kill some dysentery-causing amoeba. Besides, Halazone tablets dissolve slowly, and they lose their potency if stored longer than six months or when exposed to heat, an ever-present risk in Egypt. Although alkaline water or organic material reduce chlorine's effectiveness, neither inactivate iodine, which dissolves easily, even at cold temperatures, and works in both acid and alkaline water.

Since commercially available tablets (Globaline or Potable-Aqua) can lose their potency with extended storage or upon exposure to air, consider using crystalline iodine, which avoids these drawbacks. Before leaving home, put four to eight grams of USP-grade resublimed iodine in a one ounce, clear glass bottle with a plastic top (an ordinary medicine bottle). Once in Egypt, make a working solution by filling the bottle with water, shaking vigorously, and then letting the iodine crystals settle back to the bottom. To sterilize your drinking water, add about half (12-13 ml) of this working solution to each quart and let it stand about 15 minutes. If you have the time, you can use half this amount of working solution and let the water stand for 40 minutes. If the water is heavily contaminated, let water stand with the full 12 ml for 40 minutes. Since only a small amount of crystalline iodine dissolves with each addition of water, the working-stock bottle can be refilled nearly 1,000 times before the iodine is used up. Because pure iodine cannot lose its effectiveness, storage is not a problem. However, *individuals who are allergic to iodine should not use this system,* and people who have been treated for hyperthyroidism should check with their doctors before drinking iodine-treated water.

Although these methods sterilize the water, they don't remove sediment or eliminate mineral and chemical impurities, as does filtration; filters of small pore sizes both clear and sterilize water. The best are self-contained commercial products, such as First Need, which not only filter out bacteria and viruses, but by creating an ion-exchange screen, remove minerals. (I've even used one in Cairo to get rid of the chlorine from the city's treatment.) Equipped with a hand pump, these devices are lightweight, durable, and effective. If you use a filter that is too large to trap viruses (check the direction sheet of your system for specs), boil your water before filtering it.

Food

Like water, food is always a potential source of disease. Although most symptoms are fleeting and simply a result of diet changes, a few basic precautions can help you avoid serious diseases. The best insurance is well-cooked food; do not eat rare meat or raw fish or shellfish. Avoid cream-filled desserts and pastries, cream sauces (unless hot), and mayonnaise-type dressings, for these types of foods provide ideal homes for bacteria. Peel fruits and vegetables before eating them, or immerse them in a chlorine bleach solution (one tablespoon per gallon or per four liters) for about 20 minutes, and then rinse in clear water. This process doesn't affect the taste. The traditional potassium permanganate treatment is not as effective, nor is lime on salads. If possible, soak lettuce and other hard-to-clean vegetables, as well as roots (carrots, potatoes) which have been grown in undoubtedly contaminated soil.

Watch for sand and grit in bread, and if you cook for yourself be sure to sift your flour and pick out the rocks from the rice. The food served in most reputable hotels is safe, once your intestinal system has adapted to the fare, but beware of the roadside stands, which rarely have running water; be sure the food is well cooked. In private homes, except possibly in extreme outlying communities, Egyptian villagers take great care to carefully clean and cook the meals they serve their guests.

Medical Facilities

When looking for medical care in the larger cities, the hospitals (*mustashfa*) associated with a university provide the best care although some private facilities are also excellent. However, not all provide 24-hour emergency service. Doctors and hospitals usually require payment at the time of treatment, so try to keep a cushion of at least LE150 available. You cannot make arrangements to charge, nor will your insurance be able to pay directly; you will have to fork over the money and collect reimbursement once you're home. You will also have to pay for drugs, so get receipts, written in English if possible. Nursing is often inadequate, but you can arrange for a friend to help. You may even want outside food. Some hospitals do not supply amenities like toilet paper, soap, towels, or tissues. While the

COPING WITH HEAT

The most common medical problem for travelers in Egypt is the heat, which can produce sunburn, dehydration, prickly heat, heat stroke, and death. The best defense is to avoid going out in the middle of the day, especially in summer. Whenever possible, schedule your outdoor activities in the early morning and late evening. To prevent sunburn, protect your skin: wear a hat, dark glasses if your eyes are sensitive, and sunscreen on your nose, neck, and arms. Carry strong sunblock (SPF 9-15) and use it; even if you're dark-skinned or already tan, the desert can still fry your skin. Loose-fitting cotton clothes that cover your legs and arms not only protect your body, but keep you cooler. Don't wear nylon, especially underwear; the heat and moisture can cause vaginal infections in women and a rash for anyone. If you do break out, keep the skin aired and dry; use calamine lotion or zinc oxide talcum powder to control the itching.

Since the dry atmosphere evaporates sweat as soon as it forms, you can become dehydrated without realizing it. Drink plenty of fluids: up to eight quarts per day. If you are working in the field, take several swallows every 20 minutes by the clock; you can lose two quarts in an hour. If you prefer to drink fruit juices, dilute them with water to cut their sugar content; you may also want to add a little salt, or replace lost salt by adding three to five grams in your diet. Salt depletion and dehydration can cause muscle cramps. To relieve the cramp, stretch the muscle. If dehydration and salt depletion cause repeated bouts of cramps, supplements of 10 to 15 grams of salt and plenty of fluids will prevent recurrences. Although most salt loss can be replaced by dietary supplements, those with a history of muscle cramps or heat sickness should consider taking salt tablets; bring them from home, as they are hard to find in Egypt.

Heat injuries: In general, heat exhaustion and heat stroke can be prevented by adequate fluid and salt intake. However, people with chronic diseases such as diabetes and heart conditions, those with infections, those under the influence of amphetamines or LSD, and those not well acclimatized are more susceptible to severe heat injuries. Acclimatization to the hot environment takes about a week, and water deprivation, contrary to persistent beliefs, does *not* speed it up. However, heat injuries can occur in spite of precautions.

Heat exhaustion, caused by prolonged physical activity in a hot environment, is marked by faintness, increased pulse, nausea, and even unconsciousness. In spite of the ambient heat, body temperature is not elevated, and it may even be below normal. Sweating and skin color are variable. Treatment includes rest in a cool area and administration of salty fluids (only if the person is conscious). Recovery is nearly always rapid and without incident.

Heat stroke, in contrast, is caused by a complete breakdown of heat-regulatory mechanisms. Onset of heat stroke is rapid; body temperature quickly rises to 105 degrees or above and sweating is completely absent. Heat stroke is **a true medical emergency;** start treatment immediately. Cool the entire body—by total immersion in tepid (not cold) water if possible. Otherwise, cool by covering with wet cloths, a good alternative in Egypt because of the evaporative power of the dry air. Lightly massage legs and arms to encourage circulation. Cooling can be stopped when body temperature reaches 102, but watch that the temperature doesn't rebound. Heat stroke can usually be prevented if some relief from sweating, such as cool nights or air-conditioned quarters, is available for part of every 24 hours. Remember, untreated cases are invariably fatal due to brain damage, and residual damage in nonfatal cases is directly related to the amount of time elapsed before the body is cooled. Get suspected heat stroke patients medical help as soon as possible.

---

city hospitals are modern and staffed by excellent professionals, those in smaller towns are abysmal. If you get sick in Luxor, Aswan, or Middle Egypt, get out if you can.

Doctors

Finding medical doctors and dentists in Egypt is, like most information, dependent upon word of mouth. However, for the traveler, embassies maintain a list of recommended professionals. Another source of help is major hotels: most can recommend a doctor, clinic, or hospital, and many even have a doctor on call. Perhaps the best way to find a doctor is through membership in the International Association for Medical Assistance to Travellers (IAMAT). Participating physicians in 125 countries are on call to IAMAT members 24 hours a day. Most doctors speak fluent English, and many have trained abroad. For emergencies, you must call them at home or at their private, evening clinics. Hours begin at 1700 or 1800, though in summer and during Ramadan office hours are less predictable. Phone appointments are usually honored over walk-in patients, and fees are normally paid when you arrive.

Drugstores

Most pharmacists speak English. They stock cosmetics and toiletries—in general, the same goodies commonly found in their American and European counterparts. Most patent medicines like Tylenol and Comtrex are available in large cities, but you may have to visit several stores to find specific brand names. Egyptian druggists sell many drugs over the counter that require prescriptions in the U.S., including birth control pills. Prices usually run less than in other countries though occasionally they are higher.

Most druggists will suggest specific medicines for whatever ails you, as well as bandage minor wounds and give injections. They also sell needles and syringes. Buying your own is a practical idea, for reuse without sterilization remains a common, if lamentable, practice in parts of Egypt.

DISEASES

In Egypt, the vast majority of illnesses are innocuous if uncomfortable. Nevertheless, a few can be serious, even life-threatening. Many are intestinal infections, but you can prevent them by paying attention to personal hygiene and avoiding contaminated water and food.

Tut's Trots

The Egyptian form of travelers' diarrhea can develop from excitement and stress, changes in your diet, and the introduction of new bacteria into your system. Both individual susceptibility and travel experience seem to dictate the severity of the disease, which is usually short-lived. Symptoms normally appear in 10-12 days and disappear in two to four days, when your body

adjusts to its new regime. For the sensitive, some doctors recommend treatment with tetracycline, while others advise against antibiotics. To prevent onset, some seasoned travelers take a Lomotil tablet each morning (starting the day before they leave) for up to 10 days, but never longer than two weeks.

When symptoms of travelers' diarrhea appear, treat them quickly. Choices range from Kaopectate and Milk of Magnesia to prescription drugs. For severe cramps, try paregoric (tincture of opium), Lomotil (dipheoxylate), or codeine. (Avoid Enterovioform, still available in Egypt; it has been linked to optic nerve damage.) For those into homeopathic medicine, Podophyllium (30X) often works well. Local remedies include fasting, eating only fresh yogurt, or drinking lemon or lime juice mixed with salt. Whatever your chosen treatment, support your body with plenty of fluids (to combat dehydration) and salt (to relieve cramps). If you can find it, mix RD Sol (salt, sodium bicarbonate, potassium chloride, and dextrose) with fruit juice. If symptoms last longer than a few days, if you run a fever or develop a headache, or if you pass blood in your stool, get medical help immediately, preferably in Cairo or Alexandria; diarrhea can also be a symptom of serious infection.

Typhoid Fever

The bacteria commonly associated with food poisoning can also invade the bloodstream and give rise to the enteric fevers, typhoid and paratyphoid. These bacteria, found in water, milk, and food, can also be transmitted by flies and human carriers. In cases of food poisoning, the organisms are limited to the gastrointestinal tract; infection produces vomiting and diarrhea. If symptoms are severe, last longer than 24 hours, or are accompanied by fever, call a doctor, for the bacteria may be invading your body. All these illnesses can be treated with antibiotics. Vaccination (TAB) offers some protection against typhoid and paratyphoid types A and B.

Cholera

Endemic in much of Africa and Asia, cholera is also transmitted by sloppy hygiene. In Egypt, outbreaks are becoming rare, but occasional cases still occur. The disease is marked by *sud-*

den onset of acute diarrhea, severe cramps, and prostration. Stools are watery and flecked with spots of mucus; symptoms appear rapidly and can leave the infected person severely dehydrated and in shock within an hour or two. Cholera can kill; get help as soon as possible. Treatment includes antibiotics to kill the organism and forcing fluids to keep the patient hydrated. A vaccine, which lasts for six months, is available; consider it if you'll be traveling in the boondocks or farther south in Africa.

Bacillary Dysentery
Short, sharp, and nasty, bacillary dysentery (shigellosis) rarely lasts longer than two or three days. Marked by fever, nausea, cramps, and diarrhea, it lacks the typical "rice-water" stools of cholera. Drugs to stop the cramps and diarrhea may interfere with your ability to take fluids; try instead a hot-water bottle or heating pad to reduce the pain. Caused by bacteria, it responds well to antibiotics.

Parasites
In addition to bacterial gastroenteritis, water- and food-borne amoebas and protozoa also cause diarrhea. The most common is giardia, which (in large numbers) can cause either acute or chronic diarrhea with weakness, abdominal cramps, flatulence, and weight loss. *Endamoeba histolytica* in its early stages causes mild diarrhea and occasionally, as infection worsens, fatigue, low fever, and vague muscle, back, or joint pain. The organism can occasionally form abscesses and even invade the lungs, causing death, but early diagnosis and treatment prevents this more severe form of amebiasis. The organism can lie dormant for long periods before causing overt symptoms, so if you think you may have been infected, seek medical testing.

Bilharzia (Schistosomiasis)
Schistosomes (blood flukes) are endemic in the slow-moving waters of the Nile and even more prevalent in the irrigation canals surrounding it. This worm leads a complex life, living part of its cycle in a freshwater snail that inhabits sluggish waters. Man is infected by the cercaria in its free-swimming stage, when it can penetrate unbroken skin. Although bilharzia responds to general anti-helmenthic drugs, you're better off to avoid in-

fection. Don't swim or bathe in either the Nile or its canals (or run barefoot across irrigated fields or lawns for that matter); if you fall in, wash immediately with soap and fresh water. If you suspect you have bilharzia, which is often characterized by bloody urine or stools (without diarrhea), see a doctor as soon as possible.

Hepatitis
Viral diseases, infectious and serum hepatitis are endemic in Egypt. Infectious hepatitis is generally spread by water and food, so good hygiene prevents most cases. Typical jaundice may only develop after a bout with fever, nausea, and malaise. Treatment is bed rest; recovery is slow but usually steady. Injections of gamma globulin often give immunity for six weeks, and may lessen the severity of the symptoms up to six months. The more deadly serum hepatitis is spread only by blood-to-blood contact, usually through transfusions or use of infected needles. A vaccine is available, but it's usually reserved for health-care workers and others at high risk.

Rabies
In Egypt, as in most of the world, rabies is endemic. Invariably fatal, the virus is spread by infected saliva and occasionally by aerosol. As the virus cannot penetrate unbroken skin, the most common route of infection is through bites from infected animals although the virus can enter scratched or abraded skin as well as the mucus membranes of the nose, mouth, and eyes. Many wild animals are infected, and bats are a common reservoir, but it's unlikely that in Egypt the disease is spread through the air. Prevention is easy; avoid handling any strange animal—wild or domestic. Treatment is a series of shots given between exposure and onset of symptoms, so it's imperative to recognize the risk of infection. If you think you've been exposed, contact the Hospital of the Rabies Institute, Maahad al-Kilab, Imbaba, Cairo, tel. (02) 346-2042/3.

Malaria
Endemic in the Nile Valley, malaria is spread by *Anopheles* mosquitoes. The early stages of infection are marked by muscular soreness and a low fever (without chills); four to eight days

later, the typical, periodic bouts with chills and fever appear. Since mosquito control is good in the main tourist areas, incidence is low. However, if you plan to get off the beaten path, consider taking a half gram of chloroquin once a week, which prevents infection by most strains. Treatment is specific and must be overseen by a physician.

AIDS
While the HIV virus doesn't seem to have stormed the country, a few cases of AIDS have shown up. The government requires proof of HIV negativity for people entering the country to work, and you may have to be tested in Egypt. Tourists have no restrictions, for although prostitution exists, it's not easy for the casual visitor to uncover it.

Eye Problems
Egypt's wind-borne desert dust and Cairo's smog can produce red, stinging, itching, and watering eyes. Steroid-free, antihistamine, decongestant eye drops (Vasocon-A or Optihist) can control swelling and tearing if simple eyedrops like Murine don't give relief. More serious is the persistent irritation found in trachoma. Spread by direct contact through fingers, towels, and cosmetics, this organism produces itching and the feeling of a foreign body in the eye. Once diagnosed, the disease can be cured with common antibiotics, but if left untreated, trachoma can cause blindness.

Immunizations
Yellow fever and cholera vaccinations are required if you enter Egypt from Sudan. If you plan on visiting Sudan, you may also need a meningitis vaccination; for current information, check with your local health department. Although generally not necessary if you will be traveling with a tour group, a typhoid (TAB) vaccination is suggested for those who will be exposed to less sanitary conditions. Also consider gamma globulin for hepatitis. Especially important if you'll be wandering on your own is a tetanus vaccination; tetanus is a nasty disease, and it's totally preventable. In Egypt, you can get vaccinations at the public health facilities in the Continental Savoy Hotel, Midan Opera (open 1000-1300 and 1700-1900, ex-

cept Fri.), and at Midan al-Taawon (at Rd. 12 and Rd. 71) in Ma'adi, tel. (02) 350-3381 (open 0900-1300 and 1600-1800, except Fri.). You will need your International Vaccination Certificate (yellow card) and your passport. Meningitis vaccinations (if required for travel to Sudan) are available at the **Egyptian Organization for Biological and Vaccine Production** (see "Snakes" below).

BITES AND STINGS

Although Egypt's dry climate and sparse vegetation do not support the extensive numbers of wild fauna found in tropical Africa, the country does harbor its share of noxious critters as well as a few frankly poisonous ones: scorpions, cobras, and vipers. Obviously, those who like to poke around in village fields or traipse out to the edge of the desert to explore ruins will encounter more animals than those who confine their visits to the general tourist areas. In either case, however, risk of injury is small, especially if you use a little common sense.

General Treatment
In the unlikely event that you are bitten, wash the wound thoroughly with soap and clean water, or any other liquid that is handy. If the bite is severe, apply an antibiotic ointment and a bandage to keep out additional dust and dirt. If possible, elevate the injured area and cool it. If you use ice, protect the skin under the pack with a cloth, and remove the ice every 10 to 20 minutes to avoid freezing the tissue. (Put local ice in a plastic bag, as it may be contaminated.) If you will be away from civilization, consider taking Quick Ice, which freezes by chemical action. As soon as possible, get professional medical attention, for the mouths of all animals (including humans) harbor a vast array of bacteria that can cause nasty infections—in some cases you may even need a tetanus booster.

Anaphylactic Shock
Most bites and stings, although annoying, are harmless, but a few people are exceedingly sensitive to specific insects. In fact, deaths due to insect stings far outnumber those caused by

all other venomous animals, including poisonous snakes, spiders, and scorpions. In sensitive individuals, anaphylaxis causes muscle spasms that shut down the airways in the lungs and within minutes the entire respiratory system may collapse. Most individuals are aware of their problem and carry insect-sting kits. If you are sensitive, be sure someone in your party knows it, and show them how to use your kit. If bitten, start treatment immediately: *anaphylactic shock is a true medical emergency*—it can kill within five minutes. If epinephrine (adrenaline) is not available, use an antihistamine to try to control the reaction, and always get medical help as soon as possible.

Insects

The most ubiquitous of Egypt's insects are flies and mosquitoes. To protect yourself against their annoying attention (and possible diseases), carry a flyswatter (bring one or two with you) and perfect your aim. Alternatively, you can invest in a flywhisk, the very same kind the pharaohs and their queens carried nearly 35 centuries ago to ward off the same types of pests. Luckily, Egyptian flies tend to disappear with the setting sun.

Not so thoughtful, however, are the mosquitoes, which inhabit nearly all of civilized Egypt. Not only can certain types transmit malaria, but their bites seem to be particularly virulent. While exposure seems to lessen reactions, life is more comfortable if you can keep them from chewing on you. Out of doors, a good, strong mosquito repellent like Deep Woods Off or Muskol keeps them at bay. In your room, the blast from a strong fan discourages them from flying around, and mosquito netting keeps them away while you sleep. Even easier, burn an insect coil like Spiralette, or if electricity is reliable, buy an Ezalo, a small plastic holder that plugs into an outlet. When it heats up, a small disposable pellet gives off fumes that kill all the mosquitoes (and most of the flies) around. Both are available in most drugstores. If you're worried about the chemicals these devices might give off, run them during the day, when you're out of the room. If bitten, *don't scratch*—the bites can easily become infected. Use an antihistamine cream or other anti-itch medication.

Other Critters

Body lice can be discouraged by frequent washing—both clothes and skin. Head lice, which attach their small, white eggs (nits) to the base of hair shafts, are more persistent. Topocide, Kwell, or Eurax will destroy both nits and lice, as will Lorexane or Suleo. Five percent DDT has been used; the locals apply kerosene to the scalp, then remove the nits with a fine comb. Cheap hotels can not only harbor lice, but mites (scabies), fleas, and occasionally bedbugs. These creatures are highly infectious and spread easily in crowded situations like bus and train stations. If you find yourself with persistent skin irritation, suspect one of these blood-sucking arthropods and get medical treatment.

Scorpions

Most common in Upper Egypt, nocturnal scorpions crawl into dark holes during the day. Those that live in the dry areas hide in rocky crevices or bury themselves under the sand, while the ones living in gardens often invade houses (even plush hotels) and then hole up for the day in shoes or other hiding places. These eight-legged arachnids range in size from three to eight inches long and inject their venom through a stinger located at the tip of their slender tails. Although few deaths from scorpion stings have been reported in Egypt, the pale, slender-clawed *Buthridae* produce venom that can be more toxic than that of poisonous snakes, the neurotoxin especially affects children and older adults in poor health.

While scorpions typically inhabit dry areas, they must drink and therefore can be found near water. Although hunters, scorpions are not especially aggressive, preferring to lie in wait rather than stalk their prey. They hunt at night, but since they don't see well, they may attack humans along with crickets. Therefore, don't wander around barefoot, especially in the summer when scorpions are most active. Get into the habit of shaking out your shoes and clothes *every* morning, and don't stick your hands into rocky crevices or dig through the sand; even if scorpions are not as active during the winter, they still will sting.

The sting of the small, pale, and potentially lethal scorpion species produces a pricking sensation. Pain quickly follows, and the area becomes sensitive. The actual site of the sting usually is invisible, but tapping it lightly with a finger produces a tingling or prickly feeling that travels from the wound toward the center of the body, and in severe cases, the stung area turns numb and general shock may set in. To control the pain, cold-pack the affected area and see a doctor to get antivenin (see below). The sting of larger, darker scorpions is relatively harmless; treat it like a severe spider bite or bee sting, which it resembles.

Snakes

Cobras inject a powerful neurotoxin that can eventually cause respiratory failure; vipers, in contrast, inject a hemotoxin that destroys blood cells. Most dangerous types of snakes are nocturnal and usually shy away from heavily populated areas, although the unwary explorer can occasionally stumble upon one. Fortunately, snake bites are not as dangerous as is commonly believed. Far more deaths are caused by incorrect treatment, often for nonpoisonous bites, than by the toxin injected by the snake.

To prevent snake bites, wear heavy shoes if you go tramping around in ruins or across the desert. Turn over stones carefully, and stick your hand into dark, cool crevices at your own risk. If you happen to be bitten by a possibly poisonous snake, the first rule is to keep calm. Try to get as good a description of the snake as possible. While teeth marks at the bite site may help, remember that cobras bite with a chewing action, which may obliterate the fang marks. Wash any snake bite and administer antibiotics. Then keep an eye on the bitten area for the next three hours if there is any question about the toxicity of the snake. Nonpoisonous bites are relatively painless and cause little tissue reaction, while poisonous ones are characterized by immediate and severe pain in the bite area as well as tissue trauma and edema. The area can become numb and paralyzed. Systemic symptoms include nausea, vomiting, and vertigo.

Treat all venomous bites the same way no matter the type of venomous snake. If the bite is on an arm or leg, tie a constricting band toward the body from the wound. Under *no* circumstances should this band be a true tourniquet, which shuts total circulation from the limb, but should only slow it and therefore control the spread of the toxin. Unless you are a skilled surgeon, do not slash the puncture site; to go deep enough to be effective, you can endanger nerves and tendons, and shallow cuts only inflict additional trauma and pain and provide a perfect site for infection. To further slow circulation and control the pain, cold-pack the area. If you use ice, be sure to remove it every 10 minutes to prevent tissue damage. *Keep the patient calm,* give fluids to counteract possible shock, and get medical help as soon as possible. If hit by the venom of a black-necked spitting cobra (it can project its venom from its front teeth for up to three meters), wash the area immediately, and if the toxin came in contact with eyes or other mucus membranes, get medical help. **Antivenins** are available for most Egyptian snake and scorpion bites through the Egyptian Organization for Biological and Vaccine Production, 51 Sh. Wezarat al-Zeraa, Agouza, Cairo, tel. (02) 348-3190.

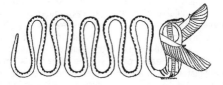

CONDUCT AND CUSTOMS

Egyptians have been raised in a social environment steeped in Islam, a background that can color their decision-making in a way difficult for foreigners to understand. Yet it is precisely this training that makes Egyptians some of the most charming and helpful of hosts. By understanding the culture and with consideration for your hosts, you can be a welcome guest in Egypt.

RELIGIOUS LIMITS

In Egypt, the line between church and state is extremely vague and ill-defined. Historically, the country was governed according to the laws of Islam, but exposure to Western thought has secularized much of Egypt's law. The modern fundamentalist movement has Egyptian adherents, and although members have caused some violence, they are, for the most part, outside the mainstream. However, in the rural areas, religious influences are much stronger than in the cities, and here you'll have to be wary not to step on sectarian toes.

Restrictions
Devout Muslims do not drink alcohol though most do not object to others imbibing in reasonable amounts. In doubt, ask. In addition to the prohibition on alcohol, the faithful do not use drugs or eat pork, which is considered unclean. Explicit sexual material—magazines, photos, tapes, or records—is illegal and subject to confiscation. Avoid getting into religious discussions with people you don't know well; proselytizing is illegal in Egypt, and foreigners actively working to convert Egyptians have been asked to leave. Remember, Islam is the state religion. (Although no longer enforced by the state, the penalty for conversion is death, and some families still exact that price from members who betray the faith.)

Moral Codes
Islamic societies segregate the sexes, although in Egypt the prohibitions on foreign women are not as strictly enforced as in some other Islamic countries. However, the more you interact with the people, the more sensitive you'll need to be. Ticket lines, for example, are often segregated; women should line up with other women (especially since the lines are usually shorter). On buses, the driver may want you to sit with other women. On the metro lines, the first car is usually reserved for women; at the end of the line, you may have to get out and change cars.

For men, speaking to an unknown Muslim woman is a breach of etiquette, and such forwardness can occasionally be severely punished. Take care in any liaisons you form because some families still follow ancient traditions, and a woman can be turned out of her home without support or even killed for consorting with a man. Although prostitutes exist, they're underground and generally unavailable to casual visitors.

If you are a man traveling with an unmarried woman friend, you may want to pass her off as your wife, otherwise small hotels and sleeper trains may not let you register in the same room or compartment. Not only does a fictitious marriage avoid upsetting numerous clerks and porters, it frees you from trying to justify your arrangement and shields her from unwelcome attention from Egyptian men, who would otherwise consider her a prostitute and fair game. (Don't worry about last names; Muslim women keep their father's family name when they marry.) Also beware of the moral watchdogs who inhabit many areas; these self-appointed guardians may follow you, watching for any "indecent activities"; if you're blatant, they may even call the police. Although most don't bother people in cars, you're safest to reserve your amour for the privacy of your hotel room.

SOCIAL MORES

In general, Egyptians are most accommodating; they will go out of their way to help you and respond to any questions you have—whether they know the correct answer or not. When asking directions, realize that many Egyptians, even educated ones, cannot read maps and have little idea of distances, so thank them politely and treat their information with cautious skepticism. Most Egyptians require little personal space and will stand within inches of you to talk. Try to keep from obviously backing away; subtle maneuvers will enable you to compromise on a mutually acceptable distance. You will find that whenever you start talking with an Egyptian, you will inevitably draw a crowd, and often the Egyptians will start arguing among themselves over the correct answer to a question.

Greeks Bearing Gifts

The welcome from most Egyptians is sincere, and if they adopt you as a friend there is little they won't do for you. However, be aware that casual acquaintances may offer you extra services or gifts and will be expecting something in return. In addition, as in every country, con artists abound wherever tourists congregate. Be on guard; some, for kickbacks, will try to steer you to certain hotels, others want to guide you into perfume shops, and yet others want to wrangle an invitation to visit your homeland. Be especially cautious of giving your address to casual acquaintances, for you may find one on your doorstep someday, and, if they've given your name to the U.S. Consulate as the person responsible for them, you could be legally held for their expenses.

Invitations

Egyptians if offered anything will refuse the first invitation; it's customary. Therefore (unless you're dealing with Egyptians used to Western frankness) you should do the same. If the offer is from the heart and not just politeness, it will be repeated. If you're invited into a home, especially in small villages, and have to refuse, the householder will often press for a promise from you to visit in the future, usually for a meal. If you make such a promise, keep it, for having foreign guests is often considered a social coup; if you fail to arrive, your would-be host will be humiliated.

To repay invitations, you can host a dinner in a restaurant, a common practice. If you issue invitations, be sure your guests understand that this is your party. If possible, arrange to pay in advance or to be billed later, otherwise you'll have trouble escaping with the check.

Baksheesh

This annoying, exasperating custom stems from the Islamic tenet that those with wealth must share it. Since most Egyptians tend to classify all Westerners as rich foreigners, they'll try to squeeze every possible piaster from you. These two beliefs have created three types of baksheesh: alms, tips, and bribes. In tourist areas you can be surrounded by beggars, and although your heart may be touched, a single gift can conjure a swarm of paupers from which you can escape only with difficulty. Children are particularly adept at begging and will descend at the slightest provocation; most often they want candy or pens and pencils. The best course of action is to ignore beggars, especially those who are not obviously handicapped. For those who are suffering, a note quickly slipped into their hand can help them.

Tips, on the other hand, are expected for minor and even unwanted services. Keep plenty of change, 25PT and 50PT notes or coins, and dispense them to those who perform minor services. Do not offer tips to professionals, businessmen, or others who would consider themselves your equals; give them gifts in return for special favors.

Serious bribing, however, is an intricate business, for there are officials who expect bribes, those who would be insulted by them, and those who would even report you to the authorities—don't attempt it. Learning to deal with the constant demands for baksheesh can be frustrating and even intimidating, but don't let it spoil your visit. Remember, the farther you get from the tourist areas, the less hassle you'll encounter.

Women Traveling Alone

In Egypt, a woman traveling alone is generally safe, but she will be noticed—less in large cities than in the country—and will attract men of all shapes, sizes, and ages. Rarely will they touch you, but they will tag along, trying to strike up a conversation; ignore them, no matter how impolite it feels to you. Remember that in their own society, speaking to an unknown woman is a gross breach of etiquette. If they continue to pester you, don't take offense, just tell them, *"Ruuh"* ("Go away"), or *"Khalas, masah lamah"* ("Enough, good-bye"). If they touch you, a real no-no, jerk away and say, *"Sibnee le wadi"*

("Don't touch me"), or *"Imshe"* ("Scram"). This last word is a tad insulting—what you say to a dog or a pesky kid—so use it sparingly. If all else fails, scream—in any language; in Egypt, you're sure to attract a crowd.

Although you probably will never be accosted, take simple precautions as you would anywhere: don't walk in deserted areas alone, don't get cornered alone in an elevator or train compartment or in tombs or monuments with the guard. Egypt is a conservative country, and becoming more so; dress accordingly: shorts and halter tops are an invitation to problems. (See "Dress" below.) Although most invitations are innocent, don't accept them from strangers. Egyptians stereotype Western women from a steady diet of "Dallas," "Dynasty," and similar television shows, and their stereotypes are reinforced by a number of lonely women who live up to the predictions. The two can lead to unpleasant surprises for some foreign women.

If you're unmarried, consider inventing a husband and wearing a wedding ring; the deception will save you countless hours of fencing. When traveling to out-of-the-way places like the oases, remember that although Egyptians usually make allowances for crazy foreigners, in their culture, the only women who travel alone are prostitutes, so be prepared for occasional unwanted attention. For trips into rural areas, consider joining up with another woman.

Red Tape

Egyptians have practiced the fine art of creating red tape for 5,000 years, creating a complex and capricious bureaucracy. Laws and departmental policies change frequently, and no one seems to bother informing the people in the field. Therefore, you can get permission or clearance from the national government and have it not honored (or have to get more permission) locally. Moreover, laws that have always been ignored may suddenly be enforced. To complicate matters, government office hours are short (usually 0900-1400).

When approached, bureaucrats tend to make the safest, easiest decisions (usually "no"), and will rarely pass you on to their boss. Appointments are often canceled, or business is frequently conducted in front of strangers who happen to be visiting. Out of politeness, officials will nearly always give you an answer (right or wrong), usually "come back tomorrow." While there are always exceptions, most bureaucrats are not creative problem solvers.

Unfortunately, visitors may have to deal with this creaking bureaucracy. To handle Egyptian red tape, you will need time, understanding, and patience. Plan ahead and allow at least a full day for any dealings with the government. Try to figure out which of three factors is motivating the worker: 1) his decisions may be based on *real* reasons, dictated directly from his bosses, and therefore he will be unable to bend or make exceptions; 2) he may be just throwing his weight around, so with proper handling, he might change his mind; 3) he could be waiting for a bribe—don't try it. Getting another department to intervene for you is not necessarily a good idea either, for considerable friction can exist between government agencies. The best approach is patience; act as if you have all the time in the world, and accept bureaucratic decisions graciously. If you need more papers or stamps, get them, but first ask the official to write down the requirements, who to see, and try to get him to sign it. On the other hand, if the answer is a flat no, hang around, talking about things in general—you can't do anything else anyway. If you're lucky, you'll be offered a cup of coffee, tea, or Coke. Always carry something with you to occupy your time while waiting, and just sit down and pull out your work as if you intend to spend the day. If you hang around long enough he may even change his mind.

Remember, Egypt is a Mediterranean country; nothing moves quickly. Delays caused by red tape are exacerbated by fatalism and a sense of timelessness, a philosophy dubbed by impatient and frustrated Westerners as "IBM": *in sha'allah* ("God willing"), *bukra* ("tomorrow"), and *mumkin* ("possibly"). The attitude is endemic, and the best way to cope with it is to adapt.

VISITOR RESPONSIBILITIES

Dress

Although few Westerners will be mistaken for natives, you can decrease the attention you draw by dressing conservatively. In cities, you can blend in with the foreigners who live there by wearing business clothes: dress shirts, ties, and either a sweater or coat for men; skirts, blouses, or suits worn with low heels for women. Formal attire is required at the Opera House, but seldom elsewhere. *Galabayyas* are worn by working men and sometimes by the upper classes for leisure; they are men's clothes, and though they are more comfortable than the woman's caftan, women should not wear them on the street in Egypt. (But buy several to take home; they make good summer- and patio-wear.) For traveling and visiting monuments, sport clothes are acceptable. Western fashions and the vagaries of foreign dress are accepted in the major tourist centers, but in rural areas, conservative dress becomes even more important.

Western men's shorts resemble the garments the Egyptians wear under their *galabayyas,* and therefore you may appear as if you're walking around in your underwear. However, the natives are good-natured and normally accept such oddities with grace. Women, however, have less leeway. Unless you're interested in a sexual liaison, reserve shorts, sunsuits, low-cut tops, and bralessness for the beaches. In fact, even on popular public beaches like those in Alexandria, wear conservative swimsuits; bikinis are for more private places like Club Med. For visiting monuments, long loose pants are okay but cover up your arms—a long-sleeved cotton shirt not only makes you "decent" but protects you from the parching sun. A hat modestly covers your head, and also lowers your body temperature. In the outlying areas, Egyptians are used to seeing foreign women in jeans and shirts. A British friend adds a black scarf to her black shirt and jeans, a practical touch that uniquely blends with Egyptian ideals. Such sensitivity politely underscores her consideration to her hosts' beliefs.

Visiting Mosques

With the exception of the Sayyidna al-Husayn in Cairo, major mosques are open to the public unless services are in progress (the main one is on Friday at noon). Unless otherwise posted, tickets to some that have been restored are sold by the caretaker for about LE3-6. All visitors to mosques, mausoleums, and *madrasas* must remove their shoes; you can take them with you (carry them in your left hand) or check them at the rack by the door. Most Muslims walk around

in their stockings, but I carry a pair of sock-like slippers to wear. Those mosques that are major tourist attractions have canvas overshoes available; a tip of 50PT to LE1 is in order for the people who put them on for you. Women must cover bare arms; if you insist upon wearing sleeveless blouses, at least carry a scarf to use as a shawl. I use it to cover my head.

Visiting Antiquities

Egypt's monuments have become increasingly damaged by the hordes of tourists who visit them every day. Avoid adding to the problem; do not to lean against walls with decorations, for you can crumble the plaster or flake away the stone. Stay within the railings set up, and don't touch the carvings or paintings. Flash photography is categorically prohibited, for it fades the paintings, but you can photograph tomb interiors in available light (use fast film) with a special permit. Although the attendants will focus sunlight into the tombs with mirrors, this practice harms the pigments even more—please don't succumb to the temptation either for photographing or to see the designs; carry a small flashlight. (See also "Photography," p.172).

Most of Egypt's monuments, museums, and other cultural sites adhere to hours set by the **Egyptian Antiquities Office (EAO).** Museums are generally open daily 0900-1600, closed Friday 1130-1300; other sites are usually open daily 0800-1600 in winter, and open at least one hour earlier in summer. You may need permission to visit the sites north of Birket Qarun (see the Fayyum or Cairo Tourist Office) and in Bahariya (see the Inspector of Antiquities at Giza Plateau).

Crime And Drugs

Crime in Egypt is nearly nonexistent, and violence is usually limited to family feuds. Unfortunately, however, Egypt is changing, so be aware of pickpockets and petty thieves—especially in areas foreigners frequent. Women must be cautious, especially in out-lying areas. Be careful with illegal drugs; if you end up in jail, the embassy cannot help except to notify your family and arrange for a lawyer's visit. Be especially cautious about cutting in on drug and black money markets; you could end up at the bottom of the Nile with a carpet wrapped around your head.

GENERAL INFORMATION

STANDARDS

Time

Cairo time is an hour earlier than most of Europe, two hours ahead of London, seven hours ahead of New York, and 10 hours earlier than San Francisco. Egypt uses daylight-saving time, but its season varies with the dates of Ramadan. Although most businesses abide by the 12-hour clock, airlines and trains run on 24-hour time.

Electricity

With the exception of some parts of Garden City in Cairo, Egyptian current is 220 volts, 50 cycles. (This change in cycles will make plug-in clocks run slow.) Sockets take European, two-pronged plugs; you will need adapters for American appliances. Some small appliances, like curling irons, will run without current converters, provided you keep them set on low and do not leave them plugged in for too long. However, to be safe, invest in a converter to drop the voltage to 110.

Measurements

In Egypt, weights and measures are metric. Instead of trying to convert exactly into the more familiar pounds, feet, or miles, learn a few equivalents and begin working within the system. For example, a kilo (kilogram) is 2.2 pounds, so if you want about a pound of anything in a shop, order half a kilo. A liter is slightly over a quart, and four liters just over a gallon. A meter is nearly three inches longer than a yard.

Temperature conversions are a little trickier: multiply temperature in centigrade by nine-fifths and add 32. It's simpler to remember that water freezes at 0° C, room temperature (70° F) is 21° C, normal body temperature is 37° C, and an outside temperature of 43° C (110° F) is just damn hot.

COMMUNICATIONS

Radio And Television

Shortwave radio sets can pick up some programs from BBC, Voice of America, and Voice of Peace; reception is best in the north. Radio Cairo broadcasts daily news in English at 0730, 1430, and 2000. In most locations where there is an appreciable foreign population, local television stations broadcast a syndicated daily news in English at 2000 or 2015. Cairo program listings are printed in the *Egyptian Gazette*.

THE MAGAZINE OF EGYPT

Print Media

Newspapers: The daily English-language *Egyptian Gazette* (called the *Egyptian Mail* on Saturday) is available at most news kiosks for 50PT. A morning paper, it's frequently sold out by noon, so buy early. Aware of the government threat of censorship, the paper prints news stories through rose-colored glasses, but is does carry the daily TV and radio schedules as well as information on movies, concerts, and special activities in both Cairo and Alexandria.

The *International Herald Tribune* provides meatier coverage, although it's usually two to four days late arriving at newsstands; it includes comic strips like Doonesbury and Peanuts. *The Guardian, The Wall Street Journal, USA Today, The London Times* and the weeklies *The Middle East Times* and *The Middle East Observer* are also available. *Al-Ahram* publishes an excellent weekly edition in English on Thursdays; it's well worth the 50 PT.

Magazines: North African editions of *Newsweek* and *Time* are available a week behind their issue dates, and in Cairo the bookstores carry many other familiar titles. In Egypt, the American Chamber of Commerce publishes the *Business Monthly; The Arab Press Review* is a biweekly compilation of political news, while *Prism* is a quarterly devoted to the arts.

The monthly *Cairo Today* is also an outstanding source of current and historical cultural information, printing a monthly activity calendar, lists of churches, museums, and regularly scheduled club meetings. In addition to its blanket coverage of Cairo, it also prints travel and event information for Alexandria and Upper Egypt. It's available in most Cairo bookstores for LE5 per issue or by yearly subscription at LE50 (foreign, US$55—delivery a month late).

Local Guides: A series of local guidebooks under a generic heading composed of the area's name followed by *Night & Day* are distributed free at hotels, Tourist Offices, and travel agencies. Currently there are four, one for Cairo, Alexandria, Upper Egypt (from Minya to Abu Simbel), and P.S.I. (Port Said, Suez City, and Ismailia). These small guides usually have a local map of unpredictable accuracy, extensive advertisements for hotels, restaurants, etc., lists of churches, theaters, banks, museums, and government offices along with their hours, but the information is often in error.

The series of guides put out by the publishers of *Cairo Today* are more reliable: *Leisure & Recreation Guide, Business Guide, Dining Guide,* and *Shopping Guide* each run about LE15 and are filled with current information.

Telephones

Egyptian phone numbers may vary from four or five digits to seven; the cities are identified by one- or two-digit numbers; from outside Egypt, dial 011 to access the international equipment, then 20 for the country, and then the city area code and number. To make long-distance calls within Egypt, add a 0 to the city code, making it either a two- or three-digit number.

Although telephone communications are improving in Cairo, service throughout the rest of Egypt is erratic. Overburdened equipment functions slowly, especially during peak hours; to avoid wrong numbers dial slowly. Local calls cost 25PT, and coin-operated phones (located in some hotels, cigarette kiosks, railway stations, and telephone offices) take aluminum piaster pieces. Many shop owners will let you make local calls from their phones, if they have them, for 25PT a call; hotels may charge up to a pound.

Long-distance and International Calls: You must place long-distance and international calls on an international line available in most hotels, businesses, telephone offices, and some private homes. Alternatively, you can now use USA Direct; dial 356-0200 and give the operator

TELEPHONE CODES	
Abuqir	55
Al Arish	067
Alexandria	03
Aswan	097
Asyut	088
Beni Suef	082
Cairo	02
Fayyum	084
Hurghada	065
Ismailia	064
Kharga	88
Luxor	095
Marsa Matruh	03
Minya	086
Nag Hammadi	096
Port Said	066
Qina	096
Sinai	062
Sohag	093
Suez	062
Tanta	040

your international number off the card. The call will be billed to your home address (U.S.) and charged as if the call was made from the U.S. You can call collect through the same service; you cannot call long-distance from coin phones.

Telephone Offices: Marked by a sign showing a phone dial, telephone exchanges handle local, intercity, and in larger cities international calls. In most large offices there is usually someone who speaks English, and major cities have at least one 24-hour telephone office. To call from an exchange, write out the number and pay for the call, either for a set amount of time or LE20-30 for an open line; when you're done settle your bill. You may have to wait quite a while for your call to go through, so bring a book. An alternate way to call is to have the exchange place the call at a specific time and then you can receive it at another number. In this case, you will have to go to the exchange and prepay for a fixed amount of time. If your call is not completed, you will have to return to the office and present your receipt for a refund.

Telex And Fax

Telexes can be sent from major hotels or telephone exchanges. Most general offices don't have minimum times, but hotels may. If you do not have a telex or fax number at home, check with your travel agent, who may be willing to let you use their number for an emergency. Egyptian businesses nearly all have fax machines which are replacing telexes. Most hotels, business centers (see "Practicalities" in "Cairo," p. 251), and some telephone offices can send faxes.

MAIL

Post Offices

Most post offices are open 0830-1500 daily except Fridays. The main office on Midan Ataba in Cairo is open 0800-1900, 0800-1200 Fridays. Postage for an airmail letter runs 70PT for either letters or postcards. **Express Mail Service** (36 hours to Europe, 48 hours to the U.S.) is available at selected post offices. International Business Associates (1079 Cornishe al-Nil, Garden City, Cairo, tel. (02) 355-0427/355-7454) handles **Federal Express** shipping.

Receiving Mail

You can receive mail at any major hotel, or if you are a member of American Express, you can get mail in care of their offices. Mail sent poste restante takes forever to sift through the system, and you seemingly spend hours in line trying to claim it. You'll have to show up in person to get it. Note: the U.S. Embassy will *no longer* accept mail for traveling Americans. If you're a member of ARCE or similar organizations you can probably make arrangements to send mail in care of their Egyptian offices. Although mail seems to be reliable, especially in major cities, like many things in Egypt it is erratic. Don't depend on it for transferring vital information; use the telex, fax, or phone. There is no reliable way of shipping packages into Egypt.

Shipping

Packages leaving Egypt must not weigh more than 20 kilos or measure more than 1½ meters in any dimension. Airmail runs about LE3/kilo; to mail packages, you will need to collect forms from various offices, so allow at least several hours. A parcel that needs an export license may be mailed from the Cairo Airport, where it will be inspected by customs officials and sewn into a cloth bag. For an additional fee you will be guided through the rest of the paperwork. Or try shipping from the post office near the train station on Sh. Ramesses. Alternatively, you can ship through Cook's, the air-freight sections of most major airlines, or shipping companies. Customs officials go through everything entering and leaving the country, and items of any value to them are regularly lifted.

TOURIST INFORMATION

ETA

The Egyptian Tourist Authority (ETA) maintains offices throughout Egypt and the world. (See p. 164.) Staffed with friendly people, they dispense information on sights, hotels, and transportation. Be aware, however, that the information is not always totally up to date or correct; if you find a local person who gives you different directions, he may be right—then again, he might not; you'll have to develop your instincts.

Tourist Police

A special detachment of the regular Egyptian Police Department, the Tourist Police wear the standard uniform, black wool in winter and white cotton in summer, but sport a green armband with "Tourist Police" written in English. Most are bilingual and are there to help tourists find their way around. They have headquarters in all major tourist sites.

Guides

All guides in Egypt must be trained in history and antiquities and pass government exams; however, not all who approach you will be so blessed. Freelance guides may be knowledgeable, but then again, they may not. I prefer a good guidebook for a visit at my own pace. If you do hire a guide, figure LE60 and up a day. The **Association of Tourists' Friends,** 33 Qasr al-Nil, Cairo, tel. (02) 742-036, is a private organization of enthusiastic volunteers (mostly students) who lurk around railway stations, bus stations, and anywhere else they might find

EGYPTIAN TOURIST AUTHORITY
(FORMERLY EGAPT)

Egypt
Headquarters
Mr. Sayed Moussa, Chairman
Egyptian Tourist Authority
Misr Travel Tower
Abasseya, Cairo, Egypt
tel. 823510/824585/831253

ETA OFFICES ABROAD

Athens
Egyptian Tourist Authority
10 Amerikis St. (6th floor)
Athens 10671 Greece
tel. 360-6906

Beverly Hills
Egyptian Tourist Authority
8383 Wilshire Blvd., Ste. 215
Beverly Hills, CA 90211 U.S.A.
tel. (310) 653-8815

Chicago
Egypthian Tourist Authority
645 N. Michigan Ave. #829
Chicago, IL 60611 U.S.A.
tel. (312) 280-4666/4693

Frankfurt
Agyptishes Fremdenverkehrsamt
64 A, Kaiser Strasse,
Frankfurt, W. Germany
tel. 252319/252153

Geneve
Office du Tourisme d'Egypte
9, rue des Alpes
Geneve, Switzerland
tel. 732-9132

Houston
Egytian Tourist Authority
2425 Fountainview Ste. 280,
Houston, TX 77057 U.S.A.
tel. (713) 782-9107/782-9110

Kuwait
Egyptian Tourist Authority
Villa 5 F Omar Ibn El Khatab St.
P.B. 27233
Safat 13133, Kuwait
tel. 240-3104

London
Egyptian Tourist Authority
168 Picadilly W1
London, U.K.
tel. 493-5282/3

Montreal
Egyptian Tourist Authority
Place Bonaventure
40 Frontenac
P.O. Box 304
Montreal P q Canada H 5-A
tel. 861-4420/851-4606

New York
Egyptian Tourist Authority
630 Fifth Avenue
New York, NY, 10111 U.S.A.
tel. (212) 246-6960

Paris
Bureau du Tourisme
Ambassade de la R.A.E.
90, Av. Champs Elysees
Paris, France
tel. 4562-9443/4562-9442

Rome
Ufficia Infirmazioni Turistiche
19, Via Bissolati, 00187
Rome, Italy
tel. 4745361

Tokyo
Egyptian Tourist Authority
Embassy of Egypt
Akasaka 2 - Chome - Annex
M - S Akasaka 2 - chome
Minato-Ku-Tokyo, Japan
Tel. (03) 5890653

foreigners in distress and rescue them. Tipping these white knights is not protocol.

Theft

Theft is uncommon in Egypt, but if you find valuables missing, contact the closest police station. These stations are manned by administrative officers 1000-1400; most are also open to the public between 2000-2200; investigations are frequently conducted at night. You must report a crime in person. If it's not an emergency, make an appointment for about 1000 hours and figure on spending at least a couple of hours. Do not expect to find someone who speaks English; if your Arabic is not fluent, find a translator, through the embassy if necessary.

Embassies

Many visitors misunderstand the role of embassies, often expecting them to somehow render them immune from Egyptian law. Consular sections can help you with student letters, visa, passport, and customs difficulties and emergencies of all types. They also handle birth and marriage certificates and will notarize documents; some services carry a small fee. You should register your passport with the consular section upon arrival in Egypt, and if you know your itinerary, leave them a copy so they will be able to reach you in an emergency. Most embassies are closed Fri., and some also close Sun.; the British Embassy closes Sat. and Sunday.

MISCELLANEOUS INFORMATION

Cultural Centers

Nearly all nations operate cultural centers, many of which offer libraries, lectures, exhibitions, and excursions. They are a good place to pick up free information. In Egypt most are located in Cairo and Alexandria; see those chapters for more information.

Church Groups

Protestant and Catholic churches form the backbone of Egyptian foreign communities, and their members are a storehouse of local information. In addition to services, they sponsor social and cultural events and offer counseling.

Counseling

Alcoholics Anonymous maintains chapters throughout Egypt, as does Al-Anon. Information is available through the U.S. Embassy Health Unit in Cairo, tel. (02) 355-7371, ext. 2351/2356. The Community Services Association offers support services including education, a newcomers' program, and preventative mental-health activities. If Egypt is getting to you, contact them Sun.-Thurs. 0900-1700 at #4 Road 21, Ma'adi, tel. (02) 350-5284.

Clubs

Clubs support numerous activities and range from running, scuba, and rugby to theater, music, ecology, continuing education, and social groups. Most are centered in Cairo and maintain formal and informal information networks. For more information see "Cairo—Practicalities," and for meeting times and dates, pick up a current copy of *Cairo Today*.

Business

Business hours can be erratic, but the larger companies and offices usually maintain set schedules. **Banks** are normally open 0830-1330, closed Fri. and Saturday. **Commercial offices** are open in summer 0800-1400, in winter 0900-1300; most reopen about 1630 or 1700 until 1900; most close Thurs. afternoon and Fri., though some close Sat. afternoon and Sunday. **Government offices** hold court 0800-1400; offices are closed on Fri. and national holidays. Hours for all businesses are shorter during Ramadan, often only in the mornings. Individuals within businesses often work varying hours, so make an appointment. **Shops** keep much less standard hours, although most modern ones such as department stores are open 0900 or 1000-1300 and again from 1600 or 1630-1930 or 2000; some stay open through midday now, especially in winter, closing about 1700 or 1800. Shops in the bazaars start opening about 0900 and, although some remain open through lunch the owner may not be around (his helper may not be helpful, although some of the larger shops are starting to train their personnel). Shops are open in the evenings, usually 1500-2000; they may close Fri., Sat., or Sunday. During Ramadan, most close for the entire afternoon, opening again after sunset.

FESTIVALS AND HOLIDAYS

Egyptians use three calendars: the Western, the Islamic, and the Coptic. Secular business and political holidays are set by the Western calendar, and banks, government offices, businesses, and schools close. Sinai Liberation Day falls on 25 April; Labor Day on 1 May; Celebration of the 1952 Revolution, 23 July; Armed Forces Day, 6 Oct.; Suez Day, 24 Oct.; and Victory Day, 23 December. In Egypt, Father's Day falls on 4 Feb.; Teachers' Day, 3 March; Doctors' and Dentists' Day, 18 March; Mother's Day, 21 March; Applied Artists' Day, 25 March; and Farmers' Day, 9 September.

Shamm Al-Nisim
This holiday descends from the pharaonic tradition of cutting the canals to let the flooding Nile spill into the fields. Celebrated on the Monday after Coptic Easter, Shamm al-Nisim means "sniffing the breeze." Egyptians flock to the banks of the Nile and parks for picnics. Private homes often open their gardens to celebrants who dine on traditional onions, fish, and colored eggs.

ALLAN HANSEN

a Coptic priest

COPTIC HOLIDAYS

The Copts do not follow the Gregorian calendar, but a solar one containing 12 months of 30 days, with five or six days extra every fourth year. Farmers as well as the Coptic Church use this calendar, which is nearly identical to the ancient pharaonic one.

Christmas Holidays
Copts celebrate Christmas on 7 Jan., which is the Western date of Epiphany. Following lengthy church services, they spend the day visiting and feasting. Epiphany, which marks both the coming of the Magi to Christ's birthplace and his later baptism by John, is celebrated by the Copts on 19 January.

Easter
Coptic Easter is set by the Coptic calendar and often falls between a week and a month from Western Easter. The Copts spend the holy week in daily prayers, beginning with Palm Sunday when they drape the churches in black. On Holy Thursday, priests commemorate Christ's washing of the feet of his apostles by anointing with holy water the feet of the men present. Good Friday is spent in prayers, and then from 2300 until sunrise, the Book of Revelation is read. Easter service is on Sat., runs from 2000 to 2400, and marks the end of the Lenten fast.

Additional Holidays
The 50 days following Easter are joyous, culminating in Pentecost, the coming of the Holy Spirit. The Apostles' Feast, 12 July, commemorates Peter's and Paul's martyrdom. The Feast of the Virgin Mary, 22 August, celebrates the Virgin's ascension. The Copts celebrate New Year on 11 Sept.; it's not a public holiday.

ISLAMIC HOLIDAYS

The Islamic religious calendar is based on 12 lunar months of about 29 or 30 days. Ten to 11 days shorter than the Gregorian calendar, it rotates forward in respect to the secular calendar.

Ramadan
The ninth month, that of Ramadan, is set aside for remembrance and atonement, much like Christian Lent. The exact beginning and end are determined by lunar sightings, so the actual dates may vary by one day from the predictions. The entire month is spent fasting between sunrise and sunset: devout Muslims don't even drink water, chew gum, or smoke until the traditional cannon fires, marking the end of the daily fast. Family and friends gather together for *iftar,* a large meal to break the fast, after which the Egyptians return to the streets; shops reopen and Egyptians party far into the night. After a little sleep, families again gather for *suhour,* the last main meal before sunrise and another day of fasting. The end of Ramadan is celebrated by a three-day feast; Ramadan Bairam or Eid al-Fitr. Visiting Egypt during Ramadan is both interesting and frustrating. Shop hours are irregular; businesses officially shorten their hours to 1000-1400, and tempers, especially in summer, grow short. To be polite, don't eat or drink in front of Egyptians during Ra-

madan. However, especially as Ramadan draws to a close, a sense of excitement permeates Egyptian life. Mosques are lighted, tents for special prayers decorate squares, movie theaters run far into the night, and vendors, especially of religious material, set up markets. You can buy special candies and desserts such as *ata'if* on the street. Ramadan is a unique time in Egypt: if you're planning to do any business, avoid it; otherwise join in the festivities.

Eid Al-Adha
Falling 70 days after the end of Ramadan, this feast commemorates Abraham's attempt to sacrifice his son to God and marks the end of the pilgrimage period. Muslims worldwide celebrate, and in so doing connect themselves with those who have completed a successful pilgrimage.

Mulids
Celebrated by both Copts and Muslims, *mulids* honor saints on dates of importance in their lives. Festivals take place throughout Egypt and include prayers, parades, and celebrations by the dervishes. If you visit one, be discreet in dress and with your camera; *mulids* are religious festivals and emotions can run high. The most famous *mulid* is Mulid al-Nubi, the prophet's birthday, which is celebrated throughout the country; nearly as famous are the *mulids* of Ahmed al-Badawi centered in Tanta and that of Sayyida Zaynab in Cairo.

SHOPPING

Shopping, like nearly everything in Egypt, is a time-consuming process. Wear sturdy shoes (you will probably be walking through areas not particularly noted for sanitation), and bring shopping bags (plastic net ones are available at most corner markets for a pound or so) and plenty of small bills and change (otherwise you may end up buying more than you had planned or waiting while a boy runs to get change).

SHOPPING TIPS

For most Egyptian items, one of the best places to shop is in the old Islamic area of Cairo around the Khan al-Khalili. Often you can see craftsmen at work in small shops and they rarely object if you stop and watch. Browsing is also acceptable; most shop owners will not object even if you stay a couple of hours and buy nothing. When you do buy, check the individual item; workmanship and quality vary from piece to piece, and in Egypt, it's caveat emptor. Some well-established stores will ship your purchases out of Egypt, but it will take at least six months by surface mail or three by airmail to get them. Even if the store is reputable, you still run the risk of never seeing these items again.

In tourist shopping areas, a "guide" may offer to show you around. He'll take you to the stores of his relatives or where he will receive kickbacks, and he'll also expect a tip from you. If you're in a hurry, these guides can lead you through rabbit-warren areas like the Khan al-Khalili and help you quickly find items you want. You can even avoid bargaining by having him ask the "no bargain price" or tell him at the outset what you're willing to pay for specific items.

Stores

Three types of stores exist in Egypt: department stores, small single-owner shops, and the *suqs* or bazaars. Department stores (as well as most small shops) have fixed prices. A clerk will help you pick out what you want, then write it up. You take the sales slip to the cashier, and while you're paying, your package, *in sha'allah,* will meet you there. Most large stores will cash traveler's checks and many now take credit cards. Small shops tend to specialize in a few items and many offer custom-made goods such as shirts, *galabayyas,* or shoes. In these cases, you'll have to order and then return anywhere from a few days to a couple of months later to pick up your purchase. Small-shop hours can be unpredictable, and they may not be open when they say they will be; you may have to make several trips before you can collect your pur-

Practice your Arabic and your bargaining skills at an open-air suq.

chase. Bazaars vary from groups of itinerant street vendors to the sophisticated shops in Cairo's Khan al-Khalili. Here, with only a few exceptions, bargaining is the rule.

Bargaining

In a tradition as old as the East, bargaining for large items is conducted over a cup of coffee or *karkaday* (in modern times, a Coke) in a leisurely, dispassionate fashion. Many visitors, however, have never encountered this ritual. Start by window shopping and asking prices from different vendors, or even better, quote the price someone else has paid. Then decide how much a given item is worth to you. Don't begin bargaining unless you intend to buy (provided a suitable price can be negotiated). Once the shopkeeper has offered you a price, make a counteroffer, roughly half what you intend to pay. The owner will make a counteroffer, and the game continues. Don't let the seller 1) trick you into going up twice in a row (it will throw off your calculations) or 2) wring an admission from you as to how much you think the item is worth; just reply that you made him an offer. Be sure you know if prices are in dollars or Egyptian pounds. If talks bog down, leave and come back later. If you settle on half the original price, you are an expert bargainer; a third off is more typical.

Antiquities

No matter where you go in Egypt, you'll probably be approached to buy "real *antikas.*" Generally these articles are as phony as their forged certificates of authenticity. Buying real antiquities or taking them out of Egypt is illegal, but copies, often good enough to make even an expert look twice, are generally inexpensive, especially in Upper Egypt.

The line between secondhand articles and antiquities is often fine, especially now that the government has taken an interest in Islamic arts and crafts; a good rule of thumb is that anything less than 100 years old is considered merely "used." During Nasser's program of nationalization, many wealthy families shut up their homes and left. These homes reverted to the government, which periodically opens one and sells off its contents. Occasionally, furnishings from these houses find their way into the open market and are available through antique dealers.

ARTS AND CRAFTS

Gold And Silver

For centuries, gold and silver markets have flourished in Egypt and today the markets remain strong. Working from ancient pharaonic, Christian, and Islamic patterns, modern jewelers have designed beautiful and unique pieces. The most popular souvenirs are cartouches with given names in hieroglyphics. The price depends on the amount of gold used and whether the letters are engraved or applied. Thin ones with glued letters are less expensive than the thicker ones with soldered letters. Other stock items include rings and cuff links engraved with hieroglyphic designs and the traditional gold bracelets collected by Egyptian women. Copies of ancient amulets also crowd jewelers' windows—the eye of Horus, the *ankh,* the scarab beetle, and the Fatma hand, a powerful charm against the evil eye. Lotus-flower pendants and earrings are among the least expensive and most appealing designs, as are disks inscribed in Arabic with sayings from the Koran or simply the word "Allah" engraved in an arabesque background.

Now all gold is stamped in Arabic numerals indicating its content, usually 14, 18, or 22 karat, and sold by the gram. Sterling silver (80 or 92.5%) is also stamped and sold by weight. Antique silver is not stamped, but then neither is older village or "tinker" silver, and these often contain only 60% silver. The best place to buy precious metals is around Cairo's Khan al-Khalili; Sh. Mu'izz al-Din-Allah, the "street of the gold sellers," lies just west of the main buildings of the Khan.

The price per gram fluctuates on a daily basis, and in the marketplace a charge is added for workmanship. Some shopkeepers, however, raise these prices, so check with several stores. However, the demise of the black market has cut into the profits of jewelers who were dealers, and the amount of gold on display is considerably less than in former years. Nevertheless, gold jewelry, because it costs relatively little for intricate workmanship, remains one of Egypt's better buys.

Other Jewelry

Jewelers work semiprecious stones into intricate designs. Although the quality of the stones is generally good, remember that you're often quoted the per-gram price of the gold settings for the entire piece. Therefore, you may want to try haggling with the storekeeper. Inexpensive costume jewelry also abounds in Egypt. Strings of scarab-shaped faience beads or copies of ancient pieces made with faience and glass beads are most typical. For a few pounds they make distinctive souvenirs.

Brass And Copper

Metalworking, begun in the pharaonic ages, still retains its ancient traditions. Today you can pick up candlesticks, molds, pitchers, and vases for converting into lamp bases, samovars, and braziers. Brass hookahs (water pipes) create unique decorative accents, but heavily inlaid brass trays mounted on wooden stands are most striking. When buying metal objects, be sure that anything you will be drinking from is lined with tin or another inert metal, because foods, especially fruit juices, can react with brass or copper to produce traces of poisonous substances. Shop around; most merchants carry similar goods, but the quality varies widely.

Wood And Inlay

Vast wooden screens called *mashribiyya* once covered nearly every window in Cairo. Made with turned beading laid down in varying designs, they're assembled with dowels and glue—no nails. Designed to filter the direct sunlight, they also allow the cool evening breezes from the Nile to circulate through houses. Antique *mashribiyya* rarely appear on the market anymore, and modern imitations do not display the refined workmanship of the old. But if you shop around you can find screens or table frames (to fit brass trays) nearly as good as older ones. Furniture and game boards inlaid with mother of pearl, bone, or wood are popular with both Egyptians and tourists. Smaller items like playing card holders or trinket boxes make nice souvenirs.

Ivory And Bone

Carved ivory and bone are available throughout Egypt. Most of the bone pieces, recognizable by their curved design and more porous texture, are inexpensive. Antique ivory is also available, but unscrupulous vendors may try to pass off plastic and bone; real ivory is more close-grained and has more veining and color than bone, and plastic melts when heated. Note: importing ivory, old or new, into the U.S. is illegal.

Alabaster

Egyptians still dig alabaster out of the southern hills and work it into affordable vases, ashtrays, and statuettes. The best prices are to be had in the "factories" in the south, where you can watch the pieces being made. Although heavy, alabaster can be fragile; pack any items you buy carefully.

Glass

Well known since the Middle Ages, hand-blown *muski* glass is still made in Egypt. Filled with numerous bubbles, it's usually turquoise, green, dark brown, dark blue, or colorless. Glasses, cups and saucers, candlesticks, and vases are all inexpensive but fragile. Much of it is made just north of Khan al-Khalili using recycled glass. The brown, for example, comes from broken Stella Beer bottles. Some jewelers are mounting pieces of antique glass, primarily from the Ptolemaic period, in gold settings; the decorative elements, which run entirely through the thickness of the glass, attest to the technical skill of the ancient glassblowers.

Basketry

The Fayyum, Siwa Oasis, and Upper Egypt produce typical basketry. Cheap, light, and easy to pack, this distinctive ware makes good wall decorations and practical gifts. The Siwan work is especially fine, often trimmed with tassels. Baskets from the Fayyum are also beautifully made, and the brightly dyed plattens available in Aswan are typical of Nubian work.

Leather

Leather items such as "poufs" (leather ottomans), sandals, purses, and briefcases are inexpensive, and you can find some well-made ones. Stores specializing in leather coats, skirts, and vests, both in Cairo and Alexandria, offer nice garments and will often custom-tailor them; you can also have shoes made. Alexandria is the center of the leather industry, and you may find the best prices there. You can also have specialty work done, like leather bookbinding.

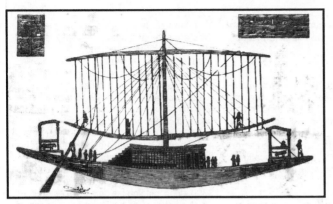

Paintings on papyrus are inexpensive and make good souvenirs.

Papyrus

The pounded stems of papyrus plants provided ancient Egyptians with a form of paper on which they recorded their history, beliefs, and experiences. Today the ancient art of papyrus-making has been reintroduced; the most famous center, the Papyrus Institute started by Dr. Hassan Ragab, produces paintings of pharaonic motifs and reproductions of ancient scenes from the Book of the Dead. Other workshops now exist, many staffed by former students of the Papyrus Institute. When buying papyrus pictures, beware of imitations on pressed banana leaves, which are darker, coarser, and lack the supple crispness of real papyrus. Most hotel shops and souvenir stands stock a selection of papyrus pictures; prices depend on size and quality.

Incense, Perfume, And Kohl

Often found around spice markets, shops specializing in incense will mix combinations of frankincense, ambergris, myrrh, or sandalwood to your specifications. Unlike Western incense, these mixtures will not burn by themselves; you have to sprinkle them over lighted coals. However, the stick variety of incense available in small street-corner kiosks will burn alone.

Egypt is also known for the perfume produced in the Fayyum, but in areas frequented by tourists, perfume sellers have become nefarious. Gambits used by shills include introducing themselves and expressing concern: "Be careful where you step." Once they've led you to a shop, they will abandon you there to the owner, where a single woman may be offered more than just perfume. Limit your perfume buying to established stores in general market areas. A fun purchase is kohl, the eyeliner used by Egyptian women in ancient times. Be sure you have the clerk show you how to apply it.

Carpets

Egyptian knotted carpets resemble the Turkish type. Many are made of Egyptian wool, and while not as finely worked (16 knots/cm as opposed to 32), they are considerably less expensive, nearly as plush, and wear well. The more expensive Turkish type made from high-grade imported wool is also available, as well as wall hangings (64 knots/cm) that are part silk. The Bedouin market rugs woven in tones of brown and beige; the price of these inexpensive rugs depends on the size. They make durable, aesthetic floor coverings.

Tapestry

The best-known local weavings come from the Harraniyya Art School, developed by the Egyptian architect Ramesses Wissa Wassef to teach village children a viable trade and to preserve local craftsmanship. Because the teachers encourage the children's own creativity, designs are primitive and most often depict scenes of village life. However, many exhibit more mature craftsmanship, subtle colors, and textures wrought within complex and sophisticated designs. Genuine Harraniyya tapestries are available only at the school itself (near Saqqara) or at

Senouhi's, their outlet in Cairo. However, a variety of other work in the same vein, some quite beautiful, is available in handicraft shops throughout Egypt.

Appliqué

Artisans of Cairo's "street of the tentmakers" still produce beautiful appliqué work. Designs reflect pharaonic or Islamic motifs, including refined and intricate calligraphy. Pieces can be made to order; most shops have pattern books or photos of their previous pieces, and some merchants will design to your specifications. Prices vary with the size of the piece.

Fabrics

Since the introduction of cotton, Egypt has become world famous for cotton fabric, and today it remains one of the best buys. If you sew, leave plenty of room in your luggage for yardage; if you don't, buy enough for a shirt, skirt, (2.5 meters) or *galabayya* (3-3.5 meters) and take it to a local shirt maker.

Silk is also a good buy, though it is not as fine or as heavy as the Chinese, and the dyes can sometimes fade. However, it's inexpensive, and you can indulge yourself in shirts, skirts, and dresses, items you might never consider having made in silk at home.

When buying yardage, watch while the clerk measures it out and check for flaws. If you'll be taking the material to a tailor, be sure to preshrink it, wetting cotton in hot water, silk in tepid. (Tailors will rarely do this even if you ask.) Preshrinking ensures the fit and enables you to handwash your silk instead of sending it to the cleaners.

Clothes

You can also buy ready-made clothes, both Western-style and native *galabayyas* or caftans. Sizes are European: men's shirts range upward from 36 (the equivalent of a 14-inch collar), with each size larger representing a half-inch increase in collar size. In ladies' dresses, a 36 equals a size 8; 38 a size 10; 40 a size 12, etc. You might want to consider buying a Bedouin dress, in which cross-stitched panels are set into a black gown. Most markets offer coarse imitations in large stitches of wool or cotton thread for the tourist trade. However, in some stores, especially in Upper Egypt, you can still find the finer silk work, but expect to pay at least $300, depending on the amount of embroidery. The embroidery on the finest dresses resembles woven panels, and they make stunning party gowns. Patterns vary for each dress, and if you're lucky you can get a shawl to match. To wear these dresses, gather them at the waist with a cord or folded scarf.

Modern Shops

Modern department stores and smaller specialized shops are springing up all over the area. While the department stores offer good deals on common Egyptian products—linens, yardage, etc., the smaller specialized shops handle better quality items. Most common in Cairo, small boutiques offer jewelry, metalwork, artwork, and designer clothes. Some larger organizations have multiple outlets, such as Safari, which makes travel clothes, and Mobaco, which specializes in all types of cotton. Prices in all these stores are fixed.

PHOTOGRAPHY

The brilliant sun playing off the stark desert, fertile farmlands, and ancient monuments makes Egypt a photographers' paradise. For nearly one and a half centuries Egypt has lured the world's best photographers and they have created photos of unparalleled beauty, their artistic eyes shaping the world's view of Egypt's monuments. But photographing Egypt's towering antiquities in her bright sun, reflective sand and sky, and dense shadows can be tricky. Don't expect your photos to rival those in books; instead, compose your shots with your own eye for beauty and concentrate on bringing back personal memories.

Restrictions

Egypt forbids photographing military installations, bridges, dams, and airports—in short, anything that might be militarily sensitive. Penalties range from verbal warnings to film confiscation and interviews "downtown." If you point your camera at something that might be sensitive, use a new roll of film in case it's confiscated. Most museums prohibit photography unless you buy a special ticket allowing you to shoot with available light but no tripod. Commercial photographers can get permission, but it costs an arm and a leg and takes forever. If you're doing research and the photos will not be used for commercial purposes, you can get permission (written right on your antiquities pass) to photograph in available light. Even then, take care to contact whoever is in charge, as many guards cannot read, or even if they can, will still take the safe way out and refuse to let you photograph.

Antiquities
Freedom to photograph monuments is limited. At most sites you can buy permits to photograph, but you cannot use a flash or lights. This restriction makes color photography in any tombs without a good supply of reflected sunlight impossible; the fluorescent lighting turns entire scenes a sickly green, a tint even fluorescent filters cannot reliably correct. Photographing details inside temples is easier, so if you find one you particularly like, buy a permit. Slides of most monuments are on sale, but the quality varies.

People
Photographing people in Egypt can be tricky; some are delighted to have their pictures taken, others pose in expectation of baksheesh, and still others flatly refuse, often for religious reasons. If possible, ask permission before you shoot. If a person asks you for a copy, get their address and make every effort to get a print to them; for many Egyptians, photos of themselves, family, and friends are rare and coveted.

To Take
For those of you who enjoy using 35 mm format, a 35-105 or similar zoom lens lets you compose and frame your shots. Also take a moderate zoom lens like a 70-120 to capture high temple details as well as a fast (2.4 or better) 50-55 mm for shade and shadows. While skylight or UV filters will help protect your camera from dust and damage, when possible you should remove them when shooting. A polarizing screen

cuts reflection (a problem in the desert) and darkens the sky, but its overuse often creates false-looking photos. Remember, you don't have to polarize completely; slight polarization cuts extraneous refracted light and still gives a natural effect. Also pack a small flash gun and use it for fill flash, especially when photographing the dark-complexioned Egyptians. A small sturdy tabletop tripod can be handy, as can extenders that increase the magnification of your lens.

Whatever equipment you take, store it in plastic bags to protect it from the dust, keep it in the shade as much as possible (the back shelf in a car can easily get up to 150 degrees Fahrenheit), and dust it every evening.

Film
The stark but intense colors of Egypt show up best on Kodachrome 64 or its equivalent, but this film gives little exposure leeway and its sensitivity combined with the tricky lighting conditions in Egypt often result in overexposed slides. High-speed color film (ASA 800-3200) produces slides well saturated with color over a wide range of exposures and also enables you to shoot from a moving vehicle in low light and still stop action. But in exchange you must be willing to accept considerably more grain than in the slower films. Films with ASA 200-400 make a nice compromise, and Egypt's colors tend to photograph true in Ektachrome. If you like shooting black and white, by all means take some to Egypt. The strong light and shadows create stark, strong compositions. Tri-X has more latitude than Plus-X, and if you develop it yourself you can control the grain. C-41 process films such as Illford 400 work well and you can push the speed considerably.

You can get black-and-white film developed in Egypt (one to two days) as well as Ektachrome and Agfacolor (10 days), but the processing is not consistent. Instead, keep your film as cool as possible and have it processed once you return. Kodachrome 25 or 64 as well as C-41 films cannot be processed in Egypt. Although most popular types of film—Kodak, Fuji, Agfa, etc.—are available, they're expensive, so take your own. No matter what kind of film you prefer, pack about twice what you think you'll need, for Egypt presents a myriad of photo opportunities that you'll be unable to resist.

Airport Security

Always pack your film in your carry-on luggage, because the strong X-ray equipment used on the checked baggage will penetrate even the lead film bags sold for protection. Most machines that screen carry-on bags will not damage low ASA film but can visibly fog ASA 400 and faster. Pack your fast film in a see-through plastic bag and pull it out for visual inspection before you send your camera gear through. Most airport security guards are cooperative, but you may have to open each canister to prove it contains only film. Don't neglect to hand carry your exposed film on the return trip. British airports will not hand inspect your film; it must be X-rayed, but one exposure probably won't hurt slow ASA rolls.

Light

Egypt's incredible sun supplies the photographer with seemingly inexhaustible variations. The source of brilliant and evocative pictures, it also creates multiple problems and challenges. Sunlight reflects off the pale desert sand nearly as strong as it does from snow, and light is scattered by innumerable fine, airborne dust particles. These factors lie to light meters, causing reflectance types to overexpose and incidence ones to underexpose. In direct sun and most broken shade you'll need to close down from a half stop to 1 full stop; to ensure good results, bracket if you can. Many automatic cameras have an adjustment where you can set it to underexpose; if yours doesn't, move the ASA speed up one setting, i.e., shoot ASA 64 film at ASA 100. While Re, the midday sun, can create beautiful, saturated color, the slanting setting rays of Re-Harakhte flood the landscape in a mellow yet brilliant golden glow. Khepri (the rising sun) washes all that his rays touch in a similar but clearer tone, and any one of these three lights can make striking photos. If you like to photograph, Egypt can hone your skills and teach you volumes about light.

TO DO

Egypt offers a myriad of cultural, sporting, and intellectual entertainment. Most visitors troop to Egypt to see the monuments, and a vast experience they are. Nothing in the world can compare to their size, preservation, and age. But hidden on the Red Sea coast lie some of the best snorkeling and diving spots in the world. Now divers and vacationers in search of water, sunshine, and warmth have invaded, and in response, resort areas have blossomed, providing any type of activity that might appeal to visitors. In addition, the dry climate invites sports enthusiasts year-round to play tennis and swim. The Opera House in Cairo and theaters in Alexandria feature music and theater, produced in Egypt and from abroad. The many universities and specialized societies offer lectures and specialized field trips. For more information on activities, see relevant travel chapters.

SPORTS

Court sports like tennis, golf, and lawn bowling are supported by sporting clubs in Cairo and Alexandria, which also maintain stables and golf courses. Some of the major hotels have golf courses available as well. Imbaba Airfield in Cairo offers gliding once a week. Shooting is under the auspices of the Doqqi Shooting Club in Cairo. Groups of runners meet in Cairo and Alexandria. Hunting is no longer permitted in Egypt.

Water Sports

Swimming is available at the hotels and sporting clubs in Cairo and Alexandria, but for the more adventurous, scuba diving and snorkeling centers line the Red Sea. Swim in and photograph the clear coastal waters and explore the color-splashed world of the reefs. The beaches of Ras Muhammad in the Sinai are now nature preserves and offer some of the best scuba diving in the world. In Hurghada, an international fishing tournament sponsored by the Egyptian Angling Federation invites fishermen to try their luck for tuna, sailfish, barracuda, wahoo, jack trevally, dolphin, and bonito. Crewing is popular in Cairo and Alexandria and is developing in Ismailia. For boating, water-skiing, and windsurfing, visit the Red Sea coast and Sinai.

Horseback Riding
Private stables in Cairo and Alexandra offer riding lessons. For the casual rider, several stables lie west of Cairo near the pyramids at Giza and at Saqqara; horses are also available in Luxor and in South Sinai.

ENTERTAINMENT

Spectator Sports
Soccer is Egypt's national sport, and the season runs from September to May. Horse racing runs a close second, and Egyptians flock to the tracks in Cairo (winter) and Alexandria (summer) on Saturdays and Sundays.

Art And Cultural Events
Both Alexandria and Cairo support special art exhibits, concerts, operas, ballets, and plays. The season in Cairo is in winter; in summer, much of the activity moves to Alexandria. Art galleries constantly appear, offering displays and sales. For current information, pick up a copy of *Cairo Today*.

Nightlife
Cairo and Alexandria offer gambling in several hotel casinos; you must be 21 to play. Bring your passport, as only foreigners are admitted, and play is in foreign cash. Nightclubs offer shows that usually include a belly dancer, and discos play taped Western music—*loudly*.

At the Giza pyramids and the temples at Karnak (Luxor) and Philae (Aswan), sound and light shows dramatize the monuments in several languages.

BOB RACE

BOB RACE

CAIRO

Al-Qahira, "The Victorious." The name was given to the city on the Nile by the Fatimid khalifs who came to rule Egypt late in the 10th century. Along with Baghdad and Damascus, Cairo became one of three powerful centers of Islamic culture and learning during the Middle Ages. Today, as the largest city in Africa, Egypt's capital is home to 14 million people.

Although the modern bazaars are but a pale reflection of former worldwide trade and the decaying slums a grim mockery of previous wealth, the city remains crossroads of Africa and Arabia as well as meeting ground of Europe and Asia—both crucible and catalyst for East-West relations. Today the city, fulfilling this role, throbs with increasing energy.

THE CITY

In spite of a thousand years of history, Cairo is young by Egyptian standards, for modern Cairo, the product of foreign invaders, only emerged with the Arab conquest of Egypt. Located at the junction of ancient trade routes, this Islamic city became the artistic, cultural, and intellectual heir to the ancient triad of Athens, Rome, and Constantinople. In al-Qahira a wealthy Muslim aristocracy made its home, and its incessant appetite for luxury supported an ever-growing population of soldiers, slaves, merchants, and concubines. Drawn by economic security and intellectual freedom, poets, historians, architects, and

physicians congregated in Cairo, creating a cultural center that, even today, dominates the Islamic world. Fleeing rural poverty, Egyptian peasants also flocked to this medieval city, establishing migratory patterns that continue to swell Cairo's modern population. With wealth seized from the land and skimmed from duties on trade, the Muslim rulers—Arab, Persian, and Turkish—created a mysterious and exotic city that served as the model for *Tales for a Thousand and One Nights*. Today Cairo still lures the visitor into narrow, twisting streets, but now the scents of spices and perfume mingle with diesel fumes.

The city sprawls over a triangular plain, bounded on the west by the cliffs of the Giza Plateau, the east by the Moqattam Hills, and on the north by the delta. The early city was constricted by the river, which ran considerably east of its present course. Not confined to secure banks, it cut through the swampy marshlands nearly at will, drifting steadily west. As the river moved, Cairenes filled the floodplains. Over 1,200 years, as habitable land emerged from the swamps, it coalesced into the modern metropolis.

This development created interlacing patterns of narrow streets and bred shifting styles of architecture. Originally, the area of Old Cairo, opposite the south end of Rhoda Island, was a pharaonic ford used by the Romans and then the Copts. A line beginning here and running north bisects Cairo, splitting it into longitudinal sections: the medieval, Islamic city to the east and the 19th century European quarter on the west. Modern areas sprawl along radiating tram lines, thrusting fingers of housing developments deep into the farmlands of the delta and the arid sands of the desert. (The oldest and best known of these suburbs is Heliopolis.)

Since the 19th century, when bridges across the Nile first provided access to the islands and west bank, builders have been subdividing these areas to provide housing for Cairo's growing middle class, while satellite communities recently built in the desert by governmental decree have created Egypt's own unique brand of urban sprawl. Yet despite such intensive development, housing shortages continue to plague the growing population.

CAIRO HISTORY

Blessed with one of the few river crossings, the area around Cairo was settled by Paleolithic peoples, and later Neolithic merchants established prehistoric trading communities, their goods passing through the Wadi Tumilat to the Red Sea and on to the Near East.

Pharaonic Cairo

At the beginning of the historical era, when King Menes united Upper and Lower Egypt, he built the city of Memphis to serve as his capital for the united Two Lands. Established about 3100 B.C.,

it lay 15 km to the south of the river crossing, its white walls rising on the west bank of the Nile. Nine kilometers to the north of the crossing, on the opposite side of the river, lay the contemporary religious center of On. Home of the sun-god Re, this ancient seat of learning was called Heliopolis by the Greeks (not to be confused with Cairo's modern suburb of the same name). The two cities were linked by a road that traversed the plain and crossed the Nile near the southern tip of Rhoda Island, where a small fortress guarded the crossing. Along the west bank, Archaic, Old, and Middle Kingdom royalty built cemeteries, raising pyramids at Abu Rawash, Giza, Saqqara, and Dahshur, peppering the horizon with the truncated forms as far south as Fayyum. Although Memphis was later supplanted by Thebes and then Piramesse during the New Kingdom, the city remained the religious center for the worship of Ptah and home to craftsmen and military units protecting Egypt's eastern border and her waterways.

The Invaders

The Persians, conquering Egypt in 525 B.C., were the first in a long line of foreign rulers. On limestone cliffs north of Memphis they established a fortress called Babylon-on-the-Nile. They controlled Egypt from this stronghold until Alexander conquered the country in 332 B.C. With the rise of the Ptolemaic capital at Alexandria, Babylon lapsed into obscurity, only to be revived by the Romans.

The Roman legions first occupied the Persian fortress, but soon built new fortifications slightly to the north bordering the river. As a military outpost, Babylon-on-the-Nile guarded Roman trade routes and controlled the native Egyptians, whose revolts were as frequent as they were futile.

To promote trade, the Roman general Trajan dug out the old Red Sea Canal (originally built by the pharaohs), which had fallen into disuse during the Persian and Greek periods. Once restored, this waterway (following the same Wadi Tumilat that the Neolithic traders had used) reopened the link between the Nile and the Red Sea. Predating the Suez Canal, it allowed ships from Arabia, Africa, and India to sail up the Red Sea, turn west toward Babylon, and then continue down the Nile to the Mediterranean.

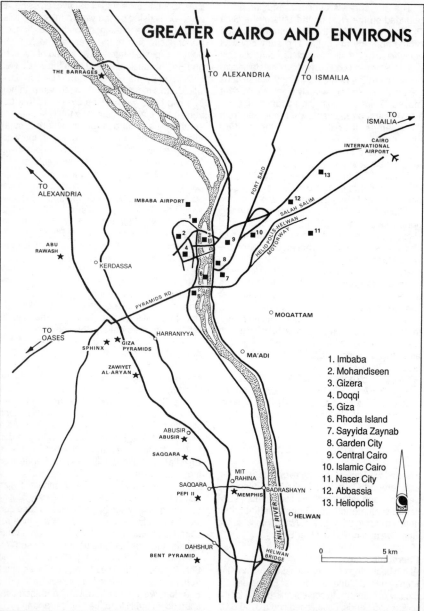

GREATER CAIRO AND ENVIRONS

TO ALEXANDRIA

TO ISMAILIA

TO ISMAILIA

CAIRO INTERNATIONAL AIRPORT

THE BARRAGES

TO ALEXANDRIA

IMBABA AIRPORT

PORT SAID

SALAH SALIM

HELIOPOLIS-HELWAN MOTORWAY

ABU RAWASH

KERDASSA

PYRAMIDS RD.

MOQATTAM

TO OASES

HARRANIYYA

SPHINX GIZA PYRAMIDS

MA'ADI

ZAWIYET AL-ARYAN

1. Imbaba
2. Mohandiseen
3. Gizera
4. Doqqi
5. Giza
6. Rhoda Island
7. Sayyida Zaynab
8. Garden City
9. Central Cairo
10. Islamic Cairo
11. Naser City
12. Abbassia
13. Heliopolis

ABUSIR
ABUSIR

SAQQARA

MIT RAHINA

SAQQARA
PEPI II MEMPHIS BADRASHAYN

HELWAN

DAHSHUR
BENT PYRAMID

NILE RIVER

HELWAN BRIDGE

0   5 km

© MOON PUBLICATIONS, INC.

Christian Cairo

During the 1st century A.D., Christianity came to Egypt, and the village that had grown up around the fort served not only as the center for the restless peasants but also as a hub of the new religion. St. Peter (1 Peter 5:13) sent his greetings from the sister church in Babylon to St. Mark, who lived and preached here in this Egyptian town. Coptic/Roman unrest continued to wrack Babylon, making it an ideal target for the Muslim forces under Amr Ibn al-As.

Arab Conquest

Amr and his troops arrived in A.D. 640 and besieged the Roman fort. After a disastrous battle the Romans arranged a truce with the Arabs. With Babylon secure, Khalif Umar ordered Amr to establish a Muslim capital in Egypt, and the general built a mosque on the east bank at Babylon, just north of the fortress. The troops' tents gave the settlement the name al-Fustat ("the Camp"), and the town eventually became known as al-Fustat al-Misr (the Camp of Egypt) to distinguish it from other "Fustats" scattered throughout the Islamic Empire.

Fustat-Misr

Amr cleared Trajan's canal (which had once more fallen into disuse) and Egypt's wealth now moved through Wadi Tumilat into the Red Sea and on to Arabia. This waterway forged chains of gold and grain that bound Egypt securely to Arabia, and allowed Fustat-Misr to develop into one of the largest trading centers of the world. The port at al-Fustat transshipped luxury goods from the Far East to wealthy markets in Europe, and the lucrative trade supported the Islamic world for centuries.

Fustat-Misr continued to grow as eastern Arabs, seeking their fortunes, moved west into Egypt. The haphazard collection of tents and huts, linked together by a chaotic labyrinth of lanes and blind allies, developed into a sophisticated commercial city. With the riches brought by trade, the citizens of al-Fustat built high-rise homes. Many were adorned with rooftop gardens, at least one of which was irrigated with water lifted by a waterwheel turned by an ox who had been carried to the roof while still a calf. The populace built public baths, diminutive models of Roman ones, which locally earned the name *al-hammamat al-far*—"mouse baths." As the city grew, the Muslims' taste for beautiful architecture increased. They looted windows, doors, and porticoes from churches, temples, and monasteries. Like the Copts before them, they treasured ancient columns and recycled them indiscriminately in their own buildings. They roofed over their streets to protect them from the scorching sun, and lit the cool interiors with lamps. The area developed spice, textile, and perfume markets which were legendary.

The Tulunids

When Ahmad Ibn Tulun came in 868 to administer Egypt for the Abbasid khalifs, he moved the capital northeast, to the hill called Yeshkur. Its mosque, which today still crowns the hill, is one of the oldest and most beautiful in the world. Behind its south wall, as was the Muslim custom, Ibn Tulun built the governmental administrative center, and around this core he laid out living quarters for the government staff and the army; the merchants, however, remained in Fustat. Thirty-seven years later, when the Abbasids retook Egypt, they sacked the Tulunid city and massacred its inhabitants. In the following years, the ruins crumbled, and today nothing of the ancient city remains but the mosque and the remnants of an aqueduct and its intake tower south of the Manyal Palace Bridge.

The Fatimids

In A.D. 969, the Fatimid general Gawhar conquered Egypt and laid out the governmental city that was to become the foundation of medieval Cairo. Lying between the Moqattam Hills and the Red Sea Canal (today filled in and covered by Sh. Port Said), it occupied a better military position than the older settlements to the south. Gawhar's original plan called for a rectangular city surrounded by walls pierced by five gates. The central street bisected the city and on either side the Fatimids built a pair of palaces and al-Azhar, the mosque-school that still stands on its original site. Although the palaces have long since vanished, the street itself (Sh. al-Mu'izz al Din Allah) and three of its gates still exist.

In spite of the Fatimids' seclusion and sporadic oppression, their economic policies were sound, and they thrived as traders. Fustat-Misr continued to grow until it stretched 2½ km along

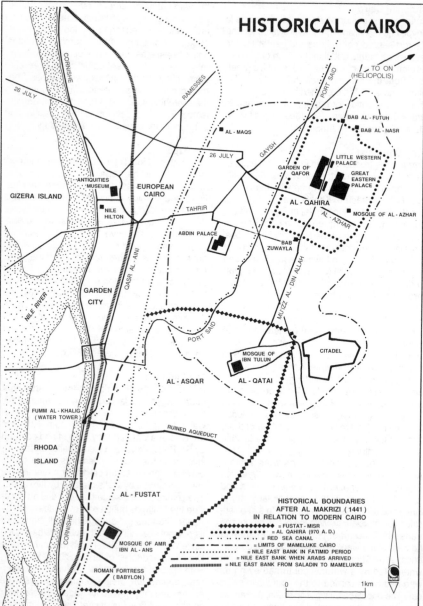

HISTORICAL CAIRO

CORNISHE

26 JULY

RAMESSES

TO ON
(HELIOPOLIS)

PORT SAID

GAYSH

AL - MAQS

26 JULY

BAB AL - FUTUH

BAB AL - NASR

ANTIQUITIES
MUSEUM

GIZERA ISLAND

EUROPEAN
CAIRO

NILE
HILTON

GARDEN OF
QAFOR

LITTLE WESTERN
PALACE

GREAT
EASTERN
PALACE

TAHRIR

AL - QAHIRA

MOSQUE OF AL - AZHAR

AL - AZHAR

ABDIN PALACE

QASR AL - AINI

BAB
ZUWAYLA

NILE RIVER

GARDEN
CITY

MUTIZZ AL - DIN ALLAH

PORT SAID

CITADEL

MOSQUE OF
IBN TULUN

AL - ASQAR

AL - QATAI

FUMM AL - KHALIG
(WATER TOWER)

RUINED AQUEDUCT

RHODA
ISLAND

AL - FUSTAT

CORNISHE

MOSQUE OF AMR
IBN AL - ANS

ROMAN FORTRESS
(BABYLON)

HISTORICAL BOUNDARIES
AFTER AL MAKRIZI (1441)
IN RELATION TO MODERN CAIRO

◆◆◆◆◆ = FUSTAT - MISR
•••••• = AL QAHIRA (970 A.D.)
··•··•·· = RED SEA CANAL
—·—·—· = LIMITS OF MAMELUKE CAIRO
············ = NILE EAST BANK IN FATIMID PERIOD
— — — — = NILE EAST BANK WHEN ARABS ARRIVED
▥▥▥▥▥ = NILE EAST BANK FROM SALADIN TO MAMELUKES

0   1km

© MOON PUBLICATIONS, INC.

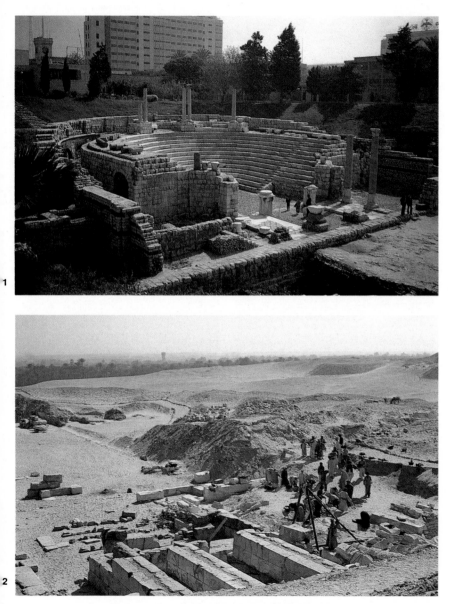

1. the Roman amphitheater in Alexandria (K. Hansen);
2. The French excavate Pepi's pyramid near Saqqara. (K. Hansen)

1. the three great pyramids of Giza (A. Hansen); **2.** faluccas at Aswan (A. Hansen);
3. Great Pyramid of Khafre (K. Hansen)

the river. It survived a massive fire triggered by the inhabitants' revolt against the oppressive policies of Khalif al-Hakim, and later, visitors claimed that its buildings, gardens, and markets surpassed even those of Baghdad. But in the middle of the 11th century, Egypt's crops failed. The Fatimid economy collapsed; Turkish troops rioted and destroyed most of al-Qahira's wealth; and famine, followed by the plague, crushed the city. Although the Fatimid khalifate survived another 75 years, the city never recovered. The southern port silted up and was replaced by al-Maqs (near modern Midan Ramesses), which lay farther north, and the traders moved from the increasingly derelict areas of the old city to build villas near the royal palaces. At that time, crusading Christians threatened to take Egypt, and to deny the Franks a toehold in unfortified Fustat the city was torched. For nearly two months the flames consumed squatters' hovels and mansions alike. The area, never rebuilt, served as the municipal dump for over 800 years. Now, however, the government is planning to clear the area and build public housing.

The Ayyubids

After Salah al-Din (Saladin) repelled the Franks in 1171, he fortified the Citadel hill, extending the Fatimid walls create a defensible area that ran from the port of al-Max on banks of the Nile to the Moqattam Hills. The fortress was the nerve center of the city and provided homes for Egypt's rulers until 1867, when Khedive Ismail built Abdin Palace. Salah al-Din's rule opened the city to orthodox Muslims, and Cairo, home to Persian professors and Spanish scholars, became the capital of Islamic learning. With the death of the last Ayyubid, al-Salah Nagm al-Din, his Armenian concubine queen Shagarit al-Durr ruled briefly before the Turkish slave troops, the Mamluks, seized power.

The Mamluks

Because succession under the Mamluks was based on strength rather than heredity, their 250-year reign was marked by constant unrest. Nevertheless, the Mamluks became great patrons of the arts and their buildings still mark Cairo's skyline. Their vast mosques and mausoleums decorate the narrow streets of Islamic

Cairo, and their burial complexes dominate the graveyards to the east of the city. Though the Mamluks prevented Tamerlane from invading Egypt, they drained Cairo's economy. With the discovery of a sea route from India to Europe coupled with plague and drought, Cairo succumbed to invasion by the Ottoman Turks under Salim, who hanged the last Mamluk sultan, Tuman Bey, from the southern gates of Bab al-Zuwayla in 1517.

The Ottoman Turks

The Ottomans ruled Egypt through a series of viceroys, but they were unable to curb the power of the Mamluks, who continued to terrorize Cairo. Famine, disease, and violence decimated Cairo's population. In spite of these hardships, the Turks built throughout the city. Their monuments tended to follow the Mamluk style, but they also endowed *sabil-kuttabs* (fountains with school rooms over them) that are unique to Cairo and decorate numerous corners of the city. Several of their houses, built around courtyards and decorated with extensive *mashribiyya* screens, still exist and are open to visitors.

Muhammad Ali

The French invasion of 1798 transformed Cairo. The Nile, which had shifted ever westward, exposed new land adjacent to the old Islamic city, and this area became the European section of Cairo. Victorian mansions graced the curving streets of Garden City; the British built barracks along the banks of the river (where the Nile Hilton now stands), and just north of them, the French erected the Cairo Museum. Broad boulevards push though the old Islamic sections and European-style stores still line streets like Qasr al-Nil, Talaat Harb, and 26 July.

Modern Cairo

Not until modern times, when the construction of sewers helped control disease, did Cairo's birth rate exceed her death rate. In 1880, Cairo's population was 400,000, and by 1927, it had grown to over a million. The influx of peasants from the countryside, combined with a steadily declining death rate, continued to push the population upward; today, over 14 million people inhabit the city, creating an occupational density higher in some cases even than Tokyo's.

Continued influx both from the countryside and through immigration has taxed available housing, and squatters occupy rooftops and the mausoleums in the Mamluk cemeteries. The rate of new building is accelerating, and country villages find themselves engulfed in Cairo's urban sprawl. Green pastures and croplands that once stood between the river and the pyramids now bristle with casinos and 10-story apartment buildings. In an attempt to unsnarl Cairo's notorious traffic jams, the government began building overpasses throughout the city. Concentration on transportation infrastructure continued with the construction of the underground Metro and additional roads and freeways serving the outlying areas. The face of Cairo is once more changing. But the profiles of the past remain in the nearly untouched sections of Old and Islamic Cairo.

Most of Cairo's immigrants are poor and crowd into these older sections of the city, where the current residents pull in their elbows to make room for them. The wars along the Suez Canal drove nearly a million refugees to the capital. At the outskirts of town as well as in any available corner, alleyway, or rooftop, the newcomers erect shanties, jerry-built of miscellaneous scavenged and salvaged material. The spacious tombs and mausoleums, invaded by the homeless, have only a few communal water taps and no sanitation. These "cities of the dead" are an urban planner's headache and a public health nightmare. Yet Cairo's masses of people give her a unique char-

acter, for despite her metropolitan size, she feels like a country village. Cairenes live in joyous crowds that surge through the streets on warm summer nights. A passionate city, she is filled with passionate people: where a resident will take 15 minutes to help a stranger find his way; where a bilingual Cairene will help a traveler order a native drink; where the residents smile and say, *marhaba* ("welcome")—and mean just that.

Cairo, though conscious of its heritage, is emerging as a vital, modern city; along with numerous museums, it boasts a symphony, opera, and ballet. Cairo's literary traditions have produced modern poets, playwrights, and novelists who have revolutionized Arabic literature, including Nobel laureate Nagib Mahfuz. Modern visual artists blend their classical heritages, Islamic culture, and modern lives; fashion designers produce creations that would be at home on the streets of London or Paris; and students flock to universities to complete Islamic and Western-style educations. Cairo's monuments to her past do not slumber, but throng with Egyptians who, aware of their history, are not slaves to it.

The roots of Cairo's people sink deep into their desert soil. On pharaonic and Christian foundations the Islamic city has grown, and for over a thousand years has continued to survive. Today, her future lies in her swelling population; the knowledge, skills, and courage of her current generations. If they choose well, al-Qahira will continue "Victorious."

BOB RACE

SIGHTS

Cairo contains early Christian churches as well as some of the world's oldest and most beautiful mosques, *madrasas,* and mausoleums. Fortified walls and gates date from the Roman period through the Middle Ages, showing many of the innovations the Crusaders incorporated into their own castles upon their return from the Holy Wars. The core of Cairo's medieval city—narrow streets and winding alleys—remains nearly unchanged from the 10th century; bazaars still occupy the same buildings they did a thousand years ago. To the west, where the Nile yielded new ground, the Victorians built shops, homes, and grand mansions in the best European style, and while many have been destroyed, the crumbling facades of others are getting a well-deserved facelift.

With the exception of the Antiquities Museum, Cairo's pharaonic antiquities lie outside the city (see "Cairo Environs"). You can see Roman and Coptic remains in Old Cairo, and prowl later Islamic sections of the city beginning with Fustat, and stretching north, or shop and eat in the modern areas along the Nile and its islands. However, this jumbled growth, coupled with Cairo's chaotic transportation system, makes seeing these areas a challenge. If you've not visited Cairo before, or aren't inured to chaos, take a couple of city tours. Be sure you check several agencies (see "Getting Around" p. 254) and get written itineraries and services provided—not all local agencies are created equal. Otherwise, branch out on your own—Cairenes are helpful, but you'll have to develop a sixth sense to sniff out the con artists.

What you'll see depends on how much time you have. The **Antiquities Museum** is a must, as is the central part of Islamic Cairo (the old bazaar of Khan al-Khalili and its southern extension of the "street of the tentmakers"). If you have time, visit Cairo's three major mosques, or take in the Islamic Museum. For an easy trip out on your own, visit Old Ciaro; its extensive museum, beautiful old churches, and synagogue are easy to reach via Metro. Or just stroll down Sh. Qasr al-Nil or Talaat Harb for shopping.

Midan Tahrir

Although no longer the administrative center of Cairo, Midan Tahrir remains its social, historical, and business heart. The long rectangle forming the *midan* lies just east of the Nile, with only the Cornishe and the Nile Hilton Hotel separating it from the river. On its north end, the turn-of-the-century sand-colored building surrounded by the wrought-iron fence houses the Antiquities Museum. From the east side of the square, just south of the museum, three streets radiate into the business district: Sh. Champollion, Qasr al-Nil, and al-Bustan. The center one, Sh. Qasr al-Nil, is the main business and shopping street. The central area of the *midan* is filled by the bus terminal, and the Metro's Sadat Station lies underground; the exits (marked by a big red M) are scattered around the *midan* and provide pedestrians a safer if less stimulating way of crossing Midan Tahrir. A second set of three streets radiates east from the south end of Tahrir: Sh. al-Tahrir, an east-west thoroughfare; Sh. Talaat Harb, which runs northeast into the business district (crossing Sh. Qasr al-Nil), and Sh. Muhammad Mahmud. Along the eastern side of the *midan* Sh. Qasr al-Aini runs south, eventually meeting the Cornishe. The curved government building (the Mugama'a) occupies the southern half of the *midan*, while the American University in Cairo stands to the southeast. The *midan* is bordered on the north by the elevated interchange that comes out onto Sh. Ramesses and on the south by Sh. al-Tahrir; both these streets continue west, crossing bridges (6 October and Tahrir respectively) to the island of Gizera.

GIZERA ISLAND

This island is modern, created by deposits of 14th century sedimentation. In the middle of the 19th century Ismail Pasha built a guest palace for the royal European visitors invited to the gala opening of the Suez Canal (1869), a palace which is now the Marriott Hotel. With the building of the first Aswan Dam (1902), Gizera's banks stabilized,

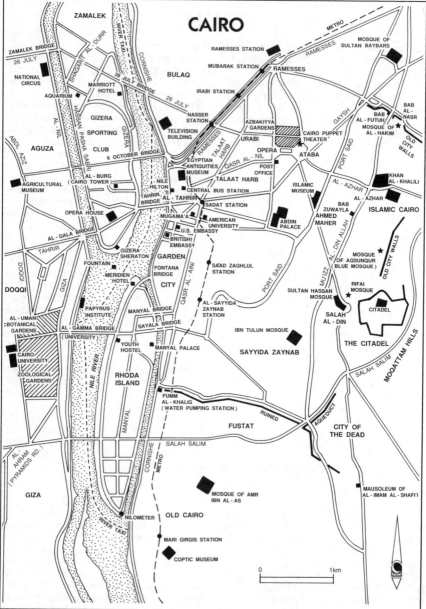

CAIRO

ZAMALEK

ZAMALEK BRIDGE
26 JULY

NATIONAL CIRCUS

AQUARIUM

MARRIOTT HOTEL

BULAQ

RAMESSES STATION

MUBARAK STATION

RAMESSES

IRABI STATION

METRO

MOSQUE OF SULTAN BAYBARS

GIZERA SPORTING CLUB

AGUZA

6 OCTOBER BRIDGE

NASSER STATION

TELEVISION BUILDING

AZBAKIYYA GARDENS

CAIRO PUPPET THEATER

BAB AL-NASR

BAB AL-FUTUH

MOSQUE OF AL-HAKIM

OLD CITY WALLS

AGRICULTURAL MUSEUM

AL-BURG (CAIRO TOWER)

NILE HILTON

URABI

EGYPTIAN ANTIQUITIES MUSEUM

OPERA

ATABA

POST OFFICE

ISLAMIC MUSEUM

KHAN AL-KHALILI

AL-AZHAR

AL-AZHAR

OPERA HOUSE

TAHRIR BRIDGE

AL-TAHRIR

CENTRAL BUS STATION

TALAAT HARB

SADAT STATION

BAB ZUWAYLA

AHMED MAHER

ISLAMIC CAIRO

AL-GALA BRIDGE

TAHRIR

MUGAMA'A

AMERICAN UNIVERSITY

ABDIN PALACE

DOQQI

GIZERA SHERATON

FOUNTAIN

MERIDIEN HOTEL

U.S. EMBASSY

BRITISH EMBASSY

GARDEN CITY

FONTANA BRIDGE

SA'AD ZAGHLUL STATION

MOSQUE OF AQSUNQUR (BLUE MOSQUE)

OLD CITY WALLS

RIFAI MOSQUE

SULTAN HASSAN MOSQUE

CITADEL

AL-UMAN BOTANICAL GARDENS

AL-GAMMA BRIDGE (UNIVERSITY)

PAPYRUS INSTITUTE

MANYAL BRIDGE

SAYALA BRIDGE

AL-SAYYIDA ZAYNAB STATION

SALAH AL-DIN

THE CITADEL

CAIRO UNIVERSITY

ZOOLOGICAL GARDENS

YOUTH HOSTEL

MANYAL PALACE

IBN TULUN MOSQUE

SAYYIDA ZAYNAB

MOQATTAM HILLS

RHODA ISLAND

FUMM AL-KHALIG (WATER PUMPING STATION)

FUSTAT

SALAH SALIM

AQUEDUCT

CITY OF THE DEAD

GIZA

AL-AHRAM (PYRAMIDS RD.)

SALAH SALIM

CORNISHE METRO

NILOMETER

RIVER TAXI

OLD CAIRO

MOSQUE OF AMR IBN AL-AS

MARI GIRGIS STATION

COPTIC MUSEUM

MAUSOLEUM OF AL-IMAM AL-SHAFI'I

0   1km

© MOON PUBLICATIONS, INC.

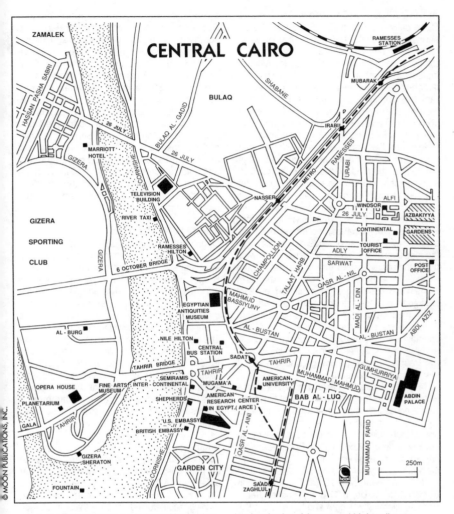

CENTRAL CAIRO

and during Cairo's boom period, wealthy foreigners and natives alike built elegant villas in its garden-like setting. Today these homes serve as clubs, embassies and the headquarters of international companies, and they comprise the suburb at the north end of the island known as Zamalek. The 26 July Bridge slashes across this northern section of the island, supporting the street of the same name, which links Cairo proper to the west

bank suburbs of Aguza and Mohandiseen.

The center and southern parts of the island are given over to the Gizera Sporting Club and the Cultural Center, which includes the new Opera House. The tip of the island is dominated by the Gizera Sheraton Hotel, and beyond it the Nile fountain stands in the middle of the channel. The landmark Burg al-Qahira (Cairo Tower), stands just north of the Tahrir Bridge.

Al-Burg Al-Qahira (Cairo Tower)
Open daily 0900 to 2400; LE9 to visit the observation deck; tel. 341-0884. Built in 1957, the tower's central cylinder rises nearly 90 meters (higher than the pyramids at Giza), its concrete latticework blossoming into a lotus. The 14th floor houses a revolving (when it works) restaurant; the 15th floor, a cafeteria; and the 16th, a viewing platform with telescopes, from which you can see most of Cairo on a clear day.

The Nile River coming down from the south widens and flows around several islands, then runs north where it splits and wanders through the delta to the Mediterranean. To the **east,** directly across the river, the blue building houses the Nile Hilton. Downstream you can see the rounded facade of the television station and the angular skyscraper of the Ramesses Hilton. Across Cairo's eastern expanse, the nearer buildings shimmer with the gray of modern concrete while the medieval quarter cuts a sandstone-tan swath along the entire eastern side of the city. On the Citadel hill rise the domes and slender minarets of Muhammad Ali's mosque; behind it, the Moqattam Hills and then desert stretch to the Red Sea.

To the **south,** at the end of the lion-guarded Tahrir Bridge, stands the Semiramis Inter-Continental Hotel, and beyond it, along the Nile bank and the Cornishe, lies Garden City, laid out on the Pasha's former palace grounds, where a few of the old villas remain.

To the **west,** directly across from Gizera lies the district of Doqqi, home to government buildings, private houses, small hotels, and the Doqqi Shooting Club. On the north end Aguza and the new area of Mohandiseen are linked to Zamalek by the 26 July Bridge. To the south of Doqqi lies Giza, named for the village where the workers who built the pyramids may well have lived. The area is home to the Cairo University, the Cairo Zoo, and Urman Gardens (see "To Do," p. 174). Two bridges, Kobre Gamma (University Bridge) and Kobre Giza, link it to the east bank of the Nile. Across the roofs of modern Giza, the pyramids stand atop the plateau that marks the beginning of the Western Desert.

RHODA ISLAND

Hugging the southern shore south of Garden City, the rocky foundations of Rhoda Island

are as old as the pyramids; pharaonic and Roman ferries may well have landed at its southern tip. The island remained agricultural until the middle of the 12th century, when al-Salih Ayyub built a fortress (which housed the Bahri [river] Mamluks) and palace on the southern half. In 1830, Ibrahim Pasha laid out gardens in the north, and then in 1903, the al-Manyal Palace was built for King Fuad's brother. Today, the northern end supports the round facade of the Meridien Hotel. Behind it lie Qasr al-Aine Hospital and Medical School as well as Manyal Palace, which is now a museum and hotel administered by Club Med. With the exception of the Nilometer on the southern end, the rest of the island is occupied with high-rent buildings.

Manyal Palace Museum
Open 0900-1400 daily; LE6; tel. 987-495. At 1 Sh. Saray al-Manyal, the museum is near Club Med just south of Kobri Gamma (University Bridge); entrance is on Sh. Sayala. The museum includes Muhammad Ali's palace, reception rooms, a private mosque, and a hunting museum. Once the exclusive haunt of royalty, it's one of the few places in Cairo that retains its beauty. The west wing is Moorish, the east, Syrian, complete with woodwork removed from the al-Azm Palace of Syria. The tiled mosque contains stained-glass windows and Oriental carpets, and the marble throne room has a golden ceiling that filters the sunlight into shimmering arabesques. The hotel next door offers a good buffet, drinks, and a swim in the pool.

Nilometer
To get in you may have to ask the children to fetch the custodian with the key. This nilometer dates from A.D. 715, but was destroyed in a storm and rebuilt in 847; the current, Turkish building reconstructed from a 19th century drawing. Some legends claim Moses was discovered here, floating in a reed basket; others maintain he was washed ashore across the river in Old Cairo. The post centered in the stone-lined pit reaches nine meters and is marked in cubits. Broken twice and mended with collars at the splices, the post sits on an old millstone. The water from the Nile roiled through the three levels of tunnels (now sealed) until it reached the

height of the flooding Nile outside. The pointed "Gothic" arches at the first level are some of the earliest known, predating the ones appearing in European cathedrals by four centuries. The four gold-on-blue inscriptions (the earliest examples of Arabic paleography in Egypt) ask for a plentiful harvest; the Muslim historian Ibn Khaldun has pointed out that the verses reflected off the surface "become lines on the face of the water when it reaches 17 cubits."

Fishermen lean over the stone wall at the south end; the islands beyond them have no connecting bridges and are still reserved for agriculture. To see a second, open-air nilometer, cross the clearing to the east; the nilometer is notched out of the bank. You can go down the stairs, sit in the cool shade, and listen to the Nile—a quiet place for a sandwich. Across the river lies Old Cairo, the Coptic cradle of Cairo's early Christianity.

Munastirli Palace
Open 0900-1400; free; tel. 986-3931. Now the Center of Art and Life, the palace was built in 1851. The exhibits inside show some nice modern pottery, textiles, and weavings. The porch of the building has hand-painted ceilings that, if you crane your neck, are worth the view.

EGYPTIAN ANTIQUITIES MUSEUM

Open Sat.-Thurs. 0900-1600, Fri. 0900-1100 and 1330-1600; LE15, the Mummy Room, LE40; tel. (02) 754-319. The museum dominates the north end of Midan Tahrir.

The Egyptian Antiquities Museum exists because of the lifetime dedication of the French archaeologist Auguste Mariette. Early in the 19th century, Egypt's treasures were taken by private collectors and European museums, and in fact, Mariette faced continued battles with Egypt's own rulers, who viewed the nation's treasures as political tools, a ready supply of gifts for foreign statesmen, to be bestowed where they would do the most good.

In 1830, the French scholar Champollion protested this looting in a strongly worded request to Muhammad Ali, and in 1835 the Service des Antiquities de l'Egypte was founded to prevent the plundering of archaeological sites by both local and foreign treasure hunters. The commission collected Egyptian artifacts and stored them in a building in Azbakiyya Garden, but when the Austrian Archduke Maximilian visited Egypt in 1855, Abbas Pasha presented the whole collec-

ANTIQUITIES MUSEUM - LOWER FLOOR

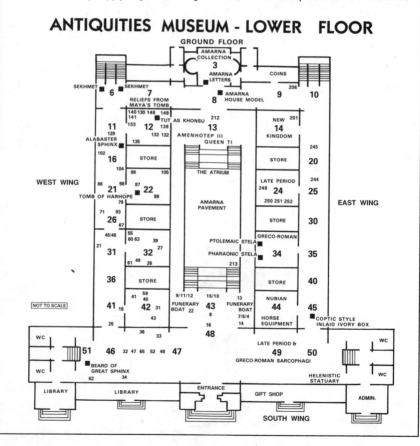

© MOON PUBLICATIONS, INC.

tion to him. With the support of the French government and the help of Ferdinand de Lesseps (the designer of the Suez Canal), Mariette convinced the pasha to appoint him Director of Antiquities. He documented the ruins scattered throughout Egypt and secured a storehouse in Bulaq for the artifacts in which he arranged four exhibition rooms. In 1878 a flood destroyed many of the objects and in the ensuing confusion, more were stolen. Undaunted, Mariette salvaged what he could and continued to display Egypt's heritage. In 1883, Ismail Pasha agreed to fund a new building, and when Mariette died, his dream of a national museum for Egypt's treasures was nearly complete. The neoclassical-style building, designed by the French architect Marcel Dourgnon, was completed in 1902. Since that time the collection of pharaonic art has grown to more than 120,000 objects—the richest in the world.

General Layout

The ground floor is devoted to large pieces, primarily stone statues, tombs, and sarcophagi; the pieces are arranged chronologically, beginning with the Archaic period in the foyer, and the Old Kingdom material in the halls to the left (west) of the entrance. The displays continue around the museum, ending with the Late Period, Ptolemaic objects, and Nubian artifacts in the right-hand (east) wing. Upstairs, the exhibits are arranged by medium, with displays of jewelry and King Tut's treasures dominating the rear (north) wing. Other galleries include wooden models, papyrus, tools, and textiles. The number codes on the objects are keyed to an outstanding catalogue prepared by the museum's director, Muhammad Salah, *The Egyptian Museum Cairo: Official Catalogue.* A must for anyone interested in pharaonic art, check to see if it's back in print in English (other languages may still be available). Numbers cited below are the same as those in the catalogue. Because the museum is stuffed with more material then even an aficionado can absorb in one trip, try to come back several times, e.g.: (1) the lower floor (west wing) of pharaonic statuary; (2) the treasures of Tut and the jewelry rooms; (3) the remainder of the upper floor.

LOWER FLOOR

Hall 43 (Archaic)

[16] Hall 43 is dominated by the statue of Djoser, builder of the Step Pyramid at Saqqara. This limestone sculpture was removed from the *serdab*, a small chamber that allowed the statue of the deceased to observe, in this case, the eternal northern constellations that never set below the horizon. The oldest life-sized statue from Egypt, it still retains traces of original paint. The statue shows that Egyptian artists already had formulated the pose and general style of pharaonic portraiture: the face (with once-inlaid eyes), is expressive yet removed from worldly concerns—a portrait for eternity.

[8] The other showpiece of Hall 43 is Narmer's palette. A decorative version of the slate palettes used to grind eye cosmetics, this piece depicts the unification of the Two Lands and the beginnings of dynastic Egypt. The sinuous entwined necks of the fantastic animals speak of Middle Eastern connections; below them, the king as a bull wrecks the walled town and tramples his enemies. The other side shows him in front of the hawk victorious and preparing to bash the head of his helpless enemy with a stone mace, a motif repeated throughout the ages. The cases scattered around the room contain yet other masterpieces of early art.

[14] This schist statue shows King Khasekhemwy (2nd Dynasty) dressed in the cloak traditional for the *heb sed* festival, rejuvenation ceremonies held after the first 30 years of the king's reign. It, too, in spite of its fragmented condition, reveals the early Egyptian artists' skill at depicting the human face.

[7] The Libyan palette shows the foundation of cities, and on its reverse, animals, already marching in registers, the head of the last ram turned back over its shoulder—a motif throughout the dynastic period.

[5] The delicate flint and obsidian knives testify to the skill of Egyptian knappers.

[4] The painted pottery shows ancient boats complete with deck cabins and registers of oars. The black-topped red ware, some of the most beautiful pottery ever produced in Egypt, was polished with a smooth stone before quite dry, and then fired to produce the red color. Inverting

the vessels on a bed of smoldering chaff created the black tops; carbonization produced the dark metallic sheen.

[13] This stone basket reproduces the lines of the reeds and tiny ropes marking its prototype.

[15 a and b] Equally beautiful are these carnelian and dolomite bowls sealed in gold.

[10] These bracelets are from the 1st Dynasty tomb of Djer; the delicate links and sure sense of color and design presage the masterworks of Middle Kingdom jewelers.

[9] This ivory plaque of Aha (Menes) labeled a jar of oil for the 1st Dynasty king, and is the oldest example of hieroglyphs.

[11/12] A series of rock crystal, faience, and limestone animals and ivory gaming pieces speak to the earliest inclusions of sacred animals, amulets, and amenities for the afterlife.

[22] The hunched figure is Hetepdief, a priest of the early dynasties, and represents the earliest example of private statuary. In contrast to the royal work, this figure appears archaic, yet follows the same principles of frontality and symmetry. Hetepdief's name, his titles, and the name of his father appear on his shoulder; the phoenix atop the pyramidal *benben* perhaps already signified resurrection and everlasting life.

Funerary Boats

On either side of the gallery stand the remains of Senwosret III's boats found at Dahshur. Their keelless sides were built up with intricate joinery, necessary because of lack of long timbers in Egypt. Like the vessels at Giza, they were buried for the king's everlasting convenience.

Halls 47 And 46

Much of the southwestern wing of the museum is devoted to sarcophagi and other large works. The center cases show off many of the figures found in Old Kingdom tombs.

[48] The double statue of Nimaatsed combines two colored images of the same man on a single pedestal. Although the meaning of such pseudo groups is not clear, they may represent the person and his *ka* or double.

[52] Dignitaries had figures of their servants buried with them, and often sculptures like this one of a female brewer, less constrained by formal canon, present insightful portraits of Egyptians at work.

[65] The painted wooden figure of Niankh-pepi, the porter, continues the same tradition; the ex-

cellent preservation of the paint reveals the intricate detail artists included in their work.

[47] This statue of the funerary priest Kaemked is the product of an excellent craftsman. The painted limestone figure was discovered in the mastaba of Urirni, a 5th Dynasty nobleman whom Kaemked served. The figure's eyes are framed in copper; the obsidian inlays give the statue a realism hard to ignore.

[32] Yet another tradition is represented by the collection of "reserve" heads, many of which were found at Giza in the entrances to subterranean burial chambers. These enigmatic portraits, sans ears and with a groove running down the back of the head, were once thought to have been models for death masks, but the recent discovery of paint on several has cast doubt on this hypothesis.

[33] Lining the hall along the north side are three schist triads uncovered at the valley temple of Menkaure. Depicting the king with Hathor on his right and a female representative of a *nome* on his left, the figures number among the masterpieces of the Old Kingdom. Four sets were discovered, the three shown here and a fourth on display at the Boston Museum of Fine Arts.

[36] The masterpiece of birds in the marshes is nearly hidden against the back wall; you can reach it by starting near the Archaic exhibit and working your way between the pieces along the wall; the effort is worthwhile. This panel from Userkaf's temple marks the first use of natural scenes as decoration in royal funerary buildings. As customary with much Egyptian art throughout the pharaonic period, the figures, without being biologically impeccable, are easily recognizable: the pied kingfisher hovers just below the butterfly, the night heron and hoopoe face the purple gallinule, and the sacred ibis walks across blossoms once brightly painted.

[34] This sarcophagus, along with others along the other side of the hall, represents good quality Old Kingdom work. Designed as eternal homes for the body, most sarcophagi were decorated in imitation of the palaces inhabited by royalty, including the vertical niches of the "palace facade" closed by rolls of matting and doors hung on peg-hinges. These coffins were carved of a single block of stone; the lid was not detached until after the sarcophagus was in the tomb.

[62] The western corner of the hall contains bas-reliefs from the 6th Dynasty tomb of Ipy. Here

we find typical Old Kingdom care lavished on the scenes destined to provide Ipy with the sacrifices and lifestyle for eternity. The various registers show estate workers slaughtering cattle, harvesting flax and grain, and transporting it on donkeys. Other panels follow Ipy on a trip in a sedan chair to inspect his ships, accompanied by his curly-tailed dog.

Hall 41

[25] The entrance to the west wing is flanked by the reliefs of the tomb of Nefer-Ma'at. Son of Snefru, Nefer-Ma'at built his mastaba tomb at Meidum. The desert scene shows a hunter stalking a leopard, while below a dog attacks a fox. The matching panel across the hall depicts hunters trapping geese with a clapnet, and below farmers plow their fields to produce eternal crops of grain. The figures, cut into the limestone walls, were inlaid with colored paste; the effect was brilliant, but the medium, unfortunately, not long-lived. The experiment was not repeated.

[18] The pair of lion tables flanking the entrance to Hall 42 date from the end of the 2nd Dynasty; they were found buried, along with an unmummified body, under the northern terrace of the Step Pyramid. Speculation continues as to their function, for huge alabaster tables have been found of nearly identical design at the Apis bull temple at Memphis. These diminutive versions were probably used as libation tables or sacrificial altars, for their tails form a bowl to catch liquid that ran from the lions' slanted backs.

Hall 42

[31] The diorite statue of Khafre, indisputably the ultimate masterpiece of the Old Kingdom, perhaps of the entire pharaonic period, dominates this hall. Khafre, son of Khufu and builder of the second pyramid at Giza, sits on a throne supported by the backs of lions, symbols of power and protection. Under their bellies, the intertwined stems of the lily (signifying Upper Egypt) and the papyrus (Lower Egypt) form the hieroglyph *sema-tawy*, symbol for unification. The workmanship, the perfection of modeling and polish, highlights Khafre who, like Djoser before him, seems to gaze into eternity. Behind him, Horus the Hawk, who manifests himself as an earthly ruler, enfolds the king in his protective wings. At the rear of the hall stand two palm columns capped with capitals of fronds that retain bindings once used on their live models to support the weight of a lintel.

[40] Nearly as famous as the statue of Khafre is the wooden figure of Ka-aper, also called the Sheikh al-Baled (Headman of the Village), for when the figure was brought to light at Saqqara, the workmen saw in his expressive features their own sheikh. This private statue, sculpted with startling realism, created a picture of Ka-aper that seems to step toward us nearly alive. While the body was carved of a piece, the arms were mortised onto the shoulders; the eyes, set into copper lids, were made of white quartz and rock crystal, the latter drilled and black paste set into the hole to form the pupil.

[41] This bust of a woman is all that remains of a standing figure found in the same 5th Dynasty tomb. Perhaps Ka-aper's wife, she wears the short wig parted in the center and the tight-fitting sheath popular in the Old Kingdom. Once gessoed and painted, she wore a wide, painted collar.

[58] The wooden false door of Ika, like its stone counterparts, was set into the walls of the tomb, enabling the deceased's spirit to emerge into his tomb to partake of ritual festivities. The plaque above the "door" shows the priest Ika and his wife Iymeret (priestess of Hathor) seated at an offering table filled with bread loaves. On either side of the jambs they appear again, now with their children. The priest himself appears in the door; above him, the wooden drum fixed above him represents the rolled matting that served as screens.

[43] This seated scribe, his reed pen long since vanished, nevertheless shows us an Egyptian ideal, for many princes and noblemen had themselves portrayed in this posture. The body is rather summarily sketched; the face with its inlaid eyes, framed by the pulled-back wig, demands all the attention.

Hall 32

[27] Yet another Old Kingdom masterpiece, the double statue of Rahotep and Nofret dominate this room. The painted figures of this son of Snefru and his wife show the realism artists of 2600 B.C. could generate. The wide straps of Nofret's dress visible under her cloak cover her breasts (in contrast to the two-dimensional depictions on walls), and a trace of her own hair is visible under her diadem and wig. These figures also testify to the Old Kingdom's artists ability to expand their view of reality. Nofret's figure, for example, shows the articulations and shapes of

her limbs under her cloak, a contrast to Djoser's nearly formless body. The chairs, which provide merely a frame for the figures and a ground on which to inscribe their names and titles, show little of the detail present in Khafre's later statue. This ability to graft new techniques onto old traditions continues throughout the Old Kingdom.

[39] This ability is nowhere better demonstrated than in the statues of the dwarf Seneh and his family. Confronted with Seneh's deformity, the artist, by filling the space normally occupied by the subject's legs with Seneh's children, fulfilled the Memphite artistic convention while portraying his client realistically. The children, as was traditional, are shown naked, with fingers to their lips; the boy wears his hair in the side-lock of youth. Their mother, Senetites, encircles her husband's shoulders; the smile on her face and the expression of contented dignity on Seneh's bespeak the happy, wealthy, and powerful family.

[26] The third unquestioned masterpiece in this room is the painted panel of the Meidum Geese. From the same mud-brick mastaba (Nefer-Ma'at) as the inlay work at the entrance to the west wing, this tempera panel formed the lower portion of an entire relief. As was typical, the composition is nearly symmetrical and is based on the doubled one-plus-two configuration popular with pharaonic artists. The artist softened the schematic design by careful selection of colors and patterns of the feathers that, though detailed enough to allow ornithologists to distinguish the types of birds, are nevertheless stylized. This ability to portray recognizable yet formalized images remained the forte of pharaonic artists throughout their long history.

[49] The *serdab* statue of Ti was removed from his tomb at Saqqara. With emphasis on the starched apron of the kilt and the sketchy rendering of the body, it lacks the quality of the carvings in his tomb. Reliefs from the walls of Saqqaran tombs decorate the walls on either side of the doorway.

[61] The scene of the musicians marks increasing interest in action and narration—in fact, these types of scenes coupled with the hieroglyphic text above the figures constitutes an ancient comic book. The musicians and singers entertain at the funeral banquet, as do the dancers below them, dressed in typical costumes with crossed straps.

[60] This boating scene, in contrast to the musicians, shows dramatic action. The boatmen atop their reed skiffs show off in front of the estate

BRUCE HANSEN

owner, but the goal of the match is lost in antiquity.

[63] This copper statue of Pepi I is one of the few surviving early metal pieces. The sheets

were hammered over a wooden core while the kilt and headdress were separate (probably of plaster) and gilded; the eyes are of limestone and obsidian.

[55] This statue of the wife of Mitri is, unlike most wooden figures of the period, carved from a single piece. Dated to the end of the 5th Dynasty, it shows the artists' ability to express creativeness and individuality within the canon of Memphite classical art.

Hall 31

[21] The wooden panel from the tomb of Hesire dates to early in the 3rd Dynasty. Chief of royal scribes, he was also a dentist—the first medical man identified in Egypt. The panel of Hesire as a scribe shows us the beginnings of the classical tradition: the combination profile and forward views of the body typical of two-dimensional Egyptian art. Already the composition is unconsciously balanced; Hesire's staff and scribal kit fill the space in front of his figure. The body itself shows lightly molded contours of the bone and muscles beneath the skin—no longer a schematic body serving only as a mounting for an expressive face, as in the statue of Djoser.

[45/46] The two statues of Ranefer continue the tradition of depicting the deceased in multiple roles. Ranefer, as high priest of Ptah and Sokar at Memphis, directed the royal workshops, a position enabling him to use the best craftsmen, creating the epitome of Old Kingdom private statuary. The figures, which differ only in the kilts and wig, have strikingly similar faces (as shown by the exhibition photos), a fact attributed to the success of individual portraiture or, conversely, the hand of the same master.

Hall 26

[67] With the black-skinned statue of King Nebhepetre Mentuhotep II we enter the Middle Kingdom. This figure's curled beard, crossed arms, and dark skin link it to Osiris. The statue itself, wrapped in a linen shroud, was buried in a tomb at Mentuhotep's funerary shrine at Deir al-Bahri (on the west bank at Thebes). Discovered by Howard Carter when his horse fell through the paving stones, the piece shows the provincialism of the southern artists at the beginning of the Middle Kingdom. This provincialism, rather than a detriment to the pharaonic art, was instead a rejuvenating force—the antidote to traditions grown stagnant on refined techniques.

[93] The statue of Queen Nofret shows similar simplicity and power, but is coupled with a more refined technique. Her fashionable Hathor wig contrasts with her traditional broad-strapped sheath. Several pectorals like the one incised on her breast occupy the jewelry exhibits on the upper floor.

[71] The sarcophagus of Dagi dates from the 11th Dynasty. Its interior contains the eyes that enabled the mummy to see, and on the corresponding outside, the false door through which the mummy could exit. Jewelry, wine, sandals, bows and quivers, and linen—the finer things for the afterworld—decorate the upper part of the interior, while the lower portions are taken up by spells for the afterworld—the coffin texts.

[79] The funerary stela of Amenemhet shows the vitality and creativity of Middle Kingdom art. In this case, Amenemhet and his wife, Iyi, embrace their son Antef, their impossibly long arms forming rhythmic, interlocking patterns echoed by the equally impossible yet artistic arrangement of the men's legs. Note the mirror handle visible in the basket beneath the bench. Beyond the offering table stands Hapy, their daughter-in-law.

Hall 22

This room is dominated by the tomb of Harhope.

[87] Ten unfinished statues of Senwosret I, which were found buried at the king's mortuary temple at Lisht (near Fayyum), surround it. The statues can be divided into two groups on the basis of the *sema-tawy* symbols carved on the sides of the thrones: one set shows the Upper and Lower Nile gods (two versions of Hapi) tying the traditional knot of unification; on the others, hawk-headed Horus and animal-headed Seth perform the ceremony, the latter still a god of Upper Egypt before his personification of sterility, foreign lands, and evil.

[88] In contrast to the expressionless faces of these stone statues, the cedarwood figure of the king with its realistic yet smooth modeling and expressive face harks back to the best of the Old Kingdom traditions. This figure wearing the white crown of Upper Egypt is one of a pair; his mate with the red crown stands in New York's Metropolitan Museum of Art.

[105] Amenemhet III's careworn face in this granite statue shows the type of portraiture in vogue during the Middle Kingdom.

[99] This severe portrait of the three daughters of Djehutyhotep from the Middle Kingdom

nomarch's tomb at al-Bersha shows slender, well-endowed figures dressed in fashionable sheaths. Heavy bracelets, anklets, and pendants balance the lotus headdresses set on their Hathor wigs. In spite of the elongated bodies and arms, the figures have a certain grace typical of Middle Kingdom painting.

Halls 21, 16, And 11

[98] Like the statue of Amenemhet, this portrait of Senwosret III delineates even more vividly the careful attention Middle Kingdom artists paid to emotion as it shaped the warrior's face. The tired, lined eyes and bitter mouth express the weight that came with the role of shepherd of his people. The granite of this statue also clearly shows the pleated *nemes* headdress with its uraeus and the asymmetrically pleated kilt looped through the belt of his royal apron.

[86] This limestone pillar of Senwosret I perfectly synthesizes the awkward vitality of Middle Kingdom art and the Old Kingdom craftsmanship inherited from Memphis. The result is an undisputed masterpiece. The king is embraced by a different god on each side: mummiform Ptah, Horus of Idfu, Amun with his feather crown, and Atum with Egypt's double crown. The symmetry, balance, and harmony gives the low relief a grandeur suitable for the gods.

[104] The double statue of the Offering Bearers of Tanis is unique. The doubled figures are personifications of Amenemhet III, who as the Nile-god brings his people fish on trays from which hang lotus and geese. The doubled figure could represent the king as ruler of Upper and Lower Egypt or as the living king in tandem with his resurrected and deified counterpart. Rarely do we see the rear of a stone figure, but this pair provides the same intricate detail that appears on the sides of the altar and the front of the figures.

[129] Hall 11 is dominated by the head of Hatshepsut, her graceful features enhanced by the color. Derived from one of her Osirian statues, the head retains the lower part of the double crown and thus must have come from a pillar on the northern side of the mortuary temple at Deir al-Bahri.

Hall 12

[138] The Hathor shrine at the end of this gallery was found in the ruined temple of Thutmose III at Deir al-Bahri. Identified with the sky-goddess Nut, Hathor had long been worshipped at Thebes as goddess of the mountain and protectress of the dead. This shrine, complete with star-studded ceiling, housed the cow form of the goddess shown emerging as reborn from the papyrus swamp. Under her protective head stands Thutmose, who is also shown as an infant suckling from the goddess. The chapel remained in use until Ramesside times when the cliff crumbled and buried Thutmose's mortuary temple. It only came to light during excavations when work triggered yet another avalanche that opened the chapel once more.

The rest of this room is crammed with masterpieces of 18th Dynasty art. Most of the statues were set up in temples as proxies for their owners. All of the pieces display unequaled craftsmanship—technical wizardry combined with elegance, idealism, and realism to produce aesthetic renderings that conveyed the idea of perfect sovereignty.

[133] The best example of this combination is the statue of Thutmose III who is shown trampling the Nine Bows (symbols of Egypt's traditional enemies) underfoot.

[137] This statue of Isis, mother of Thutmose III, was dedicated by her son to the temple of Amun-Re at Thebes. The uraei wear the crowns of Upper and Lower Egypt, and two feathers once topped her golden crown.

[132] This block statue of Senenmut, Hatshepsut's vizier, and her daughter Neferure derives from a similar tradition of block sculpture begun in the Middle Kingdom, but here it is given a new twist by incorporating the head of the princess.

[148/149] Equally interesting statues line the opposite wall, most notably those showing Amenhotep, son of Hapu as a young scribe and as an 80 year old priest. This remarkable man is one of the few who belonged to an unimportant family yet rose to prominence. As director of royal works he built the Colossi of Memnon at Thebes. He excavated a tomb for himself in the Necropolis on the West Bank and, in an unprecedented move, erected a mortuary temple among those of royalty. The memory of this wise sage remained alive for many generations and he was (in Ptolemaic times) worshipped along with Imhotep as a god of healing. Between the two statues stands King Tutankhamun, depicted as Khonsu (with the side-lock of youth), a pink granite figure removed from the classical temple of Khonsu at Thebes.

[140] This statue of Sennefer (builder of the tomb with the grape-arbor ceiling) and his wife Senay was also deposited at Karnak, enabling the Theban mayor to receive blessings and prayers. This work is one of the few signed pieces that have come down to us; the artists Amenmesse and Djed-Khonsu left their names in hieroglyphs on the left side of the seat.

[149] This wall is filled with fragments of reliefs and paintings. These two of birds in marshes are from Amenhotep III's mud-brick palace on the west bank at Thebes. Painted directly on dry stucco, the stylized figures show a considerable freedom of line—a freedom that blossomed in the Amarna period.

[130] These limestone blocks from Queen Hatshepsut's temple at Deir al-Bahri depict the Queen of Punt, who suffers from both obesity and pathological curvature of the spine, as well as her donkey, shown here with a padded saddle not unlike those still in use.

[141] The wooden statue of Lady Ibentina (in the showcase) was found in the tomb of her husband, an artist at Deir al-Medina.

[153] The ebony carving of the stablemaster Tjay reproduces in three-dimensional form the same delicacy of carvings found in Ramose's tomb. The modeling of the face, the detailing of the wig, and the texture of the golden disk collars (reward for royal service) make this figure one of the most alluring in the room.

[135] The limestone figure of Thutmose III offers *nu*-jars (filled with wine or milk) to Amun. The figure, with the kilt and *nemes* headdress, is a finely crafted model of similar life-sized statues.

Halls 6 And 7

As you turn the corner into the northern wing, you meet several of the black lion-headed statues of Sekhmet discovered at Mut Temple in Thebes. The centers of the halls are dominated by large figures of early 18th Dynasty rulers. On the heads of sphinxes appear the familiar Thutmoside features of Hatshepsut and her family. Many of the reliefs on the south side of Hall 7 were removed from Maya's tomb in the 19th century; the tomb was subsequently lost until its rediscovery in 1986 by a British Expedition working in Saqqara.

Hall 3, The Amarna Period

Dedicated to the revolutionary art of the heretic king Akhenaten, this gallery contains the art that broke with the centuries of Egyptian tradition.

[159] At its extreme, the period shows the king, not as the perfect specimen of refined masculinity, but as a grotesque, asexual being. The long, chiseled face of this colossus with its full lips and heavy hips and thighs may well have been grounded in reality, but such statues undoubtedly exaggerated the king's physique.

[160] A less extreme statue shows Akhenaten with his blue crown presenting an offering table and must have more nearly resembled reality. For unknown reasons, the royal sculptors transferred the same deformed (though less exaggerated) formula to Nefertiti and their daughters. Nevertheless, Nefertiti's features from several sculptures testify to her beauty.

[164/165] These stelae show not only the king and his wife, but also his daughters, worshipping Aton. The traces of red gridlines on [165] indicate its use as a master cartoon; black lines were used for original composition, red ones as copyist grids.

[167] The idea of a "Holy Family" appears as Akhenaten and Nefertiti play with all three daughters on a stela designed for worship in a private home. Since only Akhenaten could intercede with Aton, others could only petition him to pray for their salvation. The face of this stela shows Ankhsenpaaten (who would later wed Tutankhamun) sitting on her mother's lap. It was screened by wooden doors; the holes for the pegs are still visible on the sides of the carving.

[169] The ostraca in the same case shows one of these princesses eating a duck. The quality of Amarna art lies in its break with the stiff forms of classical canon, and the fluid lines of this sketch produce a relaxed, flowing figure.

[161] The masterpiece, however, is the unfinished head of Nefertiti. The head would have formed part of a composite statue—a separate crown resting above the smoothly finished face—a technique popular during this period. While this head portrays the serenity and beauty typical of Egyptian art, another quartzite portrait [162] blends the mannerisms of the early statues with harmony and grace. Even lacking the eyes, which would have been inlaid, this face so captures the vitality of the queen that she seems ready to speak.

[170] The fragments of marsh wildlife that hang high on the walls owe less to Akhenaten, for the tendency toward a softening of decorative canon, as we have seen, was beginning in his father's

(Amenhotep III) reign. Nevertheless, the stylized foliage and delineated textures of the birds' feathers have here given away to quick yet sure strokes of color—free compositions anticipating the beginnings of impressionism by over 2,000 years.

Hall 13, The Ramesside Period
[212] The gray granite Victory Stela of Merneptah (Israel Stela) includes the only mention of Israel in Egypt; here it's included in the list of defeated place-names.

Hall 9
In ancient Egypt, the king was always responsible for maintaining order from Chaos, and in the New Kingdom, the symbol of Apophis the serpent gave way to more human causes of disorder.

[206] (769) We thus find a block from Ramesses II's temple at Memphis showing typical iconography: the king smiting Egypt's foes, in this case three individuals representing Nubia, Libya, and Syria. He grabs their hair, a move reproduced endless times on temple walls and pylons, and with his other hand holds an ax like the one belonging to the Middle Kingdom ruler Ahmose (upstairs, Hall 3, [121]).

Hall 14
[201] (724) The statue of Seti I is an example of the massive sculptures popular during the Amarna period. The delicate face recalls that of Nefertiti, though its sensitive mouth and eyes and eyebrows are now bereft of their gold and precious stone inlay. The neck fits onto the body via a socket and the hands attach to the arms by thongs laced through holes at the wrists; a heavy collar and gold bracelets concealed the joints. The figure would have worn a *nemes* headdress, probably of gold and lapis lazuli—similar to that found on King Tut's funerary mask. From his belt hung a heavy, gold leopard-face that held ribbons bordered by uraei and sun disks; golden sandals sheathed his feet.

Hall 25, Late Period
[245] The most beautiful piece in the room is the granite head of King Taharqa, the 26th Dynasty ruler who conquered Thebes. King of the Kushites in Nubia, he is shown here with the Nubian tendency toward realism tempered with idealism borrowed from the Old and Middle kingdoms.

[244] The alabaster statue of Amenirdis the Elder is from the same period. Divine votaress of Amun, she and her successors ruled from Thebes with the support of the pharaohs, counterbalancing Amun's priests. Amenirdis is dressed in the costume of New Kingdom queens: the falcon headdress surmounted by a crown of uraei, which in turn once supported a Hathor crown of horns and sun disk. The monumental style, like that of the early dynasties, shows us a grave-faced lady who looks capable of taking on the priests of Amun.

Hall 24
Among the statues in this room are several of gods and goddesses executed in a streamlined style akin to some modern sculpture.
[248] The goddess Taweret.
[250] Isis.
[251] Hathor and Psamtik.
[252] Osiris.

Hall 34, Greco-Roman
The pieces in this gallery range from classical Hellenistic and Roman style to the objects showing the mingling of Greco-Roman realism and pharaonic symbolism. The two stelae standing near the back wall offer examples of this melding.

Halls 40, 45, And 44, Nubian
These rooms house post-pharaonic material uncovered in Nubia, including the grave goods from Ballana and Qustul. Most impressive are the saddles and bridles that once adorned war-horses, shown here mounted on models. The remaining halls on the ground floor are devoted to larger pieces of Hellenistic statuary (Hall 50) and sarcophagi (Hall 49).

The Atrium
The center of the sunken Atrium contains a large section of painted pavement from the palace at Amarna done in the same style as the fragments in Hall 3. The design, laid out asymmetrically, gives an idea of the way whole areas were covered with subjects as diverse as the traditional Nine Bows (enemies of Egypt) and ducks in a marsh.

[213] The sarcophagus of Merneptah (19th Dynasty, later usurped by Psusennes of Tanis) is surmounted by a figure of the king as Osiris, his head supported by a goddess. Inside, a figure of Nut stretches out her arms to protect the king. The body of the sarcophagus, though it contains typical New Kingdom texts, shows registers of

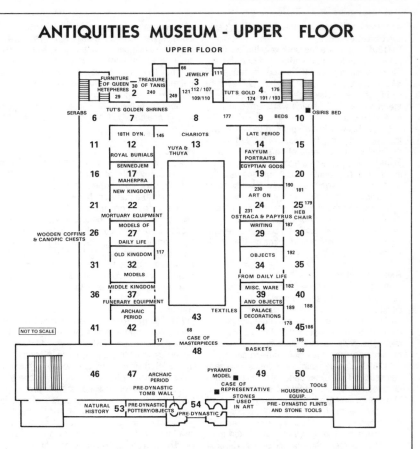

ANTIQUITIES MUSEUM - UPPER FLOOR

UPPER FLOOR

jewelry, linen, scepters, and weapons—objects typical of Middle Kingdom coffins—while the exterior is carved in the Old Kingdom palace facade motif. When discovered by Montet in 1939 in Tanis, this sarcophagus held the silver coffin of Psusennes, his mummy still covered with gold (upstairs, Hall 2).

UPPER FLOOR

Upstairs, the exhibits are grouped according to media: tools, wooden models, furniture, papyrus, textiles. But the best-known objects are the trea-

sures from Tut's tomb lining the walls of the righthand (east) hall and the jewels that occupy the three rooms (2, 3, and 4) across the back of the building. To reach Tut's treasures from the ground floor, take the southeastern staircase.

Hall 45, Tut Galleries

The pieces, beginning with this gallery, are laid out roughly as they appeared in the tomb.

[180] A pair of wooden *ka* statues guard the entrance much as they watched over the doorway to Tut's tomb. Made of wood coated with bitumen and gilded, the statues have eyes inlaid in bronze. The swollen bellies and slender legs carry over

from the Amarna canon; the Osirian black skin symbolizes rebirth.

[185] Just inside the doorway, the statue of Anubis mounted on a shrine guarded the entrance to the "treasury." The wooden statue has gilded ears and scarf, calcite and obsidian eyes inlaid in gold, and silver toenails. As protector of the dead, the god's image was carried in Tut's funeral procession.

[186] This well-known painted casket shows the king, charging into a mass of tangled bodies that, being inferior, were often shown full face. In the hunting scene on the top of the box, the animals inhabit a mountainous landscape, and the hunters, like the army below them, traverse fields of flowers painted in the Amarna style. The compositions echo the pharaonic conception of reality: the Egyptian army or hunters in disciplined registers follow their king, who conquers the jumbled mass of bodies or wild animals—the chaotic forces of the world.

Halls 40 And 35

[188] The ivory-inlaid chest nearby presents even stronger connections to Amarna art; the composition itself on the lid—Ankhesenamon, daughter of Akhenaten, offering mandrake, lotus, and papyrus to Tut—developed during Akhenaten's reign. The tender scene is surrounded by a border of cornflowers, poppies, and pomegranates.

[178] The golden shrine continues to accent domesticity: Tut reclines casually on a chair while his queen bends easily forward to touch his arm. The scenes are mixed, however, with more formal ones such as the queen (rather like a goddess) presenting the king with staffs representing millions of years. The gold leaf was worked from behind (repoussé), then attached by a thin layer of stucco to the wood. The shrine (mounted on a sledge with silver runners) is designed like the *naos* of a temple: a slanting roof decorated with flying vultures, a cavetto cornice, and double doors. It once housed statues (stolen in ancient times) of the king and queen intended to continue their relationship, providing for life and rebirth.

[189] Gaming boards both honed spiritual skills and provided practical entertainment. The 30 squares are for *senet* ("passing"), a race-game known from the Old Kingdom that had become a national obsession. Players, moving according to throws of the sticks (or dice), attempted to be the first to cast off their players at the end of the course. The game also represented the struggle of the deceased to pass into the Netherworld, so it often appeared on tomb walls. Among many, Tut took a deluxe model mounted on a sledge and a small pocket version with him to eternity.

[182] To enable the king to fulfill his labor requirements in the netherworld, he was supplied with a wide range of *shabti* figures, and one of the most beautiful is the carved wood with gold and gilt presented to the king by his general, Min-Nakht.

Hall 30

The series of statues in this room helped the king in his journey to the afterworld.

[192] The most notable is of Tutankhamun hunting with a harpoon. Made of gilded stucco over a wooden core, the statue shows the king on a papyrus skiff undoubtedly hunting down the forces of Chaos. The king's pose is familiar from tomb reliefs, but this figure translates it into a vital figure striding forward to thrust his full weight behind his weapon. The concavity of his kilt, which swings naturally along his legs, heightens the illusion of motion.

Hall 25

[179] This gallery contains furniture from the tomb, including the king's throne. Like the 4th Dynasty stone seat of Khafre, this chair is supported by lions; the legs were once connected by the intertwining lotus and sedge, symbol of unification. Unlike its prototype, this throne has arms, the wings of crowned serpents protecting the king's cartouches. The figures of the king and queen on the back, their skin and hair formed by glass inlay, are dressed in silver garments, their jewelry set with semiprecious stones. The awkward proportions of the figures and their relaxed attitude bespeak the Amarna style. The cartouches of the king and queen give the Aton form of their names, and the sun disk itself extends his life-giving rays to the king.

[181] The inlaid ceremonial chair, while a masterpiece of craftsmanship, is far less successful in its concept. The base, designed like a folding stool, is surmounted with a ridged seat and back, the resulting combination being neither functional nor aesthetically pleasing. The ebony, ivory, and stone inlay set in gold, however, is outstanding; similar inlay appears later in both Coptic and Islamic art.

Heb Chair

Far more typical of pharaonic design is the wooden chair that shows Heb, the god of eternity, with his staffs of millions of years protecting the king's cartouches. A masterpiece of functional design, this style of chair became popular in Europe during the 19th century.

[187] The prisoner cane is a beautiful example of post-Amarna craftsmanship and design. Symbolizing north and south, the Asiatic and Nubian elements provide counterpoint and symmetry yet maintain artistic tension. Inlaid with ivory (Asiatic) and ebony (Nubian), the figures are dressed in native clothes highlighted with inlaid glass. Their bodies, arched backward in the "leap of death" motif, display creative design that often stretched the canon of pharaonic art.

Hall 15

This gallery contains the beautiful alabaster work: lotus lamps (one wired with a bulb to show off the translucency of the stone) and vases.

[190] The perfume vase transforms the *sematawy* into three dimensions: the two Hapis intertwining the sedge and lotus. The missing stopper may have been a figure of the king, in which case the outstretched wings of the vulture would have protected him. Equally lovely is the antelope perfume vase, unfortunately now missing a horn.

North Halls

The northeast end of the museum is dominated by the beds removed from Tut's tomb; ceremonial ones include three dedicated to Hathor, Sekhmet, and Isis.

The Osiris Bed

Formed in the shape of the god, this flat planter was covered with Nile mud, sown with seed, and just before the tomb was sealed, watered; the seeds, symbols of rebirth, germinated in the darkness of the tomb.

[177] This golden chest held the canopic jars guarded by Selket, Isis, Nephthys, and Neith. These gilded wood deities, with turned faces and outstretched arms, show the freedom of Amarna sculpture at its most charming.

Hall 4, Tut's Gold

[174] The gold mask from Tut's mummy, wearing the *nemes* headdress, reveals the idealized face of the king confronting eternity with the same calm assurance as did Khafre over 1,000 years earlier. The gold mask is inlaid with colored glass and semiprecious stones, the eyes with obsidian and quartz.

[175] The gold coffin is equally beautiful, inlaid with the same materials. The king, his hands crossed in the Osiride position, is protected with the cloisonné feathers of Nekhbet and Wadjet. Below the vulture and cobra, Isis and Nephthys extend feathered arms—perhaps the prototypes of angels.

[191] The most impressive piece of jewelry in the room is the cloisonné corselet. Known from paintings (particularly from Ramesside tombs in the Valley of the Queens), the garment was hinged at the shoulders and waist. Perhaps originally a vest of feathers or a shirt of armor of painted leather scales, this example is of gold, glass paste, and carnelian. The pendants that form an integral part of the garment are poorly designed, showing the decline in craftsmanship from the Middle Kingdom in the crowded figures and jumbled color schemes.

[193] The pectoral, though a tour de force of workmanship, has the same problems of design; the winged scarab, clutching a lotus in one birdlike claw and a sedge in the other, labors to push not only the barque of Re but that of Khonsu over the horizon. To counterbalance this mass, the artist crowded as many pendants of gold and semiprecious stones onto the lower border as it would hold.

Hall 3, Jewelry

[66] The masterpiece in this room is the gold 6th Dynasty head of a falcon from Hieraconpolis. Worked in hammered and chiseled gold, the head was attached to a copper body (now lost) and served as the cult figure for the temple under which it was found buried. The crown appears to be an 18th century addition.

[112] The crown of Princess Khnumyt when nestled into her hair would have appeared to sprinkle brilliant stars over her head, while the diadem of Set-Hathor-Yunet takes the designs from textile crowns such as that on the Old Kingdom statue of Nofret and transforms them into gold, lapis lazuli, carnelian, and faience.

[107] The same type of delicate design appears in Khnumyt's necklaces: strings of delicate charms worked in cloisonné and set with lapis lazuli and carnelian, and another of beads and teardrops of turquoise, lapis lazuli, and gold.

[109/110] The pectorals of Middle Kingdom

princesses Set-Hathor and Mereret (found near Fayyum) show the skill with which jewelers combined design, traditional symbolism and canon, and craftsmanship.

[111] Amethysts are particularly difficult to work into successful designs because of their color, but court jewelers fashioned a belt and anklet for Mereret combining gold leopard heads and claws with amethyst beads. The double heads, outstanding examples of repoussé, brought the princes strength and amuletic protection.

[121] In 1859, Mariette discovered the tomb of Queen Ahhotep, wife of Sekenenre and mother of Kamose and Ahmose, who liberated Egypt from the Hyksos. Her tomb contained Ahmose's ceremonial ax commemorating his victory over the foreigners; the narrow head laced to the handle appears in many depictions of New Kingdom pharaohs, who use it against their Asiatic, Libyan, and Nubian enemies.

[122] The dagger blade (part of the same cache) is worked in niello, sulfide producing the black background.

[124] The queen's rigid bracelet of lapis lazuli inlaid in gold is hinged and opens via a movable pin hidden in one of the hinges.

[120] The most unusual find in her tomb, however, were the golden flies of the Order of Valor. Decorations for bravery on the battlefield, these examples with their bulging eyes and openwork bodies underlie the queen's importance in the wars of liberation.

[210] The bracelets of Ramesses II are similar in design, the gold work representing the height of the granulated technique, knowledge lost until this century.

[249] In the corner by the entrance, the mummy covering is composed of long beads crosslinked much like the bead nets of the goddesses painted on the walls of tombs such as that of Horemheb. The funerary collar, or *usekh*, is typical, rows of similar long beads interspaced with gold anchored by Horus heads. Below the collar, Isis spreads her protective arms, and the four sons of Horus guard the organs of the deceased, which at this time would have been returned to the body.

Hall 2, Furniture Of Hetepheres

Wife of Snefru and mother of Khufu, this queen was buried at the foot of her son's pyramid in Giza. When uncovered, the wood of her furniture had rotted and the gold work had collapsed onto itself. Meticulous patience produced these restorations.

[29] The sedan chair, the bed and its canopy, and the chairs all date from the 4th Dynasty, as do the graceful gold vessels [30].

[240] During the Third Intermediate Period, Tanis was the northern capital, and when the area was excavated, the unrobbed tomb of Psusennes, interred in an electrum coffin, yielded the objects that fill this annex. The gold necklace made from rows of disks is the same style shown on New Kingdom tombs.

Hall 7

The golden shrines that nested around King Tut's coffin. Stacked one inside the other, they nearly filled the burial chamber. Carter and crew had to dismantle them and carry them panel by panel out of the tomb; only then could they expose the coffin of the king.

Hall 13

The chariots removed from Tut's tomb are here, as well as the contents of the double tomb of Yuya and Thuya, parents of Queen Tiyi, wife of Amenhotep III.

[145] Of the objects from this tomb, the most beautiful is Thuya's cartonnage (linen and plaster) and gilded mask inlaid with glass and semiprecious stones.

EAST HALLS

Hall 17

This room contains material from private burials, most notably that of Sennedjem, a worker at the royal tombs in the Valley of the Kings, and Maherpra. The door to Sennedjem's tomb, which shows him playing *senet* with his wife, displays the vivacity and skill the artists used to decorate their own houses of eternity.

[218] The coffin of Isis, perhaps his daughter-in-law, shows the same creative skill.

[216] The sarcophagus of Khonsu (son of Sennedjem) contains designs popular in the workers' tombs, such as the lions of Yesterday and Today supporting the sun as it rises between the mountains of the same names. Khonsu's coffin lies on a lion-headed couch while Anubis embalms him, protected by Isis (red) and Nephthys (white).

Hall 27

This gallery houses Middle Kingdom domestic models developed from the individual figures of servants interred with Old Kingdom aristocracy.

[74] The large wooden statue of a woman with the box of wine jars on her head and holding ducks is a sculptured reproduction of the offering bearers which lining the lower walls of tombs. This lady wears an overdress of beads in the same pattern as the mummy cover in Hall 3, probably an overdress covering a linen sheath.

[75] Other groups of smaller figures come from Meketre's tomb in Thebes and include men on reed boats netting fish.

[76] Herdsmen drive cattle past their owner, who sits with his son under a sunshade while scribes count his herd.

[77/78] The discovery of workshop models like the weavers and carpenters has enabled scholars to confirm craft techniques like the use of a pull saw on timbers lashed to an upright pole. Also of note is the model of a garden—a mandatory accessory to every country estate.

[117] In the hallway outside Hall 32 stands the *ka* statue of King Auib-re Hor; the arms upraised on its head identify it as the king's spiritual double. The Middle Kingdom figure, once covered with stucco and painted, wears a tripart wig later popular with New Kingdom women.

Hall 37

Nubian archers and Egyptian pikemen represent troops assembled by a prince from Asyut. The detail in the carvings has given scholars a good idea of how the weapons shown on the walls of temples and tombs were actually made.

Halls 43 And 48

[17] This panel of blue faience tiles comes from the underground burial hall of King Djoser at his Step Pyramid at Saqqara, and clearly illustrates the construction of its prototype of reeds.

[68] This sarcophagus belonged to Kawit, wife of Mentuhotep, the Middle Kingdom ruler who reunited Egypt. The carvings, released from the confines of the classical canon, establish a simplicity and vigor typical of Middle Kingdom art. From the beautifully textured false door to the queen's slender figure, which holds a Hathor mirror while she drinks a cup of fresh milk, the spacious compositions and the assured contours of the lines create a masterpiece.

[28] The two showcases nearby contain a wonderful collection of small figures, including (on the top shelf) the only known representation of Khufu, builder of the Great Pyramid.

[90] The dancing dwarfs, actually pygmies of South Africa, are mounted on pivoting bases and could be made to "dance" by pulling a string.

[82/83] The faience hippopotamuses, symbols of fertility and rebirth, inhabited burials from Old Kingdom times until the end of the 17th Dynasty.

[144] The green steatite head of Queen Tiyi, wife of Amenhotep III, is a diminutive masterpiece that introduces the traditions of the Amarna period.

[198] The New Kingdom polychrome glass vases were molded around a clay core, decorated with applied glass rods, heated, and then combed into the pattern—early examples of a glassmaking tradition that would culminate in the famous work of Byzantine Alexandrian craftsmen.

EAST ROOMS

Hall 29, Manuscripts

[236] *The Book of AmDuat.*

[232] The illustrations of mice being served by cats.

[220] An ostracon with the beginnings of the story of Sinuhe the Sailor.

[233] The case on the east side displays writing tools: pens and their cases, ink palettes, and water jars.

[234] Artists' paints and brushes.

Hall 24, Artwork

Vibrant sketches on ostraca reveal both the awkward efforts of beginners and the breathtaking skill of the craftsman.

[230] Ostracon of a royal head.

[231] The praying scribe.

[235] The Book of the Dead made for Pinedjem shows off the talents of artists who worked in color on papyrus.

OLD CAIRO

Cairo's earliest remains are found to the south, in Old Cairo, in area intimately linked with early Christian history. The Holy Family, when escaping King Herod, fled to Egypt. They stayed at Babylon while Joseph worked at the Roman fort. By the middle of the first century after Christ, St. Mark, accompanying St. Peter from Palestine, crossed the desert to Babylon, and Coptic tradition says that Mark wrote his Gospel here for the Egyptian (Coptic) Church he had founded.

When the Romans adopted Christianity in the 3rd century, Trajan's fortress at Babylon, in addition to its military duties, became the religious center for the Roman Melkites. From here, Roman patriarchs persecuted the Copts who inhabited the surrounding village; only the coming of Amr and his Muslim armies relieved them of their misery under the rule of their fellow Christians. After Amr's victory at Babylon, the claustrophobic Muslims chose to pitch their tents on the open plain northeast of the fort, while the native Copts moved inside the fortress's sheltering walls, establishing a Christian quarter, which retains its identity even today.

The ruined fort of Babylon (Qasr al-Sham'ah —Fortress of the Beacon) is the core of Old Cairo. For visitors it offers two Roman gates, the bowels of a defense tower, and a hanging church to explore. On long narrow cobble streets stand some of the oldest Coptic churches in the world, many still in use. Young Copts often donate their time to serve as tour guides for their churches. These people will not clamor for baksheesh (like the people in the street), but a donation to the church box is certainly in order. The Coptic Museum, which includes screens, ceilings, and floors from Coptic houses, is filled with masterpieces of Coptic art. Among the churches in Old Cairo nestles the ancient **Ben Ezra Synagogue,** the center for the area's Jews, and Amr's mosque, the first founded in Egypt, lies just to the north of the walls.

Getting There

The easiest and cheapest (35PT) way to get to Old Cairo is to take the Metro south (Helwan direction); get off at the Mari Girgis stop. The entrance, directly across from the Metro station, is marked by the crosses of carved stucco and the ornate gateway. Directly ahead through the twin towers of the Roman fortress is the **Coptic Museum;** to your right behind the walls, the hanging Church, **al-Muallaka;** to your left, through the iron gate, is the old town, its lower streets lying at the old Roman ground level. Open Sat.-Thurs., 0900-1600, Fri., 0900-1100 and 1300-1600; LE8 to visit the ancient churches, and an additional LE8 for the museum. Photography is prohibited in the churches. Coptic services are held on Fridays, 0800-1100 and Sundays, 0700-1000.

The Roman Gate

The twin towers of the western gate rise in front of the gardens. When Trajan first built the circular towers, the Nile lapped at their foundations, protecting their entrance, and a bridge of barges spanned the river, linking the fortress with the southern tip of Rhoda Island. Today, the fortress's foundations are buried under 10 meters of accumulated rubble, silt, and debris; thus the street level and the interior of the compound lie nearly atop the fortress's walls.

The two towers forming this gate date from the 3rd century. The northern tower is capped by the Russian Orthodox Church of St. George; the southern one is in ruins and therefore offers a view of the interior construction. The Romans built their towers with dressed stone (some reused from pharaonic temples) alternating with brickwork. The central shaft, about 10 meters across, is supported by two masonry rings about five meters apart. The radiating ribs give the tower strength to withstand enemy siege engines like catapults and battering rams.

Al-Muallaka (The Hanging Church)

The church is called hanging because it lies suspended across the Roman towers that guarded the water entrance to the fortress. (The interior of this gate is accessible through the courtyard of the Coptic Museum.) The church, founded in the late 7th century when it served the bishop of Babylon,

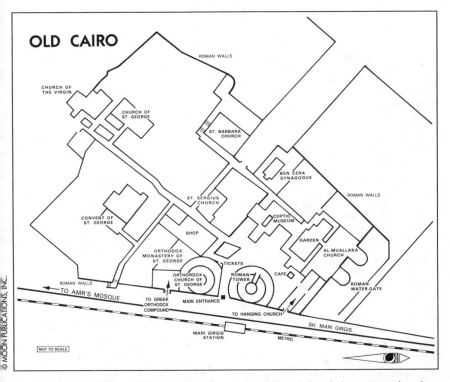

OLD CAIRO

ROMAN WALLS

CHURCH OF
THE VIRGIN

CHURCH OF
ST. GEORGE

ST. BARBARA
CHURCH

BEN EZRA
SYNAGOGUE

ROMAN WALLS

ST. SERGIUS
CHURCH

CONVENT OF
ST. GEORGE

COPTIC
MUSEUM

SHOP

GARDEN

ORTHORDOX
MONASTERY OF
ST. GEORGE

AL-MUALLAKA
CHURCH

TICKETS

ROMAN WALLS

ORTHORDOX
CHURCH OF
ST. GEORGE

ROMAN
TOWER

CAFE

TO AMR'S MOSQUE

ROMAN
WATER-GATE

TO GREEK
ORTHODOX
COMPOUND

MAIN ENTRANCE

TO HANGING CHURCH

SH. MARI GIRGIS

MARI GIRGIS
STATION

METRO

NOT TO SCALE

© MOON PUBLICATIONS, INC.

was destroyed in the 9th century. Rebuilt in 977, it continued to grow, and by the 11th century it was a center of learning and the seat of the Coptic Patriarchate. Renovation of the building continued through medieval times.

You can reach the hanging church either through the main gate—turn left in front of the cafe and walk through the opening in the walls— or from the street; there's a small entrance just south of the main gate. The clergy live in rooms under the two small, modern towers. The stairs lead to a 19th century portico. Across the courtyard the arcade forms an external narthex, an uncommon feature in Coptic churches. (The Arab tiles and ceiling are modern.) The church itself is a typical triapse design, the main, wagon-vaulted nave (a modern reconstruction) separated from its side aisles by the usual classical columns. As was customary, paintings of saints once decorated the columns but have now faded. Although the windows are modern they contain old fragments.

The 13th century marble pulpit is the typical straight-sided type, one of the finest and oldest in Cairo. It rests on seven pairs of slender columns, the design of each pair differing from all the others. Behind it, sanctuary screens (iconostasis), found in most Coptic churches, separate the *haykals* (altar areas) from the congregation. These screens in al-Muallaka date from the 13th century; the one covering the central *haykal*, which is dedicated to the Virgin, is of cedar inlaid with ivory. Although partly restored, the new work is as delicate as the original. (The trilobed tips of the Coptic cross symbolize the Trinity.) The icons at the top of the screen represent St. Paul, the Archangel Michael, St. John the Baptist, Christ enthroned, Mary, the Archangel Gabriel, and St. Peter. The inscription surrounding the pictures is a psalm of blessing and praise.

(continued on p. 208)

COPTIC MUSEUM

Open Sat.-Thurs. 0900-1600, Fri. 0900-1100 and 1300-1600; the old wing closes half an hour earlier; LE8; no bags; no cameras without a photo-ticket.

The museum, founded in 1910 and funded by private donations, stands on ground donated by the Coptic Patriarchate. The collections of the Coptic Museum bridge the time between the pharaonic and Greco-Roman eras and the Islamic period. Officials collected treasures from the old churches and Coptic houses, and received several private collections. The museum also displays artifacts from the excavations at Saqqara (Monastery of St. Jeremia) and Bawiti (Monastery of St. Appollon). In 1931, the museum came under the wing of the Egyptian government, which transferred material here from the Antiquities and Islamic museums. To house the bulging collection, the government built a new wing in 1947, and in 1983 the entire museum was renovated. The collection is displayed according to material: stone, metal, tapestries, and manuscripts occupy the new wing, wood, pottery, and glass are in the old. Throughout the museum, note the wooden details,

often from old houses, in the doorways, windows, and especially the ceilings.

THE NEW WING—DOWNSTAIRS

Entrance to the new wing is through the sculpture garden and down a set of stairs. This floor contains stonework and paintings from monasteries throughout Egypt.

Hall 1

The center of the room is dominated by a fountain from one of the old houses of the area. The walls display early carvings typical of the Coptic style but portraying classical myths. The broken pediment with the shell is typical of Coptic work, as are the figures with their large heads and stylized bodies. Note the tendency toward two flat layers that are already present in the work.

Hall 2

These carvings from Christian sites continue the same

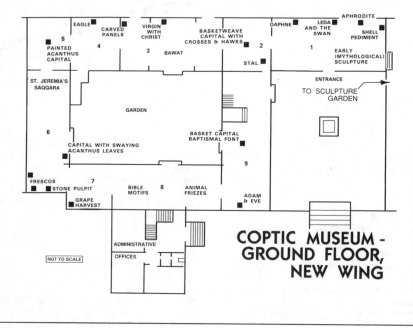

COPTIC MUSEUM - GROUND FLOOR, NEW WING

style but substitute Christian figures for pagan motifs. The work also continues, however, to show traces of pharaonic and Greco-Roman influences in the use of the *ankh* with the cross and the Horus hawk on the capital, as well as the Coptic trend toward the abstract.

Hall 3

The outstanding stonework is from the monastery at Bawiti in Upper Egypt, and the carvings span several centuries; those on the north wall mark the apogee of Coptic carving. Regular circles have displaced twining stems, and leaves, reduced to flat patterns, create compositions that nevertheless move the viewer's eye through the composition.

The fresco niche, a masterpiece of Coptic painting, shows Christ enthroned between the creatures of the Apocalypse, the moon and sun to either side. Below, the Virgin and Child (like Isis with Horus) sit between the apostles, who have their names written in Coptic above their heads.

Hall 4

In the miscellaneous collection in this room the most notable piece is the eagle. For the early Christians, this motif symbolized renewed life, as did the peacock, perhaps a continuation of the *bennu* bird or phoenix traditions of resurrection.

Hall 5

Filled with miscellaneous pieces, this gallery shows off a capital with a double row of acanthus leaves that still retains traces of paint. The motif, adapted by the Greeks for their Corinthian capitals, was quickly adopted by the Romans and carried on by the Copts, for the deeply lobed leaves will bend in sinuous forms, conforming to nearly any surface or design. In contrast to most Coptic forms, however, the plant appears to be asymbolic.

Hall 6

This room is devoted to articles from the 5th century Monastery of St. Jeremias at Saqqara. Capitals from columns march in pairs down the hall, pharaonic palm fronds and lotus mixing with Mediterranean acanthus and grapevines. The supple limestone let the artists bring out the juxtaposition of bright light and deep shadow, a theme that pervades Egyptian art of all periods. The stone pulpit, the earliest known, echoes the thrones from the nearby court of the *heb sed* festival built by Djoser in the 3rd century B.C.; perhaps such Christian pulpits influenced the design of those standing in mosques even today. The fresco beside it empha-

sizes, once again, the links between Isis and Mary.

Hall 7

This theme of reused pharaonic motifs continues with the small sphinx (between Greek columns) and the grape harvest, a perennial favorite in tombs of the pharaonic nobles.

Hall 8

Art from biblical sources includes Abraham, Isaac, and their sacrificial lamb; Christ with angels; and a scene of the fiery furnace. Mary adopts an *orans* position: facing forward and standing with her weight on one foot, her arm upraised—a stance typical of Coptic work. Animals set off in rondels formed by plants became common in later periods and the Fatimids commissioned scenes of hunters and their quarry in a nearly identical style.

Hall 9

At the entrance hangs an early painting of Adam and Eve shown both before and after the Fall, the latter scene complete with accusative serpent. The ornate basket-weave capital dominating the center of the room, complete with papyrus and lotus designs, has been hollowed out for use as a baptismal font.

NEW WING—UPPER FLOOR

This wing, devoted to fibers and metalwork, contains some of the most famous texts (like the Nag Hammadi Codex) and most beautiful textiles—both ancient and modern.

Hall 10

Cases of manuscripts stand next to the stairs. Produced by scriptoriums attached to monasteries, they were written on scrolls of papyrus. Around the 1st century, monks began to cut the scrolls and bind them into codices or books, and by the 4th century, such books had nearly replaced scrolls. Few texts appear on parchment in Egypt, but scribes continued to use ostraca (pieces of broken pottery or fragments of limestone) and bone. In addition to prayers and teachings of early Christians, the collection includes magical formulas and charms.

The Copts, however, were most noted for their textiles—the large numbers of weaves coupled with innovative designs filled demands from throughout the Roman Empire. Beginning with the 3rd and 4th centuries, Copts made extensive use of pile weave as

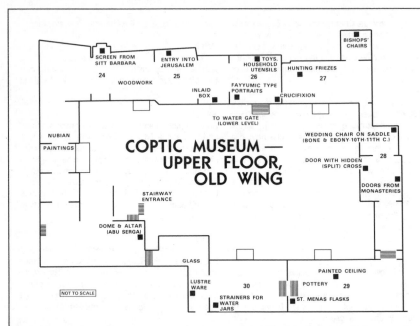

COPTIC MUSEUM —
UPPER FLOOR,
OLD WING

well as tapestry weave to create multiple designs that followed in form and feel those motifs expressed in sculpture. The fabrics on display range from ancient tunics with typical appliqués of bands and rondels to 18th century silk ecclesiastical robes.

Hall 13

Alexandrian-style delicate carved ivory stands juxtaposed against the more crude work of Upper Egypt, pieces that may have been made by the monks themselves. The ivories and jewelry are accompanied by 17th and 18th century icons that have lost the freshness of the first Coptic impulse; the motifs' complexity and the depiction of suffering were atypical of Coptic work.

The next few rooms of metalwork, much locally produced, range from kitchen utensils to patriarchal staffs, censers, and crosses. Priests use the small crosses to bless their congregation; the purpose of the fans (used early in Coptic times) is unknown, but they may represent a link to the royal fans of the pharaohs.

Hall 15

The eagle in the center of the room is from the fortress. The armor and the ornate candlestick are the products of Byzantine workshops, for Egypt remained under Byzantine control until the Arab conquest. The two gem-studded crowns were gifts from the Ethiopian emperor.

The upper floor tour ends with Nubian paintings, many the result of the Nubian Archaeological Survey. Christianity prevailed longer in Nubia than in Egypt, and many of the sites investigated by the survey had remained Christian until they were flooded by construction of the Aswan High Dam. These paintings differ from their northern neighbors in the more somber colors, more rounded heads, and larger eyes (with dark underlining).

OLD WING

The entrance to the old wing is through Hall 1 out into the sculpture garden. On either side of the porch are pagan stelae from cemeteries throughout Egypt. The mixture of classical Greco-Roman motifs and the older pharaonic ones is nowhere more apparent than in this collection. To reach the old wing, leave the porch, turn left, and climb the stairs. This wing, even more than the previous one, contains beautiful windows and ceilings—don't forget to look up.

On your left as you enter stands the original altar and dome from Abu Serga Church; although the altar is from the 4th century, the dome dates only to Fatimid times. The next halls display more Nubian wall paintings. The two lunates (half-circle paintings) are from Bawiti, the same monastery that yielded the fine carvings in the adjoining wing.

Hall 24

The museum's extensive collection of woodwork begins with the original screen from the Church of Sitt Barbara. The fragments in the following alcove, which date from the 4th-6th centuries, repeat in wood the mythological themes and the trend toward stylization found in the stonework of the same era. Once more Greek gods and goddesses mix with papyrus, lotus, and wildlife typical of the Nile Valley.

Hall 25

Here, humans appear in the decorative wood scenes. The most famous piece depicts Christ's entry into Jerusalem, a panel taken from the al-Muallaka Church.

Hall 26

The following room contains a box of the type used in homes to store linen, books, etc., and the inlay testifies to the Copts' continuing craftsmanship. The mummy portrait panels are direct descendants of Roman practices; a portrait of the deceased commissioned during his lifetime and displayed in his house was incorporated into the funerary bandages as a replacement for the pharaonic mask. Many of these are done in encaustic, but artists also used the older tempera techniques. During Coptic times several centers for this work appeared in Fayyum and Bawiti, among others. Much like the pharaonic artists before them who had molded *shabti* figures for the mass market, the Coptic painters prepared general categories of nonspecific "portraits."

The most notable carving in this hall is one of the few known Coptic crucifixes; it combines a beardless Christ with a Horus hawk and a sun disk—direct links to the piece's pharaonic antecedents. The other groups of wood carvings show both Byzantine and Persian influences: fabulous animals in addition to dancing, musical, and hunting scenes, motifs that spill over into Islamic art as well. Later pieces (13th-17th centuries) concentrate on geometric designs, undoubtedly a reflection of the restoration of Sunni Islam in Egypt. In this transition period, the inclusion of the cross marks the distinction between Coptic

and Muslim. The annex houses episcopal chairs that hardly differ from the Muslim pieces once dominating the *qa'as* of wealthy amirs.

Hall 29

This pottery is arranged not by age but rather by type. The burnished surfaces are typical, and the potters continued using the shapes (kohl pots) and motifs (fish, ducks, and plants) their pharaonic ancestors had used. Pilgrims' flasks show St. Menas between two camels, for tradition says the camels bearing his body stopped near a spring in the desert and there his attendants buried him. Water from this spring was supposed to heal and was sold to pilgrims in these flasks.

On the central dome is a painting of Istanbul. Done in the typical distorted perspective similar to Roman landscapes, the piece offsets the moored ships with the red, slanting roofs of the buildings, giving a oddly satisfying idea of the ancient town.

The pottery in the following room contains later work including lusterware pieces, a technique identified with Muslim potters, but here rendered with Christian motifs like the fish and cross. The final room contains a small collection of glass.

THE WATER GATE

Across the museum garden lies the southern gate to the Roman fortress. Once it was a land entry, but later Romans diverted the Nile into a blind quay, flooding the entrance. Still later, the Muslims drained the inlet and back-filled the entrance, making the gate once more accessible by land. Through this gate, the Christian patriarch Makaukas escaped in a boat under cover of night from Amr's advancing army.

The gate's existing walls are Byzantine, late 4th or early 5th century; only the pediments and arches of the gate itself are early Roman. The gate includes both an inner arch, closed by a door for which the stone sockets still exist, and an outer arch, once protected by a portcullis, the grooves for which are still visible. Today, the nave of al-Muallaka straddles the fortress's towers. The three stone piers supporting the back of this church partially block the hall of the gatehouse. A small gate and stairs lead deep into the bowels of the gate, a descent worth the trouble to wander around in the Gothic interior of the gatehouse. Decking above the standing water leads to the western bastion that now houses a winepress, an old mill, and other equipment.

A stepped tribune that provides seating for a bishop and the officiating clergy rises behind the main *haykal*. The center altar is dedicated to the Virgin, while the north *haykal* to St. George contains a similar screen with icons showing the saint's martyrdom. A Roman legionnaire, he defied Diocletian and was martyred in Asia, and in the 12th century the Coptic patriarch Gabriel II brought his body to Egypt. The south *haykal*, that of St. John the Baptist, is the most beautiful of the three and may have been the baptistery.

A 10th century screen, one of the finest pieces of Coptic woodworking, sits in the south wall, separating the main church from additional chapels in the south wing. If a churchman is with you, he may hold a candle behind this ivory screen, showing off its rosy luster. Behind it, on your left, stands the chapel of the Abyssinian saint Talkla Himanut, which shelters the remains of 12th or 13th century frescoes. From the window on the right you can see the ruined bastion and the quay of the Water Gate.

Abu Serga (St. Sergius)

To reach this church, go through the iron gate just to the right of the ticket kiosk next to the northern tower. (This gate is locked at 1600 hours, and sometimes during the day as well, so you may have to ask at the kiosk to have it opened.) Turn right, then left; the church is at the end of the first block on your right. The entrance is below street level, down the flight of stairs.

The oldest of Cairo's Coptic churches, it is built where tradition says the Holy Family lived while Joseph worked at the fortress. The church, however, is dedicated to the soldier-saints Sergius and Bacchus who were martyred in Syria during the 4th century. The original building, probably built in the 5th century, burned and was restored in the 8th century. Although the church has been continuously rebuilt from medieval times, it nevertheless remains a model of early Coptic churches, and due to its connection with the Holy Family, it continues to draw Christian pilgrims.

The door opens into a returned aisle, the Coptic equivalent of a narthex. Although the church remains nearly as it was first built, much of the original fresco work has been lost. The triple nave is divided by antique columns topped with Corinthian capitals supporting a continuous gallery reserved for women. The *haykal* screen dates from the 13th century, although its upper section, inset with ebony and ivory panels, is even older. The central apse contains fragments of original frescoes as well as intricate marble and mosaic decorations. Two group panels depict the Nativity and the Miracle of the Loaves and Fishes (alternately identified as the Last Supper). This 8th century carving shows Christ at a table oddly reminiscent of pharaonic offering tables.

The focal point of Abu Serga is, however, the crypt, which houses the remains of the early church founded where tradition says Joseph, Mary, and the infant Christ lived. Today a set of steps near the great pier of the north *haykal* lead down nearly 20 feet to the old Roman ground level. This lower structure dates from between the 2nd and 4th centuries and, enclosed by the walls of Trajan's fortress, was located in the heart of Jewish Babylon. Later, the larger church was erected and the original sanctuary became the crypt. Unfortunately, the crypt is now closed due to seepage that has flooded it.

Keenest Eliahu (Ben Ezra Synagogue)

To reach the synagogue, take the first right past Abu Serga and continue to the gate. The church of Sitt Barbara will be on your left, the synagogue on your right. This spot, where Elijah is said to have appeared and Moses to have prayed, has been held holy since the Jews first came to Egypt. The original Jewish temple (where Mary and Joseph must have worshipped) was apparently demolished during later reconstructions of the Roman fortress. The Christians took over the site and built a church dedicated to St. Michael the archangel. In the 12th century, it reverted to the Jews, and the synagogue was built by the Jerusalem Rabbi Abraham Ben Ezra.

The oldest synagogue in Egypt, it differs little from its Christian neighbors. The interior, however, contains the double-sided pulpit from which the rabbi reads the scriptures which, when not in use, are stored in the screened cupboard; the wood and mother-of-pearl work dates from the 12th century. Late in the 19th century, excavators turned up a cache of manuscripts including the Geniza manuscripts: the Book of Ecclesiastes, as well as numerous medieval documents shedding light on much Islamic, Coptic, and Jewish history from the 11th to 16th centuries. Renovation continues, but visitors are welcome to pick their way around the scaffolds.

Sitt Barbara (St. Barbara)

This church, one of the largest and finest in Old Cairo, stands just north of the synagogue. In 684, Athanasius the Scribe built a church here and dedicated it to the physician-saints Cyrus and John. It burned during the Fustat fire in 750, and was restored in the 11th century. The main church is dedicated to Sitt Barbara and houses her relics. Legend tells us she was the daughter of a pagan merchant and was converted to Christianity in the 3rd century. Together with her friend Juliana, she spread the gospel. For their efforts, her father, after his own efforts to kill them had failed, turned them over to the Roman governor who had them tortured, then murdered.

The main church is basilican in form, but the fresco decoration that once covered the interior has been completely lost. Note the Fatimid keel-shaped arches supporting the gallery. The current *haykal* screens date from the 13th century; earlier ones are in the Coptic Museum. The chapels dedicated to Cyrus and John occupy a wing to the north, through the door to the left of the raised altar (remove your shoes). This northern group of chapels, part of an earlier 4th or 5th century church, includes the baptistery.

Walk Through Old Cairo

If you have time, return to Abu Serga and turn right at the corner. Wander down the lanes for a glimpse of the ancient streets where few tourists go. Another small gate at the end of the northern street puts you back out on Sh. Mari Girgis. From there you can walk a few meters south to the entrance of the Greek Orthodox compound.

Greek Orthodox Church
Of St. George (Mari Girgis)

For centuries ownership of this church alternated between the Copts and Greeks, but since the late 15th century it has been Greek Orthodox. At that time, it contained a convent, a hospital, and an old people's home. In 1904 the complex burned, though most of the icons and relics were saved. The present structure dates from 1909,

and today serves as the seat of the Greek Orthodox patriarch. The entrance is inside the compound, up a curving stairway to your right.

As you ascend, you will encounter a relief of St. George and the dragon wrapped around the outer brickwork of the tower. The church itself follows the circular form of its supporting tower. Other than the oddity of being inside a round church, the interior offers the visitor little.

Amr's Mosque

LE3. Called the Old Mosque, this building still occupies the site of the Muslims' original encampment, and it's all that remains of Fustat. Tradition says that the site was chosen by Allah through a dove, for as Amr was striking his tent on his way to conquering Alexandria, he discovered a dove nesting in its folds. As Bedouin hospitality extended even to creatures, he left the tent standing. Upon his return, he decided to build his mosque on the site. Here, Amr, a man whose life nearly reached Islamic perfection, once stood and, with his companions, took actions and made decisions that determined Egypt's fate even into modern times.

The original building was small, of mud bricks, totally roofed over (undoubtedly thatch supported on palm logs), and lacking a central courtyard. This mosque served as the social, political, and the religious center of Fustat-Misr. As the Muslim population of Fustat continued to grow, the mosque was enlarged several times. In 673, the governor of Egypt introduced a central courtyard and minarets at each of it four corners. By 791 the building had reached half its present size, and in 827, Abdallah Ibn Ali doubled the mosque's area. Although it grew no larger, the Egyptian rulers continued to rebuild it, until today little of Amr's original construction remains; the mosque resembles the other beautiful courtyard mosques in Cairo.

Fustat

The old town, for centuries a garbage dump, is settled by the garbage collectors, mostly Copts, who live in shanties. Scattered among their homes are a few potters' shops that produce the jugs and decorations lining the highway. If you decide to explore Fustat, take plenty of water and watch where you step, as the ground in the old dump can be unstable.

ISLAMIC CAIRO

Perhaps the most fascinating parts of Cairo are the old Islamic sections. Except for the Khan al-Khalili area, most are rarely visited by casual tourists, giving you a chance to mingle with Cairenes. In some places you can almost revive the feel of the medieval city. Striped and scrolled stonework of Mamluk facades overlooks restless throngs of people, dogs, donkeys, and horse carts. Khan al-Khalili still houses the ancient marketplace, and behind it stands the old Fatimid city with its architectural masterpieces. At the southern gate of Bab Zuwayla, under the covered "street of the tentmakers," artisans still ply their needles. Nearby the Islamic Museum houses the best collection of Islamic art and crafts in the world. The mosques of Ibn Tulun and Sultan Hassan are world famous, and those on the Citadel and in the rest of Cairo are not far behind. Along the city's eastern edge stretches a vast Mamluk cemetery with funerary complexes dating from late Ayyubid times.

To see all the high points in only a few days, you'll need to rent a cab; otherwise you can take a week or more and really explore Islamic Cairo. You'll need at least a morning for the southern mosques—Ibn Tulun and the ones around the Citadel; or on a more leisurely schedule, you may want to spend the day at the Citadel (take a lunch and eat inside at the vista point or at the tables in the little park beside the outer walls of the entrance. The Khan and the streets north to the gates will take at least another day, and the area around Bab Zuwayla and the Islamic Museum a third.

Getting to these areas is not a problem, for most cab drivers know where they are; figure LE3-5 one-way, more in rush hours. Catching a ride back to central Cairo can be more problematic, especially from the Khan during rush hours—you may need LE10-15. Although buses also run, for those with stout legs, walking back is a less-crowded, more interesting option: head west—toward the Nile (you can't miss it). The areas, especially around the Khan and Bab Zuwayla, are safe and friendly. To get around inside the older areas you'll have to walk; the narrow streets make driving a nightmare.

Although entry to many of the mosques used to be free, they've been renovated and now you'll have to buy tickets: LE3-6 average, a few are more. Official ghaffirs will give you a ticket (tan with the amount stamped in the center of an Aton—the sun with hands); to prevent entrepreneurs from fleecing you, be sure to collect an untorn ticket printed with the name of the monument. Most of the monuments are open 0900-1400 or 1430, but the ones around Khan al-Khalili stay open later, often to 1900 or 2100. You won't be allowed in mosques during prayers, especially around 1100 or 1130 on Fridays. In some areas, especially the eastern cemeteries, women may not feel comfortable alone, but the rest of the areas are basically safe, especially if you dress conservatively. I wear a longish skirt, long-sleeved blouse, and carry a shawl to cover my head when entering. Remember, to most Egyptians, these buildings are holy; treat them with reverence.

THE MOSQUES

In Cairo all three types of classical mosques (the courtyard, the cruciform, and the Ottoman) lie within walking distance of each other, and two of the three are perfect examples of their types. The simple courtyard of the Mosque of Ibn Tulun is the oldest, and one of the most moving in the world. If you only see one mosque in Cairo, make it this one. While you're there, take in the Gayer-Anderson Museum, a restored 16th century Cairene house. The Madrasa of Sultan Hassan, built during Mamluk times, is equivalent to Ibn Tulun—the most beautiful and classical example of a Mamluk *madrasa*. The Ottoman mosque built by Muhammad Ali on the Citadel, while not as spectacular as its prototype in Istanbul, is nevertheless worth a look.

Getting There
You can visit all three mosques in a day; either hire a cab for the whole trip, or have it wait for

you at Ibn Tulun, then drop you off at the Citadel (you can walk down the hill to Sultan Hassan. If you're short of change or high on adventure, dismiss the cab at Ibn Tulun and walk to the rest; the even more adventurous can take the Metro to al-Sayyida Zaynab station, head north, and then east along Sh. Port Said (also known as Sh. al-Khalig al-Masri), to the mausoleum of Sayyida Zaynab, then east along Sh. Abd al-Magid al-Labbany (second right) to the Ibn Tulun mosque. To reach the Citadel from Ibn Tulun, go back up to this main road, which changes into Sh. al-Salbiyya and continue east where it eventually runs into Midan Salah al-Din. From the Citadel area, you can easily catch a cab or walk back to Tahrir.

Mosque Of Ahmad Ibn Tulun

Open 0900-1600; LE8. The entrance is on the east side of the building. (Don't confuse it with the towering minarets of the Mosque and the *madrasa* of Sarghatmish to the west, which are closed.) Ibn Tulun built the mosque in A.D. 876-879 to serve his administrative city of al-Qata. To protect it from the annual floods, he chose a rocky outcropping, a hill called Gebel Yashkur, and here the city flourished for 30 years. But then, sacked by the Abbasids when they reconquered Egypt and abandoned when the Fatimids shifted the capital north to al-Qahira, the city stagnated, and the mosque fell into ruin. Not until the close of the 13th century, when Amir Lagin took refuge there amid nasty rumors about his involvement in the assassination of the sultan, did the mosque's prospects change. Shocked by its decay, Lagin swore that if he ever got out of his current mess he would restore the building to its former glory.

When he became sultan, he kept his word and commissioned its restoration, which, unlike much Islamic "restoration," followed the general design and style of the original. Additions by succeeding sultans were minor, and not until King Fuad ordered the the crumbling building restored in 1882 did it receive intense work. The entrance is on the east side, and although the mosque is no longer used for services, you must remove your shoes.

Completed in 879, this building, which covers nearly 2.5 square km, has remained unchanged through the centuries. Its outer, crested walls,

the *ziyada,* protected the mosque from the crowding markets of the Tulunid city that surrounded it; the walls of the mosque itself, topped with matching crests, rise behind. The minaret, one of two built as spirals (the other is in Samarra), proclaims its Iraqi derivations. The doorways, both to the *ziyada* and the mosque, are framed in palm logs and cedar; at one time all had circular steps leading into the arcaded *riwaqs.*

Solid piers of baked brick, rather than the usual pillars cannibalized from Hellenistic churches and temples, support the arcades' arches. The vine-leafed designs on the small capitals of the nonsupporting columns embedded in the piers resemble the carved stucco of Samarra, as does similar work still visible under the arches. The designs were stamped in wet plaster with carved wooden molds.

The arcades of the *qiblah* wall rise above those of the other sides and shelter several *mihrabs,* a pair on either side of the *dikkah* (reading platform), which probably date from the 10th century, and a second pair that occupies the central columns of the second arcade, one of which was donated by Vizier al-Afdal in 1004; its mate is a copy by Sultan Lagin. To your right on the next arcade is the foundation inscription.

The wooden dome of the *qiblah* wall is Mamluk, but the main *mihrab* is more likely an Ottoman contribution. The *minbar* (made for Sultan Lagin in 1296), with its heavy carving and stalactite canopy, is one of the oldest and finest in Egypt. The door nearby once led to Ibn Tulun's Dar al-Imarah ("House of Government"), which also contained apartments where Ahmad would bathe before entering the mosque to lead Friday prayers. The *kufic* inscription just under the roof runs around the entire mosque (two km) and contains about 15% of the Koran. Legend says that some of the sycamore planks were from Noah's Ark, which was said to have landed on Gebel Yashkur. Of the window grills, those on the east wall with the arcs and circles are originals, while the rest date to Sultan Lagin's restoration.

The fountain in the center of the *sahn,* (courtyard) also dates from Sultan Lagin's restoration. Inside, a carved stalactite frieze runs along the dome drum, and above it the *naskhi* script quotes verses from the Koran on ablution (ritual washing).

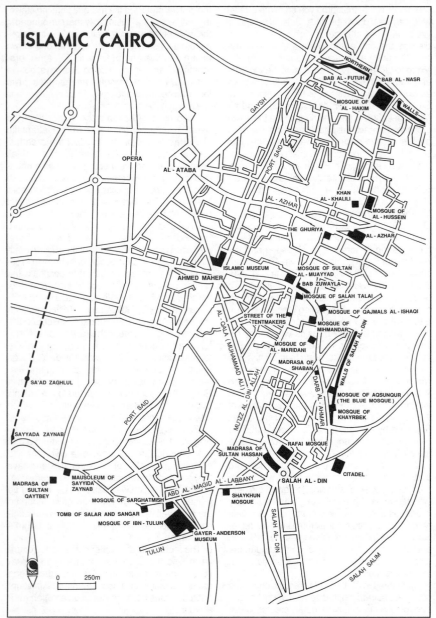

ISLAMIC CAIRO

BAB AL - FUTUH

BAB AL - NASR

NORTHERN

WALLS

MOSQUE OF
AL - HAKIM

GAYSH

PORT SAID

OPERA

AL - ATABA

KHAN
AL - KHALILI

AL - AZHAR

MOSQUE OF
AL - HUSSEIN

THE GHURIYA

AL - AZHAR

ISLAMIC MUSEUM

MOSQUE OF SULTAN
AL - MUAYYAD

AHMED MAHER

BAB ZUWAYLA

MOSQUE OF SALAH TALAI

STREET OF THE
TENTMAKERS

MOSQUE OF QAJMALS AL - ISHAQI

MOSQUE OF
MIHMANDAR

AL - QALA (MUHAMMAD ALI)

MOSQUE OF
AL - MARIDANI

WALLS OF SALAH AL - DIN

MADRASA OF
SHABAN

SA'AD ZAGHLUL

DARB AL - AHMAR

MOSQUE OF AQSUNQUR
(THE BLUE MOSQUE)

MOSQUE OF
KHAYRBEK

PORT SAID

MUIZZ AL - DIN - ALLAH

SAYYADA ZAYNAB

RAFAI MOSQUE

MADRASA OF
SULTAN HASSAN

MADRASA OF
SULTAN
QAYTBEY

MAUSOLEUM OF
SAYYIDA
ZAYNAB

CITADEL

SALAH AL - DIN

ABD AL - MAGID AL - LABBANY

MOSQUE OF SARGHATMISH

SHAYKHUN
MOSQUE

SALAH AL - DIN

TOMB OF SALAR AND SANGAR

MOSQUE OF IBN - TULUN

GAYER - ANDERSON
MUSEUM

TULUN

SALAH SALIM

0   250m

© MOON PUBLICATIONS INC.

The minaret (40 meters high) is between the mosque and its *ziyada* wall. When the mosque fell into decay, Ibn Tulun's descendants sold the building to the Fatimid khalif, al-Hakim, and began to demolish the minaret to sell the stone for scrap, claiming they'd sold only the mosque. The khalif objectd and put a stop to the dismantling. Sultan Lagin repaired the damaged lower part with the current square base, so the limestone tower retains only part of the original circular pattern of its Samarran prototype.

The minaret was once capped with a gold boat, (perhaps a folk memory of the solar barge of Re), which was blown down in 1694 during a violent storm and has since disappeared. You can climb the circular staircase, but it has no railing, so take care. The view is terrific, but not if you're acrophobic and it's a windy day. To the northeast lies the Citadel and the domes of Muhammad Ali's mosque; to the west, if the day is clear, you can see the pyramids of Giza.

Gayer-Anderson House
(Bayt Al-Kritliya)
Open Sat.-Thurs. 0900-1530, Fri. 0900-1100 and 1330-1530; LE8 (tel. 847-822). Located at the southeast corner of Ibn Tulun's mosque, two 16th-century houses are joined by an elevated bridge. The western house was built by Abd al-Qadar al-Haddad (the smith) in 1540; its two grilled windows on the southwest corner mark a *sabil* (fountain), rare in private homes. The eastern house dates from 1631, and the two were joined and furnished by Major Gayer-Anderson, who combed Cairo for Ottoman furnishings. The entrance is on the south side; the short alley between the two houses must resemble medieval Cairo streets with their overhanging *mashribiyya* balconies. The house on the right served as a *haramlik* or women's quarters; the one on the left, the *salamlik* for the men. The tour begins in the courtyard of the *haramlik*, works its way up to the roof where the women could enjoy a sitting area, crosses over the bridge, and exits through the *salamlik*.

The house includes typical furnishings for traditional rooms as well as additional ones fitted out as a writing room, a library, and a museum where the major housed his collection of pharaonic antiquities. In addition, he imported furniture, and gold and lacquer panels for one of the bedrooms, from Damascus. The *qa'a* (sitting room) on the lower floor of the *salamlik* is perhaps one of the most beautiful in Cairo, with its polychrome central fountain, opulent ceiling, and ornate *mashribiyya* screens, which shielded the ladies as they watched the action below.

The legends surrounding the house are nearly as interesting as the structure. Under the protection of their patron saint al-Hussein (grandson of Muhammad), the inhabitants of the house enjoyed his blessings. The well of the house, says another legend, taps the magical, curative waters from the Great Flood. This same well is said to be the entrance to the palace of the King of the Jinn (evil spirits) who guards vast treasures by magic; his seven daughters also sleep in his underground palace, chained to their golden beds by spells.

SIGHTS OF THE CITADEL AREA

To reach the Madrasa of Sultan Hassan and the Citadel, return to Sh. al-Habbany (Salbiyya) and head east, keeping to the main road, which will bring you out on Midan Salah al-Din; head north. The Citadel will rise to your right, the fortress-like *madrasa* of Sultan Hassan on your left.

Madrasa Of Sultan Hassan
Open 0800-1800; LE6. This 14th-century complex, built primarily of stone rather than brick, is one of the world's largest mosques. Designed to house the sultan's *madrasa* or religious school as well as his tomb, it was started in 1356 and completed four years later, after Hassan's disappearance. The design is a masterful stroke of architectural sleight of hand. The structure's outer walls as well as its inner spaces are cleverly mis-aligned to give the impression of a single square mass; however, a glance at the floor plan shows that its actual shape is bent nearly 30 degrees, making the *qiblah* of the mausoleum face Mecca, while the walls align with the street. The domed tomb on the southeast end of the building faces the square (where it would be in full view of the Mamluk parade-ground and central *midan*), lying between the worshippers in the mosque and Mecca (forcing the faithful to pray in the direction of the tomb as well).

The building's 150-meter length, emphasized by the vertical bays, and its towering height dominate the street. The clear exterior lines and the subordination of detail to the whole are hallmarks of Mamluk architecture and make it a textbook example. Its stone blocks resemble a fortress, and in fact, the mosque was used several times to siege the Citadel; cannon holes remain on the front wall of the mausoleum. The fleur-de-lis crests once circled the entire mosque, but the Ottomans removed many of them to lighten the roof's weight.

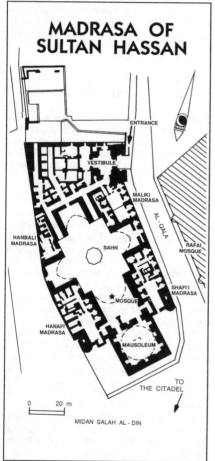

MADRASA OF SULTAN HASSAN

ENTRANCE

VESTIBULE

MALIKI MADRASA

AL-QALA

HANBALI MADRASA

SAHN

RAFAI MOSQUE

SHAFI'I MADRASA

MOSQUE

HANAFI MADRASA

MAUSOLEUM

TO THE CITADEL

0   20 m

MIDAN SALAH AL-DIN

© MOON PUBLICATIONS, INC.

The 80-meter-high minaret at the end of the western wall is the tallest in Cairo. Although the original design called for four minarets, only three were built. The west one fell in 1361, killing over 300 people; three centuries later, the east minaret fell and the following year the dome, which was riddled with holes from the Citadel guns, collapsed. Rebuilt in 1671 by Ibrahim Pasha, the dome and minaret are the only changes from the original Mamluk design.

The entrance, bent at 30 degrees from the outer wall, dominates the street, but is best appreciated from Midan Salah al-Din. Spiral-cut pilasters set into either side augment the strong vertical lines created by the panels on each side of the porch. The black stone embedded in the facade, a feature of many Cairene mosques, may represent the Kabah in Mecca. The doors are modern; the originals rest in the Islamic Museum. The ornate stalactite domes of the entryway might well frame the entrance to a magical land. Once inside, don't neglect the vestibule: take in the ornate ceiling, the beautifully finished paneling, and enjoy the bay window on your right. The corridor leads upward toward the main *sahn* and eventually emerges into the mosque's brilliant sunlit courtyard.

The interior of the *madrasa* is of brick faced with stucco, though many of the decorative details are in stone. The tall *liwans* outline the cruciform floorplan, and the doors at their sides lead to each of four schools of Islamic theology; the upper windows are those of students' rooms. The figure-eight chains hanging from the *liwans* once held enameled-glass mosque lamps, many now in the Islamic Museum; they have been replaced by reproductions. The Ottoman fountain, originally for decoration (for Muslims conceive of heaven as a beautiful garden with running water), now provides water for ritual cleansing before prayers. The eastern *liwan* serves as the mosque, and retains much of its original decoration, the marble paneling characteristic of Mamluk architecture. The *minbar* (pulpit) is of stone, its doors bronze-covered wood set into a wooden frame with a stalactite crown. The marble inlay *mihrab*, is faced with Crusader-style columns. The stucco inscription carved in monumental *kufic* surrounding the *liwan* tells of Allah's mercy and the paradise awaiting the true believer. The doors on the *qiblah* wall lead directly into the tomb chamber; the one on the right retains its original gold and silver inlay on the brass covering. The actual entrance is to the left.

The decoration inside the mausoleum continues the style of the main mosque; the marble paneling is cleated into wooden frames and Koranic inscriptions run under the dome. The mihrab, slightly smaller than the main one, has faience rather than marble decorations. The corner squinches of carved, gilded, and painted wood are the lower supports of the original dome. The recently renovated kursi (lectern) supported a huge, open Koran while the reader sat cross-legged on the platform. The central tabut (tomb) of colored marble doesn't house Hassan's body, for he disappeared one night riding his white donkey among the Moqattam Hills. His family, however, is buried here. Through the window to the left you can see the Bab al-Azab, the main gate of the Citadel. Above it, to the right, is the tower of Katkhuda al-Azab Mosque, and above it still, the mosque of Muhammad Ali.

Al-Rafai

Open 0800-1800; LE6. As an echo of the madrasa of Sultan Hassan, al-Rafai was built at the turn of the century in the Mamluk style of its older neighbor. Its designer, Hussein Fakhri, gambled on challenging Hassan's building and won. The two structures blend, each strengthening the other. Together they dominate not only the street but the entire area. The mosque itself, built on orders from Princess Dowager Khushyar, houses the tombs of two older Sufis as well as her own, plus those of Khedive Ismail, Sultan Hussein Kamil, King Fuad, and Muhammad Reza Pahlavi, the late shah of Iran. The interior, designed by Herz Bey, uses 19 different types of marble, and comprises a collection of Cairene ornamentation. The entrance lies just across the parkway from Sultan Hassan's madrasa.

Mosque Of Aqsunqur (Blue Mosque)

Cairo's other notable mosque, Aqsunqur, lies north of the Citadel along Sh. Bab al-Wazir, which becomes Darb al-Ahmar. (You can also reach the Blue Mosque from Bab Zuwayla.) Built by one of al-Nasir Muhammad's amirs, the mosque's facade is covered with blue-gray mar-

ble, but it gets its name from the Ottoman tiles installed around 1650 by Ibrahim Aga, who redecorated the mosque and used it for his own tomb. The cruciform mosque contains a good example of a Mamluk mihrab; its geometric patterns of carved and inlaid marble and mosaics reflect the soft plum, salmon, gray, and green. The Isnik tiles, however, set the tone, their blue and turquoise colors outlining plants and flowers. Coupled with the marble panels and painted ceilings they create a rich interior.

THE CITADEL

Open Sat.-Thurs. 0800-1800, Fri. 0800-1100 and 1300-1800; in winter it closes at 1700 and Fri. hours are 0800-1000 and 1200-1700; LE14. The Citadel and the Midan Salah al-Din served as the center of Islamic Cairo from the time that Salah al-Din installed his government at the Citadel until the end of Turkish rule. The Mamluks used it for equestrian practice, and the royal stables lined the square under the protective walls of the fortress. Amirs built palaces nearby, perhaps to keep tabs on the shifting balance of power within the Citadel, and the Midan became a focus for expansive Mamluk building programs.

Egypt's early conquerers did not immediately recognize the military importance of the Citadel's location, and for years the hill only provided governors a view from a sheltered pavilion, Qubbat al-Howa ("Dome of the Winds"). As part of Salah al-Din's plan to fortify the entire city, he ordered a fortress raised on the hill and encased in a wall of stone blocks, many of them mined from the smaller pyramids at Giza. Behind the western walls several layers of palaces, administrative offices, and religious buildings lay tucked into the hillside. Towers reinforced the walls and supported medieval gates that led to the Citadel's interior.

Sitting on a spur of limestone that had been detached from its parent Moqattam Hills by quarrying, the fortress guarded the only reasonable access to Upper Egypt. For nearly 700 years it housed the central government and was rebuilt twice, once when al-Nasir Muhammad leveled most of Salah al-Din's Ayyubid buildings, and again when Muhammad Ali flattened the Mamluk structures to con-

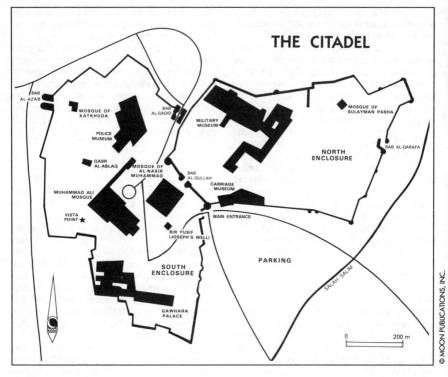

THE CITADEL

BAB
AL-AZAB

MOSQUE OF
KATKHUDA

BAB
AL-GADID

POLICE
MUSEUM

MILITARY
MUSEUM

MOSQUE OF
SULAYMAN PASHA

BAB AL-QARAFA

NORTH
ENCLOSURE

QASR
AL-ABLAQ

MOSQUE OF
AL-NASIR
MUHAMMAD

BAB
AL-QULLAH

CARRIAGE
MUSEUM

MUHAMMAD ALI
MOSQUE

VISTA
POINT ★

MAIN ENTRANCE

BIR YUSIF
(JOSEPH'S WELL)

SOUTH
ENCLOSURE

PARKING

SALAH SALIM

GAWHARA
PALACE

0   200 m

© MOON PUBLICATIONS, INC.

struct his administrative center, mosque, and palace. Today, the billowing roof and spike-like minarets of his mosque dominate Cairo's skyline, but they sit atop a jumble of Ayyubid, Mamluk, and neo-Ottoman buildings.

Bab Al-Azab

Directly on the Midan, the twin rounded towers of Bab al-Azab protected the original entrance. This gate was the site of Muhammad Ali's bloody massacre of the Mamluks whose political and economic power had caused continual unrest. As a pretense, he invited the local dignitaries to dinner, a celebration of his son's departure on a military campaign in Arabia. At the feast's conclusion, the Mamluks mounted their horses to descend into the city. As they passed between these massive towers, Muhammad Ali's followers dropped the gates, trapping the beys and massacring them. Only

one escaped (Hassan), who legend says jumped his horse off the ramparts, but scholars claim, unromantically, that Hassan was sick that fateful night and never made it to the banquet. When he heard of his comrades' fate, being a prudent man, he fled to Nubia. The gate was rebuilt in 1754, and the brass-bound wooden doors date from that time.

Getting There

Today, the Bab al-Azab is sealed and you have to go around to the east side of the Citadel to the new parking lot. Head south along Sh. Salah al-Din to Salah Salim and turn east. Or you can take minibus #54 from the Arab League building.

The Walls

Salah al-Din not only fortified the Citadel, but also ran walls around the entire city; many sections still stand, especially on the east. The approach via

Salah Salim exposes the business side of the Citadel; its watch towers pierced with arrow slits rise several stories above the ramparts. The smaller towers are the work of Salah al-Din, but the larger ones were added by al-Kamil. The walls incorporated several innovations; most importantly, the redesigned archer's slits that permitted firing at enemies storming the base of the wall, and fortified doors within the walls enabled defenders to seal off individual parts against invaders.

The interior of the Citadel is divided into two compounds, north and south: the northern enclosed the military and civic areas, the southern, the royal living quarters. Within the southern walls lie Muhammad Ali's mosque, a police museum, a courtyard-type mosque built by al-Nasr Muhammad, Yusif's well, and Gawhara Palace. The northern section houses the military museum, a small carriage collection, and the tiny Ottoman mosque of Sulayman Pasha.

Mosque Of Muhammad Ali
Built in the Turkish imperial style, the mosque is covered by multiple domes; the smaller ones and the half domes buttress the outward thrust of the massive central vault. The minarets, which rise from bases only three meters a side, soar nearly 80 meters high, piercing the Cairo skyline. The mosque, in its complete rejection of Mamluk architecture (at a time when Egyptian designs were infiltrating Ottoman and Syrian building), and in its location atop the rubble of the Mamluk administrative center, perhaps makes a stronger political statement than an architectural one.

The outside of the mosque is sheathed in alabaster, and on the south side is a sitting area; on a rare, clear day you can see the pyramids at Giza. The entrance is on the north side. The courtyard features a Turkish fountain of the same design as the popular *sabils* scattered throughout Cairo. The baroque clock on the west side was a gift of King Louis Philippe, who in 1884 traded it for the obelisk that now graces the Place de la Concorde in Paris.

The mosque interior impresses through its size and space—the specialty of Ottoman design; the domes, raised on pillars that nearly disappear into the background, seem to float weightless and massless over the warm glow of softly filtered light. Muhammad Ali is buried behind the grill to the right of the entrance, under the marble cenotaph. The large gilded wooden *minbar* is the original; the smaller alabaster one a gift of King Faruq in 1939.

Mosque Of Sultan Al-Nasir Muhammad
This jewel sits just across the road from the mosque of Muhammad Ali, all that remains of al-Nasir's massive building program here. From its double minarets with their unusual glazed faience decoration, muezzins called the faithful to prayer. Once the principal mosque of the Citadel, this congregational mosque was stripped of its marble decorations by Sultan Salim, who carried them back to Turkey. The miscellaneous columns—pharaonic, classical, and Christian—supporting the double arches of the *riwaqs* fit into a surprisingly unified whole. The restored *qiblah* is capped by a large dome, and the wooden ceiling and stalactites are worth a look.

Yusif's Well
Turn right as you leave al-Nasir's mosque and keep to the right until you reach the tower that protects the well. Built by Crusader prisoners, it plunges 97 meters to tap the natural seepage from the Nile. Normally, aqueducts below the cliffs provided water for the Citadel; it was raised from the Nile by *saqiyas*. (The remains of the aqueduct run along Salah Salim to the Nile where the old pump house still stands.) Yusif's Well was to provide water in case of a siege, but it nevertheless supplied a considerable volume throughout its working life. Its spiral stairs were once covered with dirt so donkeys could haul up the water raised by oxen on wooden platforms turning *saqiyas*.

Mosque Of Sulayman Pasha
Behind the military museum in the northern enclosure stands a tiny, intimate mosque within its garden. Built next to the Fatimid tomb of Sidi Sarya, it displays an Ottoman style tall, slender minaret and a single dome covering the entire sanctuary that rests, like the larger Muhammad Ali mosque, on triangular pendentives buttressed with half domes. The names of God, Muhammad, Abu Bakr, Umar, Uthman, and Ali appear in the large medallions, a reminder to the Sunni of their religious heritage. The floral motifs were brought by the Ottomans, but much of the rest of the decoration, the geometric patterns for example, is Mamluk in feel.

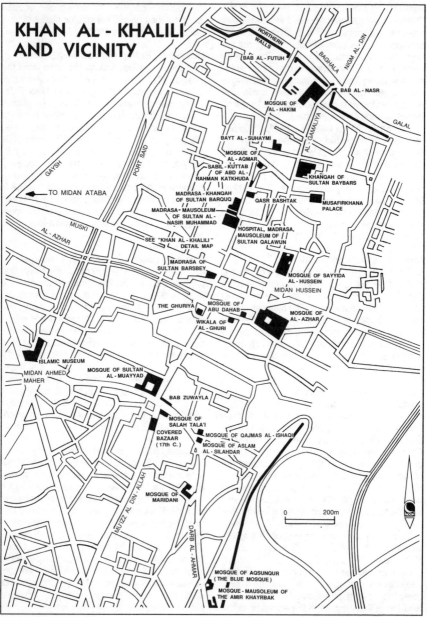

KHAN AL - KHALILI AND VICINITY

NORTHERN WALLS

BAB AL - FUTUH

BAGHALA

NIGM AL - DIN

BAB AL - NASR

MOSQUE OF AL - HAKIM

GALAL

AL - GAMALIYA

BAYT AL - SUHAYMI

MOSQUE OF AL - AQMAR

SABIL - KUTTAB OF ABD AL - RAHMAN KATKHUDA

KHANQAH OF SULTAN BAYBARS

GAYSH

PORT SAID

TO MIDAN ATABA

MADRASA - KHANQAH OF SULTAN BARQUQ

MADRASA - MAUSOLEUM OF SULTAN AL - NASIR MUHAMMAD

QASR BASHTAK

MUSAFIRKHANA PALACE

MUSKI

HOSPITAL, MADRASA, MAUSOLEUM OF SULTAN QALAWUN

AL - AZHAR

SEE "KHAN AL - KHALILI" DETAIL MAP

MADRASA OF SULTAN BARSBEY

MOSQUE OF SAYYIDA AL - HUSSEIN

MIDAN HUSSEIN

THE GHURIYA

MOSQUE OF ABU DAHAB

WIKALA OF AL - GHURI

MOSQUE OF AL - AZHAR

ISLAMIC MUSEUM

MIDAN AHMED MAHER

MOSQUE OF SULTAN AL - MUAYYAD

BAB ZUWAYLA

MOSQUE OF SALAH TALA'I

COVERED BAZAAR (17th C.)

MOSQUE OF QAJMAS AL - ISHAQI

MOSQUE OF ASLAM AL - SILAHDAR

IMUZZ AL DIN - ALLAH

MOSQUE OF MARIDANI

DARB AL - AHMAR

0   200m

MOSQUE OF AQSUNQUR (THE BLUE MOSQUE)

MOSQUE - MAUSOLEUM OF THE AMIR KHAYRBAK

Gawhara Palace

Muhammad Ali waited in the Gawhara Palace on the far side of the southern enclosure while his henchmen massacred the Mamluk beys below. It burned in 1972, but has now been reopened as a museum displaying furniture and art belonging to the family and descendants of Muhammad Ali. The other museums occupying the enclosure are fun if you have the time. The carriage collection in the northern one displays not only state carriages, but many used by the royal family. The sixth Tut chariot, found in over two hundred pieces, has been painstakingly restored and now rests just inside the military museum.

FROM KHAN AL-KHALILI TO THE NORTHERN WALLS

The bazaar of Khan al-Khalili occupies the northwestern corner of Midan al-Hussein. This heart of the Fatimid city remains a center of Cairo. During Ramadan evenings, the square in front of the mosque is packed with those who come for the concerts and performances—Cairo's own nightly celebration of the holy month. Behind the bazaar, the old road that once bisected the Fatimid city is lined with shops, mosques, and mausoleums—many of Cairo's most beautiful Islamic buildings. Here, and to the south, Egyptians ignore the touristy sections of Khan al-Khalili to surge through al-Muski, bartering and bargaining at the tiny booths for cotton and wool, plastic housewares, tennies, and the latest tapes and videos. The wealthier residents seek out the antique shops tucked into odd corners and back streets. Students congregate in al-Azhar's courtyards, just as they did 1,000 years ago, and al-Ghuriya plays host to occasional concerts, often of classical European music. The square is dominated by the mosque of Sayyidna Hussein, one of the few in Egypt closed to visitors. The Khan across the *midan*, filled with branching, covered alleys and shops tucked into dead-end halls and up twisting, narrow stairs, is a shoppers' paradise.

Getting There

Taxis are the easiest way to get to Khan al-Khalili and the surrounding areas of Islamic

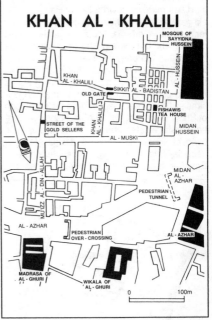

KHAN AL-KHALILI

MOSQUE OF SAYYIDNA HUSSEIN
AL-HUSSEIN
KHAN AL-KHALILI
SIKKIT AL-BADISTAN
OLD GATE
FISHAWIS TEA HOUSE
STREET OF THE GOLD SELLERS
KHAN AL-KHALILI
MIDAN HUSSEIN
AL-MUSKI
MIDAN AL-AZHAR
MUIZZ AL-DIN-ALLAH
PEDESTRIAN TUNNEL
AL-AZHAR
AL-AZHAR
PEDESTRIAN OVER-CROSSING
AL-AZHAR
MADRASA OF AL-GHURI
WIKALA OF AL-GHURI
0   100m

© MOON PUBLICATIONS, INC.

Cairo; flag one off the street; it will be about LE3-5 from Tahrir. The main street running into the area is divided, so have the driver let you off at the pedestrian overpass or use the underground tunnel at al-Azhar Mosque; otherwise the driver will have to go past the Hussein mosque and make a U-turn—a process that can consume half an hour. You can normally catch a cab back from the Khan, but the walk down Sh. al-Muski is a nice alternative; you can either catch a cab at the end or, if you're a walker, continue toward the Nile. The cheap, broke, or adventurous can get to the Khan via minibus #77 from the Arab League Building (facing the Egyptian Museum). Getting a car through Islamic Cairo takes a miracle of Allah, so plan on doing most of your sightseeing on foot.

Khan Al-Khalili

Located in the middle of the ancient Fatimid city, the bazaars of Khan al-Khalili and al-Muski (to the west) comprise one of Cairo's major shopping areas. Khan al-Khalili (or simply "the

Khan") was built in 1382, and the original courtyard lies midway down Sikkit al-Badistan; the old gate still guards the entrance. Often a center for subversive groups, it was frequently a target of raids, and thus Sultan Ghawri rebuilt much of the area in the early 16th century. Historically filled with foreign merchants, the Khan has now lost many of them, and the remaining shops tend to cater to tourists, though many Egyptians still shop here, especially in the area north of Sh. al-Badistan. The famous Fishawis's teahouse still exists, though half its former size, haunt of Nobel laureate Nagib Mahfuz. Al-Muski, especially as it runs west, is devoted more to Egyptian buyers; escape the high prices and haggling here. You can find better deals for gold and silver to the west of the Khan, along the "street of the goldsellers."

The Old City

Khan al-Khalili and the *midan* occupy the center of the old Fatimid city, its central street still runs along the west side of the Khan. Sh. Mu'izz al-Din Allah is known on the end near al-Muski as the "street of the goldsellers," and farther north, "street of the coppersmiths." Gawhar built the palaces for his rulers along this street, and where they once stood, Mamluks and Turks built some of Cairo's architectural masterpieces: tombs, schools, hospitals, and religious centers.

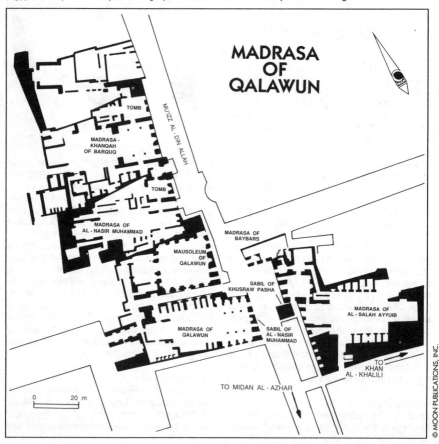

MADRASA
OF
QALAWUN

MU'IZZ AL - DIN ALLAH

TOMB

MADRASA -
KHANQAH
OF BARQUQ

TOMB

MADRASA OF
AL - NASIR MUHAMMAD

MAUSOLEUM
OF
QALAWUN

MADRASA OF
BAYBARS

SABIL OF
KHUSRAW PASHA

MADRASA OF
AL - SALAH AYYUIB

MADRASA OF
QALAWUN

SABIL OF
AL - NASIR
MUHAMMAD

TO
KHAN
AL - KHALILI

0   20 m

TO MIDAN AL - AZHAR

© MOON PUBLICATIONS, INC.

Maristan (Hospital), Madrasa, and Mausoleum Of Sultan Qalawun

An energetic ruler, Sultan al-Mansur Qalawun held off both the Mongols and Christians and founded a dynasty that lasted for three generations. He died in 1290 on his way to attack the Crusader fortress at Acre. His buildings, the earliest examples of the new Syrian styles and techniques, display typical Mamluk architecture: imposing scale coupled with delicate ornamentation. The complex occupies the west side of the street, its entrance just past the jutting corner of the *madrasa*.

The massive exterior with its columned windows appears almost Gothic, an impression undoubtedly intended, for Qalawun was familiar with Crusader churches. The doorway design of interlaced polychrome masonry *ablaq* stems directly from that area, and the square bottom and middle stories of the minaret recall Syrian designs. However, its interlacing arcades have a western Moorish feel and may well be the work of Spanish or Moroccan craftsmen. The cap was added in the Ottoman period.

The entrance to the complex is marked by a heavy wooden door decorated with bronze polygons—early examples of the geometric designs favored by Mamluks. To the left, off the corridor with its original beam-and-coffered ceiling, stands Qalawun's *madrasa*.

The **madrasa** is a courtyard with a *liwan* at either end. The school's sanctuary at the east end, with its three aisles, classical columns, and arched clerestory, recalls Syrian basilican churches, as does the *mihrab* with its glass mosaics. Little remains of the original **maristan,** which Qalawun staffed to treat all known illnesses of the age. Open to all in need, it was equipped with the most modern conveniences, including musicians and storytellers to entertain the patients. The hospital lies at the rear of the complex, and since Qalawun's time, the area has always supported medical-care facilities; today a modern eye clinic occupies the spot.

The **mausoleum** is the most beautiful part of the complex, perhaps the most beautiful building in Cairo. The entrance courtyard provides a quiet setting in which to contemplate the intricate stucco that decorates the facade and the refined joinery that screens the doorway. Inside,

the octagonal drum rises on square piers and ancient pink granite columns; the soaring dome is lighted with intense color from jewel-like glass set in plaster carved with arabesque designs. Inlaid marble strips, panels of polychrome stone, rich gilding, and the painted coffered ceiling give an idea of the visual wealth—the rich hues and shadowy stillness—that Mamluk decorative arts created. The window casements of the *qiblah* wall itself reveal their varying thickness—the common architectural trick in Egypt to align the *qiblah* wall with Mecca and the facade with the street. The *mihrab,* its hood entirely decorated with polychrome marble and its niche divided into registers of mosaic inlay and blind arcades, embodies the designs that dominate Mamluk decoration.

Madrasa-Mausoleum Of Al-Nasir Muhammad

Built by one of Qalawun's five sons, al-Nasir Muhammad, the complex is laid out along the same plans as his father's. Al-Nasir ruled intermittently between 1293 and 1340, the highpoint of Mamluk culture, and his buildings reflect their taste. The Gothic portal, stolen from a Crusader church in Acre, ranks as one of the finest in the world. Although little remains of the building itself, the four *liwans* provided homes for the four schools of Sunni jurisprudence. The minaret's square shaft of brick rising from the walls of the central corridor is covered with filigree-like stucco decoration. Al-Nasir, whose minaret was built about the same time as the restoration undertaken on that of Qalawun, undoubtedly employed the same workmen. The second story probably dates from the 15th century, and the top from Ottoman times.

Madrasa-Khanqah Of Barquq

Standing just north of the al-Nasir complex, this school and living quarters for Sufi mystics was built nearly a century after its neighbor. Barquq, the first of the "tower" or Burgi Mamluks to reign, took power in 1382. In spite of the complex's late date, the building continues the traditions of the early Mamluk style. The long, horizontal facade is lightened by the vertical thrust of the minaret and the narrow recessed panels that frame the windows. This minaret, like many of the same period, is octagonal, and its decoration combines 14th century stonework with 15th century carving—the interlaced circles a variation on the intersecting arches of Qalawun's minaret. Barquq's offset entrance boasts bronze-plated doors inlaid with silver; his name appears on the raised boss of the central star. The vaulted, bending corridor opens into a *sahn* (courtyard), the center of a cruciform plan. Four doors in the corners led to rooms for both Sufis and students. The ceiling of the *qiblah* (on the right), is supported by porphyry columns quarried along the Red Sea coast (near Safaga) by pharaonic miners.

Qasr Bashtak

Turn right at the first street past Barquq's mausoleum; the entrance to the palace is off the side alley to the right—you may need to find the guard with the key; he also has the key to Katkhuda's *sabil-kuttab*. Dating from the same period as Qalawun's complex, the palace of Bashtak is one of the most impressive secular remains of medieval Cairo. The building, recently restored by the German Archaeological Institute, was built by Amir Bashtak, who had married al-Nasir Muhammad's daughter. The palace originally stood five stories high, and all floors had running water. Today the *qa'a,* the great reception hall, gives only a glimpse of the grandeur of high society in the Mamluk period. Upstairs, the *haramlik* windows, screened in *mashribiyya* for privacy, looked out over the street, and the screened balconies over the *qa'a* gave the women of the house a chance to partake of the entertainment enjoyed by the men below.

Sabil-kuttab Of
Abd Al-Rahman Katkhuda

(The key is with the guard at Qasr Bashtak.) During the Ottoman period, rich patrons often built public fountains with Koranic schools above them. Katkhuda's fountain-school commands the corner at the fork of the street just past Qasr Bashtak. From behind the screened windows a cistern supplied water to a trough in which people could dip their cups. Built in 1744, the *sabil-kuttab* shows Mamluk traits in the joggled voussoirs of its window arches, the engaged corner columns, and the stalactite cornice, but the realistic floral patterns between the arches stem from Mongol models. The lower floor's interior is faced with Syrian tiles that, in the northeast corner, form a picture of the Kabah at Mecca. Although the modern municipal water system has closed the fountain portion, the school was used until recently.

Mosque Of Al-Aqmar

Situated just up the street from Katkhuda's *sabil-kuttab,* al-Aqmar's mosque (built 1125) is one of the few nearly intact Fatimid structures. The facade, one of the first to use stone, includes the ribbed-shell hood of the entrance with a pierced medallion—a decoration that evolved into the later cuspidate, ribbed, blind, keel-arch designs that still adorn Cairo's buildings. Shell-topped niches and panels of stalactites appear for the first time, and the decorations on the left wing— the star below the mosque lamp and the potted plant as well as the name of Ali—point to the Shi'i beliefs of the Fatimids.

Bayt Al-Suhaymi

To find this house, go north (up Sh. al-Mu'izz) for a block, then turn right; the house lies in the center of the block; a small plate marks the entrance. Dating from the 17th century, it displays the features that adapted Cairo's townhouses to the city's climate. Built around a central courtyard, the house's spaces, with the exception of the segregation between men's *(salamlik)* and women's *(haramlik)* quarters, were not divided by use, but rather by the climate, with some areas like the *qa'a* (main hall) inhabited in winter or in the chilly evenings while occupants gravitated to the shady courtyard, balconies, and roofs in the warmer weather. The thick walls, fountains, high ceilings, and marble floors kept the hot air from Cairo summers at bay, and in the evening, the north-facing *maq'ad* (wind scoop) caught the prevailing breezes and circulated cool air throughout the house. The *mashribiyya* and remaining furnishings give the visitor a good idea of a private, if wealthy, Egyptian home.

Mosque Of Al-Hakim

Located at the north end of Sh. Mu'izz al-Din Allah, on the right (east) just inside the Fatimid gate, this courtyard mosque, which covers nearly the same area as that of Ibn Tulun, was built by the eccentric Hakim. During its checkered history, the building has served as a prison for captive Crusaders, a stable for Salah al-Din, a warehouse for Napoleon, and under Nasser, a boys' school. Recently it has been "restored" (read: rebuilt) by an Ismaili Shi'i sect, which has encased the mosque in gleaming marble—destroying completely its history. Small parts of the original decoration remain only in the wooden tie-beams and the stucco carving in the clerestory. Unless you want to see what unlimited funds can do to a large courtyard mosque, don't bother visiting al-Hakim's; the people in charge are incredibly rude.

The modernization, however, didn't destroy the minarets, which, for reasons unknown, Hakim ordered encased in large square buttresses. The much smaller original bases remain intact inside these covers. The oldest surviving minarets in Cairo, they stand at the outer walls of the mosque, as did many from this period. The 1303 earthquake toppled the upper stories; the present tops date from the Mamluk period.

Northern Gates And Walls

In A.D. 1087, Cairo's original sun-dried-brick walls were replaced by stone fortifications. The Fatimid builders created masterpieces of Islamic military architecture. They insisted upon meticulous attention to details in their design and construction; the projecting towers, for example, let defenders take aim at attackers trying to scale the wall. The western **Bab al-Futuh** is the counterpart to the Bab Zuwayla; opening on either end of the main street, they mark the north and south limits of the Fatimid city. If you can find the keeper, you can go inside the gate—bring a flashlight. The more eastern **Bab al-Nasr** ("Gate of Victory") is flanked by square towers but otherwise the plan is similar to its sister gate at the west. The inscription, "Tour Courbin," testifies to Napoleon's garrisons, which occupied the fortifications (1799-1801). To return to Khan al-Khalili, walk though Bab al-Nasr and follow Sh. al-Gamaliya, which runs parallel to the Fatimid main street.

Khanqah Of Sultan
Baybars Al-Gashankir

Built in A.D. 1310, this Sufi monastery is the oldest surviving *khanqah* in Cairo. Salah al-Din introduced these structures, along with *madrasas,* during the Sunni revival following the ouster of the Shi'i Fatimids. Appearing here for the first time as part of a royal tomb complex, the *khanqah* once housed 400 Sufis. Although the monastery was closed by al-Nasr Muhammad at the time he had Baybars executed, it was soon reopened.

Entrance to the complex is over a square pharaonic column—complete with hieroglyphs—that serves as a step to the recessed copper-decorated door. The tomb lies to the left of the entrance, through a screened antechamber. Baybar's body—after al-Nasir relented—was buried in the tomb, as was that of a local sheikh (Muhammad Amin al-Husayni) who was interred in 1939.

The entrance to the courtyard of the *khanqah* is through the traditional bent entrance—an adaptation of military architecture used in civilian buildings to screen the interior from the street. The Sufis' cells flank the two *liwans,* and the decoration, including the ribbed shells, engaged columns, and ribbed, keel-arched frames, hark back to Fatimid motifs.

The minaret, which lacks the usual octagonal section, carries round tiers directly above the square; the ribbed, domed canopy (typical of Mamluk architecture) was once covered in green tiles of which only traces remain.

Musafirkhana Palace

You may have to hunt down the guard who has the key. This ornate palace was built late in the 18th century by Mahmud Muharram, a member of a wealthy merchant family. Muhammad Ali bought the palace early in the 19th century and used it for a guesthouse (Musafirkhana). A rare and complete specimen, the house offers a look at Turkish influences on secular design. The plan resembles that of Bayt Suhaymi except that it is more grand. To the left of the courtyard stands the well and *saqiya,* once powered by donkeys, which delivered water via the small aqueduct. The palace also includes the main hall with its carved ceiling and inlaid fountain, the *haramlik qa'a* with marbled panels, the bath with insets of colored glass, and *mashribiyya* throughout.

Mosque Of Sayyidna Al-Hussein

One of the few mosques barred to non-Muslims, this modern building is dedicated to Hussein, a grandson of Muhammad, and the fourth and last orthodox khalif. Today the mosque is a major center for Friday prayers; here President Mubarak and his ministers often celebrate feast days, and during Ramadan, its square is filled with tents and stalls to cater to celebrants.

Mosque Of Al-Azhar

Founded by the Fatimid conqueror Gawhar in A.D. 970 as the congregational mosque for the new city, it soon became a center of learning, a position it has maintained for over a thousand years. In the shadow of its arcades, students surrounded their instructors, learning the *hadith* (traditions), the *fiqh* (jurisprudence), and the finer points of classical Arabic. Today, the teaching remains nearly unchanged, but the addition of faculties of medicine, agriculture, engineering, and commerce has made al-Azhar a true university that attracts students from throughout the Islamic world. The school maintains nine other campuses in Egypt, and through its Academy of Islamic Research promotes the work of Muslim scholars throughout the world. The Sheikh al-Azhar remains the ultimate theological authority in Egypt, and the institution's teachings still shape Islamic beliefs abroad.

The building itself was laid out as a court-yard mosque over 100 meters square. As the center for Islamic learning, the institution at-

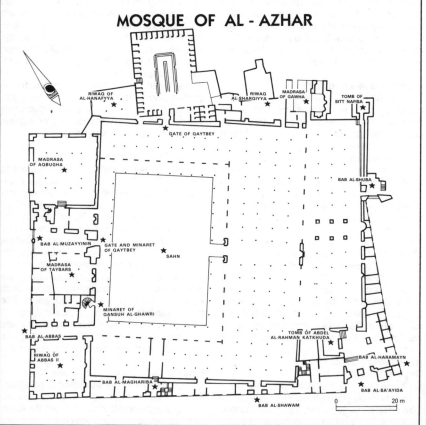

MOSQUE OF AL - AZHAR

RIWAQ OF AL-HANAFYYA

RIWAQ AL-SHARQIYYA

MADRASA OF GAWHA

TOMB OF SITT NAFISA

GATE OF QAYTBEY

MADRASA OF AQBUGHA

BAB AL-SHUBA

BAB AL-MUZAYYININ

GATE AND MINARET OF QAYTBEY

SAHN

MADRASA OF TAYBARS

MINARET OF QANSUH AL-GHAWRI

BAB AL-ABBAS

TOMB OF ABDEL AL-RAHMAN KATKHUDA

RIWAQ OF ABBAS II

BAB AL-HARAMAYN

BAB AL-MAGHARIBA

BAB AL-SA'AYIDA

BAB AL-SHAWAM

0   20 m

© MOON PUBLICATIONS, INC.

tracted the gifts, rebuilding, and additions of numerous sultans. The facade is split between the 14th century *madrasas* of Aqbugha to the north and Taybars to the south and joined by a gate installed in the mid-18th century. Originally built in the *ziyada* in front of the mosque, these buildings now house the university's manuscripts.

The entrance into the *sahn* of the main mosque is through the double gate of Sultan Qaytbey, which dates to the 15th century. This court belongs to the Fatimid period, but the rondels and keel-arched panels date from the 12th century. Occupying the right side of the *riwaq* are residential rooms for both Egyptian and foreign students.

Windows in the small dome at the entrance to the clerestory in the *qiblah* section pierce ornate stucco decorations, and the clerestory itself is typical of North African mosques. The *kufic* inscriptions and foliate stucco decorations on the hood of the *mihrab* are original; the rest are restored but capture the originals in feel. The marble, as that in al-Hakim's mosque, was added by the Ismaili sect of Bohras. Behind the *qiblah* stands the Ottoman mosque and mausoleum of Abd al-Rahman Katkhuda.

Al-Azhar contains three minarets, none of them Fatimid. The oldest, attached to the *madrasa* of Aqbugha, dates from the 14th century and is one of the oldest to be built entirely of stone rather than brick. The minaret added by Qaytbey, which stands above his gate, is a masterpiece of stonecarving. Unable to surpass the workmanship, the minaret of Qansuh al-Ghawri relies on height and unique design; its double-headed upper story is visible throughout Cairo.

Mosque Of Abu Dahab

Directly west of al-Azhar, the Ottoman mosque of Muhammad Bey Abu Dahab dominates the block. This "Father of Gold," so named because he threw gold instead of silver at his investiture as bey, built a great religious complex that included a *madrasa,* a library, fountains, and a Sufi hostel. Today only the mosque and mausoleum remain.

These buildings, rather than follow typical Ottoman design, reflect Abu Dahab's infatuation with the Mamluk period and combine elements from both periods. Shallow domes cover a portico

that surrounds the mosque on three sides, while the main room is roofed by a great dome. The polychrome marble *mihrab* is inlaid with mother-of-pearl. The shops at the ground level supply income for the maintenance of the building.

Wikala Of Al-Ghuri

Just to the south, the *wikala* (khan or caravansary) was a commercial hotel where spice merchants would board their animals in the large courtyard and lock themselves and their wares into the rooms on the upper floors. The courtyard also served as a market, but now the restored building is used by a few artists.

The Ghuriya

West of the *wikala,* Sultan Qansuh al-Ghuri built a *madrasa/*mosque and mausoleum/*sabil-kuttab* on adjoining corners. Viewed from the foot of the pedestrian overcrossing, the buildings present their decorative facades as they would have been viewed from the narrow street of the original city, before Sh. al-Azhar was widened for modern traffic. The mosque (on the west) is typical of the late Mamluk style, but the minaret reverts from the standard square/octagonal/round style to a totally square version.

Across the street, the mausoleum is now used as a cultural center that runs classes and occasionally produces plays. From the vestibule, the mausoleum takes off to the right; the arabesque carving above the wainscoting gives the wall a texture nearly as soft as textile. The little theater across the vestibule was once a *khanqah,* and Sufis came here to perform the *dikr.*

The two buildings together form one of the most impressive complexes in Cairo. The design, with the *sabil-kuttab* narrowing the street on the north and the base of the minaret doing the same on the south, provided a widened area between the two main buildings. This "square" was once covered and is the site of the silk bazaar made famous by David Robert's painting (*Silk Bazaar*). Sharia Mu'izz al-Din Allah, the old Fatimid thoroughfare, continues south to Bab Zuwayla.

Mosque Of Sultan Al-Muayyad

Just before you reach the southern gate, al-Mu'ayyad's mosque stands on your right (west), its twin minarets astride the gate. A red and turquoise framed door pierces the northern part of this huge courtyard mosque's facade. The carved arabesque above the door and the stalactite hood create a fitting counterpoint for the brass doors that once graced the *madrasa* of Sultan Hassan. The panels of *kufic* inscription on either side relate the First Pillar of Islam: There is no god but Allah, and Muhammad is his messenger. The entryway gives directly into the mausoleum and then the courtyard mosque. The rich decoration is typical for the period: the ceiling (recently restored), the *mihrab*, and the *minbar* are outstanding; the pillars, as usual, are of mixed types and date from antiquity.

Beyond the mosque, the southern tomb was devoted to the women in the sultan's family. Though Islam doesn't proscribe mixed-sex burials, the custom became ingrained during the Mamluk period. The south end of the building gives access to the roof and the minarets. The view takes in much of medieval Cairo—the northern gates to the Citadel. The eastern section of the roof looks down on the top of Nafisa Bayda's *wikala*, where families have set up homes complete with dovecotes and a porch using a classical column to support its roof. The eastern minaret is open for a climb, but the iron stair at the very top is not well-secured.

Bab Zuwayla

The southernmost gate of the Fatimids, Bab Zuwayla dates from 1092 and was named for the Berbers (al-Zuwayla) who lived in the area. From its top, musicians used to play every evening, and the Mamluks assembled here once a year to see off the caravan that took the cloth specially woven in Egypt for the Kabah to Mecca. Here, too, swung the heads of many an amir, and Sultan Salim (the Grim) hung the last Mamluk sultan, Tumanbey, from its portals. In the 19th century, however, the gate was identified with a local saint who healed the sick. Today the arch gives onto an area looking much like the medieval city must have appeared (except for cars, trucks, and bikes). To the west, where Sh. Ahmed Maher runs into Sh. Port Said, stands the Islamic Museum. To the south, continuing along Sh. Mu'izz al-Din Allah, is a section of the covered "street of the tentmakers;" where under the cool shelter, artisans still turn out beautiful appliqué—shop here for pillowcases and bedspreads. A little farther south, in the old saddlery section, you can find leather goods. The street to the east of Bab Zuwayla (Darb al-Ahman) runs past numerous beautiful islamic buildings to emerge at Aqsunqur (the Blue Mosque) and the Citadel beyond.

Mosque Of Qajamas Al-Ishaqi

To the left (east) down Sh. Darb al-Ahmar, the mosque of al-Ishaqi occupies a triangular island, the building demonstrating once again the creativity of Mamluk architects in adapting their plans to fit available space. The design utilizes both street facades, and the main mosque is joined to its *sabil-kuttab* by a second-story bridge, the *mashribiyya* indicating the family's living quarters. The mosque itself, as was traditional, was built over shops, and the building is noted for its outstanding craftsmanship. The entrance, for example, contains an exceptional *ablaq* marble panel in which leaf-forms swirl in black, white, and red.

The high level of work continues in the main mosque's carved stone walls and equally outstanding woodwork. The *mihrab* uses paste inlay, a technique that gives more freedom and control to the design and that harkens back 4,000 years to the tomb of Nefer-Ma'at. The marble floors are worth a look, especially those in the *qiblah*. The tomb chambers lie to the east, through the door in the *qiblah*.

CITIES OF THE DEAD

Beyond the Citadel a vast cemetery stretches for nearly six km along Cairo's eastern edge. Here rulers and their amirs built vast funerary complexes; domed mausoleums join mosques and *madrasas*. The cemetery is divided into two sections, south and northeast of the Citadel, respectively. The southern one holds earlier rulers, including the last of the Ayyubid khalifs and early Mamluk sultans. This area is more crowded, more rundown, and shelters much of Cairo's drug dealing. The eastern cemetery contains the more beautiful buildings—spectacular Mamluk decorative architecture laid out along spacious streets. Most of the buildings are open 0900 to 1600 or so, and you'll need to fork over LE3-6 for each; you won't be permitted in during prayers. These cemeteries (which can appear uncannily deserted in places) may make women alone uncomfortable.

The Eastern Cemetery
Known as the City of the Dead, the area was first settled in the 14th century by Sufis who sought solitude in the desolate areas outside the city's walls. Their sheikhs chose to be buried near the mystic settlements that had been their homes, and their tombs attracted devoted followers. The Mamluk royalty supported many of the orders by building and maintaining extensive *khanqahs* (Sufi monasteries). Like the pharaonic temples and Christian monasteries preceding them, the *khanqahs* supported large numbers of inhabitants who developed complex communities. The Mamluk patrons includ-

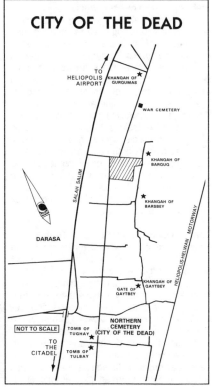

CITY OF THE DEAD

TO HELIOPOLIS AIRPORT
KHANQAH OF QURQUMAS
WAR CEMETERY
SALAH SALIM
KHANQAH OF BARQUQ
KHANQAH OF BARSBEY
HELIOPOLIS-HELWAN MOTORWAY
DARASA
KHANQAH OF QAYTBEY
GATE OF QAYTBEY
NORTHERN CEMETERY (CITY OF THE DEAD)
NOT TO SCALE
TOMB OF TUGHAY
TO THE CITADEL
TOMB OF TULBAY

© MOON PUBLICATIONS, INC.

ed their tombs within the Sufi compounds, taking advantage of the holiness surrounding the settlements. These tombs, in turn, attracted others and the area evolved into a full-fledged cemetery. Even today, families visit the area on Fridays, taking flowers and picnics to visit the dead—a custom with a 5,000-year history.

These *khanqahs* echo the style of other Mamluk buildings, but here the stone domes that crown the mausoleums stand out, their intricate shapes and decoration rising starkly against the skyline. Stone domes replaced brick ones in the 14th century. In order to raise heavier stone to grand heights, architects designed their domes with thin outer shells, upon which they carved chevron and zigzag patterns, giving the feel of the earlier ribbed domes. Ultimately, this stark decoration gave way to intricate arabesque, which, even at a distance, gives the domes a sinuous texture.

Getting There
The City of the Dead lies directly east of Khan al-Khalili where Sh. al-Azhar meets Sh. Salah Salim, and if you get tired of shopping, it makes a nice addition to a session at the Khan. As usual, a taxi is the easiest way to get there, but you can also take any bus headed for Darasa, the large stop just west of the cemetery. Or you can walk over the hill from al-Azhar; follow the main street east until you reach Salah Salim. Two streets lead into the cemetery: the southern one directly east of the underpass at al-Azhar/Salah Salim leads into the older section, which include the tombs of Princesses Tughay and Tulbayya; the large street off Salah Salim to the north leads directly into the *khanqah* of Barquq. The buildings are generally open 0900-1530 or so, and require a small (LE3-6) admission fee.

Khanqah Of Barquq
The first of the Mamluk sultans to be buried here, Barquq asked on his deathbed to be laid to rest beside the Sufi sheikhs, a request fulfilled by his son Faraj who built the *khanqah* with its double entries, minarets, *sabil-kuttabs* and great double domes. The interior of this fortress-like complex includes a teaching hall (west) and a mosque (east). The porticoes on the other sides served as the Sufis' living quarters.

The mosque, as was typical of *khanqahs* of the period, is plain, befitting the asceticism of its inhabitants. The tombs built for the sultan's family, however, show no such restraint. Beneath the breathtaking vaults of two of Cairo's largest domes, Faraj decorated the mausoleums with fine inlaid marble. He had to forego such embellishment on the domes themselves, which couldn't carry the extra weight, and content himself with painted decorations.

The view from either minaret takes in most of Cairo, and gives you a good look at the now-ruined living quarters. The square that remains served as the nucleus of the complex, which also once included mills, a bakery, a bath, and an inn for travelers. To support such a complex and to provide their families (who, under the Mamluk system, couldn't inherit) with continued security, the ruling class diverted much of their wealth into *waqfs*, trusts that the pharaonic temple estates provided for the continued upkeep of the tomb, but in addition also provided an income to surviving family members.

Khanqah Of Sultan Barsbey

Built just south of Barquq's complex, this *khanqah* lacks the unity of its older neighbor; the covered mosque, the *sabils*, and the apartment block spread out in a long facade that parallels the street. The northern portion is devoted to a duplex *rab*, the apartments inhabited by the Sufi. The four domes associated with the complex (Barsbey and three of his amirs) show a unity of style in which the chevroned patterns give way to interlocking geometric designs. The mosque, like that of Barquq, is plain, with the two parallel rows of arches supported on classical columns, but the floor's fine marble mosaics are worth asking the keeper to lift the mats covering them. The ornate Mamluk *minbar*, a 15th century donation, is the finest in Cairo. The mausoleum again shows less inhibition: mother-of-pearl and marble inlay combine in rhythmic and sophisticated design.

Funerary Complex Of Qaytbey

The jewel of late Mamluk architecture, this complex marks the consummation of the artistic refinement of previous innovations. Its striped *ablaq* exterior made famous by David Robert's watercolor, this mosque/mausoleum was the core of an active commercial center covering some six acres. It catered to a vast north-south trade with Syria and an east-west trade across the Red Sea. The old gateway to the south still exists.

To the north of the mosque are the remains of Qaytbey's *rab*, which housed travelers (the receipts went toward the complex's upkeep), and just beyond is the ornate drinking trough for their animals. Through the grand entryway of the main building on the southern corner you'll find the *sabil-kuttab*, the minaret, and the mausoleum, a unified whole. The decoration of the cruciform mosque/*madrasa*, though unbelievably rich, is nevertheless controlled and refined, the ornate windows and marble paving creating a subdued harmony. The lantern ceiling, for example, combines three major types of decoration—calligraphy, geometric designs, and arabesque—in a pleasing whole.

The tomb beyond is equally spectacular, its soaring dome seeming to vanish heavenward. The exterior of the dome is noteworthy for its delicate carving, visible from the roof. (Access is from the sanctuary—the stairway leads past some of the old living quarters.) Here you can see the dual design of intricate geometric figures intertwined with the arabesque, the flat strips contrasting with the grooved and recessed floral, lace-like designs, the different textures shifting in the reflected light as the sun advances. The ogee corners of the supporting drum contribute additional focal points, which lead to the surrounding roof encased by fleurs-de-lis. The building represents the apogee of Mamluk art, an art that could progress no further—the complex of Qaytbey marks its perfection.

Tomb Of Umm Anuk (Princess Tughay)

To the south of Qaytbey's complex stands the tomb of the favorite wife of Sultan al-Nasir Muhammad. This was the first *khanqah* built in the City of the Dead, and though much ruined, is still worth a visit if you have time. A former slave girl, she (after her husband's death), devoted her life to charitable works, among them the Sufi foundation that surrounds her tomb. Today only the ruin of a single *liwan* survives, but it still contains much fine stucco work; the peony designs and glazed tiles on the inscription of the dome drum speak of Iranian links.

The brick dome itself shows the typical ribs, which were hollow, allowing the builders to reach the heights approached by stone domes only after radical changes in design reduced their weight. Across the road lies the tomb of Princess Tulbayya, officially al-Nasir's principal wife. However, a look at the size of the tombs and the quality of work leaves little doubt as to who was the most loved.

The Southern Cemetery
Lying to the south of the Citadel, the southern cemetery holds earlier tombs of the Ayyubids. Unfortunately the area has become a haven for drug dealers, so don't visit it at night or alone. Although little random violence occurs, this is one place where a cab driver you trust and who will wait for you is worth the investment. The major monument, the mausoleum of Imam al-Shafi, lies deep in the cemetery, while two others (visit them if you have time) belonged to women: Shagarit al-Durr, who ruled Egypt briefly as sultana, and Sayyida Ruqayya who, with Sayyida Nafisa and Sayyida Zaynab, was one of Cairo's traditional patron saints.

Mausoleum of Imam al-Shafi: Built early in the 13th century by al-Kamil, nephew of Salah al-Din, the complex now contains not only the largest free-standing mausoleum in Egypt but two mosques. The older (closed to non-Muslims) dates from the late 12th century, and the other, a mid-18th century structure, is worth a visit. Imam al-Shafi, instrumental in Salah al-Din's campaign to return Egypt to Sunni Islam, founded the legal school, which bears his name. This *madrasa,* the first in Egypt, has become one of Cairo's most holy shrines, as the imam since medieval times has been re-garded as a saint. Believed to be a place of exceptional holy power, the site draws pilgrims from throughout the world, especially to celebrate the saint's *mulid.*

The mausoleum itself was extensively rebuilt in 1772 when the present wooden dome, double-tiered like that of the Dome of the Rock in Jerusalem, and layered in lead, was added. The exterior design reflects the preceding Fatimid period with interlacing strapwork designs, blind arches with ribbed hoods, and rosettes and lozenges. The spacious interior is filled with intricate design, heritage of numerous pious restorations. The imam's cenotaph, carved of teak and imported from India on the orders of Salah al-Din, still stands over the saint's grave. The marble panels date from work by Sultan Qaytbey; polychrome inlay by the entrance and the painted stalactites are 18th century renovations. The small *mihrab* was added when it was discovered that the ornate, triple-arched one was not accurately oriented to Mecca.

Tomb of Shagarit al-Durr: The last Ayyubid building in Cairo, Shagarit al-Durr's small brick and stucco tomb recalls earlier Fatimid tombs. The prayer niche, built under Byzantine influences that were strong in the 13th century, is inlaid with glass mosaics showing a branching tree. The mother-of-pearl rondels allude to the builder's name: Tree of Pearls.

Tomb of Sayyida Ruqayya: Although dedicated to the daughter of Ali, the fourth khalif, the mausoleum does not house her body, which lies in Damascus. The well-preserved Egyptian shrine is nevertheless a pilgrimage site. The original 12th century cenotaph displays fine carving; the wooden *mihrab* is a magnificent example of late Fatimid work.

MUSEUM OF ISLAMIC ART

Open daily 0900-1600, closed Fri. 1130-1330; LE8; tel. 903-930. The Islamic collection was started in 1880 by Muhammad Ali's grandson, Tawfiq; with the help of the historians Herz and Creswell, the collection soon numbered over 7,000 objects, many of them salvaged from deteriorating mosques. The pieces were housed in al-Hakim's mosque until 1902, when they were transferred to this sand-colored building. Since then the collection has steadily grown through donations, purchases, and archaeological excavations, and today its 80,000 items constitute one of the most extensive and finest Islamic collections in the world. Spanning the entire Islamic period, it contains textiles, pottery, armaments, glassware, carved wood, and metal. The exhibits, which are arranged in chronological order or by medium, trace the development of each art or craft throughout its medieval evolution.

Getting There

The museum's an easy walk from Bab Zuwayla in Islamic Cairo, and not too far from the Khan. Otherwise take a cab or try bus #75. The entrance, off Sh. Port Said, is through a courtyard at the north end of the building; the ticket booth is on your left as you enter.

The Masterworks

For those on a tight schedule, the museum has collected the masterpieces in two easily accessible spots: Halls 2 and 13, so visit these first. Hall 2 houses Umayyad (7th and 8th century) objects, many unearthed in the past years during excavations of Fustat. The bronze ewer with the crowing cockerel spout probably belonged to Marwan II, for it was found near where he was killed. Hall 13 contains a door from the Sayyida Zaynab mosque, a good representation of the various types of pottery, including Persian and Spanish, and an outstanding example of a mosque lamp, as well as the casket of al-Nasir Muhammad.

Abbasid (8th-9th Century)

Hall 3 contains Abbasid stucco panels, the earliest of which are deeply cut, juxtaposing intense shadow and glaring highlight, establishing crisp texture. The vines, leaves, and acanthus scrolls maintain much of their natural form, but as stucco decoration developed the scrolls become more abstract, their incised surfaces more tightly filled. The motifs lost their semblance of reality, creating an undulating linear style, a total break with the earlier, more classical designs. No longer carved, but molded, the panels continuously repeated identical forms.

Fatimid (10th-12th Century)

During this period, marked by the consumptive splendor of the North African rulers, Egyptian artisans consolidated and refined Islamic art. Since Islam's

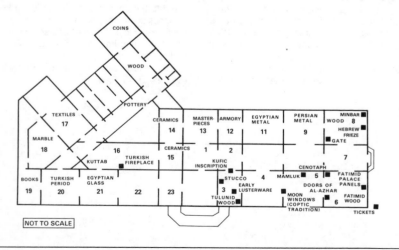

© MOON PUBLICATIONS, INC.

prohibition of figures referred to religious idols, not secular pictures (a point the Shi'i rulers exploited), figures once more inhabit Egyptian art. The figures depict daily life; the animals often appear, like in Coptic work, inside rondels with a trilobe leaf in their mouths. The entrance to Hall 4, like many of the galleries, is marked by decorated doors. The room also contains some of the earliest lusterware found; uncovered in Fustat, it argues for Egypt as the source of the technique. Don't miss the inlaid ivory and the jewelry.

Mamluk (13th-16th Century)

Hall 5 is dominated by a 12th- or 13th-century fountain, and around it is a choice collection of wood-ivory inlay, stucco *mihrabs*, and enameled *muski* lamps, which once hung in mosques. On the doorway wall, a stone plaque carries the lion of Baybars, and doors from his mosque frame the entrance; above them, colored glass set into plaster forms moon windows. The wooden *tabut* or cenotaph belonged to Hussein and dates from about 1158.

Woodworking

Halls 6-9, devoted to wood, are laid out in a chronological manner. You enter Hall 6 through the doors made in 1010 for al-Azhar's mosque. Most of the work is Fatimid and includes the *mihrab* of Sayyida Ruqayya and panels from the Western Palace. Woodworking, like stucco carving, began with the deeply incised, naturalistic forms of the Umayyads, which were replaced by the concentric circles and interlocking arches of the Abbasids, which in turn gave way to the slanting beveled style of the Tulunids' stylized animals and birds.

During the Fatimid period, secular woodcarving was more realistic, and by 1094 the compositions that had once sprawled freely over entire surfaces were now confined to smaller scales: hexagons, stars, and squares, each of which contained its own design. Decorative figures lost their realism and became silhouettes, and this trend of simplification continued into the Ayyubid period when arabesques blended smoothly into abstract decorations of line and shape. After the 15th century, due to economic decline and political unrest, woodworking, as well as the rest of the Islamic arts, started a gradual decline.

Metalworking

Halls 9-11 contain metal objects, many executed in techniques developed in Mosel. The origins of the practice of inlaying silver or copper into bronze are Near Eastern, but Egyptian craftsmen quickly became proficient at making candlesticks, ewers, and caskets. Stylized human figures, often seated listening to music or hunting on horseback, frequently appeared in rondels surrounded by arabesque designs. Hall 11 also contains astrolabes, instruments used by Muslim sailors to locate star positions.

Armory

Hall 12 houses the Mamluk Arms Collection, which includes the sword of Sulayman the Magnificent. The sword of the Mamluk commander Murad Bey is in Case 11. Captured by Murat, it was presented to Napoleon, who forgot it when he left his carriage at Waterloo. Subsequently it was presented to Wellington and then returned to Egypt. If you scrutinize the sword blades of the Mamluks, you can see faint wavy lines etched into the dull blue steel, the fingerprints of the Damascus steel from which they are forged. The hall also includes firearms and armor as beautifully inlaid as the more peaceful metal pieces in the previous galleries.

Ceramics

Islamic potters were justly famous for their work, which included a mind-boggling variety of ware: incised, sculpted, and cut-out, polychrome and luster-glazed, Persian to Chinese in design. Not limited to pots, the Muslims made tiles for decoration: Damascus type in blue, Kotyyhia with yellow accents, and Isnik with tomato red. Nor were Egyptians limited to their own productions: shards from Holland, Turkey, Italy, and Spain found in Fustat testify to the extensive trade in ceramics, a trade that continued throughout the empire period. Hall 16 also contains Fatimid *ahlaq* (chokes) from water jars. Inserted in the jar's necks, these screens slowed the water flow, preventing a slosh in a drinker's face, and kept flies, spiders, and other riff raff out of the water. The hall also contains a ceramic fireplace (the fire was built behind the tile from an adjoining room) and part of a *kuttab*.

Glass

Hall 21 is devoted to Egyptian glass. Egypt's glassmaking tradition began in pharaonic times and encompassed the master craftsmen at Alexandria who blew, molded, and cut glass for their Roman patrons. This work continued after the Muslim conquest, but enameled glass became most popular. Using this technique, Muslim glassmakers created mosque lamps with bulging bases and upper sections joined by a narrow waist. Similar enameling often decorated long narrow bottles. *Kufic* or *naskhi* script served as decoration, as did Mamluk coats of arms such as the cup or eagle set in medallions.

Books

Hall 19 is given over to the arts of the book and illuminated manuscript, many from the collection of King Faruq. Since to Muslims, art was servant of religion, the transmission of God's words elevated the art of the calligrapher above that of all others. In early manuscripts, illumination was limited to geometric forms and arabesques, but later, under Persian influence, the art of miniature painting developed. The earliest manuscripts we were written on vellum or parchment, and only in the 8th century did paper supplant animal skins. Bookbindings are of two types; a fine leather (called morocco), and lacquer. The earliest leather covers were stamped or tooled with overall geometric patterns, but by the 15th century, cut leather bearing central medallions with matching corner decorations had replaced them. Bookmakers of the 16th century transferred this medallion-corner pattern, often enhanced by colored paper filigree, to the inside of the cover (the doublures). The outsides of these books often bore panels, both stamped and gilded, as well as a triangular flap that closed over the free edges like an envelope. Lacquer bindings, made from a papier-mâché and gesso base, were decorated with watercolors, a technique that eventually spread to pen cases, mirror covers, and other small objects. In illumination, the difference between religious and secular works is striking. Note the care and style lavished upon the Korans, and compare them to the scientific and historical manuscripts. The collection includes the work of Avicena, the physician of *Canterbury Tales* fame, on botany and anatomy.

Textiles

Upstairs, the entire hall is devoted to textiles from Yemen, Egypt, Iran, and Turkey. In both design and technique, Islamic textiles followed the paths established by the Copts, and in fact, the Muslims employed many Coptic weavers. The only deviation in early textiles was the introduction of Arabic script as a decorative element. Known as *tiraz*, the Persian word for embroidery, the cloths gave their name to the shops that wove them. Beautiful cloth was a luxury item, and the government controlled the textile industry.

PRACTICALITIES

ACCOMMODATIONS

Cairo's accommodations vary from sleek, five-star hotels indistinguishable from their sterile brethren anywhere else in the world to friendly pensions and crowded youth hostels. Although Cairo once faced a critical shortage of hotel space, international corporations have built numerous new buildings. Middle-class hotels once directed by the inept Egyptian Hotels Corporation have been put under private management and are undergoing renovation; unfortunately, some of these charge exorbitant prices for individual travelers, so be sure to check prices and inspect rooms before checking in. A few of the smaller hotels are still required by the government to charge for half or full board; inquire. With the addition of minibuses to Cairo's public transportation system, the less expensive, small hotels like those in Doqqi are now much more accessible. For an introductory list see the following table, and more options can be found in *Cairo, a Practical Guide*, available in most bookstores. Like all of Cairo, hotels are struggling for their share of the tourist trade, and are in a constant state of flux. Caught between spiraling inflation, government reclassification, and increasing demands for service and facilities, they raise and lower rates.

Hotels are grouped by government ratings: five-star, $85-120 s, $100-175 d; four-star, $34-85 s, $45-125 d; three-star, $24-35 s, $35-50 d; 2-star LE35-45 s, LE45-60 d; one-star LE25-40 s, LE35-85 d. Again, these prices are approximate, and fluctuate constantly, not only within a grouping, but between hotels—what's a great deal one month may be overpriced for what it offers in the next. Always check the individual room you'll be taking and confirm its price (it should be posted), what it includes, and if taxes are additional.

SELECTED CAIRO HOTELS

NAME	ADDRESS	DISTRICT	TEL.	TELEX/FAX
DOWNTOWN: FIVE-STAR HOTELS				
Meridien	Cornishe al-Nil	Garden City	362-1717	362-1927
Nile Hilton	Cornishe al-Nil	Midan Tahrir	765-666/ 767-444	760-874
Ramesses Hilton	115 Cornishe al-Nil	Midan Tahrir	754-999/ 758-000	757-152
Semiramis Inter-continental	Cornishe al-Nil	Garden City	355-7171	356-3020
Shepherd's Hotel	Cornishe al-Nil	Garden City	355-3800/ 355-3900	355-7284
DOWNTOWN: FOUR-STAR HOTELS				
Manyal Palace/ Club Med	Qasr Muhammad Ali	Rhoda	844-524/ 854-930	363-9364
DOWNTOWN: THREE-STAR HOTELS				
Atlas Hotel	2 Muhammad Rushdi		391-8183/ 391-8311	92564 ATLOS UN
Bel Air Cairo Hotel	Moqattam Hill P.O. Box 996	Moqattam	906-911/ 906-917	922- 816
Carlton	21 26th July		755-181/ 755/022	20734 ABHAR UN
Cleopatra Palace	2 al-Bustan	Midan Tahrir	759-900/ 759-923	346-6785
Cosmopolitan	1 Ibn Taalab	Qasr al-Nil	392-3663/ 392-3845	393-3531
Continental Savoy	10 Midan	Opera	911-322/ 911-340	
Khan al-Khalili	7 Bosta	Ataba	900-271/ 900-230	
Victoria	66 al-Gumhurriya	Midan Ramesses	918-766/ 918-039	
Windsor	19 Alfy P.O. Box 2045-11111		915-277/ 915-810	921-621
DOWNTOWN: TWO-STAR HOTELS				
Lotus Hotel	12 Talaat Harb		750-966/ 750-627	
DOWNTOWN: ONE-STAR/UNRATED				
Capsis Palace	117 Ramesses	Midan Ramesses	754-219/ 754-188	
Anglo-Swiss Pension	14 Champollion		751-497	
Garden City House	23 Kamal al-Din	Salah Garden City	354-4969/ 354-8400	

SELECTED CAIRO HOTELS

NAME	ADDRESS	DISTRICT	TEL.	TELEX/FAX
DOWNTOWN: ONE-STAR/UNRATED (cont.)				
Montana	25 Sherif		748-608/ 746-264	
Pension Roma	169 Muhammad Farid		391-1088	
ZAMELEK: FIVE-STAR HOTELS				
Cairo Marriott	Saray al-Gizera	Zamalek	340-8888	340-6667
ZAMELEK: FOUR-STAR HOTELS				
Flamenco	2 al-Gizera	al-Wosta	340-0851	340-0891
ZAMELEK: THREE-STAR HOTELS				
Horus House	21 Ismail Muhammad	Zamalek	340-3977	340-3182
Newstar	34 Yehia Ibrahim	Zamalek	340-1865	340-3424
President	22 Dr. Taha Hussein	Zamalek	341-6751	341-1752
ZAMELEK: TWO-STAR HOTELS				
Al-Nil Zamalek	21 Maahad al-Swissri	Zamalek	340-0220	
ZAMELEK: ONE-STAR/UNRATED HOTELS				
Pension Zamalek	6 Sh. Salah al-Din		340-9318	
Mayfare	9 Aziz Osman		340-7351	
DOQQI: THREE-STAR HOTELS				
Concorde	146 Tahrir		708-751/ 701-873	717-033
Tonsi	143 Tahrir		348-7231	
Indiana	16 Saraya		349-3774	94144 DIANA UN
Rose	6 Iran		708-464	
Pharaohs	12 Lotfi Hassouna		361-0871-4	387-4974
King	20 Abd Rehim Sabri		710869/ 710939	22393 KIN HOUN
DOQQI: TWO-STAR HOTELS				
Commodore Cairo	10 Fawzi Ramah	Doqqi	346-0592	
GIZA: FIVE-STAR HOTELS				
Mena House Oberoi	al-Ahram	Pyramids	383-3222/ 383-3444	383-7777
Ramada Renaissance	Cairo/Alexandria	Desert Rd. Pyramids	383-8666	383-9000
Siag Pyramids	59 Maryutia	Saqqara Rd. Pyramids	385-6022/ 385-3005	384-0874
GIZA: FOUR-STAR HOTELS				
Green Pyramids	13 Helmyet al-Ahram P.O. Box 22	Giza 537-216	537-619/	93701 GPHOTUN

SELECTED CAIRO HOTELS

NAME	ADDRESS	DISTRICT	TEL.	TELEX/FAX
GIZA: FOUR-STAR HOTELS (cont.)				
Oasis Hotel	Cairo/Alexandria	Desert Rd. Pyramids	383-1777/ 383-2777	383-0916
Europa Cairo	300 al-Ahram		535-940	
GIZA: THREE-STAR HOTELS				
Lido	465 al-Ahram	Giza	727-960/ 726-655	
Sand	103 al-Ahram	Giza	855-479/ 850-113	93482 PYHTL UN
Vendome	287 al-Ahram	Giza	538-649/ 539-613	854-138
MOHANDISEEN: FOUR-STAR HOTELS				
Atlas Zamalek	20 Gamat al-Dowal	al-Arabiya Mohandiseen	346-4175/ 346-6569	347-6958
Al-Nabila	4 Gameat al-Dowal	al-Arabia	346-1131/ 3467-3384	347-5661
MOHANDISEEN: THREE-STAR HOTELS				
Cairo Inn	26 Syria St.	Mohandiseen	349-0661	93957
Caroline Crillion	49 Syria	Mohandiseen	346-4101	23158
MOHANDISEEN: ONE-STAR/UNRATED HOTELS				
Amun	Midan	Sphinx Mohandiseen	346-1434	
HELIOPOLIS: FIVE-STAR HOTELS				
Al-Salaam	61 Abdul Hamid	Badawy	245-5155/ 245-2155	245-5755
Heliopolis Movenpick	Hurriya		664-977/ 247-0077	667-347
Sonesta Hotel	4 Tayaran	Medinat Nasr	262-8111/ 261-7100	619-980
Meridien Heliopolis	51 Oruba P.O. Box 2928		290-5055	291-8591
HELIOPOLIS: FOUR-STAR HOTELS				
Novotel	Airport Rd P.O. Box 8/zip-11776	Airport	661-330/ 679-080	291-4794
Baron Hotel	Maahd al-Sahara (off Orouba)		291-5757/ 291-2467	290-7077
HELIOPOLIS: THREE-STAR HOTELS				
Egyptel	93 al-Merghany		290-2515/ 290-2516	290-7091

SELECTED CAIRO HOTELS

NAME	ADDRESS	DISTRICT	TEL.	TELEX/FAX
HELIOPOLIS: TWO-STAR HOTELS				
Helio Cairo	95 Abd Hamid Badawy		245-0563/ 245-0682	
SOUTH OF CAIRO				
MA'ADI: FOUR-STAR HOTELS				
Ma'adi Hotel	Ma'adi Entrance P.O. Box 196		350-5050/ 350-6555	351-8710
HELWAN: FOUR-STAR HOTELS				
Japan Palace	Japanese Garden		783-610/ 787-116	
SAQQARA: FOUR-STAR HOTELS				
Saqqara Palm	Sh. Saqqara	Badrashen	348-4645/ (018) 200-791	23646 PALM UN

Inexpensive Hotels

The range of services offered by these hotels can vary from air-conditioning and reliable hot water to dry-camping with bedbugs. Most of these hotels occupy the upper stories of business buildings along Talaat Harb and 26 July. Although their height somewhat blunts the noise of Cairo traffic, it also renders them vulnerable to cranky elevators and Cairo's notoriously low water pressure. Many of the managers of these hotels will bargain, especially if you don't look too hot, tired, and desperate; be sure to check the rooms first. Among the best is the **Pension Za-malek,** which is spotless, and includes full board for LE32 s, 48 d. **The Pension Roma,** downtown off Sherif, runs a close second—but you'll have to make reservations as they're nearly always full. The **Garden City House,** although it's catering more to young Europeans, still draws a few of the scholarly regulars, especially when Madame Scarzella is in residence.

Mid-range Hotels

Most of these hotels are now clean, and thanks to new standards, food and service are improving as well. Most of the best are across the river in Doqqi. Competing with each other, nearly all have a/c, TV, phones in the rooms, private baths, and many have mini-bars or even kitchenettes;

all run close to the same price; many include breakfast. The prices and quality of the ones downtown vary a little more, often trading ambience for economy. The **Windsor,** with its unabashedly British tone, offers good service; the elegant **Victoria,** renovated **Cosmopolitan,** and cleaned-up **Lotus** are also good choices.

Visiting Posh Hotels

Many of Cairo's deluxe hotels, steeped in history, are worth a visit. For even more fun, save up your piasters and splurge one night—hot water any time you wish, quiet toilets, warm (or cool) room, soft bed, softer sheets. . . . After a month in Egypt, you will be ready to kill for a night of true luxury. Many have good and not-too-expensive coffee shops, or a luxurious bar or tearoom.

Centered on the Nile side of Midan al-Tahrir, the **Nile Hilton** is the social center of the business district. Foreigners and Egyptians mix here; the press, government officials, and businessmen all seem to find their way to the garden restaurant, the rooftop bar (which moves outside to the garden in summer), or the casino. Jackie's has good music and dancing, but is expensive. The Pizzeria, on the ground floor (walk up the steps from the bus terminal to the back of the plaza—it's on your right), is a central meeting place for the less well-endowed, and the Taverne inside is a watering hole for the tired and thirsty.

Shepherd's is undoubtedly the most famous hotel in Egypt. However, the modern Shepherd's is not the original British meeting place of turn-of-the-century fame. Founded by Samuel Shepherd, an Englishman who came to Cairo in 1841, it was a small hotel that catered to European travelers. As the demand grew, Shepherd leased the palace of Alfi Bay (the former home of Napoleon's commander-in-chief) fronting on al-Azbakiyya. Eventually, the hotel was sold, but its reputation continued to grow, and its guest book read like an international "Who's Who." At the beginning of the 1952 revolution, the hotel was burned, and although relocated and rebuilt in 1956, it has never recaptured its old grandeur.

The **Cairo Marriott** occupies the old palace originally built by Ismail Pasha for Empress Eugene, who was his guest at the opening of the Suez Canal. It occupies 12 acres in the middle of Gizera Island, and was converted to a hotel in the 1960s. Although two modern towers now flank the palace (the latticework on the porticoes is original), the management has restored the older section, including furniture, wood and marble, rugs, tapestries, and art to the late 19th century. Note especially the painted ceilings and antique chandeliers.

The **Manyal Palace** is another former royal residence. Built for an uncle of King Faruq who was an avid collector of Oriental art, the palace was turned into a museum after the revolution. Now run by Club Med, it offers an inexpensive brunch which includes use of their pool for the day. Part of the palace is now a museum open to the public.

The **Mena House Oberoi,** once the hunting lodge of Ismail Pasha, lies at the foot of the Giza pyramids. In 1869 the pasha converted it into a guesthouse for his visitors to the Suez opening, and by 1880 it was operating as a hotel and became one of the most popular in Egypt. Its guests included kings, queens, statesmen, writers, and actors. Winston Churchill met President Roosevelt here, and Carter met Sadat. In 1972 the Oberoi Hotel chain of India leased the hotel and renovated it, furnishing the rooms with antique pieces discovered in a storeroom. Although the veranda from which the British

colonialists sipped tea and watched the camels trek toward the pyramids is now the enclosed coffee shop, the place is worth a visit for the quiet decor and the curry in the Mogul Room; lunch is less crowded (as well as less expensive) than dinner. And if they haven't yet raised their rates, it remains an outstanding deal.

Youth Hostel

You can reach the hostel at 135 Abdul Aziz al-Saud on Rhoda Island, 840-729, by taking the Metro to the Sayyida Zaynab station, and walking west to the Sayala Bridge, continuing past the fortress-like walls of Manyal Palace. The hostel lies across from the Salah al-Din mosque. Alternately, you can take minibus #83 from Midan Tahrir or the water taxi to the university and walk back across the bridge. Recently redone, the hostel is now clean with lockers and locks (available from the warden). Members LE5, nonmembers LE7; closed 1000-1400 and during Ramadan from 1800-2000; 2300 curfew. The hostel is often crowded, so call ahead.

Camping

Campgrounds are located near the pyramids in Harraniyya; go out Sh. al-Haram and turn left at the Saqqara road; a hand-lettered sign marks the turnoff to the grounds. For a few pounds a person, the grounds provide toilets and showers (one hot). A bar on the grounds serves typical Egyptian food: *kufta,* kebab, and grilled pigeon.

FOOD

The food available in Cairo ranges from plush European and ethnic restaurants to the foodstalls on the streets, which sell *shawirma* and *ta'miyya* for a few pounds.

Hotel Dining

All the deluxe hotels maintain fancy dining rooms and many have 24-hour coffee shops; although relatively cheap by international standards, the quality of the food can vary. Many offer lunch and/or dinner buffets—all you can eat for LE15-35. In addition, hotel restaurants often focus on a foreign cuisine for a week or so; check the current edition of *Cairo Today* for updated information. The nightclubs found in these hotels also serve dinner.

SELECTED CAIRO RESTAURANTS

NAME	ADDRESS	PHONE	HOURS	PRICE	COMMENTS
			DOWNTOWN		
Abu Shakra	69 Qasr al-Aini Sayyida Zaynab	848-881/ 848-602	1300-1700/ 1900-2300	average	great kufta/kabab, no alcohol
After 8	8 Qasr al-Nil (in passageway)		2000-0100	average	good steak; quiet dining early
Al'Americaine	44 Talaat Harb	393-7731	0700-2300	cheap	stand-up counter and coffee shop; good ice cream
Arabesque	6 Qasr al-Nil	759-896	1230-1530/ 1930-2330	average	Continental; art gallery in lobby (pictures for sale)
Brazilian Coffee Shop	38 Talaat Harb	755-722	0600-2400	cheap	fresh-ground coffee; espresso, cappuccino, ice coffee
Cafe Riche	17 Talaat Harb	392-9793	1130-2200	cheap	vintage Cairo; outside cafe; tea, coffee, ouzo, *beerk;* dining outside
Estoril	12 Talaat Harb	743-102	1200-1530/ 1900-2230	average	Continental; excellent vintage Cairo dining
Excelsior	35 Talaat Harb	392-5002	0700-2400	inexpensive	pre-revolution Cairo; restaurant, bar, and coffee shop
Fatattri al-Tahrir	55 Tahrir (off Midan Tahrir)		24 hours	cheap	good *fatiir;* clean
Felfela	15 Huda Shaarawi (just off Talaat Harb)	392-2751	0700-0100	cheap	variety Egyptian food, favorite of many Egyptian families
Fu Ching	28 Talaat Harb (passageway off street)	393-6184	1230-2230	inexpensive	Chinese
Groppi's	Midan Talaat Harb	743-244	0730-2200	average	vintage Cairo; confections; a must for every visitor
Groppi's Garden	2 Abdul Khalaq Sarwat	391-6619	0730-2100	average	made famous by British; no alcohol
Indian Tea Center	23 Talaat Harb (in passage)	393-3396		inexpensive	afternoon tea and snacks
Kentucky Fried Chicken	Abdel Khalaq Sarwat	392-9658	1000-2430	cheap	
La Chesa	21 Adly	393-9360		average	perfect place for breakfast or lunch; run by SwissAir
Le Grillon	8 Qasr al-Nil	743-114/ 764-959	1200-2400	average	outdoor dining

SELECTED CAIRO RESTAURANTS

NAME	ADDRESS	PHONE	HOURS	PRICE	COMMENTS
DOWNTOWN					
M.S. Scarabee	Cornishe al-Nil by Shepherd Hotel	355-448	Sails: 2000/2230	expensive	good buffet; show included, good deal
Paprika	1129 Cornishe al-Nil	749-447	1200-2400	average	Continental; excellent *mezzas;* haunt of Egyptian TV & radio personalities
Take Away	1 Latin America Garden City	355-4341	0800-2400	inexpensive	hamburgers, chicken, etc.
Taverna	3 Alfi		1200-1600/1900-0100	inexpensive	Greek, try the shrimp
Victoria Coffeeshop	66 Gumhuriyya (in Victoria Hotel)	918-869	0800-2400	cheap	
Wimpy's	three locations: Immobilia (off Sherif); Talaat Harb; Huda Shaarawi		0900-2400	cheap	
ZAMALEK					
Il Capo	22 Taha Hussein	341-3870	1200-0130	average	Italian; good food, prices
Justine's	4 Hassan Sabri	341-2961/340-5710	1300-1500/2000-2300	expensive	some of the best formal dining in Cairo; reservations required
La Cloche d'Or	3 Abu al-Feda	340-2268	1200-0200	expensive	Lebanese/French; live show (LE 50) Thurs. and Sat.
La Piazza	4 Hassan Sabri	341-2961/340-4385	1230-2400	average	pub; Italian food
La Terrace	President Hotel		1200-0100	average	Middle Eastern cuisine
Matchpoint	4 Hassan Sabri	341-2961/340-5710	1300-0230	expensive	nightclub
Maxie's	4 Hassan Sabri	341-2961/340-5710			
al-Patio	5 Sayed al-Bakry	340-2645	0900-0100	average	Argentinian food
Pub 28	28 Shagarit al-Durr	340-0972	1200-0100	average	
Tokyo	4 al-Maahad al-Swissry	341-0502	1800-2245 closed Sunday	expensive	Japanese
DOQQI					
Frghly Fruits	45 Midan Doqqi		1000-0200	cheap	good, fresh juices
Maha	Jasmin Hotel Gizirat al-Arab	347-2278	24 hours	average	Indian; good curries
Silver Fish	35 Mohi al-Din Abu al-Aziz	349-2272	1200-0400	average	seafood; Middle Eastern; Continental
Taj Mahal	15 Midan Ibn Affan	249-4881	1200-2400	average	Indian

SELECTED CAIRO RESTAURANTS

NAME	ADDRESS	PHONE	HOURS	PRICE	COMMENTS
DOQQI					
Tandoori	11 Shehab	348-6301	1230-2400	average	Indian; curries; no alcohol
al Tikea	12 Muhammed	711-470	1200-0300 (closed Wed.)	cheap	Middle East
MOHANDISEEN					
De Baffo	15 Batal Ahmed Abdel Aziz	346-7490 344-8468	0900-0200	average	Italian/Swiss
Flying Fish	166 al-Nil Aguza	349-3234/ 349-4084	1200-0130	average	good calamari
Prestige Pizzeria	43 Giziret al-Arab	347-0383	1200-0200	average	
Pronto Pizzeria	53 Gamat al-Dewal al-Arabia	349-0893	1200-2400	inexpensive	great pizza
Tikka Grill	47 Batal Ahmed Abdel Aziz	346-0393	2200-0100	inexpensive	Egyptian/Indian; no alcohol
GIZA					
Andrea	60 Mariuta Canal near pyramids	851-133	1300-1700/ 1900-2300	inexpensive	grilled chicken; pigeon; outdoor dining on canal; take mosquito repellent
Andrea Fish Restaurant	60 Mariuta Canal near pyramids	851-133	1300-1700/ 1900-2300	inexpensive	fish; shrimp; calamari; outdoor dining
Cafe Cairo	5 Wissa Wassef Riyadh Tower (al-Nil)	737-592	1000-0100	average	no alcohol; good snacks; 3-course menu
Il Camino	5 Wissa Wassef Riyadh Tower (al-Nil)	722-786	1300-1730/ 1930-2400	average	Italian; no alcohol
Chandani	5 Wissa Wassef Riyadh Tower (al-Nil)	737-592	1930-2400/ 1330-1630 Fri.	expensive	Indian; good non-alcoholic cocktails; jacket required; Reservations recommended
Fanous	5 Wissa Wassef Riyadh Tower (al-Nil)	737-592	1300-1630/ 1930-2400	expensive	Moroccan; no alcohol but good non-alcoholic cocktails
Felfela Village	95 Mariuta Canal near pyramids	383-4029/ 383-0574	1000-1900	average	belly dancers; dancers; dancing horses; etc.
Golden Pharaoh	docked at 31 Cornishe al-Nil	570-1000	Sails: 1430/ 2000, 2300	expensive	run by Oberoi Hotels
Madura	Cairo Sheraton	348-8600 ext. 160	1800-2430	expensive	Indonesian
Moghul	Mina House near pyramids	387-7444/ 387-4999	1230-1430/ 1930-2300	expensive	good Indian food; can select less expensive dishes
al-Mashrabia	4 Ahmed Nessim	972-602/ 972-603	1100-1600/ 2000-0100	expensive	no alcohol

SELECTED CAIRO RESTAURANTS

NAME	ADDRESS	PHONE	HOURS	PRICE	COMMENTS
GIZA					
SwissAir le Chateau	31 al-Nil (Nasr Building)	348-5321/ 348-6270	1200-2400	expensive	Continental; elegant dining; reservations recommended
SwissAir le Chalet	31 al-Nil (Nasr Building)	729-488	1000-2400	average	Swiss; good ice cream
Nile Pharoah	docked at 31 Cornishe al-Nil	738-914/ 738-957	Sails: 1500/ 2030/2330	expensive	run by Oberoi Hotels
Oasis	Mina House near pyramids	383-3444 383-3222	1200-sunset	expensive	dining next to waterfall
Sakura	5 Wissa Wassef Riyadh Tower (al-Nil)	737-592	1900-2400	expensive	Teppan-yaki table cooking; jacket required; no alcohol
MA'ADI					
Andrea	45 Road 5	351-368	1200-2400	inexpensive	
L'Egyptien	across from Pullman Hotel	925-1222	Sails: 1930	expensive	three-hour cruises (goes to Beni Suef alternate weekends)
Mermaid	77 Road 9	350-3946	1100-2330	average	good, flaky crust pizza
Pub 13	Sweet Hotel 39 Road 13	350-4544/ 359-4561			Mexican
Sultana	43 Cornishe al-Nil	351-2521	1000-0300	average	floating restaurant; good native Egytian

Small Restaurants

Independent restaurants come and go, but many remain with good and well-deserved reputations. One of the best values is **Il Capo,** located in the bottom of the President Hotel, tel. 340-1969/341-3870. This casual restaurant is an outstanding bargain with good cooking, selected wines, and great service with entrees between LE5-30. In fact, ethnic restaurants abound. For a selection at the last minute, you can head up to the top of the Riyadh Tower in Giza; the Oman restaurants offer Moroccan, Italian, Indian, and a cafe all on one floor; the food is outstanding and the service is even better; no alcohol. In Zamalek, Justine's anchors four good restaurants at the four-corners. Downtown, the Arabesque remains popular, and SwissAir has opened a delightful coffee shop (La Chesa) on Adly across from

Cairo Kodak; it continues the outstanding traditions of its double decker in Giza.

Inexpensive Cafes

Little shops line the streets of Cairo, and since the water supply in most of the city is now treated, those cafes with running water also tend to be clean and safe. You will find them all over the city; foreigners tend to use those clustered along Qasr al-Nil, Talaat Harb, in Midan Falaki, and those around the American University in Cairo.

Shopping

Grocery stores run by small, independent merchants line the residential areas. These stores sell canned goods, staples, and meats, eggs, and cheeses at set prices. The Blue Nile Grocery on Qasr al-Aini, about midway between Midan

Tahrir and the bridge to Rhoda Island, often has items like bacon and ham, imported cheese, and wines. Produce is usually sold by individual vendors, often from wagons on the street, or you can visit the vegetable *suq* in Bab al-Luq.

ENTERTAINMENT

The mystique of Cairo draws not only Egyptians, but also citizens of other Arab countries, for whom it's the center of sin. For Western visitors, the city offers glimpses into the haunting mysteries of Eastern culture. With its new Opera House serving as its focus, Cairo stands at the threshold of a revitalized cultural life, one proponents say will restore the city's place among the cultural centers of the world. For current information see *Cairo Today's* "Lists," "Arts," "Music," and "Theater" sections.

Sound And Light Show
At Giza, performances begin at 1830 and 1930 in winter; 1930 and 2030 in summer. Reservations 385-2880\385-7320 (see "Cairo Environs," p. 268). The show at Giza is not as good as those at Karnak or Philae, so if you're going south, save your money for one of those performances.

Weddings
Better shows, and ones that are free, are the weddings that dominate the expensive hotels on Thursday nights. Booked up for years in advance, the popular hotels like the Nile Hilton can guarantee a procession at about 2000 hours. The ululating wails of the celebrating women and the incessant rhythms of drummers, and trumpeters announce the procession, which often includes stick dancers and belly dancers with lighted candelabras on their heads. As the procession winds slowly up the stairs, relatives shower rose petals or, in really first-class affairs, coins. Although you won't be invited to the reception, the slow-moving and spectacular entrance provides a good half-hour's entertainment.

For Kids
Many of the attractions designed for children are equally appealing to the kid in every adult, so unwind and step back into the world of inno-cence with a visit to the circus, the zoo, or a puppet theater. The headquarters of the **Egyptian National Circus** are next to Umm Kulthum (Balloon Theater) at 26 July and al-Nil (tel. 346-4870/347-0612; tickets run about LE5 for adults, LE2 for children; the box office opens daily at 1230, the performance is at 2130) and the single ring offers kids a small but good selection of clowns, acrobats, lions, tumblers, trapeze artists, and dancing horses. Soviet trained, the troupe moves to Alexandria in July and August. The **Cairo Puppet Theater** (tel. 910-954) in Azbakiyya Gardens, Midan Opera, offers performances from October to May at 1830 Thurs.-Sun. with additional performances at 1200 Fri. and Sunday. The shows are in Arabic, but it makes little difference, for the lively action of such characters as Sinbad the Sailor, Ali Baba, or Little Red Riding Hood can be understood in any language.

The **Cairo Zoo,** open 0830-1630 (tel. 726-314/726-233; 20PT), located at the Zoological Gardens on al-Giza just south of Cairo University, is one of the oldest in the world, with an outstanding collection of international and African animals. Children can join the Friends of the Animals Club, which meets Fridays at 1330 in the club building on the grounds to learn more about the animals.

The **Gizera Planetarium** at the Gizera Exhibition Grounds (entrance on Gala Bridge side) gives nightly (1900) shows except Friday in Arabic; groups can arrange English-language performances through Dr. M. Ahmed Sulayman (tel. 341-2453).

At the **Aquarium Park,** (tel. 340-1606) Abu Feda, Zamalek (0830-1530 daily; fee 25PT), grottos hold large tanks filled with over 190 kinds of fish, and the grounds present a labyrinth of tunnels and stairs to explore; bring a picnic and spend the day.

Felfela Village on the Mariuta Canal (tel. 383-4209/383-0574 offers dancing horses, folk dancing, and good Egyptian village cuisine (see chart in "Food" section, p. 238). Daily shows run between 1300 and 1900; 1300-1800 on Fri. Sat., and Sun., between Sept. and June; the restaurant closes daily at sunset. You'll need reservations on Fridays. Or take in the ethnic dancing (2030 and 2230) at their branch in the Ramesses Hilton.

Dr. Ragab's Pharaonic Village, Jacob Island, Giza, tel. 729-053, reenacts life in pharaonic times; LE20 adults, LE10 students, for a floating ride through the canals to see a reconstructed temple with its sacred lake, and the homes of a nobleman and a farmer.

The **Heliopolis Kids Club** meets monthly (usually the second Fri.), 1200-1500, at the Baron Hotel, for ages 4-14, for programs, games, lunch, and entertainment; contact Olfat, tel. 291-5757, ext. 2034. **Ma'adi Youth Center,** 27 Road 207 Ma'adi, tel. 352-8394, offers pool, ping pong, video games, a skateboard ramp, volleyball, a VCR, and a snack bar for teenagers under 17; open Sun.-Tues. 1500-1800; Thurs. and Fri., 1500-0100; Sat., 1200-1800; closed Wednesday.

Several **amusement parks** also cater to kids. The Cookie Amusement Park near the Giza pyramids (turn right at the end of Sh. King Faisal; open at 1500 daily, 1200 Fri.) offers fun rides and challenging games. Merryland, I Hegaz, Heliopolis (Roxi), tel. 244-8003; open 0800-0100, boasts an enormous merry-go-round, a small zoo, and paddle boats. Sinbad Amusement Park, near the Cairo International Airport (open winter 1400-2300 daily, 1000-2300 Fri.; summer 1700-0200 daily), has bumper cars and a small roller coaster as well as lots of rides for small children.

Falucca Rides

Get a group of people together and you can spend a relaxing evening on the Nile under the taut sail of a falucca. Take a picnic dinner and plenty of mosquito repellent. You can rent a falucca (about LE10-15 during the day, LE15-20 in the evening, depending on your bargaining abilities) from their mooring spots near Shepherd's, the Meridien, or the Good Shot in Ma'adi. The boatman will expect a tip.

Coffeehouses

Men in Cairo often spend their afternoons in coffeehouses, a tradition that stretches back at least into the Middle Ages when coffee was introduced from Yemen. Houses used to host storytellers, performers who chanted the epic tales from *Kalilah and Dimnah,* the adventures of Abu Zeid, and *Tales For 1001 Nights.* Today the coffeehouses flourish, serving as centers where

tradesmen, intellectuals, and bus drivers congregate to smoke a *shiisha* over a cup of coffee and unwind in a game of backgammon.

Cairo's oldest coffeehouse is **Fishawis's.** Tucked back into the twisting alleys of Khan al-Khalili, the shop is not as large as it once was, but it still plays host to a number of luminaries. Nearby, **Sukaria Cafe** is often frequented by fortune tellers and magicians. Other houses where foreigners and women can visit include **Atelier,** 2 Karim al-Daoula (near Midan Talaat Harb), a small shop with garden and art gallery, its tables filled with literary types; **Cafe Riche,** where the Free Officers plotted the revolution; **Groppi's Garden,** Abdul Khalaq Sarwat, was home to British officers during the war and today serves coffee and breakfast to a number of staffers of *al-Haram* newspaper.

Hobbies

The **Heliopolis Bridge Club** meets every Monday, 0900-1330, at the Baron Hotel. New players are welcome; contact Rhoda Boraie, tel. 669-629. **Chess** is also popular in Egypt, with the Chess Federation, Gizera Sporting Club, tel. 340-6000, sponsoring local, national, and international competitions; for more information contact the federation.

Although **coin collectors** no longer meet regularly, you can contact shops in the "street of the goldsellers" or inside the markets of Khan al-Khalili, where coin dealers still informally congregate. **Stamp collectors** also meet informally at the Cafe Mukhtallat, 14 Abdul Khalaq Sarwat, near the Postal Museum, and the Philatelic Society of Egypt meets Saturday evenings at 16 Abdul Khalaq Sarwat on the 3rd floor; collectors should beware that forgeries of Egyptian classic stamps abound. A reputable dealer is Oriental Philatelic House, Continental Arcade.

After Hours

Cairo after dark offers a plethora of entertainment: nightclubs, bars, discos, cabarets (mostly for men), and casinos. Often in major hotels, they present shows usually capped with a belly dancer. Nightclubs often require dinner, and those that don't usually have a cover charge: LE5-20. Cocktail hours for Egyptians are 1900-2300; dinner doesn't start before 1730 ever, and shows at the earliest 2200. Men may be required to wear a coat and tie; often admission is for couples only, although the requirement is not always strictly enforced. You'll need a foreign passport to get in casinos; gambling is in foreign currency only. For a complete listing of night spots see "What's On" in *Cairo Today*.

Nightclubs: In Cairo, you can go dancing in romantic gardens or terraces to European or Latin music, listen to the latest international hits, or watch varied performances of foreign and Egyptian acts, nearly always including a belly dancer. Among the major hotels, the Ramesses Hilton **Two Seasons Supper Club** (tel. 744-400) has perhaps the best floor show—nightly except Mon., 2130-0230. The **Tropicana** at the Nile Hilton offers barbecue and Oriental food as well as a good dance orchestra beside the pool; it opens at 2130 but the action doesn't pick up until later. In winter (Oct.-May) it moves inside to the **Belvedere** (open 2200-0230, closed Tues., tel. 767-444/765-666 ext. 292) and substitutes French cuisine for the grill; set in 19th-century Victorian decor, you can watch the show from the bar without buying dinner. **Sahara City** on the Alexandria Desert Road occupies a tent and presents a whole string of belly dancers; the expensive price tag includes dinner. If you want to sit along the Nile, try the **Good Shot** in Ma'adi on the Cornishe next to the Ma'adi Yacht Club or the **Nile Garden** on Ma'adi Road. Both offer live music on summer weekends. **Cave des Rois,** 12 Sh. Muhammad Sakeb, Zamalek, with its dance floor and evening band, draws the locals. The family-oriented **Merryland** in Roxi, Heliopolis has a tea garden with a restaurant and nightclub with a show; no men alone. The **cabarets** that cater to men line Sh. al-Haram (Pyramids Road).

Discotheques: In Cairo, discos are actually small nightclubs, often with recorded music and sometimes a small (30-45 minute) show; prices are lower, and although many advertise for couples only, not all enforce the rule. With the trend toward conservatism, fewer young women patronize the discos. The younger the crowd, the louder the music, but even in the quietest, come with earplugs and no plans for conversation. The moderately priced **Saddle,** tel. 383-3444/383-3222 at the Mena House Oberoi is a notable exception; the Western ranch decor matches the meals; open daily from 2200. **Jackie's,** tel. 767-444/765-666, at the Nile Hilton is the chicest of Cairo's discos; open daily 2200-0330; Hilton guests are free, others pay LE20; business or dress attire. On Thurs. and Fri. 1700-2100 Jackie's offers teenagers a Discovision matinee. The **Sinbad** disco (tel. 262-8111/261-7100) is inconveniently located in the Sonesta Hotel in Nasr City, but its moderate prices and popular music draw Cairo residents.

Bars: The bars in the major hotels are plush and all are expensive, especially now with the new taxes on liquor. At the Nile Hilton, the interior of the **Taverne du Champ de Mars** was imported from Brussels and reassembled on the hotel's ground floor. The stained glass windows and Tiffany lamps make a visit mandatory; the gays who've made it their center are low-key. Open 1100-0200; snacks available. Enjoy classical quartet music in the evenings at the Semiramis **Tea Garden,** or visit **Sultan's Bar** at the Mena House, where you can enjoy drinks at the piano bar and watch the setting sun bathe the pyramids in Egypt's golden light. Cairo Marriott Hotel's **View Lounge** (open 1700-0130) lives up to its name. It has quiet surroundings at night, and 1200-1500 serves a New York-style deli buffet, LE18. Or try the Old World charm of **After Eight,** 6 Qasr al-Nil (in the passage), open at 2000. **Vito's,** open 1700-0300, at the al-Salaam Hotel, 61 Sh. Abdul Hamid Badawy (tel. 245-2155), offers Italian food and a games corner (darts, backgammon), as well as live music; open 2100-2400.

Some of the most popular bars are in Zamalek. The four-corners area boasts the **Piazza** with good Italian food and the **Matchpoint,** a video bar in the best Western tradition. Both are moderately priced and attract a mix of students and expatriates, as does **B's Corner,** open 1500-0100, 22 Taha Hussein (tel. 341-3870), which offers board games and has no cover charge. The **Il Capo** (tel. 341-3870), which shares the same building, offers good live music with a shifting cover charge, depending on the talent of the band. **Pub 28,** 28 Shagarit al-Durr, is also popular, as is **El-Patio** (tel. 340-2645), just off the same street to the right, a block north of Sh. 26 July; open 1800-0100.

Gambling for foreigners only is available at several major hotels including the Nile Hilton, the

Marriott, and the Sheraton. You must be 18, play with foreign money and possess a foreign (non-Egyptian) passport. These small casinos offer slot machines, blackjack, roulette, craps, and baccarat, and most are open from late afternoon or early evening to the small hours of the morning.

THE ARTS

In the arts, as in other disciplines of the Middle East, Egypt has taken a lead, both in classical studies and in modern innovations. Paintings and sculptures reflect Egypt's artistic history. Carienes, often avid participants in plays and concerts, make demanding and knowledgeable audiences, drawing stellar performances from outstanding international companies. Egypt is perhaps best known in the rest of the Arab world for movies; high-quality productions of original Arabic works as well as translations of Western ones. With the support of the Ministry of Culture, the Cairo Symphony, the Music Conservatory, the National Ballet, the Dramatic Arts Institute, the Folk Art Institute, and the Cinegraphic Institute all call the *City of the Arts* in Giza home; here Egypt's best teach youngsters and hone their own skills.

CAIRO CULTURAL CENTERS

NAME	ADDRESS	PHONE	COMMENTS
American Cultural Center	4 Sh. Ahmed Ragheb, Garden City	354-9601	Library (free) and films
American Research Center in Egypt	2 Midan Qasr al-Doubara (2nd floor) Garden City	354-8239/ 355-3052	Lecture series, day-trips, seminars, and library for researchers and members
Austrian Cultural Center	1103 Cornishe al-Nil, Garden City	354-4063	Music recitals, films, and exhibitions
British Council	192 Sh. al-Nil, Aguza	345-3281-4	Library (LE20; students LE10)
Canadian Cultural Center	Canadian Embassy 6 Muhammad Fahmy al-Sayed, Garden City	354-3119 354-3159	
Egyptian Center for International Cultural Cooperation	11 Shagarit al-Durr, Zamalek	341-5419	Lectures, exhibitions, films, and excursions
French Cultural Center	1 Sh. Madraset al-Huquq al-Fransia and at 1 Sh. Sabri Abu Alam, Midan al-Ismalia, Heliopolis	355-3725 663-241	Library (LE12), films, theater, and exhibitions
Goethe Institute (German Cultural Center)	5 Sh. Abdul Salam Aref	759-877	Lectures, concerts, exhibitions, and library (free)
Israeli Academic Center in Cairo	92 Sh. al-Nil, Doqqi	348-8995 349-6232	
Italian Cultural Institute	3 Sh. Sheikhal-Marsafi, Zamalek	340-8791	Lectures, recitals, and films
Netherlands' Institute of Archaeology and Arabic Studies	1 Sh. Dr. Mahmud Azmi (north of the Marriott Hotel), Zamalek	340-0076	Thursday lectures (Sept. through June)

Cultural Centers

Maintained by many European and Asian countries, these centers support the arts and sciences by sponsoring lectures, movies, and concerts. They usually have libraries, and many are open to the public, sometimes for a small fee. They mount art displays and offer classes, and in general support the cultural life of Cairo.

Performing Arts

The new **Opera House,** the centerpiece of the Education and Cultural Center on the south end of Gizera, tel. 342-0603/601-589, is the hub of Cairo's cultural life. The main stage plays host to imported shows ranging from classical Russian ballet to American musicals. The Cairo Symphony plays in a smaller hall at the center, and the complex also includes classrooms, a music library, a museum, and an art gallery. For Opera House listings, see the insert in *Cairo Today* or check the local papers. Tickets can sometimes be hard to come by; the best advice is to just keep trying. Formal attire (coat and tie) required.

Venues

In addition, Cairo is home to numerous smaller theaters, including:

The **Umm Kulthum Theater** (formally Balloon Theater), Sh. 26 July and al-Nil, Aguza (just across the Zamalek bridge, on the south side of the road), tel. 347-1718. The theater has been renamed for the most famous singer of the Arab world. Her performances attracted tens of thousands, and when she died the entire nation mourned. You can still hear her voice on Cairo radio. At the theater, folklore dance troupes perform Oct.-March; the box office opens daily at 1000.

The **Sayed Darwish Concert Hall,** Gamalal-Din al-Afghani, Giza (behind the City of Art off Pyramid Rd.) tel. 852-473, is used primarily for student performances, although sometimes the symphony and guest troupes perform here.

The **Gumhurriya Theater,** 12 Sh. Gumhurriya, tel. 919-956. When the Cairo Opera House on Midan Opera burned, this movie theater was refurbished and served as home to the opera and symphony until the new Opera House was finished. It still hosts occasional performances.

The **Sphinx Theater** at the foot of the Sphinx, Giza, tel. 856-006, hosts plays, ballets, and musical concerts in summer.

Wekalet al-Ghuri, 3 Sh. al-Sheidh Muhammad Abdul (near al-Azhar) is a restored caravansary; its courtyard serves as a stage or concert hall for visiting troupes.

The **American University in Cairo** has several concert halls and theaters: the university's theater company performs in the Wallace and Howard theaters; concerts by local and visiting artists are often staged at Ewart Hall.

Music

The Cairo Opera Company was founded in 1869, and the city built the old opera house on Midan Opera for the opening of the Suez Canal. *Aida* was specially commissioned for the opening, but as the opera was not ready, the opening was postponed. When the hall burned in 1971, the original sets and costumes were lost. The company moved to Gumhurriya Theater until the new opera house on Gizera was finished. The season begins in March.

Egyptian and Palestinian musicians as well as prominent European ones used to comprise the Haifa Symphony Orchestra frequently conducted by Arturo Toscanini. Concerts at Ewart Hall gave way to ones at Gumhurriya Theater, and now the **Cairo Symphony** performs in the Small Hall at the Opera House. Beginning in September, the orchestra invites guest artists for nearly weekly performances, and can be quite good.

The **Folkloric Orchestra of Egypt (The Nile Music Orchestra),** under the umbrella of the Egyptian Cultural Authority, performs using ancient Egyptian instruments.

The **Cairo Opera House Singers** perform regularly at the Opera House. Singers with choral experience are welcome; practice is Sat., 1800-2030. Contact Raouf Zaidan or Ashraf Sewailam; tel. 392-8244. The **Ma'adi Community Choir** rehearses on Wed., 1930 at the Ma'adi Community Church, Road 17 and Sh. Port Said. The **Cairo Choral Society** performs "great choral works" twice a year with full orchestra, usually once before Christmas and once in the spring. The **Musical Youth of Egypt,** 16 Sh. Abu Bakr al-Siddiq, Heliopolis, tel. 244-1929, holds monthly lectures on Arabic and Western music, and seminars; members give concerts both in Egypt and abroad.

Theater

Not only do professional players perform at the Opera House, but a host of plays appear yearly put on by students and local aficionados; often these sparkle. For current listings, see *Cairo Today.*

The **Cairo Players,** British Community Association Clubhouse, 2 Abdul Rahman al-Rafi, Doqqi, welcome all English speakers. They put on regular productions, readings, workshops, and impromptu performances. Contact Liz, tel. 349-8841; Jennifer, 341-3488; or Peter, 341-8404. The **Ma'adi Community Players** meet the second Wed.; contact Susan Giusti, tel. 376-8286 after 1800, or Suchinta Wijesooriya, 376-8393.

Dance

The **National Ballet** created in the 1960s by an Egyptian who trained in Russia presents performances both in Cairo and Alexandria that, although not up to strict international standards, certainly provide a good evening's entertainment. Of the large number of folk-dance troupes in Egypt, the **Reda Troupe** is best known; they perform at the Umm Kulthum Theater and in Alexandria.

Movies

Several movie theaters that regularly present foreign (non-Arabic) films cluster around Sh. Talaat Harb or 26 July. Seats are reserved and tickets are available several days prior to the performance; do buy them ahead for they are often sold out for popular movies. Most are subtitled in Arabic or French, so the Egyptians, since they don't need to hear the sound track, talk constantly, adding to the noise and distraction of vendors wandering up and down the aisles peddling soft drinks and snacks—in short, you'll probably end up doing a lot more people-watching than movie-watching.

For those serious about their movies, try the **al-Tahrir** (on Sh. al-Tahrir a few blocks beyond the Concorde Hotel) in Doqqi, which offers super stereo sound and ultra-plush seats. It screens predominantly English-language films; rules against smoking and talking are enforced. Schedules for movie theaters appear in the *Egypt Gazette,* and performances start about 2100. During Ramadan, the **Metro Cinema** of-

fers a different foreign movie every night, beginning at 2400 hours, no reserve seats; the place is mobbed. In the fall, the **Cairo International Film Festival** presents uncut foreign moves; for details see *Cairo Today.*

Visual Arts

Like music, Cairo is the center for visual arts. For current information see the "Arts" section of *Cairo Today,* which also carries a listing of the galleries and in their "Cairo Listings," a rundown of the museums (Places to See). For additional information, contact the Cairo Art Guild, c/o Women's Association, 3 Salah al-Din, Mohandiseen, tel. 346-3521/355-7371, ext. 8328. They meet the second Mon. of the month, 1830 at the above address, near al-Salaam Hospital. Anyone interested in the arts or crafts of Egypt is welcome; call for information.

Small Museums

The **Agricultural Museum** is at the end of 6 October Bridge, Doqqi, next to the Ministry of Agriculture, tel. 702-366. Open 0900-1500, closed Mon.; small fee. Founded in 1938, it's the oldest agricultural museum in the world. It contains not only mock-ups of various agricultural processes and practices, but also reproductions of Egyptian village life, all set in a quiet park with a replica of a pharaonic garden. The **Cotton Museum** next to Agricultural Museum, has the same hours/same ticket; tel. 340-3802.

The **Cairo Carriage Museum** 26 July, Bulaq, is just east of the Cornishe; a small branch is in the Citadel; same hours as above. Not limited to state coaches, this comprehensive museum set in the old stables contains the entire set of carriages used by the royal family as well as harnesses, still in their cases.

The **Egyptian Civilization Museum** is in the Agricultural Society Pavilion in Gizera Fair Grounds (opposite Mukhtar Museum); tel. 340-5198; hours 0900-1500 daily, closed Friday. It houses a collection of paintings and sculptures on the history of Egypt: prehistoric, pharaonic, Greco-Roman, Coptic, Islamic, and modern.

The **Entomological Society Museum,** 14 Sh. Ramesses (near the Railway station), contains old (1900) but well-preserved collections of insects and birds. Hours 0900-1300 daily except Fri. and 1800-2100 Mon., Sat., and Wed.; closed Friday.

The **Ethnological Museum** on Qasr al-Aini just south of the American University, tel. 345-5350, is open 0900-1300 except Friday; free. It displays village crafts, costumes, and equipment.

Mahmud Khalil Museum, 1 al-Sheikh al-Marsafi, Zamalek, tel. 341-8672; open 1000-1400, closed Fri.: Contains the original impressionist paintings and fine sculpture from the fabulous private collection of Mahmud Khalil.

The **Muhammad Nagy Museum,** contains the collections of the artist's paintings housed in what was once his studio. It's at 9 Mahmud al-Gindy, Hadaak al-Haram (off Cairo-Alexandria Rd.), tel. 387-3484; open 1000-1700; closed Monday; free.

The **Mustafa Kamal Museum,** Midan Salah al-Din, tel. 919-943, open 0900-1300 daily, contains the tomb and personal belongings of Mustafa Kamal, nationalist and political hero.

Mukhtar Museum: Sh. al-Tahrir, Gizera (just before al-Gala Bridge), tel. 340-5918; open 0900-1500 daily, Fri. 1900-1200, closed Monday. The building was built by artist and architect Ramesses Wissa Wassef and houses the works of Mahmud Mukhtar, one of Egypt's leading sculptors.

The **Museum of Modern Art** is now housed in the Opera House complex; open Sat.-Thurs. 0900-1330, Fri. 0900-1300. Contains works by Egypt's outstanding modern painters and sculptors.

The **Post Office Museum:** Midan al-Ataba, Post Office Building, 2nd floor; tel. 390-9686; open 0900-1300 daily except Fri.; free.

The **Railway Museum** is adjoining the Cairo Railway Station, Midan Ramesses; tel. 763-793; open 0900-1400 daily except Monday. It contains automated displays and a collection of railway coaches, including the plush, private train of Khedive Ismail.

Art Galleries

Opening in Cairo faster than they can be tracked, intimate galleries display the works of well-established artists as well as enterprising newcomers. A few of the most well-known follow, but for a more current update, check in the "Arts" section of *Cairo Today.* **Akhnaton Gallery** (Center of Arts), 1 Maahad al-Swissry, in Zamalek, tel. 340-8211, open 1000-1330 and 1700-2030 Sat.-Thurs., closed Friday. In an old

villa along the Nile, it has several exhibit halls for modern art and a sculpture garden. **Arabesque,** 6 Qasr al-Nil, tel. 759-896, is in the hall of the restaurant. **Atelier du Caire,** 2 Karim al-Dowla (off Talaat Harb by the Hannaux Department store), tel. 746-730, often shows the works of new artists. **Dr. Ragab's Papyrus Institute** is a houseboat on Sh. al-Nil south of the Gizera Sheraton; open daily 1000-1900; tel. 348-8676. Displays different stages of the papyrus-making process; copies of papyrus paintings are on sale. The **Egyptian Center for International Cultural Cooperation,** 11 Shagarit al-Durr, Zamalek, tel. 341-5419, also maintains a gallery, as do many of the cultural centers. Outside of Cairo, the **Aida** lies along the Saqqara Rd., next to the al-Dar Restaurant, tel. 538-141.

SPORTS AND RECREATION

Cairo offers the visitor nearly every conceivable form of recreation, from posh sport and health clubs, to horseback riding, tennis, and motorcross in the desert. For those who like their exercise with their rears planted firmly on a bench, there's soccer and horse racing. There are sailing clubs, rowing clubs, and even a diving club, which organizes trips to the Red Sea. The people involved are invariably kind, and make strangers feel welcome. The intercultural mix will make you international friends.

Sporting Clubs

Similar to country clubs, Cairo's plush sporting clubs require a steep membership fee, although you can join some for a week or month, or even use them for a daily fee. Be sure to check what facilities you'll be able to use, and if there will be additional fees (i.e. green fees). Most offer swimming pools, courts for tennis, basketball, and gym facilities. They often have good restaurants, but by law can serve no alcohol. **Gizera Sporting Club,** Zamalek, tel. 340-6000/340-2272, sprawls over 60 acres on the island. Founded by the British in 1882, it offers 23 sports, including equestrian facilities, (dressage, jumping, polo), in addition to extensive indoor and outdoor facilities; day use is LE5, but it doesn't include use of the sport facilities, and green fees are an additional LE20. The **Nation-**

al **Sporting Club (Ahly),** Gizera, (next to Gizera Club, tel. 340-2112/341-4020 and **Heliopolis Sporting Club,** 17 al-Merghany, Heliopolis, tel. 291-4800, both allow visitors for a day-use fee. **Al-Shams Sporting Club** in Heliopolis, tel. 244-1278 is the largest in the Arab world, offering extensive courts and playing fields as well as horseback riding and skeet shooting. The **Ma'adi Sporting Club,** 8 al-Nadi Square, tel. 350-5504, has an olympic-size pool and in addition to the standard sports offers movies and a computer room where kids are welcome.

Health Clubs

Now in all the major hotels, health clubs have invaded Cairo. Most have Jacuzzis, saunas, gymnasiums, and offer massage and fitness classes. Many also offer other sports, more commonly associated with the sporting clubs listed above, but without the social connotations. In addition to the ones in the hotels, several private clubs exist.

The **Community Services Association (CSA),** 4 Road 21, Ma'adi, tel. 350-5284, open 0900-1700 Sun.-Thurs., offers horseback-riding lessons and classes in general fitness. **Shaalan Fitness Center,** 1191 Cornishe al-Nil (World Trade Center), 5th floor, Garden City, tel. 740-424, has a gymnasium, bicycle theater, two swimming pools, solarium, steam bath, and sauna. **Valentine's Health and Beauty Center,** 70 Merghany, Heliopolis, tel. 291-4756, has an air-conditioned exercise/dance studio, and the standard gym equipment. Facilities include a weight-training center, aerobics, and refreshments of health food and a juice bar.

Flying

At Imbaba Airfield, glider-flying lessons are available on Thurs. and Fri.; lessons in planes are also available; make arrangements at the airfield, tel. 805-655.

Golf

Cairo boasts two nine-hole courses: the **Gizera Club** (Zamalek) and at the **Mena House Oberoi**; lessons and rental clubs are available.

Horses

Horses for rent are stabled near the pyramids: **MG Stables,** tel. 385-3832/385-1241; **AA Sta-** bles, Sh. Abu al-Hol, pyramids, tel. 385-0531; **Eurostables,** pyramids, tel. 385-5849. Private riding clubs: **Ferrosea Riding Club**, south edge of Gizera Club, tel. 800-692; **Gizera Sporting Club**, tel. 340-6000; al-Salaam Hotel, 61 Abdul Hamid Badawi, Heliopolis, tel. 245-5155; **Heliopolis Racing Club**, tel. 245-4090. Arabian horse farm of the **Egyptian Agricultural Organization**, al-Zahara Station, Sh. Ahmed Esmat (off Gisr al-Suwais), tel. 243-1733, visitors welcome daily 0800-1300. Arabian horse racing Saturday and Sunday alternating between Heliopolis Hippodrome and Gizera Racetrack, mid-Oct. through mid-May, post time 1330. The Sat. *Egyptian Mail* carries the racing form.

Motor Racing

The Pharaohs' Rally, scheduled in October, covers 4,000 km in 12 days. Starting at the pyramids, the course runs across the Western Desert from Siwa to Abu Simbel and returns to the pyramids via the Eastern Desert. The race has divisions for cars, motorcycles, and trucks; entries are due by the end of July: contact Rami Siag, tel. 285-6022, or the International Club: Fenouil SA des Pharaons, 47 rue Emile, Roux 94120, Fontenay-Dous-Bois, France.

Shooting

The **Doqqi Shooting Club**, Nadi al-Sayed, tel. 704-353, offers target, trap, and rifle shooting, as does **al-Shams Sporting Club** in Heliopolis, tel. 244-1278. For additional information you can also contact the Egyptian Shooting Federation, 37 Sh. Abdul Khalik Sarwat. Hunting is no longer permitted in Egypt.

Soccer

Soccer is Egypt's national pastime, and the season runs from Sept. to May, though you'll find pick-up games throughout the country all year. Three national leagues each field 12 teams. Cairo's Ahly and Zamalek teams play at Cairo Stadium in Heliopolis. Games are played on Fri. and Sun. afternoons starting at 1500.

Sailing

Sailing competitions are held Sept.-June by the **Cairo Yacht Club**, 3 Sh. al-Nil (beside the Sheraton Hotel), Giza, tel. 348-9415, and **Ma'adi Yacht Club**, tel. 350-5504, Cornishe al-Nil (next to the Good Shot). These clubs also provide mooring spaces for private boats. No less than 10 **rowing** clubs line the banks of the Nile around Cairo; for information contact the Egyptian Rowing Club, 11 al-Nil (behind the Giza Sheraton), tel. 348-9639.

Diving

Cairo Divers meets the first Mon. of the month at the Semiramis Inter-Continental Hotel to promote diving on the Red Sea. The group sponsors annual underwater photographic exhibits and sponsors diving classes. For information call Muhammad Shafei, tel. 258-1870.

Swimming

In addition to the clubs listed above, you can swim at any major hotel; most let non-guests use their pools. However, what used to be a reasonable charge now can vary between LE5-50, so ask before you dive in. Don't swim in the Nile, for although the water normally runs swiftly enough to discourage the snails that harbor the bilharzia larva, the risk is not worth the infection. For that matter, you probably don't want to water-ski on the Nile, either.

Running

For those who need to pound the pavement, contact the **Cairo Hash House Harriers.** They meet every Fri. afternoon about two hours before sunset for fun, non-competitive runs at the pyramids, in the desert, Ma'adi, and other popular places; runners of all abilities are welcome. Contact Mohsen al-Ashmoni, 347-5633 (h) or 341-8429 (w); Les Ross, 375-9145 (h) or 348-5913 (w); or John Hoppe, 259-0803. If you can't reach a real person, get answering machine directions from Matthew Kleinosky at 340-4932.

Tennis

Most of the sporting clubs listed above offer courts, as do the Nile Hilton and Marriott hotels. Most courts in Egypt are clay, and regulation whites are normally required. The sport is popular, and there are local as well as international tournaments. The Annual Tennis Open (late fall or early March) is held at the Tewfikia Tennis Club, Medinet al-Awkaf, Aguza, tel. 801-930.

Nature And Environment

The **Egyptian Wildlife Service** at the Cairo Zoo (tel. 726-314) takes an active part in preserving and protecting Egypt's native species, as does the **Egyptian Society for the Conservation of Nature and Wildlife,** also at the zoo, tel. 726-233, and the **Baladi Association,** tel. 743-813, which meets on the first Sun. of the month, 1700 at 47 Ramesses St., 3rd floor. The **Tree-Lovers Association** welcomes new members and interested parties; contact Muhammad Hafez Ali, 36a Road 14, Ma'adi, tel. 351-1300. If you're interested in watching Egypt's premier selection of birds, contact Ahmed Riad, 2 Granada, Heliopolis (Roxi), tel. 258-1082.

SHOPPING

Like those in much of Egypt, Cairo's shops can be divided into department stores—where prices are fixed—and dealers and *suqs*—where you're expected to bargain. The main European-type shops like Salon Vert and Omar Effendi are found along Qasr al-Nil and surrounding streets where you can buy cotton, silk, and wool. Several fabric stores offer their wares along Qasr al-Nil, toward Midan Mustafa Kamil. Just around the corner, on the west side of Sh. Muhammad Farid, is a tiny shop with beautiful embroidered caftans. Equally good are the leather and shoe stores scattered along the same area. Sharia Sarwat specializes in stationery, but has other shops as well. Surprisingly, the shops in the Hiltons (Nile and Ramesses) carry lovely items, and the clothes especially are relatively inexpensive.

For tourist items, Khan al-Khalili is the most famous, but don't limit yourself to the area of the immediate Khan—explore the surrounding streets: the gold and silver stores on Sh. Mu'izz al-Din Allah, the fabric stores behind the Ghuria, and the antique dealers and spice markets along al-Muski. You can find appliqué work (wall hangings, pillowcases, and bedspreads) as well as the old-fashioned Egyptian hat-makers *(tarboushes)* in the "street of the tentmakers." Carpets are sold in the Khan al-Khalili and at the village of Kerdassa (see p. 268), as are crafts from the Wissa Wassef School at Harraniyya (p. 280).

SERVICES

Emergency Phone Numbers
Ambulance: 123/770-123/770-018
Fire: 125/910-727/910-115
Police: 122
Tourist Police: 126/390-6028/926-028

Banks
Most international banks have branches or representatives in Cairo. In general banks are open Mon.-Thursday. **American Express,** 15 Qasr al-Nil (just off Midan Talaat Harb toward Sh. Ramesses), tel. 750-444, is open 0800-1800, and has branches at major hotels. Amex provides dollars or Egyptian pounds for traveler's checks, or if you're a card holder, personal checks. You can have mail and money sent. **Bank of America,** 106 Qasr al-Aini, Garden City, tel. 355-2747, will advance Egyptian pounds *only* against Visa and MasterCards; it may take time to confirm so bring reading material. **Cairo Barclays International Bank,** 12 Midan Sheikh Yusif, Garden City, tel. 354-2195; **Chase Manhattan Overseas,** 21-23 Giza, Giza, tel. 728-485, telex 23215 CMOC UN; **Citibank N.A.** 4 Ahmen Pasha, Garden City, tel. 355-1873/355-1877; **Commercial International Bank** (formerly Chase National), 21-23 Giza, tel. 726-132; **Lloyds Bank International,** 48 Abdul Khalek Sarwat, tel. 933-384, and at 44 Muhammad Mazhar, Zamalek, tel. 341-8366/340-6587.

Mail
The main post office (55 Sh. Sarwat, Midan Ataba, tel. 912-356) is open Sat.-Thurs., 0900-1900 (Ramadan 0900-1600); Fri., 0900-1200. Most other offices: 0830-1500, closed Fridays. Express mail service is available around the corner on Bidek (Sat.-Thurs., 0800-1900). and from: Abbassia, 127 Midan Abdul Pasha, tel. 820-469; al-Azhar, 21E Midan al-Azhar; Bab al-Luq, Muhammad Mahmud, tel. 354-6053/354-8762; Doqqi, Ministry of Land Reclamation Building, tel. 702-792; Giza, 10 Murad, tel. 724-040; Heliopolis, 3 Bosta, tel. 666-980; Ma'adi, Road 9, tel. 950-2185; and Zamalek, Hassan Sabri, tel. 340-1933.

International Business Associates handles Federal Express: 1079 Cornishe al-Nil, Garden City, tel. 355-0427. Commercial express mail may be sent through Aramex International, 85 al-Hussein, tel. 349-7119, and DHL, 20 Gamal al-Din Abul Mahasen, Garden City, tel. 355-7301/355-7118.

Telephone, Telex, Fax
Central Telephone and Telegraph offices at 8 Sh. Adly, Midan Tahrir (near Sh. Talaat Harb), 26 Ramesses, and Alfi, as well as many branch offices, are open 24 hours; others: 0700-2200. Calls within Greater Cairo as well as Helwan are local, direct-dial calls. Long-distance (within Egypt) and international calls can be handled at any phone office. You can make radio and international calls (dial 777-120) at the business centers at the hotels (see "Business Services" below), but they'll charge you a hefty 25% extra. To dial direct to the U.S. with an ATT credit card, call 356-0200 and you'll reach an American operator. Major offices will send telegrams; you will need your passport. Telex services are available at these offices, Cairo Airport, and most five-star hotels. Fax is available until 1400 at local exchanges and some post offices such as Ataba, tel. 912-356; Zamalek, tel. 340-1933; and Ma'adi, tel. 350-2185. Arabic telephone books are impossible to find, but the Ma'adi Women's Guild publishes an English-language *Cairo Telephone List* each January; it's available from the Guild, P.O. Box 218, Ma'adi, and from the Community Services Association, the American Chamber of Commerce, Ma'adi Community Church, and the Women's Association. *Yellow Pages* put out by Tele-Direct of Canada are available at most bookstores, or contact the company directly at 6 Sh. Clombaroni, Zamalek, tel. 341-2223.

Embassies
See p.122.

Health
Hospitals: Al-Salaam on the Cornishe in Ma'adi, tel. 363-8050, is good, as is the nearby **Nile Badrawi Hospital,** tel. 363-8688. Others: **Al-Salaam,** 3 Sh. Syria in Mohandiseen, tel. 346-7061-3; **Anglo-American Hospital,** next to Cairo Tower on Gizera, tel. 341-8630/340-6165; **Hayat Medical Center,** 6 Sh. Menis, Heliopolis, tel. 290-7027.

Pharmacies: For 24-hour service try **Isaaf** on the corner of Sh. 26 July and Ramesses, tel. 743-369; **Ajaz Khanat Sayfa,** 76 Sh. Qasr al-Aini, Garden City (a few blocks south of Midan Tahrir), tel. 354-2678; **Zamalek Pharmacy,** 3 Shagarit al-Durr, tel. 340-2406; and **Essam,** 101 Road 9, Ma'adi, tel. 350-4126. Other pharmacies are scattered throughout the city.

Business Services

The **American Chamber of Commerce in Egypt,** Marriott Hotel, Suite 1541, Zamalek, tel. 340-8888, meets monthly for lunch and welcomes visitors; a directory of members available. **International Business Associates (IBA),** 1079 Cornishe al-Nil, Garden City, tel. 350-1473/355-0427, provides comprehensive office services, including instant office space, messenger, courier, telex, phone, and typing. They are agents for **Federal Express,** open 24 hours a day with branches at 24 Sh. Syria, Mohandiseen, tel. 349-0986; 31 Gulf St. Ma'adi, tel. 350-7172; 21 Sh. Muhammad Ghoniem, Heliopolis; or 28 Sh. Hurriya, Alexandria (03) 420-2321. **Professional Business Services (PBS),** Osiris Building, Suite 32, Sh. Latin America, tel. 355-1913, with a branch in the Sonesta Hotel, offers similar services. In addition, nearly all five-star hotels have business centers. **Photocopying** is available at the above centers, as well as at numerous photo stores and a number of small shops around the American University in Cairo campus.

Photo Stores

You cannot get Kodachrome developed in Egypt; it must be sent to Europe. You can get one-day processing on most other films for a small fee. Like most services, film, developing, and camera supplies are less expensive outside major hotels. For film and supplies, check with **Kodak Cairo,** 20 Sh. Adly, tel 749-399; or 159 Sh. 26 July, Zamalek; open Mon.-Sat., 0900-2100. **Actina,** 4 Sh. Talaat Harb, tel. 757-236, open Mon-Fri., 0900-2000, and Sat. 0900-1230, carries Agfa and other films. **Khatchig,** 27 Sh. Abd al-Khalek Sarwat, #4, tel. 392-8747, open Tues.-Sat. 1000-1500 and 1600-1900 does excellent repair work.

Churches

Anglican/Episcopalian: All Saints' Cathedral, 5 Sh. Michael Lutfalla, Zamalek (behind the Marriott Hotel), tel. 341-839/340-2074. **Protestant:** Saint Andrew's United Protestant Church, 38 26 July (between Sh. Ramesses and Sh. Gala), tel. 759-451; Ma'adi Community Church, corner Port Said and Road 17, Ma'adi, tel. 353-2118/351-2755. **Christian Science:** Christian Science Society, 3 Midan Mustafa Kamal, tel. 350-6194/351-7850. **Mormon:** 44 Road 20, Ma'adi, tel. 350-4721. **Catholic:** Church of the Holy Family, 55 Road 15, Ma'adi, tel. 350-2004; St. Joseph's Church (Franciscan), 2 Bank Misr at corner of Muhammad Farid, tel. 393-6677; St. Joseph's Roman Catholic Church, 4 Ahmen Sabri, Zamalek, tel. 340-8902/340-8348. **Jewish:** There's a synagogue on Sh. Adly. **Coptic Patriarchate:** St. Marks Cathedral, Anba Rueis Ambolis, Heliopolis, tel. 821-274. For current times of services, call the individual churches or see the "Listings" in *Cairo Today.*

Language Studies

The following organizations teach Arabic and can recommend private tutors: **The Egyptian Center of Cultural Cooperation,** 11 Shagarit al-Durr, Zamalek, tel. 341-5419; **International Language Institute** (ILI), Muhammad Bayokumi off Merghany, Heliopolis, tel. 666-704; **American University in Cairo** (AUC), Division of Public Service, 28 Falaki, Bab al-Luq, tel. 357-6872/357-6873, 0900-1500 except Fri. and Saturday.

For French, German, Italian, Japanese, and Spanish, contact the appropriate cultural centers.

Clubs

Archaeology and History: Several clubs support the work of their national teams in the field, often organizing visits to archaeological sites and to places usually closed to visitors. These clubs are most active during the winter excavation season: **Archaeology Club (American Research Center in Egypt),** 2 Midan Qasr al-Doubara, Garden City, tel. 354-8239/355-3052; **Egyptian Exploration Society (British)**—contact Rosalind Haddon, tel. 341-5862.

Cultural Clubs: These clubs often plan trips, lectures, and other activities for their members; all welcome visitors. **The International Club** fosters knowledge about other cultures through activities; call 260-8244. The **Rotary,** is at 3 Sh. Ali

Labib Gabr (Qasr al-Nil and Talaat Harb), tel. 741-737. **The Automobile Club,** 10 Sh. Qasr al-Nil, has some of the best food in town; you'll need an international Automobile Club card; formal (coat and tie) attire required. **All Nations Woman's Group** meets the second and fourth Thurs. of the month for cultural exchange, lectures, seminars, films, and trips; call 340-8582/340-2649/341-1120. You can reach the **Women's Association** at 3 Salah al-Din, Mohandiseen; tel. 346-3521, Mon.-Thurs. 0830-1430.

Storage
Ramesses Station rents lockers (*al-khazanat*) for 15PT per day, for a maximum of 15 days. For members, the American Research Center in Egypt has limited storage available.

Laundry
Most large hotels offer both laundry and dry cleaning, mostly with next-day service. Small laundry shops are available throughout the city—ask around—but they can be slow. For delicate silks and wools, use Top-Matic Laundry and Cleaners next to the Safir Hotel, Midan al-Misaha, Doqqi.

INFORMATION

Ministry Of Tourism
The Ministry of Tourism is headquartered in the Misr Travel Tower at Abbassia, but maintains offices at 5 Sh. Adly, tel. 391-3454 (where you can get a tourist map and the best information) open daily 0800-1900. There are branch offices at Khan al-Khalili, Midan Ramesses, and at the Cairo Airport.

City Tours
Although getting around Cairo (and for that matter, the rest of Egypt) on your own is possible, it's a hassle and not always less expensive. Many travel agencies either own hotels or book numbers of rooms for large discounts and may therefore be able to arrange trips at less expense than you could on your own. For specialized tours, ask at the cultural centers (listed above), and check "What's On" in *Cairo Today*. Often these tours are not only relatively inexpensive, they often visit areas normally closed, accompanied by experts. Commercial tours are an-

other easy way to see sights, especially those "off the beaten track."

Among the more reliable **travel agents:** Eastmar Travel, 13 Qasr al-Nil, tel. 753-147/753-216; Itta Tours, 48 Qasr al-Nil, tel. 749-855. South Sinai Travel, 79 Merghany, Heliopolis tel. 672-441, at 24 Hussein Hegazi (Qasr al-Aini), tel. 355-5952, or Jeddah Tower, Ismail Muhammad, Zamalek, tel. 341-9428, arranges camping trips through the desert, including one from Siwa, along the oases, to *Darb al-arba'in;* they takes 23 days.

For trips to Siwa, contact Dahab Tours, 14 Alfi, tel. 261-3224. Although American Express maintains numerous offices throughout Cairo (like 15 Qasr al-Nil, tel. 750-444, telex 92715 AMEXT UN), their service can be erratic.

Booksellers
Booksellers are scattered throughout the city. Secondhand and obscure volumes are often to be found in the book markets in Opera Square and Midan al-Hussein. One of the best and least expensive is **Shorouk Bookshop,** 1 Midan Talaat Harb, tel. 391-2480, and at al-Borsa al-Gedia, tel. 393-8071, fax (02) 343-4814, open 0900-2000. More expensive is the **American University in Cairo Bookstore,** 113 Qasr al-Nil, tel. 354-2964-9 (ask for the bookstore); they have a new branch at 16 Sh. Muhammad Ibn Thakeb, Zamalek. The **Anglo Egyptian Bookstore** (which is piled high with English-language books—an experience), is at 165 Muhammad Farid, tel. 391-4337; **L'Orientaliste** (specializes in rare books but also has secondhand ones)—15 Qasr al-Nil, tel. 753-418; **Les Livres de France,** 36 Qasr al-Nil, tel. 393-5512, maintains a few English books; **Lehnert and Landrock,** 44 Serif and at the Cairo Museum, tel. 392-7606/393-5324, has published some of the oldest books on Egypt; **Reader's Corner**, 33 Abdul Khalaq Sarwat, tel. 748-801, and at the Nile Hilton, tel. 750-666/740-777; **Romanceia**, Shagarit al-Durr (at Ismail Muhammad); and **Shady**, 29 Abdul Khalaq Sarwat, tel. 748-168 maintains a large selection of secondhand books.

Libraries
The best library in Cairo is that at the American University in Cairo, but access is difficult; check with the head librarian about the possibility of

taking out a limited membership. The various cultural centers and a few churches maintain libraries with differing access. For an exhaustive listing, see *Cairo Practical Guide,* p. 186.

TRANSPORT

GETTING AROUND

Since the Egyptian revolution in 1952, Cairo has had little money to upgrade or expand her public transportation facilities. With 14 million people in the city, the buses and trams (also called trains, streetcars, and metros) are crammed to overflowing, especially during rush hours. At that time, it's impossible to get a cab, and even private cars are stalled in Cairo's notorious traffic jams. The truth is that to get anywhere in Cairo during rush hours (0900-1100 and 1500-1700) is nearly impossible.

The Metro

The one bright spot in Cairo's public transportation system is the Metro, which runs underground from Midan Ramesses to Said Zaghlul, where it emerges and continues through Old Cairo, Ma'adi, and on to Helwan. Tickets cost 25-50PT. The system is clean, modern, and fast, with trains running about every 10 minutes from 0530 to 0100. The stations are immaculate, well-marked, and air-conditioned; no smoking is allowed (there's a hefty fine plus questioning by police). Hang on to your ticket, as you must deposit it to get out of the station at your destination. (Not having a ticket costs LE2.50.) The trains are filled with students in the afternoons, and packed during rush hours. The women's car is at the front of the train.

The station entrances are all marked with a big red M, and at large *midans* like Tahrir, they also serve as pedestrian underpasses. The only trick to the system is that the three largest stations are named after presidents, not their location: Sadat Station (black and tan) is at Midan Tahrir, Nasser (green) is at Midan Tawfiqiyya, and Mubarak (red, white, and blue) is at Ramesses. To travel north on the line, head for al-Marg; to go south, take the Helwan direction.

The **Heliopolis Metro** is a different system, which starts at Midan Abd al-Monim Riad (behind the Egyptian Museum), and splits into three lines at Roxi (beyond Midan Ramesses): Abd al-Aziz Fahmi (green), Nuzha (red), and Merghani (yellow). Three other lines, labeled in Arabic only, run from Roxi to Medinat Nasr, Alf Maskan to Darasa, and from Mataria to Darasa; unless you speak Arabic or are good at getting around in foreign places, don't try these lines.

Buses

Cairo's public buses (red and tan, and blue and white) run fixed routes and cost about 10PT; a few are 25PT. The buses are numbered in Arabic, and the outward-bound route does not always correspond to the inward-bound one (they often make loops). The main station is in Midan Tahrir, and street stops are normally marked by a metal-roofed shed; don't hesitate to ask passengers—most are knowledgeable and helpful. Enter the bus from the back and exit through the front—but drivers rarely stop so you'll have to master techniques for boarding and disembarking the moving vehicles. Be sure to face front when you jump off, and be prepared to hit the pavement running. These buses are nearly always crowded, but lack of room never deters one more from climbing aboard—often through windows. Additional passengers hang outside the buses, sometimes only clinging to the hand of a person inside. Unless your stop is the last on the line, getting off is even harder than getting on. Although Cairo is a safe city, crowded buses tempt pickpockets, so watch your wallet or purse.

In case you're brave, here are a few major routes from Tahrir: **8** and **900:** pyramids, Mena House; **16:** Midan Doqqi, Aguza; **174:** Sayyida Zaynab, Ibn Tulun, Sultan Hassan, the Citadel; **422:** New Airport (every hour, 24 hours a day); **72:** Sayyida Zaynab, Citadel; **173:** Citadel; **63:** Khan al-Khalili; **66:** al-Azhar; **600:** 13 Zamalek. Note: the buses with the slashed numbers *do not* run the same routes as those with plain numbers.

Minibuses

The orange and white minibuses are a pleasanter option. They prohibit standing passengers so they're never crowded, and they halt at stops. The main station is in Midan Tahrir, where the bays are clearly marked with bus numbers (English and Arabic). Fares are 25-50PT.

From Tahrir in front of the Mugama'a: **59:** Ramesses, Tahrir; **52, 56:** Ma'adi, Old Cairo; **58:** Ma'adi via Dar al-Salaam; **83:** Doqqi, Giza, the pyramids (Sh. al-Haram); **82:** Qasr al-Aini, Giza (Sh. Faisal), pyramids.

From Tahrir in front of the Nile Hilton: **24:** Abbassia, Roxi; **27:** Misr al-Gadida, Airport; **35:** Abbassia, Midan Ismailia (Misr al-Gadida).

From Tahrir in front of the Arab League Building: **26:** Roxi, Tahrir, Doqqi, Giza; **76:** Ataba, Zamalek, Tahrir, Sh. Sudan; **84:** Ataba, Tahrir, Doqqi, Giza. **54:** Citadel, Cemetery, 77 Bulay al-Dakrur, Khan al-Khalili. To catch eastbound buses face the museum; to catch westbound ones, face the Mugama'a. Deluxe and large first-class hotels run courtesy buses to Midan Tahrir.

River Taxis

From Maspero Station (on the Cornishe across from the TV building), blue, glass-topped river taxis (10PT) run to University Bridge (near the SwissAir Restaurant), Manyal, Rhoda, Giza, and Old Cairo. (To get to the old churches, you'll have to climb through a maze of houses and find the pedestrian overpass to cross the tram lines; it's easier to take the Metro.)

Taxis

Cairo abounds with taxis: black-and-white sedans and Peugeot station wagons, all with the cab number written on the door (both in English and Arabic) and orange license plates. Taxis off the streets are cheaper than those outside hotels, for the hotel cabs spend much of their time waiting in line for passengers. Many drivers will tell you their fare in advance—these are often the most expensive cabs. Those drivers who speak English and hang around the tourist areas are overpaid, so you really have to bargain hard with them. You can also stop cabs on the street, even if they already have passengers, provided they're going your general direction. These drivers may not know much English. The fare depends upon the time of day and the traffic; the most hassle-free way to deal with cabs is to know how much the trip

should cost, and just hand the amount to the driver as you leave the cab. Some hotels such as the Simiramis Inter-Continental publish fixed rates; never pay more. Avoid the colored Peugeots as they charge exorbitant prices and, since some are from outside Cairo, may not even know where you want to go.

Remember, suggested fares are for one person in a cab hailed on the street, which is free to pick up other passengers. If traffic is heavy and the going slow, you might want to pay a little extra. You will also find that fares for natives run about half those for foreigners. Fares from Midan Tahrir to: Doqqi, Giza, Khan al-Khalili, Zamalek: LE5-10; to pyramids: LE10-20; to Ma'adi: LE15-30.

Taxis can be hired for full or half days. Figure on about LE10-15/hour if most of the driver's time is spent waiting for you. Figure LE40-60 for a half day and LE100 for a full day. Otherwise, agree on the cost of a specific trip. The price includes driver and gas. Some drivers are better than others, so if a driver scares you, chuck him. Your peace of mind is worth it.

Service Taxis

In Cairo, vans or Peugeot station wagons offer a fast and reliable alternative to buses. They run regular routes, and most congregate near the Mugama'a in Midan Tahrir. Fares are fixed and run from 25PT to several pounds. They can be flagged down just like regular taxis, provided your destination is on their route.

Limousines

Several companies provide limousine service on a destination, hourly, or daily basis: Bita; Gizera Sheraton, tel. 341-1333/341-1555, Marriott Hotel, tel. 340-8888; Budget, Semiramis Inter-Continental Hotel, tel. 355-7171, ext. 8991; Misr Limousine (24 hour), 7 Aziz Bil-Lah, Zeitoun, tel. 259-9813/259-8914; Egyptrav (24 hour), Nile Hilton, tel. 755-029/766-548. Prices can often be competitive with private taxis, e.g. from Semiramis Inter-Continental to the airport, so check them out.

Hiring Cars

The influx of car-rental companies now makes the luxury of renting a car to be delivered at Cairo Airport feasible. However, Egyptians drive by a

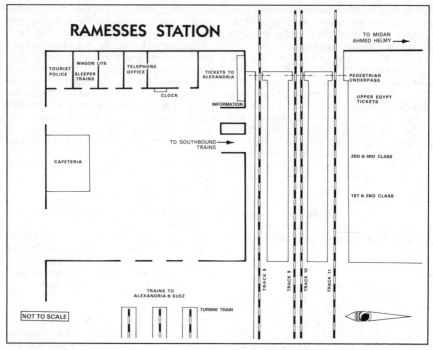

unique set of rules, and in Cairo, the games-manship rises to its peak. Fender benders are frequent, and often settled in the street (so a good-sized wad of cash is essential, and speaking a smattering of Arabic is helpful). Thus it's a good idea to put off driving until you've ridden awhile, since many street signs, with the exception of the new freeways are only written in Arabic. If you do decide to tackle this challenge and happen to be involved in an accident, get a policeman (they're on nearly every corner) right away.

International car-rental agencies have offices at the Cairo Airport and major hotels. Most rental companies will rent drivers with their cars for a small additional fee, and you can hire a car and driver by the week or longer, which will save you hassling Cairo's traffic and keep you from spending endless hours lost. To rent a car, you must be at least 25 years old and have an International Driver's License. Bring your passport and money for a hefty deposit (LE500); most companies accept credit cards for both deposits and payments.

Car Rental Companies: Avis, 16 Maamel al-Sukar, Garden City, tel. 354-8698; **Bita,** 15 Mahmud Bassiouni, tel. 774-330/753-130; **Budget,** 5 al-Maqrizi, Zamalek, tel. 341-3790; **Hertz,** 195 26 July, Aguza, tel. 347-4172/347-2238; **Max Rent Cars,** 27 Lebanon, Mohandiseen, tel. 347-4712/347-4713.

The biggest problem with driving in Cairo is parking. Three multi-level garages at Midan Ataba, Midan Opera, and off Gumhurriya near Alfi, and behind the Ramesses Hilton hardly make a dent in the problem. Many hotels allow outsiders to park in their lots provided they're not full. When parking on the street, be sure your wheels are straight and the parking brake is off: parking attendants may have to move your car to make space. Attendants should be tipped 50PT-LE1.

Carriages

Horse-drawn vehicles called calishes are available in a few areas of Cairo, primarily near five-star hotels. Prices are steep, but taking one from Shepherd's to the Cairo Tower or the Opera House makes a fun ride.

Walking
In Cairo, walking is safe and often quicker than driving. Most of the major sights lie within an hour's walk of Midan Tahrir. Take care, however, for sidewalks can be uneven and manhole covers broken. In older sections of town, the streets, originally designed for camels and donkeys, have no sidewalks, so beware of bikes, motorscooters, cars, carts, and trucks. Pedestrians never have the right-of-way, so take care crossing streets.

GETTING FROM

By Air
Three domestic airlines serve Egypt. **EgyptAir** flies to all major tourist areas: Alexandria, Luxor, Aswan, Abu Simbel, Hurghada and New Valley (Kharga). For central reservations, call 392-7444/392-7205. Cairo offices: 6 Adly, tel. 397-1256; 9 Talaat Harb, tel. 393-2836; Nile Hilton, tel. 759-806/759-703; Cairo Sheraton, tel. 348-8630, 22 Ibrahim al-Lakkani, Heliopolis, 660-399/664-305. At the airport: Terminal 1, 245-5920/245-5099; Terminal 2, 245-4400/662-630/662-488; Terminal 3, 245-9315/245-5920; Cargo, 245-1299.

Air Sinai flies regularly to Hurghada, Sharm al-Sheikh, St. Catherine's and al-Tor. Cairo office: Nile Hilton, tel. 760-948. **Zas** flies daily except Thursday to Luxor, Aswan, Hurghada, and St. Catherine's; Cairo office: Novotel, Cairo International Airport Rd., tel. 290-7836/290-8707. Zas also rents planes for national and international flights, as does **Nile Delta Air Service,** 1 Midan Talaat Harb, tel. 746-197. Tickets for all domestic flights may be paid for in Egyptian pounds without a bank receipt. Note that EgyptAir flights are not dependable, especially those to Upper Egypt, which may be canceled at any time.

By Boat
Several of the many cruise boats plying the Nile leave from Cairo at the beginning of the winter season and return in the spring. Though some tours arrange for their boats to make the entire trip, most cruises begin at either Luxor or Aswan. Be sure to book early.

Navigation Offices
Adriatica, (Mena Tours) 14 Sh. Talaat Harb, tel. 740-995, runs car and passenger ferries from Italy and Greece; **Egyptian Navigation Co.,** 20 Sh. Talaat Harb, tel. 759-166, telex 92029 ARABNAVI UN, runs the ferries between Aqaba and Nuweiba.

By Train
The Egyptian Railway connects Alexandria via Tanta, Cairo, Fayyum, the Suez Canal, and all the cities along the Nile to Aswan. Tickets are available at the main station in Midan Ramesses up to a week in advance. International Student Identity Card holders receive 50% off tickets (except sleeper trains). Ticket windows (with the number of the train posted) for various destinations are scattered throughout the station (see plan). Ticket lines are segregated: women in one, men in the other; people in line alternate at the window. The Railway Authority issues passes called Kilometre, which are similar to Eurail: 2,000 km, three month, LE52 (1st class), LE27.30 (2nd class); 3,000 km, three month, LE68.60 (1st class), LE35.60 (2nd class); 5,000 km, six month, LE101.20 (1st class), LE51.80 (2nd class); and 10,000 km, LE180.40 (1st class), and LE91 (2nd class).

Wagon Lits runs two sleeper trains daily to Upper Egypt: LE180. You will need the passport of all individuals traveling with you. If you need to make a reservation more than a week ahead, you can go to the main offices: 9 Menes, Heliopolis, tel. 290-8802/290-8804; 48 Sh. Giza, Giza, tel. 348-7354/349-2536. Wagon Lits also has an office at Shepherd's Hotel. Passengers may catch the train at Ramesses Station or Giza Station, and disembark at either Aswan or Luxor; the price is the same. This company also runs a sleeper to Marsa Matruh during the summer.

By Bus
Buses leave for all parts of Egypt from varying stations. You can buy reserve tickets on air-conditioned (doesn't always work) buses for most major cities. Bus schedules can change unexpectedly, so check locally before you plan a timetable. For some deluxe buses, tickets are

TRAIN SCHEDULE

Cairo to Alexandria (daily)

Train #	903	905**	907	911	913	915	917**	919
Cairo	0655	0810	0930	1120	1220	1310	1400	1405
Benha	0735	-	1006	1156	-	1348	-	-
Tanta	0815	-	1046	1230	1329	1433	-	-
Damanhur	0908	-	1130	1316	-	1522	-	-
Sidi Gabr	0952	1012	1213	1358	1453	1607	1602	1643
Alexandria	100	1020	1220	1405	1500	1615	1610	1650

Cairo to Alexandria (daily)

Train #	705	923	925	25	31	927**	933
Cairo	1410	1550	1750	1810	1830	1915	2130
Benha	1453	1626	1826	1852	1908	-	2206
Tanta	1530	1700	1901	1925	1944	2009	2241
Damanhur	-	1746	1948	2015	2030	-	2327
Sidi Gabr	1702	1828	2028	2058	2113	2112	0008
Alexandria	1710	1835	2035	2105	2120	2125	0015

Alexandria to Cairo (daily)

Train #	902	904**	906	910	912*	914	916**	922
Alexandria	0610	0755	0920	1030	1140	1240	1355	1530
Sidi Gabr	0621	0810	0930	1040	1150	1251	1410	1540
Damanhur	0707	-	1013	1122	-	1340	-	1622
Tanta	0803	-	1057	1207	1313	1426	-	1704
Benha	0845	-	1132	1247	-	1504	-	1742
Cairo	0920	1005	1205	1320	1420	1540	1605	1810

Alexandria to Cairo (daily)

Train #	924	26	32	926*	928	930	796
Alexandria	1710	1745	1800	1845	1910	1925	1945
Sidi Gabr	1720	1755	1810	1900	1920	1935	1957

TRAIN SCHEDULE (Cont.)

Alexandria to Cairo (daily) cont.

Train #	924	26	32	926*	928	930	796
Damanhur	1802	1840	1855	-	2005	2017	-
Tanta	1847	1926	1941	1958	2055	2107	2132
Benha	1922	2003	2017	-	2130	2142	2209
Cairo	1955	2040	2050	2055	2205	2215	2245

Cairo to Aswan (daily)

Train #	978	980	984	982	160	986-++	990	84+	86+	88	868
Cairo	0710	0730	1000	1200	1225	1400	1610	2000	2030	2000	2030
Giza	0730	0747	1017	1221	1245	1420	1627	2025	2055	2021	2050
Beni Suef	0905	0924	1115	1359	1428	-	1804	-	-	2205	2234
Minya	1038	1050	1339	1538	1600	-	1939	-	-	2348	0018
Asyut	1225	1229	1525	1723	1745	1835	2129	-	-	0144	0212
Sohag	-	1413	-	1840	1925	-	2310	-	-	0320	0343
Qina	-	1705	-	2203	2341	-	-	-	0454	0637	0755
Luxor	-	1815	-	-	0120	2310	-	0424	0645	0855	0930
Aswan	-	2320	-	-	-	-	-	0535	1045	1330	1427

Aswan to Cairo (daily)

Train #	981	987++	85+	89	87+	159	869	991	887	983	999	979
Aswan	0515	-	1725	1650	1810	-	2008	-	2035	-	-	-
Luxor	1014	0830	2126	2124	2212	0415	0102	-	2310	0515	-	-
Qina	1126	-	2237	2246	2322	0605	0237	-	0132	0704	-	-
Sohag	1424	-	-	0310	-	0937	0721	0430	-	1022	-	-
Asyut	1545	1215	-	0342	-	1205	0853	0608	-	1134	1825	1535
Minya	1728	-	-	0535	-	1348	1046	0804	-	1311	2016	1715
Beni Suef	1903	-	-	0722	-	1525	1231	0939	-	1446	2210	1850
Giza	2041	1635	0615	0906	0700	1716	1416	1116	0925	1621	2346	2030
Cairo	2055	1650	0630	0920	0715	1730	1430	1130	0940	1635	2400	2045

+ Sleeper Trains   *High Speed   **Turbini   ++Gray Ghost

BUS SCHEDULES

DESTINATION	DEPARTURE
To the Delta towns: from terminals at Kulall (by the underpass to Shubra)—fares run LE5-10	
Benha	0600-2100 every half hour
Damietta	0600-1700 every hour
Faqus	0830-1800 every half hour
Gamasa	0800-1500
Kafr Sagr	0530-2100
Mansuria	0600-1800 every 15 minutes
Mataria	0715-1815 every 15 minutes
Ras al-Barr (summer only)	0715, 0915, 1315, 1500, 1700
Zagazig	0530-1700 every 15 minutes 1700-2100 every hour

To Upper Egypt and the Fayyum: daily from Ahmed Helmi terminal—fares depend on distance: LE2-3 for Fayyum; LE7-10 for Minya; LE30 for an a/c bus to Luxor; up to LE35-45 for Aswan	
Abu Qurqas	1400, 15001745
al-Saff	0600 every 15 minutes 1730-1830 every 15 minutes
Aswan	1730
Asyut	0800, 1015, 1200, 1400 1700, 1830, 2000, 2130
Beni Suef	0600, 0700, 0815, 1015, 1115,1215, 1315, 1430, 1630 0915, 1030, 1730, 1900
Dairut	1515
Fayyum	0615-1645 every 15 minutes 1700-1845 every 15 minutes
Isna	0700
Luxor	0545, 0700, 2030, 2200
Mallawi	0715, 19301300, 1315, 1600
Minya	0630, 0930, 1015, 1230, 1330 1100, 1130, 1430, 1530, 1700, 1830
Nag Hamadi	0600, 0645, 0745 1800, 1945, 2115
Qina	0615
Samalut	1615

DESTINATION	DEPARTURE
Sohag	0630, 0730, 10301800, 1915, 2045

To the oases: daily from al-Azhar station—fares run LE20-35	
Dakhla via Baharia/ Farafra	0600
Dakhla via Kharga	0700
Kharga via Asyut	1000
Baharia/Farafra	0900
Kharga via Asyut	1800, 2000

To canal towns (Port Said, Ismailia, and Suez): daily from terminal at al-Kulali (by the underpass at Shubra)—fares run LE4-6 (to Suez) to LE10 (to Port Said)	
Fayid	0700, 1000, 1400, 1630
Ismailia	0630-1800 every hour
Port Said	0600-1800 every hour
Suez	0600-1730 every half hour

To the Red Sea: departures from Abbassia to Hurghada, daily at 0900, except Friday; daily from Ahmed Helmi, Upper Egyptian Bus Company—fares run LE16-24

Hurghada	0730, 2100, 2130, 0900

DESTINATION	DEPARTURE	RETURN
To Sinai: departures from Sinai Terminal, Abbassia—fares run LE35 (Sharm al-Sheikh) to LE45 (Taba)		
al-Arish	0700, 0800, 1500	0700, 0800 1500
Dahab	0700	2030
Nuweiba	2400	varies
St. Cath/Dahab	1030	1400
Sharm al-Sheikh	1000, 1300, 2330	0700, 1000, 1300, 2330, 2400
Sharm/Dahab	2400	2400
Taba	0700, 1630	1000

available at the station several days in advance; for others you must purchase tickets the same day, often on the bus itself. You must make reservations in person; no phone calls. Several bus terminals are scattered around Cairo.

Super Jet buses for Alexandria (about every half hour) and Marsa Matruh (twice daily, June-Sept.) leave from Heliopolis at Midan Almaza (across from EgyptAir Hospital), tel. 290-9017, stop at Tahrir on Midan Abdul Moneim Riad (across from the Ramesses Hilton), tel. 766-914/772-663/756-034, thirty minutes later, and stop again at Giza close to Midan Giza, tel. 725-032, ten minutes later. Their buses to Port Said leave from Midan Ramesses (next to the Coptic Hospital) tel. 924-877 every half hour 0600-0830 and at 1500 and 1600, stopping at Heliopolis about 15 minutes later. **Golden Arrow** runs similar buses several times daily to Hurghada, Luxor, and Aswan, leaving from the Ahmad Helmy station, tel. 574-6658, stopping in Tahrir about ten minutes later.

Standard buses for the delta towns leave from **Midan al-Kulali** (tel. 575-0570), to the side of Midan Ramesses, as do buses for the Canal cities. Buses for the Red Sea coast, the Fayyum, and Upper Egypt leave from **Midan Ahmed Helmi** (tel. 574-6658), behind the railroad station; and buses for the western oases depart from **al-Azhar Station** (tel. 390-8653) at the corner of Sh. Port Said and Sh. 26 July. Buses for Sinai leave from **Sinai (Abbasiya) Station**, tel. 824-753/839-589, at the end of Sh. Ramesses.

Alexandria: The Super Jet (luxury, a/c, refreshments, WC, and video) leaves roughly every half-hour from Cairo, 0600-0100; non-smoking buses available. The big gold-and-orange buses, which also serve the airport, take about three hours to reach Alexandria; about LE25. Their offices are at 6 Mokhtar Hussein, Heliopolis, tel. 672-262. This bus is the best way to get to Alex. You can also catch buses almost as nice run by the West Delta Bus Company from Midan Almaza (Heliopolis) and Midan Tahrir near the Super Jet. They leave about every hour or hour and a half 0530-1830 (winter), to 2100 (summer), and cost just slightly less. Offices: 15 Midan Tahrir; tel. 759-751. West Delta also runs a bus to **Marsa Matruh;** it departs 0730 daily in winter, and 0730,

0830, 0930, and 2300 in summer; fares LE25. You can also catch buses here for **Ismailia** (East Delta) and **Port Said** (Super Jet).

Delta Towns: The East Delta Bus Company (4 Tayaran, Ma'adi, tel. 261-1882-3/261-1885-6) serves the eastern delta towns from the terminal at al-Kulali.

The Canal Towns (Port Said, Ismailia, and Suez): The East Delta Company also runs buses every half-hour to every hour between 0600-1730 or 1800 from al-Kulali; fares LE-8.

To Sinai: East Delta also runs multiple buses from Sinai Terminal in Abbassia.

Upper Egypt: The Upper Egyptian Bus Company (4 Yusif Abbas, Ma'adi, tel. 260-9304/260-9297-8). These buses in particular may not be quite up to the standards advertised. They run daily from Ahmed Helmi. Far better are the Golden Arrow buses, which are air-conditioned, with WC, TV, and buffet service.

To the Oases: Upper Egyptian Company runs buses from al-Azhar Station to the various oases, but their schedule can vary.

To the Red Sea: The Upper Egyptian Bus company runs daily from Ahmed Helmi. In addition, Travco Shark al-Delta (offices at Midan Ahmed Helmi) runs a daily (except Friday) bus at 0900 from Abbassia. You can catch buses to Tel Aviv either from Sinai Station, or

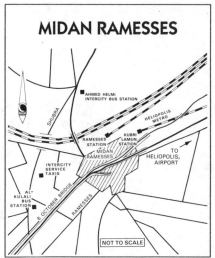

MIDAN RAMESSES

AHMED HELMI
INTERCITY BUS STATION

SHUBRA

HELIOPOLIS
METRO

RAMESSES
STATION

KUBRI
LAMUN
STATION

MIDAN
RAMESSES

TO
HELIOPOLIS,
AIRPORT

INTERCITY
SERVICE
TAXIS

AL-
KULALI
BUS
STATION

6 OCTOBER BRIDGE

RAMESSES

NOT TO SCALE

© MOON PUBLICATIONS, INC.

at the Cairo Sheraton (American Express Office, tel. 740-444).

By Service Taxi

Service taxis with fixed fares depart, like buses, from several areas. They carry seven passengers, operate on a first-come, first-served basis, and leave when all the seats are full. If you want more room than a single seat, you can buy two spaces. Service taxis are a quick way to get to distant cities, but beware that they often make such good time because of dangerous driving.

Following is a list of service taxi departure points and their destinations: Taxis from al-Kulali go to Alexandria, Port Said, Ismailia, Suez, and Sinai; from Midan Tahrir (behind the Hilton) to Alexandria and the oases; from Ahmed Helmi to the delta, the oases, Upper Eygpt (Beni Suef, Minya, and Asyut—you must change in Asyut for cities farther south); from Midan Giza to the Fayyum, the Red Sea coast, and Beni Suef; from Ramesses Station to the Red Sea coast and the oases.

BOB RACE

CAIRO ENVIRONS

Visitors who want to prowl around the greater Cairo area can explore the garden-like barrages down the Nile where the river splits and enters the delta, a petrified forest, the Fayyum Oasis, and the monasteries of Wadi Natrun. But the most famous of the outlying sights is the string of over 60 pyramids that stretches along the western border of the desert from just west of the city to the southern end of the Fayyum. The most renowned are at Giza and Saqqara. A trip to Giza to visit the Great Pyramid, its two massive neighbors, and the Great Sphinx only takes a couple of hours; add a little more time if you want to explore the tombs surrounding the pyramid. For a splurge, cap off the trip with lunch or dinner at the Mena House; or head north on the Mansuriyya Canal (west side) for a chicken or fish lunch at Andrea's and on to an afternoon of shopping at the village of Kerdassa.

Saqqara, 25 km southwest of Cairo, can take most of the day, although most tours only give it a scant couple of hours. Within the cemetery complex lie the Step Pyramid (the original pyramid) and the funerary complex of Djoser, as well as numerous tombs, two of them Old Kingdom masterpieces. On your way back, visit Memphis and stop at the native craft school at Harraniyya, where students produce weaving and pottery. Or if your craving for pyramids is insatiable, include a visit the Middle Kingdom mud-brick pyramids at the edge of the Fayyum Depression.

GIZA

Khufu, grand king of the 4th Dynasty, built his mortuary complex on the plateau at Giza, 25 km north of Memphis. From the 1st Dynasty this plateau attracted burials, and the activities of their builders shaped it. Ancient workers quarried the fossil-rich limestone for the pyramids and mastabas, leaving deep holes in some areas while leveling others by dumping refuse. Today a broad *wadi* splits the site, leaving a high area with the pyramids and surrounding mastabas (with the Great Sphinx and adjacent temples lying to the east, below the edge of the plateau), and a group of smaller, private tombs on the ridge to the southwest. South of these tombs, Egyptologists have uncovered an ancient workmen's village and its tombs. On the main plateau, Khufu built the largest pyramid ever raised, and around it he buried members of the royal family and his nobles. By the end of the era, his two sons added their own pyramids—only slightly less grand. The second of these sons, Khafre, also fashioned the Great Sphinx that sits in the old quarry on the western side of the pyramids area. On the solstices, the two great pyramids with the setting sun between them

form, on a scale of kilometers, a gigantic hieroglyph of eternity. (Note: climbing the pyramids is illegal.)

Getting There
Public transportation runs to the foot of the plateau, next to the Mena House Oberoi Hotel, a former guesthouse built by Ismail for Princess Eugene when she attended the opening of the Suez Canal. Sharia al-Haram (Pyramids Rd.) follows the route of the tram lines built at that time. Public minibuses 82 (al-Haram) and 83 (King Fisal Rd.) run to the *midan* at the base of the plateau from in front of the Mugama'a (Tahrir). Service-taxi vans leave from the side of the same building. Fares run about 25PT. A private taxi will run LE30.

CAIRO AREA PYRAMIDS

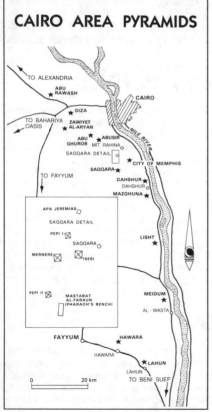

THE GREAT PYRAMID

Interior open 0900-1400; to the plateau, LE4; the pyramid, LE10; the ticket admits you to the pyramid's interior and the valley temple by the Sphinx; the Solar Boat Museum, LE27. Built by Khufu (called Cheops by the Ptolemaic Greeks), second king of the 4th Dynasty, this mammoth structure contains 2,350,000 cubic meters of stone and its base covers over 13 acres. The pyramid was once cased in limestone, of which a few blocks remain at the base. The others were stripped during the Middle Ages to be incorporated into the buildings of old Giza and Cairo. The building is accurately oriented to the cardinal points of the compass, with its entrance facing north. Specific methods used to build the edifice still puzzle investigators, but the most recent theory holds that a sloping ramp wound around the pyramid, being raised as the pyramid grew. When the core was complete, workers positioned the capstone, possibly in pink Aswan granite, which brought the pyramid's original height to 135 meters. Then the rest of the sheathing, fine-quality limestone from the Tura quarries across the river, was added, possibly from the top down; as each level was finished, its section of ramp was dismantled. Three small pyramids that stand along the southeast side of the road belonged to Khufu's queens. The narrow, stone-lined pits housed funerary boats.

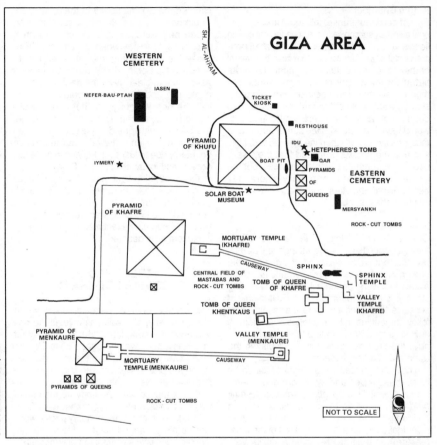

GIZA AREA

WESTERN CEMETERY

SH. AL-AHRAM

NEFER-BAU-PTAH

IASEN

TICKET KIOSK

RESTHOUSE

PYRAMID OF KHUFU

IDU

HETEPHERES'S TOMB

QAR

BOAT PIT

PYRAMIDS

OF

QUEENS

EASTERN CEMETERY

IYMERY

SOLAR BOAT MUSEUM

MERSYANKH

ROCK - CUT TOMBS

PYRAMID OF KHAFRE

MORTUARY TEMPLE (KHAFRE)

CAUSEWAY

SPHINX

SPHINX TEMPLE

CENTRAL FIELD OF MASTABAS AND ROCK - CUT TOMBS

TOMB OF QUEEN OF KHAFRE

VALLEY TEMPLE (KHAFRE)

TOMB OF QUEEN KHENTKAUS I

VALLEY TEMPLE (MENKAURE)

PYRAMID OF MENKAURE

MORTUARY TEMPLE (MENKAURE)

CAUSEWAY

PYRAMIDS OF QUEENS

ROCK - CUT TOMBS

NOT TO SCALE

© MOON PUBLICATIONS, INC.

The Interior

The complex interior of the pyramid underwent at least two changes in plan. It contains three chambers; only the Grand Gallery is open to the public. The present entrance, which lies below the original one, was cut by the Muslims in the 9th century. This tunnel connects with the descending gallery that eventually leads some 110 meters into the bedrock of the plateau. Here the first burial chamber was hollowed out, only to be replaced by one constructed within the pyramid itself. Reached from a tunnel that takes off from the descending corridor at nearly ground level, this Queen's Chamber contains a niche which perhaps was to hold a statue of the king. Left unfinished, this small room could have been a burial chamber abandoned when work began on the larger one above it.

The ascending corridor above the Queen's Chamber expands into the Grand Gallery; it's 8.5 meters tall and 75 meters long. The corbelled vault relieves the weight of the pyramid that lies above it, and the niches in the sides of the wall may have aided in handling the massive stones sealing the passage. The top of the corridor ends in a huge step that leads to a flat section sealed after the king was interred by three granite blocks set into granite slots. Of this solid mass of granite, only the slots remain.

King's Chamber
Built of solid red granite, this room now houses only a lidless sarcophagus. Above the flat ceiling lie five vertical compartments, four built of horizontal slabs, the fifth vaulted to relieve the weight of the stone above them. Engineers have debated the necessity of such measures, but though several of the blocks are cracked (possibly by earthquakes) the roof still stands. Two ducts supply air to this room. Because the shafts would have lined up with the stars Thuban and those in Orion's belt when the pyramid was built, some authors have proposed that they were used as astronomical sighting devices, but because the vents run horizontally before they bend upward, the stars would have been invisible from the chamber.

Funerary Boat
Open 0900-1400 (closed Tuesdays); LE27. Of the five boat pits that surrounding the pyramid, two still contain vessels, and of those only the one on the south side of the pyramid has been excavated. Here, beneath 40 limestone roofing slabs, lies a flat-bottomed boat. Built mainly of cedar, its 13 dismantled layers to a certain extent follow the outline of the complete boat. Restorer Hajj Ahmed Yusif worked for 14 years to rebuild the boat, which is now on display in the climate-controlled museum.

The 1,200 pieces were originally joined by halfa-grass ropes and sycamore pegs, techniques at which the Egyptians excelled. A small *baldachin* stood on the foredeck, an awning amidships, and a deckhouse (supported by palm-leaf capitals) aft. Examination of the other (eastern) boat pit has revealed a similar vessel, which remains unexcavated. Speculation as to the boats' use abounds, but the vessels' structure would have probably permitted them only one precarious trip across the Nile, if, in fact, they were used at all to bear the dead king to eternity.

The Great Sphinx
This figure sits in a depression to the south of Khufu's pyramid in what was once a quarry. 4,500 years ago, Khafre's workers shaped the stone into a recumbent lion, giving their king's features to its human face. The figure, facing the rising sun, fascinated later Egyptians, who claimed the Sphinx spoke to them, and King Thutmose IV left a stela, which still stands between the beast's forepaws, describing such an exchange. One day when still a prince, Thutmose tired of hunting and fell asleep in the shade of the Sphinx. In his dreams, the figure asked him to clear away the sand which was choking it, and the Sphinx would reward him with the kingship of Egypt. Thutmose, according to his stela, carried out the request and the Sphinx duly upheld its part of the bargain.

Actually, the long survival of the figure is undoubtedly due to just such burying in protective desert sand for much of its life. Today, exposed to the weathering wind, humidity, and Cairo's smog, the statue is crumbling. The temple in front of the Sphinx also dates from Khafre's reign, and the two structures were undoubtedly related, though the exact meaning of the unfinished temple is debated.

THE FUNERARY COMPLEX OF KHAFRE

This complex, with its pyramid, funerary temple, causeway, and valley temple, is the best example of a complete Old Kingdom layout. The king's body was brought across the river to the valley temple, where it was embalmed. When the priests were finished, the mourners gathered at this temple to purify themselves and then moved with the body up the causeway that shielded it from profane eyes. Once the king was interred, his mortuary priests would ensure his continued spiritual life by offering him the necessities of life: food and incense.

The Valley Temple
Open 0900-1400; admission with ticket from Great Pyramid. Situated just south of the temple in front of the Sphinx, Khafre's valley temple was built of limestone and faced with granite floated down from Aswan during the Nile flood. Priests responsible for mummifying the king worked at this temple, perhaps on the roof. When his body had been prepared, the participants in the rites underwent purification here, and finally the Opening of the Mouth ceremonies could well have taken place within its protective walls. After the funeral, the temple was filled

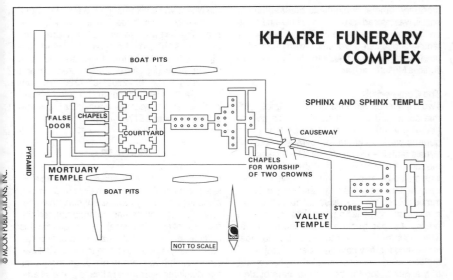

with statuary, including the green diorite masterpiece of Khafre (discovered in the pit of the antechamber) now in the Antiquities Museum. Apparently the statues once stood at the pillars within the hall, the entire temple serving as a *serdab*. This temple shows off the care ancient Egyptian builders lavished on their king's immortal estates, for example, carving corners into the individual blocks in order to interlock the walls. The door in the north side of the transverse hall leads through a passageway of alabaster to the eastern end of the causeway.

The causeway, once covered and decorated, stretched over 400 meters along a limestone ridge to Khafre's pyramid. Much of its foundation remains. Originally its carved walls were capped by slabs that didn't quite meet, leaving a central slit in the roof to admit light and allow the occasional rains to run into the corridor and be channeled into the desert.

Khafre's Pyramid

Like his father's complex, Khafre's mortuary temple lay on the east side of the pyramid; the causeway ended here and the funeral procession would continue into the pyramid. The pyramid, though slightly shorter than Khufu's, appears larger because it's on higher ground. In

addition, its intact capstone and its more steeply sloping sides bring it within a couple of meters of its predecessor.

The double entrance to this pyramid, which was robbed in ancient times, opens into double corridors that lead to two chambers, a design considerably abbreviated from Khufu's tomb. The first chamber, with the entrance cut into the ground, lies considerably north of the pyramid's center and may well indicate a change in building plans; it might have been shifted south (to better align with the causeway) or made smaller. The second chamber is located directly under the structure's center and is cut out of the bedrock.

OTHER SIGHTS

Menkaure

The smallest of the Giza pyramids and uncompleted at the time of its builder's death, Menkaure has only a few courses of granite sheathing around the base, and much of that is unfinished. Unlike the others, the corridor of this pyramid was decorated. It also contains several rooms, a more complex design that would be expanded by builders of the Middle Kingdom. The queens' pyramids that lie to the south were never finished, and the king's mortuary temple, originally to be sheathed in basalt, was instead lined with mud-brick and painted. The mud brick of the hastily finished valley temple sequestered the well-known "triad" statues ([33] p. 190) now housed in the Egyptian Antiquities Museum in Cairo.

The Cemeteries

Two cemeteries laid out around the Great Pyramid contained the bodies of Khufu's nobles (west) and family (east). Though kings and queens were buried under pyramids, private burials remained in mastabas. Once laid out in measured rows, the plan of these mastabas was disrupted by later burials at a site that had become famous for its holiness. Many of these tombs utilized the rock faces cut out in the pyramids' quarries, reshaping them into chapels and adding a superstructure to enclose the tomb. The group of tombs on the east are the most interesting for they contain life-sized statues of the deceased, and often of relatives, carved out of the wall of the tombs—forerunners of statues that would later appear in niches.

In the eastern cemetery visit the tombs of Mersyankh, Meryrenefer (called Qar), and Idu. In the western cemetery, see the tombs of Iymery, Iasen, and Nefre Ptah-Bita.

Sound And Light

Performances at 1830 and 1930; LE10. Like many pharaonic sites, the Giza pyramids sport a sound and light show. One of the first in Egypt, it's not as good as the ones at Karnak and Phi-lae where you walk through the temples, but if it's the only one you'll see, take it in. Although the recorded text may seem a bit melodramatic, the play of lights on the pyramids is worth the trip. The two daily performances are offered in several languages (see chart); be sure to confirm the schedule (tel. 385-2880/385-7320). You can take the standard transportation listed above, or check with a local tour agency for the whole package, about LE17.

KERDASSA

Known since 1400 as a weaving center, this village lies north of Sh. al-Haram (Pyramids Road), along the Mansuriyya Canal. Although the modern influx of tourists has commercialized the main street (Sh. Kerdassa), the village remains a center of quality shirts, *galabayyas,* and caftans—ready-made and made to order. Children start weaving at the age of 10, on the looms that dominate nearly every house in the village. By the time they're 20, they are designing their own patterns from the locally grown, spun, and dyed wool. (For a tour of a weaving shop check with Ahmed Eisa at 27 Sh. Kerdassa.) Some of the most innovative weaving, however, is done in town across the canal. Visit Omar Muhammad Omar's shop across from the Osman mosque on Sh. Ashmawy, or have Aref Ali al-Saman (Sh. Abu Bakr Sidiq) translate your favorite painting into a complex weaving. You can buy carpets, both woven and knotted, by the meter. Kerdassa is also a good place to find Bedouin dresses and veils; the best-quality ones will run several hundred dollars. Bargaining in Kerdassa is de rigueur.

To reach Kerdassa, go out Sh. al-Haram, turn right at the sign for Andrea's, and drive past the restaurant until you reach the covered parking area. A taxi should cost about LE20, and frequent minibuses (from Midan Giza) run about 30PT. If your adventure level runs high, try a 10PT red bus (#101 with a slash through it) to the village from Giza Station. The main shopping area is the street that runs from the parking lot; many of the workshops are behind the houses, which serve as stores. The native part of the village lies beyond the stores; just follow the main street.

GIZA SOUND AND LIGHT SHOW

	Early Show	Late Show
Saturday	English	Spanish
Sunday	French	German
Monday	English	French
Tuesday	French	Italian
Wednesday	English	French
Thursday	Arabic	English
Friday	English	French

SAQQARA

Since the founding of Memphis at the time of Menes's unification of the Two Lands, Saqqara has served as a burial ground for kings and nobility. The kings of the 1st Dynasty built mud-brick "fortresses," which, with those at Abydos, may have served as their tombs or cenotaphs. Djoser, in the 3rd Dynasty, chose Saqqara as the site for his funerary complex, the first ever constructed in stone, and here he raised his Step Pyramid—the earliest in Egypt.

In the 5th and 6th dynasties, the ruling monarchs built limestone-cased, rubble-filled pyramids, and inside them they inscribed the earliest of the pyramid texts. Their nobles constructed huge mastabas near their rulers, and at Saqqara they commissioned some of the finest Old Kingdom drawings. The Christian monks built the monastery of St. Jeremias (its most spectacular pieces are now on display at the Coptic Museum in Cairo), and Christians continued to be buried at Saqqara in large numbers until the early Middle Ages.

Practicalities

The area around Saqqara contains five separate sights: the main cemetery at Saqqara, the pyramids of south Saqqara, the pyramids at Dahshur (closed by the military), the scattered ruins of Memphis, and the sun temples and pyramids of Abusir. Of these, the most impressive sight is the cemetery at Saqqara, northern Egypt's best-preserved and most interesting area of antiquities; plan on spending a full day. Besides the step pyramid compound, be sure to see the tombs of Ti, Mereruka, and Akhethotep and Ptahhotep. The area covers several square kilometers, so wear walking shoes; drinks are available at a resthouse, but bring your own food. Take water, a flashlight, a hat, and sunscreen. Start early, especially in summer, to avoid the heat; if you have time or energy take in Abusir or Memphis on your way back.

To stay near Saqqara, contact the three-star Saqqara Palm Club, Saqqara Tourist Rd., tel. (018) 200-791/(02) 921-031, for information and reservations; LE35 s, LE45 d.

Getting There

Saqqara lies 25 km south of Cairo on the west side of the Nile Valley. No public transportation runs to the antiquities; the easiest way out there is to hire a **taxi** in Cairo for the day for LE60-100, depending on how long you stay. A less expensive option is to take the Metro to Helwan and hire a cab for the trip, LE10-20, again depending upon the time you spend. A slightly less expensive version is to take the *balidi* (village) **train** to Dahshur or Badrashayn and arrange a taxi there.

The adventurous can hire a **horse** or **camel** near the pyramids at Giza; the three-hour ride takes you past the pyramid at Zawiyet al-Aryan, the sun temple of Abu Ghurob, and the three pyramids of Abusir. Most people opt for a one-way ride (LE50 for a camel, which carries two riders, LE40 for a horse), but if you plan to ride back, you'll have to pay for the extra time at Saqqara; LE5-7/hour. This trip is not for the inexperienced; five hours in the saddle can leave you stiff, sore, and blistered.

An **organized tour** is the easiest, most luxurious way to visit Saqqara, but you'll only have a couple of hours at the cemetery and see only a few of the most interesting sights. All the large tourist agencies (see Cairo "Practicalities") run plush buses to Saqqara on a regular basis, and some day tours include Giza and lunch.

The closest that **public transportation** can get you is to the village of Abusir, north of Saqqara. A minibus (from 0600) runs from Giza Station (25PT) and also stops at the turnoff from Sh. al-Haram (Pyramids Rd.) to Saqqara; any public transportation along al-Haram will let you off at this square just west of the canal. You can get off the bus at the dirt turnoff and try to hitch to the pyramids or ride into the village, where you can hire a pickup taxi for a few pounds, hitch a ride, or walk south along the canal. The walk takes about an hour to an hour and a half and winds its way along fields and past working Egptians. When you reach the paved road, turn right; the ticket kiosk is up about 200 meters on your right. To return, you can hike across the desert to Abusir, visit the pyramids there, and catch the minibus back to town. Although hitching back to Cairo from the antiquities at Saqqara is possible in the morning, the area is usually deserted by early afternoon.

DJOSER'S FUNERARY COMPLEX

Open 0800-1700; in the summer you can sometimes get in as early as 0700, and the guards often begin locking up the tombs by 1630; LE15. The plateau at Saqqara is dominated by the fu-

nerary complex of Djoser. In this walled compound, built at the beginning of the 3rd Dynasty, stone replaced mud brick. The stones, unlike the giant ones used in the pyramids at Giza, are small—brick-sized—and the shapes of the buildings at Saqqara follow, more closely than those of any other site, the traditional forms of log roofs, slender lotus columns, and reed fences. But perhaps the most remarkable aspect of the entire complex is its preoccupation with outer form; like the sets of a stage play, the chapels in the ceremonial courts are merely rubble-filled dummies.

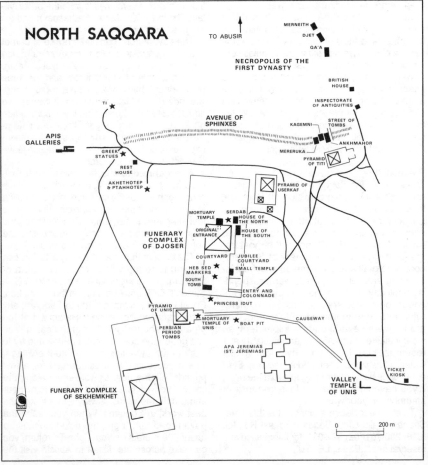

The complex was designed by Djoser's chief minister, Imhotep, a talented doctor later deified as a healing god and identified by the Greeks with Aesculapius. The eastern courtyard is a copy of a *heb sed* festival court. The ritual *heb sed* or jubilee festival, which occurred when the king had reigned 30 years and at irregular intervals thereafter, may well have had its roots in ritual "murders" of ancient kings. In these rites, which could last two months, the king underwent a symbolic death, rebirth, and a second coronation. These complex rites (often duplicated—once for Upper Egypt, once for Lower Egypt) rejuvenated the king's ruling power and reaffirmed his positive relations with the gods. The cult statues of the gods were the king's honored guests at these festivals.

Over the past 50 years, the French Egyptologist Jean-Philippe Lauer has been reconstructing the complex. The Step Pyramid dominates the compound; its temple, unlike those of Giza, was built to the north, facing the pyramid's entrance. The eastern section of the complex was devoted to the northern and southern palaces and the jubilee court with its shrines for the gods. The main courtyard to the south, with its "B"-shaped markers, may well have been the course the king ran to prove his ability to continue to rule the Two Lands. At the extreme south lies the southern tomb, its rooms filled with blue-glazed tiles imitating reed blinds and depictions of the king running his jubilee race.

Entrance Corridor
The 10-meter-high palace facade enclosure wall, which once stretched 544 meters north to south, contained several false doorways; only the one on the south end actually entered the complex. The walls, rebuilt with original blocks of Tura limestone quarried across the Nile may well resemble the walls of Memphis, which once lay to the southeast. Through doorways that stand permanently open you can see simulated log roofing with bundles of papyrus as pillars. Imhotep distrusted stone columns to support the massive weight of the stone roof so he buttressed them against the passage's outer walls. The niches these stone tongues formed (roughly corresponding to the numbers of *nomes*) may well have held statues of the king as ruler of Upper (southern side) and Lower (northern side) Egypt.

The Step Pyramid
Imhotep experimented with the design of this stone tomb, beginning with a standard mastaba like those built in mud brick at Abydos and Saqqara by the 1st and 2nd dynasty kings. Like its prototypes, a maze of passages and storage rooms and a granite-lined burial chamber were hacked out of the bedrock. Of the numerous shafts (about 30 meters deep), several led to tombs for the king's family. A panel of turquoise faience tiles, which once lined the king's chambers, now graces the upper floor of the Antiquities Museum in Cairo. The entrance to these rooms was to the north, but today, due to their dangerous condition, they are closed to the public.

Imhotep altered the design of the superstructure several times, erecting a four-stepped pyramid above the mastaba, then enlarging it to six steps. You can see these changes in the southern wall, and more so on the east where

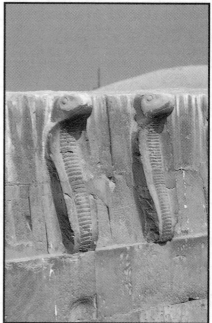

detail of cobra frieze near the Step Pyramid

ALLAN HANSEN

some of the original casing remains in place. The radical change in design from flat-topped mastaba to pyramid perhaps lies in the belief that the god-king joined his fellow gods after death by ascending a stairway to the sky. The hieroglyphic sign for stairs looks remarkably like the Step Pyramid.

The Temple
The small building that stands along the east side of the courtyard is called the temple, but from its design may have been a small palace. The upper corners carry the earliest known representations of the *djed* pillar. This strange symbol, linked to Osiris and the annual rebirth of the land, may depict the god's sacrum (base of the spine) or a pole with corn tied in tiers around its top. The pillars on the south end are original, those on the north modern reconstructions.

The *Heb Sed* Court
The jubilee court, lined with the gods' shrines, lies east of the temple. These buildings, filled with rubble cores, were only facades. The narrow, eastern shrines with their round-topped roofs echo the mud construction of Lower Egypt's earliest temples. The western buildings are modeled on the shrines of Upper Egypt, their small courtyards faced with open doors and steps leading to a throne occupied by the god. Note the reed fences between them, which, like everything in the complex, are rendered in stone. The niches probably held statues of the king or of the gods who would gather to witness the king's rebirth. At the southern end of the court, the king, in his dual rule of monarch of Upper and Lower Egypt, was twice enthroned on the double dais.

The Northern Buildings
Called the "House of the South" and the "House of the North," these two structures remain somewhat of a mystery, perhaps representing the archaic temples at Hieraconpolis and Buto. The courtyard walls are identified on the east side by the engaged columns with capitals of the heraldic lotus (south) and papyrus (north). The entrances to the chapels are bent (a device that became popular in military architecture and eventually appeared in medieval European castles), their ceilings roofed with stone imitations of

close-placed logs. The angled corridors lead to a cruciform sanctuary that probably held holy statues in niches. At the doorway to the "House of the South," a glass protects New Kingdom graffiti identifying the builder of the Step Pyramid as Djoser (his Horus name of Netjerkhet).

The Mortuary Temple
North of the pyramid, the *serdab* stands alone, a small, slanted building that housed the statue of the king that's now in the Antiquities Museum. A copy inserted in its place gazes perpetually at the constellations that, never setting, continually circle the stellar north pole—stars the Egyptians believed eternal. The mortuary temple, just to the west, is unusual in that it flanks the north rather than the eastern wall of the pyramid and that the entrance into the burial chambers under the pyramid was from its interior.

The Southern Tomb
Prototype for the auxiliary pyramids that would appear in all later complexes, the top of the tomb is decorated with a frieze of cobras and makes a perfect foreground for a photo of the step pyramid. From the top of the tomb you can descend into the cluster of mastabas and visit the pyramid of Unis.

AREA OF UNIS'S PYRAMID

Pyramid Of Unis
Once the limestone casing was stripped from the rubble-filled core of Unis's pyramid, the structure began to crumble. But the interior is worth the trip down, for the tomb is the first in which pyramid texts were inscribed on the walls, and it is also decorated with textile designs in imitation of the wall hangings that appeared in early homes and palaces. The ceilings, unlike those in previous pyramids, are not corbelled but are vaulted with massive trapezoidal blocks. The entrance's three granite blocks have been removed, allowing you to stand in the portcullis that originally held them. The entrance corridor is low; you'll have to walk much of the way doubled over.

The **mortuary temple** lies in the standard position to the south of the pyramid, but little remains except the granite false door against the east side of the pyramid and the granite gateway that once stood within the temple walls. From the temple's east end, the causeway that once linked it with the valley temple near the ticket booth stretches eastward.

To the south as you walk along the limestone flooring of the causeway you can see the **boat pits**. Lined with brick, they may have held funerary boats similar to those at Giza. Farther down the causeway, a roofed section gives you an idea of the original construction, with the central slot designed to admit light. The restored walls show traces of the numerous scenes that once decorated its stone: transportation of granite from Aswan, battle scenes with archers and shiploads of prisoners, hunting and metalworking scenes like those found in private tombs, and the famous famine reliefs—haunting depictions of starving people underscoring the country's dependence upon the Nile.

Persian Tombs

The deep shaft with a spiral staircase at the south side of Unis' pyramid houses the tombs of three Persians: chief physician Psamtik (center), Admiral Djenhebu (west), and Psamtik's son Pediese (east). These simple yet elegant tombs contain huge sarcophagi that nearly fill the tombs. Around them, the beautiful hieroglyphs invoke the same spells as those written 2,000 years earlier. The three interlocked tombs are worth the climb down the more than 300 stairs, but you may have to hunt down the *ghaffir* with the key.

Tomb Of Idut

Of the tombs around the pyramid of Unis, the most extensive is that of Idut, daughter of Unis. The scenes are typical of the type included in Old Kingdom mastabas, but those of the river and its boats are especially nice. The false door in the back is painted in imitation of granite (a common practice) and, as usual, faces the butchering scenes.

SOUTH SAQQARA

Pyramids of late Old Kingdom rulers, including those of Pepi I and II, lie south of the major complex and offer little except an excuse to go exploring. Visible from the top of Djoser's enclosure wall, the field includes the strange, sarcophagus-shaped pyramid of Shepseskaf, called Mastabat al-Faraun ("Pharaoh's Bench"). If you want to go exploring, camels and horses are rented at the resthouse. No matter what the "guides" tell you, **Dahshur** is closed; you have to get special permission from the military to see it; don't waste your time.

NORTHERN TOMBS

Other Pyramids

The pyramid of Userkaf, which lies just northeast of Djoser's enclosures, dates from the 5th Dynasty. Its mortuary temple is the only one that appears on the south side; the area around the pyramid is honeycombed with caverns and is dangerous. The interior of Titi's pyramid is open, and its ruined ceiling gives clues to its construction. Its subsidiary pyramid, just south of the mortuary temple, is in good condition.

Tomb Of Mereruka

The largest and most beautiful of the 6th Dynasty tombs, this complex mastaba was built by Mereruka, vizier and overseer of Saqqara and inspector of the Prophets of the Pyramid of Titi. He included a separate series of tombs for his wife, Her-Watet-Khet, daughter of King Titi and priestess of Hathor, and for his son Meri-titi. Already the reliefs here, though carved by excellent craftsmen, begin to show stagnation when compared to similar scenes from the tomb of Ti (see p. 277).

A series of corridors leads through the main part of the tomb to the central court, where a false door contains a statue of Mereruka striding out into the living world. Here animals were brought to slaughter, a fact testified to by the stone tether-ring set into the floor. (See tomb plan on p. 274.)

Tomb Of Kagemni

Kagemni was vizier, Inspector of Prophets and Overseer of the pyramid town of Teti. While his tomb is not as large as his neighbor's, it features some nice relief work, a stairway to the roof, and two large chambers that may well have housed funerary boats, items usually reserved for kings. (See tomb plan on p. 275.)

SAQQARA TOMBS

TOMB OF MERERUKA

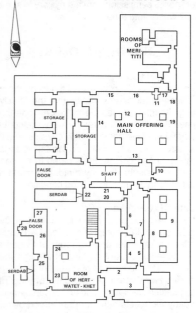

One of the most beautiful and best-preserved of the Old Kingdom tombs, this tri-part mastaba dedicated to Mereruka, his wife, and his son takes a good hour to absorb much of the incredible detail.

1. Mereruka, holding a shell and pen, paints at his easel.

2. The traditional marsh scene in which Mereruka, shown with his wife, harpoons fish and hunts birds with a throwing stick. From the smaller papyrus boats, men harpoon hippopotamuses; note the detailed wildlife, especially the grasshoppers and frogs.

3. The top register is devoted to gardening scenes, while the middle one shows cattle fording, with the traditional calf being carried across to entice the cows to follow.

4. The top part of the wall shows hunting in the desert, but the fence around the composition indicates it was on a preserve; the artist has drawn the animals less rigidly, freed from their base lines and standing on their own patch of ground.

5. Mereruka and his wife inspect goldsmiths and jewelry makers (lower rows); carpenters make beds (fourth row); and stonemasons carve vessels; in the third register, workers haul statues into the tomb.

6. Inside a columned building, perhaps Mereruka's office, farmers are beaten for not paying their taxes while scribes record the proceedings.

7. This wall shows fishermen plying their nets and hunters capturing birds.

8. In the bedroom, reliefs show servants preparing Mereruka's bed which stands beneath a canopy, the headrest lying on its side; beyond, a delicate relief shows Mereruka's wife, perhaps a daughter of King Titi, sitting on a bed playing the harp for her husband.

9. Male and female dancers entertain the deceased and his wife; note the sense of movement given by their body positions and swinging hair.

10. The lower registers show a collection of granaries and men treading grapes, which are then sacked and strained.

11. The statue of Mereruka striding out through his false door dominates the main offering hall.

12. Between pillars that carry depictions of the deceased in various dress is a round stone tether where cattle brought to slaughter for Mereruka's *ka* were tied.

13. The south wall shows Mereruka's funeral procession: mourning women, porters carrying the coffin to the boat, the funeral barque pulled by a boat under oars (note the swimmers shoving the boat off), and bearers carrying the coffin to the tomb with offerings, dancing girls, and a priest.

14. The reliefs of the boats along this wall show them under full sail, including details of their rigging and playful monkeys clambering about the yards.

15. The porters carrying Mereruka sing the song written above them, while dwarfs lead curly-tailed dogs, ancestors of the ones begging just outside the tomb.

16. Mereruka's sons support him while in the next section, workers force feed and tend to goats, oxen, antelope, ibex, gazelles, and hyenas.

17. Between the statue and door into the tomb of Mereruka's son, children play; above the door, dancers sway to the rhythm of the clappers in the shape of hands.

18. Mereruka and his wife enjoy a game of *senet*.

19. Threshing scenes in which the grain is harvested and the sheaves are loaded onto donkeys and taken to the threshing floor, where donkeys trample the heads, releasing the grain. Note the donkey leaning down to sneak a sample off the floor. Although the compositions appear active, already the scenes are beginning to set into the mold; compare the worker twisting the donkey's ear with the same picture in Ti's tomb (p. 276).

20. Women with the names of the *nomes* bring offerings to Mereruka, and scenes of counting cattle.

21. Slaughtering cattle and fishing with a pull net.

22. Feeding cranes, ducks, and pigeons. The room behind the wall contains the *serdab* where the statue of Mereruka once looked out on the offering chamber.

ROOMS OF HERT-WATET-KHET, WIFE OF MERERUKA

23. Farm scenes show the breeding, calving, and milking cattle, as well as fishing with nets.

24. Note the lion chair among the offerings to Hert-watet-khet.

25. The room off the *serdab* contains mainly offering scenes, but the dancers over the door to the following chapel show considerable life.

26. The ritual slaughter scenes, as is often the case, occur on the wall opposite the false door.

27. Hert-watet-khet sits in the lion chair (seen carried into the tomb in the outer room) to receive offerings.

28. The false door is painted to imitate granite, a common practice.

TOMB OF KAGEMNI

Although this tomb contains many of the same reliefs as those found in Mereruka's tomb, the details often differ.

1. The dancers and acrobats of Hathor are full of life, their necklaces swinging in counter-time to their movements.

2. The marsh hunting scene contains the inevitable hippopotamus hunt. Note the boys feeding the puppy to the left.

3. With typical Old Kingdom detail, the scene shows that the workers have tied the calves away from the cows so that they can milk them; note the cow with her hind legs tied to prevent kicking.

4. On this wall, we once more see prisoners brought before the magistrates.

5. The hunting scene in the marshes shows men tripping the clapnet, capturing marsh birds in lush vegetation, which the artist showed in loving detail. Above, Kagemni inspects his fowl pens.

6. Here Kagemni relaxes on his palanquin while his servants prepare cosmetic oil and tend to his monkey and dogs. Note, just beyond, the man who has his hands mounted on the wrong arms.

7. The butcher scene, once more, appears opposite the false door, and peasants bring offerings toward it.

TOMB OF KAGEMNI

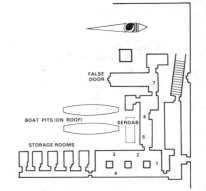

FALSE DOOR

BOAT PITS (ON ROOF)

SERDAB

STORAGE ROOMS

TOMB OF AKHETHOTEP AND PTAHHOTEP

In this double tomb, Akhethotep's chapel lies along the main axis and that of his son, Ptahhotep, takes off along the south side. This single room contains reliefs of exquisite detail and pristine color. The approach to the mastaba runs through the remains of the courtyard.

1. The agricultural scenes in this corridor show the process of cutting the figures out and then sculpting the features, shaping the flat planes into rounded forms.

2. In the chapel, the marsh scene surrounds the door; to the left, workers make papyrus boats and bring bundles of the reeds from the marsh, to the right, boatmen with crowns of lotus blossoms joust with their poles from the unsteady platforms of the papyrus boats.

3. In this chapel the butcher scenes appear around the corner from the false door.

4. The chapel of Ptahhotep is crammed with figures: examine the walls closely and you can find: winepressing, dogs attacking desert animals, a gazelle suckling a calf, panthers and wild dogs mating, lions in a cage, children playing, dancers, and Ptahhotep enjoying a feast on a boat.

Note the clapnet here; the men sit upright with the line in their hands. At a signal from their leader, they lean back, pulling the trap, which is staked to the pole at the far end, closed.

TOMB OF AKHETHOTEP AND PTAHHOTEP

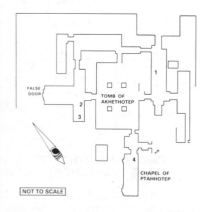

FALSE DOOR

TOMB OF AKHETHOTEP

1

2

3

4

CHAPEL OF PTAHHOTEP

NOT TO SCALE

© MOON PUBLICATIONS, INC.

TOMB OF TI

This well-preserved 5th Dynasty tomb, which includes false doors for Ti's wife and son, is the most beautiful of the Old Kingdom mastabas. The artwork shows not only the mastery of ancient artists but the freshness of design before the compositions had solidified, losing their strong link with reality.

1. The vestible shows Ti in the doorway, who asks his visitors not to desecrate his tomb, receiving offerings from women representing the *nomes*.

2. Scenes of butchering the ox; the men tie the beast, then, using the leverage of the ropes, throw it.

3. Ti, carried on his palanquin, oversees servants with his funerary furniture while dwarfs beneath his chair hold dogs and a monkey.

4. Servants feed cranes and geese the food prepared by the men above them.

5. A fowl yard fenced with woven mesh.

6. Ti in his pillared house receives accounts.

7. Ti, with his wife behind him, superintends the arrival of cargo ships and herds of animals. Behind them is the false door of Ti's son.

8. The figures of Ti, each in different dress, correspond to the many titles he held. Note that the mirror images, in order to have the ritually correct hands on the staff and baton, are mounted on wrong arms.

9. The offering bearers bringing food and animals into the tomb are carved in fine detail and are not yet stiff stereotypes.

10. Over the door through which you just entered, Ti and his wife enjoy the marshes.

11. The lower registers are dedicated to butcher scenes, while above, statues are being drawn into the tomb; a man moving ahead of the sledges pours water on the ground to reduce the friction.

12. The ships Ti used to inspect his delta estates.

13. The back wall of the storage room shows potters, bakers, and brewers, (top) as well as scribes recording the amount of corn measured by a worker.

14. Dancers appear over the doorway into the chapel. The chapel is filled with details of farming, hunting,

and fishing scenes, as well as craftsmen at work. By carefully studying these reliefs, you can begin to understand how the ancient Egyptians lived and worked.

15. Ti inspects the harvest (from the top): flax is harvested and prepared to be spun, grain is cut, sacked, and loaded on asses. Note the realism in the vignette where the man is twisting the donkey's ear to make it behave and compare it with the later, less lively one in Mereruka's tomb. The grain, taken to the threshing floor, is emptied out of the sacks to be threshed by the sharp hooves of the donkeys, winnowed with the three-pronged fork, still used, and sacked.

16. Shipbuilding scenes show the carpenters shaping tree trunks, sawing the boards, shaping, placing, and hammering them down. Ti inspects the work from one of the boats.

17. Craftsmen occupy the southeast corner (from the top): goldsmiths firing up their furnace; sculptors working in stone; carpenters making a shrine and chest, the workers using a pull saw on planks tied upright to a post, the top wedged with a rock to prevent the saw from binding; leather workers and market scenes.

18. Ti, seated at an offering table while attendants bring gifts, is entertained by musicians below.

19. Scenes of life in the delta, including the clapnet trapping birds, fishing, a hut filled with the catch, and two men at a small table cutting up fish. Below them, a cow calves, herdsmen milk others while their calves are tied up, the cow's hind legs tied to prevent kicking. The herdsmen also take them across the river, enticing the herd with a young calf (perhaps too young to cross alone), whose mother will follow.

20. A massive scene in which Ti sails through the

papyrus marsh, the gigantic reeds forming a backdrop for the three boats; Ti dominates the center one. In front of him, his workers spear hippopotamuses while behind him a single man sitting in a reed seat catches a sheatfish. The tops of the reeds are filled with nesting birds, many defending their young against stalking mongooses.

21. Men harvest papyrus and build boats, while below them sailors flail at each other with their poles in a show of prowess or a contest. Below them, a fisherman shakes his catch from a bow net into a basket. The lower registers are devoted to preparing the soil with hoe and plow, and seeding; rams, driven over the field, trample in the seed.

TOMB OF TI

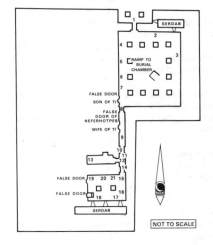

© MOON PUBLICATIONS, INC.

Tomb Of Ankh-mahor
(The Physician's Tomb)
Though containing scenes showing jewelers, metalsmiths, and sculptors at work, the tomb is most famous for its depiction of surgery: an operation on a toe and a circumcision. The funerary scene on the same wall is one of the earliest, a motif that appeared increasingly often in 6th Dynasty tombs.

First Dynasty Tombs
Little remains of these mud-brick burials the early kings erected along the edge of the cliffs. What has not been washed away by the rain and wind has been reburied by drifting sand; the best place to see the construction of the tombs is under the shed that protects the eastern wall.

WESTERN TOMBS

Tomb Of Akhethotep And Ptahhotep
The main axis of this father-and-son tomb is devoted to Akhethotep while his son's chapel occupies its southern end. The walls of the unfinished entry passage show the sequence of carving, while Ptahhotep's chapel is jammed with beautiful carvings; their original brilliant color remains. (See tomb plan on p. 276.)

Tomb Of Ti
The most beautiful example of Old Kingdom artwork, the 5th Dynasty tomb of Ti was discovered in 1860 by Mariette. As controller of ponds, stock-rearing, and arable farms, Ti drew revenues from numerous estates, eventually building himself a huge mastaba with false doors for his wife (who had royal connections) and his sons. Now nearly covered with sand, it lies down the hill and to the north of the rest area, past the circle of Greek philosophers. The tomb (entered by a modern staircase) preserves the small entrance vestibule, a court (with a modern roof), and decorated corridors leading to a storage room and the chapel. The original chapel roof is supported by pillars painted in imitation of pink Aswan granite. The entrance to the burial chamber under the chapel is through the hole in the courtyard. (See tomb plan on p. 277.)

Apis Bull Galleries (The Serapeum)
Southwest of Ti's tomb, the Serapeum is a haunting catacomb of bull burials. Although Apis bulls were buried at Saqqara from early times, these tombs date from the 26th Dynasty to the Ptolemaic period.

ABUSIR

Lying north of the main Saqqara cemetery, the pyramids of the sun-kings are rarely visited, and here you can explore the ruins away from the madding throngs of tourists. These pyramids, like most late Old Kingdom ones, were limestone-encased, mud-brick cores. With the limestone now long gone, the structures have crumbled to artificial mounds, surrounded by the shattered remains of mortuary temples and tombs. The main site is accessible by foot from

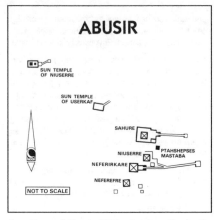

the village of Abusir (2.5 km) or from the northern end of north Saqqara (six km), from where you can see the pyramids' outline. The custodians get few visitors here and will delight in hauling you all over the site.

Pyramids
The southern pyramid of Neferefre is badly ruined. The central, unfinished pyramid of Neferirkare would have been larger than that of Menkaure at Giza; its valley temple and causeway were diverted to serve the complex of Niuserre to the north.

Tomb Of Ptahshepses
Between this pyramid and the next lie several mastabas; the most elaborate is that of Ptahshepses, relative of King Niuserre. The entrance is flanked by columns with closed-bud capitals, but access to the tomb is over a shaky ladder on the wall. The tomb is interesting in that much of the superstructure remains, giving visitors an idea of a mastaba tomb's construction. The figures inside the tomb are of the usual scenes and are not particularly well preserved; entry is from the main courtyard. To the southwest, a double room may have held boats, unusual for a private tomb; the only other known example is that of Kagemni in north Saqqara.

Pyramid Of Sahure
Although this pyramid has sunk, its interior is accessible from the north side (the *ghaffir* will

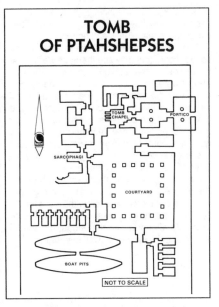

TOMB
OF PTAHSHEPSES

TOMB
CHAPEL

PORTICO

SARCOPHAGI

COURTYARD

BOAT PITS

NOT TO SCALE

show you); you'll have to crawl through the entrance corridor to reach the inner chambers. The east side of the pyramid is dominated by the ruins of the mortuary temple, and although many of the best pieces have been removed to the Antiquities Museum, enough remain to make exploring worthwhile; try to find the column shaft with the king's *serekh* with its palace facade surmounted by a Horus hawk.

Sun Temples Of Abu Ghurob

About a kilometer north of Sahure's pyramid are the sun temples of Userkaf and Niuserre, the latter being better preserved. Unlike the mortuary complexes, these buildings were designed for worshipping Re, sun-god of Heliopolis, although its location in the pyramid field at Abusir and the presence of jubilee reliefs may indicate a function similar to Djoser's courtyard at north Saqqara.

A valley temple opened onto a causeway that led to the main structure. A vestibule gives onto a great courtyard, which was dominated by the *benben,* a great obelisk, symbol of the primordial mound and the shining rays of the sun. Before this altar, priests sacrificed animals prepared in the slaughterhouse, where drains remain. The

vestibule also opens into two long corridors; the one to the north leads to magazines, while the southern one, once decorated with scenes from the king's jubilee, leads to the chapel. Scenes included the cattle count and the founding of the temple; German museums and the Egyptian Antiquities Museum now house them.

Beyond the chapel, the "Chamber of the Seasons" once held dazzling painted reliefs of "all that the solar disc encompasses." From here, the corridor leads to the obelisk. To the south lie the remains of a huge, brick model of the solar barque. The entire structure was apparently modeled on the sun temple of Re at Heliopolis. To reach these temples, walk a kilometer north from the funerary complexes at Abusir, or, if you're riding camels or horses, stop on your way to Saqqara.

MEMPHIS

The capital city founded by Menes lies southeast of its cemetery at Saqqara. Nearly as famous as its sister-city of Thebes to the south, Memphis was an administrative center throughout the history of ancient Egypt. Even in the 12th century A.D., the extensive ruins caught the eye of Arab travelers, but today the remains lie scattered throughout the cultivated fields, much of the stone long eaten away by the damp valley soil. The most accessible ruins lie just off the road to Badrashayn.

To reach Memphis from Saqqara, return to the main road, turn right, and turn left at the next bridge. Near the village of Mit Rahina, the large clear area studded with palm trees marks the beginning of the site.

Sculpture Garden

Open daily 0800-1700; LE8. Statues and architectural fragments have been collected in the sculpture garden, which occupies the southeastern part of the Ptah Temple complex, patron god of Memphis. Here the massive statue of Ramesses II lies under a roof, and the sphinx from the same period dominates the courtyard. In addition, the garden contains stelae and statues from various periods as well as some Coptic columns, identified by the dual patterns on their shafts.

Other Ruins

Beyond the garden to the east lie the remains of

Merneptah's palace. To the west along the road is the Apis bull house; the large alabaster beds perhaps served as embalming platforms. Just west of the cleared area, the road that runs along the canal leads to the old Roman Fort and the massive mud-brick platform that was the foundation for King Apries' palace; this jaunt through the village is recommended for those with extra time to kill and who are looking for an excuse to hike around the area and meet the locals.

Harraniyya Art School

Open daily 0800-1700; Saqqara Road; tel. (018) 850-403. Founded 50 years ago by Ramesses Wissa Wassef, an architect who was disturbed by the vanishing of village crafts, especially weaving. He founded a school to teach children weaving and foster their natural artistic talents. Students card and spin their own wool, dye it, and then weave it into their own original designs. Their work, well known throughout Egypt by the 1950s, has also been shown in Europe. The school has expanded to teach batik and pottery.

Adult graduates may rent studio space at the school, so visitors may see them, as well as the younger students, at work between 0800 and 1500 except for an hour at noon and on Fridays; visit the museum where huge, beautiful tapestries testify to the school's success, and buy some of the students' products. Although many schools are now imitating the school's work, the visit to Harraniyya is worth the trouble to see the lovely grounds and get a feel for well-finished mud-brick architecture.

The school lies about 2.5 km south of the Saqqara Road. Turn off Sh. al-Haram on the west side of the canal and follow the signs for the campground, turning west off the main road, then right after crossing the bridge; the school lies behind the mud-brick wall to your left.

THE FAYYUM DEPRESSION

Branching like a bud from a lotus stem, the oasis of the Fayyum lies southwest of Cairo. Unlike the other oases of the Western Desert, however, it is not fed by a spring or artesian well but by a small river, the Bahr Yusif, which ties it to the Nile. Watered by the river and fertilized by the annual flood, the Fayyum became a haven for wild animals, including ducks on their annual migration south to Africa—birds that still flock to the area every winter.

The game and fertility in turn attracted the pharaohs of the Middle Kingdom, who built their mud-brick pyramids at Lahun and Hawara, and the Greeks and Romans, who established extensive towns and irrigation works. (From their cemeteries came the famous Fayyum portraits, which now grace the Egyptian Antiquities Museum.)

Perhaps, however, the most appealing aspect of the Fayyum is its rustic tranquillity, the unique waterwheels that groan as they irrigate the lush fields, the friendly people who go out of their way to help visitors, and the quiet peace that lines the lakeshore and pervades the fields.

THE LAND

The form of the 4,000-square-km Fayyum Depression, like that of the other western oases, was dictated by the line of faults that runs across the Western Desert. The depression itself was probably carved out by wind erosion, but the soil lining it came from the annual floods of the Nile. The northern part, which holds the saline lake of Birket Qarun, lies about 45 meters below sea level.

In pharaonic times, the Bahr Yusif sliced its way through the ridge near modern Beni Suef at Lahun and watered the Fayyum directly. Today, however, the river branches off from the Nile near Asyut and, known as the Ibrahimiya Canal, runs 300 km nearly parallel to the river before it crosses the gap at Lahun to run into the center of the depression, where it radiates to feed the entire oasis. The drainage from the fields flows into two major canals and ultimately into Birket

Qarun. These waterways support the extensive agriculture for which the area is noted.

Climate

The Fayyum, more north than Upper Egypt, has milder summers, yet it is far enough south to boast milder and drier winters than Cairo. Average summer high temperatures run about 35° C, falling at night to around 20° C. Like much of Egypt, the evening heat is mitigated by the prevailing northern breezes. In winter, temperatures vary between 15-20 and 5-10° C; rainstorms are infrequent and short, though occasionally rain can fall throughout the day. In spring, strong northern winds can chill the level fields, and in March, the hot khamsins often whip across the desert from the south, enveloping the oasis with their dust. The sun, especially in summer, unfiltered by the smog and dust of the cities, can burn unprotected skin quickly and severely.

Wildlife

Birds dominate the wildlife in the Fayyum and nearly all Egypt's birds appear here. The most common are white cattle egrets and plovers, but visitors with sharp eyes can also find skylarks, wagtails, and swallows. Hooded crows, kestrels, kites, and little owls also inhabit the oasis, while grey herons and Senegal coucals occasionally put in an appearance. In winter, the Fayyum is flooded with migrating ducks, geese, quail, and doves. Shooting is no longer permitted in Fayyum.

Less obvious than the birds are the small mammals inhabiting the fields and the surrounding desert: foxes, mongooses, wolves (in the desert), and perhaps even shy field cats, gray-brown and about twice the size of their domestic cousins.

Although Birket Qarun was noted in antiquity for its fish, the lake has become too salty for most of its original species, with the notable exception of the *bolti*. In recent times, marine mullet, eel, and sole have been introduced, and the research station at Shakshuk continues to study ways of improving the catch for the 550 boats that fish the lake during its open season.

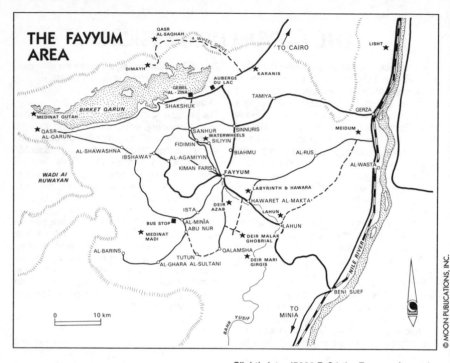

THE FAYYUM AREA

QASR AL-SAQHAH
4 WHEEL DRIVE
TO CAIRO
LISHT
DIMAYH
KARANIS
AUBERGE DU LAC
GEBEL AL-ZINA
TAMIYA
BIRKET QARUN
SHAKSHUK
GERZA
MEDINAT QUTAH
SANHUR
SINNURIS
WATERWHEELS
MEIDUM
QASR AL-QARUN
SILIYIN
FIDIMIN
AL-SHAWASHNA
IBSHAWAY
AL-AGAMIYIN
BIAHMU
AL-RUS
KIMAN FARIS
FAYYUM
AL-WASTA
WADI AI RUWAYAN
LABYRINTH & HAWARA
ISTA
DEIR AZAB
HAWARET AL-MAKTA
LAHUN
LAHUN
BUS STOP
AL-MINIA ABU NUR
DEIR MALAK GHOBRIAL
MEDINAT MADI
AL-BARINS
QALAMSHA
TUTUN
AL-GHARA AL-SULTANI
DEIR MARI GIRGIS
BENI SUEF
NILE RIVER
TO MINIA
BAHR YUSIF
0   10 km

© MOON PUBLICATIONS, INC.

HISTORY

Though linked with the Nile Valley, the history of the Fayyum is separate from the mainstream events that shaped Egypt's history. Reserved primarily for hunting and agriculture, the area was used as an administrative center only for a brief period in the Middle Kingdom. Nevertheless, the area contributed to the development of Egypt as a whole throughout its history.

Prehistoric Times

Watered by the abundant rainfall of the Pleistocene era, the Fayyum grew lush forests and swamps where gazelles, wild cattle and pigs, and diverse birdlife flourished. Birket Qarun, much larger and less salty than today, harbored fish, turtles, and crocodiles. Small bands of Stone-Age hunter-gatherers (the so-called Fayyum B people) settled on the northern shores of the lakes to exploit these resources.

Slightly later (5000 B.C.) the Fayyum A people appeared and made the transformation from a hunter-gatherer society to an agricultural one, complete with domesticated plants and animals.

In myth, the Egyptians identified this Land of the Lake with Nun, the waters of Chaos, and source of all life. On a hunting expedition here Menes was attacked by his own dogs and a crocodile carried him to safety across the lake. In appreciation, the king dedicated a temple to the crocodile-god Sobek and declared the lake a sanctuary. Sacred crocodiles were kept at Shedet (Crocodilopolis) until the close of Roman times.

Pharaonic Period

Although little remains of Old Kingdom occupation, the mines north of the lake provided stone for 4th and 5th Dynasty monuments, as well as the pavement for Khufu's mortuary temple at Giza. The Fayyum lay near the emerging Middle Kingdom powers at Herakleopolis, but the oasis did not become important in Egyptian affairs until the 12th Dynasty, when the southern king Amenemhet, to better control the delta, moved his capital north near modern Lisht, where it became the hub of the newly reunited country. Here, Middle Kingdom pharaohs built residences and scattered pyramids and temples throughout the depression. They also initiated massive irrigation projects, draining parts of the area for agriculture. They installed a series of gates that controlled the annual flood and swelled Birket Qarun, which covered twice the area of the modern lake.

Greco-Roman Period
Although the Fayyum fell from royal notice during the succeeding dynasties, the Greeks, when they came to power in 332 B.C, focused their attention on the beautiful oasis. Ptolemy I began draining the lake and reclaimed 1,200 square kilometers of land, which was watered by improved irrigation systems including the huge vertical waterwheels, which still dominate the landscape.

Increasing amounts of land were granted by the Ptolemies to Greek soldiers who settled in existing towns and built new ones. Toward the end of the period, irresponsible and inept rulers at Alexandria levied impossible taxes and persecuted those who didn't pay. Farmers fled their lands, and those who remained were forced to shoulder additional financial burdens. In addition, family battles among the Ptolemies siphoned off Greeks and Egyptians alike for personal armies; land lay uncultivated and irrigation canals silted up. Whole tracts and once-thriving towns were abandoned to the desert.

By the time the Romans defeated Cleopatra at Actium (30 B.C), the Fayyum, like much of Egypt, welcomed the new rulers. Although the cities seemed to recover under the early Roman emperors, the area eventually continued its slide. During Roman and then Byzantine rule, the people of Fayyum adopted Christianity, and when the country was invaded by the Arabs, they held out against the conquerors until after the fall of Old Cairo.

Islamic Period
In spite of the disintegration the oasis had suffered under Roman rule, the province was still quite rich at the time of the Arab conquest. Unfortunately, Muslim rule was no improvement, and the area continued to decline. The Fatimid army sacked the Fayyum in 914, and by 1245, the Syrian governor of the province found the canals useless and the Bahr Yusif so silted up that it only flowed during the annual flood. He repaired the damage and cleaned the canals. Slightly later, the new regulator at Lahun (used until this century) was constructed, but this brief attention only caused a slight hesitation in the oasis's decline, which continued under the Turkish rulers.

Modern Period
When Muhammad Ali finally took control of the country, the Fayyum's prospects began to change. His agricultural reforms, including the introduction of cotton, and later sugarcane, began to revive the province's economy. To combat the destruction of the raiding Bedouin, he settled them on the land, and in 1874, the railway reached Medinat Fayyum, linking it with the Nile Valley. By the turn of the century, the British were engaged in improving the roads, reviving the irrigation systems, and reclaiming some of the land lost to the desert. This land, with Nasser's land reforms in the 1950s, finally reverted to the *fallahin,* who had worked it for generations. The farmers' cooperatives and the rural electrification program have continued the slow climb back to prosperity, but most of the land lost under the late Ptolemies and Romans remains desert.

SIGHTS

For the visitor, the Fayyum presents a pleasing mix of pharaonic, Christian, Islamic, and modern sights. Ancient pyramids and temples mix with Christian monasteries and lush, green fields irrigated by the waterwheels that, powered by the stream itself, lift the water into the irrigation system. Many of the ancient sights have been destroyed by the encroachment of cultivation, fertilizer digging, or blowing sand. Nevertheless, they remain tantalizing, for the adventure of reaching them often introduces you to the friendly and helpful people of Fayyum. Most antiquities are open 0900-1600 and entrance fees run about LE8. Many sites are not directly accessible by public transportation, although these lie within reasonable hikes. Take care in the summer, however, because the Fayyum can be deceptively hot.

Shakshuk

Like the pharaonic kings before him, Faruq enjoyed hunting in Fayyum and built a hunting lodge along the lake, now the Hotel Auberge du Lac. Several other hotels of various classes stretch westward along the beach. The lake is the center of recreation in the Fayyum, where visitors can take a boat ride on the lake, visit ancient sights, or just relax along the beaches, swimming in the salty water, or picnicking under palm-leaf umbrellas. The lake, however, is not always placid; one storm drove six-meter waves into the garden at the Auberge, destroying it.

Medinat Fayyum

Known as Fayyum, the city dominating the oasis is pleasant if unpretentious. Cleaner than much of Egypt, this administrative hub of the oasis sits at the point where the Bahr Yusif splits into its eight branches, and the river with its low bridges flows through the city's center. Although Kiman Faris (slightly north) was the pharaonic hub of the Fayyum, Medinat Fayyum has existed since medieval times. The city center, clustered around the waterwheels, is near the railway station and the bus depot; from here you can walk to mosques, churches, and the city suq.

Mosques Of Fayyum

Since Fayyumis are not accustomed to foreigners visiting their mosques, dress appropriately (long pants for men, covered arms and shoulders for women) and ask permission of the guardian before you enter or take photos. The **Hanging Mosque** stands above five archways that once housed artist workshops; undergoing restoration, it may not be open to visitors. The **Mosque of Qaytbey** was built by the Mamluk sultan who frequently visited Fayyum during his tenure between 1468 and 1496, although some historians have suggested that he merely remodeled an existing mosque. The domed roof rises on ancient columns, some undoubtedly once standing in the pharaonic center

of Kiman Faris. Near the curtained-off section for women is the well (under the floor matting), which, connecting directly to the Bahr Yusif, once provided water for ablutions. The large minbar with its intricately carved wood and inlaid ivory is from Somalia. The dual-arched bridge near the mosque, although once named for the sultan's wife Khwand, is now called the Bridge of the Farewells, for it leads to the cemetery.

The **Mausoleum of Ali al-Rubi,** Fayyum's most popular sheikh, is worth a visit to watch the people who come to worship at his tomb. At the celebration of his mulid (during the month of Shaban) people from throughout Egypt crowd into Fayyum to celebrate.

Monasteries

Christianity came early to Fayyum and monasticism soon followed. Tradition says that St. Anthony visited the oasis in the 4th century to encourage the founding of desert monasteries, and by the 6th century the depression held 35 monastic societies. Today, the only functioning one is the modern **Deir al-Azab,** which lies south of Fayyum along the al-Lahun-Beni Suef road. Popular among Egyptian Christians, the site houses a large cemetery and the shrine for Anba Abram, bishop of Fayyum and Giza from 1882-1941. Flooded by Copts on Fridays, Sundays, and holidays, the monastery holds little interest for tourists; though founded in the 12th century, the current buildings are mostly modern.

In contrast, the **Deir al-Malak** lies outside the main track, only visited occasionally when a busload of Copts may take up residence in the rooms surrounding the monastery during feasts. The monastery was founded in the 7th or 8th century, but the church, dedicated to St. Gabriel, is only 100 years old, although its design and incorporation of older elements make it appear far older.

The monastery is reached from the Lahun-Beni Suef road; take the fork (north of Deir al-Azab) toward Qalamsha and follow it past two villages; when you come to the yellow barn in the stoneyard, turn left onto the dirt track that runs along the canal. A longer route entails staying on the al-Lahun road past Deir al-Azab and turning right at the blue and white sign for Deir al-Malak; follow the dirt road until it reaches a stone bridge (intersection of the above road), cross the canal, and continue a kilometer or so into the desert until you reach the monastery. The closest you can get with public transportation is a service taxi from al-Hawatim Station to Qalamsha, which will drop you at the barn; the walk from there is long, but pleasant in cool weather.

The Seven Waterwheels
Symbol of Fayyum, the waterwheels, which stand four to five meters tall, have lifted water since the Ptolemies introduced them as part of their extensive irrigation system. Driven by the fall of fast-moving streams, the wheels can lift water into sluices three meters above ground level. The wheels run continuously except in January, when the canals are dried for maintenance and the wheels repaired. The valley has about 200 wheels, painted with tar to retard decay, and they run for about 10 years before they need to be replaced. Although most tourists only see the set of four wheels near the Tourist Office in the center of Fayyum, the most beautiful ones lie scattered along the road to Sanhur. Follow the Bahr Sinnuris north: a single wheel lies a short way out of town at a farm; beyond is a group of four, and beyond that a pair near a rough bridge. Exploring for these wheels makes a nice walk (about half an hour), especially in the morning or evening.

a waterwheel in the lush Fayyum

Ain Al-Siliyin
The park at **Ain al-Siliyin** (open 0800-1700, 25PT), a favorite of the Egyptians, appeals less to foreigners, because its pavement and concrete enclosure have stripped the area of its native beauty. Although less crowded in winter, in summer children swarm over the swimming pool (swimming here not recommended) and soccer field; those not playing are aggressively hawking baskets. The springs no longer bubble up to the surface but flow through pipes; a walk in the nearby countryside can offer more peace and beauty.

Karanis (Kom Oshim)
The city, founded by Ptolemaic Greeks (3rd century B.C.) and later inhabited by Romans, lies at the edge of the desert, just before the Cairo-Fayyum road drops down into the depression. The frontier city, with an ancient population close to 3,000, garrisoned the desert police and served as a focus of caravan traffic. Though the town bordered the desert, its inhabitants cultivated the surrounding area, growing or trading for fruit, grains, and nuts. Expensive Alexandrian glass and Syrian perfume flasks testify to the town's prosperity, while locally made lamps (glass and terra-cotta), decanters, and statuettes indicate more than a simple agricultural society: potters, tailors, bakers, merchants, musicians, scribes, and undertakers. When the people abandoned the city late in the 5th century A.D., they left their possessions scattered about the site (many are now in the Karanis Museum), enabling archaeologists to reconstruct much of the city's life. In fact, millstones and olive presses still litter the streets.

The older part of the city lies to the south, centered on the stone temple of the crocodile-gods Pnepheros and Petesouchos. As the city grew, it spread north and west, and the people built a second temple to Sobek and perhaps Isis, although the lack of inscription makes identification little more than an educated guess. Following Greek city planning, streets in Karanis intersect at right angles; two main north-south streets run along its west and east sides, but the city had no through connecting cross streets. The pathway to the site approaches the city along the east, past many of the mud-brick houses, which in Karanis used considerable timber for lintel and window framing as well as to strengthen corners. Interior stairs reached their upper stories; private rooms were undecorated, but the more formal living areas are marked by niches and were painted. Bathrooms are scarce so the inhabitants evidently bathed at the public baths in the center of town (their stone remains marked by a large pavement and drainage pit). The street runs past a granary, with its rectangular chambers and a dovecote with nooks for pots, which served as nests.

The center of the town is dominated by the temples in an area thought to have been the agora. The southern temple contains an inscription from Nero, later usurped by Claudius. The stone foundations rest on bedrock, and the niche in the second room once held a mummified crocodile. The large altar in the sanctuary contains a hole to hide a priest acting as an oracle. The northern temple dates to the 1st century A.D. and evidence points to its abandonment by the middle of the 3rd century, perhaps because of the combined impact of Christianity and economic decline.

The sand-colored house between the temple and the museum once belonged to Sir Miles Lampson, a British ambassador and high commissioner, better known as Lord Killearn. In 1942, he ordered British tanks to surround King Faruq, who was ensconced in Abdin Palace, forcing the king to form a pro-British non-coalition government.

The **Karanis Museum** (closed for renovations) lies next to the road, just in back of the parking area, and houses a well-laid-out collection of artifacts from the city behind it, including a Fayyum portrait, delicate glassware and pottery, and the rural version of the female heads found also in Alexandria, which are thought to have been used to model hair styles.

North Of Birket Qarun

Nearly invisible, the temple of **Qasr al-Saghah** sits on a shelf backed by the sweep of the scarp. The sandstone temple, fitted together with uniform blocks, contains seven parallel shrines which open off a main, transverse corridor. A narrow passage from the outside of the southeast front wall ends in a small spyhole at the main entrance. Because the temple is uninscribed, archaeologists have long puz-

zled over its date but recently decided, based on nearby artifacts, that it dates from the Middle Kingdom and was linked to the other Middle Kingdom temple found across the Fayyum at Medinat Madi. The site offers a sweeping view of the lake below and the lakefront ruins of Dimayh al-Sib.

The ancient area of **Dimayh (Soknopaiou Nesos)** lies to the south of Qasr al-Saghah, the highly visible ruins occupying a pinnacle that once stood as an island in Birket Qarun known as the island of the crocodile-god. The city was both a caravan town and port, and the surrounding areas, irrigated by lake waters less salty than now, were cultivated fields rather than sandy waste. The old city on the west side of the ruins was founded in the 3rd century B.C., and like most of the Fayyum, saw several periods of alternating prosperity and decline, and was finally abandoned in the 3rd century A.D. The ruins, still encased in magnificent mud-brick walls, are bisected by a huge ceremonial street, which runs the length of the city. Near the lake lies a later Coptic monastery.

The sights on the north shore of Birket Qarun are accessible by car and those of Dimayh by boat from the south shore. Due to tourist looting, the sight has been closed to visitors; you may be able to get permission from the Antiquities Organization at Giza, or with the Tourist Office in Medinat Fayyum. The road that takes off just past the police station at Karanis (across from the museum) is dirt, and although it is passable without four-wheel drive, it requires a vehicle with high clearance. The 40-km road runs along the cultivation for about seven km, then takes off straight across the desert. Although it's marked in most places, follow the tracks carefully or you could spend considerable time stuck in sand. Carry food, water (for people and radiators), traction mats or a couple of boards and shovel, and plenty of gas; take at least two cars. The trip one way takes about 1½ hours. Alternately, you can reach Dimayh (not Qasr al-Saqhah) by hiring a fisherman from Shakshuk to ferry you across the lake, having him wait while you explore the ruins; the expedition, depending of course on how long you explore the ruins, should fill an afternoon. From February to April, fishing season closes and getting a boat can be hard.

Biahmu

A visit to the pedestals of the colossal statues of Amenemhet III at Biahmu makes a good excuse to get into the Fayyum countryside. Erected during the Middle Kingdom, the figures were noted by Herodotus but have continually deteriorated until today only two bases remain. Too far from the desert to be part of a funerary complex, they must have stood within a temple of some type. Petrie's reconstruction of the figures, which once sat upon the stone piles, makes them 13 meters tall. The easiest way to reach Biahmu, seven km north of Medinat Fayyum, is via local railway; Biahmu is two stops up the line (about 15 minutes). By car, take the Sinnuris road north, following the railway tracks behind the waterwheels at the Tourist Office. To reach Biahmu, you'll have to cut across the tracks Ka'abi al-Gadida (about five km south of Sinnuris) and follow the unimproved track to Biahmu, where you have to leave your car at the canal and walk about 10 minutes to the statues.

Qasr Qarun—Currently Inaccessible

Lying on the southwest side of Birket Qarun, these ruins were mistaken by early Europeans for Herodotus's labyrinth. Founded during the 3rd century B.C., the city was fortified in Roman times and finally abandoned in the 4th century A.D. The Ptolemaic temple, standing as in antiquity like a beacon in the desert, dominates the site.

Although the pylon is ruined and the Antiquities Service has shored up the entrance, the rest of the building is original. The central corridor opens into the normal three niches; the central one, being longer, probably held a crocodile mummy. Like most Ptolemaic structures, the interior is honeycombed with tiny passages and rooms (take a flashlight), which makes the temple seem larger than its outer dimensions indicate. Explore carefully; occasionally the footing is not good, and the rooms house bats, snakes, small lizards, and undoubtedly an odd scorpion or two.

Stairs lead to the roof where, on the west side, a headless king worships an equally headless Sobek. From this vantage you can see the remains of the Roman fortifications to the northwest, now mostly filled with sand. Although desert nearly surrounds the site, once Qasr Qarun stood on the shore of Birket Qarun and boasted lush gardens. Much of the domestic architecture is now buried by the sand.

If and when Qasr Qarun opens again you can reach it via service taxi (from the stand by Qaytbey's mosque in Medinat Fayyum) or train to Ibshaway, where a service taxi runs to the village of Qarun; the temple lies about an hour out of Ibshaway, just before the village. To return you'll have to flag a taxi on the road; avoid the rush hour (about 1400) as most vehicles will be full.

The trip by private car lets you enjoy the rich countryside, especially in spring when the orchards bloom. If Qasr Qarun is accessible, take the road out of Medinat Fayyum to al-Agamiyin, the center of the basket- and rope-making industry, where after a left and then a right you continue to Ibshaway, busy capital of one of Fayyum's administrative centers. In the center of town, turn right; a blue direction sign indicates Qasr Qarun. Just beyond the city, the road crosses Masraf al-Wadi, the district's western drain. Both Qasr Qarun and Medinat Qutah are accessible from Shakshuk via a good road that runs along the lake's south edge; the trip takes about half an hour.

Around Qasr Qarun

Between Ibshaway and Qasr Qarun, the unique Fayyumi landscape is half wild, half cultivated, its sandy, rocky terrain laced by a twisting stream carrying spent irrigation water to the lake. In al-Shawashna, stop for a look at the beautiful mosque, which has been compared to the Aga Khan's mausoleum in Aswan. Beyond al-Shawashna, the road winds through fields often planted in marigolds and absinthe (white daisy-like flowers), which bloom in the spring, and in places overlooks the lake itself.

After visiting Qasr Qarun, hike along the fields to the lakeshore for a picnic and a swim, or head farther west to Medinat Qutah, where ancient workers worshipped the divine twins Castor and Pollux. Although the ruins of the small tell are scanty, the top of the mound offers a spectacular panoramic view of the lake, mountains, and cultivation.

Medinat Madi

The perfect "off-the-beaten-path" destination, the focus of this site is the Middle Kingdom temple in which Amenemhet III and his son Amen-

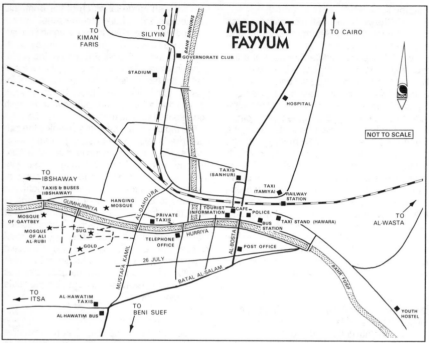

emhet IV made offerings to Renenutet, goddess of harvest, and her crocodile consort. The processional way is lined with sphinxes and lions, many of which date to Ptolemaic times. The roofed inner rooms of the temple itself contain three niches; the decorations of the left one include a portrait of the goddess in which the artist has, with typical Egyptian skill, married the serpentine head and human body. Ptolemaic additions lie back to back with the earlier temple. The mud-brick homes surrounding the temples show the same wooden reinforcements as those at Karanis.

Although the site is accessible by standard car, a high-clearance vehicle makes the trip easier. Head south from Medinat Fayyum toward Ista; a few kilometers beyond the town turn right, toward al-Minia (Medinat al-Het), and there turn south toward the canal where you'll have to jog left, and then right over the bridge. The site lies beyond the tiny village along the dusty track (see below for directions from there).

To reach Medinat Madi by public transportation, take the bus to al-Qasmiya (at 0700 or 1100) from Hawatim Station (south Fayyum); get off after about an hour's ride at Menshat Sef, by the edge of the canal. From there, turn right and walk to the first bridge; turn left and head for the stone dig-house visible on the rise ahead; the ruins lie just beyond. To return, catch the bus (going in the same direction; the route is circular) at the canal at 1200 or 1600.

Lahun Pyramid

Built by Senwosret, this Middle Kingdom funerary complex is laid out like those of the Old Kingdom, but the designs of the pyramids had evolved, and Senwosret's engineers, using mud brick, faced greater challenges than the builders before them who had built with stone. The pyramid caps a rock knoll that forms its core, and to anchor their bricks, the ancient designers constructed an interior framework of limestone pillars, which now emerge out of the corners of the eroded mud. To protect the underlying marl, the engineers dug a deep drainage trench around the pyramid, filled it with sand, and topped it with rolled stones. They then carefully angled the bricks as they built up the core so that the structure wouldn't collapse and finally sealed it with a limestone shell.

No longer oriented to the circumpolar stars, Middle Kingdom pyramids' entrances were in the south, and the underground chambers evolved into a mass of inter-branching corridors and rooms. On the north side stand the queen's pyramid and a row of mastabas hewn from the rock, the only examples of such construction known. Here visible salt encrustations relentlessly flake away the stone. Behind the mastabas, the remnant of a Middle Kingdom mud-brick wall reveals the alternating courses of headers and stretchers. In every fourth course, ancient masons inserted woven grass mats to stabilize the structure—much as modern re-bar strengthens concrete.

The mortuary temple once stood along the eastern side, and in the southern courtyard Petrie uncovered the burial chambers of the princesses of Lahun; their jewelry now graces the Antiquities Museum and New York's Metropolitan Museum of Art. Southeast of the pyramid lies the city Petrie called Kahun, the remains of houses used by the workers who built the pyramid. Beyond is the Coptic monastery of Deir al-Hammam.

To reach Lahun by car, take the Beni Suef road to the village of Lahun, recognizable by the sluices and bridges; follow the twisting main road until after it crosses a modern iron bridge, then turn left down a dust track (just before the main road swings right). On your left is the old medieval sluice, and just about opposite it, turn right; drive into the village of Lahun (notice the ornate doors and doorways) and bear left at the fork in the middle of the village. Continue for about two kilometers to the edge of the fields; turn left and follow the embankment (thought to be the remains of Amenemhet I's barrage to enlarge the lake) several kilometers into the desert. A policeman from the tent at the foot of the site may want to accompany you to the pyramid. By public transportation, take a service taxi from al-Hawatim to Lahun; it will drop you at the junction to the main road; the pyramid is about an hour's walk.

Hawara

Stripped of its protective limestone coat, Amenemhet's weathered mud-brick pyramid from a distance resembles a natural mountain. The legendary labyrinth described by Herodotus, the wondrous mortuary temple built by Amenemhet III once lay at the side of the mud-brick pyramid. Today little remains but splinters of Aswan granite and quartzite lintels and columns lying atop mounds of limestone chips. The pyramid itself, anchored to its rocky core by a limestone foundation, continued the Middle Kingdom innovations begun at Lahun. The southern entrance leads to even more complex passageways with trapdoors cut into their ceilings. West of the pyramid you can find bits of limestone turned gray and blackened lumps of slag (remains of the Roman lime kilns) mixed with grooved Roman pottery shards. Nearby stands a limestone bust, perhaps of Amenemhet himself, apparently saved from the mouth of a kiln. In the Roman cemetery north of the pyramid Petrie uncovered the Fayyum portraits now in the Antiquities Museum and elsewhere. To reach the pyramid, take the Beni Suef road south from Medinat Fayyum about 10 km to the village of Hawara; the pyramid lies about three km beyond, across the Bahr Yusif. A service taxi from al-Hawatim can drop you just beyond the village of Hawara.

Meidum

Although technically not within Fayyum, the Old Kingdom pyramid at Meidum is a nice day-trip. Isolated on a rising plain, the steeply terraced structure raises its truncated apex over 93 meters into the sapphire sky. This 3rd Dynasty structure marks the transition between the Step Pyramid at Saqqara and the true pyramids at Giza. Built of stone, it was originally designed with five steps and then enlarged to eight. The steps were filled with dressed limestone casing, now fallen, which would have given the pyramid smooth sides; traces of this perfectly fitted casing remain on the northern side of the structure. The collapse of this outer shell may have led to the abandonment of the site and the change in the angle of the bent pyramid at Dahshur, which was under construction.

Although unfinished, the subsidiary buildings are arranged in what would become standard

Old Kingdom layout: the queen's pyramid to the south, the mortuary temple to the east where the simple two-room structure still contains two uninscribed stelae, and a causeway to a valley temple. Although uninscribed, 18th Dynasty pilgrims attributed the pyramid to Snefru, first king of the 4th Dynasty.

The entrance to the pyramid is in the north, and modern visitors have to climb a steep set of stairs to enter, then negotiate a plunging corridor into the bedrock, and finally another set of vertical steps ending at the small burial chamber. This simple rectangular room is roofed by a corbelled stone vault, the earliest known, inset with a log of Lebanese cedar, which perhaps served as a fulcrum for lifting the stone sarcophagus into place. Around the pyramid, royal nobility built their mastabas, which have yielded up the treasures of the Meidum geese and the statues of Prince Ranefer and Princess Nofret.

To reach Meidum, take the al-Wasta road from Fayyum; the pyramid lies in the desert, across the railway line. By public transportation, take the train from Fayyum to al-Wasta, then a service taxi to Meidum; from the far end of the village, it's a short walk through the fields and across a couple of canals to the pyramid.

Lisht

Like Meidum, Lisht lies outside the Fayyum, but the pyramids of Lisht belong to the Middle Kingdom and were closely linked to the oases. The exact location of the Middle Kingdom capital is lost, but the two funerary complexes built by Amenemhet I and Senwosret remain. Well ruined, the pyramids and their subsidiary structures are not worth a trip unless you're a dedicated pyramidaholic.

PRACTICALITIES

Accommodations

The hotels are divided between the southern shore at Birket Qarun and those in Fayyum. The **Auberge du Lac,** Lake Qarun, Fayyum, Egypt, tel. (084) 700-002; fax (084) 700-730 (in Cairo: tel. (02) 350-2356, fax (02) 351-5717), is the nicest and most expensive hotel in the area ($46 s, $60 d). The **Panorama Shakshuk,** tel. (084) 701-746/071-314, Cairo tel. (02) 725-

848/731-480, is nearly as nice; LE90 s (double room); LE113 d; LE138 for a suite. The **Oasis Tourist Village,** tel. (084) 701-565; in Cairo, (02) 987-652; lies between the two higher-class hotels, and has been upgraded; it's now clean and neat as well as friendly: LE25 s, LE35 d, for a double room with bath, a/c, and breakfast.

In Medinat Fayyum, the best deal is the modern, clean, and friendly **Queen Hotel,** 24 Sh. Menshat Lotf-Allah, Fayyum, tel. (084) 326-819. LE45 s, LE60 d, including bath, a/c, TV, and phones in the rooms. The **Palace Hotel,** Sh. Hurriya, tel. (084) 323-641, is ideal for families and groups, for the hotel has suites with kitchens and separate double bedrooms for up to six or seven people; LE120 (including breakfast). LE25 s, LE45 d; fans in all rooms, some with a/c, no extra charge. The **Montaza Hotel** is at 2 Esmail al-Medany, tel. (084) 324-633: LE8.25 s; LE16 d; LE20.50 t. The facilities, though clean, are not as comfortable as the Palace. The **youth hostel** is at the east end of town (opens 1400). To the north, the **Ain al-Siliyin Hotel** at the park near Fidimin with no fans or a/c is overpriced at LE22.60 s; LE31 d (including breakfast).

Food

For excellent food, check in at the **Louloua,** tel. (02) 856-926 (Cairo), on Lake Qarun at the intersection of the road to Sanhur; the plush dining room exudes atmosphere and has great ice cream; in good weather you can eat on the deck next to the water. Otherwise, try the two hotels at the lake: the **Auberge** serves wild duck and charges reasonable prices. In Medinat Fayyum, the cafe by the waterwheels tends to be overpriced, although the food seems to be improving. Better is the **Mokhimar Restaurant,** about 100 meters west, where you can get good Egyptian food; also try **Kebabgi** (Mustafa Kamil between Bahr Yusif and Sh. Ramleh) and **Hajj Khaled** (Sh. Muhammadia). For Western food, visit the **Governorate Club,** Nadi al-Muhafza, north along the Bahr Sinnuris (entry fee 50PT); in good weather, eat in the garden at the back. The cafes at **Ain al-Siliyin,** if not overrun, provide a nice place to sit and have tea. For ice cream, head for **Sherif's** (across from Kebabgi); in winter treat yourself to hot *bilela* (wheat, milk, nuts, raisins, and sugar).

Information

The **Tourist Office** (open 0800-1400 or 1430, Ramadan 1000-1400) is located at the waterwheels in the center of Medinat Fayyum, and can be quite helpful. To phone them, you have to go through the main government exchange (047-322-586, ext. 177). Medinat Fayyum also has branches of major **banks** as well as the Fayyum National Bank; you can change money here and cash traveler's checks.

Shopping

The *suq* in Medinat Fayyum is for the locals, but is worth a walk through; behind it lie the gold and silver dealers, mostly Copts, who supply the Egyptian women with their dowries. The baskets hawked in the city are made in the village of al-Alam (just outside Medinat Fayyum on the Cairo road) where women weave bundles of rice straw with palm leaves into pretty and tough baskets of all sizes. On Tuesdays in Fayyum the pottery market (just off School St.) offers red, pink, and unglazed pots, many of which are made in the village of al-Nazla, south of Ibshaway. The craft center in Fidimin (north of Fayyum; Mon.-Thurs 0800-1400, children begin working about 1100) trains children in weaving, tapestry, embroidery, and beadwork; the center markets their products through fairs and exhibitions, as well as on the premises.

Transportation

Tourist information office is at the waterwheels in Medinat Fayyum; the bus and railway station are behind it, across the railroad tracks. **Trains** run north to Sinnuris, west to Ibshaway, and east to al-Wasta. Special high-speed trains connect Medinat Fayyum with Cairo, leaving Fayyum 0915, 1300, and 1630, and arriving in Cairo about two hours later; LE3.50. **Buses** for Cairo, starting 0600, leave about every half-hour (LE2-2.50) from the nearby station; those for southern destinations like Beni Suef and Upper Egypt (LE7) buses (as well as service taxis) leave from al-Hawatim Station. From the main station you can catch a bus directly to the Cairo airport at 0700 or 1500; LE50. Intervillage buses are slow, crowded, and unreliable. Far better are the **service taxis** that run from several stations in Fayyum to the outlying districts. Private taxis (LE30-40/day) are available from the stand along the river; private motorbike taxis (a thrill a minute) pick up passengers in some of the larger villages. You can rent bicycles and motorcycles at the Palace Hotel.

OFF THE BEATEN PATH

In addition to the pyramids and the Fayyum, several areas near Cairo not as well known offer getaways lasting from a few hours to all day.

WADI NATRUN

Northwest of Cairo lies a long narrow *wadi* that, like most desert playas, traps rainwater from the desert storms. When this moisture evaporates, it draws salts to the surface, carbonates of sodium the ancient Egyptians used to mummify their dead. From the 10 lakes in Wadi Natrun, the Romans extracted silica for glass, and during the Victorian period, a specially built railroad hauled the mined salts out of the *wadi*.

During the 4th century anchorites inhabited caves around the valley and eventually built monasteries. After the Arab conquest, the area became the official residence of the Coptic patriarch, and even today he is elected from Wadi Natrun monks. During the Middle Ages, the area was hard hit by plague and raiding Bedouin; the Christian population fell, and the 100 monasteries shrank to seven; today there are only four.

Throughout the history of the monasteries, hermit monks excavated caves, a practice that continues even today, for after spending 10 years as a monk, an individual can apply for status as a hermit. If his request is granted by the patriarch, he begins his quest for a cave, either finding an abandoned one or digging a new one.

The Monasteries

The foundations of all the Wadi Natrun monasteries date to the 4th century, but they were rebuilt and restored in the 8th and 11th centuries. The early churches were typical of Roman/Coptic basilicas, with a long central nave divided into three sections: the first for the communicants, the second (which often contains an old wooden pulpit) for reading the catechism, and the third for the "sinners." In this third section, a basin is sunk into the floor for washing feet, a ritual performed by the head of each monastery for all his monks once a year in commemoration of Christ's washing of his apostles' feet.

The original wooden roofs of the churches were replaced by stone and plaster, and recent work has revealed layers of early frescoes, which conservators will attempt to remove intact. Monastery complexes included refectories (often within the church itself) where the monks took their meals after celebrating communion. These compounds, walled for protection against the Bedouin, also contained a central keep (*qasr*), accessible only by an elevated drawbridge, to which the monks could withdraw in case the outer walls were breached.

The monasteries of St. Bishoi, St. Makar, and the Syrians are grouped together near the resthouse on the Alexandria Desert Rd., while the fourth, Deir Abu Maqar, lies at the south end of the *wadi* and is reached by a separate access road.

Monastery Of St. Bishoi
(Deir Anba Bishoi)

The monastery's patron saint (Bishoi), after a divine revelation, joined the hermit Saint John the Short, and both men, during the upheavals between the Monophysites and Malachites, sought refuge in Fayyum. Saint Bishoi attracted a large number of monks and founded his monastery in A.D. 340. The church refectory was built between 385 and 390 and has been restored several times since; it now serves as a museum.

Noted for his kindness, the monk was prone to wash the feet of any traveler, and discovered one day that the feet he was washing carried the stigmata (wounds of Christ), thus the icon of the church is Bishoi washing Christ's feet. Today's monks carry on his tradition by, among other things, operating medical clinics. The monastery, which has bought 400 hectares from the government, is reclaiming the land, and under their care, the desert is blooming

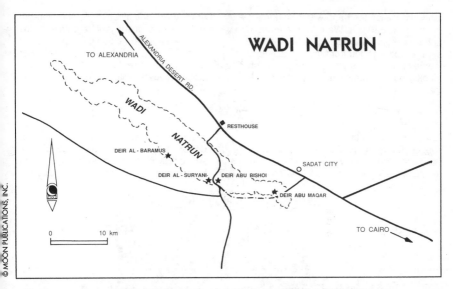

with olive groves, vegetables, fruits, and pasturage for cattle.

Monastery Of The Syrians
(Deir Al-Suryani)
Close to Deir Anba Bishoi, this monastery was bought by Syrian merchants for their monks, who inhabited the buildings until the Bedouin raids and plagues of the 14th century decimated the population. In the 15th century, Coptic and Syrian (now in the minority) monks reinhabited the complex. Well known for its extensive library, the monastery makes its collection of over 3,000 books and hundreds of manuscripts available to scholars throughout the world.

Monastery Of St. Makar (Macarius)
Living the life of a hermit in a cave, St. Makar received divine revelation in the form of a dream telling him to build this church, which became the focus of the community and eventually the official residence of the Coptic patriarch. The Church of St. Makar is dedicated to St. Benjamin and St. John the Baptist; in the same compound, the Church of the Forty-nine Martyrs holds lovely icons of St. Makar, St. Mark, St. George, and the Virgin.

Monastery Of The Romans
Named for the Roman brothers Maximum and Domitius who sought out St. Makar; after having served in the Syrian army, they retired to a cave in the desert; upon their death (within a few days of each other) St. Makar built a church near their cave to honor their memory. The central keep in this monastery, like many, lies near a natural spring; the lowest floor was used for storage, the second for sleeping, and the third was devoted to chapels, many with old frescoes still on the walls. Today this monastery is one of the largest and most prosperous in the area, farming extensive lands and incorporating modern technology.

Practicalities
The monasteries are normally open Thursdays and Fridays but may be closed during the week, so check with the Coptic Patriarchate in Cairo (Anba Reuis Building, Coptic Orthodox Patriarchate, Ramesses St. (next to St. Mark's Church), Abbassia, tel. (02) 821-274), or in Alexandria (on Nabi Daniel). The monasteries also close for holidays and fasts. If the monasteries know you're coming, they can often arrange for an English-speaking monk to guide you. Men can get written permission from the Patriarchate to spend the night at some of the monasteries;

bring your own food and water, and leave a donation (LE20-30). Wadi Natrun offers no other overnight accommodations. The resthouse, about 10 km from the monasteries, serves light snacks, sandwiches, and soft drinks; the WC works but take your own toilet paper.

Getting There
The easiest way to get to the monasteries is by car or private taxi; take the Alexandria Desert Rd. to the resthouse. Alternatively, take either the Delta or Super Jet bus to the resthouse and then pick up a later bus ei-

ther to Alexandria or Cairo: be sure you get tickets ahead for both legs of the journey, for the buses will not pick you up mid-trip without a ticket. From the resthouse you can get a taxi to the monasteries, or hitch a ride from the rash of Egyptian visitors on Fridays.

HELWAN

The industrial city of Helwan lies south of Cairo, and offers visitors a chance to see a slice of Egyptian life outside the big city. The Helwan springs once drew the rich to its sul-

phur waters and gardens, but after the revolution heavy industry moved here, and belching smokestacks of the steel mills and brick factories have replaced the palm trees and flowers.

Japanese Gardens

Once splendid, these abandoned gardens are only now beginning to be repaired. They occupy two large lots on either side of the road; the lower (left) half contains several walkways, a small lake, and a modern cafe. In the other half of the park, a statue of Buddha, elephants, and a small pavilion occupy the hill. The area, slowly turning green again, is quiet and peaceful except on Fridays.

Wax Museum

Open daily 0900-1700; 50PT; tel. 738-593. Helwan's only modern attraction, the wax museum lies near the old springs. The scenes, which show the history of Egypt from the time of the pharaohs to the revolution, are slightly the worse for the heat and dirt. A man is usually on hand to explain the tableaux; a tip is in order.

Practicalities

Getting around Helwan is easy, and the inhabitants are friendly rather than hassle-oriented. The Japan Palace Hotel lies just across from the gardens (see the "Cairo Hotels" chart). The juice stands serve up a plethora of cold, sweet drinks, or you can relax and have a Coke in the gardens.

Getting There

The easiest way to get to Helwan is by Metro (50PT), which ends at the station in the center of town. To reach the gardens, turn left as you leave the station and walk up the main street, which runs into the entrance. To reach the wax museum, get off the Metro at the Ain Helwan Station; the museum is near the tracks.

NILE BARRAGES

Sixteen km north of Cairo, the barrages span the river just before it forks. Part of the general irrigation projects to control flooding in the delta, the first dam was constructed by Muhammad Ali in the early 19th century, the second early in the 20th.

Designed with arches and turrets, the brightly painted barrages are surrounded by plush parks, and small bridges link the islands lying in the river to the banks. Here Cairenes escaping the city enjoy the river and the gardens, which are filled with cafes and casinos. The place is jammed on Fridays.

Getting There

You can reach the barrages by car; take the main road from Sh. al-Nil in Imbaba to Manruf, or follow the Alexandria-Delta road, turning off at Qalyub. Or you can take a Delta bus to Qantir (from the station behind the Nile Hilton). A ferry occasionally runs from the river-taxi station opposite the TV tower on the Cornishe, but its schedule is erratic. Alternately, you could hire a falucca; the trip by boat takes a couple of hours each way.

BOB RACE

MIDDLE EGYPT

Where the cliffs of Upper Egypt recede from the banks of the Nile, lush green farmlands dominate the river's edge. Here, Egypt's farmers cultivate the fertile soil, their techniques echo those on the tombs of their pharaonic ancestors. Although *shadufs* are giving way to pumps, browned backs still bend over *saqiyas,* nourishing the fields with precious water. Tractors are only slowly replacing oxen yoked to primitive wooden plows. Hitched to *noras,* they still thresh grain, separating it from the chaff before it's winnowed in the wind.

In pharaonic times, this section of the country was wild, often ruled by independent lords who, during the Intermediate Periods, became virtual kings. Before the Arab invasion, Middle Egypt converted to Christianity, and Coptic strongholds remain scattered throughout the area. But the truce between Muslim and Christian is not always easy, and occasional violence between the groups is not unknown—even today, Middle Egypt can be restless.

Not many tourists visit the area, but if you have an interest in Middle Kingdom art, Christian history, or like to get off the beaten path, you'll

enjoy Middle Egypt. The major northern pharaonic sites cluster about the twin towns of Minya and Mallawi and include the tombs of nomarchs at Beni Hassan—the best Middle Kingdom art available. At al-Amarna to the south, the heretic king Akhenaten dedicated his city to the worship of his only god, the sun disk Aton, and at ancient Tuna al-Gebel and Hermopolis, Greeks and Romans added their own temples and tombs.

Farther south, the traditional meeting place of Upper and Lower Egypt lies between Asyut and Sohag. While the pharaonic remains here are unimportant, the Red and White monasteries outside Sohag are two of Egypt's oldest Christian monuments. In Asyut or Sohag you can get a glimpse of how "real" Egyptians live, for these cities do not depend upon tourism, but thrive on agriculture, trading, and industry, offering a welcome respite from "antiquia" salesmen. Although religious tension in these Christian areas occasionally runs high, the Egyptians here offer visitors their traditional hospitality.

Near Luxor, the Seti Temple at Abydos, center of the Osiris cult and focus of ancient pilgrimages (for both living and dead), houses the most beautiful art in Egypt. Beyond it, outside Qina, lies the Ptolemaic temple of Dendera, cult center of the goddess Hathor since predynastic times.

The northern sites, nestled among mud-brick villages, cluster around Minya, so make your headquarters there for Beni Hassan, al-Amarna, Mallawi, and Tuna al-Gebel/Hermopolis. Because of the heat and the difficulty of getting to the sights, don't plan on visiting more than one area a day unless you have a private car; even then, you'll have to get an early start. Unless you're traveling the length of Middle Egypt, visit Abydos and Dendera as a day-trip from Luxor. The monasteries at Sohag are not worth a separate trip unless you're interested in early Christian history or architecture, but they make a delightful side trip if you're in the area. Life is slow in Middle Egypt, so take your time exploring the antiquities, prowling the countryside, and visiting friendly villagers.

MINYA AND VICINITY

With a population of 200,000, Minya is the capital of the al-Minya governorate. The city lies just east of the Ibrahimiya Canal, occupying the space between it and the Nile. The main section runs between the train station and the river. A couple of kilometers across, the town is easy to walk, its decaying turn-of-the-century architecture providing an interesting backdrop to the city.

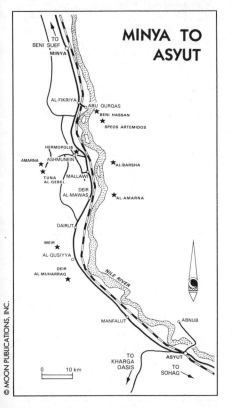

BENI HASSAN

Open 0800-1630 winter, 0700-1900 summer; LE6 plus LE3 for ferry (see "Getting There," p. 300). The tombs that Middle Kingdom monarchs built at Beni Hassan to house their souls still line the cliffs above green and golden fields. They date from late in the First Intermediate Period through most of the Middle Kingdom. Eternal homes for the governors of the Oryx Nome, they are filled with active and colorful paintings, which, though they show affinities with the Old and New kingdoms, are nevertheless different than both.

The Tomb Plans
The tombs of Beni Hassan mimic the houses in which the nomarchs lived. Steep stairs or ramps opened into a courtyard. Porches, hewn from the cliffs themselves, were raised on octagonal columns and rested on carved rafters—the entire facade suggests the later entrances to Greek temples. Inside, we see the transition from the wide floorplans of the Old Kingdom to the long, narrow ones of the New Kingdom. Middle Kingdom architects stressed the central corridor by lowering its floor and running the architraves on the columns lengthwise, parallel to the long axis

© MOON PUBLICATIONS, INC.

of the tomb. The halls and chapels cut into the cliffs, like the superstructures of the mastabas, continued to serve as focal points for the funeral rites and offerings. The mummy, encased in an elaborate coffin inscribed with funerary texts derived from the Old Kingdom pyramids, lay at the bottom of a shaft sunk into the floor. The vaulted ceilings of the cut-rock interiors are "supported" by floral (bud) pillars hewn from the same rock. The Old Kingdom *serdab* has been generally replaced by the niche in the east wall that houses a statue of the deceased.

Decorations

Motifs of the painted decorations derive primarily from the Old Kingdom tombs to the north, but the feudal lords introduced the wrestling scenes and those showing an army storming battlements—undoubtedly the predecessors of the sweeping battle scenes favored by the powerful New Kingdom pharaohs. In most of the tombs, these conflicts occupy the east (back) walls; the offering scenes appear on the south walls, the desert hunt on the north, and the rest of the tomb's walls are devoted to the funeral processions, crafts, and farming.

The Egyptian artists positioned the elements within the registers to mimic spatial perspective; the desert hunting scenes appear at the top and are therefore farthest from the viewer; valley scenes occupy the middle registers, and those concerning the river, the bottom. Thus the viewer stands at the edge of the river and gazes progressively at its bank, cultivation, and sandy steppes.

The paintings at Beni Hassan show a vitality that had died in the court art of the late Old Kingdom, and the attention to detail and the delicacy of the figures testifies to the craftsmanship of the artists, a union that produced the most beautiful of Middle Kingdom painting.

Tomb Of Khety (#17)

Four tombs are open: the 11th Dynasty ones of Baqet (#15) and his son Khety (#17), and two 12th Dynasty ones of Khnumhotep (#3) and Amenemhet (#2). Farthest to the south is the tomb of Khety, Lord of the Antelope Nome. The architraves of this tomb, which is an early one, run across the hall, dividing the cambered roof. The capitals of the columns are of lotus design (several with the remnants with their original color). The central niche had yet to appear.

[1] The papyrus harvest in the marsh; two hippopotamuses and a baby inhabit the waters.

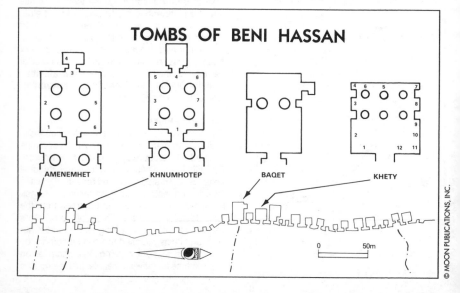

TOMBS OF BENI HASSAN

AMENEMHET   KHNUMHOTEP   BAQET   KHETY

0   50m

© MOON PUBLICATIONS, INC.

[2] The top two registers are devoted to hunting desert animals; the fence surrounding the composition tells us that Khety, like most nobles, did his hunting in a preserve, perhaps his own private one. The lower registers include barbers, linen makers, spinners and weavers, and women dancing with male partners who support them; nearby, a statue of the deceased is dragged along on a sledge. The bottom panel contains artists painting statues, carpentry, and men playing *senet*. The rows of buildings on the right side of the wall are granaries.

[3] Below the continuation of the hunting scene, musicians play before Khety and his wife.

[4] In this corner, offering bearers bring gazelles and birds, while the middle of the wall shows metalsmiths at work.

[5] The wrestling scene dominates this wall; the figures are shown in contrasting colors, but experts disagree as to whether they represent an Egyptian and a Nubian or the artist simply used the colors to show the figures clearly against each other.

[6] The lower register shows an army storming a fortress, perhaps an indication of the intradistrict fighting that occurred as the central government of the Old Kingdom lost its power. The solders carry the weapons long associated with Egyptian armies: the double-convex bows, tripletanged axes, and curved, sickle-shaped swords; the rectangular shields with rounded tops were of hide stretched over wooden frames.

[7] The grape harvest and winemaking dominate this corner, but sports and acrobatics also make their appearance.

[8] Khety rests under a sunshade with his dwarfs and a clubfooted man nearby.

[9] Cattle march sedately along the registers, while dancers perform for Khety's statue.

[10] The middle registers show agricultural scenes, with plowing taking up most of the lower panel.

[11] Butchers slaughter the bovine offering.

[12] The upper part of this wall is devoted to scenes of country life, and below them, the deceased's boats. Khety's false door is on the left.

Tomb Of Baqet III (#15)
The father of Khety, Baqet preceded his son as nomarch. His tomb is similar to the previous one, the wrestling and war scenes dominating the back wall. On the north wall, under the hunt, you can pick out the fullers beating the clothes with clubs (a practice that continues in rural Egypt), overseers stopping a quarrel, the woman spinning, and the ballplayers. On the south wall, find the scribes counting cattle and the nomarch's sheriffs beating those who wouldn't render up their taxes.

Tomb Of Khnumhotep (#3)
The builder of this 12th Dynasty tomb was not only the nomarch, but governor of the entire Eastern Desert. His tomb represents the final stage of Middle Kingdom development. The courtyard leads to an impressive entrance framed by proto-Doric columns. Although the interior is missing its four columns, the three-aisled hall sweeps the eye to the focal point of the cult niche. The long inscription around the base of the room has given historians much of their knowledge about the Middle Kingdom.

[1] *Muwu* dancers accompany Khnumhotep's shrine and the men carrying his tomb equipment.

[2] Near the door of the estate office, servants measure grain, which the scribes record, before it's stored in the granaries; below, the ground is prepared for the next crop. Underneath the agricultural scenes, Khnumhotep is shown making the journey to Abydos and back. The lower part of the wall includes a vineyard and fig orchard.

[3] Below the traditional desert hunt, the much-published scene of Asiatics with their families and animals gives us a glimpse of the foreigners who were beginning to enter Egypt. These Amu with brilliant, enveloping robes, have brought eye-paint to the governor. Khnumhotep's secretary introduces them to his employer and hands him a list of their names.

[4] The niche contains fragments of Khnumhotep's statue; above it, he watches the clapnet close in on birds.

[5] This picture, a mate with the one on the other side of the niche, shows Khnumhotep, throw-stick in hand, hunting birds from a reed skiff deep in papyrus; below him, workers fish with nets.

[6] In perhaps the same marsh and mounted on a similar skiff, Khnumhotep spears fish. The deftness of the drawing and the handling of the color place this pair of paintings among Egypt's masterpieces.

[7] Khnumhotep sits in front of an offering table and a parade of offerings, the animals of which are slaughtered below.

[8] In the top register, men launder the estate's linen; below them servants fell a palm tree for the shipwrights whom Khnumhotep inspects from his litter. The journey to Abydos appears here in the third register. Below the boats, women spin with drop spindles and weave on horizontal looms while bakers prepare bread among depictions of sculptors and other craftsmen.

Tomb Of Amenemhet (#2)

Also known as Ameni, this nomarch of the Antelope Nome was Khnumhotep's predecessor, and his tomb is similar to the previous one, except that the themes expressed here are more closely linked to those of the Old Kingdom. The long inscriptions date to the 43rd year of Senwosret I and tell of Ameni's several military campaigns and the titles conferred on him. The ceilings bear designs imitating reed mats.

[1] Leather workers and ancient armorers shaping bows and arrows are mixed among stonemasons, carpenters, potters, and metalsmiths. The lower registers show workers cultivating flax and making linen.

[2] This wall, which includes the desert hunt, is substantially the same as in the other tombs: the ceremonial dances performed before the statue of Ameni, and the bearers who offer birds and other animals. Ameni with his dogs and a military escort, receives tribute from his estates. The lowest register shows his estate office with scribes bringing defaulters to account.

[3] Below the traditional wrestling scene and the attack on the fort, the boats carry Ameni to Abydos, the sails raised on the southward leg of the trip to catch the wind.

[4] The niche contains statues of Ameni, his wife, and his mother.

[5] The offering bearers bring their goods before Ameni and his wife Hetpet who sits at her own table.

[6] Above the false door, the registers show winemaking, fishing, and the storerooms for the food. Musicians appear at the left of the false door, fording cattle and baking scenes to the right.

Speos Artemidos

For those with a yen for more, Hatshepsut's tiny temple stands up a desert *wadi,* about three km south of the tombs. The temple is small and unfinished, but it makes a nice escape if you're in the mood. The earliest cut-rock temple in Egypt, it's dedicated to the lion-goddess Pakhet. Roughed-out Hathor-headed columns decorate the facade, and above the door, a long hieroglyphic text documents the disorder under Hyksos's rule and Hatshepsut's restoration of order and her rebuilding of destroyed temples. The front hall is decorated with Hatshepsut offering to the gods, but the inner room, mostly unfinished, is dominated by the goddess's statue carved out of the rock high on the wall.

The small grotto (just before you reach the temple) on the south side of the *wadi* was decorated by Alexander II and shows him as king in the company of numerous gods. Farther into the desert, the *wadi* was inhabited by Christian hermits and became known as the Valley of the Anchorites; their cells are marked by crosses.

Getting There

Beni Hassan lies about 25 km south of Minya, roughly halfway to Mallawi. By private car, turn off at Abu Qurqas (at the blue sign), cross the bridge and follow the road through the village. After crossing a second bridge over a small canal, head north. Continue until you reach the blue sign at the paved road; turn right. At the bend in this road you get a beautiful view of the eastern hills, their dusky yellow-brown cliffs thrown into sharp relief against fields of green berseem and golden wheat. To reach the landing by public transportation, get a service taxi to Abu Qurqas and from the east side of the bridge catch a covered pickup taxi, or hike the three km to the river, or hire a private taxi from the village to the landing.

At the ferry landing, you'll have to fork over the few piasters to enter the area and LE3 (if there are more than seven of you, it costs 50PT each) for the blue tourist ferry to take you directly across the river to the site. Once there, you can walk the half-kilometer or ride the van (50PT).

At the ticket booth, you'll need another LE6 for tickets to the tombs up the steps in the cliffs. If you want to go to Speos Artemidos, you'll have to walk (three km each way) or bargain with the van driver. At the village, you'll need to find the *ghaffir* with *(in-sha'allah)* the key *(al-mufta)*. From the village, the *wadi* runs east, and the temple is about half a kilometer in, on the south side.

TUNA AL-GEBEL/HERMOPOLIS

Known to the ancient Egyptians as Khnum, Hermopolis, according to the area's priests, was the location of the primordial mound, site of the creation of the world. The area was also home to the ibis-headed Thoth, inventor of writing, patron of scribes, and god of wisdom and learning. A temple devoted to his cult once stood here, and, like most ancient holy spots, the area was continually rebuilt from the pharaonic period down to its occupation by the Copts. The site is quiet, set among grassy hills covered with pottery shards. If you like climbing around on old ruins, you can discover the Greek agora, with the old Roman cistern and behind it, a bath complete with troughs for running water from the adjoining well, and the remains of a New Kingdom temple.

Among the bizarre collection of graves found at the nearby necropolis of Tuna al-Gebel is the tomb of Petosiris, a remarkable mix of classical Egyptian, Ptolemaic, and Roman art. South of this tomb lies an extensive Greek/Roman cemetery, which dates to the first centuries of the Christian era, including the mummy of a young woman who drowned and a warren of baboon and ibis burials, the animals sacred to Thoth. Along its access road is one of Akhenaten's stelae marking the boundaries of his city.

Hermopolis (Ashmunein)

This area, sacred to Khnum, was long identified with learning. The Greeks related Khnum to their own god of knowledge, Hermes, hence the city's Greek name of Hermopolis. The original Khnum ("City of the Eight") came down to modern times through the Coptic Shmun and the Arabic Ashmunein. The city served as capital of the Hare Nome, and the early rulers were buried across the river at Deir al-Barsha. In Hellenistic times, the necropolis was moved to Tuna al-Gebel.

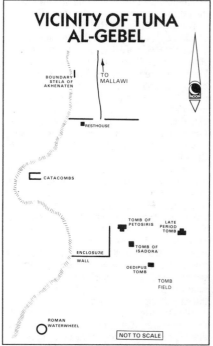

VICINITY OF TUNA AL-GEBEL

BOUNDARY STELA OF AKHENATEN

TO MALLAWI

RESTHOUSE

CATACOMBS

TOMB OF PETOSIRIS

LATE PERIOD TOMB

TOMB OF ISADORA

ENCLOSURE WALL

OEDIPUS TOMB

TOMB FIELD

ROMAN WATERWHEEL

NOT TO SCALE

© MOON PUBLICATIONS, INC.

The road leads to the old dig-house with two massive statues of Thoth in front of it; the actual ruins of the city lie over the hill to the east. The large, standing columns mark the Christian basilica built on the site of the Roman agora. To the north, the gateway beyond the ancient walls dates from the late Middle Kingdom. The pylons and hypostyle hall of the small limestone temple to the west were built by Merneptah and Seti II. Beyond them, to the north, are the remains of a temple to Thoth, unfortunately now lying in water, rebuilt by Nectanebo I and added to by later Greek and Roman rulers. To the south stand two colossal statues of Ramesses II in front of a ruined temple.

Tuna Al-Gebel

Open 0600-1700; fee LE6, plus 25PT to enter the desert. The necropolis for Hermopolis during Greco-Roman times, this area includes a number of chapels and monuments arranged in streets, making Tuna al-Gebel a true city of the dead.

Tomb of Petosiris: This small temple is one of the nicest examples of Ptolemaic art. Built about 300 B.C., it exhibits restraint and delicacy, virtues not often found in Ptolemaic artwork. Here Greek realism and pharaonic symbolism blend, creating an atmosphere later lost in the over-elaborate architecture of the later Ptolemaic period. The tomb imitates the pronaos of a Late Period temple; the vestibule is dedicated to Petosiris, chief priest of Thoth at Hermopolis, the chapel to his father Nes-Shu and brother Djed-Thotefankh.

The Necropolis: The cemetery also includes the **Tomb of Isadora** (early 2nd century A.D.), its sparse exterior opening into a chamber with a large half-shell carved over the funerary couch; the lady herself is displayed in a glass case. The **Tomb of Oedipus** is decorated with copies of scenes of the Greek Theban cycle; the originals are in the Antiquities Museum. Southwest of the tombs lie the remains of **Roman waterworks.** The wall to the north (west of Petosiris's tomb) may have formed the enclosure where the sacred ibises were raised.

Ibis Galleries: A series of catacombs lie to the west about halfway between Petosiris' tomb and the resthouse. Here excavators uncovered Aramaic papyri from the 5th century, the earliest artifacts discovered at Tuna al-Gebel. They also unearthed multiple burials of ibises and baboons, animals holy to Thoth, and of a local high priest who opted to be interred with the sacred animals.

Amarna Stela: North of the resthouse, along the base of the cliff, Akhenaten ordered carved one of the stelae that marked the limits of his city. This one, cut into the face of the bluff, is the easiest to reach, a short walk across the desert from the road. This shrine, with Akhenaten and Nefertiti adoring the Aton, marks the northwestern limit that the king claimed for his city.

Getting There

Ashmunein and Tuna al-Gebel both lie to the west and slightly north of Mallawi. Although you can reach them by car by going through Mallawi's winding streets, the easier way is to take the fork (marked by a sign for Akhenaten Tourist Village) just north of Mallawi. Turn west

and follow the road, which jogs across a bridge, through the village of Ashmunein, to where a sign points right for both Tuna al-Gebel and Hermopolis—the sign is wrong. While Hermopolis lies to the right, Tuna al-Gebel is straight ahead. On the way to the latter site, you may have to stop at the little hut at the edge of the desert and buy a ticket to the general area; it costs a few piasters. Public transportation won't take you to either site; the best bet is to hire a pickup-taxi in Mallawi for about LE20-30 and visit both. Walking and hitchhiking are unreliable, exhausting, and in the heat, dangerous.

VICINITY OF MALLAWI

Mallawi Museum

Open 0900-1300 daily except Fri. (0800-1200), and Wednesday (closed). This small museum is devoted to finds from Middle Egypt and represents a cross section of all types of objects uncovered in the area. The collection includes several beautifully painted Middle Kingdom coffins, one on which the destructive animals in the hieroglyphic alphabet have been rendered harmless by the artist who didn't complete their forms. Located on Sh. Gala (three blocks down from Bank al-Misr, the museum is on the south side of the main street that runs east-west through town.

Deir Al-Barsha

This older necropolis for Hermopolis lies across the river from Mallawi, but little remains to be seen there except for the tomb of Thuthotep II. This early Middle Kingdom tomb built for the great overlord of the Hare Nome is similar to the later tombs at Beni Hassan: the carved rock ceiling of the portico "supported" by palm-capital pillars, and the niche for a *ka* statue cut out in the back wall of the chapel.

On the west side of this chapel, which contains low-relief and painted decorations, is the famous scene of workers pulling Thuthotep's statue to the tomb. The four lines of workers are shown in registers, the repetition of the composition relieved by the different orientations of the laborers' faces. The statue has been padded with twisted cording and anchored to a sledge; a man mounted on the base of the statue pours water in front of the runners to grease the way while three more with yokes bring additional jars of water. If you want to visit this site, check with the staff at the Mallawi Museum.

AL-AMARNA

When Akhenaten decided to move his capital from Thebes, he chose a wide bay on the eastern side of the Nile ringed with the cliffs of the eastern mountains. Here, on virgin ground, he built a new city that he occupied for a scant 15 years, for when Akhenaten fell from grace, the site was abandoned. Archaeologists excavating the foundations discovered a city with several temples to Aton, palaces, villas, and the homes and workshops of craftsmen and artists. In the sculpture studio of Thutmose the famous head of Nefertiti was discovered that is now in the Berlin Museum. Little remains today, however, for the buildings had been reduced nearly to the foundations before modern times and the ever-shifting wind-borne sand has filled the excavators' trenches.

The City

As you enter the wide arc of desert, the fragmented remains of Akhenaten's main city lie to the south of the track; the ruins to the north belong to Nefertiti's palace. The city originally covered 15 km, and a central royal road parallel to the Nile ran its length. Starting at the village of al-Till, the road ran north through the northern palace, an area possibly used by Nefertiti as a private retreat. Farther south, pylons mark the bridge that linked the royal residence on the west with the "King's House" on the east. The Window of Appearances from which the king gave out the gold collars to deserving nobles occupied the middle of this bridge. The massive expanse of the main temple to Amun, surrounded by its offices and storerooms, lies northeast of the bridge. A second, smaller temple stands south of it. Its pylons and forecourts are reasonably intact although the sanctuary is destroyed. East of this temple, among the mudbrick foundations, lie the archives, the source of the Amarna letters that have given historians so much insight on international affairs during the late New Kingdom.

Houses

The houses uncovered at Amarna give a good idea of those that ancient Egyptians built throughout the country. Like all houses and palaces, they were divided into public and private rooms. The doors faced north to catch the prevailing winds, and in townhouses, porches and vestibules led to a columned hall lighted by clerestory windows where the owner entertained guests and the family met for meals. The back areas of the houses included a master bedroom with contained an alcove for the bed, a ceiling vent to catch the northern winds, and often a bathroom, complete with toilet and bathing area. The kitchen, located at the back of the villa, was open-air. The walls of the homes were plastered and painted, and scenes removed from Amarna decorate the walls of the Antiquities Museum in Cairo. The rooms were lighted by oil lamps set on pegs or in niches, and to warm them in winter, residents used open braziers.

Homes of the workmen, though much smaller, were designed along similar lines, with the vestibule leading into a living room linking to a bedroom or storage area and a kitchen. The vestibule was often used as a workshop or a stable. The living room was fitted with a permanent bench that would have been covered with

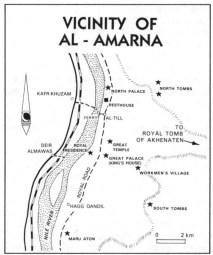

VICINITY OF AL - AMARNA

KAFR-KHUZAM

NORTH PALACE

NORTH TOMBS

RESTHOUSE

FERRY AL-TILL

TO ROYAL TOMB OF AKHENATEN

DEIR ALMAWAS

ROYAL RESIDENCE

GREAT TEMPLE

GREAT PALACE (KING'S HOUSE)

WORKMEN'S VILLAGE

HAGG QANDIL

ROYAL ROAD

SOUTH TOMBS

NILE RIVER

MARU ATON

0   2 km

© MOON PUBLICATIONS, INC.

JAN KIRK

the renowned painted limestone bust (c. 1350 B.C.) of Queen Nefertiti, found at al-Amarna

rugs. Cooking was done either in braziers in the living area or in the kitchens to the rear of the building.

The Tombs

Open 0700-1700; fee LE6, plus 50PT to enter the area and LE2 for the ferry and LE5 for a tractor ride across the desert to the tombs: total LE13.50. The tombs, however, are far more interesting than the scraps of mud-brick walls nearly covered by drifting sand. Al-Amarna's tombs, cut into the eastern cliffs beyond the city, fall into two main units: north and south. Akhenaten's tomb (between them, up a *wadi*) is in poor condition and closed to the public; normal tourist excursions only take in the two groups of northern tombs: the main cluster of four, and two later ones (Huya and Meryre II) isolated on a yet more northern spur; to visit them, you'll have to pay a few extra pounds for the additional tractor time, but they're worth the cost. Only two of the southern tombs are open; you can make the 15-km donkey ride from the north site, or you can return to the main road, drive south, and recross the river. In either case, the

keys to the tombs may be hard to locate, so if you plan on seeing this area, contact the Tourist Office in Minya beforehand.

The Amarna tombs resemble many similar, cut-rock ones, with a forecourt, facade, hall, transverse hall, and statuary niche, although in some tombs the halls have been expanded into rooms with stone columns. In spite of the ordinary plans, the artwork here is unique—softened forms coupled with extensive naturalism. The figures are executed in the mature Amarna style with soft curving lines and proportions determined by the Amarna grids, which tend to enlarge the body and head at the expense of leg length. The scenes differ from nobles' tombs of other ages as well, for although the decoration shows the deceased's achievements, it focuses on Akhenaten and the royal family—an emphasis dictated by the political and religious climate of the era. In a return to the principles of the Old Kingdom, only Akhenaten could offer to the many-handed sun disk; the rest of the population had to depend on the pharaoh for the good will of the Aton. Thus Akhenaten and his royal family dominate the scenes in these tombs: interceding with Aton for the deceased, rewarding him for service to the throne.

Tomb Of Ahmose

Fan Bearer on the King's Right Hand, Ahmose was the equivalent of a modern cabinet member or minister. The tomb contains copies of the well-known *Hymn to the Sun,* which has been compared to the 23rd Psalm. He appears over the entrance to his tomb worshipping the names of the sun; the entranceway contains the hymns. The long hall, due to the death of Akhenaten, is unfinished, revealing the methods used by the artists. On the left, the royal family banquets in the palace, serenaded by a small orchestra in a side room (behind). Above them, the army and king (in his chariot) march toward the temple. Near the false doors in the transverse hall, burial shafts were set into the floor.

Tomb Of Meryre I

Meryre was the high priest of Aton, and his tomb, though also unfinished, contains spectacular scenes in the entrance and hall. Beyond the spacious court through the doorway, the walls of the vestibule, dominated by the door-shaped stelae, show Meryre praying in front of large bouquets, and along the inner wall he's shown with his wife. In the four-columned hall beyond, the scene to the right shows Meryre carried on the shoulders of his friends to the Window of Appearances, where Akhenaten rewards him. On the long wall, the procession to the temple continues on the left half of the rear wall; priests in front of the temple await them.

The opposite wall bears similar paintings. The lower left register shows him being invested with his office, while the palace, its gardens, harbor, and barns appear on the right. To the left of the doorway, Akhenaten, Nefertiti, and two daughters offer to Aton as Meryre and a fellow priest preside. Note the rainbow below the sun disk.

Tomb Of Pentu

This tomb of the royal physician is much damaged. In the entrance, Pentu worships the sun; texts of the hymn to Aton appear before him. The chief remaining scenes show Akhenaten and one of his daughters worshipping, and Pentu receiving his office.

Tomb Of Panehsy

Panehsy was Chief Servitor of the Aton and his tomb lies slightly southeast of the others. Unlike many of the Amarna tombs, the decorated facade is preserved, although the interior was modified by the Copts who used it as a church. At the outer lintel, the royal family worships the sun; inside they appear again, including Mutnedjemet, the king's sister who would marry Horemheb, and Panehsy, at the bottom of the scene. On the entrance wall to the right, the king and queen hand Panehsy a golden collar, a reward for his service. The northern wall contains the normal visit to the temple where the king prays in the forecourt. Across the hall, the stairs lead to the unfinished burial chamber. The left half of the entrance hall shows the royal family in chariots and Panehsy again being rewarded with his collars.

The doorway to the second hall shows Panehsy as an old man; with his daughter, he worships the sun. The stairs lead to a second burial chamber. The niche once held Panehsy's statue, but it's been chiseled away. The right wall contains painted remnants of funerary offerings.

Tomb Of Huya

Huya was Superintendent of the Royal Harem and steward to the queen mother Tiyi. The scenes in this tomb reflect his employment, for depictions of the royal family include Tiyi and her daughter Baketaten. In the scene straddling the entrance, they dine with Akhenaten, Nefertiti, and some of their daughters. Akhenaten sits opposite his mother, who occupies the chair where tradition usually places the wife; Nefertiti and her daughters are behind her husband. This relief has sparked much controversy, adding fuel to the belief that during the later years of Akhenaten's reign, Nefertiti's rank was diminished, perhaps in favor of her mother-in-law. The northern wall shows Nefertiti and Akhenaten, in the 12th year of his reign, carried to the Hall of Foreign Tribute where they receive homage from their vassals. Across the hall, Akhenaten leads his mother, Tiyi, to a temple he's built for her and his father, Amenhotep III.

To the right of the rear wall, Akhenaten decorates Huya from the Window of Appearances, while below, the paintings look inside a sculptor's studio. The lintel into the transverse hall shows the three generations of the royal family. The shaft occupies the southern corner of the room; the shrine holds Huya's unfinished statue, and offerings and funerary equipment appear on its side walls.

Tomb Of Meryre II

Meryre was Superintendent of the Household of Nefertiti, and the queen, in the company of her husband, dominates the decorations. Meryre appears on the back side of the entrance worshipping the sun. The entrance wall to the right shows Nefertiti pouring a drink through a strainer for Akhenaten, who sits under a sunshade. The left side of the wall depicts Meryre receiving his golden collars from the king and queen. In the palace forecourt, the royal chariot is surrounded by fanbearers, secretaries, and servants of Meryre; below, he's welcomed home in front of his own house. The south wall shows the king and his queen receiving foreign tribute; the scene oddly echoes the Middle Kingdom reliefs at Beni Hassan. Nearby, athletes compete in their sports. The back wall of this hall shows Smenkhare (Akhenaten's co-regent and successor) and his wife Meritaten (Akhenaten's oldest daughter) rewarding Meryre; done in black ink, the figures were never completed.

Getting There

Al-Amarna lies about 11 km south of Mallawi. By private car you'll have to cross the bridge at the village of Deir Mawas. Once on the other side, double back north to Kafr-Khuzam (the second village) and then turn east to reach the ferry landing on the Nile. **Note:** there are two ferry landings; a tourist type across from the northern tombs, and a public one toward Dairut and closer to the southern tombs. You can reach Deir al-Mawas by pickup taxi from Mallawi (just south of the train station). At the tourist landing you have to buy a local governmental permit (50PT) to get into the archaeological area and board the ferry (LE2). On the other side, brave the throngs

of children selling baskets, and walk up the bank to the ticket house where you arrange a tractor/trailer ride into the desert (LE5 for about two hours at the site). Once at the foot of the cliffs you can buy your tickets to the tombs (LE6).

PRACTICALITIES

Accommodations

The only five-star hotel in Minya is the **Etap Nefertiti** on the Cornishe north of the Governorate building; tel. (086) 331-5151, fax 326-467. This hotel, while not deluxe, is comfortable, but unfortunately it's nearly always overbooked and even posh tours have people consigned to lesser lodgings; confirmed reservations here don't necessarily mean you'll get a room. Rooms run LE308 s, LE383 d, and LE464 t, with bath. The older, but clean, two-star **Lotus,** 1 Sh. Port Said (one km north of train station; tel. 324-541), is a better deal; rooms are LE22.50 s and LE33.10 d with bath; without bath it's a few pounds less.

Of the hotels lining the main street from the station to the Cornishe, the **Palace,** tel. 324-021, located on the main square, is the most unusual, as well as the best deal in town. The entrance hall is paved with black and white tiles that look as if they've been lifted from an Escher print; the reception room lies up the stairs, and the central foyer soars up several stories to a trompe l'oeil ceiling. The rooms are clean, several have attached baths with hot water, and the plumbing, though a bit cranky, works. Rooms range LE6-12; breakfasts (Egyptian style with omelets and *ful*) run a few pounds.

The newly renovated **Akhenaten** on the Cornishe (down from Sh. Gumhurriya), tel. 325-918, is runner up; LE26 s, and LE36.55 d (includes breakfast). Or try the nearby **Beach Hotel,** tel. 322-307 or **Omar Khayyam,** 3 Sh. Damaran, tel. 324-635. Just southeast of the station, the **Ibn Khasib,** 5 Sh. Ragib, tel. 224-535, is quieter and has nice gardens and a 24-hour bar; LE20.50, s, LE27.50 d; a/c is available. You can **camp** at the stadium, north of the train station, along the tracks.

Food

The Nefertiti Hotel has two expensive restaurants. The roof-top dining room of the Lotus is

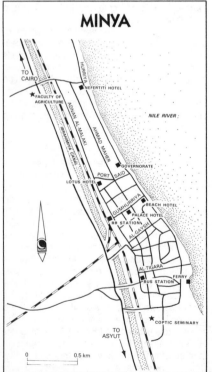

MINYA

TO CAIRO
HURRIYA
NEFERTITI HOTEL
★ FACULTY OF AGRICULTURE
ADNAN AL MALAKI
IBRAHIMY CANAL
AHMAD MAHER
NILE RIVER
GOVERNORATE
PORT SAID
LOTUS HOTEL
GUMHURRIYA
BEACH HOTEL
PALACE HOTEL
RR STATION
AL GAYSH
AL TIGARA
FERRY
BUS STATION
★ COPTIC SEMINARY
TO ASYUT
0   0.5 km

© MOON PUBLICATIONS, INC.

less expensive and offers good, if limited, lunches and dinners as well as ice cream and ice-cold Stella. The Ibn Khasib has good, inexpensive food in its downstairs restaurant and also maintains a 24-hour bar.

Information
You can change money at the Bank of Alexandria and the National Bank, both on the Cornishe. For the latest information on the sights, check with the **Tourist Office,** located a few blocks to the north of Sh. al-Mahatta (Station St.) on the Cornishe, tel. 320-150; it's supposed to be open daily 0800-1400 and 1700-2200. The area code is 086.

TRANSPORTATION

Minya lies 250 km south of Cairo and is linked to the rest of Egypt via train and the main Nile Valley road. The road is good but the traffic is thick; big, heavy trucks playing tag with service taxis will keep your attention from the beautiful green countryside. If you rent a car, consider hiring a driver as well. The trip from Cairo takes about five hours. To reach the town by car, you'll have to cross the Ibrahimiya Canal bridge (if you go around a bend and come to a bridge with arches, you've gone too far). Across the bridge, go straight until you reach the square, then bear left but do not go up the overpass; this road will take you into the train station at the center of town. Although the easiest way to get around in Middle Egypt is with a car, those more faint of heart can take the **train,** for Minya lies on the main railway line. Express trains

leave at 0710 (#978) and 0735 (#980) and are (optimistically) scheduled to reach Minya at 1038 and 1050; in fact they do usually get in before noon. The twelve o'clock express (#982) is scheduled in at 1524, and the 1600 one (#990) at 1924. Tickets start at about LE15. **Buses** from the Upper Egyptian Bus Company ply the road between Minya and Cairo hourly and fares start at LE7. Service taxis (close to the same price) also run to Middle Egypt; they're fast but mechanically unreliable and can be dangerous.

Getting Around
You can cover central Minya by walking or taking a calishe (LE3-5 for most rides). Once in Minya, you can hire a taxi to visit the sites for about LE10/hour. (slightly less if you can drive a good bargain). For directions to the sights, see individual sections.

Getting From
The bus station and service taxis to Cairo and points south are located south of the train station, near the bridge; remember, however, that service taxis on this road can be dangerous. Buses leave for Cairo about every hour (about LE10) and for Upper Egypt with about the same frequency. About 300 meters farther along (opposite the white Habaski Mosque), minibuses leave to Abu Qurqas. Trains to Cairo leave 0804 (#991), 1230 (#1348), 1715 (#979); LE15.45-19.35. To Upper Egypt, 1200 (#1050) 2348 (#88) or 0018 (868); LE13.90-23.10.90 to Luxor, slightly more to Aswan. These trains consistently run 1½ hours or more late.

ASYUT

An important commercial area from pharaonic times, Asyut was also a cult center for the jackal-god Wepwawet, and marks the crossroads of the ancient desert caravans and the major southern route into the western oases. Today, the city remains a thriving commercial center, with a major university and a large *suq;* it is the site of a British-built barrage, which supports one of the few bridges across the Nile.

The older part of Asyut lies west of the Nile, south of where the Ibrahimiya Canal takes off from the river. The barrage that diverts this water also carries a road that links the main town to its eastern extension. The Nile Valley road runs along the eastern side of the city, becoming its Cornishe, and a parallel pair of streets, al-Gala and Ragib, border the railroad tracks. They are connected to the Cornishe by a railway crossing on Sh. Salah Salim to the south of the train station, and by an underpass on Sh. Salah al-Din on the north.

The heart of the town lies at the train station; the hotels cluster at its rear, the taxis on its southern edge, and the bus station beyond them, diagonally to the southwest.

SIGHTS

The pharaonic tombs in the cliffs near the modern cemetery are closed. Although Asyut was a large administrative center in early Islamic times, few buildings from this period remain: an old inn and former camel market lie north of the *suq.* Nearby stands an old Islamic bath; its dome, rising on ancient columns, covers a marble fountain, now closed. To the north, the barrage built between 1898 and 1903 channels water into the Ibrahimiya Canal, part of the massive irrigation projects instituted by the British. The barrage sluices, designed before the complete damming of the Nile, allowed floodwaters to reach Lower Egypt, and locks allowed for navigation. On the eastern bank, the Lillian Thrasher Orphanage welcomes visitors, and the staff is happy to discuss their projects and goals. In town, a small museum at the

American School (Sh. Gumhurriya) houses a small pharaonic and Coptic collection. The shady Cornishe provides a popular promenade, and for 50PT, you can catch a falucca ferry to Gizera al-Moz ("Banana Island"), which lies off the end of Sh. Salah Salim.

To The North

The Old and Middle kingdom tombs which lie to the north at Meir are accessible from Asyut, but you'll have to make special arrangements with the Antiquities Service, for they are not always open; the hassle is not worth the trouble unless you especially want to see the tombs.

Deir al-Muharraq: Tradition maintains that the nearby monastery, Deir al-Muharraq ("Burnt Monastery"), was visited by the Holy Family where they hid in a cave. Today it's covered by

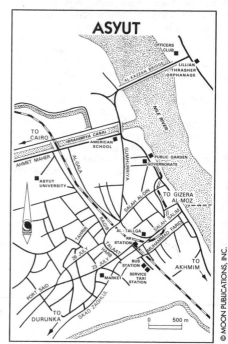

ASYUT

OFFICERS CLUB
LILLIAN THRASHER ORPHANAGE
AL-FAZZAN BRIDGE
NILE RIVER
TO CAIRO
IBRAHIMIYA CANAL
AMERICAN SCHOOL
AHMET MAHER
AL-GALA
GUMHURRIYA
PUBLIC GARDEN
GOVERNORATE
ASYUT UNIVERSITY
SALAH AL-DIN
TO GIZERA AL-MOZ
RAGIB
TAHRIR
AL-TALLGA
SALAH SALIM
26 JULY
TALAAT HARB
RR STATION
MUHAMMAD FARID
BUS STATION
23 JULY
MARKET
SERVICE TAXI STATION
TO AKHMIM
PORT SAID
SAAD ZAGHLUL
TO DURUNKA
0   500 m

© MOON PUBLICATIONS, INC.

the Church of al-Adhra (the Virgin), which is claimed to be the oldest in Egypt.

The neo-Byzantine Church of St. George, built in 1888, dominates the courtyard, while the keep, entered from a small tower and drawbridge, houses a small 16th century chapel dedicated to the Archangel Michael. The small Church of al-Adhra occupies the western side of the trapezoidal complex, its altar dating from 747. The largest and richest Coptic foundation in Egypt, the complex houses a theological seminary founded in 1905, and each June it hosts thousands of pilgrims who attend the Feast of the Consecration of the Church of the Virgin.

The monastery lies halfway between Mallawi and Asyut, near the village of al-Qusiyya, and can be reached from either town. Buses or service taxis run to al-Qusiyya, and from there, occasional minibuses serve the monastery.

Durunka

Coptic sites abound in this area south of Asyut. At Deir al-Durunka, the hills shelter the dwellings that once formed a Christian cave village. The Church of the Virgin, built in 1955, hosts an annual *mulid* in August commemorating the flight of the Holy Family. The road to Durunka is a continuation of Sh. Sa'ad Zaghlul. A service taxi from Asyut runs the eight km to Durunka and will drop you off at the road to the convent; it's a 15-minute walk uphill.

PRACTICALITIES

Accommodations

The best deal in Asyut is the new **Happy Land,** Cornishe al-Nil, tel. (088) 320-444/321-944, fax (088) 320-444; LE26 s, LE35 d. The **Badr Hotel** (behind the train station on Sh. al-Tallaga, tel. 329-811-2), while nice, charges a relatively hefty $20 s, $26 d. The nearby **Reem,** tel. 326-235, runs LE35 s, LE45 d, and LE57 t.

The best inexpensive housing is at the **YMCA** on Sh. Salah al-Din between the railroad tracks and the Cornishe, tel. 323-218; spotless rooms run LE5 s, LE7 d. If you want more comfort, you can get rooms with a bath and a/c for under LE20. The youth hostel is not worth the trouble to try to find. Visitors can **camp** at the Officers' Club, tel. 322-134, and the Asyut Sporting Club,

tel. 233-139; bathrooms and food are available. You can also pitch a tent on Gizera al-Moz, but there are no facilities.

Food

Good food is available at the **Asyut Sporting Club,** the **Officers' Club,** and the **Engineers' Club,** tel. 325-302; they lie near the ends of the barrage. Or try the restaurant in the **Badr Hotel.** In town, try the **Mattan al-Azhar,** 100 meters east of the train station along Sh. Sa'ad Zaghlul; it has no English sign, but occupies the new building with a decorative screen over the entrance. Local produce is available at the market near the train station. For a different treat, have a coffee at the **Lawyer's Club** on the banks of the Nile, across from the large Coptic church on the Cornishe toward the south end of town. The sign is in Arabic, but the balance scales are universal; entrance fee, 50PT. When you're done, wander south along the Cornishe to take a look at the beautiful old mansion where the road bends toward the edge of the river; the house is private, but the outer details were created by artisans brought from Italy—a legacy of sugarcane wealth.

Services And Information

The Bank of Alexandria, in the square west of the train station, will cash traveler's checks. The **post office** is next to the Asyut Tourist Hotel across from the train station. The **telephone** office is inside the station and is open 24 hours; the area code is 088. The **Tourist Office,** tel. 322-400, lies next to the governorate building near the Nile.

TRANSPORTATION

Asyut is a crossroads linking not only Upper and Lower Egypt but also the Nile Valley with the oases to the west. The area around the station serves as a hub for the connections.

Trains

Trains connect Cairo and Upper Egypt about every half-hour. While most are 2nd and 3rd class, two 1st-class trains (a/c) serve Cairo (LE8.40) daily (5½ hours), through Mallawi (two hours). As many run south to Sohag (two hours),

Qina (four to five hours), Luxor (six to seven hours), and Aswan (12 hours); the high-speed express trains take about half the time but don't stop in all the cities. The only train to consider, however, is the **Gray Ghost** (#986), which leaves Cairo at 1400 and regularly gets into Asyut at 1830; but the next leg of the trip to Luxor (scheduled to arrive at 2310) is rarely on time. On the trip back, the sleek train (#987) leaves Luxor at 0830 and hardly ever makes Asyut by its scheduled 1215, but from there to Cairo the trip is regularly just four hours: about LE25 either way.

Buses

Intracity buses run from the station south of the train station. They depart for Cairo about every two hours, LE12.50. Buses south to Sohag leave every half-hour between 0600 and 1800. Buses for Kharga (four to five hours) leave at 0700 and 1400; for Dakhla (eight hours) at 0630 and 0900. This schedule is erratic, so check with the station. These buses are often full, and you may not be able to buy your ticket before the day of departure, so get there early.

Service Taxis

Service taxis for Kharga leave from stand near the bus station and run about every hour or so. From other stations scattered throughout the town, they serve the rest of the Nile Valley, providing efficient if dangerous transportation.

SOHAG AND VICINITY

The administrative center of Girga Governorate, Sohag is home to a large Christian population. The Egyptians in Sohag seem especially friendly; many are anxious to try out their English. Here perhaps the impact of tourism is little felt, and more of the traditional hospitality and friendliness of Egypt remain. The surrounding area is devoted to agriculture, and the town serves as its commercial center. For visitors, the only sights are the two 5th century monasteries west of the city.

SIGHTS

Deir Al-Abyad (White Monastery)
Founded by Shenute in A.D. 440, the monastery rises from its knoll like a fortress, its gleaming limestone walls relieved only by the high row of blind windows. The monastery flourished throughout the Middle Ages, surviving 11th century Fatimid squabbles and power plays. The monastery was remodeled in the 6th century and again in the 11th, when the brick dome was erected over the center apse. The building was restored in the 13th century, again in the 19th when Muhammad Ali commissioned more work, and yet again in 1907.

The huge basilica presents an example of the fully developed Coptic church with a trilobed chancel. The entrance from the south wall opens into a long hall and then a courtyard (now open to the sky), which was once the nave of the church; the western end was the narthex. The brick pillars at the eastern end date from Roman times and were once surmounted by a second set of columns supporting galleries. Traces of pavement reveal a floor of clear white marble and red granite. The *ambon* (pulpit) lies halfway along the northern wall and is carved from a granite monolith.

The trilobed apse at the eastern chancel was walled up early in the 18th century, making it an independent chapel. The huge columns supporting the triumphal arch are now hidden by the wall. The northern sanctuary is dedicated to St. George, the central one to St. Shenute, and the southern one to the Virgin.

Deir Al-Amba Bishoi (The Red Monastery)
Built of red brick, this monastery lies three km north of Shenute's, surrounded by a small village. Founded by Besa, a follower of Shenute, the monastery must be nearly contemporary with its sister to the south and reflects similar architecture. Its Arabic name stems from the large medieval church dedicated to St. Bishoi. The oldest section of the complex is the Chapel of the Blessed Virgin in the southeastern corner.

Getting There
Both monasteries lie about 10 km west of Sohag. The best way to go from Sohag to Deir

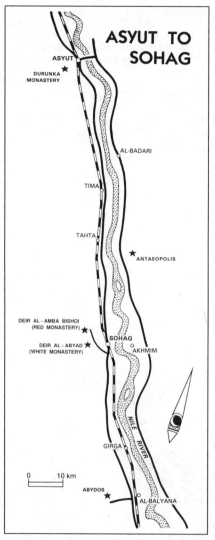

ASYUT TO SOHAG

ASYUT
DURUNKA MONASTERY

AL-BADARI

TIMA

TAHTA

ANTAEOPOLIS

DEIR AL - AMBA BISHOI
(RED MONASTERY)
SOHAG
DEIR AL - ABYAD
(WHITE MONASTERY)
AKHMIM

NILE RIVER

GIRGA

0   10 km

ABYDOS
AL-BALYANA

© MOON PUBLICATIONS, INC.

Monastery lies about three km up the road from the White Monastery.

Akhmim

A Coptic community noted for its weaving, Akhmim lies across the river. Once a flourishing provincial center, only a few cut-rock tombs and a chapel to Min remain. The excavations of the temple (with its colossal statue) are closed, but you can sit in the little park and watch the activities. You can reach Akhmim by bus from Sohag in about 15 minutes. Although best known for its weaving, you cannot buy good quality in the village; the best artists save their work for the annual show and sale, usually held in February (alternating between Cairo and Alexandria). For information contact the **Akhmin Community Center,** 85A Sh. Ramesses, Cairo, 11599, tel. 752-381, or 754-723.

PRACTICALITIES

Accommodations And Food

The best place to stay in Sohag is the **Andalus Hotel,** tel. (093) 234-328, just north of the train station, which offers clean sheets and comfortable beds: LE5.50 s, LE11.50 d; clean baths and plenty of hot water are just down the hall. The price includes a native breakfast of *ful.* The nearby **al-Salaam Hotel,** tel. 323-317, is slightly more expensive (LE10/LE15) and a little older, but it makes a good second choice. The **Myrt Amon** across the bridge in Nasr City near the Stadium, tel. 581-985/582-329, is expensive (LE55 s with bath, LE70 d, and LE80 t). It's clean enough but in need of renovation and new wallpaper, although the water is hot and under considerable pressure. Don't even try the dining room. The **youth hostel** (LE1) lies across the river, 5 Sh. Port Said, tel. 324-395; grimy but with fans; LE2, lockout 1000-1400, curfew, 2300.

Numerous cafes line the streets around the train station; al-Eman (just north of the Andalus Hotel) serves good chicken.

Information And Services

The 24-hour **telephone office** is inside the train station; code 093. The **post offfice** is on Sh. al-Nil (take the first street south of the train

al-Abyad is by service taxis that park by the bridge just before the canal. Or you can take a private taxi. In July, during the pilgrimage, special buses serve both sites. The roads are not well traveled, so if you opt for public transportation, you may do some walking; the Red station and head toward the river). Several banks, such as the **Bank of Alexandria,** have branches in Sohag; open Sun.-Thurs. 0830-1400, plus Sun. 1800-2100 and Wed. 1700-2000 for exchange.

Transportation

The **train** station lies in the middle of town (Midan al-Mahatta). Trains leave about every hour; LE5.15-9.25 to Qina, LE7.80-12.19 to Luxor; LE3.40-6.45 to Asyut, LE8.40-13.80 to Minya. Frequent **buses** leave from the station (300 meters south of the train station) between 0600-2200: Asyut (two hours, LE2.25); al-Balyana (near Abydos, one hour, LE1); Qina (three hours, LE3); Minya, LE6; Luxor, LE5; they run most frequently in the morning. Local **taxis** to Deir al-Abyad leave from about 200 meters west of the bus station by the bridge just before the canal. Catch **service taxis** headed north (Asyut, 1½ hours) about 200 meters north of the train station; those headed south (about every 20 minutes in the morning) stop at the bus station. From al-Balyana (one hour, LE1) you can pick up a service taxi for Seti's Temple at Abydos.

ABYDOS

Holy since the beginning of Egyptian history, Abydos shelters tombs built by Egypt's earliest kings, great fortress-like structures of mudbrick with palace facade walls. The area was dedicated to Osiris, and the Egyptians believed him buried here. Anyone who could built tombs or cenotaphs at Abydos, while others came as pilgrims, praying to the king of the netherworld and leaving a stela in memory of their piety. Egyptians who didn't make the journey in life often instructed their heirs to bring their bodies here; provisions for such trips appeared on tomb walls—a pair of ships, one with a raised sail for the trip upstream, a second with its canvas furled to drift downstream.

The center of the modern site contains the Seti Temple with its Osireion. Nearby lies the more ruined temple of Ramesses II, and scattered throughout the sweeping bay of sand are monuments that span the entire history of ancient Egypt.

SETI TEMPLE

The most imposing ruin at Abydos is the temple begun by Seti I and completed by his son Ramesses II. Built of white limestone, it contains the most beautiful reliefs in Egypt. The building was restored nearly singlehandedly by an Englishwoman known locally as Umm Seti ("Mother of Seti") and today stands nearly complete. Its layout is unlike other funerary temples in that it has seven parallel chapels laid out along the main axis, with three more running behind them. The wing of the L-shaped temple contains a suite of Osiris rooms and a hallway with a list of the kings who had ruled Egypt before Seti, a treasure for Egyptologists trying to sort out early chronology.

The Courtyards

Since Seti I "entered heaven" while his temple was still under construction, the two outer court-

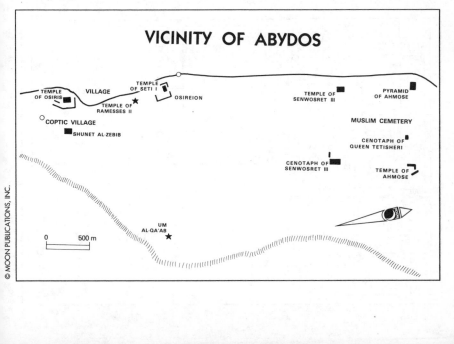

VICINITY OF ABYDOS

TEMPLE OF OSIRIS
VILLAGE
TEMPLE OF SETI I
OSIREION
TEMPLE OF RAMESSES II
COPTIC VILLAGE
SHUNET AL-ZEBIB
TEMPLE OF SENWOSRET III
PYRAMID OF AHMOSE
MUSLIM CEMETERY
CENOTAPH OF QUEEN TETISHERI
CENOTAPH OF SENWOSRET III
TEMPLE OF AHMOSE
UM AL-QA'AB

0   500 m

yards were finished by Ramesses II. The south wall of the first court (beyond the ruined pylons) carries reliefs of Ramesses' Asiatic wars, including his battles with the Hittites. The seven doors align with the chapels inside the temple, although Ramesses walled up all but the central one.

[1] The inscription of Ramesses II describes the completion of the temple. The king presents Ma'at to his father, Isis, and Osiris.

The Hypostyle Halls

The outer hall was finished by Ramesses, and the artwork is not nearly as fine as that on the inner hall. The figures of the king on the columns show him worshipping the god to whom the chapel at the end of the hall is dedicated, or members of that god's triad.

[2] Thoth and Horus pour holy water (formed by the symbols of life and purity) over Ramesses II. To the left, Wepwawet (the predynastic jackel-god of Abydos) and Horus lead the king to the temple where they hold the *ankh* (breath) sign to his nostrils. To the left, beyond Hathor of Dendera, the king hands Isis, Osiris, and Horus a case (with a falcon-head top) of papyrus.

The second hypostyle hall, decorated with the incomparable work of Seti's artists, forms the vestibule for the seven sacred chapels.

[3] Censer in hand, Seti stands before Osiris and Horus pouring holy water from garlanded vases. The king, once more with a censer, stands before Osiris' shrine which is attended by Ma'at and Ronpet (goddess of the year) in front and Isis, Amentet (goddess of the west), and Nephthys behind.

[4] The king, arrayed in the crown of Lower Egypt, adores the ornate *djed* column, which decorates the pier; its mate, worshipped by the king in the crown of Upper Egypt, adorns the complementary pier across the hall.

[5] The king, in one of the most famous pieces of Egyptian artwork, presents Ma'at to Osiris, Isis, and Horus. Presentation of the tiny figure of the goddess of balance appears in the 19th Dynasty, and may represent these kings' attempts to stabilize the country, renew the empire, and legitimize their own reigns.

The Sanctuaries

The seven sanctuaries are all roofed with false vaults, rectangular slabs with arches carved out of their lower surfaces. The chapels, with the

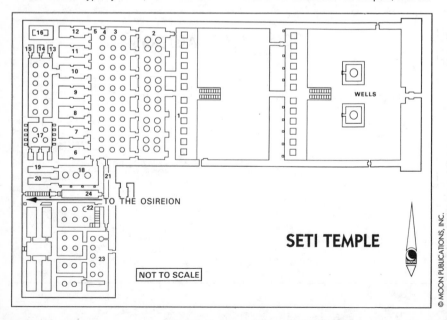

WELLS

TO THE OSIREION

SETI TEMPLE

NOT TO SCALE

© MOON PUBLICATIONS, INC.

exception of Osiris's, end in false doors. The central shrine is dedicated to Amun-Re [9], while those to the left include those of Re-Herakhty [8], Ptah [7], and the deified Seti [6], those to the right are dedicated to Osiris [10], Isis [11], and Horus [12].

With the exception of Seti's chapel (to the far south), the walls show the daily ritual of the gods. On the north wall, the king opens the doors of the shrine, offers the god sacrifices, washes it, anoints the statue's forehead, and dresses it. The south wall shows him burning incense, purifying the statue with water, and presenting it with gifts of new clothing and jeweled collars. He then offers the statue crook and flail, and jars of ointment. After his offering before the god's barque, he scatters sand on the floor and sweeps away his footprints, leaving the god in solitude until the ritual is repeated.

The carvings in Seti's chamber, however, stress his recognition by the gods. Beginning once more on the north wall, the king is led into the temple by the gods, who next ceremonially unite Upper and Lower Egypt. The king is then seated on a throne created by Horus and Thoth lashing together the signs of the Two Lands, while Buto and Nekhbet watch over him. The barque on the west end of this wall is matched by a mate on the south wall; below, the king receives a list of offerings from Thoth and Iunmutef, who wears the leopard skin and braided side-lock of hair typical of a priest. Iunmutef secures permission from the assembled gods, and the king is led from the temple, his palanquin carried by the souls of hawk-headed gods from the delta capital of Piramesse and the jackal-headed ones from the Upper Egyptian town of Nekhen. Iunmutef precedes the king, while under him are the standards of the gods of the Two Lands.

The Osiris Chambers

The doorway at the back of Osiris's chapel [10] leads to a large pillared hall and a suite of shrines to the right, which retain much of their original beauty and color. The one on the right [13] is dedicated to Horus; the central one [14] to the king; the left one [15] to Isis. The decorations in the two outer shrines show the king offering to the deities, while at the back, they bestow their blessings upon him. In the central

shrine [14], Seti receives cult implements. Behind the chapels, a sealed room [16] probably stored the treasures of the temple.

[17] The western hall walls show a variety of gods and the rituals whereby the Egyptians worshipped them. At the south end of this hall a doorway leads to a smaller hall and three chapels, all damaged.

The Nefertem/Ptah-Sokar Suite

[18] The doorway just to the left of Osiris's shrine leads to a three-columned hall dedicated to the northern deities of Nefertem and Ptah-Sokar. Nefertem, a lotus bloom that closes at night to reopen the next morning, was linked to the cycle of death and rebirth; Sokar represented the life-giving forces of the earth. Both, by Seti's time, were integrated into Osiris. The south wall of their chamber contains niches where statues once stood; the opposite wall shows Seti receiving the gods; Sokar takes a hawk-headed form while a lotus blossom crowns Nefertem's head in both his human and lion forms.

[19] This chapel, dedicated to Ptah-Sokar, shows Osiris lying on his bier. On the right wall, Osiris, with his left hand at his head and his right around his phallus, returns to life. On the left wall, Isis, in the form of a hawk, hovers over him.

[20] This mate to the previous chapel is dedicated to Nefertem, and contains beautiful and delicate sculptures.

Southern Wing

For the most part, this wing held practical rooms like the slaughterhouse [23] and storerooms [22] where the sacred barques were kept. The corridors in it, however, hold interesting reliefs.

[21] The hallway that leads from the neighboring door of the Nefertem/Sokar chapel contains a list (on the right) of all the kings, except minor ones and those in disgrace such as Akhenaten, who ever ruled Egypt. Seti and his son Ramesses II stand facing the list, which begins with Menes. Above the list, the inscription asks for the blessing of Ptah-Sokar-Osiris, Lord of the Tomb, to supply the kings with the standard offerings: 1,000 loaves of bread, 1,000 bottles of beer, 1,000 cattle, etc. The wall opposite shows the king and his son (dressed in priest's garb) offering to the gods.

[24] The reliefs from this corridor date from Ramesses II, and show him (on the right wall) with one of his sons roping a bull under the gaze of the wolf-headed Wepwawet; the bull is then sacrificed to the god. On the opposite wall, the king snares birds, which can represent evil spirits, in a clapnet. The stairway in this hall lead out the rear of the temple and the Osireion.

The Osireion
Closely connected to the temple, this cenotaph of Seti I was built along the same massive, classical lines as Khafre's funerary temple at Giza. Ancient Egyptian architects designed the building around a central room symbolic of creation. This room, exposed now that the roof has vanished, contained a mound in the center (symbol of the first land) surrounded by a trench filled with seepage, the waters of Chaos. The sarcophagus and canopic chest sat atop this island mound, the base of resurrection. The collapsed roof exposes massive, red granite pillars, and now the island and its canals are choked with reeds. The corridors and rooms surrounding the tomb are closed due to groundwater.

RAMESSES II TEMPLE

Ramesses II built his own mortuary temple at Abydos, about a third of a kilometer northeast of Seti's. More classical in design, this ruined structure was carefully constructed of fine limestone, red and black granite, and alabaster, and represents the best example of Ramesside work. The general plan is of a courtyard and two pillared halls surrounded by chapels. In these sanctuaries, the delicate low reliefs, which still retain much of their color, recall the work in Seti's Temple.

The Courtyard
The spacious outer court, now much damaged, contains a later chapel [1]. The outer walls on the north and west sides are devoted to reliefs showing the Battle of Kadesh; though in less complete detail than the depictions at the Ramesseum and Abu Simbel, the carvings are nevertheless far superior. Beyond the pylons, a courtyard with Osiride pillars sheltered scenes of offering processions.

The Chapels
Beyond the portico at the west end, four chapels lie along the temple's axis where the deified Seti [2], the royal ancestors [3], the Ennead [4], Ramesses II [5], and Onuris [6] were worshipped.

Off the second hall, shrines include those to Osiris [7], Thoth [8], and Min [9].

The chapels at the end of the hall were dedicated to the Theban Triad and associated deities [10], and to Osiris, Lord of Abydos [11]; both sanctuaries lead into decorated columned halls. Outside the main sanctuary [12] stands an alabaster stela, and inside, the gray granite re-

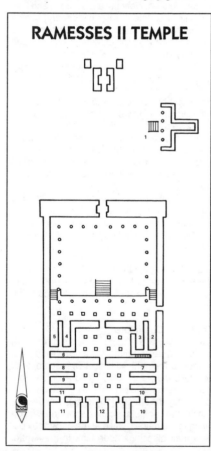

RAMESSES II TEMPLE

mains of statues of Ramesses, Seti, and two goddesses grace the room.

OTHER SIGHTS

Most of Abydos's other sights offer little to the casual tourist, for the remains are spotty and are difficult to reach. None are worth the effort unless you especially wish to visit a specific area or fancy a hike in the desert.

To The North
About a kilometer north of Ramesses' temple, the scanty remains of the ancient village include the Temple of Osiris and individual burials interred in small vaulted structures under the pavement. A half kilometer west lies the mud-brick enclosure known locally as the Shunet al-Zebib. Built in the 2nd Dynasty, the double-walled structure was long called a fort, but modern excavations have shown this enclosure with the palace-facade walls to be one of the several archaic funerary complexes in the area. The burials lie to the west, about three km into the desert at Umm al-Qa'ab (Mother of the Pots), named for the votive jars covering the graves.

To The South
The ruins of Senwosret III's funerary temple lie about two km to the south, at the edge of the desert, and another kilometer farther is a sandy mound marking Ahmose's pyramid, a few brick walls on the east indicating the mortuary temple. Across the Muslim cemetery, you can find the remains of the cenotaph Ahmose's mother, Queen Tetisheri, built. Near the cliffs lies the poorly preserved terraced temple Ahmose built for himself. Under the cliffs farther north, Senwosret built his cenotaph, now sanded up.

Getting There
You can reach Abydos from Luxor as a day-trip or from Sohag; see the relevant "transportation" sections.

*limestone funerary stela
of King Djet at Abydos
(c. 3000 B.C.)*

JAN KIRK

DENDERA

QINA

The transportation hub serving the Red Sea coast, Qina offers little of interest, except for the Temple of Dendera, nine km west of town. To the south are al-Balas, where potters make the white jars; the site of Naqada, which gave its name to the early Egyptians whose remains were discovered there; and Garagos, a Coptic community noted for its artistic, contemporary pottery.

Practicalities

If you're stuck in Qina for the night, try the **New Palace Hotel** directly across from the train station, or the **al-Salaam;** better yet, grab a taxi or bus to Nag Hammadi and check into the **Aluminium Hotel,** tel. (096) 757-947.

Transportation

The **train** station is in the middle of town and six a/c trains run daily to Cairo (12-13 hours), Luxor (two hours), and Aswan (6½ hours).

The **bus** station lies toward the Nile. Buses run hourly to Cairo between 0500 and 1500 (10-12 hours); to Alexandria, leaving at 0600 (14 hours); to Luxor (two hours); and Hurghada and Safaga, at 0930 and 1200, in addition to the two from Luxor, which come through town about 0700 and 1300; these are often crowded and you may have to stand or sit in the aisle. Buses to Suez at 0600 and 0630 also stop at Hurghada and Safaga.

Service taxis northbound leave from near the bus station to Dendera or al-Balyana (for Abydos). Southbound taxis leave from the mosque on the eastern bank of the canal: Luxor and Aswan. To reach Hurghada, take a taxi from the corner of the *midan* beyond the train station and canal.

HATHOR TEMPLE

Open 0600-1800; fee. Dendera was holy to Hathor, goddess of love and joy. The complex, like most ancient sites, has a long history. Old Kingdom tombs have been uncovered in the nearby desert, but the most recent buildings date to the Ptolemaic and Roman periods and are among the best preserved in Egypt.

The dramatic approach to the temple, across fields of berseem, shows it rising in the distance against the blue cliffs of the Western Desert. A pair of Roman fountains lie on either side of the path to the massive entrance gate; the scanty remains of their porches show where travelers could wash and rest before visiting the main precinct. The mud-brick enclosure walls date from Roman times and protect the main temple, two *mamissi,* the remains of a Coptic basilica, a sanatorium, a sacred lake, and a small temple to Isis; the Middle Kingdom chapel discovered here now resides in the Antiquities Museum in Cairo.

Like most religious complexes, the one at Dendera is oriented toward the river, but here the Qina Bend makes the river run nearly east-west, so the temple, which would normally face east, actually points north. The decorations, however, show traditional directional relationships, so the temple will be described as if its en-

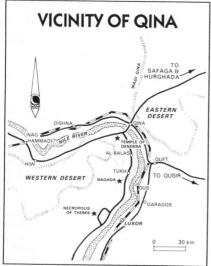

VICINITY OF QINA

TO SAFAGA & HURGHADA

WADI QINA

EASTERN DESERT

DISHNA

QINA

NAG HAMMADI

NILE RIVER

TEMPLE OF DENDERA

AL BALAS

HIW

QUFT

WESTERN DESERT

TUKH

NAQADA

TO QUSIR

QUS

GARAGOS

NECROPOLIS OF THEBES

LUXOR

0   30 km

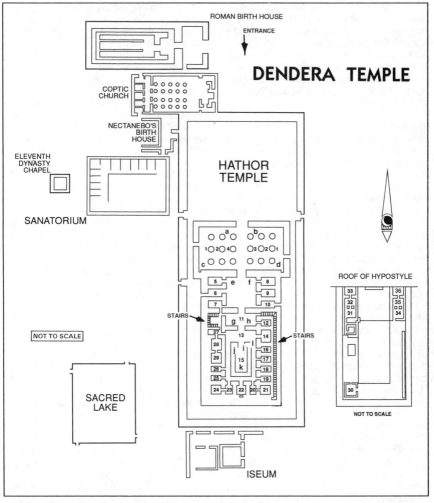

trance actually faced east. The complex was originally dedicated to Hathor, Horus of Idfu, and their son Ihy or Harsomtus, but of the main temples, only the one to Hathor remains.

Early texts refer to a predynastic temple that was rebuilt during the Old Kingdom; Pepi I was called Son of Hathor, Lady of Dendera. Fragments and texts refer to work on the temple by New Kingdom pharaohs including Thutmose III, Amenhotep

III, and Ramesses II and III. The present structure dates to the Greek and Roman periods: the sanctuary and its surrounding chapels and halls were built by the later Ptolemies, the great hypostyle hall by the Romans.

The Hypostyle Hall
The facade of the hall is closed, not by a solid pylon or wall as in earlier temples, but by a low

screen wall that exposes the ceiling and capitals. The square capitals bear Hathor's triangular face with her cow-like ears supporting the sistrum. The interior of the walls demonstrate the temple's directional awareness. The king at [a] wears the crown of Lower Egypt as he is greeted and blessed by various gods and goddesses; the similar figures at [b] wear the crown of Upper Egypt.

The Astronomical Ceiling

Maintaining much of its original color, this ceiling is one of the most beautiful in Egypt. The central corridor is decorated with flying vultures and winged disks, symbols of Upper and Lower Egypt as well as the union between Hathor and Horus. The rest of the ceiling is not a sky chart in the modern sense, but a symbolic representation of the northern and southern halves of the sky, the hours of the day and night, and the realms of the sun and moon. Therefore, the three bays to the left (traditional south) are dedicated to the stars and constellations found in that section of the night sky, while the bays to the right (traditional north) show the northern stars.

[1] The figures of Nut dominate each end of the hall, the texture of her dress representing the celestial ocean. From between her legs the sun is born at dawn, only to disappear at dusk as she swallows it. The traditional northern figure gives birth to Khepri [c], while the sun from the traditional southern one shines down on the face of Hathor and her temple (the square under her head) [d]. The barques under her body bear stars and constellations from the respective halves of the sky.

[2] The second bands show the planets, the stars of each of the 12 hours of the night, and the signs of the zodiac (introduced by the Romans); the constellations of the southern and northern heavens respectively. The Egyptians divided their 24-hour days into 12 night hours and 12 day hours; the hours of the night they calculated with stars called *decans,* which rose at 10-day intervals.

[3] The bands on either side of the center are devoted to the course of the sun (south) and moon (north). Souls depicted as jackals, birds, and human-bodied beings line the sun's course, adoring his solar barque as it passes; the phases mark the sun's daily transition from child to youth, adult, and old man.

[4] The moon's register is broken into three main scenes. The first shows the full moon. The second depicts the Eye of Re in its barque; above and below the eye are the 14 days of the waning moon. Next to it appear the 14 steps of the waxing moon, each surmounted by its own god or goddess, approaching the full disk worshipped by Thoth. Last, the moon appears as Osiris protected by Nephthys and Isis. His barque is born aloft by the sky, which is supported by its four pillars, shown here as goddesses. On either side, he is worshipped by spirits of hawks (north) and jackals (south).

Hall Of Appearances

This hall marks the beginning of the Ptolemaic section of the temple. The wall is topped by a concave cornice, and the doorway is trimmed with a round molding. Scenes on the inside of the wall [e] show the king emerging from the temple, where he breaks the earth for its foundation, lays the first stone, and dedicates the building; in [f] he presents the foundation deposit bricks to Hathor for her temple, purifies it, and dedicates it. This hall, where the goddess first appeared for her feasts, is surrounded by six rooms, their uses appearing in their decorations.

[5] The treasury housed the holy objects of precious metals. The decorations include offerings of the metals themselves as well as jewelry.

[6] The Nile room provides access to the well outside, and through this doorway priests brought the water used in the temple. The texts covering the jambs of the outer door instruct the priests in the rituals. The interior scenes show the procession of the "Niles."

[7] This room, through its side door, communicates with the interior of the temple, allowing priests to enter it without opening the large double doors between the two halls.

[8] In this "laboratory," priests made and stored the unguents, incense, and perfumes used in the temple. The decorations include recipes for unguents and show bearers bringing the exotic and aromatic materials from foreign lands.

[9] This room once sheltered temple valuables, perhaps even statues. The doorway inscriptions, which continue onto the neighboring entryway, list the festivals celebrated in the temple: a liturgical calendar.

[10] Through this room, which connects with the outside, priests brought the offerings into the temple: meat, bread, beer, and wine, as well as the ubiquitous flowers that always decorated the offering tables.

The Hall Of Offerings
[11] The entrance to the "temple proper," this hall was lighted only by the four ceiling vents. At its sides lie the two stairways to the roof. In this hall, the priests laid out the the offerings for the deities; a list of such offerings appears on the back wall **[g]**. The opposite side **[h]** shows the king offering Hathor the intoxicating drink she enjoyed.

[12] This small chapel was used for sacrificial offerings.

Hall Of The Ennead
[13] This room, immediately preceding the sanctuary proper, held the statues of the gods and kings who took part in ceremonies dedicated to Hathor. The text on the south wall (at the front of the sanctuary) contains the hymns of awakening. Light, symbolized by the sun rays streaming down, decorates the windows; the nearby texts are to the rising (theoretical east) and setting (theoretical west) suns.

[14] Priests stored the goddess's wardrobe in this small room; the decorations show the priests carrying chests that held the holy garments.

Sanctuary
[15] This holy room, the Great Seat, once housed the statue of the goddess and her barque as well as perhaps that of her consort, Horus of Idfu. The barques, raised high on the priests' shoulders with carrying poles, carried the deities whenever they ventured from their sanctuary. To travel on the river, these miniature barques were placed aboard real ones, which were then powered by ships and tow ropes pulled by her worshippers on the bank. The small barques are shown on the walls of the sanctuary. The remaining vignettes, to be read along alternating walls (left **[i]**, then right **[j]**), detail the daily awakening, bathing, anointing, and feeding of the goddess. (For a full description of the ritual, see p. 315.) On the rear wall **[k]**, the king offers the goddess Ma'at to Hathor, Horus, and Harsomtus.

Corridor Of Mystery
The dim corridor that runs around the sanctuary gives access to 11 chapels dedicated to the deities that surrounded Hathor. Over the low doorway to this passage **[l]**, the goddess appears as a cow within a wooden kiosk mounted on a barque. Along the exterior of the sanctuary march the "Niles," those representing Upper Egypt appear on the traditional south wall, those of Lower Egypt on the traditional north.

The chapels beyond are dedicated to the gods of the Dendera Nome **[16]**, Isis of Dendera **[17]**, Sokar **[18]**, and the serpent-god who was Son of the Earth **[19]**.

The standard three chapels appear at the southern end of the temple, and like similar ones at Ramesses' temple in Abydos, the corner rooms are accessible only from their neighboring chapels.

[20] The eastern shrine was the staging ground for the great voyage to Horus' temple at Idfu, which Hathor undertook each year; the hymn on the outer doors commemorates the journey.

[21] The connecting doorway leads to the Castle of the Sistrum (Hathor's musical instrument), a name by which the entire temple was also known. The niche on the north wall shows the coronation of Ihy, the god of music; that on the south shows Hathor standing on the sky (supported by four goddesses) playing a tabor.

[22] The central chapel held valuable shrines of the goddess, and from here a procession gathered before the dawn of New Year's Day for Hathor's festival. A modern ladder leads to a hidden crypt that once contained a squatting statue of the goddess like the one shown on the walls.

[23] The third chapel is dedicated to Hathor's terrible aspect, the lioness.

[24] The doorway leads to the Throne of Re, the counterpart of the Castle of the Sistrum. To protect their temple's valuables—the shrines, statues, jewelry, holy papyri, and magical implements—the priests stored them in niches and rooms hidden within the walls, and such crypts abounded in Ptolemaic temples. This suite of five rooms runs under the holy shrines: three rooms to the east and two to the west. The decorations depict the objects stored within them: musical instruments, statues of Hathor, and sacred collars. The god Harsomtus appears in the eastern room, while in the western one, a scene shows 6th Dynasty King Pepi I presenting a statue of Ihy to the goddess. The crypt also housed the statue of Hathor's *ba,* her divine spirit. This statue, on New Year's Eve, was hauled up the tortuous stairway to the suite of rooms dedicated to the festival.

The remaining two chapels (west) are dedicated to Hathor's *menat* collar [25], which was imbued with the power of healing, and to Ihy [26].

Court Of The First Feast

[27] The first room in this suite of three served as both a storeroom and hallway between the stairway, the Hall of the Ennead, and the suite.

[28] In the court beyond, priests made offerings to the statue that stood in the small kiosk.

[29] Called the Pure Place, this kiosk was separated from the court by sistrum capitals and a low screen. The reliefs show the kings worshipping the deities, and the offering bearers once more show the Egyptians' concern with direction—those on the left represent Upper Egypt, those on the right, Lower Egypt. On the ceiling, Nut gives birth to the sun, which shines on Hathor's head; her face stands poised between two hills and trees, like the rising sun, and symbolizes the temple of Dendera. This relief conveys the essence of the ritual; the statue of Hathor was taken to the roof of the temple to sit in a shrine and greet the first rays of the sun, her father, who renewed her spirit for the coming year.

THE ROOF

The steps from the suite's vestibule wind around a massive pillar to the roof. The windows carry decorations of the sun and its stylized rays; the walls show the procession that climbed the stairs each New Year's morning (outer wall) and then returned (inner wall) with the rejuvenated goddess. Similar scenes decorate the eastern stairway, which is straight and unlighted by windows. The roof, the only one open to visitors on a regular basis, contains both the kiosk, where Hathor greeted the New Year's sun, and two suites of rooms dedicated to Osiris.

The Kiosk

[30] Once up the stairs, the statue was carried to the open pavilion at the south end of the roof to await the dawn. Here, enclosed by the Hathor capitals and low walls, the goddess met her father, the solar disk, who revitalized her *ba* for the coming year.

Western Osiris Rooms

Like most temples, Dendera's rooftop rooms included a suite dedicated to the death and resurrection of Osiris, rooms representing his tomb. Like its counterpart to the east, this suite was lighted only by a slit in the roof.

[31] Isis and Nephthys mourn Osiris, who's guarded with spells cast by divinities who watch over his corpse during the 24 hours of the day and night.

[32] Knife-carrying gods guard the gates of the netherworld, while Nut stretches across the ceiling over a doubled-over figure of Geb, who is perhaps impregnating himself.

[33] The inner sanctuary or tomb proper, the decorations here show Osiris bringing himself to erection and impregnating Isis (shown as a hovering kite), who will bear Horus, the living king.

Eastern Suite

[34] The text carved on the walls of this court describes the Osiris bed of linen, filled with earth, seeded, and watered until the grain spouted—reaffirming eternal life in rhythm with nature's cycles.

[35] The home of the famous Dendera Zodiac, the original of this circular ceiling resides in the Louvre; a cast now occupies its place. The zodiac was not developed by the Egyptians but introduced by the Romans. This carving, supported by the goddesses of the four corners of the world, mimics the circular sky: Taweret is anchoring the north star and the signs of the zodiac, which (with the substitution of the scarab for the scorpion) are easily recognizable.

[36] The inner room again shows Osiris on his bier. On the ceiling, Nut encircles the stairway representing the 14 steps (days) of the waxing moon; at the top of the platform, Thoth worships the moon, while behind it, the sun rests in a chapel. Below the tortoise *decan,* Osiris strides out in his barque while Isis, as a cow, follows in her own barge.

Roof Of The Roman Hypostyle Hall

The modern iron stairway leads to the roof where, in antiquity, the pious, awaiting messages and miracles from the goddess, passed their time. The gaming boards they carved in the massive stones still remain.

The Temple's Exterior

The exterior of the temple boasts lion-headed gargoyles that served to drain water from infrequent rains. On the south end, carvings show Cleopatra VII and her son by Julius Caesar, Caesarion, who became her co-regent. The false door, carved directly behind the interior sanctuary, received the prayers of those unable to enter the temple. Much of the gigantic emblem of Hathor was destroyed by countless generations of pilgrims gouging out a little of the precious dust to take home.

OTHER SIGHTS

Sacred Lake

Lying off the southwest corner of the temple, the sacred lake provided the water for priests' ablutions. The surface of the water was reached via one of the four stairways. Today, seepage provides enough moisture to grow a good crop of reeds and attract wildlife (including a fennec family) from the surrounding desert.

Iseum

Directly south of the back wall of Hathor's Temple, the Iseum is a split temple: the sanctuary faces north but the hypostyle hall is rotated and set to the east. Within the sanctuary, a statue (now destroyed) of Osiris was supported by Isis and Nephthys, whose arms, carved in the round, reached into the niche to support him.

Sanatorium

Noted as a goddess of compassion, Hathor appealed to the sick, and the compound at Dendera developed a reputation for healing. Those waiting to receive the dream that contained the prescription for their cure inhabited rooms that surrounded a central courtyard. In this central area, priests poured water over statues inscribed with magical texts (the base of one remains), and the power passed into the water, which the patient then bathed in or drank.

Mamissi Of Nectanebo

Mamissi in Dendera celebrate the birth of Hathor's child by Horus of Idfu. The rites performed in here ensured the vitality of their child, and by analogy, the current king. This building was split by the Roman enclosure wall, and the Romans then built another mamissi beyond where the Coptic basilica now stands.

Coptic Basilica

This 5th century church was built with stone picked up from the crumbling pharaonic monuments. The plan is typical of the Coptic basilica, with the Christian builders orienting their church with the apse to the east rather than toward the river, as their pharaonic forebears had placed their temple. The western entrance opens into a narthex and baptistery, a dove occupying the half-shell niche. Niches line the walls of the nave, which leads to the tri-apsal sanctuary.

Roman Mamissi

The replacement for Nectanebo's structure, this Roman building is screened by a low curtain wall with carvings (south wall) of Trajan offering to Hathor—some of the best Greco-Roman artwork in Egypt. The graceful plant forms of the column capitals support abaci decorated with figures of the household god Bes, and architraves with alternating figures of Bes and Taweret, who worships Harsomtus (a child on a lotus blossom).

Like most mamissi the vestibule is given over to offering scenes. In the sanctuary, the standard birth scenes show the conception, the creation of the child and his ka on the potter's wheel, the birth, and the subsequent presenting of the figures to innumerable gods and goddesses. Unfortunately, the scenes here are in dire need of cleaning; take a strong flashlight and you may be able to pick out some. From the niche in the false door, framed with Hathor columns, the goddess and her child emerge.

Getting There

Dendera lies nine km west of Qina; you can catch a service taxi, minibus, or calishe from there.

BOB RACE

UPPER EGYPT—LUXOR

Luxor (Arabic: al-Uqsur, "the Palaces") rests on the site of the ancient Egyptian capital of Thebes. From here, the warrior pharaohs of the 18th Dynasty, blessed by Amun-Re and the war-god Montu, marched forth and conquered nearly all the known world. Returning to Thebes with gold and slaves, they turned their city into a wonder of the ancient world. However, foreign invasions of the 5th century B.C. stripped Thebes of her power and riches, and along with Troy and Knossos, she faded into myth.

East Bank residents, following early Christian and Roman examples, built homes inside and around her remaining temples, which over the centuries desert sand and village rubble buried up to their lotus-blossom capitals. On the West Bank, only the Colossi of Memnon, gigantic statues of Amenhotep III, shorn of the vast temple that once stood at their backs, and the crumbling ruins of a few mortuary temples and tombs remained visible. Until the turn of the 19th century, Luxor was a provincial village known only for the tomb of its 12th century Muslim sheikh, Abu al-Haggag.

Not until members of Napoleon's expedition began uncovering and recording the ruins did Egypt's imperial past reemerge. Their discoveries astonished the Victorian world, and in December of 1886 Thomas Cook inaugurated a line of steamers that brought large numbers of European tourists to view the splendor of ancient Thebes, and Luxor grew from an ill-kept village to a modern tourist center. Plush riverboats, direct descendants of Cook's steamers, still ply the waters, butting their modern prows against ancient quays.

Luxor sprawls along the east bank of the Nile. This long, narrow settlement is bounded on either end by the twin temples of Karnak (north) and Luxor (south). Between them run two parallel main streets: Sh. Bahr al-Nil or Cornishe, which lies along the riverbank, and Sh. al-Karnak, which lies to the east and roughly follows the ancient processional way connecting the two temples. Hotels, docks for the Nile cruise boats, and tourist facilities line the Cornishe.

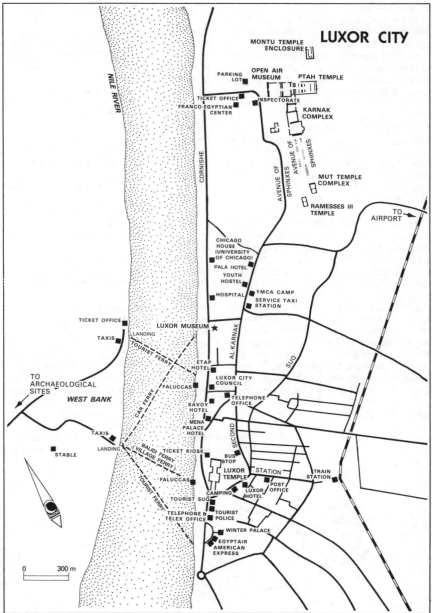

LUXOR CITY

MONTU TEMPLE ENCLOSURE

OPEN AIR MUSEUM

PARKING LOT

PTAH TEMPLE

TICKET OFFICE

INSPECTORATE

FRANCO-EGYPTIAN CENTER

KARNAK COMPLEX

NILE RIVER

CORNISHE

AVENUE OF SPHINXES

AVENUE OF SPHINXES

MUT TEMPLE COMPLEX

RAMESSES III TEMPLE

TO AIRPORT

CHICAGO HOUSE (UNIVERSITY OF CHICAGO)

PALA HOTEL YOUTH HOSTEL

HOSPITAL

YMCA CAMP

SERVICE TAXI STATION

TICKET OFFICE

TAXIS

LANDING

TOURIST FERRY

LUXOR MUSEUM

AL-KARNAK

SUQ

ETAP HOTEL

TO ARCHAEOLOGICAL SITES

WEST BANK

CAR FERRY

FALUCCAS

LUXOR CITY COUNCIL

SAVOY HOTEL

TELEPHONE OFFICE

MENA PALACE HOTEL

TAXIS

STABLE

LANDING

BALIDI FERRY (VILLAGE FERRY)

TICKET KIOSK

SECOND

BUS STOP

STATION

TRAIN STATION

FALUCCAS

LUXOR TEMPLE

CAMPING

POST OFFICE

LUXOR HOTEL

TOURIST SUQ

TELEPHONE & TELEX OFFICE

TOURIST POLICE

WINTER PALACE

EGYPTAIR AMERICAN EXPRESS

TOURIST FERRY

0   300 m

© MOON PUBLICATIONS, INC.

Itinerary Notes

In Luxor, you'll have to coordinate your sightseeing to fit in both the East and West banks, especially if your time is limited. Since the West Bank is hot, especially during the summer, many of the monuments close in the afternoon, so it's best to reserve mornings for the "Land of the Dead." In the evenings, after a siesta, visit Luxor Temple, perhaps even at night, when the moonlight may conjure up pharaonic ghosts. Luxor Museum (only open evenings), is an air-conditioned jewel that displays treasures from predynastic to Islamic Egypt. Even a visit to the Karnak complex, which sprawls over several acres, can be split into several evenings. Don't miss the Sound and Light show at Karnak; it's the best in Egypt.

Although Thebes served as Upper Egypt's capital for over 1,500 years, little remains of her former glory. The mud-brick palaces of her kings and nobles have long since vanished, leaving only the stone temples. To the north, the main temple in the Karnak complex was dedicated to Amun-Re, the invisible god of air, wind, and later, sun. In the south, Luxor Temple, known as the Southern Harem, was home to Amun's fertility aspect, Amun-Min. With his consort Mut and their son, the moon-god Khonsu, they formed the holy triad of Thebes. The two complexes were linked by a sphinx-lined avenue, along which the yearly Opet, or fertility festival, brought Amun from Karnak to visit Luxor. These temples, although rebuilt and enlarged, still reflect the classical canon of New Kingdom religious buildings.

LUXOR MUSEUM

Open daily 1500-2100 in winter and 1700-2200 in summer; fee LE8; downstairs exhibit, LE10; no tickets sold after 2030. Located along the Cornishe, near the Etap Hotel, this modern museum (1975) has a limited collection, but its premier artifacts are displayed with the care usually reserved for jewels. The clear labeling and expansive historical notes make the displays self-explanatory. Don't miss the garden: north of the entrance is a pink granite slab of King Nebhepetre-Mentuhotep enthroned between Seth and Horus. Opposite, the sporting King Amenhotep II shoots arrows through a copper target. Of the remaining royal statues, most date from the 18th Dynasty; at the southern corner of the building, a carved block shows Amenhotep III with an ithyphallic Amun—the style, in contrast to the carvings at Luxor Temple, is bold and detailed.

The lower gallery is now open, having been specially designed for the "Luxor Temple Cachette." In 1989, 26 statues were uncovered in the courtyard of Luxor Temple while workmen were stabilizing the colonnade court. Displayed with the same austere emphasis as the artifacts above, the statues are in almost perfect condition. The focus of the display is a statue of Amenhotep III which, upon careful examination, turns out to be a "statue of a statue"; ancient statues were mounted on sledges, and this statue includes such a sledge. The gallery also includes statues of King Horemheb offering to Atum, as well as one showing him with Amun-Re. Statues of the goddesses Hathor and a rare depiction of Inuet, wife of Montu, are in nearly pristine condition. The detour is worth the LE10.

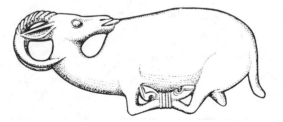

LUXOR TEMPLE

Open daily in summer 0700-2100, in winter during Ramadan 0700-1830 and 2000-2300; fee LE10, after 1700, LE5. Luxor Temple, dedicated to the triad of Amun-Min, Mut, and Khonsu, was planned by the 18th Dynasty pharaoh Amenhotep III. Located on the site of an earlier sanctuary, the temple was only half finished when Amenhotep IV (Akhenaten) succeeded his father and suspended construction. He ordered the name of his father erased and built a sanctuary dedicated to Aton at the side of the temple. He then moved the seat of his government north to al-Amarna. Not until Tutankhamun returned the royal residence to Thebes was the colonnade finished and the wall decorated. Ramesses II built the great double-colonnaded court in front of the original structure and erected the pylon gateway. Alexander rebuilt the sanctuary; later, the Romans remodeled portions and held services in the temple. Finally, the Muslims built a mosque at the northeast corner of Ramesses' courtyard.

The temple's artwork, executed in the middle of the 18th Dynasty, is some of the best in Egypt; because the temple's walls were deeply buried, the carvings are also well preserved. Unfortunately, the reliefs have not fared so well once exposed. A rising water table forces salts into the stone. They eventually crystallize onto the surface of the temple walls and then flake off layers of stone, taking their designs with them. The temple itself is compact; a quick tour takes only an hour. However, if you spend extra time studying the carvings, the New Kingdom will come to life.

Outer Courtyard

The entrance lies north of the complex; access is from the Cornishe. The walkway takes you through a small garden. Once the entire complex was surrounded by great *temenos* walls; now it lies amidst the mud-brick ruins of a Roman town. To your right, down the hill, are the remains of a Roman fort, and beyond, to the south, two chapels nestle next to the temple's walls. Modern steps descend into a Late Kingdom (circa 350 B.C.) courtyard, the work of Nectanebo.

[1] This Roman mud-brick chapel still contains a Greco-Roman style statue of Isis.

[2] The courtyard's western wall opens into the Avenue of Sphinxes, which once connected Luxor Temple with Karnak. Between the statues of human-headed lions, archaeologists uncovered holes that once held the trees that shaded the 2½-km paved way.

The Pylons

In front of Ramesses II's towers (their faces notched for flag poles), six colossal statues (two sitting and four standing) of the pharaoh once guarded the entrance. Behind them rose a pair of obelisks. Today only a single obelisk and four statues (the others are in the Louvre) remain. The other obelisk, all 230 metric tons of it, stands at the Place de la Concorde in Paris, a gift from Muhammad Ali to King Charles X.

On the walls of the pylons is inscribed a depiction of the Battle of Kadesh against the Hittites (1285 B.C.). Although now much decayed, the general outlines of the scenes are visible (best in the morning sun or at night under the lights). (The same story is more clearly visible at Abu Simbel, p. 398.) The windows near the top of the pylons admit light and fresh air to rooms in the towers. The reliefs on the inner walls of the gateway were added by the Ethiopian king Shabaka of the 25th Dynasty. The pylons open into a large peristyle court surrounded by two rows of papyrus-bud columns and filled with relief scenes and inscriptions.

Great Court Of Ramesses II

[3] Thutmose III built his barque shrine with granite pillars and panels reused from Hatshepsut's earlier building. The deities' barques rested in these three chapels dedicated to Amun (center), Mut (west), and Khonsu (east) during the opening of the Opet feast.

Around the once-roofed ambulatory stand statues of Amenhotep II, which were usurped by Ramesses II; others show Ramesses himself as a young man, with his wife Queen Nefertari standing at his calf.

[4] The drawings here show part of the tem-

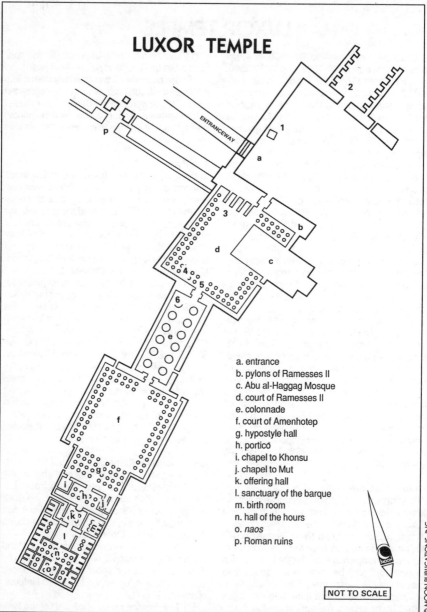

LUXOR TEMPLE

a. entrance
b. pylons of Ramesses II
c. Abu al-Haggag Mosque
d. court of Ramesses II
e. colonnade
f. court of Amenhotep
g. hypostyle hall
h. portico
i. chapel to Khonsu
j. chapel to Mut
k. offering hall
l. sanctuary of the barque
m. birth room
n. hall of the hours
o. *naos*
p. Roman ruins

NOT TO SCALE

© MOON PUBLICATIONS, INC.

ple's major feast, the Opet. The procession of the festival of ithyphallic Amun approach the temple itself, complete with flying flags, from the right. At the Opet festival, which took place at the beginning of the harvest season, Amun-Min received offerings of long, slender lettuce, symbol of his fecundity. The pharaoh himself offers to Mut and Montu, while his queen and 17 of his sons look on. The deposits on the lower part of the pylon and walls are salt encrustations.

The entire northeast corner of the courtyard remains buried under accumulated debris that marked the general ground level before the French archaeologist Maspero began clearing the temple. Archaeologists have been unable to get permission to move the mosque that stands atop the ruins, its mud-brick minaret standing on a stone lintel of the ancient temple.

Mosque Of Abu Al-Haggag

Although most of the mosque is 19th century, the minaret dates to 1077, and was erected by Badr al-Gamali to mark his victories over the Nubians. Sheikh Yusif Abu al-Haggag, a descendant of Khalif Ali, came from Baghdad in the middle of the 12th century to settle in Luxor. One of Upper Egypt's greatest sheikhs, his tomb lies in the mosque. The entrance is outside the mosque, and the quietly lighted interior is worth a trip up. Here, faux marble is painted on the pillars, but it somehow imbues the shrine with a more powerful, holy feeling.

Colonnade

[5] Two black colossi of Ramesses II flank the entrance to the colonnade, with bound prisoners from Asia (north) and Nubia (south) decorating the bases. At this point, the temple's main axis bends, marking the junction between Amenhotep's original design and Ramesses' additions. Limestone statues of Amun and Mut bear the cartouches of Ramesses II. The colonnade, built by Amenhotep III, is over 50 meters long, and seven pairs of papyrus columns, still supporting their architraves on calyx capitals, line this processional way.

On the walls, beginning on the west side, carvings added by Tutankhamun and Horemheb repeat the Opet festival procession from Karnak Temple to Luxor, a journey of the gods that kicked off 24 days of merrymaking.

[6] Tutankhamun offers sacrifices to Amun (top), Mut, and Khonsu within the temple sanctuary. To the left, at the bottom, stands the king's barque. Priests, carrying the idols' barques high on their shoulders, emerge from the temple's third pylon (its front at the time the carvings were executed); led by musicians, the procession moves to the river, where the gods embark upriver for Luxor. (The barques are clearer on the other side—on the return trip to Karnak, you can see the decorations on bow and stern.) Priests, soldiers, *fallahin,* and foreigners follow along the riverbank, adding their muscle to tow ropes attached to the barques, while musicians and dancing girls provide entertainment. Oxen, their turned-up hooves indicating life in a fattening pen, are led to slaughter (lower register). Continue around the courtyard, and you can follow the gods' return trip to Karnak.

Court Of Amenhotep III

The open courtyard is edged with pairs of papyriform columns. The artwork includes decorations from the time of Amenhotep to that of Alexander and Philip; the eastern and western sides even preserve some of the original colors.

Hypostyle Hall

The south end of the courtyard blends imperceptibly into the hypostyle hall. Four rows of papyrus columns once supported a roof, but now only the architrave remains. On the left side of the central aisle (between the last two columns) stands a Roman altar dedicated to Constantine. Beyond this hall lies the temple proper.

Portico

Beyond the hypostyle hall, on either side of the central axis, were shrines for the barques of Mut and Khonsu. The central, eight-columned hall was transformed into a chapel by the Roman legion, which took up residence in Luxor. They plastered over the pharaonic reliefs and erected a shrine, complete with Corinthian columns, which closed off the temple's portal. Traces of imperial figures still remain near the tops of the walls.

Long believed to be a Christian church, it was instead a chapel dedicated to Rome's emperors. In fact, as William Murnane has pointed out (in *The Penguin Guide to Ancient Egypt*), "It was probably here that local Christians were offered the choice between martyrdom and sacrificing to the imperial cult." The present door was cut into the shrine in modern times, and as the chapel gradually sheds its stucco layers, Amenhotep's fierce figure emerges once more.

The Sanctuary

South of the chapel lies a four-columned offering hall where priests collected sacrifices to the god. Along the walls, reliefs show priests carrying the divine barques into the sanctuary, and the god's "wife" accompanies him.

Directly behind this offering hall is the sanctuary of the barque. Amenhotep's original square room was supported by pillars, the bases of which remain in the center of the floor. Alexander the Great added the chapel that now surrounds the granite pedestal for the barque. On these walls, Alexander, dressed as a pharaoh, presents offerings to Min. The carvings on the sanctuary walls show Amenhotep receiving the double crown of Egypt with the ennead of gods as witness.

Birth Room

To the east, the "birth room" contains the story of Amenhotep's divine conception. Hatshepsut, to legitimize her claim to the throne, had already used the same motif on her temple at Deir al-Bahri. However, in this case some anthropologists feel the scene represents a yearly ritual performed by pharaoh as Amun-Min and his wife as Mut to ensure, through a sacred marriage, the continuing vitality of the ruler and the renewal of the land.

Although the scenes are now quite damaged, you can still make out many of the figures. From the bottom right, Amun and Hathor (defaced) embrace Mutemwia, Amenhotep's mother; Amun with Thoth; Amun with the queen sitting on a bed; and Amun watching Khnum, the ram-headed potter, fashion the double souls of Amenhotep on his wheel. In the center, Thoth informs the queen that she is to bear a royal son; Hathor and Khnum conduct her to the birth room where, seated on a birthing chair, she delivers. On the right, the newborn *ka* is held by an attendant. Hathor then presents the young king to his father, Amun.

In the top register, Amenhotep, after being suckled by 13 goddesses, joins his *ka,* and they are conducted by the gods of magic and the Nile to meet Horus, who then presents them to Amun. The assemblage of gods determines the length of the young king's reign, and Seshat, the scribal goddess, duly notes the decision.

Back Rooms

The small rooms along the back wall constitute the *opet,* or private apartments, of the gods. The central *naos* or "holy of holies" held the image of the god, which rested on the pedestal that still remains. The long room, which serves as a hall between the back of the sanctuary of the barque and the central *naos,* is an unusual variation on traditional design. The 12 columns stand between drawings (on either end wall) of the day-barque and the night-barque of the sun, and represent the 12 hours of the Egyptian night.

Exterior Walls

You can exit the temple through the south chapel. Walk around the end of the temple to the west wall (toward the Cornishe) and you can still make out the incised figures of Ramesses II's armies campaigning in Asia. The pharaoh captures Tunip in Nahrin, the king's lion hurls himself against the Hittites of Dapur, and a bear seizes the leg of a Syrian who is climbing a pine tree to escape from pharaoh's destruction of the hill-fortress of Satuna.

KARNAK COMPLEX

Built on a scale for giant gods, the Karnak temple complex at Thebes sprawls across much of northern Luxor. The massive pylons and pillars of the Temple of Amun loom above the ruins of smaller chapels scattered throughout the enclosure. The main structure grew from a 12th Dynasty core (the open rubble-strewn courtyard beyond the obelisks) **[J]** undoubtedly an ancient holy site. As each succeeding ruler added to the original plan, the temple expanded like ripples in water from a thrown stone. Early Thutmoside kings built a large court, a colonnade with Osiride pillars, and the fifth pylon, now ruined. Hatshepsut added a rose granite sanctuary and commissioned two of the largest obelisks ever erected, and later Thutmose III erased her name wherever he found it, appropriating her works. Akhenaten built a chapel to his sun-god Aton, which Horemheb dismantled and used for filler blocks for the pylons he erected, while Seti and the Ramesside kings who followed him built yet more pylons and added the famous hypostyle hall.

Practicalities

Open daily 0700-1700; fee LE10 (be sure to get a ticket to the open-air museum—same hours; LE5). Karnak lies about three km north of Luxor proper and is accessible by taxi, calishe, bicycle, or foot, though you may want to save your feet for the extensive ruins. Of the two routes, the Cornishe (rather than Sh. al-Karnak, which follows the ancient sphinx-lined avenue), is the easiest, for it brings you right to the ticket booth (on your right); beyond it lies the main entrance to the Temple of Amun.

Sound And Light Show

Two performances every evening 1800 and 2000; fee. The hour-and-a-half show at Karnak, one of the best in Egypt, starts at the first pylon. With lights, music, and narration, it takes you back into Theban times, walking you through the temple to the sacred lake. Here, seated in the grandstand, you view the second half of the show, with the lighted monuments throwing their reflections into the pool. Confirm the schedule at

KARNAK SOUND AND LIGHT SHOW

	Early Show	Late Show
Saturday	English	French
Sunday	French	German
Monday	English	French
Tuesday	French	English
Wednesday	English	German
Thursday	Arabic	English
Friday	French	English

the Tourist Office or any hotel; come early, as there is usually a line for tickets.

General Plan

The Temple of Amun dominates the compound; its two series of pylons connect the ancient quay and the processional way, linking Karnak with the Temple of Mut and Luxor Temple. In addition to this main building and its sacred lake, the complex houses an outdoor museum (including the Middle Kingdom chapel of Senwosret) **[T]**, a temple to Ptah **[V]**, the festival hall of Thutmose III **[K]**, several auxiliary temples to hear the prayers of the population **[L and M]**, and a temple to Khonsu **[S]**.

The Processional Way

[A] In front of the first pylon stands the ancient dock from which the Opet procession departed. A fragment of the processional way, lined with ram-head sphinxes that shelter statues of Ramesses II, spans the distance from the dock to the first pylon. The landing stage itself, surmounted by a sandstone platform, bears several inscriptions marking the Nile's level during exceptionally high floods. Of two small sandstone obelisks, only the one on the right, with the name of Seti II (19th Dynasty), remains.

[B] To the right stands the chapel of Achoris.

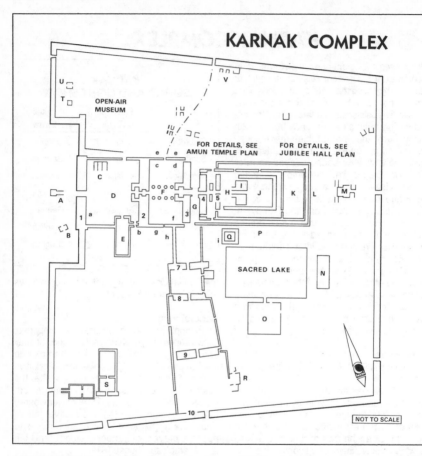

KARNAK COMPLEX

OPEN-AIR MUSEUM

FOR DETAILS, SEE AMUN TEMPLE PLAN

FOR DETAILS, SEE JUBILEE HALL PLAN

SACRED LAKE

NOT TO SCALE

© MOON PUBLICATIONS, INC.

Dating to 390 B.C, this riverbank shrine provided a resting spot for Amun's barque during his trips from the temple. Mercenaries in service of the 29th Dynasty carved numerous inscriptions in Cairian script.

First Pylon

[1] This, the largest and latest of Karnak's pylons, was built in regular courses of sandstone, a technique favored by the rulers following the 21st Dynasty. The towers may well have been built as late as the 30th Dynasty by Nectanebo I when he erected the mud-brick enclosure walls. The pylon is unfinished; the northern tower remains lower than the southern one, and neither is decorated. High on the right tower inside the doorway, the French under Napoleon inscribed survey notes and the distances to other temples of Upper Egypt.

Great Court

This court, a late addition, encloses an area that was once part of the processional way. As a result, three earlier buildings now lie within its walls: Seti's barque shrine **[C]**, the one remaining pillar of Taharqa's kiosk **[D]**, and Ramesses III's temple **[E]**. Along the colonnade, the ancient builders stored spare sphinxes, brothers to those still standing outside the first pylon; these ram-headed figures were moved when the processional way was shortened to accommodate the new court. The disintegrating pile of dirt in the southwest corner [a] was part of the scaffolding used to erect the southern tower.

[C] This shrine of Seti II provided a resting place for royal barques. The three chambers housed (left to right) Mut, Amun, and Khonsu when they paused in their journeys to and from the temple. The square doorways are of rose granite, the rest of the building gray sandstone.

[D] Ten papyriform columns marking the kiosk of Taharqa were once linked by low walls open at either end. Although there is no evidence that the structure ever had a roof, the pillars may well have been topped with statues. The priests would have carried Amun's image to the alabaster block in the pavilion's center for its yearly union with the solar disk of Re. In this yearly resurrection ritual the priests had to be sure that the first rays of the New Year's sun would touch the statue. Dawn was followed by sacrifices and feasting, rejoicing at the god's renewal.

Nearby stands the sphinx of King Tut, its surface darkened by countless caressing hands. Behind the kiosk, two striding colossi of Ramesses II flanked the entrance, but of the northern one, only the feet remain. In front of the latter, a third statue of the king grasps the crook and flail, badges of his office. Between his legs stands his queen holding a fly-whisk, still the badge of Luxor's residents.

[E] Ramesses III Temple, though built to serve the same purpose as the simpler shrine opposite, was designed as a classical temple. Behind the two colossi, Ramesses added a small pylon that screens the festival hall of the front court. The walls of this court, lined with mummiform pillar-statues of the pharaoh, carry carvings of the yearly procession of Amun-Min. Beyond lie the portico and the hypostyle hall, and, in the darkness, the three shrines to house the barques of the Theban Triad.

[b] The carvings of the Shoshenq relief show Amun presiding over the ceremonial slaughter of captives by King Shoshenq I (Shishak of the Bible; I Kings 14:25-26). The rings behind Amun spell out the locations raided in Palestine, providing corroborating details of the biblical account. Unfortunately, the figure of the king is nearly invisible because it was only lightly carved in plaster, which has fallen away. The gateway, called the Bubastite Portal, was built by the kings of the 22nd Dynasty from the delta town of Bubastis.

Second Pylon

[2] These towers, in poor condition in spite of restoration attempts, were begun by Horemheb and Ramesses I, but construction was not completed until the time of Seti I. The dark streaks along the face date from a fire in antiquity, which destroyed the wooden flagpoles and doors. In more modern times, workers restoring the crumbling towers discovered sandstone blocks that were once part of Akhenaten's temples to Aton. Figures on the vestibule wall show Ramesses II defeating the foes of Amun, and just inside the doorway, you can pick out the cartouches of Ramesses I, Seti I, and Ramesses II.

ram-headed sphinx at Karnak

GREAT HYPOSTYLE HALL

[F] Beyond the second pylon looms the pillared forest of Egypt's most famous hypostyle hall, which, at 102 by 53 meters, could house Paris's entire Notre Dame Cathedral. Begun by Ramesses I, the actual construction was completed by his son Seti I and his successor, Ramesses II. It was restored at the turn of the century after several columns collapsed. The central columns supported a raised roof with their open capitals; elevated nearly a meter above the bud-style pillars filling either side of the hall, they provided room for clerestory windows (the stone grills of several remain in position). Supplying the only light to the hall, these few windows would have only dimly illuminated the interior, like the depths of the papyrus swamp the hall was designed to mimic.

The Pillars
Like those at Luxor, the sandstone columns are built up of circular drums, but because of their size, the builders eliminated the three lateral ridges that denoted the bundled stalks of the plant. The leaves at the foot of the shaft are nearly obscured by decorations, but the sepals (rounded triangular shapes) are clearly visible under the umbels of the open capitals. The sunk-relief carvings show pharaoh making offerings to various gods, below which are the king's cartouches. Divinities' cartouches (surmounted by two feathers and a sun disk) ring the columns both above and below. Seti I decorated the northern columns in the beautiful bas-relief for which he was noted; Ramesses II had those on the south carved in sunk relief. Their original bases, plundered from Akhenaten's heretical buildings, were removed to the Luxor Museum, and the columns now stand on cement replacements.

The Inscriptions
Like the columns, the hall decoration is divided between the bas-relief decorations of Seti and the incised ones of his son, Ramesses II. On the western wall, nearly symmetrical decorations show the procession of Amun's barque with the king worshipping it.

[c] On the north wall (where Seti had engraved the finest decorations of the temple), depictions of the barque appear again, first veiled, then unveiled.

[d] To the east of the doorway, in the upper corner, Seti appears with Thoth at the sacred persea tree, where the length of his reign is recorded on its leaves.

[e] The "battle reliefs" of Seti appear outside the northern door. Here, the king recorded the chronicles of his great battles with the enemies at Egypt's borders. The carvings have weathered poorly and are best viewed by the slanting rays of morning or afternoon sun. The carvings on the exterior wall serve as a "road map" of Seti's campaigns to rebuild the empire wasted by the neglect of Akhenaten. Following in the steps of Thutmose III, Seti conquered Palestine to the banks of the Orintes.

Although the doorways are flanked by the ritualistic scenes of massacre before Amun, the drawings on either side show the foreigners sensitively drawn, often in full-face view. In the upper register, Lebanese fell their famous cedars to supply lumber for the pharaoh's sacred barques and flagstaffs; in the lower one, Seti launches his chariot against the Bedouin while above to the left, the Canaanites pull their fleeing countrymen into the safety of their walled city. Seti defeated the Hittite king and conquered Yenoam and Bethshael, cities known through biblical references. The king returns, captives in tow, to present them to his patron god, Amun, where they will become slaves of the temple.

[f] Echoing Seti, Ramesses II commissioned similar scenes. Particularly notable is the carving (second register) where Ramesses, enthroned between Wadjet and Nekhbet, has Horus and Thoth steadying his crowns. The fluidity and movement of this composition are unusual even for post-18th Dynasty monumental artwork.

[g] Outside the wall Ramesses II battles the Hittites, but this piece, executed in the stereotyped monumental style, has none of the charm of its predecessor on the other side. In the center, the Egyptian camp, fortified by its own shields, is attacked by the Hittites; on the right, Ramesses launches his chariot against the enemy, chasing them to their walled city of Kadesh. At the far left, the Hittite king turns in surrender toward Ramesses. The tablets uncovered in Kadesh carry a different version of

the story, and historians figure the battle was probably a draw.

[h] The text of Ramesses' treaty with the Hittites covers most of this wall, the earliest such document known. Beyond it, below the scene of Ramesses leading his prisoners, is a poetical account of the battle. To continue through the main temple, return the way you came and turn right.

Third Pylon

[3] The south wall of the hypostyle hall is formed by Amenhotep III's pylon. Conceived as a monumental gateway fitting for Amun's glory, it is now a gutted shell. Behind this facade excavations revealed the remains of over a dozen other buildings used as filling for the towers. Now removed, the blocks have been reassembled into structures now standing in the open-air museum at the northern corner of the compound. Although the decorations have deteriorated badly, you can still see pharaoh riding on Amun's barque on the northern tower, while on the southern one, several columns list the offerings he has made to the god.

Beyond the pylon's gateway, a corridor fills the narrow space between the third and fourth pylons. Once four obelisks, the first pair erected by Thutmose III, the second pair by Thutmose I, filled the narrow space. Today, only one remains.

TEMPLE OF AMUN

Fourth Pylon

[4] Continue directly east along the main temple axis through the ruined gateway of the fourth pylon. Beyond it, Thutmose I erected two obelisks. The bases of columns that once supported the room remain, as do the Osiride pillars along the third pylon. Toward the center of the temple, two more pylons (4 and 5), progressively smaller, separate colonnaded halls.

[i] In the first of these halls, Hatshepsut set up rose granite obelisks, quarried in Aswan, commemorating her 16th jubilee. The northern one still stands, the second-tallest obelisk in the world. The southern one lies shattered on the ground. The long inscription running the entire length of the monument records the dedication as well as the information that they were made in only seven months.

The upper reliefs show "King" Hatshepsut, her father Thutmose I, and her nephew Thutmose III offering to the gods. When Thutmose III came to power, he had the lower parts of the monuments encased in walls. Although many Egyptologists claim the move was to hide the name of his hated aunt, the upper portions would have still been visible for miles. Simple destruction would have made more sense. Whatever Thutmose's reasoning, the walls undoubtedly protected the monuments from the vandalism of Akhenaten's reign.

[j] A granite statue of Thutmose II kneels, extending an altar in front of him. At the time he walled up the obelisks, Thutmose III added a stone roof supported by papyriform columns.

[k] The granite bas-relief against the passage wall shows Amenhotep II target shooting from a moving chariot.

Fifth And Sixth Pylons

[5] Beyond the fifth pylon, two small antechambers partially screen the colonnaded courtyards behind them. Erected by Thutmose I, the 16-sided columns and Osiris statues are the remnants of a larger courtyard, which once surrounded the Middle Kingdom temple.

[6] The sixth pylon has nearly vanished, but the walls on either side of the granite doorway still contain Thutmose III's lists of conquered peoples (southern lands to the right and Upper Retenu, now modern Syria, to the left). Directly ahead lies Amun's sanctuary, the center of his ritual cult.

The Sanctuary

[l] In the courtyard beyond the last pylon, two tall pink granite pillars carry the heraldic flowers of Upper (papyrus) and Lower (lotus) Egypt.

[m] To the north, the large statues of Amun and his consort Amaunet were dedicated by Tutankhamun when he restored the old religion following the Amarna heresy.

[H] On the temple's central axis, the granite shrine built by Philip Arrhidaeus, Alexander's half brother, replaces an earlier one of Thutmose III. The sanctuary itself is divided into two sections: in the first the god held audiences, while the room behind contained his sacred barque (its pedestal still remains). The decoration, bas-relief on the inside, sunk relief on the outside, carries the Greek-style refinement of Ptolemaic carving. The interior shows offerings to Amun in his various guises.

The outer drawings, especially those to the south, still carry traces of the original paint. The upper register traces the coronation of the king: his preliminary purification by Thoth and Horus, his coronation, his presentation by Atum and Montu, Thoth's declaration of welcome, and finally, his confirmation (under the canopy) as Amun, seated, sets the white crown on his head. To the right, Amaunet suckles the small phar-

aoh. The lower registers show Amun's barque leaving Karnak for two "station chapels," and below, its return is accompanied by the king in the barque's *naos*. To the right, note the grids the artists used as guides for their work.

Hatshepsut's Chambers
[n] Along this wall, Thutmose III inscribed records of his military victories; he's also shown dedicating gifts, including two obelisks, to Amun.

[l] In the chambers beyond, when archaeologists removed Thutmose's covering wall

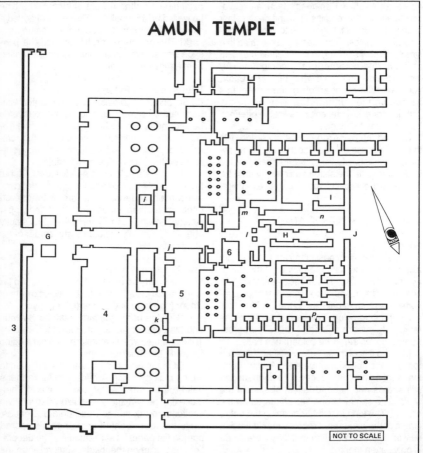

AMUN TEMPLE

NOT TO SCALE

(which ironically had preserved the queen's work) they discovered original paintings dating from Hatshepsut's reign. On the north wall, the figures of the queen have been hacked out, but much of the original coloring remains. In contrast, on the south wall, Thutmose had totally removed the queen's figures, replacing them with offering tables or bouquets, and in their cartouches, he substituted his father's and grandfather's names. The ironic result of this attempt to erase the evidence of his aunt's reign is to have named the replacement flowers and vegetables as his ancestors. Amun's figures suffered the usual disfigurement during Akhenaten's reign, and the 19th Dynasty restoration was careless.

Southern Chapels

Although the sandstone rooms on either side of the granite shrine were originally built by Hatshepsut, they were heavily redecorated by Thutmose III. He also added the walls around the shrine itself and altered (some say vandalized) the outer walls of his aunt's chambers.

[o] The rose granite false door is again the work of Thutmose III, and its figures once carried inlays of precious metals and gems. The chapels beyond are dedicated to Thutmose and Amenhotep I.

[p] The rows of hieroglyphs cut on this northern wall list the offerings devoted to Amun. The corridor was once a processional way to the jubilee hall of Thutmose III.

Original Temple

[J] This area served as a limestone quarry in antiquity, and little remains; only the patchwork pavements testify to its complex history. At the east end of the court, three granite doorsills lead to an alabaster pedestal where the god's statue once stood. The walls, the original back of the building, now lie in ruin. The jubilee hall beyond them was not originally part of the temple.

JUBILEE HALL OF THUTMOSE III

[K] At the back of the Middle Kingdom complex, Thutmose inserted a building devoted to his own ancestral cult, a personal mortuary temple in the center of Amun's religious compound. In addition to the main hall, the temple contains a chapel to Sokar, the god of darkness, an altar in a raised room on the north side aligned with the rising sun, a sanctuary of Amun decorated by Alexander the Great, and the botanical halls of Thutmose III.

The Entrance

The building's main axis runs north-south. To enter along the ancient processional way, cut right across the courtyard to the steps at the southwest corner; the old entrance [q] lies between the two statues of the king in jubilee dress. Storage chambers lie along the south wall, their reliefs in various states of preservation. The carvings on the north wall show Thutmose celebrating his jubilee festival.

[r] The "chamber of the ancestors," to your left around the corner, contains reliefs showing Thutmose making offerings to the kings who

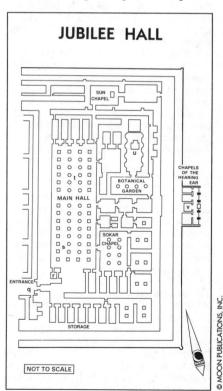

JUBILEE HALL

NOT TO SCALE

© MOON PUBLICATIONS, INC.

preceded him, whom Thutmose considered ancestors by virtue of their common royalty. The list, of course, excludes the embarrassing name of Hatshepsut. The original reliefs, which were removed in 1843 to the Louvre, have been replaced with casts.

Main Hall

The round columns running down the center of the hall create a clerestory roof above the central aisle. These tentpole-style columns, although rare in stone, were common in wooden buildings, and perhaps indicate the translation of a fragile festival tent into eternal stone. But the building also shows its human side, for when a new processional barque proved too long to make the sharp turns from the entrance to the central aisle, the priests had notches cut out in the stone columns [s] and their round bases cut away. The hall's outer roof is supported by square pillars decorated in bas-relief, which has retained much of its original color.

In Christian times, the hall was used as a church, and traces of painted saints [t], complete with gold halos, still grace several of the pillars. Here in this colonnaded hall, with its clerestory roof, the link between pharaonic temple and Christian basilica seems overwhelming. At the north end of the main hall are three shrines, the left one with figures of Amun and Mut on either side of Thutmose.

Chapel Of Sokar

A miniature temple to the god of darkness, these rooms are unfortunately not well preserved. Its columned hall leads to the three shrines at the south end which housed the god's statue, barque, and paraphernalia. This shrine, when paired with the sun room (no longer accessible), represents the forces of darkness coupled with the rejuvenating power of the sun.

The Botanical Garden

While in Syria-Palestine, Thutmose collected native plants and animals, which he then dedicated to his patron god. But since the plants and animals themselves were perishable, he had them drawn on Amun's wall as a perpetual offering. With the exception of the goose on the west wall (possibly defaced by a zealous follower of Akhenaten, since the goose was sacred to Amun) the reliefs are in good condition.

[u] North of these rooms, a long sanctuary is dominated by the raised dais at the end. Here, the *naos* held the god's statue on the immense pedestal that occupies this niche, and in front of it stands a huge offering table. Perhaps it represents the primordial mound and some Egyptologists speculate that it could be "On of the South" mentioned in the texts.

Chapels Of The Hearing Ear

[L] East of the jubilee hall, beyond the outer walls of the complex, lay Thebes. Although the temples dominated the city, her population was not permitted into the hallowed precincts. To accommodate them, small shrines dotted the enclosure, miniature temples dedicated to lesser gods who heard the petitions and duly passed them on to the great gods within the temples. The first of these small chapels built by Thutmose III centers on a large, alabaster statue of Thutmose and Amun. On either side, bases for another pair of Hatshepsut's obelisks stand shorn of their needle-like shafts.

[M] To the east lie the halls and colonnades of another, the Temple of the Hearing Ear built by Ramesses II. At its back stands the base to the highest (31 meters) obelisk known. In A.D. 357, Emperor Constantine had the obelisk moved to the Circus Maximus, where it stood until removed to Lateran Square in Rome in 1587.

OTHER SIGHTS

Eastern Gateway

Beyond these chapels, the great brick enclosure wall, begun by Nectanebo I (4th century B.C.) and completed by the Ptolemies, encloses and fortifies the domain of Amun. The gateway stands nearly 20 meters tall and is now permanently closed. Beyond it once lay Akhenaten's temple to Aton, demolished by Horemheb and used as filler for the ninth and tenth pylons. To the north, inside the wall, lies the 22nd Dynasty Temple of Osiris and the remains of several contemporary "listening" shrines.

Sacred Lake

[N] Under the modern grandstand that provides seating for the Sound and Light show lie the remains of priests' mud-brick houses. The sacred lake provided holy water for the priests' ablutions.

[O] The remains of the fowlyards for Amun's sacred geese are buried in the mound on the south side of the lake. The stone tunnel set into the rough-hewn stones lining the pool allowed them to be driven to the lake for their daily swim.

[P] A Nilometer runs along the northern side of the lake, east of the refreshment stand.

[Q] The Temple of Taharqa, a square platform, surmounts underground rooms whose inscribed texts depict the sun-god's nightly journey and his daily rebirth as a scarab beetle. In fact, this temple may have been the site of that journey's reenactment, rather like a passion play, to ensure the sun's continual victory over Chaos, which he battled nightly. Such a religious focus would also explain the huge, granite scarab [i] erected by Amenhotep III (18th Dynasty), which now stands at the north edge of the pool. Just to its north lies the tip of Queen Hatshepsut's obelisk, depicting the queen being crowned by Amun himself.

Southern Wing

Formed by a series of four pylons, this wing served as a processional way leading to the Avenue of Sphinxes, which connected the Karnak precinct with that of Mut. The entrance lies directly west of the scarab, and the courtyard in front of the seventh pylon joins the main axis of the Temple of Amun at its central court between the third and fourth pylons.

[7] This pylon is the work of Thutmose III, though the walls are 19th Dynasty. The western one bears reliefs of Merneptah battling the Libyans and the Sea People. At the south end of the courtyard, archaeologists between 1902 and 1909 discovered a buried hoard of nearly 25,000 statues from the Temple of Amun. Most of the wooden ones had been destroyed by ground water and the nearly 17,000 bronze ones were considerably damaged, but 800 stone figures were in good condition. Examples from this cache are set in front of the pylon, and the remainder now swell the Egyptian Antiquities Museum's collection.

The pylons in the remainder of this wing are being restored and are closed. The eighth pylon was built by Hatshepsut, the ninth and tenth by Horemheb. As filler, he used stone from Akhenaten's temples to Aton, and archaeologists have removed these blocks during their renovations, hoping to reconstruct parts of these temples.

[R] The small chapel in the center of the east wall commemorated Amenhotep II's jubilee; its central hall, decorated with fine low relief, retains much of its original color. Damage to Amun's figures inflicted by the Atonists was repaired by Seti I. From the 18th Dynasty onward, the tenth pylon formed the south entrance to the complex. Beyond these towers, a sacred way lined with sphinxes leads to a gate in the outer enclosure wall, and from there to the precinct of Mut.

Temple Of Khonsu

[S] Dedicated to the moon-god Khonsu, the son of Amun and Mut, this temple was started by Ramesses III but the decoration and perhaps actual construction of the courtyard and pylon are later. Not only is this temple a nearly perfect representative of classical architectural canon, its reliefs offer unique political insights into the conflicts that ultimately ended the New Kingdom. The high priests of Amun, taking advantage of a weakening central government the Ramesside kings had shifted north to the delta, became virtual rulers of Upper Egypt. The decoration shows the first of such priest-kings, Herihor, making offerings with Ramesses XI, but by the time the courtyard was decorated, "King" Herihor stood alone as pharaoh. On the pylons, Pinedjem, a later high priest, worships the gods as a king would.

The twin towers of Euergetes' Ptolemaic gateway pierces the mud-brick enclosure wall, its decoration showing the Greek ruler sacrificing to the Theban gods. Beyond the gate, under its winged sun disk, the sphinx-lined avenue stretches toward Luxor, the beginning of the sacred way. The courtyard separating it from the pylons of the temple is strewn with the remains of yet more sphinxes; the round bases are from columns that once supported a wooden-roofed porch.

The temple pylon, complete with windows and grooves for flagstaffs, is particularly well built of fitted masonry. The reliefs are of "King" Pinedjem I (21st Dynasty) and his wife Henttewe sacrificing to Theban deities.

The center portal, with reliefs added by Alexander II, opens into a colonnaded court with a double row of bud-capital papyriform columns. The shafts and walls carry representations of Herihor, as pharaoh, offering sacrifices; on the right wall—incense to the sacred barques of Amun (ram's head), Mut (human head), and Khonsu (falcon's head). The four side exits are original.

The incline at the rear of the court leads to the vestibule, and beyond, to the hypostyle hall. Even in this small temple, the hall has a raised central roof, borne on calyx-capital columns, providing light through stone clerestory grills. The king in the reliefs is Ramesses XI, while Herihor is shown here in his role as high priest. However, on either side of the northern doorway, he makes offerings before the barque of the Theban Triad, a role traditionally reserved for the pharaoh.

The sanctuary is open at both ends, and in the central section sat Khonsu's barque. The statue of Khonsu with Tutankhamun's features, which is now in the Antiquities Museum, was found in this area. Around the central core of the temple lie seven smaller rooms; the reliefs on the two on the right are well preserved and deserve a look.

On the north wall of this eastern room, you'll find the pharaoh accompanied by Hathor offering flowers to the falcon-headed Montu and his consort, Sun of Both Lands, Eye of Re, who sits in a chapel. On the west wall, he offers incense and holy water to Khonsu and ithyphallic Amun, who here is strangely lion-headed.

The corner room was dedicated to Osiris and contains a carving showing him lying dead on his bier while Isis and Nephthys mourn. The next room, which lies on the temple's main axis, housed the *naos* of the god's statue in the back niche, which was once closed by double doors.

Open-air Museum

Returning to the main Temple of Amun, visitors can see the open-air museum, which nestles into the northwest corner of the first pylon. Here archaeologists have reconstructed two Middle Kingdom temples excavated from the third pylon and the cache in the floor in front of the seventh. The red granite blocks are the remains of Amun's chapel built by Hatshepsut. While some of Hatshepsut's figures have been destroyed, others still show her offering before the gods, her young co-regent, Thutmose III, following her with Amun's barque.

[T] The delicate barque shrine of Senwosret I stands in the northwest corner of the museum. The roof is supported by pillars set on a raised floor, and the fine carvings on this shrine, both scenes and hieroglyphs, depict Amun in his ithyphallic and anthropoid forms. This chapel, built as a way station for the king's jubilee, offers a tantalizing glimpse of classical Middle Kingdom architecture, much of which has been lost.

[U] The alabaster barque shrine of Amenhotep I is simpler, its spare rectangular structure open at both ends. Inside, the king offers to Amun and the barque. The building was also intended for a jubilee, but Amenhotep died before the festival, and the south wall was completed by Thutmose I. The rest of the courtyard is filled with smaller fragments dating from the Middle Kingdom, which suggest that Amun's temple was once smaller, more refined than the present structure.

Temple Of Ptah

[V] Of the buildings to the north of the main temple, only the ruins of Ptah's temple are worth a visit if you have time. Built by Thutmose III, this temple to the patron god of Memphis was enlarged and restored by Shabaka (an Ethiopian) and several of the Ptolemies.

The entrance, which sits amid the palm trees, runs through a series of five pylons dating from late pharaonic, Ptolemaic, and Roman eras. Beyond the four-columned vestibule (note the flowered capitals) with screened walls lie three chapels dedicated to Ptah and his consort Sekhmet. A statue of Ptah (missing its head) remains in the central chapel, and a lion-headed statue of Sekhmet stands in the southern one. With the modern wooden doors to the chapel closed, the only light is from a small hole in the chapel roof, which focuses eerily on the central figures. The atmosphere that must have pervaded all pharaonic temples still clings to the sanctuary of this nearly intact temple. The roof is one of the few accessible, but there is little to see but the view.

WEST BANK SIGHTS

Luxor's West Bank has two types of monuments: mortuary temples along the Nile devoted to the cult of the dead pharaohs, and tombs, both royal and private, hidden deep in the hills. The mortuary temples are designed much like Karnak and Luxor, but the focus of worship is the former king, whose Osiride statues grace the temple and occupy its chapels.

Frustrated by the pillage of earlier, more visible tombs, New Kingdom pharaohs, beginning with Thutmose I, cut their tombs deep into the sandstone cliffs, away from public view, divorced from their mortuary temples. The move proved fruitless, for the gravediggers themselves returned to the sites, especially in troubled times, and plundered the pharaohs' treasures. The only tomb to escape nearly intact was that of a minor king, Tutankhamun, its entrance buried beneath the rubble of another, later tomb. Here, in 1922, Howard Carter, digging beneath foundations of ancient workers' huts, uncovered undreamed-of treasure, adding invaluable knowledge to our understanding of ancient Egypt.

Over the ridge to the south, a smaller valley houses the tombs of queens, while nobles' tombs, which are built on a less grand scale yet contain equally fine artwork, are scattered among the cliffs. Of the mortuary temples, Hatshepsut's, at Deir al-Bahri, is the most famous, but the Ramesseum and Medinat Habu are also worth a look.

What To Take

Days on the West Bank are usually long, hot, and tiring, so plan ahead. Wear comfortable, sturdy shoes, as you'll be climbing around over sand and shale. Cover up with cool (cotton) loose-fitting clothes to prevent sunburn (even on overcast days) and dehydration. Take sunscreen, a hat, a strong flashlight (many of the tombs are poorly lighted) and, if you're allergic to dust, a mask. Several resthouses are scattered throughout the various sites, but they are normally crowded, service is often slow, and they never seem to be handy when you're the thirstiest, so take your own snacks and water or juice.

Photo Notes

The monuments are open to photography; tomb interiors require a photo permit (you can get one at the ticket kiosk). However, officials worried about fading pigments have now banned flash photography. Enforcement is sporadic, and although a little baksheesh will often get the caretakers to look the other way, consider before you snap off a flash. The cumulative effect of innocent flashes can fade the ancient pigments. Even worse are the guards who will set up mirrors to concentrate the strong sun on the walls; discourage this practice if you can. In addition, unless you have multiple strobe units fitted with diffusers and are equipped with a flash meter, the results are dismal; hot spots wash out detail and color in the center while leaving the edges of the photo underexposed and dark. Unless you have fast film, shooting tomb interiors is useless.

Tickets/Itinerary Notes

Most of the sites on the West Bank are open daily 0700-1700. You must buy tickets at one of two ticket kiosks: one by the landing at the tourist ferry, the other near the Antiquities Office—*no tickets are available at the sites*. Students with an ISIC card can get 50% off, but they must buy their tickets at the valley kiosk. You must have a ticket for each of the following areas: (for any three tombs)

Valley of the Kings	LE10
Valley of the Queens	6
Tombs of the Nobles	6
(for each area)	
Nakht and Menna	6
Deir al-Bahri	6
Medinat Habu	6
Deir al-Medina	6
Ramesseum	6
Temple of Seti I	6

The Graffiti Cavern in the cliffs at Deir al-Bahri is closed, as are the tombs of Seti I, Thutmose III (#34), Tutankhamun (#62), Horemheb (#57), and Ramesses VI (#9) in the Valley of

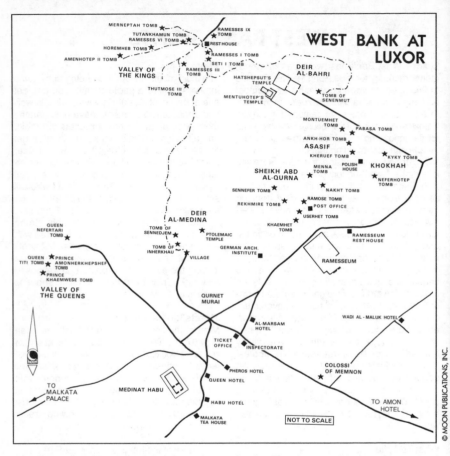

WEST BANK AT LUXOR

MERNEPTAH TOMB
RAMESSES IX TOMB
TUTANKHAMUN TOMB
RAMESSES VI TOMB
RESTHOUSE
HOREMHEB TOMB
RAMESSES I TOMB
AMENHOTEP II TOMB
SETI I TOMB
VALLEY OF THE KINGS
RAMESSES III TOMB
HATSHEPSUT'S TEMPLE
DEIR AL-BAHRI
THUTMOSE III TOMB
MENTUHOTEP'S TEMPLE
TOMB OF SENENMUT
MONTUEMHET TOMB
PABASA TOMB
ANKH-HOR TOMB
ASASIF
KHERUEF TOMB
KYKY TOMB
POLISH HOUSE
MENNA TOMB
KHOKHAH
SHEIKH ABD AL-QURNA
NEFERHOTEP TOMB
SENNEFER TOMB
NAKHT TOMB
REKHMIRE TOMB
RAMOSE TOMB
POST OFFICE
USERHET TOMB
DEIR AL-MEDINA
KHAEMHET TOMB
QUEEN NEFERTARI TOMB
TOMB OF SENNEDJEM
PTOLEMAIC TEMPLE
GERMAN ARCH. INSTITUTE
RAMESSEUM REST HOUSE
TOMB OF INHERKHAU
VILLAGE
RAMESSEUM
QUEEN TITI TOMB
PRINCE AMONHERKHEPSHEF TOMB
PRINCE KHAEMWESE TOMB
VALLEY OF THE QUEENS
QURNET MURAI
WADI AL-MALUK HOTEL
AL-MARSAM HOTEL
TICKET OFFICE
INSPECTORATE
COLOSSI OF MEMNON
TO MALKATA PALACE
MEDINAT HABU
PHEROS HOTEL
QUEEN HOTEL
TO AMON HOTEL
HABU HOTEL
MALKATA TEA HOUSE
NOT TO SCALE

the Kings, and Nefertari in the Valley of the Queens. They are undergoing conservation and reopening dates are uncertain, so check locally. Since tickets are valid for a specific site, and only for the day issued, plan your visits—the easiest way is geographical: Deir al-Bahri, the Valley of the Kings, and a few nobles' tombs, followed by the Ramesseum, Deir al-Medina, Medinat Habu, and the Valley of the Queens, will take two full days, longer if you don't hire a taxi. Start early, especially in summer. To really enjoy the West Bank takes several days.

Getting There

For LE2, either of the tourist ferries (which leave from in front of the Winter Palace or the Savoy) will take you directly to the ticket booth. They tend to run slowly so you may end up waiting nearly an hour. The local ferry (25PT) departs opposite Luxor Temple (down the bank). However, it docks about one-half kilometer above the ticket booth, so you'll have to hike down or stop by the Antiquities Office. If you hire a taxi, the driver will usually buy your tickets for you.

Getting Around

The sites are too far and too scattered to walk between, so if you don't rent a bike and bring it across (local ferry only), you'll either have to hire a car and driver or a donkey and owner. Donkeys are picturesque but slow and uncomfortable. Cars are more expensive and, depending on your bargaining abilities, run about LE50 for a half day, LE100 for a full day. Some driver/guides speak more English than others, so if you're planning on visiting the private tombs, be sure the driver understands where you want to go; many of the nobles' tombs are locked, and your driver will have to find the caretaker. A hassle-free option is to take the American Express tour of the West Bank—LE85, which includes a guide, an air-conditioned bus, and entrance tickets for the Valley of the Kings, Valley of the Queens, Medinat Habu, and the colossi; you can stay after the tour if you want.

Hiking: The trails that run over the *gebel* (mountain) make nice hikes. The most popular path is from the Valley of the Kings to Deir al-Bahri. A branch of this trail forks off at the top of the mountain and, following the path the ancient tomb artists used, runs south to Deir al-Medina and the Valley of the Queens.

COLOSSI OF MEMNON

This pair of gigantic statues (nearly 18 meters high) dominates the road that runs to the ancient sites. Statues of Amenhotep III, they once graced the entrance to his immense temple, a massive structure built to the same scale as these giants. Today, little but the colossi remain, the temple having served as a quarry during the New Kingdom.

The figures' yellow sandstone blocks (a strange choice of material—it is hard to shape yet crumbles on exposure to the elements) were brought from Idfu, 115 km to the south. On the sides of the thrones, figures of the Nile-god Hapi tie Upper Egypt's sage with the papyrus of Lower Egypt in the hieroglyphic knot of unification. The king's wife, Tiyi, and the queen mother stand at his legs. The figure in front of him is unrecognizable.

In 27 B.C., an earthquake shook the area, apparently damaging the northern (far) figure, which began emitting a tone as the sun rose, perhaps due to the cooling of the stone during the cold desert night and its subsequent warming at dawn. Greek travelers named the figure Memnon, fallen hero of Troy, who was greeting his mother, Aurora, the dawn. Greek and Roman tourists flocked to the site, often waiting several days to hear the statue sing. Graffiti, especially on the statue's left leg, testify to illustrious visitors, including Emperor Hadrian, who, with his wife Sabina, spent several days here. Alas, Septimius Severus, perhaps in an attempt to pacify the god, crudely repaired the figure, and it fell silent. Beyond the colossi, a quartzite stela proclaiming the king's devotion, his tribute, and temples, now overlooks a flat, cultivated field.

DEIR AL-BAHRI

The narrow gorge of Deir al-Bahri, which is honeycombed with ancient tombs, opens into a semicircular amphitheater formed by the sheer cliff faces of the Western Mountains. The temple, although dedicated to Amun, Hathor, and Anubis, serves as a huge private chapel built by her majesty "King" Hatshepsut so that offerings might be made to her *ka* and to that of Thutmose I, her father. A tour of the temple takes at least an hour. The site, unshaded and heated by the surrounding rocks, which reflect the searing sun, swelters at midday, so plan your visit for early morning.

Hatshepsut

Queen Hatshepsut has generated nearly as much controversy as the heretic Akhenaten. Daughter of Thutmose I and wife of Thutmose II, she was widowed without producing a male heir to the throne. Upon the death of King Thutmose II, the heir apparent, teenaged Thutmose III (son of a secondary wife) was too young to assume the throne, so Hatshepsut ruled as coregent. However, within a few years, she assumed the headdress, beard, and kilt of the royal ruler and declared herself pharaoh, the only Egyptian queen to rule as a king.

Although elaborate tales have been woven about her power politics, personality, and death, known facts about her reign are few. She retained sole control of the country until her apparently natural death, in spite of the fact that Thutmose III, then grown, commanded the Egyptian army. She ruled with the advice of Senenmut, a commoner who became the most powerful official in the country, until the last six years of her reign, when he abruptly disappeared from the records. She restored many of the temples that had fallen into disrepair during the Second Intermediate Period and sent a trading expedition to the land of Punt, probably somewhere along the coast of East Africa.

When Thutmose III ascended the throne at her death in 1458 B.C., he effaced depictions of the queen-pharaoh—supposedly in a fit of repressed anger. But not all Hatshepsut's figures disappeared under his workmen's chisels, and this selectivity has puzzled and intrigued Egyptologists for decades.

The Site

The semicircular notch in the cliffs of the Western Desert first housed the remains of 11th Dynasty royalty, including the mortuary temple of Mentuhotep-Nebhepetre I, its excavated ruins now visible to the south of Hatshepsut's main building. The queen's construction, halted at her death, left several parts unfinished, and Thutmose III had nearly all references as well as her figures erased, often substituting his father's cartouches for the queen's. Thutmose then built a third temple between and behind the first two, a singularly unhappy choice of location, for ancient landslides soon buried his monument.

At the time of the Amarna heresy, Akhenaten defaced Amun's images, which were then repaired by Ramesses II. The Ptolemaic King Euergetes II added a shrine for Imhotep and Amenhotep Son of Hapu at the top of the temple, and in Christian times, this area became a home for Coptic monks, giving the area its modern name. Although the temple was crumbling, careful restoration and conservation over the last 100 years have stabilized the structure and restored much of the original appearance.

The Temple

The wide line of the building contrasts starkly with the towering vertical cliffs that form its backdrop. Designed in three levels, the temple is hewn into the foot of the cliff, its flat courts buttressed by dressed limestone walls and linked with ascending ramps. Each terrace is separated by colonnades of pillars, which, with their dark shadows, echo the vertical lines of the sheer rock behind.

A variant of New Kingdom temples, Hatshepsut's building nonetheless contains much of the same symbolism of creation. The rising terraced courtyards lead to a hypostyle hall and beyond to the sanctuaries. The chapels for the queen and her father, as well as an open-air shrine to Amun-Re, lie nestled in the top tier back in the rock of the cliff. Separate chapels to Hathor (south) and Anubis (north) flank either side of the middle terrace.

In direct sun, the designs carved on the surfaces fade in the glaring light, and the temple stands stark, reduced to harmonious masses of light and dark, its elegant proportions seemingly wrought from the cliff's face. This integration (although blunted by the modern retaining

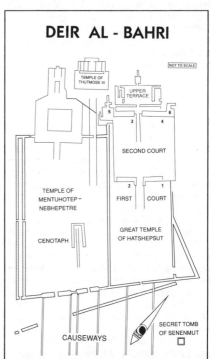

DEIR AL - BAHRI

NOT TO SCALE

TEMPLE OF THUTMOSE III

UPPER TERRACE

SECOND COURT

TEMPLE OF MENTUHOTEP-NEBHEPETRE

FIRST COURT

GREAT TEMPLE OF HATSHEPSUT

CENOTAPH

CAUSEWAYS

SECRET TOMB OF SENENMUT

© MOON PUBLICATIONS, INC.

wall erected behind the temple to protect it from rock slides) is unique in Egypt. It also appeals to the modern eye, and the temple is justly considered one of the world's architectural masterpieces.

Entrance And Lower Court
The approach to the temple enclosure was along a sphinx-lined causeway to pylons, now long vanished. The courtyard, today desert sand and rock, once bloomed with exotic trees and flowers brought to the queen from the land of Punt. Archaeologists uncovered the remains of myrrh trees, their roots still boxed in the soil that nourished them.

The colonnades on either side of the inclined ramp are supported by square pillars in front and 16-sided columns behind. Carved on the rear walls of these porticoes are scenes of northern marshlands [1] and the quarrying and transport of Hatshepsut's obelisks to Karnak [2]. The central ramp leads to the middle terrace, which, like the lower, is bounded by colonnades.

Punt Wall
[3] To the south of the ramp, the story of the queen's expedition to Punt lines the walls behind the colonnades. Unfortunately, the shallow relief has succumbed to the elements in many places and the details are difficult to follow. The story begins on the short wall to your left with Amun commissioning the journey. After their sea voyage, the Egyptians are welcomed by the king and queen of Punt (complete with the local dog). The block with the queen's figure was stolen around the turn of the century and has been replaced with a cast of a similar block in the Antiquities Museum. The queen's strange physical appearance may have been due to elephantiasis, a common infection in Africa.

In spite of the restrictions of formal registers, the ancient artists succeeded in creating the impression of a coastal settlement scattered among the trees, complete with local details like the rounded-topped African huts with their ladders. The registers show both Semitic and African people, as well as a collection of plants, animals, and produce impossible to locate together geographically, so ancient Punt's exact location remains disputed.

Moving to the right, the scene unfolds with

trading between the two peoples, the Egyptians offering trinkets in exchange for exotic plants, animals, gold, and incense. Note the natives cutting the branches of the myrrh trees to collect the aromatic gum, their axes, Egyptian style, newly received gifts. The expedition culminates with the Egyptians loading their ships with precious cargoes and sailing for home. In places, the carvings show exceptional detail such as the boats' rigging (complete with loose baboons) and the saltwater species of fish under the vessels.

Upon arrival home, the Egyptians greet their queen, who then dedicates the spoils to Amun. Note the cattle in the lower register. In the center of the wall, Horus, watched by the Nubian god Dedun, weighs gold, while Seshat records the results. Below, beside the myrrh trees, Thoth records the measuring of incense. To the right, Thutmose offers the aromatic resin to Amun's barque, while near the corner Hatshepsut offers to Amun himself. The space between them once contained a long inscription, now erased. The north wall shows the queen, again defaced, beneath a canopy, her guardian spirit behind her. This relief, which replaces the battle scenes typical of her ancestors' temples, has led to a pacifist interpretation of the queen's political policies. Whatever her usurped male prerogatives, she apparently did not personally lead her army and therefore did not conquer barbarous forces and offer Amun the customary spoils of war.

Hathor Chapel
[5] The square entrance pillars of this shrine, dedicated to Hathor, goddess of joy and love, take the form of a sistrum, the ritual rattle played during the goddess's rites. Above Hathor's triangular face, complete with cow-like ears, lies the naos-shaped sounding box with scroll clappers on either side. In the hall beyond, the column shaft forms the handle of the sistrum, and the naos above the mask makes a double-faced capital.

Large reliefs on the facade show Hathor as a cow licking Hatshepsut's hand. The same scene is repeated inside the vestibule (on the north wall) along with another showing the goddess suckling the queen, whose figure is not defaced—hardly an oversight. In the hypostyle hall beyond the vestibule, the delicate carvings on the north wall have retained much of their color. This procession, accompanied by dancing Libyans and soldiers with the branches borne on festival days, is remarkably fresh. Within the artistic conventions (or perhaps because of them), the artists blended human activities into the order and harmony of a sacred festival.

The western walls repeat the familiar scenes with the goddess as a cow. Entrance to the three shrines of the chapel proper are now closed. Beyond the gateway, no longer accessible, stand the two small figures of Senenmut, carved where the open doors would hide them, so that he could accompany his queen into eternity.

The Birth Wall

[4] Figures of the queen, her features effaced, and Thutmose III with Amun decorate the square pillars supporting the portico's restored roof; the birth scene is carved into the rear walls. This sequence may have served as the model for the similar scene at Luxor Temple. The reliefs show Amun with the queen mother Ahmose on a raised couch, surrounded by romantic poems. Their facial expressions speak to an unmistakable and abiding love. The following registers show Khnum fashioning Hatshepsut and her *ka* on his potter's wheel, her birth accompanied by Bes and the frog-deity Heqet (a consort of Khnum), the nursing of the boy-child Hatshepsut by the goddesses, and the recording of her reign.

The purpose of such scenes has been debated by scholars, some claiming purely political motivations. However, the entanglement of religion in pharaonic secular life, as well as the sequestered position of the reliefs (especially at Luxor) and the archaic tone of the language, argue for a more esoteric motivation. While the divine nature of pharaoh was apparently accepted in the Old Kingdom, later royalty may well have enhanced their sacred rights by such magical scenes. Similar iconography and beliefs accompanied the stories of Christ's holy conception, a continuation of this theme. Whatever their purpose, the fine lines and delicate expressions make this relief one of Egypt's best.

Chapel Of Anubis

[6] At the north end of the colonnade, three steps lead back into the cliffs and Anubis' temple. The slight widening of the central aisle draws the visitor forward, a device that would later invite guests into Greek temples. The vestibule roof is supported by two rows of colonnades, which, with their soft lines and simple capitals, create a soft rhythm and harmony—a style that would flower under the Greeks.

To the right, above the niche, stand Thutmose III and the falcon-headed sun-god, assimilated to Amun, to whom the main temple is dedicated. Hathor occupies the left wall.

The familiar food offerings, set with elegant precision before the jackal-headed god of the dead, fill the remaining walls. The delicately curving lines of the gazelle's horn, the grape tendrils, and the winding stem of the lotus bud as it curls around the vase anticipate the later 18th Dynasty fondness of such curves. The sanctuary at the back of the colonnaded hall was never finished; the niches at the back may have served for gods of the underworld. Note the false arch of the roof, carved into the rock, its graceful lines lacking the tension of load-bearing arches like those at Medinat Habu.

Upper Terrace

The ramp leading to the upper level is flanked by sinuous serpentine coils, which end in a vulture head, symbolizing the union of the Two Lands. Originally the top floor was framed by Osiride pillars, which Thutmose destroyed, and in later times only the granite portal re-

Anubis

JAN KIRK

mained. However, modern restorations have reerected the columns. The upper terrace, currently closed, houses the main sanctuary, chapels dedicated to the mortuary cult of Hatshepsut and her father, and a miniature sun temple.

Temple Of Thutmose III

From the south side of Hatshepsut's temple you can look down on the building of Thutmose III. Destroyed by a landslide in antiquity, the excavated remains offer little of interest; the painted relief from the temple is in Luxor Museum.

Temple Of Mentuhotep-Nebhepetre

Unlike the later New Kingdom temples, this 11th Dynasty complex contained the royal tomb. The deep trench cut into the floor of the first courtyard housed an empty coffin and a linen-wrapped statue of the king, both now in the Antiquities Museum. The tomb was converted to a cenotaph when the temple was moved back against the cliff.

This building is one of the earliest Theban temples and is remarkable for its simplicity. Like Hatshepsut's later monument, it was constructed in terraces bounded with square pillars. A pillared facade encloses three sides of the upper terrace. The square filled area in its center was once thought to be the base of a pyramid, but modern archaeologists interpret the structure as a tall, mastaba-type tomb. The ruined northern side included separate chapels for the king's wives.

Secret Tomb Of Senenmut

Before leaving the area, ask the guard for the key to Senenmut's shaft tomb. Although he built a perfectly good tomb in Qurna, he sunk a second here. The entrance descends steeply, and on the wall opposite it, a bust of Senenmut portrays his alert, if aging, features.

At the bottom of the stair a second chamber is crowned with an astronomical ceiling, the earliest and perhaps most beautiful of its kind. The great stars of the northern and southern constellations (and the monthly festivals) lie within in their 12 circles of 24 hourly compartments. The walls are inscribed with extracts from the Book of the Dead. The stairway leads to the empty and unfinished burial chambers.

VICINITY OF DEIR AL-BAHRI

Tombs Of Asasif And Khokha

Across the road, several tombs lie in the plain below the old dig house of the Metropolitan Museum expeditions. (Tombs are designated with a Theban (Th) number in the order in which they were recorded.)

Pabasa (Th #279): The most noticeable of these tombs belongs to Pabasa, Steward of the Divine Votaress. The massive mud-brick gateway of this 26th Dynasty tomb leads into several rooms with carvings, which, typical of the Saite period, imitate the style of the Old Kingdom. The scenes in the vestibule show the voyage to Abydos and the funeral procession. In the courtyard, the usual domestic scenes of fishing, hunting, and viticulture appear, but here many of them have been transferred from the walls to the pillars. Note the rare beekeeping scene on the central column and the preparation of the bedroom.

Kheruef (Th #192): A steward of Queen Tiyi, Kheruef lived during the Amarna period and the reliefs in his tomb rival those of Ramose. This tomb lies across a courtyard and its spectacular carvings make it a worthwhile visit. The reliefs depict parts of the *heb sed* festival, a procession showing the queen and her husband, Amenhotep III, and multiple scenes of dancers, musicians, and numerous animals.

Three more recently opened tombs include Ankh-Hor, Neferhotep, and Horiuf. Neferhotep (Th #49) was the Chief Scribe of Amun, and his Tut-period tomb contains an unusual range of subjects including temple, industrial, herding, and gardening scenes. Ankh-Hor (Th #414) was Chief Steward of the Divine Votaress of Amun, and Overseer of Upper Egypt during the time of Psamtik. His tomb has been meticulously restored by the Austrian mission, although little of the decoration remains.

The Trail To The Valley Of The Kings

To the north of Hatshepsut's temple several trails zigzag up the mountain. All meet at the top of the cliff and head west, skirting the curve that frames the temples below, rewarding you with an incomparable view of the valley. The path over the hills is well worn, making it nearly impossible to get lost. However, if you feel more comfortable, hire a boy (plenty hang around the temples) for a few pounds to guide you. (If you don't want to make the half-hour hike, hire a donkey—it will also come with a guide.)

VALLEY OF THE KINGS

North of Deir al-Bahri, the desert mountains close around a narrow defile. Here the pharaohs of the New Kingdom, in the futile hope of foiling tomb robbers, sunk their tomb chambers deep into the limestone cliffs of this desolate wilderness. From the pyramid-shaped heights of the towering mountains, the silence of the mountain-goddess Mertseger permeated the still valley. Only hyenas and jackals visited the desolate hills, leaving solitary tracks on the windswept gravels. Only the gravediggers, like moles, burrowed deep into its parched outline. Only the occasional funeral processions (followed by the inevitable tomb robbers) brought life to this area, which had become the Valley of the Shadow of Death.

Itinerary Notes
Ancient funeral sledges carrying mummified pharaohs followed the same path now taken by the modern road that snakes up Wadi al-Maluk. Excavated by various archaeological groups, the royal tombs have been shored up and lighting installed. Paved pathways between the 62 tombs, now cleared of rubble, make access easy. Small signs give both the name of the tomb's occupant and its number (in its order of discovery, not location).

The Tombs
The two best examples of the early-style tombs are those of Thutmose III and Amenhotep II. However, Thutmose's tomb is closed for restoration.

The two transitional tombs, those of Tutankhamun and Horemheb (currently closed), were built at the close of the Amarna period. The first, small and cramped, was not designed for the royal figure it housed. Perhaps begun by Ay before the capital moved north, its atypical design actually lies outside the main development of royal tombs.

From the transitional form of Horemheb's tomb, you can trace the evolution to the straight-corridored Ramesside tombs. For the adventurous, other tombs are marked on the map. Note: the most beautiful tomb in the valley, that of Seti, is closed indefinitely for restoration.

The Plans
At first, the royal tombs followed the general patterns inherited from the Middle Kingdom. Entrance hallways led far into the rock to a deep well. A trap for rainwater, an obstacle to grave robbers or the symbol of Sokar's tomb, or perhaps all three, it blocked passage to the remaining chambers. Beyond, through a doorway sealed at the funeral, workers excavated a columned vestibule, its walls covered with divinities. In the early tombs this vestibule lay at right angles to the corridor, but in later ones, it ran parallel to the entrance hall. Behind the vestibule, the burial chamber contained the king's sarcophagus and small niches; in later times, larger rooms stored possessions the king would need in eternity.

The Decorations
In spite of New Kingdom skepticism, Egyptians continued to decorate royal tombs with magic rituals for pharaoh's journey through the Duat (underworld). Instinctively, they still believed his successful battle with the forces of darkness ensured their own continued existence. The daily appearance of the sun was likened to the dead king emerging into eternity and finding his place among the stars.

The Texts
Funerary texts date from the Old Kingdom, but the best known of the New Kingdom comprise the Book of the Dead. This early literature, like the modern Bible or Koran, is a collection of texts providing guidelines and magic spells to assist the soul in its spiritual journey through the underworld. In these tombs, the texts spread across the walls as if they were a gigantic, unrolled papyrus. Although the several books all show the voyage of the sun-god on his solar barque along the celestial river of the netherworld, each text seems to emphasize a different aspect of the life/death/rebirth doctrine. (This literary selection includes the: *Book of Amduat,*

Book of the Gates, Book of Caverns, Litany of Re, Book of Aker, Book of Day, and *Book of Night;* see pp. 68-69.) In these books, Re as the sun travels through the 12 hours of the night to his rising at dawn while Re as the incarnate flesh (pharaoh) reemerges at the end of the journey as human spirit. The dead king, assimilated to Osiris, is avenged by Horus. Khepri, the scarab beetle of Re, grows from egg to winged adult, to emerge at sunrise between the mountains guarded by the lions of Yesterday and Tomorrow. The strange pictorials are not a departure from but an outgrowth of the ancient texts.

Tomb Of Thutmose III (#34)

Currently closed, this tomb lies at the upper end of the valley. (If you've come down the path from Deir al-Bahri, it's on your left.) The entrance, reached by a steep metal stairway, lies at the end of the path, and only Amun-Re knows how the Egyptians wrestled the heavy sarcophagus up this cliff. Several descending corridors lead to the well, its star-studded ceiling symbolic of night. Beyond it, at nearly right angles, lies the vestibule, its walls painted with 741 different deities, many of which we'll meet again in the burial chamber. At the room's end, yet another corridor leads to the burial vault.

The stick-like figures, the work of skilled artists, reduce terrible demons and monsters of the Duat to dry abstractions. The text begins on the left, and the first two hours are broken into four registers. The stick-figure format, which dates from the end of the Middle Kingdom, imitates that used on papyrus rolls and was applied to all early 18th Dynasty tombs. As usual with royalty, scant reference is made to the tomb's owner; on the north face of the western pillar, the king's mother stands behind him in a divine barque, and in the register below, three wives and a daughter follow him. To the right, the divine tree called Isis suckles the young king.

In the center of the oval, nearly cartouche-shaped chamber stands Thutmose's quartzite sarcophagus mounted on a cracked limestone podium. (His body was found at the Deir al-Bahri cache.) On both the lid and box the sky-goddess Nut stretches protective wings over the areas once occupied by his limbs. The space

around his sarcophagus suggests that this coffin, like Tut's, may have been encased in golden shrines. The small chambers on either side of the main room stored the funerary objects buried with the king.

Tomb Of Amenhotep II (#33)

This tomb, when opened in 1898 by Loret, still contained Amenhotep's mummy. In a side chamber off the burial room, excavators discovered nine more mummified bodies—New Kingdom royalty rewrapped after their tombs had been robbed and hidden here by priests of the 21st Dynasty. These mummies were moved to the Antiquities Museum, leaving Amenhotep to enjoy his solitude, but after a modern robbery attempt, he too was moved to the safety of the museum.

In spite of being unfinished, the tomb's steep, uneven corridors plunge farther into the cliffs than any other. Like the previous tomb, the descending corridors (over 90 steps) lead to the well and into an antechamber. With the exception of the well, which, although unfinished, is painted like that of Thutmose III, these rooms are undecorated; the vestibule hadn't even received its final smoothing.

From the vestibule, a right-angled corridor leads to the square burial chamber. In the "pillared hall" the blue ceiling is studded with yellow stars; its walls, painted yellow in imitation of papyrus, carry a shortened version of *Amduat*. The delicate, sure sketches on the pillars showing the king receiving the sign of life from Osiris, Anubis, or Hathor were never completed. Unfortunately, the glass panels (erected to protect the walls from tourists' questing fingers, which had begun to damage the paintings) glare in the primitive lighting. The king's sarcophagus, now empty, still lies in the sunken area at the back of the hall. The reburied mummies along with some funerary equipment were found in the second chamber on the right.

Tomb Of Tutankhamun (#62)

Currently closed. Undoubtedly the most famous tomb in the valley, this tiny vault contained a profusion of 18th Dynasty chariots, beds, statues, and jewelry—in all, some 1,700 items, most now housed in the Antiquities Museum. When the size and value of Carter's discovery in 1922 was realized, several archaeologists, including staff from New York's Metropolitan Museum, offered to help in clearing the tomb, assistance Carter was delighted to accept. (For Carter's own version of the discovery, read his book, *Tomb of Tutankhamun.*) Because the pieces were moved only after they had been carefully drawn, documented, photographed, and wrapped, the task took nearly 10 years. Items were then taken to the "laboratory" at the tomb of Seti II, where Arthur Mace, associate curator of the Egyptian Expedition, cleaned and stabilized them. Many pieces, the victims of early grave robbers, had so deteriorated that Mace found his work as taxing as it was exciting.

The tomb was documented by the superb photographic work of Harry Burton, whose prints still dominate the literature. Burton shot over 1,800 photos in Tut's tomb, and from his plates came the huge blowups that decorated the walls of the touring Tut exhibit. If electricity was unavailable, Burton devised systems of mirrors to reflect sunlight into the dark caverns. He hung blackout curtains in an empty tomb to create a darkroom, for in those days the heavy glass plates had to be developed directly after exposure.

Unfortunately, the tomb's small interior and average artwork don't match the splendor of its furnishings. Since the tomb was never intended for a royal burial, its architecture is atypical, and its arrangement, with its right angles, marks a transition between those of the early 18th Dynasty and the straight Ramesside tombs. Its entrance hall goes straight into the earth (the first few steps are original, offering Carter his first glimpse of the tomb). The short corridor leads to the antechamber where the animal-headed beds, the chariots, the throne, footstools, and chests lay jumbled together. The small burial chamber is dominated by the quartzite sarcophagus, which still contains Tut's outer coffin and his mummy. When Carter discovered this tomb, the three golden shrines on display in the Antiquities Museum encased the sarcophagus, filling nearly all available space. The burial chamber is the only decorated room in the tomb. Although its pigments are fresh, its designs, which were recovering from the Amarna period, exhibit neither the grace of their predecessors nor the skill of their descendants.

On the north wall, Ay stands before Tut's mummy performing the Opening of the Mouth ceremony, for by burying the dead king he established his own right to the throne. In the other scenes, Nut greets Tut, and the king with his *ka* embraces Osiris. On the west wall, artists painted the first Hour of the Amduat. Along the entrance wall, but nearly impossible to see, Tut, followed by Anubis, stands before Hathor, who gives him life. The eastern wall drawings of the dead king's sarcophagus dragged on a sledge are common in private tombs, but unusual in the mythological context of royal monuments.

The treasury, location of the smaller shrine with its jars and golden protective goddesses, lies off the burial chamber, through the small doorway on the right. Its entrance, when discovered by Carter, was guarded by the prone black jackal with the gold-lined ears. Beyond the burial chamber is the short doorway to the annex, now closed with bars. Here, Carter found even more goods heaped in the orderly confusion created by ancient robbers and the consequent tidying of contemporary priests.

Tomb Of Horemheb (#57)

Currently closed, this tomb is typical of the transitional architecture that followed the Amarna experiments. Its descent, long and steep, is through undecorated halls to the well room, where figures of the king and the various gods to whom he offers appear bright against the blue-gray walls. The room beyond, decorated to mimic a burial chamber, was left unfinished, and the entrances to the tomb beyond sealed. Note the traces of painting around the doorway, an extension of the wall designs that once covered the plastered entrance. Thieves, not convinced they had broken into an unfinished tomb, discovered the stairway that led downward into the main part of the tomb buried in the chamber floor. The corridor plunges deep into the rock toward the antechamber and is a stylistic duplicate of the well room above.

Ma'at guards the entrance to the burial chamber, which continues along a straight line. On the unfinished walls you can see the artists' work in progress, from the layout of grids to the final carvings. In this tomb, the stick figures metamorphose into rounded, detailed forms. The *Book of the Gates* begins to your left and runs around the chamber walls. In the second storage chamber (on your left) the figure of Osiris before a *djed* pillar is worth the short side trip.

Tomb Of Merneptah (#8)

Tomb architecture changed radically with this chamber of a grandson of Seti I. The central corridor plunges straight into the cliff, and its rooms, with one exception, all lie on the original axis. Although many of the decorations were destroyed when the tomb flooded, those of the false burial chamber are worth the trip down if you have the time and enjoy exploring.

Over the entrance, Isis and Nephthys worship the familiar sun disk with its sarcophagus and ram-headed sun-god. The paintings in the false burial chamber are intact. About halfway down the second corridor lie the remains of a gigantic sarcophagus, its lid bearing sections of both the *Book of Amduat* and the *Book of Gates.* At the bottom of the corridor, the pillared chamber is dominated by the burial vault; the side aisles are covered by flat roofs. The inner, anthropoid sarcophagus still rests in the burial chamber; Merneptah's body was recovered in Amenhotep II's tomb. This huge tomb, with its ruined gloom, creates a haunting atmosphere against which ancient grave robbers must have steeled their nerves.

Tomb Of Ramesses III (#11)

This tomb, also known as the Tomb of the Harpers from one of its paintings, offers scenes of daily life unique in a royal tomb. The entrance steps are split by an inclined plane to facilitate moving the sarcophagus. Two figures of Ma'at kneel at the entrance, protecting those who enter with sheltering wings; the *Litany of Re* decorates the corridor walls.

[1] The first of the small storage rooms is filled with kitchen scenes: slaughtering, cooking, baking the rounded loaves of bread.

[2] Across the hall, ships with sails furled and others with canvas set sail along the walls.

[3] The armory shows weapons, standards, and armor. Note the black bull of Meri (right), who stands on the "Southern Lake," and the black cow of Hesi on the "Northern Lake."

[4] The treasury includes drawings of utensils, furniture, and elephants' tusks. The tall couches were mounted by steps, the false-necked vases

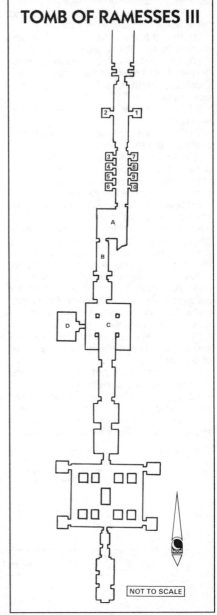

TOMB OF RAMESSES III

NOT TO SCALE

© MOON PUBLICATIONS, INC.

under them imported from Greece.

[5] Here the king sails through the sacred fields, where he inspects the activities.

[6] The 12 forms of Osiris shown here are possibly linked to the 12 *decans* of the night.

[7] Hapi, personification of the Nile, blesses grain-gods and offers to the serpent-headed goddess Napret (corn) and uraeus-snakes fitted with aprons.

[8] Female and hermaphroditic deities reminiscent of private tombs bring offerings.

[9] Oars and sacred cattle dominate the decorations in this store room.

[10] Two harpists sing to Shu and Atum, while Anhor and Harsomtus receive the king. The text of the song covers the entrance wall, and the tomb was named for this scene.

[A] Beyond these rooms, the corridor widens. The dead-end tunnel to the left marks the point where ancient excavators broke into the neighboring tomb (#10), an indication that even the priests did not keep track of tomb locations. At this point, the original builder, Sethnakht (founder of the 20th Dynasty), abandoned the tomb. Under Ramesses III, construction resumed; the axis was shifted to the right and digging continued. The goddess on the rear wall raising the water jar represents the south.

[B] The corridor is lined with paintings from the fourth (left) and fifth (right) hours of the *Book of Amduat.*

[C] On the left wall is the fourth chapter of the *Book of Gates,* and below it, the four races of men: Egyptians, Asiatics (with pointed beards and colored dress), Negroes, and Libyans (wearing feathered headdresses). On the right wall appears the fifth chapter of the *Book of Gates.*

[D] The small room to the right shows scenes from the *Book of Amduat.*

Tomb Of Ramesses VI (#9)

Currently closed. The number of inscriptions, their size and excellent state of preservation, as well as the handy location (immediately above Tut's) make this tomb one of the valley's most visited. Called by the Greeks the Tomb of Memnon, its corridors, filled with Greek and Coptic graffiti, attest to hundreds of years of tourist visits. Begun by Ramesses V, the tomb was usurped and enlarged by Ramesses VI. The debris from this construction, as well as the huts erected by his workers, covered the entrance to Tut's tomb, preserving it from subsequent robberies.

The six long corridors of Ramesses' tomb are broken only by the pillared false burial chamber [B]. The well room [A] is a vestige of its former self, and the streamlined false burial chamber only dimly echoes the complex chambers seen in earlier tombs. The corridors beyond, rather than being offset, continue directly through this chamber on their way to the tomb's end. Although the style and exactness of the artwork are inferior to that of the 18th and even 19th dynasties, the bright pigments and simple elegance of the sunk relief as well as the large selection of texts unavailable elsewhere spotlight many of the changes that actually occurred as early as Merneptah's reign.

The outer lintel carries the standard ram-headed Re and scarab; to the left lie a stylized mountain and figures of Isis and Nephthys. Beginning at the entrance of the first corridor, just beyond the figure of Ramesses presenting a

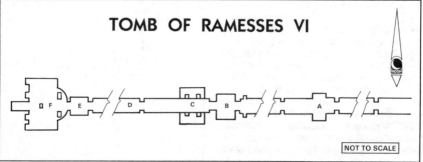

TOMB OF RAMESSES VI

NOT TO SCALE

© MOON PUBLICATIONS, INC.

lamp to Horus of the Horizon, stretch the oval co-coons of the *Book of the Caverns*. On the other side runs the *Book of Amduat*. Both texts are complete and decorate the wall well into the false burial chamber.

[C] The far wall of this room shows a double scene of Ramesses VI offering to Osiris. On the pillars, the king offers to Khonsu, Amun-Re, Mertseger, Ptah-Sokar, Ptah, and Re-Herakhty. The astronomical ceiling is repeated and better preserved in the burial chamber.

[D] The next corridor is guarded by four winged serpents, the goddesses Mertseger and Selket (right), and Nekhbet and Neith. The passage walls are filled with the hours from *The Book of Amduat;* the ceiling supports the barques from the *Book of the Day* and the *Book of the Night.*

[E] The small vestibule contains texts from the *Book of Coming Forth by Day,* which includes (left) the Negative Confession. The ceiling depicts the resurrection of Osiris: in the first register, the king sails in the barques of day and night, in the second, Osiris rises from his bier.

[F] In the burial chamber, the *Book of Aker* occupies the rear and right walls (next to the mummy on the mound). The black granite sarcophagus now lies broken and scattered, the victim of treasure hunters who believed it contained gold. The ceiling bears the beautiful, back-to-back versions of the *Book of the Day* and the *Book of the Night.*

Tomb Of Ramesses IX (#6)

This unfinished tomb contains some of the most enigmatic drawings in the valley. The artwork, which follows the themes and style of the Ramesside tombs, becomes yet more opulent. Only the first three corridors and the false burial chamber had been finished at the time of the king's death, so the corridor beyond was widened and hastily finished to receive the sarcophagus, and its artwork suffered.

Many of the scenes in this tomb are now familiar—*Book of Amduat, Book of Caverns,* and the *Litany of Re*—Yet the portraiture in this tomb takes on greater likeness of the king, and some of the mythological scenes have been described as "hardly conventional." Note the bull- and dog-headed figures (right) in the first corridor. In the next corridor, in a scene that has captured the attention of mystics and archaeologists alike, the mummified king, with his head lying in a hillock, stretches out his arms; once ithyphallic, he lost his penis to a prudish visitor. Above him the scarab beetle pushes the solar disc across the sky. Just as the sun's rays revive biological life laying dormant in the netherworld of Sokar, so does it warm the dead Osiris, initiating his rebirth into eternity. This richly symbolic scene, which fixes the dead king's relationship with the living, is a premier example of the multiple metaphors used with unerring touch by Egyptians in their religious art.

TOMBS OF THE NOBLES

In contrast to the ritual scenes appearing on kings' tomb walls, paintings and carvings in nobles' tombs show the deceased in an idealized version of his home and estate, often with his family and perhaps friends gathered in a banquet in his honor.

Both decoration and layout of the nobles' tombs were adopted from earlier Old and Middle kingdom tombs. The entrance was through a courtyard while the doorway led to a transverse hall, which was usually painted with scenes showing the tomb owner's career, scenes of daily life, and offerings brought to him. Beyond this hall, a corridor—often with burial scenes—led into the burial chamber; the actual grave was down a shaft or steeply sloping corridor. The statue of the deceased, no longer confined to a sealed chamber (the *serdab*) or positioned as if emerging from a spiritual false door as it was in Old Kingdom mastaba tombs, stands at the end of the burial chamber in a cut-out niche. The false door, the focus of earlier tombs, still appears, although less obviously than in former ages.

Decorations include depictions of the deceased's funeral procession and scenes that show him hunting or fishing. Offering bearers bring him sacrifices, and workshops supply goods ranging from gold collars and leather sandals to boats for shipping the products of his estates. Workers sow and harvest grain and slaughter cattle. The Egyptians believed these scenes, when animated by the correct magical formulas, would come alive to supply the deceased with food, drink, laborers, and entertainment.

The nobles' tombs are grouped within the sweeping arm of the road to the Valley of the Kings and the turnoff to Deir al-Bahri primarily in two groups: Sheikh Abd al-Qurna, named for the Muslim holy man whose tomb rests on the summit of the hill, and Asasif. For those at Asasif, see p. 347. Of the ones nestled around the village at Qurna, only the most popular tombs are covered below; check with the guides for others that may be open, if you have the time and desire.

Tomb Of Ramose (Th #55)

The most beautiful private tomb in the valley belongs to Ramose, vizier under Akhenaten. The tomb's artwork was executed both before and after Akhenaten's brief reign, and here you can easily compare the two styles. The delicate carving on the entrance walls has produced breathtaking portraits of refined style and sure touch, typical of the relaxation of strict artistic canon that began under Amenhotep III.

The painted scene of the funeral on the southwest wall shows (in the swaying bodies of the mourning women) the lyrical movement in figures that was emerging at the same time. These tendencies, combined with the heretical pharaoh's demand for naturalism, created the new style referred to as Amarna art. The two sides of the door directly opposite the entrance carry work of the classical style (left as you face it) and the exaggerated style of Amarna (on the right) where Ramose is receiving golden collars in thanks for his service.

Tomb Of Sennefer (Th #96)

Up the hill, next to the villagers' houses, is the tomb of Sennefer, mayor of Thebes during the reign of Amenhotep II. The well-known grape arbor ceiling makes this tomb worth the climb. These beautiful paintings, rendered on the undulating surfaces of the chambers, still retain their freshness, and the quality of the drawing makes the visitor feel as if he could practically pick the ripe fruit. The scenes on the walls are no less beautiful.

[a] Sennefer's funeral procession and Hathor and Osiris.

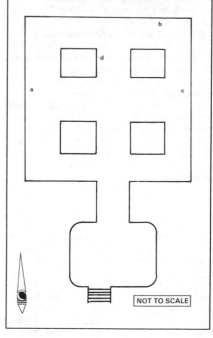

TOMB OF SENNEFER

NOT TO SCALE

© MOON PUBLICATIONS, INC.

[b] The boats transporting the deceased to Abydos.

[c] Sennefer as a mummy lies on his couch, ministered to by Anubis; his *ba* is between Isis and Nephthys.

[d] The sacred tree-goddess.

Tomb Of Rekhmire (Th #100)

The paintings in the nearby tomb of Rekhmire, vizier under Thutmose III and Amenhotep II, are one of the richest sources of insights into ancient Egypt.

[a] Foreign tribute comes to Rekhmire's office: Sub-Saharan animals—giraffes, monkeys, and a tame lion—as well as Cretans with their vast vases decorated in nautical motifs, and Syrians bring chariots and horses.

[b] The entrance hall shows Rekhmire in his office as vizier collecting taxes from Upper Egyptians.

[c] On the other side of the door, the paintings show him collecting from Lower Egyptians.

[d] Beyond, he inspects temple workshops and the chariotry, as well as the standard agricultural scenes.

[e] The grapes, harvested from the supporting arbors, are trod in big tubs; the crushers hang onto ropes suspended from a frame for support. The juice is strained and then jarred.

[f] Rekhmire goes hunting in the desert.

[B] The long corridor, which slopes to the rear niche, is covered with rarer scenes of daily life and the methods applied by artists, goldsmiths, leather workers, and carpenters.

[g] These scenes show workers preparing food; slaves store grain in round-topped silos, to be dispersed later, often as wages.

[h] Views of industrial workers, including armorers, carpenters, and sculptors.

[i] Scenes from Rekhmire's funeral procession, and the offering lists.

[j] This pond shows the Egyptians' use of

perspective, for the trees edging the garden on the right wall are drawn in profile and thus appear to lie on their sides, as do the fish in the pool, while the ducks swim upright.

[k] The banqueting scene.

Tomb Of Userhet (Th #54)
Southeast of Sennefer's tomb lie two additional tombs worth visiting. The closest is that of Userhet, a royal scribe who was brought up in the court with the king's children and who served under both Seti I and Ramesses II. A large variety of beautifully rendered scenes set off this tomb: agriculture (winemaking, cattle), marsh lands, military, and funerary. Note the details of design and shading.

Tomb Of Khaemhet (Th #57)
Next door is the tomb of Khaemhet, a royal scribe who was overseer of the granaries of Upper and Lower Egypt during the time of Amenhotep III. One of the best-carved tombs in Egypt, its style is more firm, less feminine than that of Ramose. Its beautiful scenes of harvest, market, and freight ships contain a multitude of human touches, such as the sleeping chariot driver and the flute player following the harvest. Ships show the deceased making the pilgrimage to the holy city of Abydos, goal of every pious Egyptian; and in paradise, the deceased is welcomed to the Fields of Yaru. The tomb is also noted for the sequence depicting the surveying of fields.

Tomb Of Nakht (Th #52)
The tomb of Nakht dates from the beginning of the 18th Dynasty, and while the scenes show no particular sweep of history, they do contain interesting details. In one, Nakht supervises his farmhands; note the worker drinking from the water skin hanging from the tree and another cutting down a tree. In the harvest scene, two women, one who lacks an arm, are gleaning. Nakht and his wife sit among scenes of offerings, hunting, and winemaking. The false door at the end of the corridor was painted to imitate the pink granite from Aswan; the picture shows the statue that once stood in the niche but was lost at sea on its way to the U.S.

Menna (Th #69)
Scribe of the Fields of the Lord of the Two

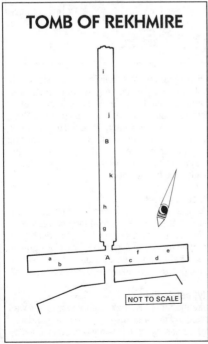

TOMB OF REKHMIRE

NOT TO SCALE

Lands, Menna was a powerful man, and he obviously made enemies, for his eyes have been damaged, his throwing stick cut through, and the balance in the judgment scene has been tampered with. The paintings do, however, maintain their beauty, especially behind the protective glass wall. Like Nakht's tomb, the details here are especially human: the quarreling girls, and another group in which one girl removes a thorn from the foot of another.

THE RAMESSEUM

Built by Ramesses II to house his mortuary cult, this sprawling ruin is perhaps the most romantic in Thebes. Ramesses II designed his works on a massive scale, even by Egyptian standards, and the Ramesseum is only one of numerous building projects he sponsored. The complex includes not only the massive main temple, but also a royal palace, a mortuary temple of Seti I, and numerous mud-brick magazines. The temple itself, which faces southeast, follows the main outlines of classical design, with two pylons and courtyards.

The modern entrance opens into the second court, which is strewn with rubble, including the shattered remnants of a statue of the king, which measured seven meters between his shoulders; additional pieces, including the feet and hands, have tumbled into the depression below. This statue, many believe, was the model for Shelley's poem "Ozymandias." Undoubtedly carved by gangs of workmen, it testifies to the ancient sculptors' training, both artistically and in their ability to work together to produce a unified whole.

First Court
The depression beyond was once the first court. At its end lie the ruins of the first pylon, which collapsed with the continued flooding of the courtyard and the eroding of its foundations. The trees here, growing around the shattered remnants of sculpture, make it an ideal place for a picnic lunch.

The Palace
Against the southern side of the first court stood the audience hall of the king's royal palace. Like

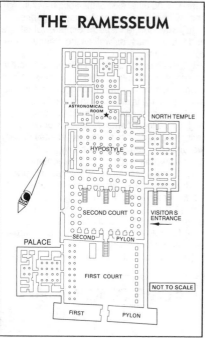

THE RAMESSEUM

ASTRONOMICAL ROOM

NORTH TEMPLE

HYPOSTYLE

SECOND COURT

VISITOR'S ENTRANCE

PALACE

SECOND PYLON

FIRST COURT

NOT TO SCALE

FIRST PYLON

© MOON PUBLICATIONS, INC.

private homes, this building was divided into public rooms (including a Window of Appearances set into the outer wall and a reception or throne room) and private apartments. Such buildings were invariably attached to New Kingdom temples at the southwestern corner and may not only have served as a home for the king when he visited his temples, but also for his spirit once he had died.

Second Court
Dominated by the Osiride pillars, this court contains incised reliefs of an offering procession to Min (top) and part of the Battle of Kadesh (bottom) on the remaining pylon. The black granite head belongs to one of a pair of colossi that once guarded the entrance to the hypostyle hall.

Hypostyle Hall
Like the one at Karnak, the hypostyle hall was designed to mimic the primeval forest and was lighted only by the clerestory windows formed by

the tall central rows of columns. The ceiling of this hall was decorated with the flying vultures, and the eastern wall shows the king and his sons attacking the fortress at Dapur; the Hittites attempt to repel the Egyptians scaling the walls protected by shields slung over their backs.

Astronomical Ceiling

Beyond the great hypostyle hall are five rooms, rather than the customary three. The first is a small hypostyle hall with an astronomical ceiling. The drawings, which include the Egyptian forms of the northern constellations (see "Dendera," p. 320), contain the oldest 12-month calendar known, but whether the months are lunar or solar is debated. The figures also link the helical rising of Sirius to the Nile inundation.

On the western wall, the king sits under the persea tree while Atum, Seshat, and Thoth record the years of his reign. The small rooms beyond (the second was a library) led to the now-ruined sanctuary.

North Temple

Long a puzzle, modern excavations have revealed that this building served as a small mortuary temple for Seti I. Its two sections indicate it was dedicated to both Seti and Ramesses I (Seti's father) in their deified forms, which were linked to Amun.

Magazines

These well-preserved buildings covered about three times the area of the temple, their mud-brick vaults among the earliest known. Built against a standing wall, the grooved bricks, thinner than those of the walls, were canted back against the rear support. Several examples of these arches remain in the northern corner of the enclosure.

DEIR AL-MEDINA (THE WORKMEN'S VILLAGE)

Home for the workmen who fashioned the royal tombs, the remaining foundations of this village lie on the path between Deir al-Bahri and the Valley of the Queens. The nearly identical houses are all small and most share common walls. The entrance vestibule was supported by a single column, with the main chamber lying behind it; the mud-brick divan is a feature still found in village homes. The stairways led to long-vanished roofs, and the kitchens occupied the open courts behind them. Within the confines of the village, the houses do vary; the largest, most spacious belonged to the chiefs of the crews.

The Tombs

These artists, who walked each day to the Valley of the Kings to build the beautiful tombs, also prepared their own houses of eternity. Their tombs date mostly from the Ramesside period, and although the subjects encompass the standard themes, here the skill of the artists, unfettered by rigid canon, shows in the ease of the drawing and the delicate textures and shading of the figures. The tombs of Sennedjem and Inherkhau are open and the delicate, fresh artwork repays the short climb up the hill to the necropolis, for here the tombs are built and decorated on a human scale.

The Temples

To the north of the village, in the cut that led to the Valley of the Kings, stand several temples, the most noticeable one built by the Ptolemies and dedicated to Hathor. The columned hall opened into a narrow portico in front of the three sanctuaries. The left one shows the Judgment; the crocodile-monster, the Devourer of Souls, looms unexpectedly large. Just beyond, the temple of Amenhotep I rises on the upper terrace, that to Hathor, built by Seti I, on the lower. Across the valley stands the remains of a temple to Amun built by Ramesses II where the Theban Triad was worshipped. The huge pit was excavated in Greco-Roman times, perhaps to supply the temple with water.

VALLEY OF THE QUEENS

West of Deir al-Medina, in a small but beautiful valley, lie the tombs of the pharaohs' queens and princes. These tombs, less pretentious than those of their husbands and fathers, are equally lovely. The decorations are devoted to offerings and rituals, and in the princes' tombs, their father leads them through the dark hours of death, introducing them to the gods and ensuring that their correct answers will admit them to Duat. The most famous of these tombs, that of Nefertari, wife of Ramesses II, is closed for restoration studies. In addition to the following well-known tombs, that of Sethirkhopshef (#43) is also open, but you'll have to ask to see it; take a strong flashlight, as it has no lights.

Tomb Of Prince Khaemwese

This little-visited tomb of Khaemwese, a son of Ramesses III, lies up the hill behind the souvenir booths; its brilliant murals are worth the short climb. Most of the paintings show Khaemwese with his father offering to the gods and then accompanying him past the corridor, filled with the guards, to the Fields of Yaru. The boy is shown with his hair cut in the side-lock of youth. The princes were allowed to play with their companions while selected officers taught them to swim, drive, and shoot. When old enough the prince would serve a military apprenticeship along with the sons of foreign rulers who had been brought to Egypt to be trained in Egyptian ways. The crown prince was often wed to a sister (as Osiris had married Isis) or half-sister, although such marriages were not common among other Egyptians.

In the first corridor, the king offers to the deities in the name of his son, while in the side rooms, he worships the mortuary gods, the four sons of Horus and Anubis. Isis and Nephthys greet Osiris (or Sokar) on the back wall. The second corridor carries inscriptions from the *Book of the Gates,* the strange, knife-wielding figures their guardians. In the burial chamber, the king appears for his son before Osiris; note the four sons of Horus perched upon the lotus blossom.

Tomb Of Queen Titi

This Ramesside tomb built by Titi contains beautiful artwork, the delicate colors vibrant against their white or gold backgrounds. The most noticeable mural is that showing Hathor (the cow) appearing from between the Mountains of East and West. Beside her, a human-form Hathor pours the water of the Nile from a persea tree—magic fluid that will rejuvenate the queen, who casually sits on a cushion across the room.

Tomb Of Prince Amonherkhepshef

Another son of Ramesses III, this prince's tomb is easily accessible and well preserved; its paint-

ings are equal to those in the tomb of his brother. In the first rooms the king leads his son, who carries the fan of his office, before the deities, while in the corridor he leads him past the keepers of the gates. At the rear chamber stands a granite sarcophagus that contained the mummy of a child. The prince, though he died in infancy, was accorded a royal burial.

MEDINAT HABU

The farthest south of the mortuary temples, Medinat Habu was built by Ramesses III. "Sacred since the beginning of time," the site was originally occupied by a small temple to Amun built by Hatshepsut and Thutmose III, which stands to the east of the modern gateway. Ramesses, who ruled between 1182 and 1151 B.C., built the Great Temple and then settled numerous war prisoners around it; with its enclosing wall and massive storage magazines, the area grew into a city that maintained its population well into Coptic times, when it was known as Djeme.

The fortifications, which followed New Kingdom military design, offered the citizens of the West Bank shelter from the raiding bands that roamed the countryside during the turbulent years of the Late Period and from the Bedouin attacks that followed.

Entrance

[A] The modern road ends at the quay, which was connected to the Nile via a canal. The entrance to the complex is through the fortified towers of the Great Gate, a forerunner of those adorning castles in Europe during the Middle Ages. In the southern recess [a] the statue of Ptah served the commoners who came to pray, transmitting their messages to the Great Amun, who resided within.

The Towers: Now closed to visitors, the upper levels of these gates once served as a royal retreat, for scenes show Ramesses surrounded by slender young women who offer him food, drink, and flowers. At least some of these ladies were the king's children, but others may well have been members of the royal harem. The rooms, too, seem to have been the site of an attempt on the king's life. The literature

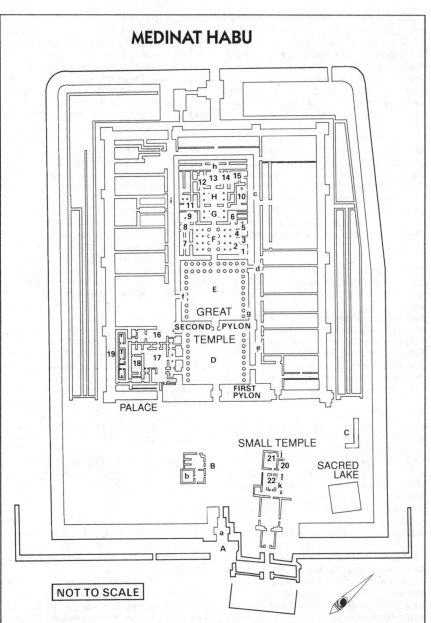

MEDINAT HABU

NOT TO SCALE

© MOON PUBLICATIONS, INC.

tells us that during the "god's arrival" at the Feast of the Valley, Amun's yearly visit to the West Bank, the king was attacked by conspirators. The plot had been hatched in the harem, and although many of the instigators were uncovered and punished, the entire scheme caused a great scandal, not least for the discovery that some of the judges sitting on the case had been carousing with some of the ladies on trial.

Chapels Of The Divine Votaresses

[B] The small chapels to the south were built during the 25th and 26th dynasties for the mortuary cult of the divine votaresses of Amun. These daughters of the king "wed" Amun and ruled Thebes in their fathers' names. The artwork in Amenirdis' forecourt and shrine [b] show precision and skill lacking in the other chapels. The votaress was buried in a crypt under the sanctuary.

The Enclosure

The mud-brick foundations within the walls are the remains of the Coptic town of Djeme; settlers originally occupied the heavily fortified enclosure to escape from marauding Bedouin, but they abandoned their village in the 9th century.

The far southeastern corner houses the remains of the sacred lake. Here, village women who want children still come to bathe at night in what is left of the sacred waters and to pray to Isis for conception. Behind it is a nilometer [C].

The Great Temple

Like other mortuary temples, this building, named United-With-Eternity, served as the focus for the king's cult, and was linked spiritually with his tomb in the Valley of the Kings. At the yearly Festival of the Valley, Amun, Khonsu, and Mut visited from Thebes; probably only at this time did their statues occupy the sanctuaries, but other deities lived in the remaining shrines and received daily offerings.

Designed along the same lines as the Ramesseum, this temple is better preserved. The two courtyards, the palace, and the layout of the sanctuary rooms all are familiar. Although many of the religious decorations were also copied from the temple's predecessor, the battle scenes were contemporary and have provided historians with numerous details.

Northern Reliefs

The best time to view these long-exposed scenes is in the morning. Damaged by long grooves cut by people seeking dust from sacred places for charms, and interrupted by doors cut by the Copts, the walls nevertheless distinctly show the battles, both on land and sea, of Ramesses repelling the Sea Peoples. The scenes actually begin on the back wall of the temple with an unimportant Nubian battle; the famous scenes run from the west end of the north wall toward the front of the temple.

[c] The Libyans: These western tribes, who had joined with the Sea Peoples (on the move throughout the Mediterranean area), hoped to establish a toehold in the delta. Repulsed by Merneptah, the Libyans tried again early in Ramesses III's reign. The first scene shows the Egyptian army, led by the king (with his lion) and the standard of Amun ("opener of the way"). Following the battle, scribes tote up the enemy losses, counting severed hands and genitals; rewards of gold, land, and slaves will follow for soldiers who have contributed to the count.

[d] Sea Peoples: Three years later, in his eighth regnal year, we find Ramesses III again at war, this time with the Sea Peoples, who, determined to settle in Egypt, have brought their families and household goods in oxen-drawn carts. Over the next seven scenes, Ramesses once more mobilizes his army and defeats the invaders on land and sea, and then celebrates by going hunting in the desert. The main scenes close with Ramesses presenting his captives from these wars to Amun-Re, Khonsu, and Mut.

[e] The Libyans, Again: The reliefs between the first and second pylon document yet another attempt by the Libyans to invade Egypt. This army was again defeated, but their descendants would eventually succeed and rule Egypt as the 23rd and 24th dynasties.

First Pylon

The scenes decorating the pylons' exterior depict the traditional smiting of the king's enemies; the round shields with foreign heads, which name subjugated countries, show the extent of Egypt's New Kingdom empire.

Stairways inside the pylons lead to terraces on the top, areas where the king (or his representative) came each morning before dawn to ensure that the sun rose on schedule.

[D] Behind the first pylon, the courtyard is dominated by the pillars with engaged statues of the king. The decorations essentially reproduce those on the outer walls. Behind the columns on the southern wall stands the palace.

The Palace

A royal resthouse rather than a true palace, this building not only accommodated the live king on his visits to his temple, but also, as the false door indicates, housed his spirit. Although built of mud-brick, the building was decorated with stone and glazed tiles (now in the Antiquities Museum). In the middle of this wall was the king's window of appearances; the reliefs at either end show the king with his chariotry, a fast, mobile, and indispensable arm of his military. Access to the palace is from the outside (see below).

Second Courtyard

[E] This courtyard was converted by the Copts of Djeme into a church; traces of the conversion remain in the Coptic crosses incised on the walls and the traces of the apse, an octagonal font, and roofing, which shows that the entire courtyard was covered.

[f] Reliefs on the west wall show the procession of the Festival of Min. Opposite it **[g]** we find the Festival of Sokar, god of the necropolis at Memphis, identified by his strange barque. The walls on either side of the western door show the king being crowned and purified.

Hypostyle Hall

[F] On the east wall, artists carved mirror images of the preceding scenes on the other side of the wall. The five chapels along the northern wall belonged to the deities that "shared" the temple with the Theban Triad: the cult of the king **[1]**, Ptah **[2]**, Osiris **[3]**, Sokar **[4]**, a courtyard and chapel that seem to have been used for offerings **[5]**, and a chapel to Ramesses II **[6]**.

[7] On the opposite side of the hall, the treasure chambers show the weighing of gold, harps and golden statuettes of the king, myrrh, stacks of gold and electrum, pieces of lapis lazuli and turquoise, and copper ingots.

[8] This room served as the sanctuary for Ramesses II's barque.

[9] Chapel to Montu, the Theban war-god.

Second Hypostyle Hall

[G] Like most mortuary temples, the suites of side rooms are dedicated to the solar-god (north) and Osiris rooms (south).

[10] The northern open court had an altar to Re, and the decorations show the king offering to the sun; on the architraves, he's joined by baboons, which, as they arise at dawn, were considered by the Egyptians to worship the sun.

[11] The suite of Osiris rooms are prefaced by a vestibule in which the king was purified and crowned for his role in the afterlife. Decorations in other rooms show similar ceremonies, excerpts from the Book of the Dead, and an astronomical ceiling.

Sanctuary

[H] Beyond the third hypostyle hall are the three sanctuaries of Mut **[12]**, Amun **[13]**, and Khonsu **[14]**.

[15] The nine rooms to the north of Khonsu's chapel may well have been dedicated to the Ennead.

[h] The false door behind the main sanctuary was for the use of Amun-Re United-With-Eternity, who was the dead and deified Ramesses III, the god of the temple.

The rest of the rooms are too ruined to deduce their purpose, though some, like the two rooms with the low, easily concealed entrances, may well have hidden treasure. The southern wall **[i]** contains a listing of the temple festival days.

Palace Interior

[16] The public rooms include a front hall where petitioners could conduct business with the king, who was enthroned in the small room behind.

[17] The large reception room opened to the stairways to the Window of Appearances, which looked into the first courtyard.

[18] At the opposite end, the formal throne room forms the living area of the king's suite. East of this room lies the king's bath, lined with stone to prevent the water from crumbling the mud walls. To the west was his bedroom.

[19] Behind the main rooms, three suites may have housed women of the family.

The Small Temple

The oldest building at Medinat Habu, this small temple southeast of the main building was originally a simple pillared cloister surrounding the barque chapel of Amun and the storage rooms at its rear. The decorations of much of this sanctuary were done by Hatshepsut, but Thutmose III, when he finished the temple, replaced her name with those of Thutmose I and II. Unconnected with the mortuary cult of the king, the rites celebrated in this temple centered on Amun, who was linked with the eight primeval creator gods, the Ogdoad.

The Sanctuary

[20] This room, dedicated to the king's cult, was probably used for purification.

[21] The actual sanctuary of the god, as shown by the huge *naos* **[j]**, which was introduced in antiquity by dismantling the back wall; the blocks were numbered to facilitate their reassembly.

Barque Shrine

[22] Built by Thutmose III, this shrine is surrounded by an ambulatory porch with reused limestone blocks mixed in with the new sandstone ones.

[k] On the north side of the sanctuary, six scenes (running from front to back) show Thutmose III presiding over the founding ceremonies. Wearing the *atef* crown with its long twisting horns, he "stretches the cord" (across two upright standards) with the goddess Seshat. The next panel shows him "scattering the gypsum," pouring the white chips into the trenches surrounding the temple. In the third scene he is "hacking the earth" before ithyphallic Amun, excavating the foundation trenches. The remaining scenes show the king molding a brick, offering wine, and presenting sacrifices.

The small entrance pylons belong to the Late

JAN KIRK

the "stretching of the cord," from the barque shrine at Medinat Habu

Period, the courtyard to the Roman era, and the great pylons set into the wall, to Ptolemaic times.

MALKATA

Amenhotep III, perhaps seeking solitude from the rigors of life on the East Bank, built a luxurious mud-brick place south of Medinat Habu. Here he excavated a giant T-shaped lake for Queen Titi, a feature that still stands out when viewed from the surrounding hills; the levees are now occupied by villages and the depression is cultivated.

Little remains of the palace but eroded and windswept mud-brick walls. While a walk through them may be nostalgic, the nearly buried foundations reveal little of their original plan.

PRACTICALITIES

ACCOMMODATIONS

Cost and availability of rooms varies with the time of year, the winter being the most expensive. This "season" runs from November to May, and the more popular tourist hotels are booked well in advance. In fact, many overbook, so if you have reservations, be sure to bring vouchers as you may have to fight for your room. In summer, however, many hotels drop their rates considerably.

Many hotels no longer require half-board; ask before you check in. Tourist facilities in Luxor are improving; even the small hotels are clean. Not only have new, expensive chain hotels invaded Luxor, but many of the medium-priced ones have been renovated; all have been cleaned up and offer good accommodations. Mid-range and inexpensive hotels are mostly in the center of town; the newer, plush ones occupy either end, and on the West Bank, the small hotels there—both old and new—offer friendly, amazingly clean (if simple) accommodations. As in most cities, local taxes and service charges are added to your bill, so make sure the price quoted is for the total charge, not just the basic rate. Rooms in the front may overlook the Nile, but the back ones, often above a garden, are quieter.

Hotels

Luxor now boasts a crop of five-star hotels including the new Hilton and Sheraton, but the slightly more expensive **Jolie Ville,** sequestered on a natural island, is a real haven from the hassles of Luxor. The two grandes dames of Luxor, the **Luxor Hotel** and the **Old Winter Palace,** have now been rescued; completely renovated and under new management, they are once more worth inhabiting. The **Novotel,** at $44-48 s and $55-60 d, complete with Nile-side garden and pool, is perhaps the best deal.

Of the mid-priced hotels, the **Pola** is outstanding; its surgically clean rooms and baths are offset by the friendly, courteous staff; the

rates, $25 s and $31 d, make seeking out this jewel well worthwhile. Of other, similar hotels, all with a/c, private baths, and many with swimming pools, the renovated **Savoy** is perhaps the best value; the **Windsor** is a bit more upscale as well as expensive; the rest, all good, run about $35 s, $45 d.

The **Mena Palace** stands right next to the river and represents the rest of the hotels in its class; all are clean with a/c, private baths, and rates run about LE35-45. Of the low-end hotels, the most outstanding is the **Venus;** LE8 s, LE15 d, and LE18 t includes a/c, free laundry, a kitchen for guest use, and good hot water. The rest run about the same but without, for example, a/c, though the **Nobles** is slightly more expensive. Into this group goes the difficult to classify **Rezeiky Camp,** which includes not only the campgrounds, but clean, modern bungalows, and a few rooms with a/c and spotless, private baths; LE10-55 depending on the class of accommodations.

Pensions

A number of small pensions cluster around the southern part of Luxor; most are clean and run LE10-15. Start at the circle at the south end of town and work your way toward the train station.

Youth Hostel

Located at 16 Sh. al-Karnak, tel. (095) 382-139, across from the YMCA camp, the hostel tends to the grimy and is inconvenient, but it does have lockers for backpacks and a flexible lockout, usually 1000-1400, 2300 curfew. LE3 s dorm bed, LE12 d; nonmembers must buy a guest card, LE1, or a membership for LE18. Breakfast is LE1.50.

Camping

You can camp (with permission) in the garden in front of the Luxor Hotel. You can also pitch a tent at the YMCA campgrounds, Sh. al-Karnak, tel. 838-2425. For LE3 pp and a slight charge for vehicles you can use the hot showers and toilets. The walled camp is attended 24 hours a day, and often shows movies. **Rezeiky**

SELECTED LUXOR HOTELS

NAME	LOCATION	DISTRICT	TEL.	FAX
FIVE-STAR HOTELS				
Isis Hotel	Sh. Khaled Ibn al-Walid	South Luxor	382-750	
			Telex: 90278 ISTEL UN	
Luxor Hilton		New Karnak	384-933	386-571
Luxor Sheraton	Sh. al-Awameya		384-544	384-941
Movenpick Jolie Ville	Crocodile Island, south of Luxor		384-855	384-936
FOUR-STAR HOTELS				
Akhenaten Club Med	Sh. Khaled Ibn al-Walid	South Luxor	580-850	580-8057
Etap Hotel	Cornishe		580-944	383-316
Luxor Hotel	opposite Luxor Temple		580-018	580-623
Novotel	Sh. Khalid Ibn al-Walid		580-925	580-972
Winter Palace	Cornishe		580-422	384-087
THREE-STAR HOTELS				
Emilio's Hotel	Sh. Yusif Hassan		383-570	
Hotel Philippe	Sh. Nefertiti		382-284	
Nile Hotel	Sh. Nefertiti		382-859	382-859
Pola	Sh. al-Taktet al-Ekieme by sevice station		580-551	580-552
Savoy Hotel	Cornishe		382-200	
Windsor Hotel	off Sh. Nefertiti		384-306	383-447
TWO-STAR HOTELS				
Horus Hotel	Sh. Suq		382-165	
Mena Palace	Cornishe		382-074	
Ramoza Hotel	Sh. al-Mahatta		382-270	
ONE-STAR HOTELS				
New Karnak Hotel	across from train station		382-427	
Nobles	Sh. Yusif Hassan (Midan Ahmos)		382-823	
Rezeiky Camp	Sh. Karnak Temple		581-334	383-447
Sphinx Hotel	Sh. Yusif Hassan		382-830	
Venus	Sh. Yusif Hassan		382-625	
WEST BANK HOTELS				
Abdul Kasem Hotel	Qurna		384-835	
Amon Hotel	village by people's ferry		382-354	
Habu Hotel	across from temple		382-477/382-677	
Memnon Hotel	across from colossi		382-502	
Mersam Hotel (Sheikh Ali's)	opposite Antiquities Office		382-403	
Pharahos Hotel	on the road to Medinat Habu		382-502	
Queens Hotel	between Habu and Pharahos hotels		382-502	
Wadi al-Maluk	near canal on road to Valley of Kings		382-798	

Camp, just down the road (north) behind the gas station offers the same facilities but in a nicer setting.

West Bank
The most notable changes in Luxor hotels however, are those on the West Bank; all are clean and comfortable; prices include breakfast, often full board. Most have roof gardens or terraces, fans, and hot water at least part of the day. The most upscale is the **Pharaohs Hotel,** where some rooms have private baths: LE60 d, LE90 t, hot water all day and a good restaurant. A better deal, however, is the new but small and beautiful **Amon Hotel,** in the village just up from the people's ferry; ask at the pharmacy for Ahmed Mahmud Soliman; LE30 s, LE50 d, with private baths. The **Abdul Kasem** offers clean rooms with private baths, fans, and meals: LE25 s, LE50 d. The **Wadi al-Maluk** has beautiful new baths, fans, and a quiet setting along the canal with a nice rooftop terrace; LE20 s, LE30 d, LE35 t, meals included.

FOOD

Most of Luxor's best food is in the hotels. The Jolie Ville has superb Continental and Oriental food, and the Isis's La Terrazza produces a good Italian meal. Try the new rooftop terrace at the Horus for less expensive fare.

Restaurants
The independent restaurants are unpretentious. One of the best is the **al-Hatey,** Sh. al-Mahatta, tel. 382-210, serving cheap, good Egyptian food from 2000-2400. For breakfast, try **Restaurant Limpy,** next to the New Karnak Hotel, or have lunch at the neighboring **Salt and Bread Cafeteria. The Amun Restaurant,** on Sh. al-Karnak just north of Luxor Temple, serves full meals for about LE10, as does the nearby **al-Patio.** The only upscale restaurant, the **Marhaba,** on the terrace over the tourist pavilion, offers a spectacular view, and its moderately priced food is good.

ENTERTAINMENT

Old Luxor
Other than visiting the archaeological sites, Luxor offers little entertainment, although you can once more spend the afternoon drinking cold beer on the terrace of the Savoy. Or if you prefer, order up tea, coffee, or soft drinks, and relax and take in the river and the Cornishe.

You can visit the beautiful gardens at the Luxor Hotel and afterwards sip cold lemonade on their terrace. A stroll through the Victorian Winter Palace public rooms used by Lord Carnarvon and Howard Carter in the 1920s can end with a luncheon buffet in the dining room or a sandwich (expensive) at poolside. Even nicer is a morning cup of Egyptian coffee (or tea if you'd rather) on their front patio, overlooking the Nile.

To Do
Swimming: All of the large hotels have pools available for a fee; the Novotel and Windsor charge LE8, the Winter Palace a whopping LE35.

Shopping: The main tourist shopping is behind the hotels, along Sh. al-Karnak; some of the shops are starting to deal in fixed prices, a real joy. Otherwise, you'll have to bargain and look carefully at the quality of the merchandise.

Horseback Riding: Horses are available on the West Bank, just south of the village where the local ferry lands. For more information, check with American Express office.

Crocodile Island: Spend a relaxing day in the Jolie Ville's surroundings. Explore the trails and birdwatch (a guide booklet is available). Hire a falucca (LE8-11/hour) and cruise on the Nile; a good time is sunset. Or watch the sun go down on the Nile from the Jolie Ville's terrace to the accompaniment of classical music, which starts in the winter around 1700. Inquire about their astronomy telescope and star maps for nighttime stargazing, or check with them (or the Hilton) about hot-air balloon rides. A shuttle bus runs to the island about every hour from the Winter Palace.

Nightclubs And Discos: Check out the Fellah's Tent or the Sobek Tent nightclubs at the Jolie Ville. The Winter Palace nightclub show includes a belly dancer and Oriental music, as well as a local folk dance troupe and snake handlers. The young flock to the loud music at the Sabil Disco in the Etap.

SERVICES

Police
Tourist police can be found in the Tourist Suq on the Cornishe, tel. 382-120, and in the train station, tel. 382-018; both open 24 hours. The regular police station is off Sh. al-Karnak, tel. 382-006.

Passport Office
You can register your passport or extend your visa in the foreigners' office located next to the Isis Hotel, on the Cornishe at the south end of town, tel. 382-318. Open daily 0800-2200; visas in mornings only.

Banks
The Misr Bank, on Sh. al-Karnak (near Hotel Philippe), is open daily 1000-1330 and 1700-2000, except Friday. The Cairo Bank in the lobby of the Etap is open 0800-2200.

Post Office
The main post office is midway down Sh. al-Mahatta (Station St.), and a branch is in the Tourist Suq; both open Sun.-Thurs. 0800-1400.

Telephone Office
Telephone code: 95. The central telephone office is on Sh. al-Karnak (behind the Etap Hotel); international and domestic calls. Telephones are also available next to the EgyptAir office, in front of the Old Winter Palace. Better if more expensive services available from the large hotels.

Medical Help
The emergency phone number doesn't work. The al-Amiri Hospital on the Cornishe, tel. 382-025, is open 24 hours and has English speakers on staff, but it's pretty grim; try to get back to Cairo. Ahsraf Pharmacy, on a small street near Horus Hotel, tel. 382-834, is open 24 hours.

INFORMATION

Tourist Office
The Tourist Office is in the Tourist Suq on the Cornishe, tel. 382-215; open daily 0800-1400 and 1500-2000. A branch office at the airport, tel. 382-306, is open 24 hours.

Travel Agents
Most travel agents have offices in the semicircle in front of the Old Winter Palace Hotel. **American Express,** tel. 382-862, is open daily 0800-2000, closed orthodox (Coptic) Christmas; they sell traveler's checks to cardholders, change money, and send money-grams. They will also arrange tours to the West Bank and trips to the outlying temples both north (Dendera and Abydos) and south (Isna, Idfu, and Kom Ombo).

Bookstores
The best stocked store in Luxor is **Aboudi's,** tucked into the south corner of the Tourist Suq near the Tourist Office. **A. A. Gaddis** in the northern arcade by the Winter Palace runs a close second; prices are a little cheaper and the store has a stock of old prints of Luxor done by Emile Gaddis's father.

TRANSPORTATION

Getting Around
Although Luxor is relatively small, it's long, 2½ km from temple to temple. If you're in good shape, you may want to walk. Otherwise you can catch a calishe. Also called *hanturs,* they are everywhere, but tend to congregate outside the Etap and Luxor hotels. Fares for either a calishe or taxi should run LE3-5 for the trip from the center of town to either end. Private cabs charge about LE8-10 to the airport and about the same to the hotels on the outskirts of town. Small pickups travel fixed routes through the back of town, but the route is off the beaten path.

Bicycles: Available all over town, bikes rent for about LE5 per hour; Venus Hotel rents them for LE2. Boulos' Bicycles, 52 Sh. al-Mahatta; Ahmen Kamal Amin, Sh. Yusif Hassan (near

Dina Hotel); and the Bike Shop, Sh. Nefertiti (near Hotel Philippe), all have bikes to rent, as does nearly every major hotel. You may have to leave your passport or student identity card. If you're in shape, you can even haul one over to the West Bank (*balidi* ferry) for the day—take plenty of water.

Ferries: The tourist ferries (LE2) leave from in front of the Etap and Old Winter Palace hotels. They are faster than the local ferries and dock at the tourist landing by the ticket kiosk but you may have a long wait, over an hour. *Balidi* ferries (25PT) used by the villagers leave from in front of the Etap and Winter Palace hotels. Plenty of taxis haunt the dock, so even if you want to sightsee, riding the *balidi* ferry is a fun option. They run from sunup to the wee hours of the morning. The car ferry makes frequent trips, docking near Luxor Museum.

West Bank

Most people opt for private taxis (LE35-70/day) to visit the West Bank sites. If you have plenty of time, you can go by donkey or horse (stables are near the *balidi* ferry dock), or if you're really intrepid, hire a bike (LE5). The archaeological sites are too far apart for most people to walk between. The little covered pickups serve the villages; you can flag them down on the main roads if your destination is near one of them. A hassle-free option is to take the American Express tour of the West Bank—LE85; see p. 343.

Getting From Luxor

The hub of the Nile Valley, Luxor is a major destination for all planes, trains, and buses.

By Air: The airport, tel. 828-486, lies 11 km northeast of town. Bus service is instituted on an on-again off-again basis; inquire. Otherwise, you'll have to take a taxi (LE10). **EgyptAir,** at the Old Winter Palace, tel. 382-040, runs flights to Cairo at 0800, 0945, 1330, 1630, 2030, and some days 2215; LE282 one-way (return 10%

less). They also have several flights a day to Aswan with some connecting to Abu Simbel. Flights are crowded (make reservations early) and subject to multiple delays and cancellations. **Zas Airlines,** tel. 383-308/384-872, also runs regularly scheduled flights to the same destinations.

By Train: The train station, tel. 382-018, is on Luxor's southeast edge, at the end of Sh. al-Mahatta. Wagon Lits sleepers stop on their way through from Aswan at 2126 and 2322. Frequent passenger trains depart throughout the day; check locally for the schedules and prices.

By Bus: The main bus stop is in the center of town opposite the Horus Hotel; you can buy your tickets on the bus. To Cairo (13 hours), express buses leave at 0600, 1900 (Golden Arrow), LE30, and 1600 (a/c, LE13). Buses south to Isna, Idfu, Kom Ombo, and Aswan leave every half-hour from 0600 to 1530. Buses north run every couple of hours, 0600-1500. Two daily buses from Aswan to Hurghada (four hours, LE10) stop in Luxor, at 0600 and 1030.

Service Taxis: The station is on Sh. al-Karnak behind the museum. They leave about every 15 minutes in the early morning and late afternoon for: Qina (one hour), Isna (45 minutes), Idfu (1½ hours), Kom Ombo (two to three hours), and Aswan (three to four hours). These drivers are fast and dangerous; use them at your own risk.

Private Taxis: To wander up or down the river taking in the sights figure (roundtrip): Abydos and Dendera, LE100; Isna, Idfu, and Kom Ombo, LE150; Isna, Idfu, Kom Ombo to Aswan, LE200 (LE120 one way); to Qina on the Red Sea coast, LE150 (you may be able to get the driver to take you on into Hurghada for that as well).

Faluccas: You can rent faluccas all along the East Bank for the trip to Aswan. However, it's quicker (and therefore cheaper) to go downstream, so consider making the river trip from Aswan.

BOB RACE

UPPER EGYPT— ASWAN AND ENVIRONS

LUXOR TO ASWAN

Between Luxor and Aswan, the Nile river runs in gentle, lazy curves. About midway between the two towns, the limestone typical of northern Egypt begins to give way to the older, Nubian sandstone; farther south, the granite backbone of the desert mountains pushes through its sand cloak. The Nile's banks are higher here, firmer, and the rocky canyon walls confine the river more closely. With the exception of the eastern plain at Kom Ombo (the remains of an ancient lake), the narrow strip of arable land often shrinks to nothing, the desert hills encroaching on the river. On these banks, the Egyptians founded settlements at Isna, al-Kab, Idfu, and Kom Ombo; the Ptolemaic temples in these towns are some of the best preserved in Egypt.

Ptolemaic Temples

Though they follow the traditions of New King-dom temples, these Greek and Roman com-plexes, in addition to the *mamissi,* enclosed the hypostyle hall with partial screens rather than full walls, decreased the emphasis on pylons and, in a few cases, eliminated the columned court-yard. In general, Ptolemaic temples have more rooms: libraries with their catalogs carved into the walls, laboratories with recipes for incense and other potions, repositories for offerings, and robing rooms where the priests donned their vestments for temple ceremonies. These auxil-iary rooms usually open off the vestibule rather than at the rear, behind the *naos,* where they lay in most New Kingdom temples. In the space formerly occupied by storerooms and two flank-ing chapels (devoted to the triad worshipped in the area), later builders inserted 11 or 12 chapels dedicated to lesser gods.

In addition, the numbers of enclosure walls increased; they were often extensions of the vestibule, hypostyle hall, and/or courtyard, and typically the corridors that separate these walls are narrow and covered with decoration. Crypts, the small, blind rooms either dug beneath the floor or set into walls, were used for storing valuable statues or relics, and in some temples, the secret hole in the wall of the temple from which priests could answer questions put to the god still remains.

Getting There

The easiest way to reach the following sites is by private car or hired taxi (al-Kab is nearly inac-

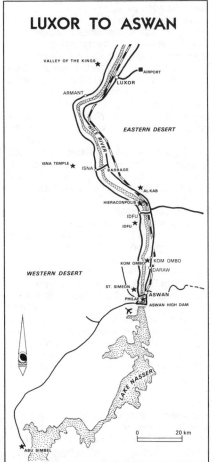

cessible any other way). Alternately, you can take service taxis between the towns and pick up a cab or calishe in town. You can also ride the buses, but they only run until early afternoon, so you'll have to plan carefully.

ISNA

Isna was known to the Egyptians as Te-snet, which became Sne to the Copts and Isnah to Arabs. The British built the barrage at Isna 1906-09; the lock on the west side lets boats ply the river as they had in ancient times. In the center of town stands the temple to Khnum, the goat-headed river god, and is noted for its astronomical ceiling.

Isna Temple

The temple lies in a depression about nine meters deep surrounded by the rubble of the intervening centuries. Rebuilt over ancient foundations by the Greeks, the temple was embellished by the Romans. It was shared by Khnum and Neith, a goddess of war who wore the red crown and was symbolized by two arrows crossed on a shield.

The area has never been completely excavated, but all that remains of the temple today is the hypostyle hall, which appears to be original and complete. Perhaps the most beautiful aspects of the building are the varied designs of the column capitals. The small room abutting the screen just to the left of the main entrance is a feature repeated at Idfu, perhaps a robing room for the priests. At either end of the screen wall, the pillars carry esoteric hieroglyphs composed only of rams (left) and crocodiles (right). Directly opposite the entrance is a portal which, resembling a pylon crowned with a concave cornice, once gave access to the interior of the temple. To the right of this doorway, Khnum receives offerings of a potter's wheel. The scene on the northwest wall, which shows the netting of fowl and hostile spirits, retains the elegance of earlier Egyptian work.

The astronomical ceiling at Isna is incomparable, except perhaps with that of Dendera Temple to the north, which it resembles. As you walk into the hall, the register second from the north shows Orion (Osiris) and Sirius (Isis) above the northern constellations, which included Taweret, the hippopotamus-goddess, and a listing of the *decan* stars. The southern register is filled with recognizable signs of the zodiac; the east wind intrudes between Gemini and Cancer. Planets appear here as well: Mercury may be the walking sphinx.

AL-KAB

Site of the ancient town of Nekhen, this walled fortress was home to the vulture-goddess Nekhbet, patroness of Upper Egypt. The 12-meter ramparts are the most impressive remains of this city, but the site is closed due to continued excavations. The New Kingdom tombs across the road, however, are open. But perhaps the most beautiful sight is the Amenhotep III chapel, a tiny jewel buried deep in the desert.

The Tombs
The New Kingdom tombs are provincial, interesting mainly for the comparisons of the scenes. That of Pheri is the nicest, and includes a scene where he, as tutor of Prince Wedjmose, holds him on his lap. On the unfinished wall of the tomb of Ahmose, Son of Ebana, you can still see many of the artists' grids; the eastern wall of the tomb contains the text of the war against the Hyksos.

Eastern *Wadi*
The Ptolemaic temple and the little chapel near it are not especially interesting. Beyond it, Vulture Rock is covered with drawings and inscriptions from prehistoric times to late Old Kingdom. But the temple of Amenhotep III, which lies at the end of the road, is worth the four-km trip. The tiny building seems to magically expand, the Hathor columns soaring to the painted ceiling. The brightly colored figures on the walls are vintage 18th Dynasty work, only marred by the awkward Ptolemaic figures on either side of the *naos* and the numerous turn-of-the-century graffiti.

IDFU TEMPLE

Known to the ancients as Tbot, Idfu was the traditional location of the battle between Horus

and Seth. In Coptic times the town was Atbo, from which the Arabs derived Idfu; it was the capital of the second *nome* of Upper Egypt. In ancient times, the people of Idfu celebrated the annual festival of the sun's (Horus's) victories, for they left a description of the rites inscribed on the inner side of the enclosure wall of the temple of Horus, which dominates the modern town. With the ritual of 10 harpoons (the slaying of a hippopotamus), triumphant Horus (and thus the current pharaoh) secured his earthly inheritance for the following year. The festival took place on the sacred lake to the east of the temple, now covered by the village.

In another ritual, the Horus temple was ceremonially linked with the Dendera complex dedicated to Hathor. In the third month of summer, the two temples celebrated the "Feast of the Beautiful Meeting." The festival began at Dendera, where the statue of Hathor, bedecked in her finest regalia, entered her barque. Accompanied by celebrants, she sailed up river to Horus's temple at Idfu. When the goddess arrived, on the afternoon of the new moon, she was met with joyful celebrations. During the day, the twin barques of the god and goddess probably shared the sanctuary. Each night, until the festival's conclusion at the full moon, the god and goddess retired to the *mamissi*.

The Temple Complex
Idfu Temple, the most complete and best-preserved example of pharaonic architecture in Egypt, occupies an ancient holy site. The current Ptolemaic building replaces a New Kingdom temple that originally faced east, toward the river. When Greek architects reconstructed the temple, they changed the entrance so that the building faced south, but a remaining New Kingdom pylon testifies to the earlier orientation. Thanks to inscriptions on the girdle wall, we know that the present building was started under Ptolemy III in 237 B.C., but the decorations, due to Egyptian uprisings, were not completed until 57 B.C.

Mamissi
This building still preserves the entrance colonnade, its screens between the pillars decorated with a curious blend of pharaonic and foreign motifs. The birth room itself is surrounded by

an ambulatory of columns linked by low walls, and in places, the reliefs still maintain much of their color.

The Main Temple
Unfortunately, the modern entrance to the temple compound is at its rear, so the modern visitor has no grand avenue from which to view the massive complex, though even the close view at the south entrance is suitably awesome. To the south of the temple, lies an old portal to a ceremonial way.

The main temple generally follows the plan of early New Kingdom buildings, and here visitors leave the bright reality of the outside world to walk through the pylons (the great Mountains of East and West) and into the colonnaded courtyard, the covered vestibule, and then into the increasingly dark and mysterious sanctuary where the god, in all his splendor, sat in state.

The Pylons
Like most New Kingdom pylons, these carry scenes of the pharaoh smiting his enemies; this example is stiffly designed.

[R] Scenes show the Feast of the Beautiful Meeting; Horus' barque tows Hathor's along the canal to the temple, and the deities, after suitable greetings and rituals, retire to the sanctuary.

[S] The end of the festival, when Hathor and Horus emerge from the temple, embark, and drift (sails furled) downstream to the edge of Idfu Nome, where they part.

Hypostyle Hall
[A] The offering scenes include the temple foundation ceremonies, familiar from Medinat Habu. The two small chambers on the front wall were a library **[1]** for ancient texts and a robing room **[2]**, where the king or his priestly representative dressed for the rituals.

Second Hypostyle Hall
[B] Like the temple at Dendera, the eastern door of this room leads to the well. From here, the god formally appeared; note the barques of Horus and Hathor on either side of the north doorway.

[3] The laboratory with recipes inscribed on the walls.

[4] The offerings were kept in this storeroom.

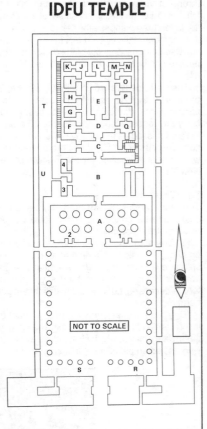

IDFU TEMPLE

NOT TO SCALE

© MOON PUBLICATIONS, INC.

The Sanctuary
[C] The offering hall.

[D] The vestibule.

[E] The sanctuary proper, complete with a huge granite *naos* dedicated by Nectanebo II. Here, each morning the priest would unseal the doors and open them to the god, whom he then washed, dressed, anointed, fed, and entertained.

The Chapels
Leading off from the vestibule, the rooms surrounding the sanctuary are: **[F]** chapel of Min,

[G] chamber of the linen, [H] chamber of the throne of the gods, [I] chamber of Osiris, [J] tomb of Osiris, and [K] the chamber of the West; the latter three comprise the Osiris Suite. In [L] the chamber of the victor (i.e., Horus), a reconstructed barque looms out of the darkness. The next rooms belong to Khonsu [M] and Hathor [N].

The east side finished up with [O] the chapel of the throne of Re, and [P] the chapel of the spread wings, dedicated to the deities, especially the lioness Mehit, who guarded the path the soul passed on its journey toward resurrection. The sun court [Q], like that at Dendera, was undoubtedly used for the Festival of the New Year.

The Walls

The entire area between the temple and the outer wall is decorated; the most notable scenes occur on the west wall.

[T] The king and god pull closed a clapnet on birds, animals, and men that represent evil spirits, evidence that perhaps similar scenes from Old Kingdom tombs not only supplied food for the deceased, but held the spirits that might harm him at bay.

[U] These scenes show the annual ritual of the Triumph of Horus (and the reigning king) in the mystery play in which Horus slays evil Seth who has taken the guise of a hippopotamus.

KOM OMBO

Most spectacular of all the river temples, Kom Ombo lies right on the riverbank, retaining the solitude and grandeur visitors expect in Egyptian monuments. The temple stands on a plateau once crossed by two streams, now reduced to dry *wadis*. Remains of prehistoric cemeteries testify to the antiquity of the site.

Kom Ombo has long served as a meeting point for the Egyptians and the Nubians. Surrounded by a fertile plain formed by an ancient lake, the town became prosperous during the Ptolemaic period when it was designated the capital of its *nome* and housed the training center for African elephants destined for the army. Since then, a large irrigation pumping station has enabled the population to convert the desert into fertile farmland where many of the Nubians displaced by the Aswan Dam have settled. A sugarcane refinery processes local produce, shipping it downriver to Cairo.

The Temple

The temple's position was not so precarious formerly, but a shift in the river washed out the bank and some of the buildings, including much of the *mamissi* that stood in front of it. Modern stonework has stabilized the shore, so the temple is no longer threatened.

boys playing along the Nile, near Aswan

ALLAN HANSEN

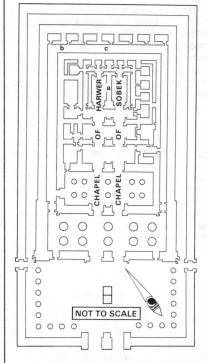

KOM OMBO

NOT TO SCALE

© MOON PUBLICATIONS, INC.

Not only is Kom Ombo unique in its riverbank setting, but also in its design—a double temple dedicated to Harwer (Horus the Elder) and Sobek, the crocodile-god. Once, the sand banks where the river bends back to the west must have harbored basking crocodiles, and a large

cache of their mummified remains is housed in a small chapel near the temple. Pilgrims to Kom Ombo came to Harwer, the Healer, to be treated, waiting in the corridors, playing games with stones on boards scratched into the pavement.

The temple, built of local sandstone by the troops garrisoned here, is divided between the two gods and their respective consorts. The design of the building reflects this duality in its double gateways, ceremonial hallways, and shrines. Decorations followed a similar division with Sobek dominating the east side, Harwer the west. At the end of the Late Period, when the temple fell from use, sand drifted in and protected much of it from the chisels of fanatic Christians and stone-hungry builders.

The temple itself is honeycombed with crypts and secret passages, the most noticeable of which lies between the double walls joining the two sanctuaries **[a]**. Connected to a tunnel that runs under the floor and to another room, this space was actually a priest's hole—the source of the gods' human voices.

Rear Of The Temple
[b] This controversial carving may well show medical instruments, but they are more probably ritual implements or maybe both.

[c] This chapel of the "hearing ear" has been expanded beyond the usual false door. Here, the figures of Sobek (left) with his lion-headed wand and Harwer (right) with his two-legged knife frame a niche that once held a cult statue. The carvings of ears heard pilgrims' prayers while the sacred eyes symbolized wholeness and health for which the petitioners wished. Above the images, a hymn links Harwer and Sobek to the cosmos, its four winds (represented by a bull, a lion, a falcon, and a snake—which the Christian apostles oddly echo), and Ma'at, goddess of truth, who supports the sky.

ASWAN

Lying at the southernmost border of Egypt's ancient empire, Aswan is truly the jewel of the Nile. Pink and gray basement granite thrusts upward through the Nubian sandstone forming mountains, cliffs, and jagged outcroppings. The river runs clear and cold, splashing and swirling around the jutting granite that marks the first cataract. At Aswan, the Nile has lost its buffer of cultivated land, and endless waves of golden sand swirl against its banks. Islands, some inhabited since before the time of the pharaohs, dominate the river; the town, with its sheltered gardens and tree-lined avenues, entices the visitor with cool shade—a quiet, relaxing haven from Luxor and Cairo.

The pharaonic center of the first *nome,* Aswan today remains the capital of the district. A boomtown during the construction of the dam, it now has about 250,000 people. Modern Aswan lines the east bank of the Nile; its three parallel streets—the Cornishe, Sh. al-Tahrir, and Sh. al-Suq (market street)—run lengthwise through the narrow town. The modern shopping district stretches nearly 2½ km along the Cornishe, and Sh. al-Suq houses a native bazaar (one of the best outside Cairo), which still betrays its mixed African and Oriental heritage. At the south end of the Cornishe, atop a granite promontory, rise the Cataract Hotels, Old and New.

Just downstream from the hotels, the southern tip of Elephantine Island splits the river like the prow of a four-km barge. The ruins of the ancient fortress capital sprawl over its southern end, native villages cluster under tall palm trees in its middle, and the modern tower of the Oberoi Hotel looms over its northern end. Kitchener's Island, screened by Elephantine, lies to the west, a legacy of the general who retired there and developed extensive gardens now open to the public. On the west bank, the modern mausoleum of the Aga Khan tops the hill above his white winter villa. To the north, nearly vertical stairways from the tombs of local Middle Kingdom grandees drop down the steep hillside.

The historical First Cataract lies about three km upstream from the town, and above them is the old dam. In the lake behind this barrage

stands the reconstructed island of Philae and its Ptolemaic-period temples. Construction of the New High Dam six km farther upstream flooded Nubia and led to the rescue of over 30 Nubian monuments and temples (including Abu Simbel, 270 km to the south) that were threatened by the rising water. The entire area is populated with modern villages built for the Nubians displaced by Lake Nasser.

Climate

Close to the Tropic of Cancer, Aswan is hot and dry nearly year-round. Winter daytime temperatures range from 23-30° C, while in summer they average 38-40° C and can go as high as 54°; temperatures drop rapidly in the evenings. The ideal time to visit is winter, when some days are warm enough for swimming; summer is also pleasant, due to low humidity, widespread air-conditioning, and habitual siestas.

HISTORY

Ancient Egyptians believed the Nile gushed up from subterranean caves just south of Aswan. These caves, they thought, housed the goat-god Khnum, a potter who fashioned men's bodies and *kas* on his wheel. From the earliest periods, the cliffs surrounding the river supplied pharaohs with pink granite to decorate their temples and tombs. The ancient town was a fortress called Yebu located on the southern tip of Elephantine Island, and it became Egypt's gateway into the African heartland, the jumping-off point for trading, mining, and military expeditions. At Yebu, pharaoh's priests measured the level of the Nile's annual inundation; by predicting its height, they could calculate the taxes to be levied on the farmers.

A large colony of Jews settled on Elephantine in the Late Period and built a temple to Jehovah, but no traces of it remain. In the Ptolemaic era, the Alexandrian geographer Eratosthenes (276-196 B.C.), upon hearing that the sun on the summer solstice cast no shadow in a well, realized that this town (called Syene by the Greeks) lay on the

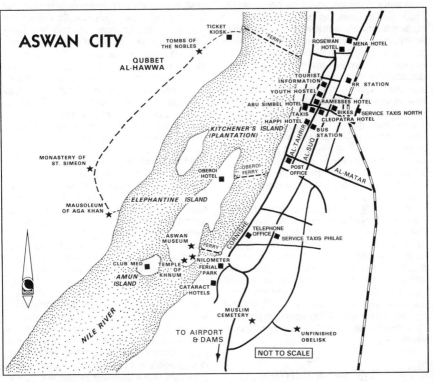

ASWAN CITY

TICKET KIOSK
TOMBS OF THE NOBLES
QUBBET AL-HAWWA
ROSEWAN HOTEL
MENA HOTEL
TOURIST INFORMATION
RR STATION
YOUTH HOSTEL
ABU SIMBEL HOTEL
RAMESSES HOTEL
TAXIS
BIKES
SERVICE TAXIS NORTH
HAPPI HOTEL
CLEOPATRA HOTEL
KITCHENER'S ISLAND (PLANTATION)
BUS STATION
MONASTERY OF ST. SIMEON
OBEROI HOTEL
OBEROI FERRY
POST OFFICE
AL-MATAR
MAUSOLEUM OF AGA KHAN
ELEPHANTINE ISLAND
CORNISHE
TELEPHONE OFFICE
SERVICE TAXIS PHILAE
ASWAN MUSEUM
FERRY
CLUB MED
TEMPLE OF KHNUM
NILOMETER
FERIAL PARK
AMUN ISLAND
CATARACT HOTELS
NILE RIVER
MUSLIM CEMETERY
TO AIRPORT & DAMS
UNFINISHED OBELISK
NOT TO SCALE

© MOON PUBLICATIONS, INC.

Tropic of Cancer, and he used the distance between it and Alexandria to calculate the circumference of the earth with nearly modern accuracy.

The Christian And Muslim Periods

During the Christian era Aswan became a bishopric, and the Copts built the Monastery of St. Simeon on the Nile's west bank. Under the conquering khalifs, the town enjoyed prosperity based on continuing African trade, marred only by raids from the Bedouin—harassment that did not stop until 1517 when Sultan Salim stationed a garrison here. At the turn of the 19th century, when the British became active in the region, Aswan became not only their southern base for operations in Africa, but also a winter vacation land, the favorite resort of Europe's delicate and ailing rich who flocked to the city for its dry winter heat and healing sand baths.

The Modern Period

In modern times, the old dam or barrage built by the British from 1898-1902 has been displaced by the High Dam, completed by the Soviets in 1971. To escape the inundation, whole Nubian villages were moved to the Aswan area, where Nubians now make up a large segment of the population. Not only has the dam shifted Aswan's population, it has also changed the climate, increasing the humidity. In addition, cheap electricity from the dam has led to more industrialization, fertilizer factories, and foundries, as well as the reopening of ancient stone quarries. Nevertheless, these changes seem compatible with Aswan's role as a winter vacation area. The ruins and gardens remain, enticing the visitor to stay yet another day, to visit the *suq* once more, to explore the Nile again under a taut falucca sail, or to simply relax under Aswan's verdant trees.

Aswan's sights range from the pharaonic period to modern times, though they are neither as numerous nor as monumental as those elsewhere. In fact, Aswan's major sights can easily be seen in three days. Perhaps best known for its High Dam, Aswan is also the modern point of departure for tours to Abu Simbel. Visitors can tour the museum on Elephantine and poke around in the remains of the ancient fortress covering much of its southern tip or walk through the Nubian villages lining its western shore. Guests can visit the quarries, which supplied pharaohs with Aswan's famous pink granite, delight in the cool shade and delicate foliage of Kitchener's Island gardens, or view the entire area from the tranquil hilltop mausoleum of the Aga Khan.

Aswan is also the place to indulge a bent for clambering around isolated ruins. Investigate the west bank's ancient decorated tombs (many contemporary with Beni Hassan) built for the town's governors, or scramble around in the Monastery of St. Simeon. Visitors interested in architecture can explore the Fatimid tombs, and those inclined to relaxation can sail to Sehel Island, at the First Cataract, and find ancient figures cut into the desert patina of the rocks as well as explore a modern Nubian village.

EAST BANK SIGHTS

Aswan's east bank has few sights right in town; the Temple of Isis (LE3) and the public park with pharaonic inscriptions are both at the south end of town. You can hike to outlying attractions, such as the Muslim cemetery and the unfinished obelisk at the north quarry, which lie only about a km or so outside of town on the road to the airport and dam.

Northern Quarry
Open 0700-1600; LE5. The quarry, about a km southeast of the Cataract hotels, contains a great, but unfinished, obelisk. If excavated, it would have been the world's largest, but when it cracked it was abandoned, along with numerous quarrying tools, which have enabled archaeologists to deduce actual mining methods. Pharaonic miners used stone, copper, and

bronze tools, often in conjunction with a slurry of quartz sand for an abrasive. To extract the obelisk, they cut the stone back from its top and with dolerite balls pounded out channels underneath. Workers then chiseled notches into the seams with the mother rock, hammered wooden wedges into them, and wet the wood. The subsequent swelling caused the rock to split away from its ground. As the stone was being loosened from its bed, the miners polished its exposed sides, leaving the smooth surface you see under your feet.

Muslim Cemetery
Lying south of town, the cemetery contains several hundred mausoleums, including an extensive collection of 9th century Tulunid as well as more modern tombs. This collection of structures not only illustrates the evolution of Muslim building styles but also exhibits all the known ways of mounting a dome on a square base. Some of the oldest tombs, now open to the sky, lie to the north of the road to the airport, on the hill near the caretaker's house.

The earliest of these structures are walled enclosures which were sometimes filled with earth and represent a direct continuation of the Coptic traditions; later styles contain a low brick vault. The domed cube, a style that appeared in the 11th century, at first rested on pillars, forming an open canopy. Later models were built with a solid *qiblah* wall; eventually, tombs were constructed with four solid walls with a door in the northwest side. Still later forms were rectangular, the central dome flanked by two tunnel vaults, and these evolved in the same way; the earliest buildings were open pavilions, superseded by those containing a closed *qiblah* wall. The latest tombs were entirely enclosed and often contained a forecourt.

Ferial Park
Aswan is built on an ancient quarry, and Aswan's Ferial Gardens perch on pink granite slabs, complete with inscriptions. The public park is located next to the river on the hill just north of the Cataract Hotels. The trees offer plenty of shade, but you'll have to compete with the locals for space, especially down near the swimming hole.

ELEPHANTINE ISLAND

Lying just offshore at the south end of Aswan, Elephantine Island (2½ km long by ½ km wide) is Aswan's largest island. Eminently defensible, the area was occupied from predynastic times. During dynastic times, this fortified capital of the province dominated the island's southern tip, serving as both an administrative and trading center. Although the island was considered the home of the Nile-god Hapi, the great temple built here honored Khnum, the ram-god who was worshipped throughout the cataract area. During the Persian period, Jews quartered on Elephantine built a temple to their own Jehovah, but it was later destroyed on orders of Khnum's priests.

Today, the island offers a variety of activities. Modern villages sprawl across Elephantine's center, bustling with activity. A small museum entices visitors to view its collections and to linger in its cool green garden. Below this garden, at the edge of the water, you can still explore the ancient nilometer where the ancient priests as well as more modern Romans and Muslims measured the height of the all-important inundation. Although little remains of the ancient buildings, you can stand on the site of ancient Egypt's last civilized outpost, atop the sweeping platform of the Temple of Khnum and look south—like the armies of the pharaohs once did, trying to see the dangers lurking deep in hostile Nubia.

Museum

Open Sat.-Thurs. 0730-1600, closed 1130-1330; Fri. hours are 0730-1300; LE5. You will need your museum ticket to get into the nilometer and the ruins on the south end of the island; if it's hot, you may want to buy your ticket and visit the ruins first, returning to the sheltered galleries and ending your visit to Elephantine with tea in the cool gardens.

The museum, which contains pharaonic artifacts found in the Aswan area, is in the white clapboard house at the top of the hill. The building's four wings form a square around a skylight that illuminates the basement gallery. As you enter, note the statues on the porch: Amenhotep III in the company of goddesses.

To see the galleries in roughly chronological order, start with the predynastic materials on your left. Note the sophisticated jewelry in Room 2. Don't miss the basement gallery, with one of the royal rams that were discovered in the vaulted tombs near the Temple of Khnum.

Nilometer

As you descend the museum steps, the path forks. Take the southern branch, which leads to the nilometer and the fortress's ruins. About 300 meters southeast of the museum, beneath a sycamore tree (a pharaonic symbol of the bountiful earth-goddess) lies the Aswan Nilometer. Crafty *ghaffirs* usually keep the barbed-wire gate shut and will expect baksheesh to open it and guide you to the site.

Elephantine Island

KATHY HANSEN

Built into the ancient quay, the steep staircase plunges down the bank to the river. This nilometer, described by Strabo, was used from pharaonic times. Here the priests would measure the height of the inundation and calculate the effects of the flood. The steps used to be roofed, for only the initiated had access to the sacred information. The nilometer was rebuilt by the Romans, and in the 19th century the Muslims pressed it into service; thus Arabic as well as Roman numerals appear on the steps.

Temple Of Khnum

To reach the ancient city of Kom, return to the path and continue south; you'll emerge on the platform floor of the massive Temple of Khnum, which once dominated the city's center. The town was well established by at least the Old Kingdom and in the Middle Kingdom nearly doubled its size, growing northwest from the central focus of the temple. The area continued to expand throughout the Late Period and into the Roman era, spilling across the city's granite walls and eventually occupying nearly two square kilometers. Excavations have uncovered private houses to the southwest that must have been mansions, homes of the governors and princes who are buried in the rock tombs across the river.

The temple's axis runs east-west, and Roman paving stones abut the column bases, which were originally installed by Ramesses II when he rebuilt the temple. The large expanse of flooring is all that remains of the front section. Below you, to the east, are the massive blocks of the Roman quay that used to serve this temple. If you walk to the north side, you can see remains of pillars painted by the Romans and several altars with Greek inscriptions. The edge of the floor reveals that it was built upon filler blocks placed on the old level. To the west, isolated against the sky, stands the main temple entrance; built by Alexander II, its carvings show him worshipping Khnum. Beyond it, the jumble of ruins illustrates the temple's many transformations, but the only other structure is the large granite *naos* begun by Nectanebo II. The preliminary designs were painted, but the decorations were never finished.

Other Ruins

To the north lie the mud-brick vaults (Late Period) that once housed the bodies of the royal rams; one of the mummies recovered here is on display in the museum. Beyond and slightly northeast lies the New Kingdom Temple of Satis, (consort of Khnum), which is currently being rebuilt and is closed to visitors. To the northwest is a **shrine to Hekayib**, the governor whose tomb was cut into the west bank. His cult flourished in the Middle Kingdom, and statues excavated from this shrine are on display in the museum. Just visible to the west is a 3rd Dynasty granite **step pyramid.**

At the south end of the island, blocks discovered at Kalabsha Temple have been reconstructed into the sanctuary of a small **Ptolemaic temple.** The singleroom had decoration added by the Nubian Pharaoh Arkamani in the 3rd century B.C. and was completed by the Romans. The reliefs on its outer walls name Caesar Augustus, the Roman. Fragments from the vestibule (which was not reconstructed) lie in front of the chapel.

Native Villages

Several interesting native villages cluster along Elephantine's western edge. The inhabitants are friendly, and the narrow, twisting alleys fascinating. Here you can see painted *hajj* houses, and others with lintels carved with crocodiles, fish, and men. These villages are separated from the northern tip of the island by the high wall at the back of the Oberoi Hotel. Since the hotel grounds are walled off, you'll have to return to Aswan via the public ferry.

Getting There

A public sailing ferry runs to Elephantine (60PT) from 0600-2400, leaving about every 15 minutes from the bank of the Cornishe just north of the EgyptAir office. You can reach it by walking down the steps before the road turns at the park. On the island, the ferry docks just below the museum, to the north of the ruins and the nilometer. At the other end of the island, the Oberoi Hotel's ferry, a garish imitation of a pharaonic boat, connects the north end of Elephantine with the east bank; the ferry is free, but the hotel grounds are walled off from the surrounding area.

KITCHENER'S ISLAND

Open daily 0600-sunset; fee LE5. Hidden behind the northern tip of Elephantine, Gizirat al-Nabatat ("Plant Island") or Gizirat al-Bustan ("Plantation Island") was deeded to Lord Kitchener as a reward for his campaigns in Sudan. A passionate botanist, he retired here and turned the island into a garden wonderland, importing shrubs and trees from tropical Africa.

The Egyptian government, which now owns and maintains the island, has continued to preserve it as a botanical garden. Tourist stands and a small resthouse occupy the southern end of the island; the duck ponds beyond them are managed by a biological research station. The rest of the island is devoted to the plants; the bookstalls at the quay usually sell a small guidebook. Although Kitchener's cannot compare to European gardens, a stroll along the shaded paths makes a welcome conclusion to a morning spent either on the west bank or Elephantine. An afternoon visit, however, will give you a closer look at the many birds that make the island their home, as rays from the sinking sun filter through the vegetation, spotlighting the garden with their golden glow.

Getting There

To visit Kitchener's Island, LE5, you'll need to hire a falucca. Figure on LE20 for a two-hour sail around the islands. Since there is no set price, you'll have to bargain; again, a group splitting the cost lowers the per person price. If you like adventure, you might be able to induce (with a pound or so) a boy from one of the villages on Elephantine to row you across the short stretch of water to Kitchener's; if you stay until about 1700 hours, you can catch a ride on the rowboat that brings employees back to Aswan; otherwise, you'll wish you'd brought a sleeping bag.

ACCOMMODATIONS

Aswan's hotels line the banks of the Nile, making them easy to find and giving their rooms spectacular views. The hotels here seem cleaner and their food tastier than in other towns of Upper Egypt. In general, management is ge-nial and accommodating, and most hotels will let you leave your baggage behind their desks if you come in on the early train.

Accommodations are tight during the winter high season, so try to get confirmed reservations; in summer rooms are more plentiful and cheaper; reductions range from 25 to 40%. Many have a/c, but it may be on for limited hours (but it's usually all you need). All the smaller hotels include breakfast, and some still require half-board. Those in the lower price ranges usually have fixed menus, and in these smaller establishments you may need to arrange meals ahead of time.

Hotels

Of the hotels in Aswan, the **Old Cataract** is the best known. An ancient watering place for the Victorians, the hotel had nearly disintegrated when it was ordered renovated by Mubarak; the facade, rooms, and gardens have had extensive facelifts; the terrace overlooking the Nile once more serves traditional tea, and the garden nook plays classical music at sunset. The site for filming in Agatha Christie's *Death on the Nile,* its view, gardens, and ambience will run $96 s and $119.30 d. The **Oberoi** tower on the north end of Elephantine Island stands amid beautiful gardens and quiet luxury, fees just sightly less than the Old Cataract. The new **Basma** includes spacious rooms and a luxurious pool with a bar in the center for $58 s, $76 d, and $94 t. Aswan is the place to enjoy a small, intimate hotel; everyone seems to have their favorites. I enjoy the **Cleopatra,** which has added a swimming pool on the 5th floor and good food and a grand view from the top floor dining room. The more expensive **Isis** ($64 s, $84 d, and $100) is spotless and modern.

The **Hathor** is perhaps the best deal in town at LE15 s, LE26 d, and LE34 t; the price includes access to their new pool and an international phone line. The **Abu Simbel** runs it a close second with rooms with private baths, and nice gardens at LE23 s, LE30 d. The **Rosewan** trains its staff to European customs, and prides itself on making women comfortable. You can write to them for reservations at P.O. Box 106, Aswan, Egypt; they will respond. Very clean rooms, at LE10.44 s, 19.60 d, make this cozy hotel north of the train station (left after the gas station) a great deal.

Youth Hostel

The hostel, 96 Sh. Abtal al-Tahrir, (west from the train station one block, then left), tel. 322-313, is clean, with hot water and a/c or fans, but no food is available. The entrance for non-Egyptians is around the north corner of the building. Closed 1000-1400 and at 2300; LE3.

Camping

Aswan's campgrounds are inconveniently located near the unfinished obelisk on Sh. Sharq al-Bandar. For LE3 you can pitch a tent on grass and use the water and bathrooms at this large campground. As in Europe, the grounds charge for each vehicle: motorcycle, LE1.50; car LE5; RV LE7. You can buy firewood from the locals. Since this area caters to trans-African safaris in addition to individuals, you can meet interesting campers here, but you'll also be a target for hustlers. You can also camp across the river on the west bank.

FOOD

Aswan offers three eating choices: hotels, street-side cafes, or your own supplies bought in the *suq*. Hotel dining rooms, for the most part, offer good, hearty fare, and plenty of it, for surprisingly reasonable prices. For a night of true luxury, sample the Continental cuisine or East Indian fare under candlelight at the **L'Orangerie** at the Oberoi; entrees run LE35-50. The **al-Marsi** on Sh. al-Matar (up from Sh. al-Suq) serves excellent food in a good atmosphere; it's a favorite of the Egyptians.

Riverfront cafes now stretch southward along the Cornishe; most have a relaxing terrace view of the Nile and specialize in Egyptian food. Try the **Monnalisa** at the south end of the Cornishe for baked fish or kebabs. The **Aswan Moon** next door is less expensive and even serves

SELECTED ASWAN HOTELS

NAME	LOCATION	TEL.	FAX
FIVE-STAR HOTELS			
The Aswan Oberoi	Elephantine Island	323-455	323-485
Old Cataract	Abtal al-Tahrir	323-222	323-510
FOUR-STAR HOTELS			
Basma	in front of New Nubian Museum	310-901	310-907
Isis Hotel	Cornishe al-Nil	324-905/324-744	328-893
Kalabsha Hotel	Abtal al-Tahrir	322-666	325-974
THREE-STAR HOTELS			
Cleopatra Hotel	Sh. Sa'ad Zaghlul	322-983 324-001	326-381
TWO-STAR HOTELS			
Abu Simbel Hotel	Cornishe al-Nil	322-888	Telex: 23602 PBASW UN
Happi Hotel	Sh. Sa'ad Zaghlul	322-028	Telex: 23602
ONE-STAR HOTELS			
Al-Salam Hotel	Cornishe al-Nil	322-651	
Hathor Hotel	Cornishe al-Nil	322-590	
Mena Hotel	North of Railway Station	324-388	
Rosewan Hotel	(P.O. Box 106)	324-497	

mahallabiya (the green soup typical of Egypt) and good ice cream, but when it's crowded the service can be terrible.

Farther north, the **al-Nil** serves a delicious selection of *kufta*, fish, and chicken, but they specialize in shish kebab grilled on their patio. Just up the street, the **al-Shati**, in addition to the general menu, has fresh fruit juices and *karkaday*. South of the train station on Sh. Abtal al-Tahrir (across from the Cleopatra Hotel), the **Madina Restaurant** is a local favorite.

The little shop just south of the Hathor Hotel make wonderful ice cream. In winter a special treat is tea on the veranda of the Old Cataract Hotel. Chocaholics should visit the **Karmi Nuts Oven** under the Mickey Mouse sign on Sh. al-Suq. Coffee shops are scattered throughout the downtown area; several lie along Sh. al-Suq, including the **al-Nasa Club.**

You can buy fresh food in the local *suq,* which lies along the back streets paralleling the Cornishe; they sell fresh fruits and vegetables; buy early in the morning, because as the day progresses the selection of quality goods shrinks.

ENTERTAINMENT

As in most of Egypt, evening entertainment is designed primarily for foreigners. The Oberoi, Cataract, and Abu Simbel hotel **nightclubs** offer Nubian and Western entertainment; cover charges vary with the season, but drinks are expensive. The only **disco** is on the third floor of the Ramesses Hotel, and is open only in winter.

At nightfall, the *suq* comes alive. Join Egyptians as they wander in and out of shops and coffeehouses. Watch the bargaining, buy a few things for yourself, or simply sip coffee at **al-Nasa Club** (north of Sh. Saida Nafisa).

Sound And Light Show
On Agilkia Island, the Philae Sound and Light show (LE15) is set among the Ptolemaic temples (see p. 391). Shows are at 1800 and 1930, but confirm times and schedule with the Tourist Office or the larger hotels.

Nubian Folk Troupe
The Aswan Cultural Center, tel. 323-344, sponsors a genuine Nubian music and dance troupe.

Nightly (except Friday) performances are held at the Aswan Palace of Culture (on the Cornishe near the Abu Simbel Hotel) from Oct.-May at 2130. Tickets (LE15) can be purchased at the door; however, since the show is popular, it's wise to buy them ahead of time.

Swimming
The Cataract, Cleopatra, Hathor, and Oberoi hotels let non-guests swim; fees range from LE5 (Hathor) to LE25 at the Oberoi. The municipal pool is no longer open to foreigners.

Camel Market
At Daraw, toward Kom Ombo, the Darb Arba'in ends and the camels that survive the trip are sold here, often to be trucked to Cairo and sold yet again. Although there is some activity all week, the main market day is Tuesday, and most of the action is in the morning. You can reach Daraw by public transportation to Kom Ombo and from there take a service taxi to the town. Or you can hire a taxi in Aswan. The village is a good place to explore as well, and if you haven't already done so, finish up with a visit to the temple at Kom Ombo.

Shopping
The Aswan bazaar that fills the streets behind the Cornishe is one of the best shopping areas outside Cairo. Wandering through the unpaved shops you can still sense the nearness of tropical Africa. Here, bone and ivory, ebony and spices compete for shoppers' pounds with woven blankets and rugs, baskets and colorful reed platters. Shops are open mornings and evenings. The south end of the *suq* has the more fashionable and expensive fixed-price shops. For Nubian crafts, the **Cultural Center** maintains a shop. If you explore the surrounding villages you can often find goods for less, but again, be prepared to bargain.

Just down from the Abu Simbel Hotel is the **government store,** and beyond the Hathor Hotel are several **photo supply shops.**

INFORMATION AND SERVICES

English-speaking **Tourist Police,** tel. 323-163, are on duty 24 hours. Their office is on the south side of the train station.

The **Aswan Passport Office,** tel. 322-238, is open daily 0800-1400 and 1800-2000; sometimes hours are shorter on Friday. It's on the Cornishe under the large, yellow sign near the Continental Hotel. Here, you can register your passport, or during the morning hours, extend your visa.

The **post office** is on the Cornishe just south of the Rowing Club Restaurant, and the **poste restante** is off the Cornishe, a block behind the Bank of Alexandria. Hours for both are 0900-1400; outward-bound mail often gets there quicker if posted from a major hotel.

The **telephone office,** open 24 hours, is two doors south of EgyptAir; you can make international calls. A branch office is in the train station and is open daily 0800-2200; code is 097.

The Egyptian **hospital,** tel. 322-855, is in the Said area near the eastern edge of town, but is crowded and understaffed. A better option is the **German Hospital,** tel. 322-176, at the south end of Cornishe; open 24 hours. You can use insurance for their quality care. Of the several pharmacies, Pharmacy al-Saad al-Ali, 41 Sh. Saad Zaghlul, tel. 323-516, is open 0800-2300.

The **Tourist Office,** tel. 323-297, is open Sun.-Thurs. 0900-1400 and 1800-2000, Fri. 1000-1200 and 1800-2000, Ramadan 0900-1400. Nearly hidden behind a small park, the impressive modern office is two blocks north of the Abu Simbel Hotel, half a block off the Cornishe. Here you can find a listing of government rates for faluccas and taxis; the staff can help you arrange travel to Kalabsha and Sudan. It's one of the few efficient ones in Egypt; don't confuse it with the State Information Center, which is a press service and not for tourists; beware of enterprising Egyptians who lurk in the area and give out false information.

American Express, tel. 323-222, is in the lobby of the Old Cataract Hotel (the lobby is open even when the hotel is closed). Open 0800-1400 and 1700-2000, Ramadan 0800-1400.

TRANSPORTATION

Getting Around
You can walk the two km from one end of Aswan to the other in about 30 minutes. For longer distances, biking is an ideal way to travel. **Bikes** are available from Nahas Yahia, one and a half blocks off the Cornishe for about LE5/hour; bargain. You'll have to leave your passport or other collateral. **Calishes** or **taxis** run about LE2-5, depending on where you want to go; the white taxis run along the Cornishe for about LE1. Service taxis to the Old Dam leave from the square by the main mosque; 25PT. The ones by the Abu Simbel Hotel run to the nearby villages. **Private taxis** cost about LE2-5 to the train station, LE10-15 to the airport. They will also take you sightseeing; figure LE40-80, depending on the distance and time. You're in a better position to bargain if you flag them down away from the hotel; for long trips, fix the sights and the price before you leave. Local **trains** run out to the New Dam/Wadi Halfa Docks. **Buses** run to the Old Dam and along the Cornishe. **Faluccas** cost about LE18/hour for general cruising. The Tourist Office suggests the following prices for specific trips: Kitchener's Island (two hours), LE20; the above plus Elephantine Island (2½ hours), LE25; Sehel Island (three hours), LE40. Motorboats run about 15% more.

Getting From Aswan
Aswan's **airport,** tel. 480-320, is 20 km southwest of town; taxi fare to or from the city is at least LE10. It's served only by EgyptAir (tel. 322-400; open 0830-1800), which has offices on the Cornishe at the south end of town. There are frequent flights to Cairo (LE338), Luxor (LE109), and Abu Simbel (LE295); fares are roundtrip.

The **train station,** tel. 322-007, on the northern end of Sh. al-Suq is open 24 hours, but the ticket window is only open from 0800-1400, 1900-2200, and an hour before departures. Lines for tickets are shortest from 2000-2200. Wagon Lits sleepers leave at 1725 (#85), and 1810 (#87)—includes a nice coach car; LE216. Express coaches (such as they are) with stops in Luxor leave at 0515 (#981, arrives Cairo supposedly at 2255), 1650 (#89, arrives Cairo 0920), and 2035 (#887, arrives Cairo 0940); LE40.60, 1st class; LE22.80, 2nd class (to Cairo). Make reservations up to seven days ahead. Although the station is an easy walk from the Cornishe, if you have baggage or your hotel is in the center of town consider hiring a calishe or taxi, LE2-5.

The **bus station** (open 0530-2030) on Sh. Abtal al-Tahrir is near the Ramesses Hotel. To the northern towns, buses run from 0545-1500. To **Cairo:** three buses a day (all with a/c and video: 0600, LE35; 1530 via Hurghada, LE27 and Suez LE30, to Cairo LE43; 1600 alternates through Hurghada or Luxor depending on the day, check, LE43. Buses to **Luxor** (3½ hours, LE5) begin at 0630 and run north about every 40 minutes; they all stop in Kom Ombo (45 minutes, LE1.50), Idfu (two hours, LE2.25), and Isna (2½ hours, LE3.25). To **Hurghada:** in addition to the 1530 Cairo bus listed above, one leaves at 0800 (seven hours, LE16). To **Abu Simbel:** two buses a day leave Aswan 0800 and 1600, returning 0700 and 1345; they are supposed to be air-conditioned, but they aren't always.

Service taxis to the north depart from a covered stand west of the railroad tracks, near the large overpass. Kom Ombo, LE1.50; Idfu, LE2; Isna, LE3, and Luxor LE7. Southbound taxis leave from the square at Sh. Mahmud Yakoub and Abtal al-Tahrir (about two blocks south of the bus station).

Falucca trips down the Nile let you stop at the sites along the way. Figure LE25 (one day/one night) to Kom Ombo; LE45 (two days/two nights) to Idfu; LE50 (three days/three nights) to Isna; and LE60 (four days/four nights) to Luxor. Prices do not include food. You'll need to make arrangements directly with the captains of the boats. The boats take six people, and there is usually a list of people wanting to team up for a ride at the Tourist Office, which also keeps a list of captains. You'll have to register your passport, LE5, before you leave. Be careful sleeping on the banks, as tourists have been known to have their loads lightened as they dozed.

To Sudan
If you want to continue south from Aswan you can take a steamer/ferry across Lake Nasser. Make arrangements with the Nile Navigation Company, tel. 323-348; the offices are next to the Tourist Office; Sat.-Thurs. 0800-1400. You can book individual tickets at their offices at Ramesses Station in Cairo: open daily except Fri., 0900-1400. Boats sail on Mon. and Sat., although occasionally they run an extra ship during the week. The trip takes 20 hours; the ferry lands at Wadi Halfa and is supposed to connect with the train to Khartoum—don't count on it. Fares run LE125 1st class and LE75 2nd class. The trip is long and the schedule erratic; be sure to take food and a warm sleeping bag—the deck is cold steel. This trip is only for the hardy; flying out of Cairo into Khartoum is quicker and easier. However, the road past Abu Simbel now continues into Sudan and is quite good much of the way; confirm conditions in Aswan.

Geb, Nut, and Shu

VICINITY OF ASWAN

TOMBS OF THE NOBLES

Open daily 0800-1600; LE6. The pharaonic local gentry built their tombs into the cliffs tucked beneath the small round Dome of the Winds. Far from the center of culture in Memphis where the best craftsmen worked, these tombs are, by comparison, modest, their artwork considered by some to be crude. Nevertheless, the paintings are infused with life, for this is the work that led to the Middle and New Kingdom revivals.

The path from the ticket kiosk runs to the center of the caves; turn right and follow the path downward toward the tomb of Sarenput I. However, if you only have a short time, be sure to see the tomb of Sarenput II, which lies in the other direction. (See below.)

Tomb Of Sarenput I (#36)

This tomb, belonging to the 12th Dynasty prince who was mayor of Elephantine and the overseer of the priests of Satis, has fine limestone reliefs on the entrance. The six pillars of the vestibule, which once supported a ceiling, bear figures of the owner and biographical texts. On the right wall, scenes include the deceased with his bow-bearer and a dog; above them, Sarenput sits in a garden with singers and his mother, wife, and two daughters; the lower register shows men playing a board game. The left wall includes the deceased watching bulls fighting, in his papyrus raft spearing fish, and with his sandal-bearer, his three sons, and a dog; the side and rear walls of the west niche show him receiving offerings.

The stucco murals on the hall are badly damaged, but on the lower right wall (facing the doorway) you can still make out fowlers with a large net. On the left wall, the fine hieroglyphs relate Sarenput's biography; on the right at the rear of the chamber are the remains of a marsh hunting scene. Beyond lies the chapel, supported by two squared columns, with a false door set into the niche at the rear wall. The corridor to the left leads to the burial chamber.

Tomb Of Pepynakht (Hekayib) (#35)

As you return along the path, you'll encounter a jumble of several tombs. The two rooms to the left belonged to Pepynakht (also called Hekayib), the man who was deified and had a cult building at Kom on Elephantine. He was overseer of foreign troops in the 6th Dynasty during the long reign of Pepi II. On either side of the door (left room), this caravan leader and scribe tells of his adventures in Nubia and Asia (where he was sent by Pepi II to subdue the natives). In the small courtyard, the right wall depicts offering bearers; the entrance to the neighboring room (the left passageway) shows the deceased officiating. The room behind runs into the tomb of Hekayib's son, Governor Sibni II.

Tomb Of Harkhuf

The next major tomb to the south belongs to Harkhuf, Overseer of Foreign Soldiers, who lived during the reigns of Pepi I, Mernere, and Pepi II. This tomb is most noted for the biography inscribed at the entrance which, because it's carved in soft limestone, is now in poor condition. Hieroglyphs above the entrance spell out standard offerings and prayers as well as a catalogue of virtues, but the 26 lines to the far right comprise a letter written to Harkhuf by the boy-king Pepi I, with directions concerning the pygmy Harkhuf was bringing him from Yam. With typical boyhood candor, the king writes, "Come north to the residence at once! Hurry and bring with you this pygmy whom you brought from the land of the horizon-dwellers live, hale, and healthy, for the dances of the god, to gladden the heart, to delight the heart of King Neferkare who lives forever!" The rest of the rather small, four-pillared chapel contains little but two false doors.

Tomb Of Khunes

The large tomb just before you reach the steps by which you ascended belongs to the 6th Dynasty chancellor and lector-priest Khunes. The eight-pillared chapel stands open to the path. This tomb was plastered over by the Copts, an act that preserved the ancient paint. The left side of the chapel is painted with scenes of cat-

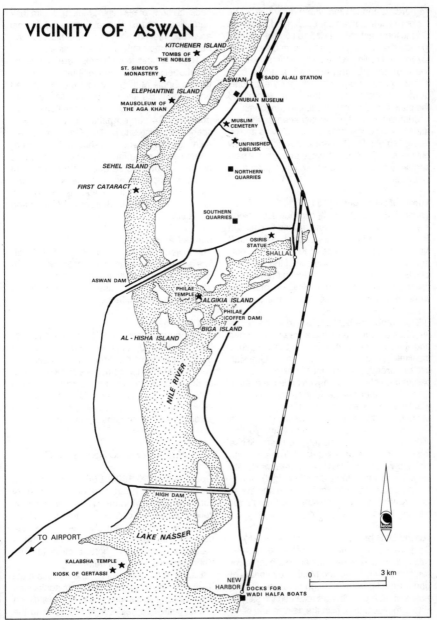

VICINITY OF ASWAN

KITCHENER ISLAND

TOMBS OF
THE NOBLES

ST. SIMEON'S
MONASTERY

ELEPHANTINE ISLAND

ASWAN

SADD AL-ALI STATION

NUBIAN MUSEUM

MAUSOLEUM OF
THE AGA KHAN

MUSLIM
CEMETERY

UNFINISHED
OBELISK

SEHEL ISLAND

NORTHERN
QUARRIES

FIRST CATARACT

SOUTHERN
QUARRIES

OSIRIS
STATUE

SHALLAL

ASWAN DAM

PHILAE
TEMPLE

ALGIKIA ISLAND

PHILAE
(COFFER DAM)

BIGA ISLAND

AL - HISHA ISLAND

NILE RIVER

HIGH DAM

TO AIRPORT

LAKE NASSER

KALABSHA TEMPLE

KIOSK OF QERTASSI

NEW
HARBOR

DOCKS FOR
WADI HALFA BOATS

0   3 km

© MOON PUBLICATIONS, INC.

tle herding and fowling with a draw net. In the lower register, servants prepare food and beer. On the fragment of front wall (to your left) scenes include a scribe, offering bearers, and a scene of fowling and fishing, while on the bottom there are more offering bearers, plowing, and a bull. These figures are particularly good examples of the provincial art liveliness that revitalized the stale formulas of the late Old Kingdom.

Just to the right of the last scenes, Khunes and his son appear before Khunes's wife and offering tables. The bottom two registers show butchers and cooks. Continue through this passageway to a small room, which served as a Coptic cell.

Tomb Of Sarenput II (# 31)

To reach Sarenput's tomb, continue south along the path, past the steps and around the bend in the cliff. Grandson of Sarenput I, Serenput II was Overseer of Priests of Khnum and Commander of the Frontier Garrison of the Southern Lands under Amenemhet II during the 12th Dynasty, when Egypt's Middle Kingdom pharaohs were extending their control to the Second Cataract.

This tomb, the best preserved in the cemetery, has an offering table between the second and third pillars on the right in the vestibule. Inset into niches in the hallway are Osiride statues of Sarenput, their paint still intact. The best part of the entire tomb, however, is the chapel. Its roof is supported by four pillars decorated with his portraits; the work rivals that produced in Memphis. At the rear of this chapel, the paint in the niche scenes is still fresh looking, glowing with color. If you look closely, you can still see the grid lines the painters used. The paintings that show Sarenput with his son (rear wall), with his wife and son (left), and mother (right) with offerings equal those at Beni Hassan and therefore rank as some of the best of Egypt's remaining Middle Kingdom art.

Tombs Of Sibni And Mekhu (#25 and 26)

Continue south to the tombs with the doubled causeways, which mark the adjoining tombs of son and father, Sibni and Mekhu, overseers of Upper Egypt during the reign of Pepi II. On the facade of Sibni's tomb, he's recorded the story of his trip to Nubia to punish the natives and bring back the body of his father, Mekhu, whom they had killed. The text also tells of the royal burial accorded Mekhu; King Pepi sent his own embalmers to mummify his valiant officer.

The entrances to both tombs are marked by small obelisks. The two vestibules, however, form a single rectangular room, distinguished only by the size and number of pillars and the two false doors. Sibni's large vestibule (supported by 14 carved pillars) is painted with scenes of fishing and fowling. On the front wall, paintings of the deceased show him with attendants receiving animals; across from it, in a niche, is Sibni's false door. In the center of Mekhu's 18-columned vestibule is an offering table. The back wall, contiguous with Sibni's tomb, contains the false doors of Mekhu and his family.

Qubbet Al-Hawwa

This tower, tomb of the local Sheikh Sidi Ali, offers a splendid panoramic view of the Nile and its islands, but is hardly worth the climb unless you're itching for exercise or continuing on to St. Simeon's Monastery.

Getting There

A village motor ferry (50PT) leaves every half-hour (0600-1800) and every hour (1800-2100) from just north of the Abu Simbel Hotel. Buy your ticket to the tombs at the small kiosk south of the landing site and then take the winding path that starts behind the building, a climb less steep than the straight causeways used to haul sarcophagi to the mouths of the tombs.

MONASTERY OF ST. SIMEON

Open daily 0900-1600; LE6—if and when a monk from the nearby modern monastery comes to collect. A monk will also make an excellent guide and can let you into the locked keep—be sure to tip him. But even without access to the keep, the ruins of Deir Amba Sama'an are worth the short walk from the Aga Khan's mausoleum (see below).

Begun in the 6th century, the fortress must have stood as a comforting bastion against the fierce landscape; situated on the side of a desert hill, its cultivated fields once ran down to the

Nile. The monastery was in constant use until its abandonment in 12-13th centuries.

Under the fragmented domes you can find remnants of Coptic art, and the structure itself, although late, is typical of early Christian fortress monasteries common in Egypt. The monastery's central keep demonstrates early use of the arch, not only as a structural element but as a vent for a passive air-conditioning system. But the real draw of St. Simeon is its isolation and the chance to climb around timeless ruins without constant "help" from greedy *ghaffirs*.

Lower Level

Originally surrounded by a 10-meter wall, the monastery is built on a pair of rock plateaus; religious functions were centered in the lower level, living quarters in the upper. The entrance is in the northeast, through a covered vestibule, and opens into the lower level nearly opposite the old church. To the left, visitors' lodgings line the wall. Beyond them a stairway rises, giving access to the upper stories of the tower where guards watched for Bedouin raiders. The rooms to the right, tucked into the corner under the tower, include the remains of a kiln. Although the buildings' lower stone stories are nearly intact, the upper ones of mud brick have vanished.

Fragments of paintings exist in the rooms next to the main church. The large courtyard with the bench set into the wall was probably used by the monks for recreation or to entertain visitors. At the northwest corner of the church, the ruins of the baptistery nestle in the shelter of the cliff, and a stairway leading to the upper levels climbs its northern side.

The Keep

The thick-walled keep (tower) dominating the upper area stood as a fortress within a fortress, serving the monks as a last defense if raiders breached the outer walls. The lower door is locked, so you'll need a guide to visit the monks' living quarters housed in a wing off its northern side. The ducts in the tops of the arches that span the hall provided the ventilation. To the east of the long corridor, which gives access to the monks' cells, lies the refectory, with shallow stone basins set in the floor; wooden tables that once lined the center vanished long ago. Farther east, bordering the refectory, is the kitchen.

The Upper Level

Directly south across the courtyard are the remains of the mill; behind it were workrooms and a water-filtration system that served the monks' bath and privies. In the southwest corner are work areas that include ovens, water-cooling systems, and even a winepress. The large set of ruins in the center of the courtyard were storage magazines and the northern end had equipment used in salt extraction. The bent entrance in the middle of the western wall gave exterior access to this upper level; the small building against the wall just south of it was the stable, the building farther south the grooms' quarters. The foundations in the northwestern corner are the remains of granaries and perhaps, in the corner, a weaving workshop.

For a short taste of desert hiking, return to the mausoleum's harbor via the gully that drops off to the left in front of the gateway.

Getting There

The Monastery of St. Simeon is about a 10- to 15-minute walk west along a nearly level paved path from the Aga Khan mausoleum, or you can hire a donkey or camel at the foot of the hill for about LE10. If you want to combine these sights with the nobles' tombs, start early with the nobles' tombs, then climb to the top of the cliffs (near the dome of Qubbet al-Hawwa). From there you can see the monastery, a walk of about 40 minutes across the sand—take plenty of water. If you're not a hearty walker, you can rent camels (best) or donkeys. If you want a detour, a quarry lies about halfway between the two sites; follow the path over the hill and turn right near the little tent. You can return via the mausoleum, either taking your chances on catching a falucca back or having made arrangements for one to meet you there.

MAUSOLEUM OF AGA KHAN

Open Tues.-Sun. 0900-1600; free admission; tipping is forbidden. Dominating the desert hill across from the south end of Elephantine Island, the pink granite mausoleum was built in the late 1950s to house the body of Aga Sultan Muhammad Shah (1887-1957), leader of the

Ismaili sect of Islam. Educated in Europe, he succeeded his father in 1885, becoming the 48th imam; after political exile from Pakistan, he continued to guide his faithful. Members of the sect believe themselves to be the direct spiritual ancestors of the Fatimids, which explains the resemblance of the Aga Khan's tomb to the Mosque of Giyushi, which nestles at the foot of the Moqattam Hills near Cairo.

The Aga Khan selected his own burial site, reached by a paved path from the base of the cliff, about a 10-minute climb, which is steep but has good footing. Giant brass doors open onto an airy courtyard; the marble sarcophagus lies beneath a dome at the far end of the mausoleum. It's covered with inscriptions from the Koran, except for the place where the name and dates of the Begum (his wife) will one day be added. Each day, according to his wishes, a fresh red rose is laid on the sarcophagus. The clean lines and imposing grandeur make the mausoleum worth the short climb. The Aga Khan mausoleum is easily accessible by privately hired falucca and is best included on a sail to the islands.

SEHEL ISLAND

Just north of the Aswan Barrage, Sehel marks the northern end of the First Cataract. The ancient Egyptians who were headed south stopped here to cut their prayers into the patina of the island's rocks, while those returning offered their thanks to the deities of the cataract for their safe trip. In fact, from the top of the west side, you can see the remains of the once-fierce First Cataract, now tamed by upriver dams. If you're hankering for a sail longer than just across the river, Sehel is an ideal destination—about an hour each way with a good wind. Pack a meal and spend the afternoon or early evening.

The inscriptions are found south of where you land, incised on jumbled mountains of boulders. The tan figures, even after 3,500 years, still stand out against the dark desert varnish. As you land, youngsters will undoubtedly swarm toward you, offering to show you to the rocks. Many are endearing and can guide you all over the island, including the Nubian village on the west side; your tip will help their families.

The inscribed rocks form two hills, and both piles are worth the climb. Of special note (on the top of the eastern hill) is the Ptolemaic-period stela (#81)—back-dated to the reign of King Djoser—telling how Khnum ended a catastrophic famine during the 3rd Dynasty. Undoubtedly, the priests, in an attempt to strengthen their god (and thus themselves), used the authority of age and put it in the center of Khnum's own territory.

Getting There

To reach Sehel, hire a falucca (LE40) from Aswan; you can combine this sail with a trip to Aga Khan's mausoleum and St. Simeon's Monastery and/or Kitchener's Island for another LE20.

THE DAMS

Note: both dams are *off-limits* to photography. The road south to the airport and the High Dam crosses the Aswan **Barrage,** or old dam. Built by the British between 1898 and 1902, it was for many years the largest in the world. Raised in 1912 and 1934, this granite dam now stands 50 meters high, 2,000 meters long, 30 meters thick at the base and 11 meters at the top. Its 180 sluice gates, which were opened during the inundation and then gradually closed as the river level dropped, preserved a semi-natural flood cycle.

High Dam

Open 0700-1700; LE2. Allow about an hour for a hurried visit, half a day if you intend to include Kalabsha Temple. The Aswan High Dam, built between 1960 and 1971, rises 111 meters high, is 980 meters thick at the bottom and 40 meters at the top, and stretches 3.6 km across the river. Lake Nasser backs up for nearly 500 km and averages over 10 km wide and 180 meters deep.

At the time the dam was built, Egypt was unable to feed her growing population, but with the impounded water, the country has now converted 700,000 *feddans* from the ancient basin irrigation system to perennial irrigation. In addition, the dam generates electricity for the country's emerging industries (increasing production by 30%), nourishes a fledgling fishing industry in

Lake Nasser, and protects the land from the vagaries of the Nile floods. In fact, without the High Dam, Egypt would have been hard hit by recurring droughts.

The dam, however, has also brought problems. Lake Nasser has raised the water table and increased humidity, thereby threatening the ancient limestone monuments with both dampness and salt encrustation. And the dam's effect on agriculture has not all been favorable: the land has lost the cleansing floodwaters of the Nile, and its annual layer of silt, now trapped behind the dam, can no longer renew the cultivated soil, forcing farmers to use chemical fertilizers. The change in irrigation systems has led to increased soil salinity, which requires extensive drainage projects to keep fields arable. A concurrent increase in standing water has allowed insect pest populations to explode.

The entrance is on the west side of the dam. To the south rises the modern lotus blossom tower, the visitor center. Originally a monument to Soviet-Egyptian accord, it now symbolizes general friendship; Soviet bas-reliefs illustrate the dam's benefits. Elevators run to observation towers above.

At the center of the road across the dam, the turnout contains diagrams and cross-sectional drawings of the dam. The power station dominates the east side, and if you walk across to it, you can see, on the south side of the dam, the protective gate that channels excessive water from the lake into the desert. From this side, you can also see across the lake to the granite promontory capped by the Temple of Kalabsha.

With the completion of the High Dam, much of ancient Nubia was flooded. In order to save both monuments and archaeological information, UNESCO, the Egyptian government, and numerous other countries mounted a salvage program that put over 40 international teams into the field. Massive amounts of anthropological material were excavated and recorded. Monuments that could not be moved were documented; the rest were cut up and transported piece by piece to higher ground or given to participating countries. (Entire temples, for example, are on display at New York's Metropolitan Museum and at Leiden, Netherlands.) The most famous moving job involved the Ramesses II

temples at Abu Simbel. The collection at the High Dam is less well known, but includes the well-preserved Kalabsha Temple, the granite chapel of Dedwen, the Roman kiosk from Qertassi, and the temple of Beit al-Wali.

KALABSHA COMPLEX

Kalabsha Temple

Open 0800-1700; LE5 for the temple; LE5 for the launch; permission is no longer required to visit the complex. The temple was dedicated to Merwel, known to the Greeks as Mandulis, a Nubian solar deity. Built in the Ptolemaic period, the temple follows the classical design: pylons, courtyard, hypostyle hall, and three-room sanctuary. The pylons run the entire width of the temple, but they're skewed from both the causeway and the front of the building. To rectify this error, the gateway (although it is aligned with the pylons) pierces the wall at less than 90 degrees. (A similar device of angling rooms within squared walls appears 1,000 years later as a design element in Cairo's mosques.)

[A] As a result of the slanted pylons, the open courtyard, which was once columned on all three sides, forms a trapezoid rather than a square; it is shorter on the southern side where the pillars are set closer together. Stairways at either end lead to the upper floors, which run through the pylons and offer a sweeping view of Lake Nasser. Stone screen-walls separate the courtyard from the hypostyle hall or vestibule and are decorated with reliefs of the king with Ibis-headed Thoth and falcon-headed Horus [a], who are pouring water, represented by the hieroglyphic signs for life and purity. There also appears a Greek decree [b], issued in A.D. 249 by Aurelius Besarion, the governor of Ombos and Elephantine, forbidding swineherds with their pigs to approach the temple.

The horseman in Roman dress receiving a crown from a war goddess [c] is perhaps the 5th century Nubian King Silko, who conquered the fierce Nubian tribe of Blemmyes.

[B] On the back wall of the vestibule, its roof supported by ornate flowered capitals, scenes show a Ptolemaic king presenting offerings to Isis and Mandulis [d], and Amenhotep II, founder of the temple, offering a libation of wine to Min

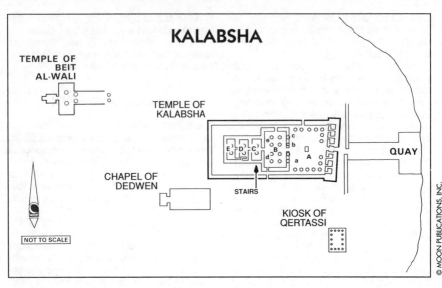

KALABSHA

TEMPLE OF
BEIT
AL-WALI

TEMPLE OF
KALABSHA

CHAPEL OF
DEDWEN

STAIRS

QUAY

KIOSK OF
QERTASSI

NOT TO SCALE

© MOON PUBLICATIONS, INC.

and Mandulis **[e]**. The Coptic painting to the left of the doorway shows the Hebrews in the fiery furnace.

[C] In the first chamber, the *pronaos,* the figures in the lower register personify the nomes; the large figure directly following the king is that of Nubia. Above them, gods, including Mandulis and the cobra-goddess, face the inner rooms; the king, surrounded by the goddesses of Upper and Lower Egypt as well as Amun-Min and Ptah, who is seated in his shrine, receives holy waters from Thoth and Horus.

[D] The *naos* decorations in the second room contain Augustus's name in several places; the figures, though quite well carved, have lost much of their color. In the bottom row, figures of the Nile-god form a decorative wainscoting; above them the king presents offerings to Osiris, Isis, and Mandulis, and he is also shown in the presence of such divinities as the lion-headed Nubian god Dedwen and Imhotep of Saqqara.

[E] The decoration of the third room, the *adyton,* is similar: the king offering Osiris and Mandulis a vase of water and a bouquet of flowers, symbols of inundation and fertility. This room, the third of the sanctuary, once housed the cult statue of Mandulis.

The Roof

Steps to the roof ascend from the south side of the *pronaos,* then downward into a small chapel set into the wall. The remains of a statue nearly fill the first room, and a passageway leads to a crypt. The whole complex is an abbreviated form of the Osiris temples in similar locations in other Ptolemaic temples.

Outer Walls

Outside the temple, on its back wall, Mandulis stands at either end of the scene: on the right in his royal form with pharaonic crown, holding the scepter and *ankh* sign, on the left in his divine form, complete with ram-horn crown surmounted by the uraeus, a solar disk, and ostrich plumes (a headdress designed to intimidate any divinity who might challenge him); his vulture-feather cloak unfurls wings that entwine across his body.

Kiosk Of Qertassi

To the south of the temple, this kiosk was moved at the same time as Kalabsha. Similar to Trajan's kiosk at Philae (see p. 395), the composite capitals were once linked by decorated screens. Of the entryway, only the two large Hathor columns remain. The light, almost delicate structure offers a little shade and a view of both the temple and lake.

Rock Temple Of Beit Al-Wali

Located behind Kalabsha, around the hill to the northwest, this temple was originally carved out of its native mountain in the time of Ramesses II. The narrow court of the cruciform temple is decorated with contemporary battle scenes. On the left, the king with his eldest sons in their chariots battle the Nubians, who flee back to their camp; the king, in victory, sits on his throne beneath a canopy while Ethiopians bring their tribute. Amenemope, viceroy of Nubia, who probably led the campaign, receives his reward of rings and skins from the king. The opposite wall shows battles against the Libyans and Asiatics and the king's sons dragging prisoners before him.

The interior transverse hall is supported by two proto-Doric columns, while the remarkably preserved walls depict Ramesses II worshipping before Isis and Horus of Buhen, as well as the local deities of Aswan: Khnum, Satis, and Anukis. In the Christian period, the vestibule was roofed with a vault and converted into a church.

Getting There

Local trains run out to the High Dam (Sadd al-Ali Station) about eight times a day (outward-bound from 0630 to 1945, inward-bound 0800-1230) and cost 25PT. However, the station is at the docks—not at the dam itself, so you'll need to hike back (about 4½ km) to the structure. A far better plan is to catch a bus out (about every 40 minutes, 20PT), or better yet, bargain with a cab for a half-day tour, about LE30, including a stop at Philae and time at Kalabsha.

If Lake Nasser is low, you can reach the temple from the road that runs along the back of the dam; about two-thirds of the way down, cut off to your right and cross a ravine filled with boat-building equipment; it's then a short walk up to the temple wall. If the water's high, you'll need to take a launch (LE5 roundtrip) across this stretch.

PHILAE TEMPLE COMPLEX

Open 0700-1500, winter 0700-1400; LE10 plus LE10 for the whole boat—you can usually find someone to split it with you if you want. This Ptolemaic temple complex dedicated to Isis was built on the island of Philae, but when the Aswan Barrage was constructed, many of the temple buildings were partially flooded. When the High Dam (which would have raised the lake level so much as to completely submerge the island complex) was proposed, the buildings were moved to the higher neighboring island of Agilkia. Agilkia, blasted and relandscaped to duplicate Philae's topography, became modern Philae. Today, the island floats like a jewel in a pool of royal blue; the best time to see it is early, when the lake is glassy calm and the slanting rays of Khepri turn the island complex richly golden.

Although ancient Egyptians came to the sacred islands late in the New Kingdom, the area's mystique developed during the Greco-Roman period. Most of the present buildings date to the Late Period and the Ptolemaic era. Though the construction spanned over 800 years, some of the structures are still incomplete.

So powerful was Isis' cult throughout the Roman period that pilgrims from the farthest reaches of the empire traveled to Philae to invoke the goddess's healing powers. When Rome lay in ruins and sheep were grazing in the abandoned Colosseum, long after the rest of Egypt had converted to Christianity, this temple remained open for pagan worship. Not until the reign of Justinian in A.D. 550 was the temple finally closed, ending the 40-century reigns of Re, Isis, Horus, Osiris, and the other pagan

PHILAE SOUND AND LIGHT SHOW		
	Early Show	Late Show
Saturday	English	French
Sunday	French	German
Monday	English	Italian
Tuesday	French	English
Wednesday	English	Spanish
Thursday	Arabic	French
Friday	English	French

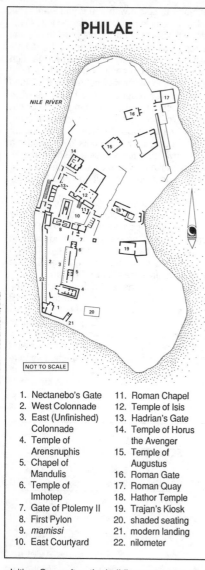

PHILAE

NILE RIVER

NOT TO SCALE

© MOON PUBLICATIONS, INC.

1. Nectanebo's Gate
2. West Colonnade
3. East (Unfinished) Colonnade
4. Temple of Arensnuphis
5. Chapel of Mandulis
6. Temple of Imhotep
7. Gate of Ptolemy II
8. First Pylon
9. *mamissi*
10. East Courtyard
11. Roman Chapel
12. Temple of Isis
13. Hadrian's Gate
14. Temple of Horus the Avenger
15. Temple of Augustus
16. Roman Gate
17. Roman Quay
18. Hathor Temple
19. Trajan's Kiosk
20. shaded seating
21. modern landing
22. nilometer

Biga Island

In ancient times, the cults were centered on the neighboring islands of Philae and Biga. Located just west of Philae, Biga to the southern Egyptians was the sacred mound, the first island of earth created from the Chaos of Nun. Like Abydos, it was a burial place of Osiris, and elaborate rites centered on the Osirian shrine, from which all but the high priests were banned. The Greeks named it Biga Abaton, the Forbidden. As a result of these ritual prohibitions, Philae became the center for public cult activities.

Although the exact site of the sacred shine has never been determined, remains of a Ptolemaic vestibule and *pronaos* cap the promontory. If you like to walk, hike to the southeast corner of the island, where you'll find New Kingdom graffiti: large-scale inscriptions of Khaemwese, son of Ramesses II, commemorating his father's jubilees. Farther south are the cartouches of King Apries. The mud-brick ruins atop the hill to the south are the remains of a Christian monastery.

Philae Island

Island from the Time of Re, Philae was the last link with the ancient religion. The temple's art and architecture represent a fusion of Egyptian, Greek, and Roman civilizations; the buildings, unsurpassed in their harmony, nestle in one of Egypt's most beautiful settings. The remarkably intact temple and its complex cover most of the southern tip of the island. To the north, the remains of a Roman mud-brick village were reduced to amorphous mud by the repeated soaking of the lake, so only the stone remnants of a temple, a convent, an old quay, and a gateway were moved to Algikia.

If you approach Philae from the eastern side, you will pass the arches of Diocletian's Roman gateway and then beyond them, the looming pillars of Trajan's kiosk, also known as Pharaoh's Bed, the most photographed of all Philae's monuments. As you approach these monuments, take photos, for the boatman may well make the return trip along the western side of the island.

Kiosk Of Nectanebo

[1] The launches land at the ancient quay at the southern tip of the island. Begin your ex-

deities. Soon after, the buildings were occupied by Christians who defaced the images, carved memorial crosses in the walls, and held services in the temple courtyard.

ploration of the ruins with the small kiosk of Nectanebo I (30th Dynasty). In ancient times, this entrance to the temple was reached by a double stairway that ascended both sides of the quay. The kiosk, dedicated to Nectanebo's "Mother Isis" was originally formed of 14 columns, but today only six remain. Note the double capitals composed of the traditional flower shapes and the sistrum-Hathor squares, an addition that supported the architrave. The screens that once formed the walls are crowned with cavetto cornices and rows of uraeus serpents, architectural details dating at least to the 3rd Dynasty nearly 3,000 years earlier.

The Colonnades

[2] Two colonnades link the kiosk to the gateway of the first pylon. The one on the west, which follows the natural curve of the island, is the more complete. Here, the capitals, of which no two are alike, demonstrate the Ptolemaic artisans'

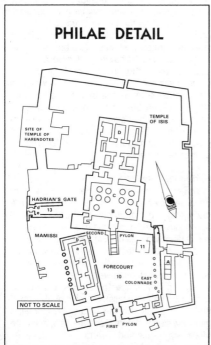

PHILAE DETAIL

TEMPLE OF ISIS

SITE OF TEMPLE OF HARENDOTES

HADRIAN'S GATE

D

C

B

13

MAMISSI

SECOND PYLON

11

FORECOURT

10 EAST COLONNADE

NOT TO SCALE

FIRST PYLON

© MOON PUBLICATIONS, INC.

capacity for creating intricate, natural detail. The windows piercing the wall behind the columns once faced Biga, Island of Osiris. Between 12 and 13 are steps to a nilometer.

[3] The eastern colonnade was never finished, but its back wall shelters several important structures.

[4] At its southern end lie the ruins of the Temple of Arensnuphis, an obscure god of the Late Period who was worshipped as the Goodly Companion of Isis. Little more than the foundations of the kiosk-like forecourt, its three vestibules and the sanctuary protected by a wall remain.

[5] Slightly north, entered by a door in the colonnade wall, is the ruined chapel of Mandulis, the Nubian god to which Kalabsha Temple is dedicated.

[6] At the north end are the well-preserved remains of the Temple of Imhotep, the physician/sage who built Djoser's Step Pyramid at Saqqara and in later times was deified as a god of healing. On the walls of the forecourt (the interior was never decorated) Ptolemy IV appears before Imhotep; Khnum, Satis, Anukis, Osiris, and Isis also adorn the walls.

First Pylon

[7] Outside the southeast wall of the first pylon and set at right angles to it is the gate of Ptolemy II, possibly a remnant of an earlier layout. The eastern pylon wall (along with its partner to the west) was built by Ptolemy XII and contains traditional scenes of offerings and of the pharaoh massacring his enemies.

[8] The main portal is older, dating to Nectanebo I; to the right, inside the lintel, are inscriptions carved by Napoleon's French army, commemorating their victory over the Mamluks in 1799. Two granite obelisks once graced the front (one of which contained Cleopatra's cartouche, which was recognized by Champollion), but now only a pair of granite lions remains.

The eastern pylon is split, the door in its center leading to the *mamissi*. The entrance is covered with images of the gods who will partake in the rituals conducted in the *mamissi*, and below them march the personified districts of Nubia. The two rooms inside the pylon on either side of the entrance once housed guards. The back of the pylon has scenes of priests carrying Isis' barque.

The Mammisi

[9] Built by Ptolemy IV, this birth house is similar to those at Dendera and Idfu, where pharaoh linked his ancestry to Horus and Osiris. The building is surrounded by a screened colonnade whose capitals are similar to those on Nectanebo's kiosk. A columned forecourt leads into two vestibules and the sanctuary; traditional birth scenes cover the second vestibule.

[a] On the back wall, the triumphant Horus, wearing the double crown, rises from the marsh where Isis brought him up. [b] The exterior decorations are not outstanding, but the back of the mammisi is notable for a scene (lower register) showing Isis nursing the infant Horus in the swamp—a poignant counterpoint to the triumphant Horus on the opposite (inside) of the wall.

East Courtyard And Colonnade

[10] Beyond the elegant plant columns, the east wall is covered with scenes of the king performing rituals, including dragging the barque of Sokar [c]. Behind the wall are five service rooms, their original functions uncertain. The fourth [A] is called the library and is dedicated to Thoth, whose images in both his baboon and ibis forms cover the walls.

Roman Chapel

[11] Built on a natural outcropping of granite, the eastern pylon incorporates rock smoothed and inscribed by Ptolemy IV recording his deed in the temple to Isis. In front of this inscription, the Romans built a small chapel.

Second Pylon

Set at an angle to the first pylon, this gateway changes the complex's axis. On the right upper corner of the passageway between the pylons are remains of Christian paintings. The gateway leads into the hypostyle hall of the Isis Temple.

Isis Temple

[B] The main outline of the Isis Temple follows the classical layout, but typical of Ptolemaic construction, the second pylon opens onto the hypostyle hall, the front portion being left as an uncovered courtyard. Like the columns in the western colonnade, the work on the capitals here is unusually fine.

[C] The eight-columned vestibule, originally separated from the courtyard by screen-walls, leads to the temple's interior.

[D] The main axis is divided into three serial antechambers and, adjoining them, three side rooms. The sanctuary, with two tiny windows in the roof to admit light, still contains the pedestal, dedicated by Ptolemy III and his wife Bernice, that once supported Isis' royal barque.

Occasionally you might find the gate (west side) to the roof open; otherwise inquire about getting it open. Once up, be careful not to step onto the screens covering the skylights of the sanctuary below. Steps lead downward to the vestibule of the Osiris rooms. Here you'll find gods bewailing the dead Osiris or offering to Isis, Nephthys, or Osiris-Wenennefer. The actual scenes vary from temple to temple, but most correspond to the various rituals enacted. The inner room depicts the gathering up of Osiris' limbs and his revival and impregnation of Isis, who would later give birth to Horus. Osiris, on his bier, lies naked and ithyphallic, his phallus crudely obliterated by later Christians. Mourned by Isis and Nephthys, he revives; his dismembered, headless body is then reconstructed by Selket and Douait, preparing him for his solar rebirth in late July or August, when the Nile began its rise.

Identified with the hawk-headed Sokar, Osiris is carried out by the four sons of Horus to a papyrus marsh, where a priest pours holy water on him. Anubis attends the bier, while Isis and Nephthys kneel beside it. The entire sequence seems to have no beginning, no end—an endless cycle of death and rebirth. Return to the ground floor, turn right and leave the Isis Temple by the western door.

Hadrian's Gate

[13] Set into a section of the girdle wall that once encircled the island, this gateway is the main standing monument west of the temple and is joined to the remains of a vestibule, with reliefs depicting rites of Osiris. Perhaps these rituals are shown here because the gateway once faced Biga, Osiris's special sanctuary. Over the lintel, Emperor Hadrian stands before the gods; on the left jamb is the sacred relic of Abydos, and on the right, the fetish of Osiris. At the top of the wall, Marcus Aurelius, who embellished the gateway, stands before Osiris and Isis; below he offers Isis grapes and flowers.

horizon, Osiris sits enthroned with his heir, Horus. The scene is framed by a canopy of stars, the sun, and the moon.

Through the gate to the west are the remains of another ancient quay, and farther south, near the side of the *mamissi,* lie the remains of a nilometer.

Temple Of Hathor
[18] In the restored colonnade of Hathor's small temple, the columns are decorated with musical scenes: Bes playing a tambourine or strumming a harp, an ape playing a guitar-like instrument, and the king rattling a sistrum before Hathor in her guise as the lion-goddess Sekhmet. The plant columns, which were once joined to the bearing walls by screens, mark the entrance to the temple proper, which was never decorated. Of the sanctuary beyond, all that remains is the pavement.

Trajan's Kiosk
[19] The majestic floral-capped columns of Trajan's kiosk are linked by screen-walls pierced both east and west to provide a gateway for formal processions emerging from the quay below and approaching the temple precinct. The kiosk, much of which was permanently underwater on Philae, was removed block by block by a team of British navy divers. Today the kiosk's majestic effect is produced by the sheer massiveness of its simple design.

Getting There
If you hire a cab (LE15-25) to explore the Aswan area, include the island temple complex of Philae on your itinerary. Although an organized tour usually offers enough time to visit the temples, it doesn't give you the flexibility to choose the time of your visit or the option of landing on neighboring Biga Island for a hike over the rocky hills.

Trajan's kiosk, Philae

[d] This wall (which was never completed) depicts the origin of the Nile. Here, a vulture and a falcon sit atop the rocky pile of Biga; beneath, in a cave, the Nile-god Hapi (encircled by a protective snake) pours forth the two streams of the Nile. To the right, Isis, Nephthys, and others adore the young falcon as he rises from the marsh.

[e] The top register depicts the sisters presenting the crowns of Upper and Lower Egypt to Horus, whose name is being inscribed on a palm branch by Thoth (left) and Seshat (right). Farther to the left, a goddess plays the lyre. Below, Isis stands outside her temple watching a crocodile bear the corpse of Osiris across the water to a rocky promontory that could only be Biga. Above, inside the disk rising between the hills of the

ABU SIMBEL

Nubia, Land of Gold to the ancients, lies between Aswan and Khartoum in modern Sudan, an area that supplied Egypt with gold, incense, wood, ivory, mercenaries, and slaves. Old Kingdom pharaohs sporadically sent trading, mining, and military expeditions into Nubia, but Middle Kingdom pharaohs methodically subdued the natives and built a series of mud-brick forts that also served as trading posts along the Nile from Aswan to the Second Cataract.

New Kingdom rulers extended Egypt's borders to the Fourth Cataract, and Ramesses II, in a gesture of piety and self-aggrandizement (and also to flex political muscle in Nubia), ordered two sun temples carved from the limestone mountains at Abu Simbel. Here, on the face of the cliffs, stonemasons hewed giant figures of the king that (to the ancients) radiated power, dominated the landscape, and with their ceaseless stares subjugated all who dared to enter Egypt.

History

The desolate stretch of the Nile near Abu Simbel was venerated from prehistoric times, and Ramesses' temples occupied the site of an earlier shrine. The main building, dedicated to the gods Ptah, Re-Harakhte, Amun-Re, and Ramesses' own deified form, faces east, and twice each year (22 Feb. and 22 Oct.) the rising sun streams nearly 200 meters into the heart of the rock to bathe the statues of the sun-gods occupying the temple sanctuary. Nearby, around to the side of the cliff, Ramesses ordered a smaller temple built, one which angles more southward; although nominally dedicated to Hathor, it, in fact, immortalizes his Great Wife, Nefertari.

The temples were used well into the Christian period until they were ordered closed. When rituals ceased, the priests abandoned the buildings to the desert. Filled with sand, walled off from the world, the temples were forgotten until 1813, when they were discovered by the Swiss explorer Burckhard. They became a must-see site for Victorian visitors, who crossed the desert to reach the gigantic temples which stood above the Nile, dominating the barren landscape.

In modern times, the two temples of Abu Simbel were threatened by the waters that would rise with the completion of the High Dam. A campaign to save them was organized and funded by UNESCO. The plan was to cut the temples into blocks, raise them piece by piece, and then reassemble them in their new position; but the massive job presented numerous difficulties. The brittle stone had to be stabilized with injections of synthetic resin. Then, when workers started to cut into the limestone with water-cooled saws, the water dissolved the stone and special saws had to be developed. In addition, stonemasons had to cut and move not only the giant figures at the fronts of the temples, but cut into the cliff behind them and extract the rooms ancient carvers had tunneled deep into the hill. The project took over two years (1966-68), during which time workers cut the temples into blocks weighing up to 30 tons, numbered them, and hauled them to the top of the cliff. Being careful to preserve the temples' original orientations, they reassembled the structures 70 meters above and 200 meters behind their original position on the riverbank. The temples were then encased in a cement-and-steel mountain, replicating their original topography; the waters of Lake Nasser have risen at the new site to nearly the level of the former river, so the temples once more look south over the water.

Visiting The Site

Open daily 0500-1700; LE21, including an obligatory guide fee. The false mountain rises to the north of the ticket stand; to reach the temple entrances, walk past the stand, down the slight hill, and head left around the shoulder of the mountain.

To best photograph the temples, schedule your visit before noon, for by afternoon the passing sun plunges the temple face into shadow. To bring out the detail, underexpose the reflective face of the temples by 1-1½ stops. If you want to photograph the temples from the air, sit on the left side of the plane and use a telephoto (at least 200 mm) with a haze filter.

THE SUN TEMPLE OF RAMESSES II

The temple, not executed with the most careful of craftsmanship, nevertheless succeeds in its majesty of design. The facade of the temple is dominated by four giant colossi, which, at 20 meters, are taller than the Colossi of Memnon at Luxor. Ramesses II's cartouches appear on the pendants suspended from the figures' necks and are carved into the upper arms and between the huge legs. Appreciation of the statues depends upon individual taste: some claim that calm and introspective faces rise above well-proportioned figures, while others feel that stylized and empty visages top awkwardly carved, overly massive bodies. But no one disputes that the temple facade, in its sheer size, is awesome.

Between the colossi, members of Ramesses' family stand at his knees. To the left of the headless figure is his mother, Tuiy, on his right, Nefertari, and between his legs, Prince Amonherkhepshef, whose beautifully painted tomb lies at the top of the hill in the Valley of the Queens. On this same colossus, a Greek inscription on his left leg identifies mercenaries sent by Psamtik II from Aswan to the Second Cataract. On either side of the two colossi framing the entrance, the prisoners carved on the bases display the ancient artists' sense of geography: the captives appearing on the south side are Nubian while those on the north are Asiatic. Above them, the two Hapis of Upper and Lower Egypt entwine the papyrus and sedge around the hieroglyph "to unite."

The Facade

The face of the cliff replaces the pylon of an ordinary temple; the cornice sports cartouches of Ramesses II surrounded by uraei. Along the top, a troop of baboons face east as if to greet the rising sun. Above the doorway, set into the rock, stands a falcon-headed sun-god. In his left hand the god holds a *was*-scepter and in his right, a figure of Ma'at; the entire figure forms a pictorial play of words on the king's prenomen User-Ma'at-Re, who therefore appears as the central figure of the temple and its principal divinity.

On either side of this figure, the king, executed in sunk relief, presents images of Ma'at to

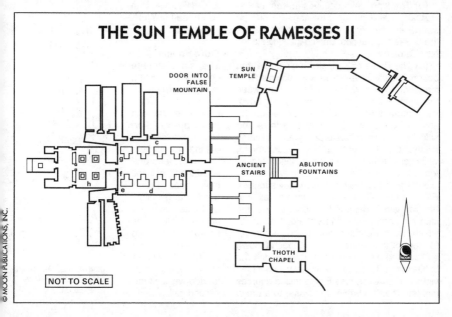

THE SUN TEMPLE OF RAMESSES II

DOOR INTO FALSE MOUNTAIN

SUN TEMPLE

ANCIENT STAIRS

ABLUTION FOUNTAINS

THOTH CHAPEL

NOT TO SCALE

the god and therefore to his own deified name. On the door lintel, Ramesses is shown laying the foundation stone of the temple before Amun and Mut (left) and Re-Harakhte and the lion-headed Wert-Hekew (right).

Grand Hall

The door, bearing Ramesses II's cartouches, leads into a large pillared hall cut from the rock, and beyond it, a second cut-rock hall connects to the sanctuary with its statues of the gods. Long rectangular storage rooms branch off at right angles to the temple axis: two on the south, four on the north. As in other temples, the floor gradually rises and the roof lowers, narrowing focus to the sanctuary.

Corresponding roughly to the open court with a covered portico, this hall is supported by eight pillars carved with Osirian figures of Ramesses II, wearing short kilts rather than mummy bandages. Those on the south side of the hall wear the white crown of Upper Egypt, those on the north, the double crown. The wall paintings testify to the king's prowess in battle.

[a] The king slaughters captives in the presence of Amun-Re.

[b] The king slays captives in front of Re-Harakhte who hands the king the curved sword—a shape typical of Egyptian arms since the prehistoric periods. Behind the king stands his guardian *ka*.

[c] The Battle of Kadesh. Beginning at the bottom left, the Egyptian army is shown marching toward the city. The next scene (between the doors of the storage rooms) is of the Egyptian encampment, which is protected by shields—the camp life complete with resting soldiers, unhitched horses being fed, and camp followers. To the right, the king sits enthroned, while below him, captive spies are tortured for information.

Acting on the misinformation they supplied, Ramesses attacks the city and thereby falls into the trap laid for him. In the upper panels, the king singlehandedly fights the enemy army, which has surrounded him. In the center, defenders of the fortified city of Kadesh (shown surrounded by the Orontes River) watch the battle, which Ramesses claims as an unqualified victory. (However, less Egyptianized sources indicate that the battle was closer to a draw,

the king cutting himself out of the Hittite trap but failing to take Kadesh.) The far right scene shows the king in his chariot supervising his officers who count the severed hands of the dead enemies and bring fettered prisoners.

[d] In more battle scenes, the king, followed by his three sons, storms a fortress, while below, a herdsman flees. Although the king's double arm has been touted as an attempt to show animation, it more probably is an artistic error not completely obliterated—and no matter what the guides tell you, Egyptian chariots only work with *two* horses.

[e] The triumphal return of the king with captured Negroes. In the top register, the king kneels under the sacred tree before Re-Harakhte as Thoth and Seshat stand nearby, perhaps to record his reign.

[f] Ramesses II presents Negroes to Amun, himself, and Mut. Between the last two pillars, the stela commemorates Ramesses II's building program in Memphis.

[g] Ramesses leads captured Hittites before Harakhte as well as his own deified figure and the lion-headed Wert-Hekew.

Store Rooms

The eight storage chambers adjoining the hall were probably used to stow temple treasure and cult objects. The scenes are religious, but the artwork here is cruder, less polished than that in the main rooms. (You'll need your flashlight as these room are not illuminated.) The rooms' positions and the use of connecting hallways eliminated the need for doorways off the second hall.

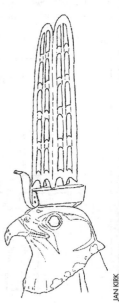

gold and obsidian head of Horus, 6th Dynasty (c. 2350 B.C.)

Second Pillared Hall

The second hall corresponds to the hypostyle hall of freestanding temples.

[h] The king and his wife Nefertari, holding two sistra, offer incense before the sacred barque and shrine of Amun, which is carried by priests.

[i] A similar scene before Re-Harakhte's barque.

The Sanctuary

Beyond are three chapels, the central one containing the four deities worshipped in the temple: Ptah, Re-Harakhte, Amun-Re, and the king. Interestingly, the figure of Ptah is situated so that the sun does not strike it when its rays pierce the inner chambers.

Exterior Monuments

[j] The stela that commemorates Ramesses II's marriage to a daughter of the Hittite king; at the top of the plaque, Ramesses II sits enthroned between two gods under a canopy as the Hittite king and his daughter worship him.

Sun Chapel: Within this open court dedicated to the sun stand two pedestals with cavetto cornices. The southern one (with steps) once held four praying baboons; the northern one had a chapel enclosing images of Khepri and baboon-Thoth (now in the Antiquities Museum in Cairo). On the north wall, Ramesses sacrifices to Re-Harakhte in a sun boat drawn by jackals.

HATHOR TEMPLE OF NEFERTARI

To visit the queen's Hathor Temple, walk north through the gate in the wall that joins the courtyard. The facade of this temple, like that of Ramesses' temple, is hewn from the cliff-face to imitate a receding pylon; its cavetto cornice has, however, fallen. On either side of the entrance, colossi of Ramesses and the deified Nefertari seem to stride from the rock; like the figures at the larger temple, these too are surrounded by their children. The temple doorway is protected by a frieze of cobras.

Hypostyle Hall

The Hathor Temple is simpler than Ramesses', having a single columned hall, a vestibule with the two ancillary rooms forming niches at either end, and a single sanctuary set into the center of the back wall. The columns show Hathor on the side facing the central aisle; the royal couple, gods, and goddesses adorn the other sides. The wall scenes show the queen participating in the ritual as an equal to her husband. On the entrance wall, she accompanies Ramesses as he slays Egypt's enemies.

The northeast wall has scenes of offerings, while the southwest one portrays Ramesses' crowning by Horus and Seth, beyond which he presents Ma'at to Amun. The presentation of Ma'at appeared at the beginning of the 19th Dynasty and was perhaps related to an attempt of the Ramesside line to restore order after the upheavals caused by Akhenaten and the instability of the short reigns that followed. The back wall shows the queen before Hathor (left) and Mut (right).

Transverse Chamber

Three doors lead to a transverse chamber, and over the doors of the lateral storage rooms (barely begun) are a pair of reliefs depicting a Hathor cow perfectly framed by the reeds of the marsh; in one she is worshipped by the king, and on the other by his wife.

The Sanctuary

Its roof supported by sistrum capitals, this room contains a high relief of Hathor the cow, and under her chin, the recipient of her protection, is the king. Above it, vultures guard the queen's cartouches. On the left wall, Nefertari offers incense to Mut and Hathor; on the right, the king worships before his own image and that of his wife. Two spaces have been left for doors to chambers planned to flank the sanctuary. The reliefs in this temple appear more delicate, more carefully drawn than those in the larger temple, and the figure of the queen is markedly slender. The predominance of yellow in the paintings may allude to Hathor, who was also known as The Golden.

The False Mountain

Return to the ticket kiosk via the interior of the false mountain. Rather than passing through the gate in the ancient wall, veer right and enter through the gray door. An inside landing supports a display explaining how the temple was moved.

The "Solstices"
On 22 February and 22 October, (and a day or so either direction) the temple is aligned so that the sun, upon rising, streams directly through the temple to touch the face of Ramesses. The place is a zoo, however, with crowds packing the aisles and officials keeping the lights on until the darkness has already faded, diluting the impact of the moment. The days are becoming a festival time for the town however, with folk dancing and sporting events. If you're interested, check with the Tourist Office in Aswan for the schedule.

PRACTICALITIES

Abu Simbel City nestles near the temples, and its few streets make exploring easy if you wish. Recently, new development has occurred several km out the road to the airport. The Police Station and the post office are on the main road from the temples before you get to the "Y." The telephone code is 097.

Accommodations
The **Nefertari Hotel,** (tel. 324-836 or in Cairo 757-905/837-472) charges $48 s, $68 d, complete with a/c and baths. Within easy walking distance of the temples, the hotel offers a swimming pool (LE10), which overlooks the lake and tennis courts. Out by the airport is the clean, simple **Nobaleh Ramesses,** Abu Simbel City, tel. 324-736, ext. 294; in Cairo: 348-5592/348-7761, fax 348-4821; $25 s, $31 d.

You can camp along the lakeshore in front of the temples; no facilities.

Getting There
Abu Simbel lies on the west side of Lake Nasser, 270 km south of Aswan. The quickest and easiest way to reach the site is by air. EgyptAir runs two flights daily during the summer season (more in winter) that also connect with Luxor and Cairo. The roundtrip fare (LE295) from Aswan includes bus transportation from the Abu Simbel airport to the monument and back. The flight is popular, so make reservations; if the Cairo offices of EgyptAir report that the flight is filled, often you can still get seats in Aswan the day before, but if your schedule is tight, don't take the chance.

The flight from Aswan takes about half an hour, but since the seats aren't reserved, plan on getting to the airport an hour to an hour and a half early, especially if you want to get a left-side seat, which is best for photos. The plane schedule gives you about two hours at the temples, which is usually sufficient; if you wish to stay longer, you can catch a later flight back, although airline officials usually discourage it.

The new road and improved accommodations have increased the tourist flow to Abu Simbel, and now sunrise at Abu Simbel, once a nearly private time, is overrun with busloads of tourists. Daily a/c (at least sometimes) **buses** ply the road along Lake Nasser between Aswan and Wadi Halfa on the Sudanese border, stopping at Abu Simbel; 0800 and 1345 to, and 1600 and 1900 back, LE19. The trip takes three hours, so pack a lunch. Service taxis congregate across from the Ramesses Hotel; LE10 to Aswan. The road is an easy drive for private cars; gas is available toward the airport.

uraeus of Sesostris II, 12th Dynasty (c. 1897-1878 B.C.)

JAN KIRK

THE DELTA, ALEXANDRIA, AND THE MEDITERRANEAN COAST

THE DELTA

In pharaonic times, five tributaries of the Nile fed the vast marshlands of the delta. Thickets of papyrus and tangles of reeds isolated the land; only in flood stage could the light reed skiffs of the ancient Egyptians penetrate the growth. But pharaonic farmers cultivated the borders, for where the rich soil was exposed at the edge of the desert, the marsh mellowed into savanna. As the climate dried over the centuries, the Egyptians penetrated ever deeper into the sloughs, their irrigation works draining and drying the land for cultivation. Eventually, silt filled in all but two branches of the Nile, the western Rosetta and the eastern Damietta. The Egyptians reclaimed the entire area and today the delta supplies the vast majority of Egypt's crops.

History

The general hostility of the delta, like the desert, tended to repel invaders, who skirted the area and headed for Memphis. Nevertheless, foreigners, especially from the east, filtered into the great green triangle, establishing homes and villages. As the land dried and the population grew, the area became more inviting, eventually providing a base for the Hyksos who invaded in the middle of the 17th century B.C.

Although the pharaohs of the early New Kingdom ruled from Thebes in Upper Egypt, to protect the delta they maintained a strong military presence at Memphis. When the Ramesside kings inherited the throne, they moved their capital north to Tanis in the eastern delta, from where they could both control their Middle Eastern subjects

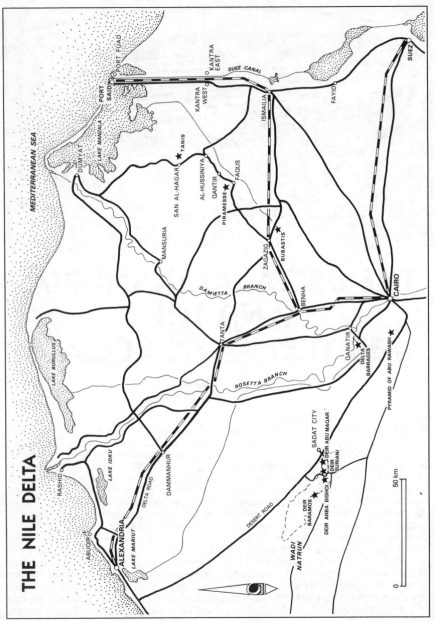

THE NILE DELTA

MEDITERRANEAN SEA

PORT SAID
PORT FUAD
KANTRA EAST
KANTRA WEST
SUEZ CANAL
SUEZ
ISMAILIA
FAYID

LAKE MANZALA
DUMYAT
TANIS
SAN AL-HAGAR
AL-HUSSINIYA
QANTIR
FAQUS
PIRAMESSE

MANSURIA

BUBASTIS
ZAGAZIG

DAMIETTA BRANCH
BENHA

LAKE BURULLUS

TANTA

QANATIR
DELTA BARRAGES
PYRAMID OF ABU RAWASH

CAIRO

ROSETTA BRANCH

LAKE IDKU
RASHID

DAMMANHUR

SADAT CITY
DEIR ABU MAQAR
DEIR SURIANI
DEIR ANBA BISHOI
DEIR BARAMOS

DELTA ROAD
DESERT ROAD

ALEXANDRIA
ABUQIR
LAKE MARIUT

WADI NATRUN

50 km
0

© MOON PUBLICATIONS, INC.

and guard against intruders. When Alexander founded the city that bears his name along the Mediterranean coast, he solidified the shift of power north, where it remained until the conquering Arabs moved the capital of Egypt to Fustat.

SIGHTS

Although a number of cult centers and ports flourished throughout the delta, the moist soil has reduced most to a few foundation blocks and pavements. But for those who want to get off the beaten path, the ruins are a good excuse to go exploring.

Eastern Delta

Near Zagazig lie the ruins of **Bubastis,** ancient capital of the 18th *nome* and home of the cat-goddess Bastet, whose feast, according to Herodotus, was the largest in Egypt. Today the ruins of Tell al-Basta span the road; the remains of Late Period temples built by Osorkon II and Nectanebo II lie to the south, and to the north, behind an Old Kingdom structure dated to Pepi I, are the catacombs where the sacred cats were buried. The ancient Hyksos capital of **Avaris** lies toward Qantir at Tell al-Dabba, and at Qantir are the remains of **Piramesse,** the Ramesside capital of the 19th and 20th dynasties. Little remains at either of these sites.

In contrast, **Tanis** is one of the most imposing sights in the delta. Located on Lake Manzala, the city became Egypt's commercial port, a position it held until replaced by the Greek settlement at Naucratis in the west. The great temple dominates the ruins of Tanis (known in the Bible as Zoan); located within a double-walled enclosure, the main temple has been reduced to fallen obelisks and superbly carved blocks. The adjoining temple dates to the 30th Dynasty; in the smaller, granite temple outside the enclosure, Ramesses II and Osorkon II reused Old Kingdom columns. The royal tombs of the 21st and 22nd dynasties lie at the southern corner of the inner enclosure wall. The decorations make a visit worthwhile; ask permission to see them.

Tanta

This small town, which anchors the Delta Road, plays host each October to three million people who flock to the *mulid* (saint's day) of al-Sayed Ahmed al-Badawi, a Muslim visionary and miracle worker. The celebration is launched by the *zaffa,* a procession leading to the saint's mosque, and culminates with *leyla kabyra,* the big night. The Arafr Hotel in Tanta (tel. 26-952) sits on the main square; if you want to come during the *mulid,* you'll have to make reservations far in advance.

ALEXANDRIA

Second-largest city in Egypt, "Iskandariah" has always been more Mediterranean than Arab. Although facing the problems of large cities everywhere, Alexandria clings to her civilized mien; her elegant, if faded, turn-of-the-century buildings remain the outward sign of her refined tranquillity. Quieter, cleaner, and less hectic than Cairo, the city, with its elegant restaurants and hotels, temperate climate, and international flavor, exudes a unique charm that attracts visitors year-round. In planning your itinerary, however, avoid Easter week (both Western and Orthodox), for during this time Egyptians and Europeans alike flock to Alexandria. Summer is as bad, for millions seeking to escape Egypt's heat flock to the seaside.

Land

Alexandria occupies a limestone ridge rising between the waters of Lake Mariut and the Mediterranean. Originally, the coastline swung inward at the village of Rhacotis, forming a bay, with the island of Pharos occupying the center of this rudimentary harbor. Alexander connected the island to the mainland with a 1,300-meter artificial causeway (the Heptastadion), forming two well-protected anchorages. The causeway has long since silted up, creating the arm of land between the city's Eastern and Western harbors. The modern city strings out along the coast for several miles, but the main business section lies over the ruins of the town founded by Alexander. The most popular public beaches run out to the east from just past the modern breakwater to Montaza Palace. Although less crammed ones lie west of the Western Harbor, these too are becoming increasingly crowded. In fact, resort development is invading the coast nearly to Marsa Matruh.

Climate

Spring and fall are the most pleasant times to visit Alexandria. Due to the influence of the Mediterranean, Alexandria is nearly 10 degrees cooler than Cairo in summer, and then a million people invade its beaches. If you want a taste of native Alexandria, visit in the winter,

when the city is warmer, though wetter, than Cairo. But even in the middle of the summer season, when the city's resorts and hotels are jammed and social life moves into full swing, the coast is worth a visit for those who want to taste its culture, swim in the crystal waters of the Mediterranean, or lie on beaches basking in the clear sun.

HISTORY

Alexandria was founded by Alexander the Great at the site of a modest fishing village. On his way to visit the famous oracle at Siwa Oasis, he was attracted to the natural harbor near Rhacotis, and here he built a fortified port. The town was laid out, according to Greek tradition, with its wide streets following a rectangular grid. The main east-west street roughly paralleled the modern Sh. al-Hurriya; the corresponding north-south road ran close to Sh. Nabi Daniel. The Pharos Lighthouse, one of the Seven Wonders of the Ancient World, dominated the end of the Heptastadion, its giant mirrors reflecting firelight far out to sea. Alexander did not live to see his city completed, but his general, Ptolemy, brought his body here and buried the young ruler at the city's center.

The Museum And Library

Under the Ptolemies, the city grew rapidly, displacing Tyre and then Carthage as the Mediterranean's international center of trade, culture, and learning. Ptolemy built the Serapeum, the great temple to Serapis (his personal god, which combined Apis with Osiris) and the museum/school that became famous throughout the world. Following the example of Aristotle's Athenian academy, this forerunner of today's universities fed and housed the scholars who came and worked here. This museum and its affiliated library attracted the cream of ancient philosophers, artists, poets, doctors, geographers, and mathematicians.

Founded as a part of the museum, the Alexandrian Library contained the largest collection of books in the ancient world. Callimachus, one of its early librarians, catalogued the collection, dividing it much like the subjective sections of modern libraries. A second, smaller branch was built on the hill near the Serapeum. The original library burned during the Alexandrian Wars when Julius Caesar set fire to the fleet in the harbor. Though rebuilt by Mark Antony, it was finally destroyed by the Emperor Aurelian in A.D. 270. At that time, some scholars fled the country, while others moved to the branch library at the Serapeum, a seat of pagan learning later destroyed by the Christians. By the time of the Arab conquest, even this library had vanished.

Ancient Learning

Zendotos of Ephesis, writing at Alexandria, created the first scholarly texts of Homer's *Iliad* and *Odyssey*. Apollonius composed an epic based on the expedition of the Argonauts, which fellow poet Callimachus promptly attacked, triggering one of the oldest and fiercest literary quarrels known. Euclid, whose *Elements* serves as the foundation of modern geometry, created a school of mathematics lasting several centuries.

Archimedes came to Alexandria during the reign of Ptolemy II (285-246 B.C.), and in addition to his discovery of the buoyancy of water and numerous mechanical inventions, he developed the Archimedes screw, a device still used by the *fallahin* to raise irrigation water. Hipparchus, the father of astronomy, who watched the progression of the stars from Alexandria, determined the revolution of the moon, calculated the magnitudes and distances of heavenly bodies, and, by using the equinoxes, established the length of the solar year.

Eratosthenes, in addition to tutoring the son of Ptolemy III, wrote extensively on history, astronomy, geometry, philosophy, and grammar, served as chief librarian, and in his spare time calculated the diameter of the Earth. Perhaps, however, he is best known for his three-volume *Geographica,* which, now unfortunately lost, was extensively quoted by later classical writers such as Strabo.

Claudius Ptolemy, geographer, mathematician, and astronomer, created a map of the ancient world, now one of our primary sources of classical geography. The physicians Herophilus and Erasistratus studied anatomy and physiology at Alexandria (the former discovering that veins carried blood, not air or ether), and their work has left us many terms still used in anatomy, physiology, and medicine.

Roman Period

In 48 B.C., Julius Caesar laid successful siege to Alexandria, bringing the city under nominal Roman control. Upon his death, Cleopatra allied herself with Mark Antony, heir apparent to the Roman Empire, and built the temple called the Caesareum near the modern area of Ramleh. At its entrance stood two obelisks known as "Cleopatra's Needles," now in New York and London. Antony and Cleopatra ruled successfully from Alexandria until Octavian defeated their army at Actium (30 B.C.), and with their suicides, Alexandria fell under overt Roman control.

As residence of the Roman prefect, Alexandria remained a great cosmopolitan city, home to some 500,000 Greeks, Egyptians, and Jews. Although a Jewish revolt during Trajan's reign caused extensive damage to the city, it was repaired by Hadrian.

The close of the Roman period was marked by violence in Alexandria, when the populace openly revolted and the Roman emperors themselves had to come and quell the riots. Caracalla (A.D. 211-271), infuriated by his reception at the hands of the Alexandrians, dissolved the Academy and allowed his troops to sack the city, murdering many of its youths. By this time, Christianity was well established and part of the unrest was due to the tensions created first by Rome and then by Constantinople in their attempts to impose state religions on the Egyptians.

The Christians

According to tradition, Christianity was brought to Alexandria by St. Mark in the middle of the 1st century. He was martyred in A.D. 62, and buried where St. Mark's Cathedral now stands. Although early worshippers met secretly, by the middle of the 2nd century Alexandria's growing Christian community surfaced, founding a catechetical school, which, under Clement and his successor Origen, produced brilliant scholars and teachers. Introducing scientific study of the scriptures, it produced a Greek translation of the Hebrew Bible, the Septuagint (named for the 70 scholars who, according to tradition, worked in isolation to produce identical versions). This work became the definitive source for all succeeding translations.

Once established in Alexandria, Christianity spread throughout the Nile Valley and by the 3rd century Alexandrian dioceses were playing a central role in Egypt's Christian community. During this period, pagan emperors intermittently persecuted Egypt's Christians, but with Constantine's conversion, Christianity finally triumphed, and in the 4th century, Emperor Theodosius demolished the Serapeum, destroyed the pagan statuary, and sacked the library.

Under the Byzantine rulers, the Alexandrian bishopric became active in the politico-religious turmoil of the 4th and 5th centuries. Two Alexandrians, Athanasius and Arius, argued opposite sides of the Monophysite question at the Council of Nicea (A.D. 325), an issue finally decided in 451 at the Council of Chalcedon when the Copts left mainstream Christianity. Viewing the Copts as heretics, Byzantine rulers appointed Cyril patriarch of Alexandria, and under his leadership Egyptian Christians once again faced martyrdom. In the 6th century Justinian (527-565) closed the remaining temples and pagan schools. The beacon of intellectual light that had shone from Alexandria to the rest of the ancient world flickered out.

The Arabs
Persecuted by their fellow Christians, Alexandria's Copts welcomed the Arab invasion. The city was taken by Amr in summer of 642, and in September the remains of the Byzantine Empire's army sailed out of the harbor. Amr, enchanted with the culture and beauty of Alexandria, wanted to convert it to the Arabic capital, but his khalif refused, concerned that the Nile created a barrier between the city and Mecca. The Arabs left the city to decay; the Canopic branch of the Nile silted up, closing the shipping lanes, and Alexandria lost even her lingering trade. By the 18th century, the port at nearby Rosetta had supplanted it, and Alexandria had shrunk to a small village of a few thousand inhabitants.

Modern Period
Alexandria's resurgence began with the Napoleon's invasion. Aware of Alexandria's strategic importance, he landed forces west of the Old Harbor and took Alexandria nearly at once. The British, however, were equally aware of the city's position, and a month later Nelson defeated the French fleet at Abuqir. Deprived of their maritime supply route, the French left Egypt by the turn of the century.

Alexandria really began to recover when Muhammad Ali (who ruled 1805-1849), built the palace of Ras al-Tin on Pharos, developed the naval dockyards at al-Mex, and dug the Mahmudiya Canal, which provided irrigation water as well as a water link for trade via the Nile to the rest of Egypt. During the British occupation, the city continued to grow; the Western Port area of al-Mex expanded its dock facilities, cotton warehouses, and factories, and plush houses and businesses developed, filling the eastern part of the city. In 1860 a rail line linked Alexandria to Suez, and that, coupled with the rebuilding of the docks in the 1880s, made the city again a major port. This progress was only briefly interrupted by the uprising in 1882 led by Ahmed Urabi and the resulting British bombardment of the city.

During the Second World War, the port of Alexandria became a prime target for the Axis forces. To defend it, British General Montgomery took on Rommel, the Desert Fox, at al-Alamein (west of Alexandria), and the Allies' victory spared the city the upheavals of war. In 1952, upon the successful revolt of the Egyptian army officers, King Faruq took refuge at Ras al-Tin before he abdicated.

Alexandria, now an important commercial center, stands at the trading crossroads between Africa, Asia, and Europe. In addition to this strategic position at the eastern end of the Mediterranean, her climate and culture have made her Egypt's summer playground.

The City
The modern city stretches out 10-15 km along the coastline, but its heart lies near the harbors, much of it built on ancient ruins. The shoreline Cornishe is known as Sh. 26 July downtown, and as it runs east, it changes into Sh. Gaysh. The Victorian section of Alexandria centers on

Midan Sa'ad Zaghlul (with its standing statue of this leader). At neighboring Ramleh Station to the east, blue trams runs east, yellow ones to the west and south. On the *midan's* southern side, Sh. Nabi Daniel runs in front of the Cecil Hotel and south, crossing Sh. Al-Hurriya and on toward the train station. The central district of Alexandria is called al-Manshiya, while to the west lies al-Gumrik and then (at the tip of the peninsula) al-Anfushi. Along the Cornishe to the west, the Midan al-Manshiya is composed of Midan Tahrir, which centers on the Tomb of the Unknown Soldier, and Midan Orabi with the bus station. From its southeastern side, Sh. Sa'ad Zaghlul heads back east, running south of the *midan* for which it's named.

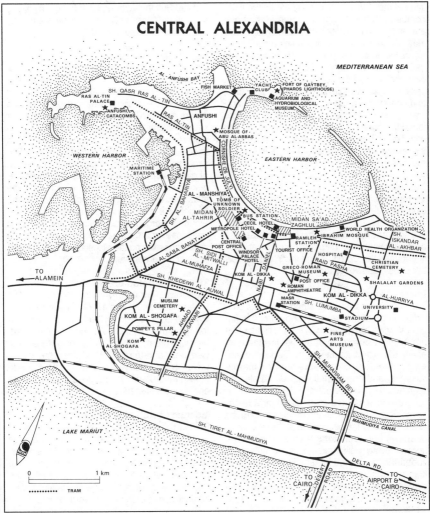

CENTRAL ALEXANDRIA

SIGHTS

Much of the ancient city of Alexandria has sunk into the harbors or been built over by succeeding generations. On the hill that was the site of the original village of Rhacotis stands the oldest part of Alexandria. Here the Greeks built the Serapeum, and today the area is a small park where visitors can see Pompey's Column, the foundations of the library annex, and nearby, the catacombs of Kom al-Shogafa, some of the best-preserved tombs in Alexandria. Although the ruins may not be impressive after a sojourn in Upper Egypt, the areas, now planted and cleaned up, are usually quiet with few visitors. Downtown, the outstanding collection of the Greco-Roman Museum introduces you to Egypt after the pharaohs, and nearby, excavators have uncovered the remains of a Roman theater, the only such structure found in Egypt. Of the Islamic monuments, you can visit the beautiful mosque of Abu Abbas and the restored fort of Qaytbey, which stands on the site of the ancient lighthouse.

Pharos
The island of Pharos, along with the Heptastadion, has silted up, forming a long isthmus that forks into the sea like the horns of a bull. If you'd like to wander in the older, less prosperous areas of town, then the streets on the peninsula between the Cornishe and the Western Harbor should suit your fancy.

Pharos Lighthouse
The lighthouse that once stood here was considered one of the Seven Wonders of the Ancient World. Completed in 279 B.C., its four stories rising 135 meters, it dominated the east end of the island. Its ancient builders surrounded its limestone blocks, granite and marble columns, and ornamental work of marble and bronze with a pillared courtyard.

The lowest, square stage sat over a freshwater cistern and contained primitive lifts (used to haul wood to the beacon fire at the top), living quarters, and fuel-storage areas. Above the second, octagonal stage, the third, circular floor supported the domed lantern. Here attendants kept a signal fire burning for the lighthouse's polished glass mirrors, which reflected its welcoming beacon. Some accounts say a man sitting under the lantern could see ships invisible to the naked eye, a reference to the increased visibility due to the height of the tower and the curvature of the Earth or possibly to an early lens.

The lighthouse continued to function after the Arab conquest until about A.D. 700, when the lantern fell. Although repaired by the Arabs in 800 and again in 980, earthquakes in the 11th and 14th centuries finally destroyed the building. In 1480 Sultan Qaytbey built a fort on the site, a coastal defense restored in modern times by the Antiquities Department.

Fort Of Qaytbey
Open 0900-1500, Fri. 0900-1200; fee LE6, students LE3; tel. 809-144. Standing at the eastern end of the island, the squat mass of Qaytbey's fort was built with some of the original limestone blocks from the lighthouse. A good example of secular Islamic architecture, it incorporates military features developed by the Muslims and later exported to Europe by the Crusaders. The minor museum inside includes a small collection of guns, models, and dioramas of warfare beginning with pharaonic times. Unfortunately, the titles and explanations are only in Arabic and French, but language is no barrier to wandering around the grounds, exploring cannon bays and residential apartments, or clambering atop the walls and watching the Mediterranean surf crash against the breakwater.

The Hydrobiological Museum (Aquarium)
Open 0900-1400; fee 10PT. The Aquarium, which stands just down the Cornishe from the fort (past the Yacht Club) maintains 50 aquariums with creatures from the Mediterranean, the Red Sea, and the Nile. Next door, the Museum of Hydro-Biology (same hours; the ticket to the Aquarium admits you) boasts boat models and a whale skeleton.

Mosque Of Abu Al-Abbas
Built in the 13th century, the mosque was restored in 1767 and stands, with its four domes and tall minarets, as a masterpiece of Islamic architecture. This clean and quiet mosque, about a km south of the fort (at the first right turn off the Cornishe and not far from the fish market), contrasts those of Cairo and is worth a visit.

Ras Al-Tin

Now closed to the public, the palace of Ras al-Tin, which occupies the western horn of Pharos, was built 1835 by Muhammad Ali, who used it as a summer residence. When King Fuad chose Montaza (to the east) as his summer residence, he rebuilt Ras al-Tin as a summer seat of his government. Here, King Faruq signed his abdication and from the dock he boarded his yacht and sailed into exile. The rooms, left as they were in 1952, now serve as a navy base and a residence for visiting statesmen.

Anfushi Cemetery

Open from 1000 to however long the *ghaffir* sticks around; fee LE6, students LE3. Off the beaten track for most tourists, the catacomb-like tombs are located up the hill from Ras al-Tin, in a small park southwest of the palace grounds and above the tram stop. Walk straight up the hill and enter through the nearly invisible gate in the brick wall.

Cut into the limestone during the 2nd and 3rd centuries B.C., each of the two pairs of tombs opens off a sunken atrium; individual tombs consist of a vestibule and a mortuary chapel. Decoration is limited to the Greco-Egyptian style of the Ptolemies: a few traditional figures and scenes, and fragments of painting that imitate marble or alabaster paneling. The architecture too is mixed; the builders combined cobra friezes and cavetto cornices with the Greek tympanum.

The right-hand tombs are the more interesting. At the first landing of the stair into the atrium, a painting shows Anubis leading the deceased to Osiris and Isis, and at the bottom of the stairs Horus presents the tomb owner to Osiris and Anubis in the underworld. In the archway, the paint now faded, a dog turns back its head, an echo of the pharaonic paintings where cattle or donkeys looked over their shoulders. At the entrance to the burial chamber, below the solar disk carved on the cornice, lie two sphinxes. The burial chamber is finished with two coats of plaster, and some of the more recent has fallen, revealing the original. The black and white squares once contained mythological scenes and if you look closely you can still see traces of the original designs.

The plan of the left-hand tombs are similar but the decorations are not as interesting. The benches in the vestibule accommodated mourners or held grave goods. The ceiling is painted with rectangles imitating the carved wooden panels of a coffered ceiling; a rose granite sarcophagus dominates the burial chamber. The other suite (to the left of the sunken courtyard) contains subsidiary burials introduced during Roman times.

The Roman Amphitheater
At Kom Al-Dikka

Open 0900-1700; fee LE3. The only non-funerary Roman site in Alexandria, the theater occupies the park at the corners of Sh. Amir Abdel Munim and Sh. Nabi Daniel (about a block north

fort of Qaytbey

ALLAN HANSEN

of Midan al-Gumhuriyya) behind Cinema Amir. When the area (the site of an old fort) was being cleared, excavators discovered a series of Muslim (9-11th century) tombs concealing the remains of a Roman theater. Built in the 2nd century A.D., the theater was of the odeum type with a stage intended for theatrical performances. Later the stage was replaced with arches, forming a circle, which was roofed with a dome, and plays gave way to political activities. Graffiti about the Blues and Greens (ancient horse-racing teams) link the theater with the hippodrome to the west. The walls, not designed for the weight of the dome, bulged, and within about 50 years of its construction the dome collapsed.

The 13 rows of seats accommodated 700-800 spectators; the structure was built of white and gray marble imported from Europe, while the columns in the double colonnade at the rear of the theater are of Aswan granite and green marble from Asia Minor. Below and in front of the theater, excavators have uncovered the remains of an even earlier Roman street and villas that date to the 1st and 2nd century. North of the theater lie brick remains of Roman baths. Built in the 3rd century, they were reconstructed in the reign of Justinian and have given excavators vital clues to the intricate mechanics and functional designs. Unfortunately, the excavations are currently closed.

Serapeum And Pompey's Column

Open daily 0830-1600, Ramadan 1000-1500; fee LE3, students LE1.50. If you wish, bring a lunch (sodas are available from vendors) and eat on benches under the shade of the trees. Among the statues is the colossal limestone statue of Isis Pharia (the goddess associated with the lighthouse), which was recovered from the sea off Qaytbey's fort.

The temple to Serapis stood at the top of the hill and contained a statue of the god, whose right hand rested on three-headed Cerberus, the dog of Hell. The building was oriented so that the rising sun entered the *naos,* bathing the statue in light. Of the temple proper, little remains but a pink granite column popularly known as Pompey's Column.

Pompey's Column: After the destruction of the Serapeum, this column was reerected about A.D. 300 in honor of Diocletian, either for quelling

riots or saving the city from famine. In any case, the 22-meter-high pillar probably carried an equestrian statue of the emperor, thus accounting for its Arabic name, al-Ambid al-Saware, or the Column of the Horseman, but by the Middle Ages the statue had disappeared.

The Library: Northwest of the pillar a tunnel leads down to the subterranean vaults (under the temple of Anubis) where sacred jackals were buried. Another gallery contains shelves, the only existing reminder of the library annex that once stood here. In an attempt to revive the splendor that was once the Alexandrian Library, the General Organization of the Alexandria Library was formed by the Egyptian Government in 1987. With support from UNESCO, the new facility will occupy a 40,000-square-meter site near the University of Alexandria overlooking the Mediterranean. Open to the public, it will contain unique collections covering the Mediterranean region. But the plan has floundered on specific questions on the details, so currently the project appears to be on hold.

Catacombs Of Kom Al-Shogafa

Open daily 0830-1600, Ramadan 1000-1500; fee LE8, students LE4. To get there, walk out the Serapeum gate, turn right, and follow the street until you reach the site at the top of the hill on your left. The most interesting tombs in Alexandria, they were built around the 2nd century A.D. Younger than those at Anfushi, their decorations combine Egyptian and Greco-Roman iconography. Originally the tomb was probably built for a wealthy Alexandrian family. However, the complex was taken over by a corporation of dues-paying members who agreed to give each other decent burials. In its final form, the warren of passages contains burials on three levels that are linked by steps. Unfortunately, the lowest chambers are flooded

Greco-Roman statue of Petosiris, 2nd century B.C.

JAN KIRK

due to water seepage from nearby Mahmudiya Canal. (The planks laid down for visitors often flex and tilt, so take care.)

The Tomb: Visitors enter by the mourners' spiral staircase, which ends in a landing. The dead were lowered by ropes down the central well and the coffins passed through large openings at the bottom. The benches in the vestibule were for the infirm; note the half-shells carved in the niches above them, a motif that would dominate much of later Coptic art. Another stairway and landing, built around a second well, opens into the rotunda with a domed ceiling supported by eight pillars. The portrait heads are reproductions of those unearthed at the bottom of this shaft; the marble originals are in the Greco-Roman Museum. To the left of this landing is the triclinium or banquet hall, with benches carved from the rock lining three sides of the room. Here members of the funerary party feasted in memory of the deceased. Guests reclined on the benches piled with mattresses and pillows, dining off a wooden table in the center of the room.

The Central Chapel/Tomb: From the rotunda, stairs lead down to the porch, which is supported by papyrus columns with elaborate capitals, miniatures of those in massive temples in Upper Egypt. In side-wall niches stand statues of a man and woman in Egyptian dress, possibly the tomb's original owners. At the entrance to the inner room, two serpents, with the double crowns of Egypt, coil around the pine cone of Dionysius and the serpent staff of Hermes. The motifs in this mixed iconography all appeal to various gods' abilities to protect the dead; the gorgons' heads carved on shields above them may also repel evil influences. The portal above them is surmounted with the winged disk and cobra frieze.

The mock burial chamber is flanked at its entrance with statues of Anubis (right) and Seth (left), both dressed in Roman armor. The lids of the three sarcophagi, festooned with grape leaves, gorgons' heads, and ox skulls, do not lift off; the interiors are reached by cavities in the back, for these sarcophagi were only temporary repositories for the dead during funeral ceremonies. The chamber walls, carved with Egyptian funerary scenes, include the painting on the back wall of a mummy lying on a lion-headed couch protected by Horus, Anubis, and

Thoth. Note that only three canopic jars stand under the couch. The side walls depict a priest officiating before the deceased, a generic male and female. The side niches are similarly decorated, with the king in front of an Apis bull on a pedestal and a winged goddess. The galleries surrounding the central chamber are lined with shelves cut into the rock for bodies or cinerary urns placed there after services.

Upper-level Tombs: Additional tombs are reached through a breach in the rotunda wall that brings you into another access well. Along the left corridor, a large tomb with paintings lies to your right. At its back, Isis and Nephthys protect the mummy of Osiris in the presence of two horned figures. The side walls are now faded, but the pilasters preserve their color, showing a human-headed *ba* bird, and on its outer face, a falcon-god (one of the four sons of Horus) standing on a lotus. To the right of the well is the long hall of Caracalla, named after the emperor of the massacres for the quantity of horse and human bones found here. The walls of this and adjoining chambers hold shelves for bodies.

Tombs Of Chatby

Open 0830-1600; LE3. Alexandria's oldest tombs, these date from 300 B.C. On Sh. Port Said facing St. Marks College, the remains of tombs similar to those at Anfushi lead off the courtyard, now sunken by the city's gradual deposition of debris.

Gardens

Long known for its gardens, Alexandria continues to maintain several; most are open 0800 to 1600 and entrance fees run 10-25PT.

To the East: The complex containing **Nouzha Gardens and Zoo** is on Sh. Smouha near the Mahmudiya Canal. The zoo, built and stocked early in the twentieth century, was expanded in the forties, and still houses animals. The adjoining gardens offer several picnic spots. The area was an ancient suburb of Alexandria and the poet Callimachus, head of the Library around 200 B.C., lived here. The nearby **Antoniadis Villa and Gardens** were originally owned by a wealthy Greek family who gave them to the city.

(CONTINUED ON PAGE 416)

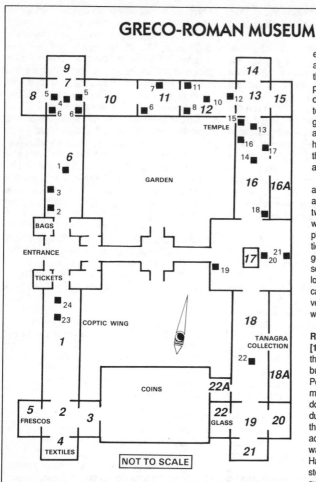

GRECO-ROMAN MUSEUM

ered, and its craftsmanship and images were exported throughout the Roman Empire. The museum also devotes several rooms to extensive collections of glass, coins, and Coptic art and textiles. Most exotic, however, are the sculptures that meld Greek naturalism and Egyptian symbolism.

The building is laid out along several wings, forming a figure eight that surrounds two large central gardens where larger items are displayed. The coins and Coptic textile sections are undergoing renovation, so check to see if they're open yet. To follow approximate chronological order, when you enter the vestibule, turn left and start with Room 6.

Room 6

[1] The hall is dominated by the diorite statue of the Apis bull. Found to the west of Pompey's Column, the fragments of this idol were undoubtedly buried with others during the Christian sack of the Serapeum. The statue, according to its inscription, was set up in the reign of Hadrian (A.D. 117-138). Restored by the sculptor Marcucci in 1898, this bull represents perhaps the most successful imposition of Greek realism upon an Egyptian image.

[2] Note the fine mosaics, an Alexandrian specialty, including this one of a ship sailing, done with colored pebbles set in cement, the earliest type of mosaic made. The idea may have been imported to Alexandria from Greece, but the city made the artform her own, and eventually produced outstanding pieces from cubed bits of marble, stone, glass, and even shell.

[3] The Serapis head, sculpted of fine, white marble, was found near Pompey's Column. Invented by

Open 0900-1600, closed Fridays 1130-1330; fee LE8, tel. 482-5820. Located just off Sh. al-Hurriya (Sh. Musée), the museum was founded in 1891 to accommodate artifacts removed from local excavations. The collection soon outgrew its quarters and moved to its present location in 1895. The bulk of the artifacts are from the Greco-Roman era, and link the pharaonic work found in the Antiquities Museum to that of the Coptic Museum in Old Cairo. In addition, the Greco-Roman Museum displays several mosaic pavements, for in Alexandria the artform flow-the Ptolemies, the god was a blend of Osiris and Apis, but is here shown with curly hair and a beard, wearing the Kalathos or sacred basket of mysteries as a crown.

Room 7

Most of the artifacts in this room were unearthed at Abuqir (ancient Canopus), east of Alexandria, in 1891.

[4] The colossal red granite statue of a pharaoh in the center of the room now carries the cartouche of Ramesses II, and the princess on his left is Hut-Ma-Re, his daughter, who, according to tradition, saved the infant Moses.

[5] The two headless sandstone sphinxes were carved under Amenemhet IV (12th Dynasty) and one still bears his name; the other was recut for Ramesses II.

[6] The two headless black basalt statues of Isis in the niches flanking the doorway show particularly clear examples of the Isis knot. Egyptian dress characterized by this knot was formed by three pieces: an under-wrap, a cloak, and a fringed shawl, which, tied into the cloak, served as a counterweight.

Room 8

This room is devoted to mummies and sarcophagi. Note the difference between the gilded and painted cartonnage of the pharaonic mummies and the ornate diamond bandaging of the Ptolemaic ones, for in later times, the techniques of mummification waned and the artistry of the wrapping became more important than the preservation of the body. The Fayyum portraits, done in encaustic on wood panels, appear to have been cut down to fit the size of the mummy and may, in fact, have been hung in the deceased's home during his lifetime.

Room 9

The primary pieces in this room are from a shrine in the Fayyum dedicated to the crocodile-god Pnepheros. (The stone chapel from which this shrine came, complete with its three pylons, is set up in the northern garden.) The wooden door displayed in the museum is from the first pylon and was dedicated (according to its Greek inscription) by Agathodoros, an Alexandrian citizen, in 137 B.C. On the other side of the room is the stretcher that carried the live crocodile during processions; its place is now held by a mummy. The smaller pieces in the room include an ancient set of panpipes and a figure of Sekhmet, the lioness-goddess.

Room 10

This room contains late pharaonic items, primarily from the collection donated by Sir John Antoniadis. The small statues distributed in the glass cases represent the gods and goddesses of Egypt; the scribe sitting cross-legged is the deified Imhotep, the architect, minister, and physician of the 3rd Dynasty king Djoser, builder of the Step Pyramid. On the other side of the room, amulets of gold, bronze, stone, glass, and faience were concealed within the mummy's wrappings to protect and aid the dead in his journey through the netherworld. The case of funerary equipment at the far corner contains a nice ebony folding stool, its inlaid legs in the shape of ducks' heads.

Room 11

This hall contains some of the most interesting statues, in which Egyptian scenes and techniques are overlaid with Greek influences.

[6] Images of divine serpents (the Agathadaimon stelae) and their worshippers.

[7] Along the north wall stand limestone fragments from a temple at Athribis (Benha). The god Tutu (right), wearing a crown of sacred animal heads and birds, faces Horus and Athribis (left) with a broken inscription of Greek between them.

Room 12

This hall, along with rooms 13 and 14, contains statuary of the Greco-Roman period.

[8] This colossal red granite head of Ptolemy IV was found at Abuqir, the eyes inlaid according to Egyptian canon. Wearing the double crown of Egypt, the head lacks a beard but shows the curly side whiskers also found on his coins.

[9] [Temporarily removed] The mosaic of Medusa, once a pavement, originally showed Medusa's entire head, but now only the ends of her serpent hair can be made out at the edges of the damaged portion. Note that the darker cubed tesserae are set lower in the cement to reflect less light, aiding the artist in creating the dark areas.

[10] The most striking piece in the hall, however, is the colossal white marble statue of Marcus Aurelius (A.D. 121-180), which was uncovered under the foundations of the modern Sayed Darwish Theater. The bareheaded emperor wears the imperial cuirass decorated with a commander's scarf. Below the Medusa head and winged griffins, the cuirass was once adorned with an eagle, which was removed and replaced with the cross during Christian times. The em-

peror stands on his right leg, a classical pose copied in later Coptic art but where the realistic feeling of a balanced mass in touch with terra firma is replaced by figures floating apparently weightless.

[11] The nummulitic limestone head with the crown of uraei is thought to be Cleopatra VII, last of Egypt's Ptolemies.

[12] This marble shows Isis as goddess of the Nile reclining against a sphinx. Her left hand holds a vessel for the Holy Water, and the eight children climbing over her represent the eight cubits the Nile rises for a perfect flood. The awkward proportions and heavy arms of this statue presage the emergence of Coptic symbolism.

Room 13

In the middle of the room stands a colossal statue of a Roman emperor; the head of Septimius Severus is a later addition.

Room 14

This gallery is filled with the busts of famous Romans: Hadrian, Vespasian, and Augustus. One wonders if such portrait heads descended from those included in Old Kingdom tombs.

Room 15

This room houses paintings that once formed part of a tomb cut into a course-grained limestone. The largest fragment shows a saqiya or waterwheel. The pole turned by a yoke of oxen drives a horizontal wheel geared to the large wheel with the jars; this last wheel, by means of its containers, raises the water. Such wooden saqiyas continued in operation until just a few years ago; now they've been replaced by metal wheels, although the gearing remains nearly identical. The entire impressionistic piece marks a sharp division from the studied forms of ancient Egyptian and realistic Greek painting.

Room 16

[13] In the center of the hall rises a colossal forearm holding a ball. Note how well the straining muscles and swelling veins are depicted on this Ptolemaic work.

[14] The large eagle of the same period was found on the island of Thasos in the Aegean and this finely wrought piece may indicate the spread of Egyptian religious ideas (such as Horus) throughout the Mediterranean world.

[15] This headless statue, the personification of the Nile, lies on a rocky throne, with his left arm resting on a hippopotamus, his hand holding a cornucopia. The two boys beneath him indicate the peak of the Nile flood on a scale that is scarcely visible. The marble statue was found in Middle Egypt near Minya and is of provincial workmanship from the late Roman period, most probably a copy of a Hellenistic original.

[16] The haunting expression of this bust of Demeter-Selene is heightened by the two horn tips projecting from her forehead.

[17] An old man reclines on the sarcophagus lid, his careworn face eloquently conveying great weariness. This gray marble portrait found at Kom al-Shogafa may well have been of a priest of Serapis.

[18] In this stela, a composite god Chronos has the head of a lion and the body of a goat. He's equipped with four wings, and in his hands he holds the tails of two snakes, two keys, and a thunderbolt, while a torch rests against his right shoulder.

Room 16A

This room contains some of the finest Hellenistic statuary in the Greco-Roman Museum. The torso of Aphrodite is especially graceful, a good example of pure Greek sculpture. At the end of the hall, a couple of male torsos, a female, and a seated male probably belonged to a group of statues carved for a pediment in the palace area near the Eastern Harbor. The figures date from the 3rd or 2nd century B.C. The missing pieces were carved separately; you can see the sockets for the dowels. Note especially the sumptuous arrangement of the folds over the lady's legs, one of the finest examples of carved draperies surviving from ancient times.

On the east wall is a bust of Alexander the Great, a Roman copy of a high-quality original. The torso and nose have been restored. The marble frog in the same case was probably an accessory of a fountain in a private house. Between cases 1 and 2 stands a small marble of Bellerophon mounting his winged horse Pegasus.

Room 17

Sarcophagi, both the box and bathtub types, are scattered around the room. The black stone examples were first used as baths and later converted to caskets. Most of the box styles are decorated with garlands, Medusa heads, satyrs, and fauns—similar to the types seen at Kom al-Shogafa. [19] The best-preserved and most elaborate one is unique in Alexandria, being carved with mythological scenes. The front is divided into two scenes; the larger, right side shows Ariadne asleep on the island of Naxos.

The god of sleep (Hypnos) stands by her head, and behind him lies the boat that brought her from Crete. In front of her stands Dionysius, whom she marries, along with his retinue. The left third of the facade, in an unrelated scene, shows a drunken Heracles helped homeward.

[20] The mosaic pavement is of the type that may have developed as a durable alternative to patterned rugs. The outer border resembles the egg-and-dart pattern, which appears on the cornices of classical Greek temples.

[21] The huge headless statue of an enthroned emperor that dominates the center of the east wall is the largest found in Alexandria and the largest known done in porphyry.

Room 18

Among the lamps on the eastern wall is one built as a model of the Pharos Lighthouse. The Athenian black-figure amphorae across the room contained olive oil and were presented to the winners of the Olympic games. Athena or Nike is depicted on one side, and on the other, the event for which the vessel was rewarded.

[22] The funerary amphora from Chatby, which dates to the end of the 4th or early 3rd century B.C., still has its artificial wreath of green leaves and golden berries around its neck.

Room 18A

This hall is devoted to a collection of clay Tanagra figures, named after their city of origin in northern Greece; their polychrome paint appears against a white background. The Alexandrian collection spans the 3rd century B.C. to the 1st century A.D. and provides information about ladies' fashions—hairstyles, hats, and dresses—in the ancient world. Most come from burials of children or young women, and so it's possible they held sentimental rather than religious meaning. The remainder of the cases contain heads, animals, gods, and masks used in the theater. Note the Roman lamp in the western case, which shows a reed boat in a papyrus swamp in front of a fort.

Room 19

This room, together with the next two, is devoted to stone and pottery. The center of the room is occupied by a mosaic found at Chatby that dates to Roman times.

Room 20

Many of the cases contain multiple figures of Bes, but in Roman times the jolly household god who loved music became more warlike, a sword replacing his tambourine. The southern case contains a bone flute.

Room 21

This room contains more pottery and a few statuettes: Hercules with a club in his left hand and his lion-skin coat in his right. Idols of the fertility god Min continued to be made throughout the Greco-Roman period; this one shows him in his boat. However, the collection of most interest to historians is the amphora handles in the cases, which are stamped with the name of the potter and his place of origin. The pots were imported from Greece and contained oil or wine, and the stamped handles represent one of the earliest examples of commercial labeling.

Room 22

With the exception of a few ivory pieces, this hall is dedicated to colored glassware. Early in Egypt's history, the people learned how to make glass, perhaps a chance discovery of the fusion of soda and sand. By the dynastic period, artisans drew out rods of blue, green, red, and yellow to cut up for beads. Though craftsmen had been decorating jewelry, amulets, and vases with enamel (liquid glass) from the earliest periods, the oldest glassware known dates from the reign of Thutmose III (18th Dynasty). The vessels were made over a wet sand core wrapped with a cloth and tied to a stick, lowered into a vat of liquid glass, and rapidly spun to coat the outer surface. Artisans then decorated these vessels with thin rods of different-colored glass, which they spread on the still-hot surface with a comb-like tool. Then the glass was rolled on a stone tile to produce the smooth, even finish; the edge, base, and handles were added later.

Glassblowing was unknown until introduced by the Syrians in the 1st century A.D., and the technique revolutionized the glass industry, increasing production and lowering cost. The first pieces imitated marble and stone, but later pieces were in all colors and forms. Alexandria became a center for glassmaking, and artisans skillfully assembled small pieces of polychrome mosaic glass into flower designs that were demanded throughout the Roman Empire. In addition, Alexandrians made a millefiori ("thousand flowers") glass by combining rods of differing colors into bundles; the pattern was exposed when the bundles were cut horizontally and displayed in cross section. The iridescence of ancient glass is caused by its decomposition rather than its original color.

Room 22A

This room, devoted to metal, contains the beautifully realistic bronze head of Hadrian (A.D. 76-138), its eyes inlaid with glass and ivory, which was found at Dendera in Upper Egypt.

Room 3

This hall is also devoted to metal—silver and gold. The silver torso of Aphrodite dates from the 2nd or 3rd century, and was probably made in Alexandria. The gilded silver cup shows winged cupids gathering grapes, while others stand under the vines, cups upraised to catch the juice; yet another carries a full cup to Dionysius. The side cases show a varied collection of gold jewelry, one necklace of scarabs, another with pearls, and several beautiful cameos—the artist utilizing the colors of the different layers of stone to make the design stand out from its background. The golden leaves found on a mummy at Kom al-Shogafa protected individual parts of the body; other cases include silver bracelets that end in the shape of female busts and the foundation deposits of several temples from the Serapeum.

Room 2

The rest of this wing is devoted to Coptic art, much of it similar to that found in the Coptic Museum in Old Cairo. This hall contains many architectural elements from early Christian buildings, the central basket capital being typical of Coptic work.

Room 4

This gallery is devoted to Coptic textiles, for the Copts were some of the finest weavers in the Christian world. Most of the early designs shown here are not yet Christian, but continue the pagan motifs of the Greeks and Romans. The east case contains patches and rondels that decorated tunics like the one to the right. The south case displays an entire cloth in which riders alternate with dancers, both framed in undulating borders; the outlined figures, although still showing their links to Greek black-figure ware, have

already become stylized. The western case contains fabrics with both low nap and shag, a loop weave invented by the Copts. The triangular face in the design to the right is typical of Coptic stylization.

Room 5

In the center of this room, the pottery maze may represent a model of the Labyrinth of Minos or a water-cooling system. The large slippers were coffins, their exteriors decorated with patterns representing mummy wrappings. The painted stucco fragments around the walls come from the monasteries west of Alexandria and date from the 5th century. The figure on the west wall has a tunic under his cloak that shows an example of the rondel decorations in the textile room next door.

Room 1

The fragments along the west wall continue to show Greek subjects; at the center is a "broken pediment" that often enclosed early Coptic niches. Beyond it, the grapevines still show their natural form, only beginning to become flattened and abstracted.

[23] The alabaster Good Shepherd was found at Marsa Matruh, and with its large eyes and flat, regular folds of the robe is perhaps typical of the developing Coptic style.

[24] This capital, probably from the Church of St. Mark in Alexandria, is from the same school; its hollow interior may well have been used as a baptismal font.

The northeast wall is devoted to artifacts from the Monastery of St. Menas, west of Alexandria; the most numerous are the pilgrims' flasks with the depiction of the saint between two camels, which the devout filled with the sacred, healing water of the spring. Just south of the saint's artifacts are more pagan reliefs, including several of Leda and the Swan, good demonstrations of Coptic style and Greek motif.

Sculpture Garden

The Sculpture Garden is filled with delightful surprises; most are well labeled. Don't miss the small temple to the crocodile-god erected at the north corner.

The house, now reserved for state functions, is closed, but the beautifully maintained gardens are open, offering peace and tranquillity in the heart of Alexandria.

City Center: The **Shalalat Gardens**, east of the Roman theater and the train station, en-

closes 36 *feddans*. The fountain midan and its flower clock separate the area into north and south gardens. Marking the eastern gate of the old city, its hills and valleys send water cascading into its lake.

Outside the City: Currently the government

is developing a new **International Garden** on 110 *feddans* near the entrance to the desert road. Although not yet easily accessible by public transportation, the area is appealing.

Small Museums

The **Museum of Fine Arts,** 18 Sh. Menasce, Moharrem Bey, tel. 493-6616, houses its own art collection, stages special exhibitions, and hosts concerts. Open 0800-1400, closed Fridays; free.

The **Royal Jewelry Museum,** 27 Ahmen Yehia, Glym, is open 0900-1600, closed Fridays between 1130 and 1330; LE10, students LE5. Royal jewelry from the time of Muhammad Ali to King Faruq is housed in the palace of Muhammad Ali's great-granddaughter.

PRACTICALITIES

Accommodations

Like Cairo, where you choose to stay in Alexandria depends upon what you plan to do. If you want to see the city, pick a downtown hotel; though some are noisy, they put you in the center of the transportation hub. Several of the old Victorian hotels downtown have been renovated. If you just want to escape, choose an outlying beach hotel. The cost of rooms varies, with those on the sea with a view more expensive than those facing the city. For **camping** information, see Abuqir, p. 426.

Downtown Hotels

All the downtown hotels include breakfast. The best deal is the **Metropole,** which offers renovated old world charm and service for $20 s, $24 d. The high-ceiling rooms come with French doors and some of the baths even have clawfooted tubs—with plugs. The baroque splendor of the **Windsor Palace,** at $27 s, $34 d, is a good second choice. The renovated **Cecil,** is nice, but unless you want the ambience of staying there, it's overpriced at $66 s, $75 d.

Of the smaller hotels, the spotlessly clean and restored **Acropole** is a bargain for LE7-15 s, LE20 d, and LE30 t. Across the street, the **Hotel Ailema** and **Hyde Park House** are nearly as nice at about the same price; the main difference is smaller rooms and about eight floors. The **Piccadilly** is slightly less expensive. The

hotels clustered around Midan Orabi are cheap but tend to be grimy.

Beach Hotels

Beach hotels are strung out along the Cornishe with a few clustered near Montaza. Of the latter, the **Palestine** offers a private beach, an indoor pool, and peace and quiet; it's well worth the $68 s, $86 d. The other chain-type hotels range $90-97 s, $115-120 d. Back toward town, the **Landmark** sits right at the end of the tram line, and offers the best deal: $59 s, $74 d. The **San Stefano** is showing its age, and for $30 s and $37 d, the three-star hotels are a better deal. The new **Regency** offers excellent service and clean rooms, all with an ocean view for $32 s, $38 d. As nice, the **San Giovanni** sits right on the beach, $33-40 s, $44-47 d.

Youth Hostel (IYHF)

32 Port Said, tel. 597-5459, just off the Cornishe in Chatby. You can reach it from the center of town by taking the eastbound tram from Ramleh Station; the hostel is opposite the large red-and-white dome of St. Mark's College. Beds are LE4.50 in clean rooms. Members only; it often fills in summer so make reservations. Open 1400-2300—strict curfew.

Food

In Alexandria, as in much of Egypt, the cheapest food for those with hardy digestive tracts is found at the local *ta'miyya* and *ful* stands located throughout the city; they are the only option in the old city area around Pompey's Column and on the west side of the peninsula. Otherwise, Alex offers a wide variety of restaurants that serve excellent food at reasonable prices. Many small restaurants lining the Cornishe specialize in seafood, which you can often select live from aquariums or purchase by the kilo. Prepared by the restaurant's chef, a kilo of seafood serves three people, or two with hearty appetites. Recommended restaurants in Alex include the **Sea Gull** housed in an imitation of Qaytbay Fort with a playground for kids, the waterfront **Tikka Grill, La Pizzeria, Taverna,** and **Chez Gaby.**

Alexandria's tearooms reflect her Old World charm, and rising late for a pastry breakfast or spending an afternoon in one of these genteel establishments is a special Alexandrian delight.

SELECTED ALEXANDRIA HOTELS

NAME	ADDRESS	DISTRICT	TEL.	TELEX/FAX
DOWNTOWN: FOUR-STAR HOTELS				
Cecil	16 Sa'ad Zaghlul	Ramleh Station	807-055	807-250
Delta	14 Champollion		482-9053	482-5630
Windsor Palace	17 al-Shohada	Ramleh Station	808-256/ 808-123	809-090
DOWNTOWN: THREE-STAR HOTELS				
Metropole	52 Sa'ad Zaghlul	Ramleh Station	482-1465	54350 METRO UN
Semiramis	80 26 July	Ramleh Station	482-6837/ 483-0824	
DOWNTOWN: TWO-STAR HOTELS				
Admiral Hotel	24 Amin Fikri	By Greco-Roman Museum	483-1787	54320 AMRIL UN
New Capri Hotel	23 al-Minya al-Sharkiya (above tourism office)	Ramleh Station	809-310	
DOWNTOWN: ONE-STAR HOTELS				
Acropole	1 Gamal al-Din		805-980	
Hotel Ailema	21 Amin Fikri (7th floor)	By Greco-Roman Museum	482-7011	
Piccadilly	11 Hurriya (at Nabi Daniel)	By train station	430-802	
Hyde Park House	21 Amin Fikri (8th floor)	By Greco-Roman Museum	483-5666	
BEACH HOTELS: FIVE-STAR				
Montaza Sheraton	al-Cornishe	Montaza	548-1220	872-848
Palestine	on Palace Grounds	Montaza	547-3500	547-3378
Ramada Renaissance	544 al-Gaysh	Sidi Bishr	548-3977	549-7690
BEACH HOTELS: FOUR-STAR				
Landmark	163 Abdl Salam	San Stefano	586-7850	54246 LARKA UN
Plaza Metropole	al-Gaysh (at Sh. Zinzinia)		587-8714	587-5399 54772 SAFA UN
San Stefano	Midan San Stefano	San Stefano	586-3580/ 586-3589	586-5953
BEACH HOTELS: THREE-STAR				
Hotel San Giovanni	205 al-Gaysh	Stanley Beach	546-7774	546-4408
Regency	696 al-Gaysh	Miyami	871-547	
BEACH HOTELS: TWO-STAR				
New Swiss Cottage	346 al-Gaysh	Glym	587-5830/ 587-0455	

Entertainment

Alexandria's numerous **cinemas** offer nearly as many foreign films as Cairo's. English-language movies play at several theaters around Ramleh Station, including the Zaghlul, the al-Hurriya, the Royal, and the Amir. Check listings in the *Egyptian Gazette,* or scan the billboards for current offerings. Late summer brings Alexandria's International Film Festival, and unlike the regular films, these are uncensored.

Nightlife: As in Cairo, most **nightclubs** serve a late dinner, which is included in the price, but they charge no cover fee; drinks are extra. The higher-priced hotels all have nightclubs that offer live entertainment, often with a belly dancer. Check the latest issue of *Cairo Today* for up-to-date information. The **Crazy Horse** on the Cornishe east of Midan Sa'ad Zaghlul near Ramleh Station features live rock music, and next door, the **Athineos** offers live, loud, and very Greek entertainment—if you throw plates, you'll have to pay for them.

Just down the street to the west, the **Ala-Kayfak's** third-floor bar offers friendly service, a good view, and excellent pizzas from the restaurant below. **The Baudrot,** on the south side of Sa'ad Zaghlul just before it ends, has a peaceful garden tucked behind the tearoom; it's ideal for a quiet beer. Slightly farther west and across the street, the **Spitfire,** with its loud rock music, comes close to a European bar. The **Cap d'Or** (rue Adib, around the corner south off Sa'ad Zaghlul), founded in 1898, retains the grandeur and extravagance that attracted wealthy cotton merchants and politicians. Or try the **Havana Bistro** on al-Hurriya.

The **Belvedere,** on the second street west of the Cecil Hotel, commands a spectacular view of the harbor and offers late-night drinking and dancing, and the **Santa Lucia Restaurant** has a bar with live, but quiet, music, as does the **Au Prive** restaurant. Two **casinos** at the Cecil and on the Montaza Palace grounds are smaller than the ones in Cairo. Play is in foreign currency, and you may need your passport for entry. Open 1600-2400.

Performing Arts: During the summer season, the **Cairo Symphony** moves to Alexandria, giving concerts on Fridays at the Sayed al-Darwish Theater, Alexandria's old opera house, 22 Sh. Fuad (facing Cinema Royal), tel. 482-5106/483-9578. Beginning in July the **Reda Dance Company** performs nightly at the open-air Firquit Reda Theater, located on the Cornishe a few blocks east of Midan Sa'ad Zaghlul.

Beaches

East of the Eastern Harbor, a series of public beaches strings out along the coastline: Chatby, Sporting, Ibrahimiya, Cleopatra, Stanley, Glym, San Stefano, Sidi Bishr, Miami, Asfara, and Mandara. You can reach them by the buses that run east along the Cornishe. Umbrellas and chairs are available to rent, and many small shops along the Cornishe carry suntan lotion and other sundries. Since these beaches are free and easily accessible, they tend to be dirty and crowded.

Beaches Farther East: Several less-crammed beaches lie farther east. Three inviting stretches of sand occupy the grounds of the **Montaza Palace.** The first is for the use of Palestine Hotel patrons only. The second, for visitors who rent the cabanas lining the shore, is often nearly deserted. Next door is the public beach which includes a snack bar and small shop, but it's well known and well used in summer. To avoid the crowds, you can move farther east, toward the bridge to the Tea Island Palace. In summer, beach fees run LE2 pp in addition to the entrance fee to Montaza. Beyond Montaza lies Mamoura, a popular beach with a full range of services within walking distance; fee LE1.10. (For beaches west of Alexandria, see p. 427.)

Sports

Sailing buffs can contact the **Yacht Club,** tel. 802-563, at the tip of the peninsula just before the fort of Qaytbey; the club offers lessons (sailing, surfing, and diving) and slips, sponsors a yearly regatta, and takes part in the International Fishing Competition in the Red Sea. Members can bring guests for LE10.

Sporting Clubs: The extensive grounds of Alexandria's private **Sporting Club,** tel. 853-627/853-628, east of downtown Alexandria, include a large clubhouse and several smaller ones, and facilities for golf, tennis (clay courts), swimming, lawn bowling, and horseback riding; in summer, horse racing is held at Sporting's track. Entrance fee is LE10 and you'll need a

SELECTED ALEXANDRIA RESTAURANTS

NAME	ADDRESS	PHONE	HOURS	PRICE	COMMENTS
PHAROS AND WEST					
Andrea's Armed Forces Club	Agami	433-9227		inexpensive	
Michael's Bliss Area	Agami	433-0241		expensive	Swiss/French good everything
Qadoura	Beyram al-Tonsi Anfushi			inexpensive	set price before eating
Sea Gull	Agami Rd. al-Max	445-5575	1200-2400	average	in "castle" with playground
Tikka Grill	al-Gaysh, halfway along the peninsula toward Qaytbey	480-5119	1300-1630/ 2000-0100	average	excellent entrees, bread, alcohol served
DOWNTOWN					
Calithea	82 26 July (Cornishe)	482-7764	1200-2100	average	good fish and shrimp
Chez Gaby	Sh. Rue al-Bakhete (north off 22 al-Hurriya)			average	liquor served
La Pizzeria	14 al-Hurriya	483-8082	1900-1530/ 1930-1300		good pizza and pasta, liquor served
Muhammad Ahmed Ful	a block south of Midan Sa'ad Zaghlul on the little street between Nabi Daniel and Safiya Zaghlul	483-3576	0600-2400	cheap	takeout downstairs, cafeteria style; sit-down restaurant upstairs, good Egyptian food
Rang Mahal	Cecil Hotel Sa'ad Zaghlul			expensive	good Indian food
Restaurant Elite	43 Safiya Zaghlul			inexpensive	good moussaka, espresso, liquor served
Santa Lucia	40 Safiya Zaghlul	482-0056/ 482-0332	1200-1600/ 1900-2200	average	classy atmosphere, French cuisine
Taverna	6 Midan Tahrir	804-907		inexpensive	good fried or grilled fish, squid, or shellfish
Wimpy's	3 locations: Montaza, Mamoura, and Rush				
EAST					
Al-Saraya	al-Gaysh near San Giovanni Hotel	485-0884	1330-1630/ 2030-2400	average	good variety of meals, outstanding view of the Mediterranean Sea
International Sea Food	808 al-Gaysh near Montaza Sheraton	873-951	1200-2330	expensive	outstanding seafood
Lord's Inn	12 Muhammad Ahmed, al-Afifi/San Stefano	586-5664	2000-0200	expensive	European, disco after 2300
New China	802 al-Gaysh (Corail Hotel)	548-0996	1200-1600/ 1800-2300	inexpensive	Chinese food: spicy beef, sweet chicken, hot pepper shrimp

SELECTED ALEXANDRIA RESTAURANTS

NAME	ADDRESS	PHONE	HOURS	PRICE	COMMENTS
EAST					
San Giovanni	San Giovanni Hotel 205 al-Gaysh	840-984 842-213	1200-1600 2030-2400	expensive	good seafood, oriental and continental; overlooks the bay
Taverna	Montaza Grounds	860-056		average	beach-front dining
TEAROOMS					
Delices	46 Sa'ad Zaghlul	482-5657			
Grand Trianon	east end of Midan Sa'ad Zaghlul	482-8539			wonderful coffee, chocolates, pastry
Pastroudis	39 al-Hurriya, by the Roman amphitheater	492-9609			famous, but service and quality slipping

member to sign you in. To use the facilities will run another LE5-12 depending on the sport. **Smouha Club,** tel. 420-4668, entrance is LE3. The emphasis here is on horseback riding, but other sports are also available. For **runners,** Alexandria's Delta Hash House Harriers run (jog, stroll, amble, limp, or lurch) about an hour before sunset on Fridays; contact Ben Goulding, tel. 849-344. For fishing and shooting, contact the **Fishing Club,** next to Fort Qaytbay, tel. 422-3510; they also have a supervised children's playground and swimming pool as well as lighted tennis courts. Diving and sporting equipment are available on Sh. Nabi Daniel just north of al-Hurriya.

Shopping

Alexandria's shopping area lies to the south and west of Midan Sa'ad Zaghlul. The main street for shops is al-Hurriya, and along its length lie several government stores such as Salon Vert (which carries beautiful silk and cotton material), Sednaui, and Omar Effendi (general merchandise). Good-quality leather goods and clothes are available from Sarkis Vartzbedian, 32 Salah Salim (upstairs), tel. 482-4471, open 0900-1300 and 1700-1930 except Sundays. A mixture of small shops lies just off the Cornishe beyond the Tomb of the Unknown Soldier, where you can browse for rugs, tapestries, and tourist items.

Services And Information

General Emergency: tel. 123; **police,** tel. 122; both numbers operate 24 hours. The **Tourist Police** main office is at Montaza Palace (tel. 547-3395/547-3814 in the a.m., but call the Tourist Office number in the p.m.). A branch office of the Tourist Police is located above the Tourist Office, open daily 0800-2000; Fri. 0800-1400. The **Tourist Office** is located on Midan Sa'ad Zaghlul at Sh. Nabi Daniel, tel. 807-611/809-985; open daily 0800-1700, Ramadan 0900-1600 except Friday. Branch offices at the train station and at the port keep the same hours.

Communications: The main **post office** is on Sh. al-Sahafa (open 0900-1500), off Sh. Sa'ad Zaghlul near the bus station (Midan Orabi); the entrance is beside the colored mailboxes. Nicer and more reliable branch offices are at Masr (open 0800-2000) and Ramleh stations. Alexandria's **postal code** is 21519; the **telephone code** is 03. The main **telephone/ telex** office in Ramleh Station is open 24 hours; the two branches at Masr Station and at the west end of Sh. Sa'ad Zaghlul are open till 2300.

Government Offices: The **passport office,** 28 Sh. Talaat Harb at the corner of Sh. Falaki (tel. 482-7873), is open Sat.-Thurs. 0800-1300 and sometimes 1700-2100, Fri. 1000-1300. The **customs office** is at the port and is open when boats dock.

Consulates

The **U.S. Consulate,** 111 Sh. al-Hurriya (tel. 482-1911), lies about one block west of the roundabout and parks and is open Sun.-Thurs. 0900-1200, closed Fri. and Saturday. This office provides limited service so it's best to conduct most of your business in Cairo. The **British Consulate,** 3 Sh. Minya Kafr Abdu, Rusdi (tel. 546-7001), is about six km east of downtown, several blocks south of al-Hurriya; open Sun.-Thurs. 0800-1300, closed Fri. and Saturday. **Israel,** 453 Sh. al-Hurriya, Rushdi, tel. 586-0492.

Banks

Bank of America, tel. 493-1115, lies across from the soccer stadium on Sh. Lomomba; **Citibank,** tel. 483-4363, is at 95 26 July (Cornishe); and **Barclay's,** tel. 492-1307, at 10 Sh. al-Fawatem.

Travel Agents

The **American Express** office, at 26 al-Hurriya (Eyress Travel Office), tel. 483-0084, is open Mon.-Thurs., 0830-1300 and 1700-1830; Fri. and Sat., 0830-1300. The **Thomas Cook** offices, 15 Midan Sa'ad Zaghlul, tel. 482-8077, four blocks east of Ramleh Station (near Ibrahim Mosque) provide similar services. **Menatours,** on Midan Sa'ad Zaghlul (next to the Cecil Hotel), tel. 808-704, handles reservations for Adriatica boats, which call at Piraeus and Venice. The **Tourist Friends Association in Alexandria,** tel. 596-2108 (Essam al-Melahy) or 586-6115 (Hany Shaarawy) is a group of volunteer students who want to improve their language skills (most are already quite good) and help tourists. They will also arrange multi-lingual guides.

Medical Facilities

Khalid Pharmacy, on Alexander the Great off Sa'ad Zaghlul, is open 0900-2000, or check along Sa'ad Zaghlul. If you fall ill, ask for assistance at your consulate or any five-star hotel, or contact the Medical Care Advisory Team (MECAT) at 97 Sh. Abel Salam Aref, tel. 586-2323, about eight km east of downtown at Glym Beach, or call the privately run **Smouha Medical Center,** 14 May Rd., Smouha, tel. 420-2652.

Books And Newspapers

The library at the American Cultural Center (see information below) offers a good selection of books. Otherwise you can buy books at **El Ma'arif,** 44 Sh. Sa'ad Zaghlul, at the nearby **Center Books,** 49 Sa'ad Zaghlul, or the **Library Mustakbal,** 32 Sh. Safiya Zaghlul. Both of the latter stores carry a good selection of books in English, including modern paperbacks, as does **al-Haram,** 13 Sh. al-Hurriya opposite the Piccadilly Hotel. Newspapers, including British dailies, *The Egyptian Gazette,* and the *Tribune* are on sale at newsstands throughout Alexandria, as are *Time* and *Newsweek.*

Photography

Kodak, 63 Safiya Zaghlul (across from the Rialto Cinema), is open Mon.-Sat. 0900-2100. Additional small shops are on Sa'ad Zaghlul.

Alexandria skyline from the beach at Montaza Palace

KATHY HANSEN

Cultural Centers

Many of Alexandria's cultural centers present evening programs, so call for information. The **American Center**, 3 Pharana, tel. 481-435, is open Mon.-Fri 0900-1600; has a good library, both books and video. MacNeil-Lehrer News is on daily 1300; ABC World News is Mon. and Fri., 1200. The **British Council**, 9 Batalsa, Bab Sharki, tel. 482-9890, has library services, film programs, and language classes. The **French Center**, 30 Nabi Daniel, tel. 491-8952/492-0804, is open 0900-1300 and 1600-2000, closed Friday and Saturday. At the **Goethe Institute**, 10 Ptolemy, Azarita, tel. 483-9870, the library is open Mon.-Wed. 1000-1700, Thurs. 1100-2000, and Fri. 1000-1400; there are films, lectures, concerts, and exhibitions.

Several Egyptian ones include: **Anfushi Cultural Center**, Sh. Ras al-Tin, Eastern Harbor, tel. 804-805; open daily 0930-1330 and 1730-2030 except Fri. afternoons. **Hurriya Cultural Palace**, 1 Sh. al-Hurriya, tel. 492-4533; open daily 0930-1330 and 1730-2030 except Fri. afternoon. **Shatby Cultural Center** for artistic and literary appreciation, Sh. Port Said (facing St. Mark's College) tel. 597-2379.

Clubs

The **Archaeological Society of Alexandria**, 6 Mahmoud Mukhtar (behind the Greco-Roman Museum), meets the first Monday of the month at their library and the third Wednesday at the Goethe Institute. Their library is open Sat.-Thurs. 1700-1900, tel. 482-0650. **Friends of the Environment** meet at the Sporting Club; call Adul Abu Zahra, tel. 595-3094. The **International Ladies' Club of Alexandria** meets the 1st and 3rd Tuesdays, 1030; trips on the 2nd Tuesday; contact Kudsieh Mitwali (tel. 517-4151) or Kismet Leheta (tel. 842-000). **Les Amis de la Musique et des Arts** promotes classical music and plastic arts, and arranges lectures and performances; call Adl Abu Zahra (tel. 595-3094) or Magda (tel. 546-7221). The **Rotary** meets every Tuesday at the San Giovanni Hotel for dinner at 2000, and Wednesday, at the Alexandria (Syrian) Club for lunch at 1400.

Churches

The **Alexandria Community Church**, Protestant interdenominational worship, is at the Schutz American School, 51 Sh. Schutz, tel. 857-525; services are Friday at 1030, there is a church school for children. **All Saints' Church**, Anglican/Episcopal, Stanley Bay, and **St. Mark's Anglican**, Midan al-Tahrir, alternate services; contact Howard Levett, tel. 840-720. The **Synagogue**, is at 69 Nabi Daniel, tel. 482-1426; temporarily closed.

TRANSPORT

Getting Around

Walking is the best way to get around downtown, for the central district is small and the city narrow, so it's difficult to get lost; besides, Alex is safe and the people are friendly and helpful. The business section centers on Midan Sa'ad Zaghlul and Ramleh Station.

The three main east-west streets are the Cornishe (Sh. 26 July) along the shore, Sh. Sa'ad Zaghlul, a block inland (it does not intersect the *midah* of the same name), and Sh. al-Hurriya, which is inland. North-south arteries include Sh. Nabi Daniel, which borders the west side of Midan Sa'ad Zaghlul and runs into the train station, and Sh. Safiya Zaghlul, which bisects Midan Sa'ad Zaghlul and Ramleh Station. The city's public transportation system is easy to use and is relatively uncrowded except during rush hours, when visitors may want to avoid the trams and buses.

Trams: The easiest way to travel long distances in Alexandria is to ride the trams, which leave from Ramleh Station east of Midan Zaghlul; pay the conductor on board (10PT). The car in front is the women's car; when the tram reaches the end of the line, you'll have to get off and switch. The blue trams run east and branch before the Sporting Club; #1 follows the main road, which starts as Sa'ad Zaghlul and, changing its name frequently, runs to al-Nasr College; #2 runs south to Sidi Gabr Station and rejoins the line near San Stefano Hotel. The yellow trams run out to the peninsula, near Ras al-Tin. Number 16 runs south to Pompey's pillar. Number 15 takes you through Anfushi, near Pharos, and then on to Ras al-Tin. You can walk up the hill and catch the old yellow trams that serve the older sections of the city; #5 goes to Pompey's column.

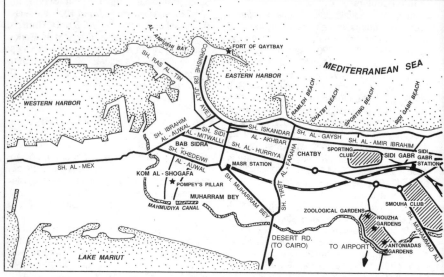

Buses: The city buses run out of three main terminals: Midan Sa'ad Zaghlul, Midan al-Manshiya, and Midan Gumhuriyya (by the train station). Buses run roughly from 0530 to 2400 or 0100 and cost 10-50PT. Numbers on the buses and at the stops are in Arabic, and the stops are posted with these numbers. The numbers change frequently, so check with the Tourist Office for the numbers and then confirm them with the Egyptians at the stop. The slightly more expensive (50PT) blue and white buses run up and down the Cornishe serving the beaches; some eastbound ones turn inland about halfway down, but just get off and catch the next one. These buses take only as many as they have seats, so indicate the number in your group by holding up your fingers; they have stops by benches, but most will stop if they have room between stations. Number 303 serves the airport.

Taxis: Like the taxis in Cairo, Alexandria's black-and-orange taxis are supposed to run off their meters so most trips around town should be a pound or two out to Montaza or Abuqir, LE5-10. However, since the rates are unbelievably low, most meters are "broken"; if your driver does run off the meter, give him a good tip. Single-colored Peugeot taxis are more expensive.

Service taxis, like those in Cairo, ply set routes, primarily along the main streets. Chauffeur-driven limousines are available from **Alexandria Limousine,** 25 Sh. Talaat Harb, tel. 482-5252, telex 54388 ATON UN. **Carriages** provide service to downtown Alexandria. You'll have to negotiate fares (LE5-10) with the driver.

Cars: Although the traffic within Alexandria can be hectic, it's not like Cairo. Parking, however, can be difficult to find so try to find a hotel that can provide parking. The ease of reaching the beautiful areas outside Alex makes having a car an attractive option. **Rental cars** are available from Avis, at the Cecil Hotel, tel. 807-055/807-532, and Budget, 59 Sh. al-Gaysh, Ibrahimiya (tel. 597-1273), which is east of the youth hostel in Chatby. Fees and conditions for rental are similar to Cairo's.

GETTING FROM ALEXANDRIA

Two main roads link the city with Cairo: a heavily traveled road that winds through delta villages, and a good toll road that runs through the desert. The latter is quicker (about 3½ hours) and safer, although the delta road offers more

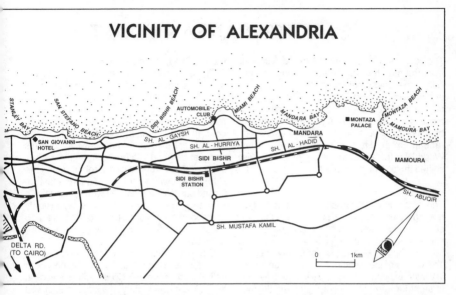

VICINITY OF ALEXANDRIA

native sights. **Hitchhiking** is nearly impossible and would cost as much as a service taxi since you would be expected to share gas expenses. For additional information, see "Cairo—Getting From" on p. 257. **Bus** line offices are on Midan Sa'ad Zaghlul: Super Jet on the south side and Delta on the west, across from the Cecil Hotel. Many are non-smoking—enquire. The latter also runs to the west, connecting Alexandria with Marsa Matruh, and now runs to Siwa at 1200 on Mon., Wed., and Sat., returning at 0900 on Sun., Tues., and Thurs; LE17. Super Jet connects to Cairo (LE12) and the airport (LE20), as does West Delta, for slightly less. In Cairo, you can transfer at Midan Tahrir for Port Said; avoid the local buses unless you want an up-close and personal view of Egyptian village life.

Trains linking Alexandria to the delta cities and Cairo run through the countryside, often following the large canals and giving passengers a glimpse of the rural life. Trains depart from 0600 to 2000 (winter) or 2130 (summer) from Masr Station, Midan al-Gumhuriyya at Nabi Daniel. They reach Sidi Gabr Station (on Sh. al-Hurriya (five km east of the main station) about 10 minutes later; from there, they leave via Tanta for Ramesses Station in Cairo. The best

are the three-times daily turbini that depart at 0755, 1355, and 1845; about LE17/11. You should buy your tickets ahead as these trains are popular. Otherwise, you can pick up an air-conditioned tourist train, which is slower and not as plush; again you must reserve ahead. Local trains serve the delta and the towns east and west of Alexandria.

Taxis: Intercity taxis to Cairo leave from the taxi stand by Masr Station at the south end of Sh. Nabi Daniel. Most cabbies take the delta road and drive like crazy—the ride will give you enough adrenaline to last your entire stay in Egypt. Taxis for Marsa Matruh and other points west leave from the same area.

Cars: Driving between Alexandria and Cairo is easy; the desert (toll) road is straight and has little traffic, but the delta road is treacherous with its four lanes of fast trucks and slow donkeys, horses, and camels.

Planes: Alexandria is also linked to Cairo by plane, but considering the time spent going through the airport, the flight takes nearly as long as a drive. Both EgyptAir and Air Sinai offer several daily flights to Cairo. The airport lies a few km to the southeast along the delta road; bus #303 (Midan al-Manshiya) and local taxis service it.

THE MEDITERRANEAN COAST

The beaches on either side of Alexandria stretch from the mouth of the Rosetta branch of the Nile to the Libyan border. While visitors bathe and bask in the hot sun, fishermen ply the waters for the justly famous catches, and the best place to eat them is at Abuqir. To the west, the beaches and blue-green waters of the Mediterranean rim the Libyan Desert where, during World War II, the Allies' victory over the Axis shifted the tide of the conflict.

Climate

The entire coast is cooled by the north wind, making it pleasant even in summer, but the sun still burns incessantly, so cover up if you're sensitive. In summer, the nights can be cool, so take a wrap; in winter, the entire day is cold. The waters of the Mediterranean, though harsh in winter and early sprlng, are warm and inviting in summer and fall. Native Egyptians fleeing Alexandria's crowds have discovered the western coast and now jam the beaches from Agami to Matruh, so the best time to visit the area is in early fall, after the crowds have left and before the weather and the water cool off.

EAST OF ALEXANDRIA

Abuqir

On 1 August 1789, at this small town about five km past Montaza, Nelson trapped and destroyed a French squadron anchored in the Abuqir Bay. Cutting Napoleon's supply route from France, the victory forced the French to withdraw from Egypt. Nearby lie the ruins of Canopus, which was one of the most important trading towns during the closing eras of the pharaonic period. Little now remains of this city where Hadrian often stayed (and attempted to recreate at his villa near Rome). Today Abuqir is most famous for its seafood, including the small Abuqir shrimp. Visitors to Alexandria routinely troop out to the headland for a seafood dinner. **Nelson Island** lies about 25 minutes from Abuqir (LE40, roundtrip) and offers quiet beaches for swimming or fishing. Pick up a fish meal in Abuqir

(LE20-40) and have a picnic.

The most noted restaurant is the Zephyron, which has served fish dinners since 1929; open 1200-2400 (to 0200 in summer); from the main square walk straight toward the sea. The restaurant next door is slightly cheaper and nearly as good. In the summer, Egyptians grill fish right on the beach; it's cheaper than in the restaurants and just as good. To get to Abuqir, take bus #129 or #109 from Midan Zaghlul (Cornishe side); check with your driver as to the last returning bus to Alex (about 2130 in winter, later in summer). You can also take the train (pretty gruesome) from Masr Station (about every 15 minutes) for a few piasters, or go by local taxi (LE5-10).

Camping: Abuqir also offers the only campground near Alexandria. Abu Kir Camp, about half a kilometer south of Zephryon Restaurant, tel. 560-1541, will rent you a large tent, or you can pitch your own for under a pound. With permission from the police, you can camp on the beach for free.

Rashid

This town is best known as the site where the French Lieutenant Bouchard, while working on Fort Rosetta, uncovered the trilingual Rosetta Stone. The modern town, however, was founded in the 9th century A.D. and enjoyed a thousand years of prosperity as Egypt's primary western port. Possessed of large baths and a famous market, it was a center for shipping dates. Favored by Turks, it reached its zenith in the 17th and 18th centuries; only in the last 200 years has it declined, falling once again in the shade of growing Alexandria.

But the town is still filled with medieval buildings, including several merchant houses with reused ancient stones, capitals, and columns: the al-Amaciali house, the al-Fatatri, and the Arab Keli, which is now a museum. The mosques, too, are notable, their simple lines offset by faience tile decoration; the Zaghlul Mosque and the al-Abassi are two of the more outstanding. Take a picnic lunch and hire a falucca to visit the Mosque of Abu Madur, which lies along

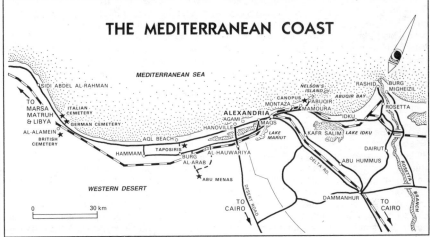

© MOON PUBLICATIONS, INC.

THE MEDITERRANEAN COAST

MEDITERRANEAN SEA

SIDI ABDEL AL-RAHMAN

TO MARSA MATRUH & LIBYA

ITALIAN CEMETERY

GERMAN CEMETERY

AL-ALAMEIN

BRITISH CEMETERY

AQL BEACH

HAMMAM

TAPOSIRIS

BURG AL-ARAB

AL-HAUWARIYA

ABU MENAS

WESTERN DESERT

NELSON'S ISLAND

CANOPUS

MONTAZA

ABUQIR

ABUQIR BAY

RASHID

BURG MIGHEIZIL

ROSETTA

ALEXANDRIA

AGAMI

HANOVILLE

MAQS

MAMOURA

IDKU

KAFR SALIM

LAKE IDKU

LAKE MARIUT

DAIRUT

ABU HUMMUS

DELTA RD.

DAMMANHUR

TO CAIRO

DESERT ROAD

TO CAIRO

ROSETTA BRANCH

0   30 km

---

the river about five km south of town. Or visit Edfina Park with its dam (Qanater), or just spend the day on the hills overlooking the Nile.

Few visit this fishing town of 25,000 people, which means a refreshing lack of "touristic pursuit." You can reach Rashid via the coast road, by train from Sidi Gabr Station (change in Mamoura), by bus from al-Manshiya, and by service taxi.

WEST OF ALEXANDRIA

Between Alexandria and the Libyan border, the restless amethyst and sapphire Mediterranean beats against shell-white beaches. This stretch of sea coast contains the Abu Menas Monastery (the oldest Christian basilica in Egypt), the World War II memorials at al-Alamein, and the spectacular beaches at Sidi Abdel al-Rahman and Marsa Matruh. Beyond the limestone ridge that runs parallel with the beach, the desert *reg* dips southward toward the salt-encrusted Qattara Depression. In the center of this inhospitable landscape lies Egypt's most beautiful and unique oasis—Siwa. (See p. 448.)

Practicalities

Because of the proximity to the Libyan border, the military presence along the coast increases as you head west. You may be subject to military stops at any time, so be sure to carry your passport. Foreigners are not permitted off the roads without permission, as unexploded land mines await the unwary.

Like Alex, the west coast is a summer resort, and developers are splashing tourist villages all along the beaches. Prices are higher from May to October, and hotel accommodations can be tough to get. In winter, prices lower, but some hotels and restaurants close. Camping on the beaches is permitted only with permission from the military (see p. 432) and this rule is strictly enforced.

Transport

Situated at either end of the western coast, Alexandria and Marsa Matruh are the area's main transportation terminals. **EgyptAir** flies from Cairo to Marsa Matruh twice a week. During the summer (1 June to 31 Oct.) **Wagon Lits** sleeper trains connect Cairo to Matruh (see p. 258). Note that this train does *not* stop in Alexandria. **Bus** service between Cairo, Alex, and Matruh is good, with both the Super Jet (summer only) and Delta's blue buses running throughout the day. Service taxis also connect Cairo, Alex, and Matruh; they are slightly more expensive than the buses, but they will get you to your destination faster; that is, if they get you there at all.

Unfortunately, to reach the intermediate sites along the coast by public transportation is difficult. The buses and service taxis that run from Alex to Marsa Matruh are more than happy to let you off wherever you wish, especially since you have to pay the full fare to the end of the line. However, catching another one later that is not already full is difficult. Thus the easiest way to visit the coast is to get a group together and rent a cab or to hire a private car.

Western Beaches

The beaches of Agami and Hanoville lie about 20 km west of Alexandria. Long the refuge of wealthy Egyptians, the beach at Agami is becoming increasingly crowded and has unfortunately borne the brunt of pollution from Alexandria's Western Harbor. Farther west, Hanoville is cleaner and less crowded. Amenities such as beach chairs and umbrellas are available, but only during the summer.

Accommodations: During summer, when accommodations are tight, be sure to phone ahead. The newly redone **Admiral Hotel,** tel. 430-8465, fax 430-3038, offers rooms with private baths, TV, a large refrigerator, and a sink area for sandwiches, for LE100, sea view; it also has a private beach, gardens and patio. Both the **Agami Palace,** tel. 433-0230, and the **Hannoville,** tel. 430-3258, are more expensive. Use the **Costa Blanca,** tel. 430-3112, as a last resort.

Beach Resorts: From here west, plush resorts gobble up the beach, imposing multiple story hotels attended by scattered "chalets" and "villas," complete with swimming pools, tennis courts, health clubs, shopping centers, and golf courses. You can swim, water-ski, or sailboard in the Mediterranean, or simply laze under beach umbrellas. All are closed in winter. The **Aida Beach,** 77 km out the Alexandria-Matruh Road, tel. 990-850 or Cairo (02) 348-1512, fax 990-867, is representative, and to partake of their goodies will cost you over $100 a night, better than half that for day use of the beach and a cabin for two.

Transport: Unlike most of the rest of the western coast, Agami and Hanoville are easily accessible by public transportation. **Bus #500** (Agami only) and #600 (both beaches) leave daily between 0600-2400 from Masr Station and *midans* Ramleh and al-Manshiya. The ride to either beach is 50PT, but if you wish to visit both get a transfer for an additional 15PT. **Service taxis** run out for a few pounds, and **private cabs** charge LE10 one way; be sure to make arrangements to have the driver pick you up if you want a ride back.

Deir Abu Menas

If you have a car, a pleasant side trip is to the Monastery of St. Menas, dedicated to the Christian soldier who died in the 3rd century fighting in the East for his faith. His last wish was to be buried in his homeland. Accordingly, his body was loaded on a camel that, when it reached the springs that mark the site of the present monastery, laid down and refused to move. This action, taken as a divine sign, dictated the burial place of the saint, and a cult grew up around his tomb. The nearby spring gained a reputation throughout the Christian world for its miraculous cures, and the monastery became the center of a thriving town that catered to pilgrims until the 8th century. Excavations have uncovered several churches, baths, catacombs, monks' cells, and the remnants of the town. The Basilica of Arcadius, the oldest surviving Christian structure in Egypt, was built by the Roman emperor in the 5th century in thanks for the spring waters' cure of his son.

Getting there is easiest with a private car or taxi. The turnoff to the monastery is 48 km from Alex, at the village of Burg al-Arab. Seven km south lies the village of Bahiq, and here you can hire a villager to guide you to the ruins, for they lie 15 km out into the desert. But the roads are good, so if you speak a little Arabic, you can get directions.

Taposiris Magna

Near Burg al-Arab at the city of Abusir are the ruins of ancient Taposiris Magna. The area is most noted for its model of Pharos Lighthouse built to a 1/10 scale; the wooden staircase lets visitors to climb to the top. The gate only looks shut. To the west lie the two pylons of the old limestone temple; of the interior, extensively changed by the Christians, only the foundations remain. To the south, ruined houses overlook the wild edges of Lake Mariut.

AL-ALAMEIN

This desolate piece of desert marks the turning point of the African campaigns of World War II. Here, Montgomery took his stand, barely 100 km from his headquarters in Alexandria, and faced Rommel, the German Desert Fox. Many Egyptians viewed Rommel as a hero for freeing them from the hated yoke of the British. But their freedom was short-lived. Between 23 October and 4 November 1942, Montgomery's Eighth Army defeated Rommel's Africa Corps in a battle that marked the beginning of the Allies' sweep through Tripoli, Tunis, and on to Italy. The stark landscape is still littered with rusting hulks of tanks and trucks, and several memorial cemeteries document, in eerie reality, the blood shed on this forsaken wasteland. Do not wander off the roads; live mines from the battle remain.

The British Cemetery

Located on the south side of the road just before the village of al-Alamein, this graveyard names the nearly 11,000 Allied soldiers who died here. The approach is through a black iron gateway, and the memorial and graveyard lie 100 meters to the south, at the foot of the ridge. Memorial lists of soldiers who were never found are mounted inside the archway. Through this arch and beyond the haunting gardens lie row upon row of tombstones, some with only a name and date of death, others with personal inscriptions from families and friends.

The Village

Al-Alamein village lies just 100 meters west, where a resthouse on the north side of the road serves as a bus stop. Just beyond is the small military museum with a courtyard display of various tanks and armored vehicles. For an idea of what combat must have been like, climb in one of the tiny tanks. The museum proper is closed for restoration. It contains additional equipment and models that show the battle's strategy. The museum also contains a section showing detailed construction of the Israeli Bar Lev Line and outlining its subsequent smashing by the Egyptian army. Though they ultimately lost the war, Egyptians view this battle as a major victory.

Practicalities

The rest stop at al-Alamein provides light food (good beef and fries as well as spaghetti) and tea for a few pounds. A vendor across the road usually has fresh fruit for sale. The only hotel is the al-Alamein Rest House (LE18 s, LE21 d), is clean if simple.

Transport

Visiting al-Alamein by **train** is not feasible, since the tracks lie nearly two km across the desert from the village; in summer it's a sweltering walk, in winter a bitingly cold one. **Buses** and **service taxis** traveling between Alex or

*the British cemetery
at al-Alamein*

KATHY HANSEN

Cairo and Marsa Matruh make about a half-hour stop in al-Alamein. This stop should give you enough time to walk down to the British cemetery or take a quick trip through the museum, but you'll not be able to visit the other memorials. If you want to spend more time, before you leave, buy an additional seat on a later bus from either Alexandria or Marsa Matruh. (The last bus usually arrives about 1630.) Otherwise, you may try to hitch to your destination (not recommended for females alone), as most Egyptians are willing to share, especially if you're willing to pay a few pounds; ask at the resthouse. To visit al-Alamein with the least hassle, hire a private car or a taxi (about LE100 for the day).

Italian And German Memorials

These two additional memorials lie about 10 km west of al-Alamein proper, and both, although difficult to reach without a private car or taxi, are worth a visit. Perched on the ridge overlooking the Mediterranean, the memorials are different yet similar fortresses against the living world.

The German memorial, a fortress enclosing a courtyard, stands just down the road. Inside, around its perimeter, lie coffins symbolizing the divisions that fought in the battle, while in the center, an obelisk surmounts the tomb of an unidentified soldier.

The Italian one, reached along a sand track lined with shrubs, reaches skyward like a medieval tower. Its soaring interior is lined with marble; its huge window looks through a grid emblazoned with division insignias across the desolate sands. Outside, the stairway curled around its base leads to a platform with a spectacular view of the sea. By the main road, an archway screens war equipment displayed in its courtyard and a small museum. Just west, a mosque commemorates the Libyan dead.

Sidi Abdel Al-Rahman

About 20 km from al-Alamein and a couple of kilometers off the main road lies the seaside resort of Sidi Abdel al-Rahman. Blessed by white sands and aqua-blue water, the area is breathtakingly beautiful. In spite of its isolation and the small gobs of oil (the result of offshore spills) it's inundated with bathers during the summer.

The four-star **Azur al-Alamein Hotel** (tel. 492-1228; telex 55372 ALMTL UN) is simple, comfortable, and now run by Pullman. Access to the public beach is the turnoff before you reach the hotel. The public toilet facilities are dismal. There is no camping on the beach.

MARSA MATRUH

Known as the Egyptian Riviera, Marsa Matruh nestles in a cove of white sands facing a small, sheltered bay. From antiquity, the town has catered to bathers, sun worshippers, and beachcombers. Cleopatra sojourned here, and during World War II, Rommel used the area as his headquarters, from which he directed the battle at al-Alamein. Today, the town's beautiful coastline, honeycombed with lagoons and caves, invites the visitor to idle away peaceful hours. In summer, the area is besieged by Egyptians escaping from the throngs at Alexandria, hordes that make Matruh's spacious beaches nearly as crowded as the better-known resorts to the east. To have the area to yourself, visit in fall or spring, but you'll also find many of the hotels closed and Matruh's social scene and nightlife at a standstill.

The Alexandria road enters the small town from the east, curves and runs north to the Cornishe. At this junction lie the government buildings, and to the west, along the Cornishe, are the newer hotels. Sharia Alexandria is the main shopping street, though small shops occupy the parallel streets to the west and south. Visitors can buy good-quality Siwan silver jewelry and Bedouin rugs here. The beach known as the **Lido** stretches in front of the more westerly hotels, and during the season, you can rent chairs and umbrellas. Beyond the Lido, **Lover's Beach** lies in the western curve of the bay. At the eastern end, **Rommel's Beach** is named after the cave where the Desert Fox headquartered. This cave, nearly at the end of the spit, has been converted into a museum (open daily 0900-1500; fee 50PT); it's closed in winter but check at the Tourist Office to see if they can open it.

Townspeople use the bayside beach, but over the hill lies a nearly deserted sea beach with a strong surf. You can reach Rommel's cave by driving, or by hiring a *tuf tuf* (donkey cart), bike, or boat. In summer, the adventurous can rent a surf kayak at the Beau Site Hotel.

Western Beaches
The road to the western beaches that lie outside the town proper is a continuation of the Cornishe, which turns south at the end of the Lido and then winds westward. About five km out a sign in both English and Arabic indicates **Cleopatra's Bath.** The road follows the western curve of the bay, ending at a strip of beach. The calm shallow waters, however, are deceptive; beware of the sharp dropoff a few feet from the shore. Across the sand dunes, across from the walled compound, lies Cleopatra's Bath, a hollow, roofless rock with a landward doorway, which is hidden in the clefts. Legend says that it was created for Cleopatra so she could bathe away from heavy surf, which, like today, pounded relentlessly against the rocks. Waves constantly force water into its interior, and if you look closely you can see traces of carvings. Other than in the bath, the shore is treacherous—the rocks are slippery and sharp and the surf is heavy—so if you swim, do so with care. A ferry runs to Cleopatra's Beach sporadically from the Old Harbor.

Farther west, **Ubayyid Beach,** although now populated with summer homes, offers a pleasant though slightly rougher surf than the sheltered Lido. During the season, a couple of resthouses serve refreshments and rent chairs and umbrellas. They also supply showers and changing rooms free for those who have rented equipment, and at a small fee for others.

Agiba Beach: Beyond Ubayyid, about 15 km from town, lies the most stunning beach on the west coast. In Arabic, *agiba* means astonishing or beautiful—and either name is applicable. The road ends at a cliff top, and you have to walk across it to the coast. Here, the vista stretches out across a small inlet framed with clean, white sand. Protected by the cliffs and a small reef, this beach is a perfect place to swim or sunbathe. Beyond it rises a companion cliff, strangely weathered by the repeated onslaught of the waves. You can climb down the slope, cross the beach, and walk around the headland where there lies a natural shallow cave fronted by a small beach—a good place to relax and contemplate the sea. Agiba is crowded much of the time, and although facilities are developing, it's still a good idea to bring your own equipment and food. If you want to escape the crowds, try the small stretch of beach just east of the large cliff.

Accommodations
With the "discovery" of the western coast, and Marsa Matruh in particular, prices have skyrocketed. Even with new development, during the tourist season (May-October) and Ramadan hotel space can be tight. However, in the off-season, those hotels that don't close drop their prices and often their requirements for full board.

The best hotel in town, and perhaps in Egypt, is the **Beau Site,** tel. 934-011/922-066, fax 933-319, on Sh. al-Shati' (on the Cornishe about two km west of Sh. Alexandria). In Cairo, you can make reservations at 6 Sh. Osman Ahmed Osman (tel. 259-9480, fax 256-4464—open daily 1700-2100). $55 s, $70 d includes compulsory full board, but the service and food make this a place to splurge. The hotel also rents chalets (three or four people) and can provide accommodations for up to eight. Make reservations well in advance, for the hotel is popular. It's closed 1 Nov. to 30 April.

The government-run **Arous al-Bahr** on the Cornishe, tel. 944-420, east of the Beau Site, is adequate; the food, like the rooms, is clean if not inspired. Inexpensive rooms (LE15.40 s, LE19.50 d, without breakfast) make it a good deal.

The **Riveria,** on the main street, tel. 930-004, offers good rooms with TV, phone, and refrigerator for LE31.25 s, LE43 d, and LE55 t, all with private bath and breakfast. The **Royal Palace** on the Cornishe, tel. 930-004, offers a good view of the sea; LE25 s, LE40 d, and LE50 t, all including breakfast. The similar **Adriatika** (go past the Greek restaurant, turn right at the *midan,* and then follow the sign down the alley), tel. 935-194, is similar. Rooms at the **New Lido,** also on the Cornishe, tel. 944-515, are expensive, but the bungalows on the shore (complete with refrigerators) for four people (two beds) run less.

Several less-expensive hotels lie east of Sh. Alexandria. Of these, the best is **al-Ghazala,**

Sh. Alma Rumm, tel. 942-086. This well-run and clean hotel charges LE5 per person in shared rooms with three beds. If it's full (often in July and Aug.) try the the nearby **Al-Dest**, tel. 942-105.

The **youth hostel** (IYHF), 4 Sh. al-Galeh, tel. 942-331, is located west of Sh. Alexandria and two blocks in from the Cornishe. New and relatively tidy, it's the cheapest place in town. Shared rooms and baths run LE2 members, LE5 non-members.

You can **camp** free of charge on the bay beach with *permission from the military office* (open 0900-1500 and 1700-2300) on Sh. Galeh, east of Sh. Alexandria. Do not camp on the beaches without a permit. The other option is to rent a beachside tent at **Badr Camp** at Ubayyid Beach.

Food
Other than the Beau Site's dining room, Marsa Matruh offers little in the way of fine dining. Elegant buffets (breakfast LE10, lunch LE17.50, and dinner LE19.25) are served on the hotel's porch. Several clean if simple cafes occupy the center of town; try the chicken at **Mattam Shatti Matruh**, about four blocks up Sh. Alexandria, across from the okay **Greek Restaurant**. The **Haniel-Onda** is east on Sh. Gamal Abd al-Nasser and the **Mansour Fish Restuarant** is two blocks east of Sh. Alexandria. The cheapest, and perhaps the most fun, way to feed a group is to visit the local *suq* about three blocks east of Sh. Alexandria and north of Sh. Gamal Abd al-Nasser.

Entertainment
Nightlife in Marsa Matruh is based in the hotel bars, notably the Bamboo Bar at the Beau Site or the small independent nightclubs along the bay like Disco 54 in the Radi Hotel or J.R. Club.

Services And Information
Tourist Information, tel. 933-192 (open daily 0800-1400 and 2000-2200), is behind the government building at the junction of Sh. Alexandria and the Cornishe. **Bank of Cairo** has offices a block east of the Ghazala Hotel; open 0830-1400 and 1800-2100. The larger hotels will cash traveler's checks. The **police station,** tel. 943-063, lies two blocks east of Sh.

Alexandria, a block south of the Cornishe (open 24 hours). The **post office** is next door (open Sat.-Thurs. 0800-1500) and the **telephone office** is across the street (open 24 hours; code is 03). The **Military Investigations Office,** where you get permission to camp, lies at the end of the street behind the green gate; ring the bell, and someone will eventually show up; open 0900-1300 and 2000-2200—helpful, English-speaking staff.

Transport
Marsa Matruh is small enough to walk around. Donkey-drawn *tuf tuf* drivers have discovered tourists, and they will try to stick you for several pounds for a jaunt around town; as in Cairo, just give them LE1 for most rides. Rent **bicycles** next to the Riveria Hotel; LE7/day; open 1800-2400. To reach the beaches, take a service taxi or the minibus that leaves from the bus station (LE2-3/person) to Agiba. In summer, both the taxis and minibuses run about every 10 minutes from 0900-1500. Alternately, you can catch a public bus (50PT) to Cleopatra, Ubayyid, or Agiba. In summer, the Beau Site runs irregularly scheduled boat and car tours to the beaches. You can rent a taxi for a couple of hours at the beaches for about LE25. In summer, the number of visitors and the holiday spirit make hitchhiking feasible.

EgyptAir flies between Cairo and Marsa Matruh on Sun. (1500), Fri. (1000), and Wed. (1500); the ticket office in Matruh is on Sh. Galah next to the National Bank.

Trains connect Alexandria with Marsa Matruh, but are 3rd class and not recommended except for the most intrepid travelers. However, from 1 June to 31 October, Wagon Lits runs a sleeper from Cairo to Matruh; trains leave Matruh on Sun., Tues., and Thurs. at 2215. The train station is at the south end of Sh. Alexandria, about two km from the Cornishe.

Bus service links Matruh with both Alexandria and Cairo. Super Jet runs buses to Cairo at 1100 (LE28) and Alexandria (LE20) at 1400. West Delta leaves at 0730 (LE13) for Cairo and again at 1400 (LE22); to Alexandria at 1700 (winter) or 1900 (summer), LE10. The buses of both lines connect Marsa Matruh with Midan Tahrir in Cairo (five hours); for any of these trips, make reservations a day or two ahead. The bus station in Marsa Matruh is about seven blocks from the Cornishe and one block west of Sh. Alexandria.

Service taxis also link Alexandria and Cairo with Marsa Matruh. Using service taxis means you don't have to book in advance, are always assured of a seat (such as it is), and will get (God willing) to your destination sooner—provided, of course, you don't die of fright on your way: LE15 to Cairo, LE8-10 to Alexandria. In Marsa Matruh the service taxis gather next to the bus station.

To Siwa

The daily bus to Siwa leaves at 0730 and 1500; the earlier one is better, for the late bus, which starts in Alex, is often full by the time it gets to Marsa Matruh, and it puts you into Siwa at 2000. West Delta runs a special a/c bus on Sat., Mon., and Wed. at 1530; LE8, arriving in under five hours; you must book ahead. Service taxis leave from the northwest side of the bus station early in the morning and late afternoon. Both stop at the resthouse at the halfway point; coffee and tea are available. No restrooms.

BOB RACE

THE WESTERN OASES

To escape the Nile Valley's press of tourists and hawking vendors, follow old caravan routes through the Western Desert and its varied oases. Restless dunes stalk the countryside, alternately covering and revealing the geological pages of their history: giant limestone mushrooms shaped by vast, ancient seas, and cliffs painted by steaming deposits of iron and sulfur. Scoured by the winds, the desert's sands and rocks yield up ancient fossils as well as flints and pottery shards discarded by early inhabitants of now dry springs. Ancient seas, howling winds, and torrential rains not only shaped the land but deposited minerals—iron, potash, sulfur—and created a vast underground aquifer that today feeds the oases.

In these fertile depressions verdant with trees and fields, the villages remain little changed from the Middle Ages. Hot springs still sooth arthritic joints and frayed nerves. Walk through ancient *suqs* and collect needles of calcite from Crystal Mountain. Go camping in the White Desert and listen to traditional Arabic music under a clear, starry sky. Buy handcrafted pottery and carpets. Wallow in hot springs where

water gushes from the bowels of the earth. Walk well-trodden paths between gardens, and eat food fresh from nearby fields. Take time out from modern Egypt's pressures to explore a land that time has kindly forgotten.

Isolated, the oases have maintained much of their tranquil appeal. Only a few hardy visitors who wanted to escape the hassles of the Nile Valley came here with backpack and sleeping bag. Now, however, in an effort to strengthen their economies, the areas are turning to tourism. Hotels are springing up, and tour buses are invading the quiet countryside. While some areas, such as Dakhla, are trying to integrate increasing numbers of visitors without sacrificing their rural lifestyle, change seems inevitable.

THE LAND

The western oases lie in a series of geologic troughs stretching in a south-north arc beginning in Nubia and ending at Siwa. Egypt's five main depressions lie at Kharga, Dakhla, Farafra, Bahariya, and Siwa (for the Fayyum and Wadi

Natrun, see "Cairo Environs" p. 281 and p. 292.) Unlike the stereotypical small pools fringed with a single rim of palm trees, Egypt's oases stretch for kilometers. Once fed by copious prehistoric rains now trapped in the porous rock, the artesian wells that occupy these sinks tap into water reserves stored in the underlying Nubian Sandstones. Although pharaonic Egyptians considered the oases mere outposts of civilization, the Romans, early Muslims, and now modern Egyptians have mined the water—liquid gold that erupts into lush green.

Geography
The oases of Egypt's Western Desert continue the southeast to northwest line begun by similar depressions in Sudan. Kharga, the largest and most southerly of Egypt's oases, occupies a north-south depression that extends 220 km, widening in places to 40 km. To the northwest, the Dakhla depression runs east-west along the southern edge of the central Libyan Plateau. To the north, Farafra lies enclosed by cliffs on three sides; yet farther north, beyond a high white ridge, lies Bahariya. Unlike the other oases, this 1800-square-km area is encased by escarpments, and its oval depression contains several hills. Between them lies the brooding Black Desert and the limestone White Desert with its mushroom-shaped pediments sculpted by long-vanished oceans. Siwa, the oasis farthest to the north, lies just west of the Qattara Depression and is more closely linked to the Mediterranean than the others. In all of them, however, the water nourishes verdant crops: olives and dates in the north, rice and berseem in the south.

Geology
In early geologic times, much of the Western Desert lowland was flooded; in fact, the Cretaceous period witnessed four major transgressive cycles. Shallow seas flowed southward, swamping central Egypt, their intertidal zones and estuaries depositing marine sediments that formed limestones. During the water's retreat, sand from higher areas washed into the basin, creating layers of sandstone. At each transgression, the shoreline moved north, and by late Miocene, these inter-fingered sediments some 3,000 meters deep emerged to become the plateau of the Western Desert.

The Oases
The oases lie in great hollows in this plateau. Although earlier geologists felt that the wind excavated them, increasing evidence indicates they were created by a system of late-Miocene rivers that drained the Western Plateau and ran into the early Nile. The Qattara Depression, for example, once part of an ancient stream bed, was cut off from its outlet by tectonic movement, then scoured by water and wind. The oases dip close to the aquifer that underlies the Western Desert.

BRUCE HANSEN

The deities of the Nile Valley, such as the baboon-god Thoth, were also recognized and worshipped in the western oases.

The Nubian Sandstones slope down toward the Mediterranean, and gravity forces the confined water north, putting it under considerable hydrostatic pressure. Where the land is low enough, the gradient forces this "fossil" water upward into artesian springs. Where it's tapped by wells, it gushes from standpipes as if pumped.

The Wells
Ancient depressions in the Arba'in Desert testify to a long history of spring activity. As the springs dried up, the land, no longer buoyed up by the water, sank, forming circles and ovals 15-100 km in diameter and up to 40 meters deep. In Kharga and Dakhla, more recent activity formed conical mounds ranging from a few meters to 20 meters high. Their central, cylindrical vents oozed water laden with clay, ocher, sand, or carbonates that solidified. Today, similar wells pour forth iron-rich or sulfurous waters that are often warm, if not frankly hot.

Water And Development
The water that feeds these artesian wells was trapped during local, heavy rains during the time when Egypt was more tropical. Although some new water filters down from Sudan, it cannot fully replenish the aquifer that man

tapped from prehistoric times. As the water table dropped, the Persians introduced gravity-driven wells, and the Romans perfected them, irrigating extensive areas of the ancient playas. Such old Roman wells, now dry, lie 10 meters above modern ones, and these too, with new development, are running dry. Groundwater is being overdrafted at ten times the rate that it can be naturally replenished. Although the Nubian aquifer system gives Egypt an enormous groundwater supply, it's non-renewable; it would take Sudanese water several hundred thousand years to reach New Valley.

Climate

Away from even the small, tempering influence of the Nile, the Western oases feel the full force of the desert. Temperatures, unmoderated by the dry air, reflect daily extremes. Since the oases are cool in winter, their nights bordering on cold, and summers are unremittingly hot, fall is the best time to visit the oases, although spring can be nice if the khamsin winds don't blow. Rain is negligible and storms may be decades apart at any given site. When they do hit, they can drop huge amounts of rain in short periods, creating flash floods kilometers from their source, so be wary of camping in dry wadis. Winds seem ever-present, ranging 4-20 km/h throughout the year at Kharga and Dakhla.

HISTORY

In prehistoric times, these fertile hollows supported bands of hunters who harvested the big game of the surrounding steppes. As early as the Old Kingdom, the people of the Nile Delta established trading links with those in the oases, and by the Middle Kingdom, pharaohs actively Egyptianized the areas. The string of oases provide the only alternative route across Egypt, and the pharaohs, recognizing their strategic importance, garrisoned the areas. The lonely assignment was not relished by army staff, and in fact, political opponents to the rulers at Thebes were banished to Kharga.

During the New Kingdom, the prosperity of the oases grew, and the pharaohs tapped the area's agricultural and mineral wealth. Nevertheless, the oases, especially in times of political unrest,

sheltered bands of marauders who attacked the settled areas linked to the empire. Late in the New Kingdom, the Libyans invaded Egypt from the west, and the assaulting armies must have used the oases as a base of operations. During the Late Period, the Libyan kings, having found the oases desolate, spent considerable effort upgrading them.

Greco-Roman Period

With the exception of Siwa, and perhaps of Bahariya, the Greeks left little evidence of activity, but the Romans, apparently recognizing the potential fertility of the ancient playas, established settlements along the line of depressions. They cleaned old wells and dug new ones, improving the water-delivery systems. But as the Roman Empire declined, the Egyptian peasants suffered. The outlying oases lost their economic base, and the villages became easy targets for bandits. The sand encroached on the fields and filtered into the wells. The oases constricted and continued to decline. The isolation, however, sheltered them from early Christian conflicts, and the churches flourished.

Islamic Period

Although soon after the Arab conquest, Islam found its way to the oases, Christianity remained strong until the 14th century, when the Coptic Church ceased appointing bishops to the area. The cycle of high taxes and lack of maintenance or protection for the inhabitants continued during the Middle Ages, and many families fled. Although the settlements remained important stops for the caravan that carried pilgrims from North Africa to Mecca, the areas of cultivation shrank and the population fell. With the exception of a brief revival under the Mamluks, life in the oases was dismal until the time of Muhammad Ali. As in most of Egypt, the 19th century ushered in a period of growth. Today, with new water, money, and immigrants, the people of the oases are digging new wells, planting more fields, and building accommodations for a healthy influx of tourists.

SIGHTS

While guides in the oases are quick to point out their pharaonic remains, most are Ptolemaic and Roman, often hard to reach, and tickets average LE8; in short, they're hardly worth the effort. The Temple of Hebis in Kharga is now closed, and you must get permission from the Antiquities Inspector at Giza to see the tombs at Bahariya. In Wadi Gadid, you'll need to cough up LE2.50 for a tourism tax that's supposed to go toward development of the local sights. The real appeal of the oases, however, lies in the slow, relaxed way of living. You can visit villages out of the past—their mud-brick architecture echoing pharaonic and Islamic traditions. See the desert in all its myriad faces, under the burning skys or in the shifting light and shadows of cumulus clouds. Its ranks of dunes march across level, stony plains, and jutting boulders and scarps reflect in vast mirages.

PRACTICALITIES

With the oases' increase in agriculture and mining development, they have become more closely linked with the Nile Valley. Roads following the historical caravan routes are now paved, and a new highway from Luxor to Kharga should be completed soon. (You cannot drive west of these main highways without permission) To get through the main checkpoints, you'll need your passport; usually these checkpoints come in groups of two: one military, the other manned by police. You no longer need special permission to visit Siwa.

Bed And Board
Although improving, the oases remain a destination for the hardy traveler. Accommodations range from the outstanding three-star (with five-star service) **Mebarez Hotel** in Dakhla to questionably clean resthouses in Farafra. Most of the other resthouses are more or less clean, if primitive. Your best bet is to take a sleeping bag and plan on camping out. The food is native and good, but only for stomachs accustomed to street fare; take reasonable precautions about fruit (peel it) and take plenty of bottled water and food for between stops.

Transportation
You can reach the oases from three areas. Siwa is accessible through Marsa Matruh on the Mediterranean Coast (p. 430); centrally located

Bahariya and Farafra are both easily reached from Cairo (p. 260); and the Wadi Gadid (Dakhla and Kharga) from the Nile Valley at Asyut (p. 309) and soon from Luxor. You can make a loop through the southern four in either direction, either by car or bus; facilities get more primitive from south to north. If you want to include Siwa in the loop, you'll have to use a car, and the road only allows private cars from Bahariya to Siwa, not from Siwa to Bahariya; no buses run between Bahariya and Siwa.

The roads between the oases are paved, more or less, but are not super-highways. The shifting beds of sand buckle the road base, the scouring wind and pounding traffic builds pit-snares in the blacktop, and the crews continually repairing them create hazards and detours of their own. The shifting dunes frequently cover the roads (especially around Dakhla), and you'll be side-tracked by detours of varying quality. After a dune moves on and uncovers the main road, it has often deteriorated. With the exception of the road between Bahariya and Farafra and a stretch between Kharga and Asyut, most are currently in good shape.

By Car: This is the most convenient way to visit the oases, but you'll need to prepare for the desert. You can either rent a car in Cairo (p. 255; or Alexandria for Siwa, p. 424). Smart travelers carry extra gas, as well as spare parts, tools, and plenty of water (for radiators and humans), for the country between the oases is as unfriendly today as when King Cambyses lost an entire army somewhere between Kharga and Siwa. In summer, don't plan on using your air-conditioning much, as it will quickly overheat the car. Most people drive at night, but if the roads are covered with sand, navigation can be tricky. If you break down, wait in the shade of your car: **Do not attempt to walk for help.** The desert can and will kill you. Gas is available (although not always on the last day or so of the month) except in Farafra, so you'll need to carry enough to cover the 500 km between Bahariya and Dakhla. If driving cross-country daunts you, you can hire a car and driver in Cairo (or Alexandria), or you can take a bus (or fly into Kharga) and hire a local car and guide in the oases.

Public Transportation: Daily **buses** link the southern four oases to Cairo, Asyut, and to each other. With the exception of Wednesdays, buses run daily between the oases, often continuing on to either Cairo or Asyut. Times fall into several patterns, usually on staggered days, so check with the locals in the oases. From Cairo, daily buses (some with a/c, some so dilapidated you'll wonder how they survive the trip) run from al-Azhar station to Bahariya, Farafra, Dakhla, and

Kharga; every morning a special bus with a/c leaves from Midan Ataba. Local buses also run daily from Asyut. You can make reservations a day or two ahead. Costs run from LE7 between oases to LE25 into Cairo. **Service taxis** follow similar routes. **Planes** scheduled by EgyptAir fly into New Valley Wednesdays and Sundays.

KHARGA

The most visited of the western oases, Kharga is the center of the government's improvements in the Wadi Gadid (New Valley). The main town, Kharga, lies about 250 km from Asyut. Having grown into a near metropolis, the city retains little of its ancient flavor. The largest town on the oases loop, it has the best facilities.

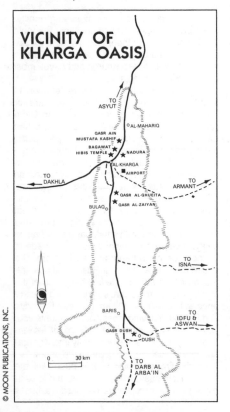

SIGHTS

Kharga's ancient remains are split into two groups: one stands to the north near the main city of Kharga, while the others string out along the road south to Dush. The northern sights, which lie within walking distance (several km) of the Kharga Hotel, include the well-preserved Temple of Hibis, the Christian cemetery at Bagawat, and the ruins of a Roman temple and the spectacular view from the hill of Nadura.

Temple Of Hibis
This classical-style temple was begun by the Persian King Darius (5th century B.C.) and Nectanebo II added the colonnade. The ancient builders used local limestone, its speckled color giving Amun's temple a warm coloring. The artwork displays an unusual boldness, perhaps a local influence. The temple gives a good idea of the mood of Egypt's ancient religious buildings. Unfortunately it's shifting, and the Antiquities Service has closed the interior. Discussion centers around whether to try to shore up the unstable walls or move the temple north to the dry sands of Bagawat.

Although the ancient lake that once surrounded the temple is now gone, the palm groves remain, making the temple still worth a stop. The approach, past the old quay and a row of sphinxes, is through four gateways into the colonnade, the colonnaded court, the hypostyle hall, and the sanctuary.

Nadura
Across the road, the hill of Nadura supports the remains of a Roman temple and the mud-brick remnants of the ancient city of Hibis. The scattered ruins are probably not worth the climb, but the view is.

Christian Cemetery Of Bagawat

Open 0800-1800 (1700 winter); LE10: Half a km north of Hibis Temple, the brick tombs dating to the banishment of Bishop Athanasius (7th century) are the remains of a large Christian community that once inhabited Kharga. Standing on either side of a broad avenue, the domed chambers, many with an eastern apse and vestibule, resemble miniature basilicas; the triangular recesses once held oil lamps. The tombs appear as a continuation of those at Tuna al-Gebel, and forge the link with later Coptic artwork. The interior paintings surround biblical scenes with Alexandrian-style allegorical figures, vine-leaf decorations, rosettes, and foliage (#80); the most notable painting remaining is of Daniel in the lion's den in the Chapel of Exodus. Enjoy the elaborate decorative molding and false windows; explore the crumbling vaults and domes, with their painted plaster still clinging to the mud bricks of their burial chamber. In the center of the necropolis, only traces of the church that once dominated the hill remain.

Old Kharga

Centered on Midan Showla, the old section of town (off Sh. al-Nabawy al-Mohandis) lies a few km to the southeast. In the *suq* you can shop for food with the locals or buy handicrafts and then wander down to visit the "underground city" of Darb al-Sendediya—walk down Sh. Salah Salim, turn right at the large intersection, then left after about 50 meters. The 9th century Muslim inhabitants built their homes underground, taking advantage of the earth's natural air-conditioning. Still inhabited, this village welcomes visitors.

Pottery And Carpet School

On the road toward Dakhla, just before the turnoff to Baris, the Project of Developing Textiles and Handicrafts maintains a school. Here you can photograph potters running their kickwheels and weavers seated at rows of looms turning out rugs and hangings. The fixed-price shop is a good place to get an idea of the going prices, and if something strikes your fancy, pick it up.

Sights To The South

Those with plenty of time and a hankering after adventure can head south down the old caravan route toward Baris. Several temples (*qasrs* to the locals) stretch along this 100 km, along with a couple of wells complete with palms and resthouses.

About 25 km south of al-Kharga, the stone temple of Qasr al-Ghueita stands surrounded by mud-brick outbuildings; begun by the Nubians of the 25th Dynasty, it was finished in Ptolemaic times and dedicated to the Theban Triad. The Greco-Roman temple to Amun at Qasr al-Zaiyan lies about five km farther south.

The Wells: Along the road to Baris, both Nasser and Bulaq have resthouses. **Bulaq Tourist Wells** (about 30 km south of al-Kharga) offers a bed for LE3.30; water from 0600-0800, 1200-1400, and 1600-1800; electricity, 1800-0200; no hot water, but the wells are warm. The manager can arrange for meals. **Nasser Wells** (about 17 km south), slightly more upscale, has recently been renovated. Its bungalows stand back behind the wells in a grove of palms, their backs to the desert; the two rooms and bath run LE4.

Baris: If you decide to go, you can reach Baris (about 55 km) by bus from Kharga twice a day (1200 and 1400) for LE2.50. If your stomach is cast-iron, you can dip into local *ful* and *ta'miyya* and stay at the government resthouse just south of the never-finished Hassan Fathy complex. You'll have to make arrangements for the resthouse, which is reasonably clean, with the manager: (across from the police station in town) LE3/bed, electricity sunset to 0100, water during the day only.

Temple of Dush: Open 0700-1700; LE8 (the *ghaffir* has no change). The temple at Dush lies about 35 km beyond Baris, and you'll need an approved guide who will have to get you permission (he'll need a copy of your passport) to get through the military checkpoint. The building sits behind the hill about 4½ km past the village of Dush. (This restriction may soon be lifted.) Reconstructed by the French, the temple has a barrel-vaulted sanctuary approached by several gates; the entire structure is surrounded by a mud-brick fortress. Frankly, unless you're really into temples, this Roman example to Isis and Serapis is hardly worth the trouble.

PRACTICALITIES

Accommodations

Ranging from two-star hotels to government resthouses and the youth hostel, the accommodations in Kharga offer more choices than any other town in the oases. My favorite is the **Hamadalla Hotel,** tel. 900-638, off the main street at the blue sign near the mosque, just up from the gas station. LE25 s with bath, without, LE15; LE32.50 d with bath, without, LE23.55. Lunch runs LE8.55; dinner LE9.90. Not quite as nice is **Kharga Hotel,** tel. 901-500, the former government resthouse located at the north end of town. Rooms, all with private baths but no air-conditioning, run LE25-30, and reservations can be made through the Victoria Hotel in Cairo. The **Waha,** tel. 900-393, at the south end of Sh. Nasser, offers clean accommodations and plenty of hot water: LE11 s, LE14, and LE1.35 for an extra bed. Known locally as Metalco, the **New Valley Tourist Homes** (Metalco), tel. 900-728, Sh. 23 July, offers bed and breakfast for LE3.65 a person, double occupancy in clean rooms but no hot water 1100-1700. Turn left at the first *midan,* then right two blocks later; it's the green building on the left.

Food

Kharga offers little in the way of specialized food; both the Hamadalla and the Kharga hotels serve adequate lunches and dinners for under LE10. The smaller hotels offer a better deal, but you'll have to make arrangements with the manager ahead of time. The *suq* carries fresh produce in season and several small restaurants and stands nearby serve cheap, tasty Egyptian fare.

Information And Services

The **Tourist Office** is open Sun.-Thurs. 1000-1500 and 1900-2200, Ramadan 1000-1700 and 2000-2300; it's located in the round, white build-ing across the plaza from the Kharga Hotel; tel. 901-205/901-206. The police, tel. 900-700, occupy the same building.

The **Tourist Police** are open daily 0800-1400, across from the Tourist Office; tel. 901-502.

Banks: The Misr Bank, open Sun.-Thurs. 0800-1400 and 1700-2000, Fri.-Sat. 1030-1330 and 1700-2000, opposite the Cinema Hibis, and the Cairo Bank (same hours) both change money and cash traveler's checks; no credit card advances.

The **post office** is open Sat.-Thurs. 0900-1500; the main office is off Gamal Abd al-Nasser (behind the Cinema Hibis) and there's a branch in Sh. Showla, Old Kharga.

The **telephone office** is open 24 hours, next to the main post office; code 88; international service is available intermittently, or you can use the phones at the hotels for a fee.

The **hospital,** tel. 900-777, off Sh. al-Nasser south of al-Nabawy, is open 24 hours.

Transportation

To get around in Kharga, use taxis; LE20-30/day; service taxis run to the Kharga Hotel. A trip to Baris and Dush costs LE40-50. Buses south to Baris (one hour) leave the bus station on Midan Showla at 1200 and 1400 (LE2.50).

Getting From: Planes from Cairo to Upper Egypt swing by Kharga on Wednesdays and Sundays. Good roads link Kharga with both Asyut and Dakhla, though the first 25 km of the Dakhla road may be covered with drifting sand, requiring the use of detours, which are normally safe. Half a dozen **buses** leave for Asyut (four hours) between 0630-1530, and at 1900 and 1200 (LE5); for Cairo (nine hours), 1600, 0900, 1900 and 2000 (LE15-18); to Dakhla (3½ hours) 0600, 1700; the two through buses from Cairo/Asyut stop in the afternoon. **Service taxis** across the street from the bus station run frequently to Asyut (LE7), but only rarely continue to Cairo. A private taxi to Dakhla will run LE70.

DAKHLA OASIS

Lying northwest of Kharga, Dakhla is the farthest oasis from Cairo. Surrounded by the pink cliffs of the depression, it remains one of Egypt's most beautiful oases, noted today, as in ancient times, for its greenery. Residents are primarily farmers who carry on the neverending battle with the encroaching dunes that hover around the fields and orchards. In Dakhla, in contrast to the ugly modern sprawl in Kharga, the infusion of government money and technical training seems to have revitalized the population, which is absorbing change without allowing it to disintegrate the culture.

In hopes of keeping control, the Mut Tourist Office is training villagers as guides and hosts. They are also attempting to set rates and fees, thus avoiding the types of hassles visitors to Luxor receive. To help them, they request that you check with their office for going rates and report any problems.

The Dakhla depression runs southeast to northwest, and contains three population centers: Balat, Mut, and al-Qasr al-Dakhla; of the three, Mut, named for Amun's consort, who had a temple in the area, is the functional capital.

SIGHTS

The temple that once graced the city of Mut has been engulfed by the sands, but ruins along the main road at Balat and at Dakhla are open to visitors. In Mut proper, only the **Dakhla Ethnographic Museum** is of interest. It's located next to the Hotel Dar al-Wafden (eastern Mut), and examining the wooden locks, gazelle trap, and dioramas of village festivities is worth the LE1 admission. Make arrangements through the Tourist Office or with the curator, Ibrahim Kamel Abdalla at the Ministry of Culture, tel. 940-311 (or at home, tel. 940-769). In addition to the museum, there are some late pharaonic tombs and several of the outlying villages are worth a trip.

East
Bashendi: About 40 km east of Mut, Bashendi is known as the "pharaonic village." Its supple curving walls and rounded outlines sit atop an old temple. The **Tomb of Ketenus** mixes pharaonic gods with Roman-style painting. Next to it, the village's patron erected his tomb, an Islamic dome atop Roman foundations. The village streets, some of which run underground, are sprinkled with sand and the whole place is immaculate. Home to the Bashendi Carpet Works, you'll ultimately end up there, watching the youths learning to weave; prices are fixed in the associated store.

Balat: Old Kingdom governors made Balat their capital. Lying about 35 km east of the main town of Mut, the well-preserved mastaba lies half a km north of the road, down the drive between the red-brick posts. The modern Fathi Hassan complex houses the French Expedition excavating the huge Old Kingdom Mastabas. The skimpy remains of the ancient town are several kilometers to the northwest, at Ain Asul, accessible only by four-wheel drive or on foot—the remains are hardly worth the trouble unless you want the hike.

Across the street and back toward Bashendi half a km, the Islamic village lies up the hill. Here again, you can enjoy a clean, quiet set-

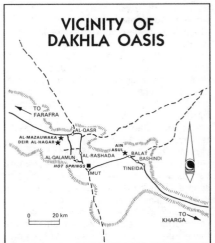

VICINITY OF DAKHLA OASIS

TO FARAFRA

AL-QASR

AL-MAZAUWAKA
DEIR AL-HAGAR

AL-QALAMUN
HOT SPRINGS

MUT

AL-RASHADA

AIN ASUL

BALAT

BASHINDI

TINEIDA

TO KHARGA

0   20 km

© MOON PUBLICATIONS, INC.

ting, exploring the underground passageways and gardens.

North And West

Al-Qasr: This village was built around a medieval Islamic core; enjoy walking around the town and perhaps climbing the minaret of the old *madrasa*. Pottery works lie on the outer margins of the Old Town.

The best monuments in Dakhla lie to the west of Mut, out the road to Farafra at al-Qasr where, at al-Mazauwaka, two brightly painted tombs of the Hellenistic period show a blend of native and classical styles; the mythological scenes in the tomb of Petosiris include a zodiac ceiling. The Roman temple at Deir al-Hagar, a few kilometers beyond, dates to the 1st century A.D.; the unrestored remains conjure up images of the "romantic ruins" described by the early European travelers to Egypt.

If you have a private car, you can return to Mut via al-Mushiya, a nice drive through prosperous farmlands, or take a detour to the springs at Bir al-Gebel; the turnoff lies a km east of al-Qasr. Top off your sightseeing with a dip in the **Tourist Wells** hot springs three km north of Mut. Water bubbling up out of the ground at 42° C is piped into swimming pools. The color is from iron oxides, not dirt.

PRACTICALITIES

Accommodations

The only worthwile hotel in Mut is the **Mebarez** out Farafra Rd. toward the hot springs, tel. 941-524. Excellent service, spotless rooms, and good food make this oasis an unbelievable deal with rooms going for LE15-30. Otherwise use the resthouses, which charge a few pounds a night. Within Mut, the **Government Resthouse,** tel. 941-758, on the *midan* with the new mosque (next to the bus station), is newly renovated, and is now clean as well as convenient. About 3½ km from Mut out the Farafra Rd., the complex at **Tourist Wells Resthouses** has two government hotels near the hot springs. The **Roadside Resthouse** (The Villa) near the springs offers clean rooms (with fan); a kitchen is available. Rooms at the **Poolside Resthouse** (the Bungalows) are smaller; although they have no fans, they do have pri-

vate baths; both run LE4.25. **Government resthouses** in Balat and nearby Bashendi will do in a pinch; check with the Tourist Office as they are sometimes closed. **Camping** is permitted at the Tourist Wells Resthouses. You can also camp in the rest of the oases, but the police are not used to it and they may ask you to move.

Food

Other than the Mebarez Hotel, Mut has no good restaurants, but a couple masquerade as such along the main highway between Old Mut and New Mut. Food stalls cluster around the *midan* at the new mosque, and government stores provide staples and bottled water.

Information And Services

Tourist Office: Open daily 0800-1400, sometimes 2100-2300 (winter, 0800-1100), it's located at the Tourist Rest Home (2nd floor), New Mosque Square, Mut; tel. 940-407.

Tourist Police: Open daily 0800-1400 and 1900-2100; they're located in Liberty Square (on the Kharga-Farafra road), tel. 941-500; you must register here your first night in Dakhla unless the hotel does it for you.

Banks: Bank Misr, (tel. 940-063/941-518), open Sun.-Thurs. 0830-1400 and 1700-2000. The bank will change hard currency and major banks' traveler's checks.

Post Office: Open Sat.-Thurs. 0800-1500; New Mosque Square, Mut.

Telephone Office: Open 24 hours; international lines available. Located in New Mut, west of Sh. Wadi Gadid (New Valley) and about a km northeast of New Mosque Square. Code 088.

Hospital: Located on the edge of Mut, tel. 941-332 (ambulance, tel. 941-333); there is also a small clinic in each village.

TRANSPORTATION

Getting Around

Local **buses** leave from the station in New Mosque Square in Mut. Three a day (from 0600-1600) serve the eastern villages of Balat and Bashendi (30PT) and return an hour later. Six a day run north to al-Qasr (30PT) and return to

Mut half an hour later. **Taxis** will take you sightseeing; for current rates, check with the Tourist Office. **Service taxis** in the form of pickups run between Liberty Square and the villages, but the government is discouraging tourists from using them. (In fact, they're trying to discourage the Egyptians from using them, as they're dangerous.) **Bicycles** can occasionally be rented at the shop in New Mosque Square (LE2-3/day—a bargain).

Getting From

Buses leave from the station at New Mosque Square. Four a day serve Kharga (3½ hours, LE5-6), and connect with Asyut (7½ hours, LE9-11) and Cairo (14 hours, LE19-25). The 0830 bus connects with the train to Luxor in Asyut at 1830. On Mon., Thurs., and Sat., an 0600 bus connects to Farafra (4½ hours, LE6.50), Bahariya (7½ hours, LE10), and Cairo (14 hours, LE19). Book a day ahead.

Private Car: The roads to both Kharga and Farafra are nominally paved. The road from Dakhla to Kharga is good; the other direction, however, to Farafra is nearly non-existent in places. The trip will take the whole day, although it's passable for a passenger car. **Gas** is available from the station on the Kharga road (eastern Mut), which is open 24 hours. This is the only gas between Dakhla and Bahariya (500 km).

BRUCE HANSEN

FARAFRA

The smallest of Egypt's oases, Farafra was once an idyllic jewel, but modern development has spoiled the pristine effect. The village, however, still offers hospitality and, outside the construction areas, quiet isolation.

SIGHTS

The monuments, clustered around the capital of Qasr Farafra, are composed for the most part of poorly excavated, unfinished cemeteries. In Farafra, a local artist, Badr, has started a private museum of his own work as well as a local artifacts and natural history collection; hours are sporadic, and the museum is free, though he welcomes small donations. Sa'ad, who owns the restaurant at the top of the hill, will show you around the wells—good places to camp and hang out. He can also arrange trips into the White Desert complete with a campfire, music, and a night under the crisp stars—an experience not to be missed.

PRACTICALITIES

Accommodations
Rooms in Farafra are grim; most visitors choose to camp out. However, the two government **resthouses** will put up foreigners for a few pounds; bring your own sheets and drinking water. Electricity is available only between 1900-0100; no hot water. You can **camp** near the hot springs in town, or at the small, green, wide spot in the road south of town at Bir Abu Minqar.

Food
Farafra's best cafe, **Sa'ad's,** lies up the hill from the main road. Here you can lounge on the roof and have a good omelet and coffee. Take a look at the knitted stoles and vests, soft and warm at a reasonable price. Otherwise, you can take your chances with the cafes on the main road. Several small government stores carry supplies and a limited amount of bottled water.

Transportation
Farafra is the most isolated of the oases. The three weekly **buses** (Mon., Thurs., and Sat.) stop in Farafra around 1000 and continue to Bahariya (three hours, LE10) and Cairo (eight hours, LE19). The bus from Cairo stops in Farafra on Sun., Tues., and Fri., and continues to Dakhla (LE10). Buses may have standing room only when they reach this small oasis. **Service taxis** from Bahariya arrive every few days, and might take you on the return trip (LE7), or a private taxi may be willing to take you to Bahariya for LE140; to Dakhla, LE200.

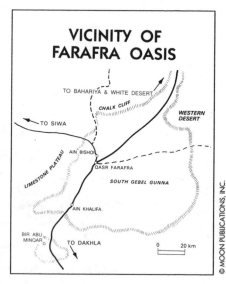

VICINITY OF FARAFRA OASIS

BAHARIYA

Along with the rest of the oases, Bahariya catered to caravans that took the western trail through the desert from Sudan to the Mediterranean. Several villages occupy the depression, but the main one is al-Bawiti, which nearly runs into the neighboring village of Qasr al-Bahariya. The gas station, police station, and bus station all lie on the main road. A major route since pharaonic times, the road between it and Farafra covers some of the most beautiful desert in Egypt. The most spectacular is the **White Desert,** which was formed when inland seas transgressed the area; the fantastic pediments were sculpted by the action of water and wind. Farther on lies Crystal Mountain, where you'll find long needles of nearly clear calcium carbonates. Nearby, the brooding **Black Desert** is relieved by brilliant pastels of limestone formations.

The oasis itself is large and enclosed by limestone cliffs. On the Cairo side of the oasis you'll pass a few pharaonic ruins (you need permission) and a small field of classical dunes and palm trees. Hot springs lie scattered throughout the depression, which is also marked by mountains. An Englishman in the 1940s built his stone house atop one near Bawiti; he holed up during the war, determined to resist the Germans if they came on from Siwa. There's a good path up to it (from the east side) and the view from the top is spectacular. A road suitable for cars leads to a *wadi* below (don't go off the road unless you have four-wheel drive); the trail runs up the *wadi* to your right as you face the house.

SIGHTS

The monuments near al-Qasr al-Bahariya (at the northern end of the depression), include a ruined 26th Dynasty temple. The chapels built by King Apries are located near Ain al-Muftilla (a few kilometers west of the modern village), which was part of the extensive ancient city. The decorations show the king, with the governor behind him, presenting offerings to the various gods and goddesses; the four chapels include one of the few known dedicated to the household deity and god of music, Bes. Little remains of the Roman arch, the principal mid-19th century sight; today most of its blocks have been incorporated into local houses.

Al-Qasr

The city adjoining Bawiti, Qasr al-Bahariya, houses an old Roman spring. Once a large pool fed by several underground springs, it is now, due to the falling water table, a mere trickle. In Roman times, however, the surrounding rock made a large ring, and the water came to the top. Now erosion and man have broken down the end and the rivulet escapes into the fields.

Qarat Hilwa

Cemeteries of the ancient town lie on the surrounding ridges, and the only tomb worth visiting is that of Amenhotep at Qarat Hilwa. This Empire Period tomb contains the traditional courtyard and two pillared halls. Although Amenhotep claimed to be a native of the oases, he undoubtedly imported the artists for his tomb from

VICINITY OF BAHARIYA OASIS

TO SIWA

TO CAIRO

RESTHOUSE

QASR AL-BAHARIYA

QARAT HILWA

AL-BAWITI

HOT SPRINGS

AIN AL-HARRA

IRON MINES

QASR ALLAM

QASR AL-MIGYSBAH

AIN AL-HAYZ

TO FARAFRA

0   20 km

© MOON PUBLICATIONS, INC.

the sophisticated schools in the Nile Valley. Much of the artwork, though increasingly damaged, still shows its original color. Courtyard scenes scenes show Amenhotep seated on a stool supervising the filling and storing of his wine, while his son, Menna, sits in front of him. In the fragmented banquet scene, his wife Ourly lies at his feet, while in the remains of the funeral wall (north) drawings show that his tomb was once protected by a pyramid. In the second chamber, the east wall shows workers harvesting grain and filling wine jars. On the north wall, Amenhotep and Ourly pray to Hathor, who emerges from the hillside and papyrus plants. You will need permission to visit from the Inspector of the Antiquities Organization at Giza.

Springs

Near the resthouse, a warm spring (about 25° C) lies within a couple minute's walk. The hot springs (35° C) at Bir al-Ghaba lie in a grove about eight km away; head for the mountain that looks like a pyramid; follow the left side of the grove, following the road through the long-leafed pines, eucalyptus, and palms until you come to the intersection at the canal. Turn left and follow the road as it circles back to the springs.

Al-Bawiti

Lying about five km south of Bahariya, the tombs all date to the 26th Dynasty and appear in two areas: Qarat al-Subi and Qarat Qasr Salim. Of the several decorated tombs, the most worthwhile to see is that of Bannentiu. The chapel has vanished but the paintings underground still retain much of their beauty. The notable scenes on either side of the entrance to the burial vault show the journey of the moon and sun, prototypes for the ceiling decorations later executed in the temples of Dendera and Isna. On the right, Shu holds aloft the sky; the rays stream down in the form of linked *ankhs*. Nephthys and Isis cast their protective spells over the sun disk, while the frog-headed gods and goddesses of the Ogdoad march along the lower register. The companion scene shows Shu again holding the sky, which supports the barque of the sun, the disk occupying its center while the *ba* bird sits on the stern. The inner burial chamber contains a judgment hall, a scene often found in papyri and coffins.

Qasr Allam

Noted primarily for its Alexandrian temple, Qasr Allam lies 16 km south of Bahariya; the site is known to the locals as Qasr al-Migysbah. The chapel itself is two chambers surrounded by a vast wall. Behind the sanctuary stood two priests' houses, and the rest of the area was filled with service rooms and magazines.

Ain Al-Hayz

Classed as a separate oasis in antiquity, Ain al-Hayz stood on the caravan route between Farafra and Bahariya and flourished during the post-pharaonic period. The 5th or 6th century church is the only well-preserved one in the Western Desert. The two-story basilica was plastered and decorated with religious figures; one (now vanished) of a mounted saint may mean that the building was dedicated to St. George. Across the road lies a palace, its size and richness suggesting that the inhabitants cultivated vast areas of the oases and that the center flourished for several centuries.

Hot Springs

The Bir Mathar gushes out lightly sulfurous water about six km from al-Bawiti, a setting straight from the movies; only men can swim here during the day; mixed groups can use it at night. Bar al-Ghaba offers both cold and hot springs and is co-ed; the springs lie 15 km from al-Bawiti and make a good day-trip or overnighter.

PRACTICALITIES

Accommodations And Food

The best place to stay in Bahariya is the **resthouse** at the Iron Mines, about 40 km northeast of al-Bawiti, by the guard station. They have large suites with kitchens and hot water for LE33; food is available in the restaurant in the club. Make reservations in Cairo, tel. 910-681—they have a radio-phone connection with the mine. Mine staff can arrange guides for the oasis.

The local hotels have all been closed, so the only accommodations in town are at the government resthouse about five km outside of town at Bir Mathar; it's relatively clean but has no hot water; it costs only a few pounds. A bus to the resthouse meets all intra-city buses; a cab to the hot springs will cost you LE10. You can camp anywhere, but women should not camp alone here. Hot springs are favorite spots, and about seven km down the road, women as well as men can swim in the Bir al-Ghaba.

Several stores provide staples and bottled water. Al-Bawiti boasts several coffee shops for meals and evening entertainment. Take care however, and set the price before the meal, or you may have a nasty surprise. The people in Bahariya, in contrast to the rest of the oases, tend to imitate those in Luxor.

Transportation

For day-trips or overnight expeditions to the various sights around Bahariya make arrangements at the iron mines or talk to Max—he meets most buses.

Buses leave daily from Bahariya to Cairo (seven to eight hours) 0700, another leaves about 1300; to ensure a seat, book a couple of days ahead. On Mon., Thurs., and Sat., the bus from Dakhla stops at 1330, but it's usually full. The Cairo bus on Sun., Tues., and Fri. continues on to Farafra and Dakhla.

A few **service taxis** make the trip between Cairo and Bahariya, usually in the evenings, but they rarely continue on to Farafra. The road is good between Bahariya and Cairo, but dismal to Farafra. It's good to Siwa but you'll have to arrange special permission to drive it; there is no public transportation to Siwa. Gas is available both at the iron mines resthouse and in al-Bawiti.

SIWA OASIS

In the center of the sand sea that forms the Libyan Desert, Siwa Oasis shelters numerous hot springs and hectares of palm and olive groves. The people, although once hostile to foreigners, are now receptive to visitors. Isolated until well into the 19th century, the area has preserved its own customs, language, and dress. The people still speak Siwan, a Berber dialect, as their first language, and their dress is distinct from that of the Nile Valley and the other oases.

Only 50 km from the Libyan border, the oasis is heavily guarded by the Egyptian army. Now, however, connected to the outside world by the paved road to Marsa Matruh and television, and subject to increasing numbers of tourists, the oasis may not retain its charm long. Nevertheless, since there are still few visitors, the inhabitants will take the time to show you through their gardens and invite you to taste Siwan dates, famous even in antiquity, directly from the trees. To fully appreciate the quiet beauty of the place, plan on spending several days.

Land And Climate

Winds have scoured a crater 17 meters below sea level that is 82 km long and varies from three to 28 km wide. This trough is filled with date and olive orchards, warm springs and salt lakes, and mud villages—all wind-weathered and salt-encrusted.

Like the other oases, Siwa is cool in winter and hot in summer. The best times to visit Siwa are in fall (when the harvests are coming in) and winter.

HISTORY

Siwa shows little common culture with the other oases. It apparently had little connection with the Nile Valley until the Late Period, for the oldest monument dates to Ahmose of the 26th Dynasty. Even before this time, however, the oasis had been a stop on the caravan route that carried African goods across the desert to Cyrene and the Mediterranean coast for transshipment.

With their increasing wealth, the Siwans built several temples, one which housed the oracle that became famous throughout the Greek world.

Foreign Rule

When Cambyses took Thebes, he dispatched 50,000 men to Siwa to destroy the oracle; the army reached Kharga but then vanished into the desert. No traces have ever been found—a demise that must have enhanced the oracle's prestige. Two hundred years later, after laying the foundations of Alexandria, Alexander the Great pressed on to Siwa where the god Amun, so legend says, received the king as his own son. Whether or not Alexander truly believed himself to be divine, he nevertheless has the royal horn of Amun, nearly invisible in his unruly curls, coiling neatly around his ear on coins minted with his portrait.

During the Roman period, the oracle declined, replaced by other methods of fortune telling, and by the 4th century, Christianity had come to Siwa, the worship of Christ and his God replacing that of Alexander and Amun. Later, Roman control slipped; the Berbers harassed the trading caravans, and Siwa may have been their stronghold. When Muslims invaded Siwa, the people held out for a while in their fortress-like homes, but by the end of the first century of Muslim rule, the oasis converted. The caravan routes continued to pass through the oasis, which marketed dates, olives, and olive oil. The trade kept Siwa in touch with Fezzan, Alexandria, Fayyum, and Cairo. Nevertheless, the area remained independent, only succumbing to Muhammad Ali in 1820, and unrest continued until 1904 when the area was visited by Abbas II.

Modern Siwa

In 1928, King Fuad finished the mosque started by Abbas II, ordered stone walls built around the springs, and commissioned modern oil presses and a factory for packaging dates. He appointed an imam from Cairo to the mosque and started schools. During World War II, when the Axis forces took Siwa, Rommel was welcomed and had tea in a local garden. The army treated the villagers well, and after the battle at al-Alamein, the retreating troops sold the villagers their supplies, alleviating a threatened famine. In 1945 King Faruq visited the area and at the request of the people, paved the road to Marsa Matruh.

The increasing use of cars helped Egyptianize Siwa, but the conservative population has retained its own language and many customs and traditions. The people themselves are mixed, their Berber blood diluted with that of the Arab Bedouin from the east and the Nubians who came north with the caravans. The villagers divided themselves into the Westerners and the Easterners, and bloody battles often occurred between the factions, but now this animosity is dying out. Today the Siwans welcome visitors, but still, for all their hospitality, are reluctant to give up their privacy.

SIGHTS

The main city of the depression is Siwa, which lies slightly west of the center, where the hollow begins to narrow, near numerous springs and several salt lakes. Here the road from Marsa Matruh runs past the government hotel on the left and ends at the new mosque. Behind the mosque, jumbled over the acropolis, lie the mud ruins of the fortifified town, al-Shali. The main part of the village, populated by some 6,000 people, lies to the left, around two squares. The main road runs through the village and out to the old fortress and temples.

The original village was at Aghurmi where the temple of the oracle still stands. Not far away are the temple of Umm Ubaydah and the necropolis of Gebel al-Mawta.

Aghurmi

The temple to the Siwan oracle is four km from the main town, standing amongst crumbling ruins of the town destroyed in the same storms as al-Shali. The path enters the fortified city via the old gate which is strengthened with palm-tree logs; the benches served as seats for the elders when they gathered in the evenings. The mosque was built over the gate, but its floor has

fallen; the square minaret is accessible via a narrow winding stair (watch your step) on the right at the end of the passage. The old well, sheathed in dressed limestone blocks, stands to the left as you enter the enclosed spaces of the courtyard. To reach the temple, which stands on the northwestern side of the clearing, you'll have to climb up the ledge. The stone temple itself stands at the edge of the crumbling rock bluff—take care as the friable rock is continually sloughing away and threatens the building.

The temple foundations date to the 26th Dynasty, and the plan follows the normal layout, with a forecourt, a vestibule, and a sanctuary. During Ptolemaic times, the Greeks erected a second, Doric-style facade; the base of the western fluted column remains. The narrow corridor to the right of the sanctuary may have been used by the priest who played the part of the oracle. The decorations of the temple show King Ahmose (26th Dynasty) offering to the gods, while on the other side, the Siwan governor holds the same position, lending credence to the idea that Siwa was remote enough from the Egyptian Empire for her leaders to rule as kings.

Temple Of Umm Ubaydah
This second temple to Amun stands a kilometer from Aghurmi, its fallen lintels nestled in palm groves. Built by King Nectanebo in the 30th Dynasty, the structure may have been a funerary temple for the legendary King Wenamun who ruled Siwa during this time. The temple stood nearly intact until the 19th century when an earthquake damaged it; the remainder was blasted apart by a government official in 1897 for blocks, which he used as stairs to a police station and for his house.

Tombs Of Gebel Al-Mawta
The conical hill about 1½ km from Siwa known as Gebel al-Mawta is honeycombed with tombs, small and large, decorated and plain. The earliest date to the Late Period and most were reused by the Romans, who cut niches for their coffins, destroying much of the earlier artwork. The tombs were robbed repeatedly and often served as houses for Siwans and Bedouin. These repeated uses have taken their toll, but enough of the painting remains in the four major decorated tombs to be worth a visit.

Tomb of Si-Amun: The largest and most impressive of the tombs is near the top of the hill; its entrance is to the north. The main chamber is reached by a flight of stairs that opens into a long corridor, which ends in the burial chamber. The quality of the plaster and the skill of the artists indicate that they may have been imported from the Nile Valley. Si-Amun had no titles, but he may have been the wealthy son of a Greek merchant. The Romans robbed the tomb and then cut niches in the walls for their own burials, damaging several of the scenes.

Along the west wall, the top register once contained the judgment scene with Anubis weighing the deceased's heart against the feather of Ma'at before Osiris, but the three crypts cut into the wall have nearly destroyed it. Below, Si-Amun sits before his youngest son, and the goddess Nut stands before a sycamore tree, holding a tray of offerings and pouring the water of everlasting life into a pond. On the south wall, Anubis tends the mummy while Isis and Nephthys guard the head and feet; behind Nephthys stand the four sons of Horus. One of the most interesting paintings is the funerary boat, here lacking the highway of the Nile River, mounted on wheels; the deceased's mummy lies in the shrine while the *ba* bird and Wepwawet, the jackal of the dead, appear on either side. The ornate ceiling includes painted imitations of wood as well as a beautifully drawn vulture and hawk with outspread wings, clasping a feather in each talon.

Tomb of Mesu-Isis: Located about 20 meters east of Si-Amun's tomb, this unfinished tomb is decorated only on the south wall. The name of the man for whom this tomb was built has been lost, so it is named for his wife. The most striking aspect of the tomb is the entrance; the cornice is decorated with uraei cut in relief and brightly painted. Beneath them, the spread wings once held gold or gold-plated disks to symbolize the sun. Osiris and Isis sit at either side of the entrance.

Tomb of the Crocodile: Named for the image found in the decorated chamber, this tomb lies in the northeastern corner of the terrace. Dating to Ptolemaic or Roman times, this tomb reinforces the idea that Siwa maintained cultural links with Fayyum, home of the crocodile-god Sobek. The focal point of the wall is the niche, where the red-scaled crocodile lurks under the seated owner of the tomb, who is guarded by the ram-headed Amun, a knife in each hand. The painting of the grapevines with the foxes nibbling at the fruit shows Hellenic influences, while the images of the goddesses protecting the sun-god seated on a lotus and the tomb owner worshipping Osiris are more traditional.

Tomb of Niperpathot: Built by Niperpathot, prophet of Osiris, this tomb's scenes include the deceased worshipping Osiris and Hathor with her cow's head, and Niperpathot holding the lines to the four calves: red, white, black, and spotted. This tomb makes no mention of Amun, so Egyptologists speculate that Osiris was worshipped here first; only later did Amun appear in the rituals, and still later, the deified Alexander.

The Fortress Of Al-Shali

Built by the few inhabitants who had escaped Bedouin depredations, the fortress dates to the beginning of the 13th century. The town, which once stood eight stories high, clings to the slope of the hill; protected from desert raiders, the Siwans living here prospered. The oasis was ruled by the heads of the several families who lived in the fortress, making the population more or less independent of the Egyptian government. With the security offered in modern times, the Siwans gradually moved out of the fortress town, spreading out in the village of stone-block homes below. The rains have turned the old houses into romantic ruins, perfect places from which to view a glorious Siwan sunrise.

PRACTICALITIES

The mayor of Siwa greets all the guests that he can, and he or one of the guides to the area are most helpful. Check with them about any of your needs or check with the helpful, newly instituted Tourist Office.

Accommodations

The best hotel is the **Cleopatra,** tel. 103, which is attractive and clean, with hot water and some rooms with private baths; LE12-20; breakfast, LE3.50. The government's **Hotel Arous al-Waha,** at the entrance to Siwa, offers rooms with private baths but no hot water; the rooms are hot in summer (but you can sleep on the balcony), for about the same price. The best budget place is the **Bawadi** about a km north of town; clean and simple, it runs LE3 a bed (you may need proof of marriage for a double). The **Social Rest House,** also run by the government, is just down the street; dorm-like rooms with a shared bath run LE3. The **New Siwa Hotel** and the **Hotel Medina** are less inviting as well as less expensive. **Camping** is permitted near Cleopatra's bath; otherwise be sure to check with the Tourist Office before you pitch a tent, since much of the area is off limits.

Food
The Cleopatra Hotel serves good food, as does the Arous Hotel, but you may have to order ahead of time. At the small cafes along the squares, rice, *ful,* and chicken are staples. The local stores normally have good supplies of canned foods and the wonderful Siwan dates.

Entertainment
Unless you happen to visit during a festival, there is little to do in Siwa other than walk through the quiet countryside. The people will not, in general, disturb you. During the day, you might want to swim in one of the warm springs. The Pool of Cleopatra lies about two km south of Aghurmi, and here the men swim. More private, however, is the Pool of Fatnus, which lies across town on an island linked by a causeway that runs across the salty lake.

Shopping
The handicrafts of Siwa are distinct from others throughout Egypt. The finely woven platters and baskets (traditionally decorated with tassels) make unique and inexpensive gifts, as do the small embroidered shawls. The blue, full-length veils worn by the Siwan women are more difficult to come by, and when new ones are

offered for sale, they're expensive, much of the cost attributed to getting the material from where it's made in Kerdassa. The small shops also sell silver and silver-alloy jewelry that adorn Siwan women.

Collectors of ethnic costumes can still buy a few wedding outfits of embroidered pants and tunic. The main shop lies on the square to the left of the mosque, but a number of small dealers may approach you for private showings—they tend to be honest, and you can spend a lovely evening at one of their homes.

Information
The **Tourist Office** sits off the main square, around the corner from the post office and down the street; open Sat.-Thurs., 0900-1300 and Fri. 1800-2000. All other services in Siwa are handily grouped in modern buildings across from the Arous Hotel: The **police station** (open 24 hours) and the **post office** (open Sat.-Thurs, 0900-1400) are in the modern building on the square. The **telephone office** (open 0700-2200) is across the street and has the only phone in Siwa. **Electricity** is available from 2000-0300.

Transport
Around town you can catch a *caretta* (donkey cart) for a pound or two, but they can be difficult to find. **Bikes** are available at the Hotel Medina, LE4/day. To reach the Bedouin town of al-Maraqi, take the local bus (50PT roundtrip); check with the Tourist Office or the mayor for times. To return to Marsa Matruh, take a daily bus at 0500 or 1400, or take the bus directly to Alexandria, Sun., Tues., or Thurs., 0900, LE17; they stop at Matruh, then continue to Alexandria. The bus leaves from the central *midan* and stops at the Arous al-Waha, but by then most seats are taken. Service taxis leave from the town market, and most go early in the morning or late afternoon.

SUEZ, THE RED SEA COAST, AND SINAI

Fifty million years ago, a geological fault fractured the Eastern Desert, splitting the Red Sea mountains. Fresh lava rose steadily, prying Africa from Asia, forming the Red Sea and creating a triangular thumb of wasteland: Sinai. Bounded on the east by Israel, the north by the Mediterranean, the west by Suez, and the south by the Red Sea, the land is an extension of the Eastern Desert and its Red Sea mountains.

Sinai, linking Africa to Asia and the Near East, provided the sole land route out of Africa. Only for the brief time that the Strait of Gibraltar was dry could mankind and animals migrate directly north to Europe; otherwise they had to move northeast through Sinai and the Near East, then west into Europe or east into Asia. Ancient civilizations sent trading caravans and armies over this bridge, and Moses may well have fled east from pharaoh across its shallow waters. Christ's apostles brought the holy word to Egypt through its corridors, and the Muslims stormed the isthmus to conquer Egypt, northern Africa, and Spain. Mamluk warriors rode out from here to defend Islam against crusading Christian knights and protect their empire from marauding Mongols. Even with improved transportation, the area remained strategic, and during WW I the British and Germans shed their blood on its sands. Throughout WW II, the Allies used it as a buffer, and the Israelis in sporadic conflicts with Egypt quickly took possession of the area, heavily mined the western coast, and erected the defensive Bar Lev Line on the eastern side of the Suez Canal. Even today, it remains the only land link with the east; cars, buses, and trucks roar under the Suez Canal through the modern Ahmad Hamdi Tunnel.

THE LAND

The Red Sea follows the geological fault that runs north from Africa's Rift Valley toward the southern tip of Sinai where it splits, the arms of its "Y" framing the east and west sides of the peninsula. The main fracture continues north through the Gulf of Suez to the Mediterranean, numerous lakes and salt marshes filling its depression. To the south, the Red Sea flows over shallow straits of Bab al-Mandab at Yemen, filling the rift and creating a warm, sequestered, ocean basin where coral reefs, both fossil and living, abound. These reefs fringe the coasts, edge the sea's numerous islands, and line the waters of the gulfs of Aqaba and Suez.

The Sinai Peninsula, more wilderness than desert, is dotted with luxuriant oases populated by Bedouin. Its mountains hold vast treasures of copper and turquoise, which the pharaohs mined. Today, the Red Sea's spectacular reefs attract visitors from across the globe. Blue waters wash over vast, offshore oil reserves the government is just beginning to tap. In the north, the Suez Canal continues to funnel trade north and south, maintaining its ancient role of Mediterranean crossroads.

Climate

In the north, the Mediterranean Sea tempers the climate, making it warmer and damper in winter, cooler in summer. As you move south, the desert is blistering hot in the summer, cold in the winter, and windy nearly all the time. No matter what time of year you visit Sinai, be prepared for wide swings in temperature; even in summer, the evenings grow cool. In winter, the nights are cold; the mountains even get occasional snow. Fresh water is scarce, limited to the oases dotted throughout the area and occasional underground reservoirs. Date palms, scattered acacia trees, and scrub relieve the barren sands and gravel plateaus. In the south, ridge upon ridge of naked, jagged mountains reveal shapes sandblasted by the relentless wind. *Wadis,* gouged by torrents of water from cloudbursts, lace the northern desert, central

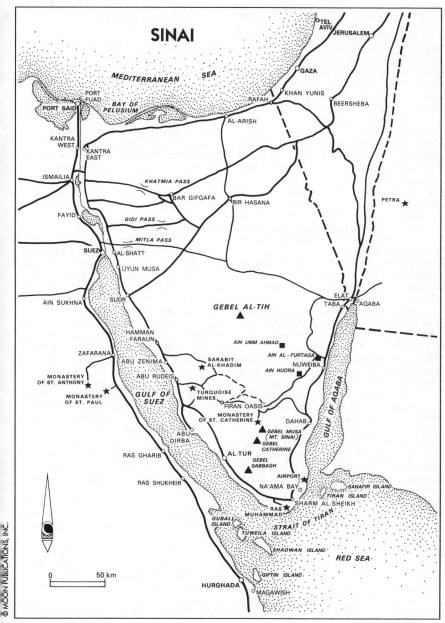

SINAI

MEDITERRANEAN SEA

BAY OF PELUSIUM

PORT FUAD

PORT SAID

KANTRA WEST

KANTRA EAST

ISMAILIA

FAYID

SUEZ

AL-SHATT

UYUN MUSA

AIN SUKHNA

SUDR

ZAFARANA

MONASTERY OF ST. ANTHONY

MONASTERY OF ST. PAUL

HAMMAN FARAUN

ABU ZENIMA

ABU RUDEIS

GULF OF SUEZ

TURQUOISE MINES

ABU DIRBA

RAS GHARIB

RAS SHUKHEIR

KHATMIA PASS

BAR GIFGAFA

BIR HASANA

GIDI PASS

MITLA PASS

AL-ARISH

RAFAH

KHAN YUNIS

GAZA

TEL AVIV

JERUSALEM

BEERSHEBA

PETRA

GEBEL AL-TIH

AIN UMM AHMAD

AIN AL-FURTAGA

NUWEIBA

AIN HUDRA

SARABIT AL-KHADIM

FIRAN OASIS

MONASTERY OF ST. CATHERINE

GEBEL MUSA (MT. SINAI)

GEBEL CATHERINE

GEBEL SABBAGH

AL-TUR

AIRPORT

NA'AMA BAY

DAHAB

GULF OF AQABA

ELAT

TABA

AQABA

SANAFIR ISLAND

TIRAN ISLAND

SHARM AL-SHEIKH

RAS MUHAMMAD

GUBAL ISLAND

TUWEILA ISLAND

SHADWAN ISLAND

STRAIT OF TIRAN

RED SEA

GIFTIN ISLAND

HURGHADA

MAGAWISH

0   50 km

MOON

plateau, and rugged mountains. Snow falls regularly on Mt. Sinai. Although the Red Sea is warmer than the Mediterranean, it nevertheless can be chilly in winter, often with strong winds. While the sea does temper the atmosphere, making it less hot and dry in summer, the area still heats up. Cover up, especially when snorkeling or on the beaches, and drink plenty of water.

Flora And Fauna

On land, desert fox, lizards, scorpions, and snakes prowl the sands in the mornings and evenings, but hide themselves away in rocky crevices and cool holes when the air begins to heat up. In contrast, the marine world teems with life. Separated geographically from the Mediterranean Sea by the Isthmus of Suez and further barred by the muddy brine of the Bitter Lakes, aquatic life in the Red Sea seldom mixes with that of the Mediterranean. In fact, the fauna more closely resemble that found in the mid-Pacific, and only a knowledgeable eye can easily distinguish Red Sea fish from those some 20,000 km to the west.

Coral reefs form the backbone of the Red Sea's ecology. Built by generation after generation of tiny polyps extracting calcium from the sea water and laying down sturdy limestone exoskeletons, a healthy reef can grow four to five cm per year. But bruising, in some cases even brushing against the organisms, can retard growth, and even kill the coral. To protect it, swim rather than walk whenever possible over the shallow reefs; the intense salinity (nearly five percent) makes it easy to float gently over the surface of water, gently undulating the tips of your fins until you're into the deep areas. Don't break off coral (it loses its color within hours of leaving the sea) or kill the marine life. Take only photos, and try not to leave even footprints.

Aware of the unique marine environment, the Egyptian government has set aside the southern tip of the peninsula at Ras Muhammad as a natural preserve, where taking fauna or flora is strictly prohibited. Unfortunately however, rampant development and the massive influx of tourists continue to stress the fragile desert and marine communities. To report any wildlife violations, call (066) 726-233.

HISTORY

Sinai and the Red Sea coast, historically more verdant than today, were home to prehistoric nomads who left Mediterranean shells to be discovered on the western Sinai coast at al-Tur. From earliest times, the major trade routes funneled African goods through Egypt to the Near East. Neolithic traders established posts near modern Cairo, and 400 Bronze-Age jars with Palestinian seals have been uncovered at Abydos in Middle Egypt. Early Bronze-Age Semites from Mesopotamia, attracted to Sinai by the copper ores and turquoise, were the first in a long progression of conquerors to overrun the peninsula.

Pharaonic Era

Under 3rd dynasty pharaohs, the Egyptians colonized the area, securing the northern desert as a buffer fortified against invaders, sending goods and military expeditions along the trade routes, and working the copper and turquoise mines in the mountains across the Gulf of Suez. By conscripting the vanquished Semitic population for slaves, they expanded their lucrative mining operations during the 3rd and 4th dynasties, mines that continued producing until the end of the Middle Kingdom, when the Hyksos invaded Egypt.

By 1570 B.C., New Kingdom rulers had driven out the Hyksos and once more sent expeditions to these wastelands. During this period, Hebrew slaves, revolting against the pharaoh, fled east to wander the 40 years of Exodus in Sinai. Although Biblical scholars wrangle over place names, chronologies, and routes, most feel the Jews crossed the Sea of Reeds (just north of Suez City) rather than the Red Sea. However, recent computer simulations indicate that a steady 40 mph wind blowing over the Red Sea at one of its shallower points could have stacked up the waters and exposed its bottom.

Throughout the Empire and Late periods, when Egypt colonized the East and was colonized in turn, a grand succession of invasions and retreats ravaged Sinai. Assyrians, Hittites, Babylonians, Persians, and Greeks invaded Egypt, controlling the all-important trade routes to the East. The Ptolemies sent expeditions into the peninsula and built ports along the Mediterranean coast. In the south, they encountered the Semitic Nabateans who, from their base in Petra, had seized Aqaba and opened a land route across Sinai into Gaza. Ultimately, both were conquered by the Romans.

Romans And Christians

From 30 B.C. to A.D. 640, the Roman Empire and its Byzantine successor developed the area, increasing Sinai's military and commercial importance. As far south as Bernice, they lined the Red Sea coast with ports where they offloaded goods to ship overland to the Nile Valley. To the north, along the Mediterranean coast, they established chains of garrisons within a day's march of each other (about 20 km) stringing out from the ancient Egyptian stronghold at Pelusium. They strengthened the foundations of Rhinocolorum, which would develop into al-Arish, the largest modern city in Sinai, and Raffia (modern Rafah), the gateway to Gaza and Palestine. But these fortresses didn't seal the area; Mary and Joseph escaped from Herod across Sinai, and returned by the same route after his death.

When Roman persecution intensified, Christians fled into the desert. Off the coast in the Red Sea mountains, Anthony laid the foundations of monasticism, followed soon by Paul who established another monastery to the south. On the peninsula, anchorites believed the oasis in Wadi Firan was the life-given Elim of Exodus, and revered the nearby Gebel Serbal as Mt. Sinai. In spite of continuing conflicts with the Bedouin, the area prospered, becoming a cathedral city and the site of a bishopric.

Following their conversion, Emperor Constantine and his mother Empress Helena turned their attention to the Holy Land and Sinai. They built a cathedral, monastery, and convent at Rhinocolorum, and cathedral cities developed at Ostracine, Pelusium, and near Kadesh Barnea, where the wandering Hebrews had spent much of their 40 years. When the Empress visited the settlement at Gebel Musa in 327 A.D., she ordered a chapel to the Holy Virgin built to the traditional "burning" bush she found growing there. Like many Christian settlements of the era, its inhabitants fortified the chapel against incessant attacks of marauding Bedouin. As the area drew more pilgrims, Gebel Musa replaced Gebel Serbal, eventually becoming known as Mt. Sinai.

The Muslims

The Arabs, infused with the verve of Islam, swept across Sinai, destroying Constantine's northern cathedral-cities. In the south, the natives who found the new beliefs tailor-made for their own nomadic existence assaulted the desert monasteries. These Bedouin, among the earliest soldiers of Islam, were charged with protecting the *hajj* (pilgrimage) routes across the area. The covenants with Christians reestablished peace, and for a period the monasteries prospered.

With Fatimid control of Egypt and the Holy Land late in the 10th century, the uneasy truce between Muslim and Christian started to unravel, and by the end of the 11th century, the West, for religious, economic, and political reasons, mounted a series of attacks—the Crusades—to free the Christian holy shrines. By 1100, the Christians had taken Jerusalem, and the kingdom they established included a slice of Sinai from Rafah to Aqaba. They erected outposts at the head of the Gulf of Aqaba, the largest on Fara'un (Pharaoh's) Island, and barred the Muslims from crossing Sinai on their *hajj*.

Following a wave of Crusader invasions of Egypt, Salah al-Din invaded Sinai, his howling armies retaking Aqaba and driving the Christian knights back to Gaza. By the end of the 12th century, the Crusades had collapsed, and Sinai was ruled by the Mamluks who reopened the east-west trade routes. In 1517 the Ottoman forces of Salim brought Sinai under Turkish control.

The Modern Period

Napoleon in 1798, and then Muhammad Ali in 1831, took Sinai, but in both cases the British retrieved the peninsula and returned it to the Turks (although they maintained administrative control over the strategic Suez Canal area). With its completion in 1869, the Suez Canal became one of the main arteries for British trade and communication throughout the empire. By 1892, the British had established outposts in the area and forced the Turks to cede a buffer zone that ran from Rafah to Aqaba.

By the outbreak of WW I, the Turks, backed by Germany, attacked Sinai, with the canal as their major objective. The British held Suez, but realized that the once-formidable desert buffer of Sinai, now laced with German roads, railways, and water lines, was vulnerable. During the war, the Bedouin (armed with discarded weapons and ammunition) found that they could pretty much run things their own way. After the fighting ended, Britain ruled Sinai as a separate province, but the Bedouin, with dreams of Arab nationalism, glory, and plunder, took to raiding and smuggling hashish from Turkey and Syria to Egypt, giving the British police forces fits. With the outbreak of WW II, the British augmented their forces, but the peninsula was the site of little fighting, serving only as a buffer protecting the Suez Canal from Axis powers. At the conclusion of the conflict, Egypt, with British blessing, took over Sinai.

The Arab-Israeli Wars

In 1948, after much international wrangling, the United Nations General Assembly endorsed a plan to partition part of Palestine for the Jewish immigrants pouring in from post-Holocaust Europe. The British, faced with Arabs who rejected the plan and threatened to drive the Jews into the sea, opted out of the discussion. The state of Israel was formed and immediately attacked by the Arabs; Egypt sent troops through Sinai to occupy the Gaza Strip. The Israelis not only held their own, but went on the offensive, and by January of 1949 were poised to take Rafah and al-Arish. The stunned Egyptians signed an armistice in February. The agreement did little to quell the animosity between the two nations, however, and border skirmishes and terrorist attacks continued to heighten tensions, which have thus far erupted in four armed conflicts.

In 1956, Egypt blockaded the Gulf of Aqaba, closing it to Israeli shipping. Nasser built up Egyptian forces in Sinai and nationalized the Suez Canal, effectively abolishing British military presence in Egypt. These moves, coupled with increasing Arab terrorism, again triggered Israeli action. Their forces ripped through Sinai, devastating the Egyptian military, lifting the blockade at Sharm al-Sheikh and approaching the eastern parts of the Suez Canal. The British, hoping to win back the canal, invaded Port Said, but world opinion forced both them and Israel to withdraw. United Nations peacekeeping forces established a buffer zone in the Gaza Strip and reestablished maritime routes in the Gulf of Aqaba, but these actions did little to stem the increasing Arab demand for a *jihad,* or holy war, against Israel.

In 1967, Nasser precipitated the Six Day War by ordering the U.N. forces to withdraw and moving his own troops into Sinai to close off the Gulf of Aqaba once more. Thus provoked, Israel struck again, wiping out the Egyptian air force while it remained on the ground, and sweeping Sinai of Egyptian troops. Still facing Arab hostility and feeling the need of for a buffer, Israel refused to relinquish Sinai, heavily fortifying their side of the canal by building the Bar Lev Line.

In 1969, skirmishes broke out into the War of Attrition, basically a continuation of the Six Day War. Facing heavy shelling, the populations of the Suez area decamped for Cairo. The Egypt-Israeli stalemate was finally broken in August 1970 with a U.S.-sponsored cease-fire agreement. Although the Suez Canal remained blocked with sunken ships, the agreement reopened the Gulf of Aqaba to Israeli shipping. Israel took advantage of the peace to settle Sinai and build tourist villages along its southeastern coast.

Three years later, Sadat, following up on his repeated threats to retake Sinai, invaded on 6 October 1973, the Jewish holiday of Yom Kippur. His troops breached the Bar Lev Line while, at the same time, Syrian forces stormed the Israeli-held Golan Heights. Taken off guard, the Israeli defenses fell back, but by the third day they recovered and took the offensive. On the 10th day, the Israelis poured across the central part of the Suez Canal, cutting off Egyptian forces in Sinai from water and supplies.

By January 1974, with the aid of U.S. Secretary of State Henry Kissinger, Egypt and Israel agreed to a cease-fire: Egypt was given a five-mile-wide buffer strip east of the canal; a second strip was manned by U.N. forces; the third served as Israel's buffer. In 1982, the entire peninsula reverted to Egypt, and in exchange Egypt agreed to clear the Suez Canal and to permit worldwide shipping. Since then, the canal cities have embarked on a rebuilding program, and Egypt proved to the world she could run the canal in an efficient and politically neutral manner. Although the Red Sea coast, especially at Hurghada, has become over-developed (with concurrent damage to the reefs), the government and private groups are trying to prevent the same damage to the shores of South Sinai.

THE SUEZ CANAL AREA

Bordering the Biblical land of Goshen, the Suez area lies between the Gulf of Suez and the Mediterranean Sea. The depression houses Small Bitter Lake, Large Bitter Lake, and Lake Timsah (Crocodile Lake), now joined by the Suez Canal. Running nearly 200 km, the waterway links the area's three major cities: Port Said, gateway to the Mediterranean; Ismailia, the midway garden city; and Suez, the industrial port to the south.

Suez was shaped by the trade routes that crossed its land. The earliest ran from the Gulf of Suez through the Bitter Lakes where goods were off-loaded and transshipped across the desert to the Nile, and then loaded once more on ships and sent either north to the Mediterranean or south to the Pharaonic interior. As early as the New Kingdom, the Egyptians tried to replace the overland caravans by linking Cairo via the freshwater channel of Wadi Tumilat. It was repaired by Necho II in 600 B.C., but soon fell into disuse. The Persians under Darius reopened it, and Ptolemy II extended it, but by early Roman times it had been abandoned. Repaired by Trajan in the 1st century A.D., the canal facilitated trade between the Roman Empire and the East; but as Roman rule faltered, it once more silted up.

Islamic Period
The canal was briefly revitalized by the Arabs under Amr Ibn al-As so that Egyptian foodstuffs could be shipped by sea to Mecca, but by the 8th century it was no longer in operation. Although medieval spice traders began to seek quicker, easier links to the Red Sea and Indian Ocean, not until Napoleon's expedition did serious work begin to link the Red Sea directly to the Mediterranean. However, due to a miscalculation, his engineers thought the Red Sea was nine meters above the Mediterranean, an error not corrected until the Frenchman Ferdi-

nand de Lesseps proved that the two waters were equal and convinced the Turkish governor Said Pasha that a canal was feasible.

The Suez Canal
Work began in 1859 and the canal, largely financed by foreign money and built by Egyptian labor, was opened amid great fanfare in 1869. Ismail Pasha hosted European royalty with lavish entertainment and housing, but the opening was one of his last extravaganzas. By 1876 he was nearly broke. The British gained control of the Suez Canal Company and a 99-year lease on the canal itself, but the Egyptians nationalized it in 1956. During the Six Day War of 1967, trapped ships and mines blocked the canal; Israelis dug in on the east bank, and the people fled the towns. Closed for eight years, the canal was finally reopened in June 1975.

The channel is 200 meters wide and can accommodate ships with up to a 53-foot draft. The crossing takes 15-20 hours, and traffic is one way: north in the morning and south in the afternoon. Perennial plans to widen the canal for two-way traffic are still in the works.

SUEZ CITY

Located about 130 km south of the Mediterranean coast, Suez City was founded in the 15th century, but it only developed with the building of the rail line from Cairo, which served the Peninsular and Oriental Company's shipping services to India. The city, which gave the canal its name, still serves international trade, as does Port Tawfiq (Suez's sister city), which lies across the causeway. The canal city most damaged by the Arab-Israeli wars, Suez has been nearly completely rebuilt. Today, except for one of the nicest views of the canal and southeast coast, it offers little to interest tourists. In Port Tawfiq

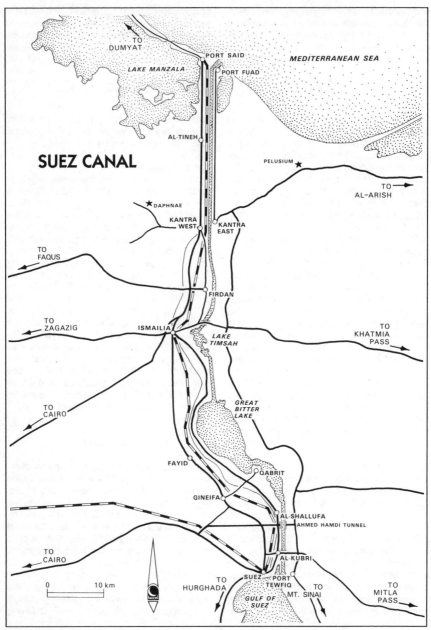

SUEZ CANAL

MEDITERRANEAN SEA

TO DUMYAT

LAKE MANZALA

PORT SAID

PORT FUAD

AL-TINEH

★ PELUSIUM

TO AL-ARISH

★ DAPHNAE

KANTRA WEST

KANTRA EAST

TO FAQUS

FIRDAN

TO ZAGAZIG

ISMAILIA

LAKE TIMSAH

TO KHATMIA PASS

TO CAIRO

GREAT BITTER LAKE

FAYID

QABRIT

GINEIFA

AL-SHALLUFA

AHMED HAMDI TUNNEL

TO CAIRO

AL-KUBRI

0   10 km

SUEZ

PORT TEWFIQ

TO HURGHADA

GULF OF SUEZ

TO MT. SINAI

TO MITLA PASS

© MOON PUBLICATIONS, INC. / 2

you can enjoy the quiet charm of the Victorian homes that once housed the canal workers. At the end of the peninsula, watch the ships head into the canal or view them from the top floor dining room of the Red Sea Hotel over breakfast and coffee.

Accommodations

Port Tawfiq: Quieter than Suez City proper, Tawfiq has several hotels. The best is the **Red Sea Hotel,** 13 Sh. Riad, tel. 223-334, fax 227-761. Rooms run $35 s, $45 d, suites $52-57; all rooms have baths, a/c, and TV. On the other side of the peninsula, the **Summer Palace,** tel. 224-475, offers good clean rooms on the beach for LE74 s, LE89 d, and LE117 t, including breakfast and use of the beach-side swimming pool.

Suez City: Suez City boasts the new **Green Hotel** on the Suez end of the causeway to Port Tawfiq, tel. 223-330, fax 223-337. All the amenities in a plush atmosphere (including pool) for

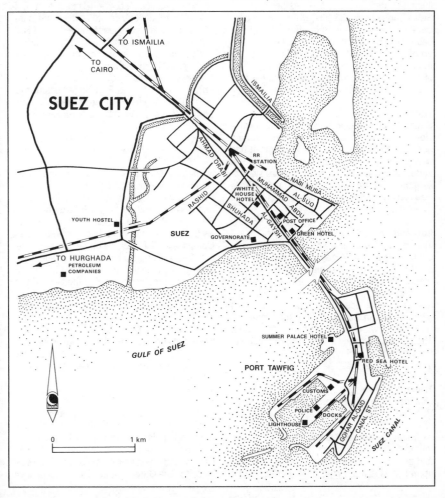

$26 s, $32 d, and $43 for a suite, make this new addition a good deal. But the best deal in town is the newly renovated and clean **Bel Air** on Sa'ad Zaghlul, tel. 223-211, fax 225-781, which has a beautiful balcony area and patio dining in summer. Rooms run LE38 s, LE58 d, suites LE7, including all the amenities and breakfast. Nearly as good, rooms at the **White House Hotel,** 322 Sh. Salaam, tel. 227-599, telex 55102 SWSIT#UN, run LE26 s, LE33 d; private showers, TV, a/c, and breakfast. Those less flush can try the nearby **Misr Palace Hotel,** 2 Sa'ad Zaghlul, tel. 223-031, which covers bare bones accommodations but has a/c, private baths, and breakfast for LE11 s, LE22 d. The **youth hostel,** tel. 3145, lies west of town near the stadium. This inconvenient location, coupled with chronic overcrowding, make this less than desirable, even at LE4-6.

Food
Several good restaurants cluster near the White House Hotel. The **Champs Elysees** serves good, inexpensive food. The **Magharbel** has been redone, and now caters more to the tourist trade; the prices have gone up (but are still reasonable) and the food is good. The **Sea Side** also has good food; the **St. James** has become more of a pub.

Information And Services
The **Tourist Office** is in Port Tawfiq; open daily 0830-1430 except Friday. **Tourist police** are in the bus station off al-Salaam, as is the office of the **Friends of Tourists,** dedicated student volunteers who will help you with travel arrangements and tips on food and entertainment (such as it is in Suez). The **post office** is on Hoda Sharawi; open Sat.-Thurs. 0900-1500. The **telephone office** is on al-Salaam, north of the White House Hotel; open 24 hours; code 011.

Transportation
Minibuses run a fixed route between Arbaeen Bus Station and Port Tawfiq along al-Salaam (25PT).

Trains run between Cairo and Suez on two routes: four direct express trains (three hours) and five slow ones (via Ismailia—six to seven hours). This is not a high priority option, but if you're stuck, trains depart at 0555, 0950, 1530, and 1840 to Cairo (Ain Shams Station); or through Ismailia at 1505 and 1730.

Suez is the hub of the **bus** service, and coaches run to Cairo (LE4.50) every half hour from 0600 to 1800 plus two additional (LE6) at 1900 and 2000. They run to Ismailia (LE2.25) every fifteen minutes from 0600 to 1600, and to Port Said (LE5.50) at 0630, 1200, and 1530. Into Sinai they head for Sharm al-Sheikh (LE12) at 1030 with stops at Dahab (LE14), and Nuweiba, or you can catch additional buses to Nuweiba (LE15.17) at 0630 or 1400, which go via the central Sinai and continue to Taba (LE15/17). A bus leaves for St. Catherine (LE14) at 1230.

Service taxis run similar routes and cost slightly more than the buses.

The Egyptian Navigation Company runs two **ships** to Jeddah and Port Sudan about four times a month; check with their offices in Suez on Sh. Nabi Musa or in Cairo or Alexandria.

ISMAILIA

Named for Egypt's ruler during the canal's construction, this most attractive of the canal cities sits on Lake Timsah, its waterfront a beautiful series of parks and gardens. Halfway between Suez and Port Said, Ismailia was founded by de Lesseps to accommodate the Suez Canal Company staff. In fact, his home, filled with mementos, is used as a government guesthouse; arrangements to visit it may be made with the public relations department of the Suez Canal Authority. Targeted as a new resort area, the town has several new building projects underway.

The main street, Sh. Muhammad Ali (Sh. Port Said), runs parallel to the canal and the lakeside parks; the main body of the town lies west. Sharia Orabi connects the main train station with the parks.

Sights
The **Ismailia Museum** (Sh. Muhammad Ali), open daily 0830-1600, displays artifacts from prehistoric to modern times, including information on the ancient navigable canals that ran to Ismailia and a beautiful collection of 4th century mosaics. The **Garden of Stelae,** one block west

of the museum, boasts plaques, statues, and sphinxes from the age of Ramesses II; inquire at the museum about permission to get in.

The **home of Ferdinand de Lesseps** is supposed to be open Wed.-Mon. 0900-1600 (free), but you may have trouble getting in; sometimes permission from the public relations department of the Suez Canal Authority helps.

To Do

Egyptians come to Ismailia to relax on the beaches of Lake Timsah. The resort clubs (along the beach by the Etap Hotel) charge LE5-10 daily use fee, but the price often includes buffet meals. In addition to swimming, the new Etap Hotel offers water-skiing, windsurfing, sailing, and tennis.

For a change of pace, drive out toward the Etap and up the hill to the residential area of Nemrah Sitah, which is filled with stately French homes. From the top of the hill there's a spectacular view of the canal.

Accommodations

Plush accommodations can be had at the **Etap,** Forsan Island, tel. 322-274, fax 222-220, with rooms for $60 s, $77 d, $90 t, and a suite (four

people) $145, all with breakfast. You can make reservations in Cairo, tel. (02) 765-322/768-802. A better deal is the **Crocodile Inn,** centrally located at 179 Sh. Sa'ad Zaghlul, tel. 324-377; LE32 s with bath, LE45 d, LE54 t. Reservations can be made in Cairo through the Caroline Crillon, tel. (02) 374-7570. A step down is the clean but simple **Nefertari Hotel,** 41 Sultan Husayn, tel. 322-822; LE20 s, LE26 d, LE32 t; baths, a/c, TV, and breakfast included. Several inexpensive hotels crowd around Midan Orabi, and the best of these is the **Burg,** down the street from the train station, tel. 326-327. Newly renovated, the old rooms still have their high ceilings, and comfortable sitting rooms make this hotel the best choice for the money. It offers a/c, telephones, TV, and private baths for LE15 s, LE25 d, and LE35 t; no breakfast. Across the *midan,* the **Isis,** tel. 227-821, is nearly as good; rooms are LE12 s, LE20 d, and LE20 t; breakfast is LE3.

The **youth hostel** is in the suburban area of Sheikh Zayed, and is as beautiful and friendly as it is remote; spotless rooms run LE3.65. Sports teams (usually soccer) often stay here. **Camping** on the beach at Lake Timsah is permitted.

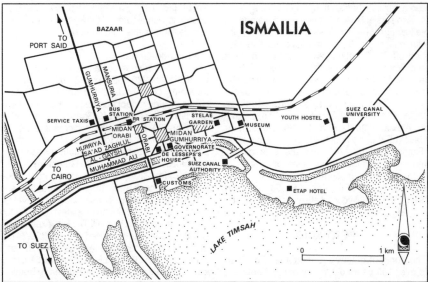

Food

The **Etap** has a French chef in the main dining room, and the food is great; in warm weather they run a nightly barbecue at 2100. The 24-hour coffee shop at the Crocodile Inn is a good deal. The locals eat at **George's,** just down the street from the Nefertiti Hotel. The paneled **King Edward Restaurant,** 171 Tahrir, tel. 325-451, offers entrees for LE12-20 and they occasionally are worth the price. **Groppi's,** across the street and down from the Nefertari Hotel, has sweets for dessert.

Information And Services

The **Tourist Office** is in the Governorate Building and is open daily 0830-1500 except Friday. The **police station** is also in the same building; **emergency phone** number is 122. The **post office** and **telephone office** (24 hours) are both on Midan Orabi. The code is 084.

Transportation

The **train station** is on the north side of Midan Orabi. Trains between Cairo and Suez run through Ismailia, but they're slow and grubby. However, express (two hours) trains link Ismailia to Port Said at 0540, 0905, 0930, and 1100; LE3.50 (1st class, a/c), LE1.30 (2nd class). You can get tickets half an hour before departure.

Two sets of **buses** link Ismailia, the standard yellow and green wrecks and the East Delta blue buses. The former run out of the **bus station** off Sh. Gumhurriya. Buses linking Suez and Port Said stop in Ismailia. Service to Cairo is available hourly—the buses are supposedly air-conditioned but it rarely works. Far better are the ones from the **East Delta Kiosk** on Midan Orabi, near the train station. They leave for Alex at 0700 (LE8) and 1430 (LE8.30); for Cairo (LE5) every hour between 0630 and 1900 (Ramadan, 0700-1700). **Service taxis,** across the street from the main bus station, cover the same routes at a slightly higher cost: Cairo, LE3.75; Tanta, LE5; Suez, LE2.56; and Port Said, LE2.75; get your tickets at the green booth.

PORT SAID

The northern gateway to the canal, Port Said is over 100 years old; many of its streets are lined with buildings dating to the last century, their pillared-porch facades looking like New Orleans's French Quarter. Nearby, the Mediterranean's sweeping beaches are less crowded than those at Alexandria.

The rectangular town is bounded by two main streets: one along the beach (the New Cornishe), the other along the canal docks (Sh. Palestine). The main shopping area is in the southeastern corner of town, for here lie the duty-free shops and restaurants. Port Said's sister city, Port Fuad, lies across the canal, linked by a free ferry.

Sights

Port Said, primarily a commercial city, offers the casual tourist little except a view of port workings and the beaches. You can rent a chair, sit on the northern beach, and watch the ships go by.

The **Port Said Museum,** currently undergoing renovation, contains a beautifully displayed collection that spans Egypt's entire history. A small **military museum** on Sh. 23 July is open daily 0800-1500 (LE2) and shows pharaonic and Islamic battles, but concentrates on the 1973 war against Israel.

If you have the time, take the free ferry to **Port Fuad;** you'll get a magnificent view and a chance to wander around the less touristy shops and gardens of this smaller port.

Accommodations

The four-star **Helnan** lies on the east end of the Cornishe, tel. 220-892, fax 223-762; rooms go for a hefty LE240 s, LE295 d, and LE361 t; facilities include a pool and health club. A better deal is the **Akri Palace,** 19 Ghandy St., tel. 239-450/239-490, fax 239-464, which offers rates of $30 s, $39 d, LE66 for suites, all with baths, a/c, and breakfast; rooms without a sea view run $4 less. The **Holiday,** Sh. Gumhurriya, tel. 220-710, fax 220-710, offers equally good accommodations in the commercial area: $20 s, $24 d, and a suite for $35.70, includes private baths, TV, and a/c, but no breakfast. Use P.O. Box 204 for inquiries by mail. The less expensive **Crystal,** 12 Mohammed Mahmud, tel. 322-747, has new, clean rooms with private baths, hot water, and a/c: LE34 s, LE44 d, and LE51 t, including breakfast. Of the less expensive hotels

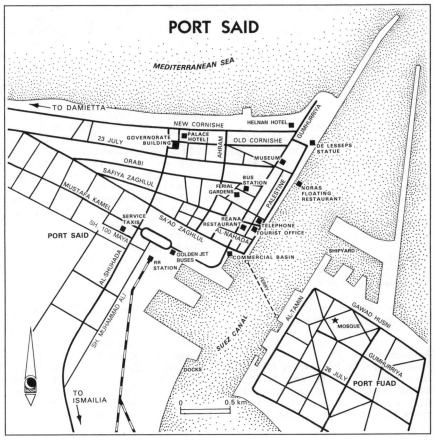

PORT SAID

MEDITERRANEAN SEA

TO DAMIETTA

NEW CORNISHE
HELNAN HOTEL
GUMHURRIYA
23 JULY
GOVERNORATE BUILDING
PALACE HOTEL
AHRAM
OLD CORNISHE
DE LESSEPS STATUE
ORABI
MUSEUM
SAFIYA ZAGHLUL
BUS STATION
PALESTINE
NORAS FLOATING RESTAURANT
MUSTAFA KAMEL
FERIAL GARDENS
SH. 100 MAYA
SERVICE TAXIS
SA'AD ZAGHLUL
REANA RESTAURANT
AL-NAHADA
TELEPHONE
TOURIST OFFICE
PORT SAID
AL-SHUHADA
RR STATION
GOLDEN JET BUSES
COMMERCIAL BASIN
SHIPYARD
SH. MUHAMMAD ALI
FERRY
AL-TANIM
SUEZ CANAL
GAWAD HUSNI
MOSQUE
GUMHURRIYA
TO ISMAILIA
DOCKS
26 JULY
PORT FUAD
0   0.5 km
© MOON PUBLICATIONS, INC.

(those with fans), the **Hotel de la Poste,** 42 Sh. Gumhurriya, tel. 224-048, offers rooms with TV, refrigerator, private bath, and a/c, (without breakfast) for LE15 s, LE18.25 d, and LE23 t; rooms facing the side rather than main street run about LE3 less. The **New Swiss,** 6 Orabi, tel. 225-887, occupies an old building with high ceilings, fans, and telephones; clean rooms; some rooms with private baths; LE12/15 s, LE16/22 d, and LE24/28 t, including breakfast. Although a bit dilapidated on the outside, the **Abu Simbel Hotel,** 15 Gumhurriya, tel. 221-150, charges LE20 s (with bath), LE30 d; a/c is available in some rooms. The **Akri Palace,** 24 Sh. Gumhur-

riya, tel. 221-013, is a great deal for those with thin pocketbooks. The **Regent,** tel. 223-802, offers rock-bottom but clean rooms (some with private bath) for LE11.50 s, LE18.50 d, and LE24 t; includes breakfast.

The **youth hostel,** tel. 228-702, is in the Sea Rangers' building at Sh. al-Amin and the New Cornishe; members only, LE3. In addition to its inconvenient location, the place has an unfriendly atmosphere; you may want to avoid it.

Food
The best Taiwanese food in Egypt is prepared at the **Reana Restaurant,** diagonally across from

the Akri Palace and up the stairs; inexpensive. The **Akri Palace** serves good Greek food; **Popeye's Cafe** opposite the Hotel de la Poste offers Western fare; the **Soufar,** at the corner of Degla and Gumhurriya prepares outstanding Lebanese food. You can just pick a seafood restaurant; I like the **Seahorse** on the Cornishe. The **Noras** floating restaurant will give you a good dinner and a cruise of the bay for about LE25.

Information And Services
The **Tourist Office,** 43 Sh. Palestine (south end), tel. 223-868, is open Sat.-Thurs. 0800-1400 and 1500-2000. The **Tourist Police** are in the Customs building (south end of Palestine, next to the bus station), tel. 228-570, with a branch office in the train station; both are open 24 hours. To **change money,** try Thomas Cook on Gumhurriya; open daily 0900-1800. The **post office** is on the southeast corner of the Ferial Gardens; open daily 0700-1700.

The **telephone office** is next to the Tourist Office on Sh. Palestine; open 24 hours. Code is 066. **Al Isaaf Pharmacy,** on Safiya Zaghlul near Shuhada, tel. 228-888, is open all night. **The American Consulate,** tel. 223-886, is on Sh. Tarh al-Bahr, but it's a commercial branch that deals only with shipping.

Transportation
The train station is on the south side of town. Frequent **trains** serve Cairo throughout the day, but they are slow and dirty. If you decide to use them, buy your tickets ahead, especially in summer and on holidays. The 135-km trip takes about 4½

hours, for most stop in Mansuria and Ismailia; tickets are about LE10 for 2nd class, a/c. The only exception is the 1530 1st-class special, which takes 4½ hours, to Cairo (LE12). The tickets are around the corner to the left as you face the main entrance; the main building is worth a trip inside to look at the murals on either end.

The bus station is off Sh. Orabi; the Customs building is next door. **Buses** to Cairo (LE10) leave hourly from 0600 to 1700 (window #2); to Ismailia (LE3.50), same hours (window #4); and to Suez (LE5.50) at 0600, 1000, 1300, and 1500 (window #1). Buses to the canal cities to the south leave regularly. The **Super Jet,** based in the red kiosk across from the train station, also serves Cairo (six hours, LE10), nearly hourly with several non-smoking (NS) buses: 0700 (NS), 0800, 1200, 1300, 1400 (NS), 1500, 1600 (NS), 1700, 1750, and 1800 (NS). Buses to Alexandria leave at 0430; LE17.

Service taxis leave from a square on Sh. 100 Maya, off Sh. al-Shuhada: Cairo LE6.30, Ismailia LE2.75, Suez LE5.50, and Alexandria LE11.

As for **boats,** you won't be able to hire on the commercial ships, but you can try the private yachts in Port Fuad.

Good **roads** connect the canal area with Cairo, Sinai, and the Red Sea coast. Gas is available at the resthouse halfway to Cairo. The road south along the canal is good and gas is available in major cities. The Ahmed Hamdi Tunnel crosses the canal just north of Suez City; a bridge spans it at Ismailia. The ferry at Kantra runs on an erratic schedule.

THE RED SEA COAST

Linked geologically to Sinai, the western coast of the Red Sea mirrors its reefs and aquatic life. Hemmed in by the Red Sea mountains, which run its length, the coastal plains often disappear, the granite cliffs dropping straight into the turquoise waters. The beaches near Hurghada are blossoming with resorts, plush mini-villages where temporary residents fish, scuba dive, snorkel, beachcomb, or just relax on the soft white sand. As the resort became more crowded, divers and visitors in search of solitude pushed south, and now plush hotels are starting to follow, invading Safaga and Qusir. Farther north, the undeveloped beach at Ain Sukhna, close to Cairo, hosts day-trippers, while the ancient monasteries of St. Anthony and St. Paul draw both Christian and Muslim visitors. During the Israeli wars, the Egyptians heavily mined the Red Sea coast, and many live mines remain in the hills. *Do not wander from the public areas of the beaches without a guide.*

THE RED SEA MONASTERIES

The oldest monasteries in Egypt, these two complexes present a study in contrasts: St. Paul's is a small, primitive compound, while St. Anthony's is a modern, rich, and vigorous stronghold of the Coptic faith. Marking the beginnings of the monastic movement, these sites also maintain many of the original features of the ascetic life: to daily perform the divine office, to fast, to practice chastity and penance—in short, to live like the angels of God.

St. Anthony's Monastery

Saint Anthony, a founder of Egyptian monasticism, found himself an orphan at the age of 18, and in A.D. 285 he moved to the Eastern Desert; finally, to escape the attentions of followers, he retreated to a cave high in the mountain. He was buried here, and shortly thereafter, his followers formed a settlement with a community refectory and chapel.

The monastery, enclosed by a fortified wall, contains several churches, the monks' cells, a permanent spring, flour mills and ovens, and a large garden. English-speaking visitors will be given a guided tour by a monk fluent in the language, like Father Zakariya.

St. Anthony's Cave

The cave in which St. Anthony made his home involves an exhilarating ascent up Mt. Clysma, a climb best done in the early morning. The first stage, the climb to St. Paul's cave, takes about 35 minutes; St. Anthony cave takes only about another 15 minutes but the trail is steeper. From the nearly hidden entrance terrace, the narrow tunnel runs back to a small altar set over the stone the hermit used for his pillow. Solitude and peace exude from the very walls.

St. Paul's Monastery

Considered the first Christian monk, St. Paul the Simple was born in Alexandria in A.D. 228, but at the age of 16 he fled to the Eastern Desert to escape the Roman persecutions. Here St. Anthony visited him. Icons show St. Paul in a simple tunic receiving his daily half loaf of bread from a raven, but tradition maintains that when his neighboring hermit visited, the raven presciently brought a whole loaf.

Saint Paul's Monastery, covering about five acres, is more idyllic than its larger neighbor, its neat gardens and curving paths offering a soft and luminous peace. The main door is rarely used; follow the path to the left around the corner of the building and up a slight hill.

Note: The monasteries do not receive visitors during periods of fasting; Coptic fasting periods are more extended than Western ones so check with the Coptic Patriarchate in Cairo (see below).

Accommodations

The monks at both monasteries will put up guests (men only at St. Paul's) but you must have permission from the Coptic Patriarchate in Cairo, tel. (02) 917-360. The monks will supply drinking water, but you must bring your own food; there are no showers or cooking facilities. There is no fee, but donations of staples (tea, oil, rice, jam, sugar) or money (to be put in one of the locked boxes) are welcome.

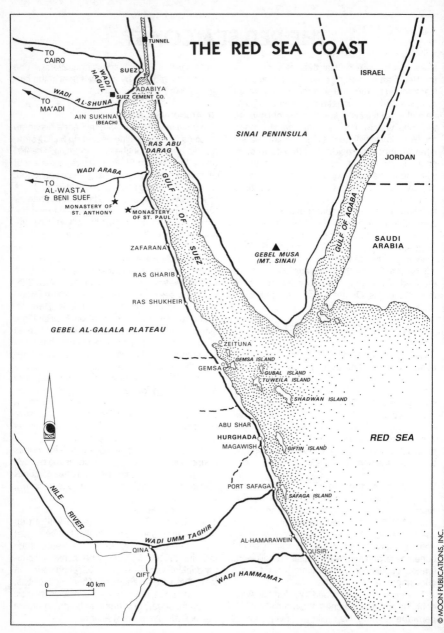

THE RED SEA COAST

Getting There

You cannot reach the monasteries by public transportation; private cars, taxis, or a tour are the only options. For tour possibilities, contact the Coptic Church of St. Peter and Paul, 22 Ramesses St., Abbassia; the YMCA, 27 al-Gumhurriya, Cairo, tel. (02) 917-360; or the Egyptian Center of International Cultural Co-operation, 11 Shagarit al-Dorr, Zamalek, tel. (02) 341-5419. The roads are paved to both monasteries and the turnoffs are clearly marked.

HURGHADA

Hurghada lies about 600 km south of Suez; the climate here is mild nearly year-round (except for the occasional winter winds). To accommodate the fishermen and divers who come to explore the spectacular underwater scenery of the off-shore islands, the villagers developed small hotels, restaurants, and shops. However, opportunistic developers have now built up the whole area, even shoving dirt out over the reefs to create fill for new buildings.

The main town of Hurghada lies about two km northwest of its port; at the north end of the main north-south street lies the al-Dhar Mosque and opposite it, the tourist bazaar. To both the north (along the plateau) and the south, along the coast road, stretch the resorts.

Sights

Other than the beaches, Hurghada offers little except a tiny marine museum (free, but if the caretaker shows you around, a tip is in order) about four km north of town. You can catch a bus (25PT) at the traffic circle at the port or on the main street of town; get off at the sign to the Aquarium on the east side of the road. The larger and better stocked Red Sea Aquarium is open daily 0800- 2200, LE4. Or you can see the real thing close up with a ride in the submarine run by the Sinbad Amusement Park.

For adventure on your own (but you'll need to take a guide) rent a four-wheel drive from Hill Hoppers, next to the service station in the main town, tel./fax 446-704. They'll arrange for a guide to the interior ruins or along the coast fishing and snorkeling.

Diving And Snorkeling

The hotels or tourist flats will arrange trips to the outer reefs and the numerous islands, as well as to the beaches and dive spots to the south. Day-trips to the islands often include a fish lunch on the beach. You'll have to reserve a day ahead; make sure all the numbers are copied correctly from your passport and visa to the form or the dock authorities may not let you go. Take a hat, sunscreen, water, and clothes to cover your body in the afternoon.

Dive boats run to other destinations as well; check with local dive shops or your hotel.

Dive Centers

Diving near Hurghada is not so good anymore, but the offshore islands remain good spots; to the south, dive sites are less crowded and disturbed, so you'll get some of the best diving here. Of the centers, the best known is the **Red Sea Diving Center.** It's just that—a center, not a school. To dive with Rudy and his crew, you'll already have to have considerable experience under your belt and you'll have to plan ahead, for all their facilities are booked from abroad. For a week on one of the plushiest dive boats in existence, contact Red Sea Aquarians at 59 London Rd., Hackbridge, Surrey, SM6 7BJ, England, tel. 081-669-0086, fax 081-669-6531. Otherwise you can dive with **Subex** at the harbor junction, the **Barakuda** behind the Giftun Hotel, or **Arabaya** along the beach north of Abu Rudeis. Prices, often quoted in deutsche marks, run about the same as in Sinai.

Beaches

The best beaches in Hurghada are south of town, toward the resorts. The free beach beside the Sheraton is usually overrun by Egyptians, but the semiprivate Shel-Ighada a little north of the hotel is less crowded and more Western; you can drink up to your entrance fee in soft drinks and use the freshwater showers. Giftun Island also has a beautiful beach.

Fishing

Hurghada is the center of Egypt's sportfishing, and every year the town plays host to an international deep-sea fishing tournament between May and July. For current information and dates, contact the closest ETA office (see chart, p. 164).

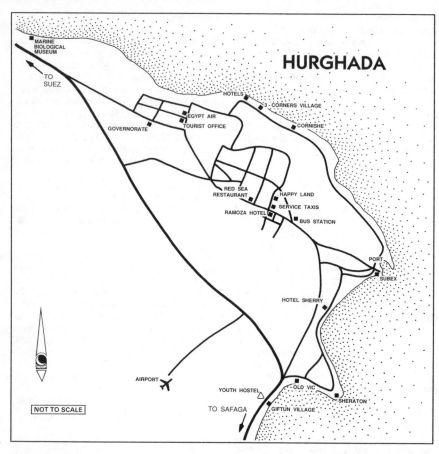

HURGHADA

NOT TO SCALE

© MOON PUBLICATIONS, INC.

Accommodations

Hurghada has downtown hotels, and resorts stringing out along the beach to the south (they now fill almost the entire area between Maga-wish and the port); hotels run up the plateau and spill out between the old town and the sea, along the coast.

To the South: This area is anchored by the tall, round Sheraton, tel. 440-785, fax 348-8217, and rooms here run $80-95. The newly redone **Giftun,** tel. 442-667/-674, fax 442-666, offers a better deal with TV, phones, water all day, and refrigerators for $50.82 s, $71.61 d, and $90.90 t, including half-board. The resort has

an excellent dive center and good water-sports equipment for rent. You can make reservations in Cairo through the Victoria Hotel, 66 Gumhur-riya, tel. 910-771. The **Jasmine,** beyond Maga-wish, tel. 442-442, fax 442-441, offers plush rooms with beautiful grounds and atmosphere; $50 s, $70 d, and $92 t, including half-board.

Private Homes: For a group, one of the best deals is the private homes that line the beach south of the Sheraton. Known collectively as the **Old Vic,** tel. 442-235, they are available when the owners are not using them. Each is individual (some have a/c, some just fans) but all have at least two or three bedrooms, a couple of baths, and kitchen facilities (the staff will shop for you). They run between LE150-500, averaging about LE200/day. You can make reservations in Cairo with the manager, Dr. Ibrahim, tel. (02) 350-1036.

From the Sheraton to the Port: Numerous hotels shoulder their way between the mountain and the beach. The best deal here is the **Hotel Sherry,** which sits back off the main beach road, tel. 442-087, fax 442-709, and offers newly renovated rooms with a/c, private baths, phone, and a choice of half-board or full board: LE43.34/52.86 s, LE66.45/85.49 d, and LE90.75/119.30 t; Cairo reservations are available at 5 Ali Gamal al-Din, Giza, tel. (02) 866-257, fax 860-985. Divers flock to the **Scuba Doo,** where they can get clean, well-designed rooms with half-board: LE66 s, LE99 d. The Swiss run **Moon Valley,** tel. 442-811, offers rooms with fans, a balcony with a view, and good food (half-board included): $25 s, $30 d, and $45 t; a private beach is across the road. Slightly less expensive, the **Pharos** behind Subex, tel. 447-577, has large, light, inviting rooms with fans, balconies, and shared baths for LE15 s, LE25 d, including breakfast—on your balcony if you want. Divers can now get rooms at **Subex,** $12 pp including breakfast; this is a great place to met people.

North of the Port: A string of medium-priced hotels line the Cornishe on the plateau north of the port. The best deal here, in fact the best deal in Hurghada, is the **Three Corners Village,** 2 Cornishe, tel. 447-816, fax 447-514; it's spotless and has great food, a/c, and a pool. Rooms (most with a view), including half-board, run $35 s, $70 d. The **Sand Beach** on the Cornishe, tel. 447-821-2, fax 447-992, has all the amenities (but no lift): rooms with breakfast/half-board run $42/52 s, $63/71.40 d, $84/97.60 t, suites $81.90/94 (two people), $94.50/107 (three). Toward the port, the **Arabia Beach Hotel,** tel. 443-790, fax 443-792, offers plush accommodations, including total wheelchair access, a private beach, and all the amenities including half-board for $53.13 s, $76.23 d, $97.02 t, $19.06 for a child.

Downtown: Most of the small and inexpensive hotels cluster in the downtown area, some down toward the *suq* and beaches. The best deal is the **Ritz,** on Sh. al-Dahar (next to the tourism office) tel. 447-031, which lives up to its name, offering simple but spotless rooms with private baths, hot water all day, telephones,

fans, and some a/c: LE29 s, LE40 d, and LE52 t. Second choice for the money is the **Ramoza,** off al-Orabi behind the service taxi (minibus) stand near the book shop, tel. 446-608, with hot water and fans, (although no private baths) for LE12 s, LE14 d, which includes breakfast.

In Town: The hotel provides bikes and transportation to the beach for guests. The **Abu Nawas** lies at the edge of the harbor almost down to the port, past Red Sea Divers, tel. 446-704. It offers lovely, quiet rooms with ocean views, fans, and hot water. Shared baths are new; this simple but very clean hotel runs LE15 s, LE25 d, and LE30 t, including breakfast.

Tourist Flats: The remnants of the early days of Hurghada's unexpected tourists, these homes still take up to a dozen or so guests. Most are blending with the smaller hotels, and many have changed their names to reflect this shift. They do not include breakfast, but it's available for a few pounds extra. The **Happy Land Hotel,** on Sh. al-Sheikh Sebak, tel. 447-373, has rooms with balconies, some with a sea view, fans, some with private baths (all baths are new), and hot water all day: LE12 s, LE20 d, LE21 t, without bath; LE15 s, LE25 d, with bath. The hotel has a private beach 6½ km north of town and runs minibuses to it. The **St. George** in the bazaar area has very quiet and clean, if basic, rooms with fans, some with private bath; LE20/25. The **Gobel Hotel,** Sh. al-Sheikh Sebak (at Abel Aziz) tel. 446-623, is also a good bet, clean with all-new shared baths, hot water, and fans: LE12.50 s, LE20.50 d, and LE30.50 t.

Youth Hostel: The YH is across the road from the Sonesta; you'll need a card (LE24 for a card and six stamps), lock-out 1000-1400 and curfew at 0200; spacious dorm rooms run LE5 pp. Sheets and blankets are available, along with solar-heated hot water as long as it lasts, kitchen facilities, and lockers; you'll need to bring a lock and soap.

Camping: Camping is increasingly limited. For the beach, check with the Tourist Office for the current information, and with the Tourist Police next door. For LE5 pp you can camp behind the Geisum Village where you can have hot showers, use of the pool at the Sand Beach Hotel (next door) and a good view. You can also camp between the Mashribiyya and the Giftun. Also check with the **Moon Valley Resort,** tel. 40-074, four km southwest along the coast; a campsite with toilets and showers runs LE6 pp. Because of possible minefields, camping can be risky.

Food

The best restaurant is **Arleen's**, Sh. Dr. Said Korayem (Hospital St.), no telephone, open 1200-2400, where you can get great food for moderate prices. Italian food across the street at the **Portofino** falls into the same category. For Korean food, try the **Korean Palace** in the Gobal Hotel. **Pirates**, downtown, is good if slightly more expensive; the **Red Sea Restaurant** across the street (burned and now rebuilt) is equivalent and has a rooftop garden, but no longer serves alcohol. For great food and lots of it, hit the buffet at the **Three Corners**, LE25. For coffee and light snacks, visit **Cheers** on the Cornishe, open 1000-0200. Many of the hotels have rooftop bars; the one at **La Bambola** has a pool table nestled in its Tudor decor. The only real disco is the **Chu Chu**, next to the Three Corners.

Information And Services

The **Tourist Office**, tel. 446-513, on Sh. Governorate, is open daily 0900-1400 and 1800-2000, with a branch at the bus station; it has current information on the dive sites and costs of island trips, as well as excursions to Luxor, St. Paul's and St. Anthony's monasteries, desert safaris, and other current tourist information. Both the **post office** and **telephone office** (open Sat.-Thurs. 24 hours) are on the *midan* near the mosque toward the north of town; telephone code: 065. The **Bookshop** behind the service station is limited to a couple of shelves; far better is the one by the Aquanaut Divers out on the Cornishe. **Bank Misr**, on the main street, is open daily 0830-1400 and 1700-2000, as is the neighboring **National Bank of Egypt**.

Getting Around

The public transportation system in Hurghada consists primarily of minibuses, which run from the Aquarium through the town and the harbor, and out to the resorts (75PT), and local buses, which run from the town to the port (20PT). You can ask for the beaches (*shot*) or the hotels (*fondo*); for the harbor, say (*mina*). The Jasmine Hotel runs a bus from their parking lot into town at 1000 and 1330, returning at 1300 and 1530, LE5. Private taxis, according to the governorate rates, should run LE5/hour (waiting time, LE3/hour); to the airport, LE10-15; to the beaches, LE10-20. You can rent a car at Giftun Village. You can rent bikes for several pounds per hour at a shop just north of the al-Dhar Mosque (return hours, 1900-2100) or several nearby shops; by the harbor, La Bambola Hotel rents them for LE5/hour. If you fly in and have reservations at one of the resorts, the resort bus will meet you.

Getting From Hurghada

By Air: The airport lies 15 km west of town. The EgyptAir/Air Sinai Office, tel. 440-788, is in the tourist bazaar near the mosque and is open Sat.-Thurs. 0900-1400 and 1800-2000, Fri. (partial service) 0900-1400. The Zas offices are in the Giftun Hotel. EgyptAir runs two to four daily flights to Cairo. Air Sinai connects Hurghada to Cairo, Sharm al-Sheikh, and St. Catherine several times a week, as does Zas. Check with their offices for current schedules and fares.

By Bus: The bus station lies on the main road heading south. Book seats at least a day in advance; the office is open 0600-2000. Buses to Cairo run at 0500 (LE16.50), and 0700, 1000, and 1300 (LE24.50); to Luxor at 0600 and 1130 (LE6.50), and 1500 and 1600 (LE5); to Safaga at 0600, 1100, 1500, and 1700 (LE3); and to Qusir at 0500 and 1500 (LE5). At Suez, you can connect with the buses to Sinai.

By Service Taxi: The service taxis park on the main street and, for slightly higher prices than the buses, serve the same cities: Safaga, LE2.50; Qina, LE7; Luxor, LE10; Qusir, LE5; Marsa Alam (you may have to wait), LE10; Suez, LE15; and Cairo, LE20. Multiply the price by seven and you can have a private taxi to any of these areas.

By Car: The roads between Hurghada and Cairo, Suez, or Luxor are good, but there is no gas en route. The trip to Cairo takes about five hours, Suez about the same.

By Boat: The Spring Tours ferry (tel. 443-003, LE60) to Sharm al-Sheikh (five hours) leaves at 0900 on Sat., Mon., and Wed.; Sea Cruise's *Golden Sun* leaves at 0900 on Sun., Tues., and Thurs., same fare. Get tickets at least a day in advance beside EgyptAir at the mosque for Spring Tours, and across from the bank for Sea Cruises.

TO THE SOUTH

As the dive sites have gotten more crowded around Hurghada, visitors have headed south. Developers have not been far behind, and plush resorts of the type that mar the Hurghada coastline are budding along the virgin beaches.

Safaga

Accommodations: Originally a port for the phosphate mines, the area is being discovered, with a bevy of expensive resorts springing up south of town. The **Safaga Paradise**, tel. 451-631-9, fax 451-630, offers villas scattered amongst pleasant gardens, some with a beach view, all with private bath, a/c; rooms are $53.55 s, $73.78 d, $82.11 t, including breakfast. In Cairo, get reservations at 33 Sh. Husni Saleh (by Sudan), Mohandiseen, tel. 347-1015. Amenities include an attached dive center and standard recreational opportunities: sailboarding, health club, tennis, etc. The less expensive **Lotus Bay** has clean, nice rooms with half-board for $25 s, $50 d, and $65 t, making this hotel with its private beach a good deal. Reserve rooms from Cairo at 2 Sh. al-Qarum, Mohandiseen, tel. 360- 5987, fax 701-782. A step farther down is the clean but older **Elokby Village**, tel. 410-414, which offers fans, hot water all day, and a swimming pool. Rooms with private baths and breakfast run LE25 s, LE50 d, and LE75 t; chalets include two rooms (four people), a stove, a refrigerator, and a sitting area for LE100.

The best deal in town is the **Cleopatra**, downtown, which has spotless rooms with new private baths for LE40 s, LE50 d, and LE55 t, including breakfast. The **Maka Hotel**, tel. 541-621, offers clean rooms with baths outside; LE6 s, LE12 d. Reserve the neighboring **Maro-Fioz** for emergencies.

Camping: You can camp on the beach at **Sun Beach Camping** near the turnoff to the Lotus Bay Hotel, tel. 451-811. Showers with hot water are included in the LE5 pp. Or you can sleep in the bungalows for LE60 s, LE90 d, which includes half-board. If you opt for an outdoor bath, it runs about LE15 less. Breakfasts are available for LE5, dinners for LE15.

Transport: The **bus** station lies at the south end of town where the two roads meet; both East Delta and Upper Egypt lines stop here. Two deluxe buses serve Qusir: 0545 (LE3) and 1545 (LE4); third-class buses run to Hurghada all day, but the deluxe ones (LE5) leave at 1700, 1830, 1930, and 2030; to Cairo at 1500 (LE27); to Suez at 0745, 0815, and sometimes 0900 (LE11); and to Luxor at 0645 and 1245 (LE5). **Service taxis** hang out at the other end of town above the soccer pitch: Qusir, LE3; Hurghada, LE2.50, Qina, LE6. **Private taxis** to Qusir run LE45; to Hurghada, LE40, and to Luxor, LE120. **Gas** is available at the service station on the main road.

Qusir

Beyond Safaga, mangroves start appearing along the beaches, and the Red Sea mountains send jagged, saw-tooth ridges skyward. The medieval port of Qusir lies 85 km south of Safaga and about 160 km east of Qift, which is on the Nile River. A port since Roman times, the town was a thriving trade and export center as well as host to numerous pilgrims to Mecca. With the completion of the Suez Canal, the town shriveled, and today little remains but an old fort in the center of town (worth a quick look), a small *suq*, and a snorkeling beach about 5½ km north of town. To the south, check with the Red Sea Diving Safari for dive information.

Practicalities: The only place to stay is the **Sea Princess**, toward the south end of town (around the bend at the fortress), tel. 430-044. Very clean, small rooms with fans and shared baths run LE9 s, LE14 d, and LE24t; there's a rooftop garden and a restaurant below. The **bus** station lies down the road, around the corner to the left; it's across from the restaurant on your left. Buses to Safaga leave at 0500 and 0800 (LE4) and on to Hurghada (LE6); to Marsa Alam, on Mon., Tues., Fri., and Sun. sometime between 1500 and 1700 (LE5). **Service taxis** stand south of town: to Safaga, LE3; to Hurghada, LE5; to Marsa Alam, LE5; to Qurna, LE7.

Marsa Alam

To the south, the desert *reg* marches right down to the sea. Plants and bushes become more numerous. The town is little more than a crossroads, a fishing village grown up around the road to Idfu. There is little but a small store and a gas station; foreigners are not permitted beyond here without special permits.

THE SINAI PENINSULA

As the "great and terrible wilderness" of Exodus, Sinai was the early home of Jehovah, the birthplace of monotheism and much of Western law, and where Moses is said to have received the Ten Commandments. But mostly, Sinai has been used as a military corridor and buffer, its history dominated by wars, most recently the Arab-Israeli conflicts of the past four decades.

Peaceful once more, however, Sinai beckons modern tourists and pilgrims. The southern coastline offers clear water and clean beaches, kilometers of coral reefs and shelves, and some of the best snorkeling and skin diving in the world.

A triangular thumb wedged into the north end of the Red Sea, Sinai covers about 37,600 square km. The peninsula's northern coast sweeps along the Mediterranean in a 240-km arc from Egypt's Port Said to the Gaza Strip in Palestine. A broad plain extending inland about 25 km south rises slowly from the coast; the flat surface once washed by ancient seas is now classic desert marked by silken, shifting dunes, which are steadily creeping south.

In the central part of the peninsula, the sand stops abruptly at the forbidding gravel and limestone escarpment that marks the beginning of the al-Tih ("The Wandering") Plateau. Cleaved by the Gidi and Mitla passes, this harsh landscape, rich in minerals, is dotted with only an occasional oasis. As the peninsula narrows, the irregular tableland tilts gradually upward, finally erupting into startling brown, gray, and red craggy granite mountains. The tallest of these is Gebel Catherine, rising nearly 2,600 meters; neighboring Gebel Musa (Mt. Sinai) where tradition says Moses received the Ten Commandments, soars 2,250 meters into the clear sky.

Nearly 400 km to the south at Ras Muhammad, the peninsula ends. The eastern coast is separated from Saudi Arabia by the Gulf of Aqaba. Above the gulf, the northeastern angle of Sinai joins the southern end of Israel's Negev Desert, and at Taba, Egypt joins Israel and Jordan.

PRACTICALITIES

Sights
Sinai offers rugged, starkly beautiful terrain, beaches for swimming and sunning, and some of the most spectacular dive sites in the world. In addition to underwater activities, visitors can rent sailboarding equipment, water-ski, or take boat trips to offshore islands. Inland, visit the Monastery of St. Catherine and, if you're driving, the Oasis of Firan. Bedouins can take you camel (or jeep) trekking to visit the desolate beauty of the interior, an experience without equal.

Regulations
Visitors to Sinai must have a valid Egyptian visa, either regular or for Sinai only. If you'll be leaving Egypt and returning, even for a jaunt into Elat, be sure to get a reentry visa before you go. Because of leftover mines, visitors are not permitted off the main road without special permits. Be especially wary of uninhabited beaches, for people have been killed by old mines. Camping is prohibited on some beaches, most notably Na'ama Bay; the areas are often not posted, so ask before you make camp. Nude bathing is illegal.

To import a car you will need a triptych or *carnet de passage en douane*. Be sure to get one *before* you enter Egypt; it is nearly impossible to get one once you're in the country. (See p. 121.) You will also need a valid international driver's license. Bringing rental cars across the border is difficult, especially for a one-way trip; be sure you check with the rental company; most prohibit it. If you will be returning to Saudi Arabia, customs there may strip-search your vehicle, looking for alcohol, pork, or pornography.

Accommodations
In response to increasing demand, Egyptians have scrambled to add more hotel space in Sinai, especially in the south. Unfortunately, new building has simply focused on expensive hotels complete with swimming pools and health clubs. Inexpensive accommodations are rare: a few places with rush bungalows or pre-pitched

tents. Such tents, however, have been banished from Na'ama Bay. Camping gear is not readily available here, so bring your own.

Food And Supplies
Although the major towns have "supermarkets," you may not be able to get exactly what you want. Supplies are more expensive than in Cairo, so bring most of what you'll need.

Food: These stores stock a limited selection of canned goods, so you'll either have to stock up before your trip or avail yourself of the local restaurants. Some areas have quite good establishments, but in general, you'll have to subsist on hotel fare.

Water: Along much of the southern coast, water is scarce. In Sharm al-Sheikh, water is only available for a couple of hours in the morning, and occasionally at night. Most hotels have tanks to get through the day, but wherever you can conserve on water, do so. Some water supplies may be brackish, for the wells are shallow and the salts seep in.

Warning: Do not swim off the coasts, either Mediterranean or Red Sea, at night. Police are on the watch for smugglers and you could be shot on sight. Night dives with a licensed diving center are safe.

TRANSPORTATION

The easiest way to visit Sinai is on a tour, but such trips cannot capture the nearly unspoiled wilderness. Far better is to travel in a small group of your own, preferably by car, which will enable you to get around easier once you're on the coast. If you've been itching to rent a camper, a trip to Sinai is a good excuse; the roads are good and gas is available. If possible, take two vehicles and caravan, for much of Sinai is unpopulated and desolate, and traffic is light; car trouble can make life exceedingly uncomfortable.

By Plane
Air Sinai flies into Sharm al-Sheikh, St. Catherine's, and Hurghada, as well as to al-Arish, Tel Aviv, and Elat. Check with their offices, any travel agent, or the reception desks at the major hotels for flight times and current prices. **El Al** also flies the same routes, as does **Zas**.

By Bus
East Delta Bus Lines connects Cairo with north and south Sinai. The main Cairo office is near Midan Abbassia, the Sinai Terminal (Mahattat Seena), tel. (02) 824-753/824-999. Buses link all the major towns, and often have a/c and video. They run along the coast or cut through the center of the peninsula to serve St. Catherine. Buses run to Cairo directly, leaving at 0700, 1000, 1300, 1630, 1730, 2330, and 2400 (the last three have a/c). The trip takes 8-14 hours and you can buy your tickets 24 hours ahead of time at the office in Sharm; it lies down the hill from the main town, is usually open during the day and an hour or so before the buses leave, but its hours can be erratic. **Super Jet** runs buses directly into Jordan; for prices and schedules, inquire in Cairo.

By Car
To reach al-Arish and the northern coast, you must cross the canal (at Ahmed Hamdi Tunnel is easiest) and head north to Kantra East. To get to south Sinai, go through the Ahmed Hamdi Tunnel, and then head south along the coast; road signs are in English as well as Arabic. If you want to see St. Catherine, take the Firan Oasis road at Abu Rudeis, otherwise continue south to Sharm; from Cairo figure two hours to the tunnel and four more to the tip of the peninsula. The roads are all hardtop and generally good; gas is available at most towns, though hours may be erratic, so keep your tank topped off. There is no 90-octane gasoline in St. Catherine. The speed limit is 90 km/hour, and the Egyptian police are enforcing it. You can rent cars from Europcar (Max) in the Gazalla Hotel, tel. 600-686.

To And From Israel
Entry to north Sinai from Israel is at Rafah, to the south at Taba; remember, Egyptian border stamps from these borders are evidence you've been to Israel. If you're traveling by public transportation, you will have to hike over the border; on the Egyptian side, officials will stamp your passport and issue a visa if you need one. You'll have to visit the bank to change money (US$150 for a regular visa, US$6 for a Sinai-only visa) and then pay a tourist tax of LE6. Service taxis from Midan Ahmed Helmi serve al-Arish and Rafah. Trans-

portation within Israel is available over the border.

By Boat To Jordan
The terminal lies about eight km south of Nuwei-ba (any Nuweiba bus will drop you off if you ask, or you can catch a cab from town). Two daily ferries leave somewhere between 1000 and 1200 and 1400-1600, but the schedule is notoriously erratic. Show up about an hour before embarking for customs searches. Be prepared for customs and immigration hassles at either end; you're traveling with the locals now; it's a lesson in how they have to deal with their own governments. You will be leaving the country, so you'll have to show bank receipts that you changed money legally, or change more on the spot. **Remember:** if you have evidence of a visit to Israel in your passport, you may be allowed on the ferry, but you will *not be allowed to disembark in Jordan*. Normally you can buy tickets when you arrive, unless it's an Egyptian holiday, when the buses and ferries will be crammed with workers. You can get a Jordanian visa on board, but it's easier before you go. Your passport will be held during the trip; retrieve it in Aqaba.

To Hurghada
Ferries run daily except Fri. between Sharm al-Sheikh and Hurghada (five to six hours), leaving at 0900 from the bay just north of Sharm al-Sheikh; LE60.

Getting Around
Once in Sinai, getting around without a private car can be time-consuming. Buses run along the southern coast, leaving Taba at 1400 (but in practice anywhere from 1300-1530) and servicing Nuweiba, Dahab, and Na'ama and Sharm al-Sheikh. From Sharm al-Sheikh, buses leave for Dahab (LE4) at 0800, for St. Catherine (LE8.59) at 0800, for Na'ama (LE1), Dahab, Nuweiba (LE6), and Taba (LE8) at 0900; for Nuweiba at 1700. **Taxis** are not a good way to travel here, especially for women alone; you'll spend long, isolated hours in the company of a stranger. Use them en masse and bargain hard. **Hitchhiking** is chancy, for the wide expanses of desert have little traffic; don't accept a ride unless it's all the way to your destination (or to a place where you can wait in the shade for a bus). Although most people will stop, military personnel are prohibited from picking up riders. Women should not hitchhike alone.

AL-ARISH

Blessed with beaches nearly as beautiful as Alexandria's, al-Arish is turning itself into a tourist resort. This capital of Sinai still offers a look at the Egyptian Bedouin's life as well as beaches yet uncrowded by tourists. The town's main thoroughfare, 23 July, runs north-south, from the bus station to the coast, where it meets Sh. Fuad Zakry.

Sights
The museum, which lies along the road toward Rafah, shows life (human and animal) in Sinai; displays range from stuffed birds to Bedouin handicrafts. The Bedouins gather for their weekly *suq* on Wednesday, but the beaches are the main attraction here.

Accommodations
The new **Oberoi al-Arish,** tel. 351-323, offers the most upscale rooms at $72 s, $91.20 d. The low end includes the **Moonlight Hotel,** tel. 341-362, which offers a good view of the beach for LE10-15; call ahead. The **al-Salaam Hotel,** tel. 341-219, on Sh. 23 July for LE4-8, is similar but not quite as nice.

    Camping: Possibly the best choice in al-Arish is camping. Several campgrounds string west out along the beach; two beds in a large tent run about LE6-10, or a few pounds for just a site. With permission from the police station (which may not be granted) you can camp on the beach closer to town.

Food
The town has several good local cafes: the **Aziz** and the **Sammar**, both on Sh. 23 July, are popular. The **Sinai Rose** and the **Mashribiyya** cafeterias, both on the beach, have bars and serve good salad and fish. Groceries are easily available here.

Information And Services
The **Tourist Office** is on Sh. Fuad Zakry (nearly a kilometer west of Sh. 23 July), tel. 340-569,

Sinai was a crossroads for Semitic peoples traveling from the Middle East into Egypt.

Resorts

The beaches at Ras al-Sudr make ideal swimming. The Sudr Tourist Village offers apartments and chalets (unfortunately near the refinery) for LE40 per night.

South lie the springs of Hammam Faraun (Pharaoh's Bath) where boiling waters, according to the Bedouin, cure rheumatism. In the hills beyond, accessible by four-wheel-drive vehicles only, is the Middle Kingdom temple dedicated to Hathor. Slightly south are the Old Kingdom turquoise, malachite, and copper mines at Wadi Maghara.

SOUTH SINAI

The Aqaba coast supports four main settlements: in the south, Sharm al-Sheikh and its nearby resort area of Na'ama Bay (also known as Marina Sharm after the original hotel); Dahab; Nuweiba; and the three border towns of Taba (Egyptian), Elat (Israeli), and Aqaba (Jordanian). As south Sinai's popularity increases, the government is expanding visitor facilities within these towns.

Snorkeling And Scuba

As the peninsula narrows, granite ridges thrust upward from the limestone bedrock, their windward sides scoured clean. The coast's jagged coastline, ringed by rugged and desolate mountains, is blessed with miles of reefs that often extend 30 meters straight down into the clear waters of the Gulf of Aqaba. Separated from the Indian Ocean by the 100-km shelf at Bab al-Mandeb, the Red Sea forms a nearly enclosed basin. Surrounded by desert, the sea lacks river drainage, and evaporation far exceeds the area's slight rainfall, conditions that produce an unusually warm and exceptionally salty sea.

You can rent snorkeling equipment in Sinai at the major dive centers in Na'ama Bay and Dahab. You'll need a mask, snorkel, and set of fins, preferably with full feet to protect your soles from the jagged coral or the painful spikes of the black sea urchin. Otherwise, wear tennis shoes.

To protect your body from the coral, wear an old pair of jeans; a T-shirt will save your back from severe sunburn. Although a wetsuit isn't necessary, some people like to use them in win-

open Sat.-Thurs., 0800-1400 and 1900-2200. The **Tourist Police** are next door, tel. 341-016. The **hospital,** tel. 340-010, is on Sh. Gaysh, east of Sh. Suq. The **post office** (open Sat.-Thurs. 0900-1500) and the **telephone office** (open 24 hours, international calls) share the same building just south of Sh. Fuad Zakry two blocks east of Sh. 23 July; code is 068. **Pharmacy Fuad,** a couple blocks north of the bus station on Sh. 23 July, (open 0800-2400) can put you in touch with a doctor. For emergencies, call the ambulance, tel. 340-010, or the local police, tel. 340-220.

Transportation

The bus station is on the central Midal Baladiya. Minibuses run from the bus station north to the beach; taxis charge 50-75PT. Buses from Cairo to Rafah stop in al-Arish. You can go directly to Cairo or Ismailia, but for Port Said, you must change buses in Kantra. There is no direct connection between al-Arish/Rafah and the Aqaba coast.

THE WESTERN COAST

Uyun Musa

The Springs of Moses lie in a palm grove where Moses is said to have rested with his flock. Several of the original springs remain, but the water is now undrinkable. Camping is permitted, and several of the Cairo/Sharm al-Sheikh buses stop at the resthouse.

ter when the water is a little colder, or as protection against the coral. To keep a fog from forming on your mask, cover it with saliva; if it leaks, try to reseat it, but don't open your eyes—the salty water will burn for hours. With full-face masks that leak, you can take a breath in through your nose to form a partial vacuum. When you're not swimming, protect your feet from the coral with shoes, use sunscreen liberally, keep your head covered, and drink plenty of water—even if you don't feel thirsty; drinking five to six liters per day is not excessive.

To rent scuba equipment, you have to be certified. Sinai dive shops will take you for an introductory dive for US$40 (dive shops quote prices in dollars) or for $225-250 give you a full certification course.

Accommodations

New building is most noticeable in Na'ama Bay, although resorts are springing up all along the coast. The most obvious are the plush new hotels that are turning the bay into a small Miami Beach. A few less expensive but clean and nice hotels are appearing for between LE35-60. Huts and tents (fine as long as the wind doesn't blow) run between LE10-25.

Camping: Tents are available already set up (about LE10-25), or you can bring your own (rented in Cairo), but canvas keeps out neither wind nor heat. Another option, especially for a family or group, is to rent a camper or RV in Cairo.

Food

The towns all have restaurants that serve a variety of cheap dishes, and at the hotels, nonguests can dine on fixed-menu meals, which run LE25-50. Although the selection of canned foods is limited, they're available; the supermarket in Na'ama Bay has the most varied supply as well as good-quality cheese and fresh produce. Toiletries, on the other hand, are plain scarce; take what you'll need, including toilet paper and tampons. The water is good at the tourist hotels; otherwise, stick to bottled water or use a purifier.

Services

There are **banks** only at Taba and Sharm al-Sheikh, though U.S. dollars are accepted by dive shops and hotels, and many of the new, larger hotels will change money. Mail is slow and the only **post office** is at Sharm al-Sheikh, although you can mail from most hotels. There are hospitals in Sharm and St. Catherine. The **telephone office** is in Sharm, but only for calls within Egypt; code is 062. The office will also send telegrams and telexes. You can make international calls from the large hotels in Na'ama Bay.

SHARM AL-SHEIKH

The town sits just east of the southernmost tip of the Sinai Peninsula. Apart from services, it offers little; the best diving is either just west at Ras Muhammad or at Na'ama Bay, east of Sharm. To commute between Na'ama and Sharm, catch the Ramada Residence Bus which runs every hour between the Fayrouz Village in Na'ama Bay and the Ramada Residence Hotel on the plateau at Sharm, LE1.

Accommodations And Food

The **Clifftop Village,** tel. 770-448, sits on a promontory overlooking the sea. The main building is a log cabin; the rooms are twin bungalows with a/c and private baths; $32 s, $40 d, including half-board. The **youth hostel** is good: LE11.50 includes a/c, showers, use of the kitchen, and breakfast. It's next door to the Clifftop (through the green gate), but is open to members only (open 0630-0900 and 1400-2300 in summer, 1400-2200 in winter; 2300 curfew). **Safety Land Camping** lies down the hill, tel. 600-373. You can make reservations in Cairo, 78 Sh. al-Sawra, Heliopolis, tel. 664-800/290-7866, fax 664-800. You can get rooms with a/c and breakfast for LE43 s, LE76 d; bungalows, LE25 s, LE36 d; a tent for LE13 or a camping site for LE8. Clean facilities, with plenty of hot water and a place to do your laundry, make this a good deal. Otherwise you can camp at Ras Muhammad.

Besides the hotel dining room, there are a couple of **cafes** off the main square, and near them, a **supermarket** (open 1000-1400 and 1800-2200). The best food is at the **Clifftop;** dinners run about LE20.

Practicalities

The outskirts of Sharm start at the intersection

where the Cairo road meets the Taba road. To the east of this junction, several buildings house markets; to the west, there is a gas station, the **hospital,** and a **police station.** The **main police station** is down the west branch of the road—toward the port. You'll have to go here to register your passport, if you haven't already done so. The **bus station** lies at the foot of the hill, behind the gas station and near Safety Land Camping. The buses from Cairo stop in Sharm al-Sheikh at the bus station, at the square on top of the hill, at Clifftop Village (near the youth hostel)—if you ask (and remind) them. In Na'ama Bay they stop at the Marina Sharm and Ghazala hotels, and sometimes others if you ask. The main town is on the clifftop to the south; the **Tourist Police** are halfway up the hill.

To reach the center of town, continue to the top of the hill, turn right, then turn right again; you'll end up in the main square, which has two **banks** (open Mon.-Sat. 1830-1330, Sun. 1000-1200), a **post office** (open daily, 0900-1500), and a **telephone office** (open 24 hours for calls within Egypt; code is 062). The **airport** is to the northeast, beyond Na'ama Bay toward Dahab.

NA'AMA BAY

Just northeast of Sharm, folded within a sheltered bay, is Na'ama (also called Marina Sharm); it's a diving center, and its hotels, camping spots, dive shops, restaurants, and supermarket make it the ideal spot from which to explore the area's reefs.

Dive Shops

The **Sinai Divers** at the Ghazala and the **Camel Dive Club** have the best diving equipment safety records. The **Red Sea Divers** (at the south end of the bay, next to the Marina Sharm Hotel) and the **Aquamarine,** near the hotel of the same name, offer water-skiing and sailboarding, and Red Sea Divers runs glass-bottomed boats to the reefs near the harbor.

The long-awaited medical center specializing in diving accidents is about to become reality. A director has been appointed, the land bought and fenced (between Na'ama Bay and Sharm), and the contract for the decompression chamber signed. The advanced "Hyperbaric Medical Center" should be up and running within the next year or so. The center will offer an inexpensive insurance plan for divers and will give first aid and treat traumas. A physician will be on call 24 hours. Long-range plans include a small outboard rescue boat and research facilities specializing in diving sicknesses and accidents. Currently, victims of diving accidents are flown to Israel if they are foreigners; Egyptians are sent to Cairo, so a competent local facility will be welcome.

Dive Sites

Na'ama offers two sites within walking distance at the north end of the bay. The **Near Gardens** are just beyond the shoulder at the northeast end of the bay (past the Aquamarine Hotel and the end of the beach), but unfortunately much of the reef has died off here. The **Far Gardens** lie about a half-hour's walk farther northeast. The corals harbor undersea foliage and fish of

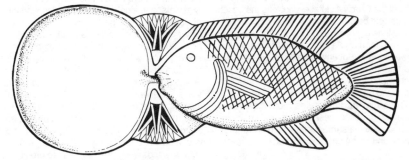

The varied fishes of the Red Sea appeared as motifs in Egyptian arts, as in this carved wooden spoon.

exquisite colors. If you tire of these areas, the local dive shops will take you to the more distant and even more beautiful **Tiran Island** and **Ras Muhammad**. Although these sites offer the most wildly beautiful, incandescent-colored fish and coral, you can take shorter trips to nearly as exotic **Ras Masrani, Ras Umm Sidd,** and other reefs. Trips start at US$35 and up.

Accommodations

Once only the fiberglass geodesic domes of the three-star **Marina Sharm Hotel** dominated the south end of the bay; the more traditional rooms occupy the long building behind. Now the entire shore stands shoulder-deep in hotels; the Movenpicke spills across the road and claws its way up the *wadi*. Among the high-priced hotels, the Hilton's **Fayrouz Village**, tel. 769-400, in the center of the bay's curve is the nicest for the money, with private bungalows scattered in a garden. The neighboring **Ghazala Hotel** dominates the center of the bay's curve and is nearly as nice. Behind it, the **Sanafir Hotel** is not only as inexpensive ($40 s, $52 d) but offers rush huts ($11) that have access to good, clean baths; it's an inexpensive way to go if it's not cold or windy.

Gafy Land, which was once a tent enclave, has blossomed into the best deal in Na'ama Bay: spotless rooms with private bath and a/c run LE39 s, and LE51 d. You cannot camp on the beach.

Food

The hotels offer good, fixed-menu meals and evening buffets; inquire at the Fayrouz Village about their Bedouin dinner under the stars. The patio at the Ghazala Hotel overlooking the beach serves cold beer and good food, if you don't die by the time it gets to you. The Sanafir has good Egyptian food and a smattering of other ethnic cafes; none are overly expensive. Even better and less expensive is the little cafe next to the supermarket, off the beach road at the south end of the bay.

The **supermarket** carries a good selection of canned goods, cheese, yogurt, and fresh produce, as well as suntan lotion, skin cream, toiletries, and some snorkeling gear.

Entertainment

Where once only the discos at the Marina Sharm and the covered deck in the middle of the shore and the occasional underwater slide show put on by a dive club provided entertainment, now the resorts' mission is to never allow you a bored moment. They all have programs and activities, including everything from horseback riding and treks into the desert for a Bedouin dinner, to flying over the bay. Check in any lobby for their programs. For free, you can walk down to the docks beyond the Marina Sharm Hotel and watch the dive boats come in around 1600; listen to the waves and relax.

RAS MUHAMMAD

The acute angle forming the tip of the peninsula is coated by a coral wall that drops vertically into the salty sea. The reef, now a national park protected by the 1983 Nature Conservation Law, is difficult to reach without a car; the easiest way to get there is through one of the dive clubs. The turnoff to the park is up the west coast road beyond Sharm heading for Cairo.

The swimming and diving area is the coral shelf just west of the shark lookout. Here, a nice, if small, beach runs into a pale coral shelf where crabs and sea anemones bask in the clear, warm water. Where the shelf plunges into the blue depths you enter a world of brilliant blue, turquoise, and yellow-gold fish swimming among pink, green, yellow, and red corals—staghorn and lace. The limestone cliffs, scooped out by centuries of surf, offer some shade, but otherwise the area is hot and barren; take plenty of water and food, towels, umbrellas, and a lot of sunscreen. The park now boasts rangers who patrol the land and dive to take care of the new underwater nature trails. The rangers themselves, most with university degrees, hauled rock to mark the roads, and they spend considerable amounts of time cleaning up the debris that still washes in from the Red Sea. Their efforts, however are paying off. The mangroves, their roots now freed from trash and plastic, are reproducing. The animals benefit too; the beach is closed while turtles lay their eggs, and the shallow sands where the eels live are protected. Fox, osprey, ibex, and gazelle are returning.

ALLAN HANSEN

*the rugged
Red Sea Coast
at Ras Muhammad*

To dive here, you must anchor your boat to a permanent mooring; do not risk damaging the fragile bottom with an anchor. By limiting each mooring to one boat, the management effectively controls usage. A new visitor's center with a small buffet overlooks the sea; the management promises *no music.* From the terrace you can see Saudi Arabia (use the free telescopes if you wish) or walk down the short path to the shore, crossing from ancient coral to modern. In addition, a gallery hangs changing displays of Red Sea art, and a public library will soon open; all facilities are fully handicapped-accessible.

Campsites, open to the public with permission from the management, are along the beach in secluded niches, making camping an almost private affair. The necessary boat dock was designed to accommodate the natural flow of the water, control erosion, and blend with the surroundings. Sunshades for the beaches blend into the cliffs, and these areas are spotless. The rangers are educating their visitors, and it shows. If Ras Muhammad isn't careful it may become an international example of what a national park can and should be.

MONASTERY OF ST. CATHERINE AND VICINITY

The Monastery of St. Catherine nestles at the foot of Mt. Sinai, buffered only by the lush gardens tended by the monks. Traditional site of the burning bush and Moses' reception of the Ten Commandments, the fortress dates from the 6th century and is the oldest unrestored basilica in continuous use. The monastery is open 0900-1200 except Fri. and Sun., when it's firmly closed. It's also closed on feast days; check with the Greek Orthodox office in Cairo (see below).

The village of St. Catherine lies about two km down the road from the monastery turnoff. The hotel complex of St. Catherine's Village lies at the circular *midan,* and the monastery is up the paved road nearly two km. The airport is 12 km out of town.

History

Founded in the middle of the 4th century by Empress Helena (Constantine's mother), its oldest buildings included a chapel at the site of the burning bush, where God revealed himself to Moses, ordering him to return to Egypt and bring the Children of Israel into Sinai. In the 6th century A.D., Justinian ordered the present basilica built and had it and the older buildings enclosed by a fortress wall to protect monks and pilgrims from raiding Bedouins.

Throughout the ensuing centuries, this fortress, known as the Monastery of the Transfiguration, was singularly undisturbed by the wars fought in the rest of Sinai. Muhammad, at the request of a group of monks that traveled to Mecca, granted his protection and patronage; a copy of his document still resides in the monastery's library. Nevertheless, many of the inhabitants either converted to Islam or fled, and the monastery's population gradually dwindled until by the 9th century only about 30 monks remained. In the 11th century, probably to placate less benevolent Muslim rulers, the monks added the mosque within the compound.

In the Middle Ages, the monastery experienced a brief resurgence when both its monks and pilgrims came under the protection of the Sinaite Order of Crusader Knights. With the Christians' defeat however, the monastery weathered a difficult time until Sultan Salim I, in 1517, brought the monks protection once more.

During the 17th century, the monastery maintained extensive properties and schools throughout the Mediterranean and Europe. When Napoleon conquered Egypt he extended his protection to St. Catherine's; the documentation is also preserved in the monastery library.

the belltower at St. Catherine's Monastery

Although in the 19th and 20th centuries the monastery lost most of its foreign holdings, it nevertheless has remained viable and in 1966 celebrated its 1,400th anniversary.

St. Catherine
The monastery takes its modern name from the early martyr, St. Catherine. A daughter of an aristocratic family, she was born Dorothea at Alexandria in A.D. 294. The beautiful young woman was educated in philosophy, rhetoric, poetry, music, physics, mathematics, astronomy, and medicine. When a Syrian monk converted her to Christianity, she was baptized as Catherine.

In the reign of Maximus (early 4th century), she publicly accused the emperor of sacrificing to pagan idols. Although 50 wise men tried to change her persuasions, she instead used her classical education to convert them to her own beliefs. Maximus, resorting to torture, ordered her bound to spiked wheels, but she was unrepentant, converting members of the Roman aristocracy as well as some of the emperor's own family, until she was finally beheaded.

After her execution, her body vanished— transported by angels, it's maintained, to Mt. St. Catherine in Sinai. Here, in the 9th century, monks from the monastery, guided by a dream, found her body miraculously preserved and brought her to rest in the basilica. She became a major saint, and since the 11th century the Monastery of the Transfiguration has also been named after her.

The Monastery
The plan of the monastery is simple, its four walls forming a rough square. Buildings line its walls, jutting outward, creating a jigsaw puzzle of structures that fill the interior courtyard. The monastery orchards line the entrance road, which leads to a set of steps giving onto an outer courtyard. Today the entrance is to your left, down the ramp and around the corner, near the original door, set into the southern towers. The entrance goes by a small shop, then opens into the courtyard. The basilica is straight ahead; the burning bush is down the walkway to your left.

The Basilica
Constructed in A.D. 542, the granite building incorporates St. Helen's Chapel of the Burning

Bush. The walls, pillars, and roof date from the original construction, but the ceiling, floor, iconostasis, and the interior decorations are all 17-18th century. At the entrance, the painting of the transfiguration on the tympanum below the granite arch was added later, as was the glass door installed to protect the 12th century wooden (Crusader) doors that open into the narthex.

The narthex: A miniature museum, it displays some of the monastery's 2,000 icons. The collection spans 15 centuries, and embodies, both historically and stylistically, the trends and techniques of Byzantine art. The earliest (6-10th century) icons are done in encaustic, a technique in which wax and vegetable pigments are mixed at high temperature and then spread, still hot, onto wood, or more rarely, marble. The paint penetrates the pores and when cool becomes indelible. The technique, known from antiquity, was replaced around the 10th century, when tempera became more popular.

The doors opening into the church proper are original, dating from the days of Justinian and carved by a Byzantine artist who cut reliefs of birds, animals, flowers, and leaves into the four-part panels of Lebanese cedar. The central aisle is flanked by monolithic granite columns, whitewashed and bearing the icons of saints venerated each month. The capitals, which are reminiscent of the Ptolemaic composite ones, have crosses, flags, grapes, and lambs worked into their curving leaves. The 18th century ceiling has openings in the shape of the sun and crescent moon, through which the sun and moon are said to shine on Easter. Unfortunately, a rope stretched across the near end of the church prevents visitors from examining the iconostasis of gilded wood, carved in Crete in 1612. The massive library of ancient theological manuscripts and its icons are off-limits except to experts who have made proper application to the monks.

The North Side

The old bell tower dominates the northwest corner of the basilica. Built in 1817 by a Sinai monk, the tower has nine various-sized bells presented by Russia. The *talanton* (wooden bell) is rung for daily vespers; the metal ones are reserved for communion and holy days. Directly north is Moses' well, now fitted with a hand pump. At the back of the basilica grows the thorny, evergreen burning bush.

The Gardens

The work of tireless monks who brought in the soil and made tanks to provide irrigation from rainwater and melted snow, the long, triangular gardens push back the desert. From this oasis amid granite mountains and barren wilderness the monks coax olives, apricots, plums, and cherries into bloom. They also grow their own vegetables, the main part of their diet.

The Sinaite Monastic Order

Since the 6th century, the religious order that occupies St. Catherine's Monastery has been independent, although it observes the canon of the Eastern Orthodox Church. As independents they are completely self-governed. Members arise at 0400, attend matins and holy liturgy until 0730, when they split up to work. They meet again at 1500 for evening prayers, after which they partake of their one communal meal of the day.

The Bedouin who help the monks and guard the monastery are members of the Gebeliya tribe, but they trace their families to the Greek slaves originally brought from Anatolia and Alexandria in the time of Justinian and therefore consider themselves Greek, not Arab. Though Muslim, they have retained some of their Christian heritage, celebrating the feast of Moses on the mountain peak, believing in St. Catherine, and looking to the archbishop to settle their problems and disputes.

Gebel Musa (Mt. Sinai)

A hike up Gebel Musa, traditional site of the biblical Mt. Horeb where Moses received the Tablets of the Law, is worth the trek, but the climb is for the hardy; start in early morning or late afternoon, avoiding the heat of the day. Camping is forbidden, but the restriction is not always enforced; if you insist, be sure to bring warm clothes and a sleeping bag—there is little room at the top and no place to pitch a tent.

The Holy Peak is a 2½-hour hike from the monastery. The easiest route is the camel path. It's wide and has good footing; it starts 50 meters behind the monastery's back wall and is clearly marked by stone curbs. The only junction in the path occurs at the top of the ridge about two-thirds of the way up (beyond the stone cleft), where the path from the stairs connects. It will come in from your right, the peak lies to the left, up the rudimentary steps.

At this fork, look downhill to the small plain. A 500-year-old cypress tree marks the area where the prophet Elijah heard the voice of God (I Kings 19:9-18). Two chapels, one dedicated to Elijah, the other to his successor Elisha, occupy the site. The area makes a nice rest stop.

At the summit, the chapel dedicated to the Holy Trinity was built in 1934 of stones from an earlier church first erected by Justinian. To the north lies a cave within which God sheltered Moses: "I will put thee in a cleft of the rock, and will cover thee with my hand while I pass by." (Exodus 33:22).

To descend, you can take the 3,750 **Steps of Repentance,** which make a short but steep path. Rather than returning through the cleft, go straight down, past Elijah's chapels; bear slightly to the right, and head down the steps. Built by a pious monk fulfilling his pledge of penitence, they are arduous and tricky by day and treacherous by night, so take care.

Gebel Catherine

Named after the saint discovered at the top, this mountain is the highest in Egypt. A pathway, which starts at in the village rather than at the monastery, is more secluded and beautiful than the one up Gebel Musa. At the top is a chapel that marks the position of St. Catherine's remains. You will need to contact the mayor (sheikh) in St. Catherine's Village, who will give you permission and hire a guide. (It is illegal to hike in Sinai without a local guide.) The climb is more arduous than Gebel Musa, but the path is clearer and the peak is higher—from it you can see from the Red Sea coast of Egypt to the mountains of Saudi Arabia on a clear day.

Accommodations

Accommodations vary in St. Catherine from the primitive dorms at the monastery to the relatively upscale tourist village. To ensure a room at the monastery, check in early: 0800-1430 and 1700-1900; the gates are firmly closed at 2130. Cost is LE25 for bunk beds in clean dorm rooms (mixed sexes), but they have no fans or showers.

At the end of the monastery road is the **St. Catherine Tourist Village,** Wadi Raha, tel. 770-221, which rents chalets with twin beds, a/c, private baths, and small verandas; the place is way overpriced at $100-130. The smaller hotels toward the village are better. The neighboring stone bungalows of **Farouz Village** are spotless but without a/c: LE56 gets you the whole thing, including a private bath. Or opt for a room in the hostel, LE11.50, or a tent, LE5.25. Across the road, the **Daniela Village** offers rooms with a/c and a private bath for $24 s, $31 d, and $37 t; meals are available.

Camp at **Zeitouna Camping,** about five km down the road to Nuweiba. Tents run LE12 pp; communal showers (cold) and toilets.

Food

You can eat at the hotel's dining room, or try the little village restaurant next to the bus stop. Next to the restaurant is a small supermarket; a larger one (Katreen) behind the gas station a little way down the road carries canned goods and other supplies. A series of well-stocked markets occupy a long metal building on the left as you go into town. Or try the inexpensive **Cafeteria al-Ekhlas,** open 0600-2000.

Services

The town itself lies down the road from the bus station. The **police station** is at the end of the town's only square. The 24-hour **hospital** is close by. The **post office** is open Sat.-Thurs., 0800-1400; the **telephone office,** open 24-hours, offers international service; code is 062. There are gas stations both at the fork where the monastery road branches off and in the town of St. Catherine; there is no 90-octane gasoline available.

Transportation

The airport at St. Catherine lies 12 km from the village. The bus station lies on the outskirts of the village, near the hotel. Schedules are erratic, but buses are supposed to leave for Cairo at 0600, 0900, 1330; for Dahab and Sharm al-Sheikh at 1300; and for Nuweiba and Taba at 1330. If you want to visit the monastery on your way in, ask the driver to drop you at the turnoff before town. You can occasionally get service taxis into Dahab. If you're traveling by car, you can reach the monastery either from the turnoff to the Firan Oasis on the west coast or from the interior road (now well paved), which leaves the east coast near Dahab.

DAHAB

In Arabic, *dahab* is gold, and in truth, the village is perhaps Sinai's most treasured spot, cradled by spectacular mountains and fronted by fringes of palms set into glittering beaches; and beyond, the clear blue waters harbor coral reefs. The best of these are at the north and south ends of the cove of which the tourist village occupies the center. The native Bedouins live in a village to the north, off the road just past the MFO base and blue gateway. But like many areas in Egypt, it's becoming tarnished with development and the unhappy chemistry that changes visitors into rude invaders and Egyptians into aggressive hawksters. The tourist village is now run by Pullman and the renovations are reflected in the hefty price tag. The Bedouin village, once a welcoming and relaxing place to escape, now feels ominous; drug dealing is rampant here. The bright spot is the Dive Center and the nearby hotel. Make these your centers for exploring Dahab. Some of the most beautiful dive sites lie tucked into the scalloped coast here, and the bay's steady wind and sheltered cove make it one of the best sailboarding areas in Sinai.

Diving
The **INMO Dive Shop,** P.O. Box 15, Dahab, tel. 770-788 (ask for INMO), lies between the Bedouin village and the tourist village. It's equal to the best in Na'ama Bay; competitive prices are quoted in US$, but you can pay in LE. If you order ahead you can get a super diver's lunch: vegetarian LE7, with meat LE10. The dive sites are located on the map in the shop, or you can just walk to either end of the cove to where the surf breaks over the coral, but better sites lie outside the town itself. Some of these areas, such as the Blue Hole, are technically difficult and can be dangerous; ask at the shop, and if they recommend a guide, take one.

Camel Trekking
The Bedouin in the northern village run camel treks into the interior. A good day-trip is to **Wadi Gnay,** a small oasis and village (pay when you return).

Accommodations
The **Dahab Holiday Village** by the beach, tel. 770-788/290-8802, fax 258-7490, is not quite running full speed, although their recreational programs are starting. Rooms come in several flavors and run $28-35 s and $38-50 d. The best hotel for the money, however, is the simple but clean **Gulf,** the white and blue building south of INMO Dive Shop. Rooms with a separate shower, LE28; with a private shower, LE38; hot water on request.

At the **Bedouin village** you can rent thatched or stone huts for about LE6 pp; some have cold showers. The cleanest appear along the southern end of the camp. Ask before you photograph people here. Egyptians are not permitted to stay at the village.

Food
At the bus station, the small cafe sells bottled water and sandwiches. The hotel restaurant is behind the kiosk, or you can eat in the hotel; check in the main lobby for hours and prices. For cheaper fare, try the Bedouin village, which has good native foods, along the street that turns into the *suq* at the northern end.

Practicalities
The town is split into three parts: the tourist village area, where the bus stops; the central business area that lies up the hill; and the Bedouin village to the northeast. In the central town, the **telephone office,** open 24 hours, has no international lines. The **post office** is open Sat.-Thurs., 0830-1500. The **supermarket** is open 0800-2200 (1700-2000 in winter).

By the tourist village hotel, the **police** are across the parking lot from the **bus stop.** Several buses a day pass through Dahab linking it to Sharm al-Sheikh (a.m. and p.m.); to Suez (a.m.); to Cairo (a.m. and p.m.); to Taba via Nuweiba (a.m.); to Nuweiba directly (a.m. and p.m.); and to St. Catherine (a.m.). Buses load up and leave after they arrive; drivers do not adhere strictly to departure time. Although they are usually late, they've been known to leave up to 30 minutes early. Several **service taxis** are based in the

Bedouin village, but they're expensive; you'll have to bargain hard.

NUWEIBA

Located some 85 km north of Dahab, Nuweiba sits in a plain between the Gulf of Aqaba and the high desert mountains, its reefs offering delights as beautiful as its sister towns to the south. The holiday village is similar to the one in Dahab, built by the Israelis. The Bedouin who run most of the tourist facilities live in two nearby villages: Nuweiba Tarabin, two km north of the town, and Nuweiba Muzayana, seven km to the south, the location of the port and several adequate hotels. The tourist village lies slightly north of the main town. The town itself contains a fish restaurant, the kiosk and bus station, the bathroom and shower facilities, and beyond them a series of fish and chip shops.

Water Sports
You can rent masks, snorkels, and fins from the **sailing club** on the north end of the beach, as well as kayaks and canoes; no scuba gear. The beaches lie along shallow coves and make good swimming areas, especially for children. The diving is better to the south.

Camel Trekking
The best trips to the interior start from Nuweiba; you can get a Bedouin guide for one or several day trips, either by jeep or camel. The road to **Ain Furtaga** runs through a *wadi* cut by the freshwater springs at the oasis, and the scenery is spectacular. Another day extends the trip to **Ain Hudra,** which is well worth the time and money. Or visit the Colored Canyon or Ayn Umm Ahmed; take several days and travel deep into the interior of the Sinai mountains by camel or jeep. To find a guide ask at the fish and chip shops or at the villages. Your guide will have to take your passport to the police the day before and get permission to take you into the interior. Once your route is planned, don't ask your guide to deviate; he could get in serious trouble with the government.

Accommodations And Food
Nuweiba Holiday Village, tel. 770-395, fax 392-2228, has rooms for $61 s, $78.50 d, and $89.50 t, including breakfast; lunch runs $21 and dinner $22.50. They also have small bungalows: $31.50 s, $40.50 d, and $50 t. Both let you use the pool and private beach. You can make reservations in Cairo: 32 Sh. Sabry Abu Alam, tel./fax (02) 768-832. A less expensive option, to the north through the dumpy end of town, is the clean and typically Egyptian **al-Salaam Village,** tel. 392-8830, telex 93939. You can have a room in the modern "caravans" (portable housing) for LE40 s and LE52 d; in the main building for LE38 s and LE52 d; all include breakfast.

Camping on the beach is no longer permitted, but the tourist village runs a campground with permanent tents and bungalows. Showers and toilets are in a separate building, open 0700-2000.

Several small restaurants offer fish meals and drinks; the quality varies but is usually okay. Canned food is not easily available.

Practicalities
The services center on the holiday village; to change money, make international calls, or ask about extended trips into the Sinai mountains, inquire at the main reception desk. The **Tourist Police** are near here; the regular **police** are down the road near the camp.

Transportation
The **bus station** is in the center of the town, toward the road rather than the beach, but buses usually stop at the entrance to the tourist village in the north. Buses run north to Taba (0630, 1000, 1200, 1530), south to Sharm al-Sheikh via Dahab (0700, 1400, and 1600), to St. Catharine (0630, 1100, and 1400), west to Suez (0530, 0630, and 0730) and to Suez continuing to Cairo (1100 and 1400). A bus directly to Cairo leaves from the port at 2300.

The Port
The one main road that leads from the north into the port will be lined with cars and trucks waiting for the ferry. Along this road, you will find a *suq,* two banks, and the bus station. The **Barracuda Hotel** is clean and neat if simple, and offers rooms for LE41 s, LE53 d, and LE70 t. You can make reservations in Cairo: 10 Sh. Talaat Harb, tel. 354-8754, fax 354-0598. This

central hotel's a good place to spend the night if you're coming off the ferry. About three km southwest of the port, the more upscale **Sayadin Village,** tel. 757-398, offers quiet, clean rooms for $38.55 s, $50.45 d, and $60.75 t, including breakfast, a private bath and a/c. You can make reservations through the Nile Hilton.

Toward Taba

Between Nuweiba and Taba, the road dips close to the coast, threading its way between the brilliant mountains and azure waters. Lots of easily accessible beaches offer diving and snorkeling, or you can just throw out a sleeping bag. Several new and creative developments are springing up along the road north of Nuweiba. Family-style camping at **Basata** (about 20 km up the road) lets you sleep in bamboo huts or pitch a tent. Use the kitchen and pay only LE5-12/day for the food you use. Showers are available, but not hot water. You can rent snorkel equipment or arrange camel (LE65/day) or jeep (LE45/day) treks to the interior.

More luxurious, and perhaps the best deal, is **Sally Land,** tel. 743-689; rooms with private baths and a/c run LE33 s, LE45 d, and LE60 t, including breakfast. The quiet, private beach opens outside the modern stone buildings. Good service, food, and amiable atmosphere make this isolated jewel an inexpensive getaway. You can make reservations in Cairo between 1730-2200 at 743-689.

Taba

Taba marks the border with Israel and includes a couple of hotels and **Pharoah's Island,** site of a medieval fortress built by Salah al-Din and restored by the Antiquities Organization. It lies about five km south of Taba and is reached by a launch (LE3.50), which runs on demand from 0900 to 1700. The island (LE8) offers a great view and a place to clamber about on the ruins.

Accommodations include the **Taba Hilton,** on Taba Beach in the city itself, tel. 768-200, fax 707-044, which charges typical Hilton prices for its activities, including a private beach and a swimming pool complete with a central island bar. Across from Pharoah's Island, the **Salah al-Din,** tel. 771-345, offers nice accommodations for considerably less.

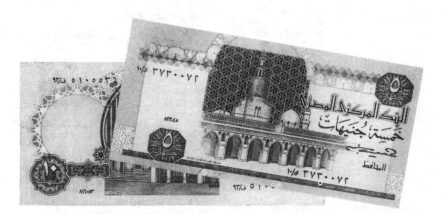

BOOKLIST

ANCIENT EGYPT

Aldred, Cyril. *Egyptian Art.* New York: Oxford University Press, 1980.

Badawy, Alexander. *A History of Egyptian Architecture: From the Earliest Times to the End of the Old Kingdom.* Berkeley: University of California Press, 1948. This readable series is the best source for understanding the development of ancient Egyptian architecture.

————. *A History of Egyptian Architecture: The First Intermediate Period, the Middle Kingdom, and the Second Intermediate Period.* Berkeley: University of California Press, 1966.

————. *A History of Egyptian Architecture: The Empire (New Kingdom).* Berkeley: University of California Press, 1968.

Baines, John, and Jaromir Malek. *Atlas of Ancient Egypt.* New York: Facts on File, 1980. A good description of the pharaonic monuments along the Nile.

Bowman, Alan K. *Egypt after the Pharaohs.* Berkeley: University of California Press, 1986. A good summery of Greco-Roman Egypt.

Chubb, Mary. *Nefertiti Lived Here.* New York: Thomas Crowell, 1954. A charming account of a season digging at Akhenaten's city at al-Amarna.

Brewer, Douglas & Renee F. Freedman, *Fish and Fishing in Ancient Egypt.* Cairo: American University in Cairo Press, 1989.

Cott, Jonathan. *The Search for Omm Sety.* New York: Doubleday, 1981. A biography of the Englishwoman who nearly singlehandedly restored Seti's temple at Abydos.

Davies. W.V. *Reading the Past: Egyptian Hieroglyphs.* London: The British Museum Publications, 1987.

du Bourquet, Pierre M. *The Art of the Copts.* New York: Greystone Press, 1967.

Edwards, I.E.S. *The Pyramids of Egypt.* New York: Penguin Books, 1985. Covers all the pyramids, including the Middle Kingdom mud-brick ones.

Fakhry, Ahmed. *The Oases of Egypt; Vol. I, Siwa.* Cairo: American University in Cairo Press, 1973. The definitive works on these oases.

————. *The Oases of Egypt; Vol. II, Bahariya and Farafra.* Cairo: American University in Cairo Press, 1974.

Frith, Francis. *Egypt and the Holy Land in Historic Photographs.* New York: Dover, 1980. This collection of Frith's outstanding photos shows Egypt as it was in the Victorian era.

Greener, Leslie. *The Discovery of Egypt.* New York: Viking Press, 1966. Traces the visitors to Egypt who have come to discover its past.

Harris, J.R. *The Legacy of Egypt.* 2nd ed. Oxford: Clarendon Press, 1971.

Herodotus. *The Histories, Book II.* Baltimore: Penguin Classics, 1954.

Hoffman, Michael A. *Egypt Before the Pharaohs.* New York: Alfred A. Knopf, 1979. The only good survey available on Egypt's prehistory and the development of Archaic Period Egypt.

Houlihan, Patrick F., *The Birds of Ancient Egypt.* Cairo: American University in Cairo Press, 1986.

James, T.G.H. *Pharaoh's People: Scenes from Life in Imperial Egypt.* London: Bodley Head (Chi), 1984. This slim easy-reading volume by the former keeper of Egyptian Antiquities at the British Museum offers insights into the daily lives of the ancient Egyptians.

————. *An Introduction to Ancient Egypt.* London: British Museum Publications, 1979.

Katan, Norma Jean. *Hieroglyphs: the Writing of Ancient Egypt.* London: British Museum

Publications, 1985. A good short introduction to reading hieroglyphs.

Keating, Rex. *Nubian Rescue*. London: Robert Hale, 1975.

Kees, Hermann. *Ancient Egypt: Cultural Topography*. Chicago: University of Chicago Press, 1961. This 1977 translation not only gives the reader insight into the ancient culture, but also covers the development of numerous important ancient cities.

Krupp, E.C. *In Search of Ancient Astronomers*. New York: Doubleday, 1977. This survey not only explains basic astronomy terms but also includes an extensive chapter on the ancient Egyptian monuments.

Lichtheim, Miriam. *Ancient Egyptian Literature: Vol. I, The Old and Middle Kingdoms*. Berkeley: University of California Press, 1973. This author not only translates the best-known inscriptions into modern English that nevertheless maintains the feel of the original Egyptian, but also includes extensive discussions of the literature, its styles, and development.

———. *Ancient Egyptian Literature: Vol. II, The New Kingdom*. Berkeley: University of California Press, 1976.

——— *Ancient Egyptian Literature: Vol. III, The Late Period*. Berkeley: University of California Press, 1980.

Lurker, Manfred. *The Gods and Symbols of Ancient Egypt*. London, Thames and Hudson, 1980. This illustrated dictionary offers a clear and concise look at the religion of ancient Egypt.

Mertz, Barbara. *Red Land, Black Land: Daily Life in Ancient Egypt*. New York, Dodd, Mead, and Co., 1978.

———. *Temples, Tombs, and Hieroglyphs: A Popular History of Ancient Egypt*. New York: Dodd, Mead and Co., 1978.

Russmann, Edne, and David Finn. *Egyption Sculpture: Cairo & Luxor,* University of Texas Press, 1989.

Trigger, B.G. et al. *Ancient Egypt: A Social History*. Cambridge University Press, 1983.

ISLAMIC AND MODERN EGYPT

Abu al-Izz, M.S. *Landforms of Egypt*. Cairo: American University in Cairo Press, 1971.

Abu-Lughod, Lila. *Veiled Sentiments: Honor and Poetry in a Bedouin Society*. Cairo: American University in Cairo Press, 1987.

Ammar, Hamed. *Growing Up in an Egyptian Village*. New York: Octagon Books, 1966.

Amoun, Denise, *Crafts of Egypt*. Cairo: American University in Cairo Press, 1991.

Anderson, Robert and Ibrahim Fawzy, *Egypt Revealed: Scenes from Napoleon's Description de L'Egypte*. Cairo: American University in Cairo Press, 1987.

Ansari, Hamied. *Egypt: The Stalled Society*. Cairo: American University in Cairo Press, 1986.

Atiya, Nayra. *Khul-Khaal: Five Egyptian Women Tell Their Stories*. Cairo: American University in Cairo Press, 1984.

Baz, Farouk al-. *Say it in Arabic*. New York: Dover, 1968.

Bernstein, Burton. *Sinai: The Great and Terrible Wilderness*. New York: Viking Press, 1979.

Boulos, Loutfy. *Medicinal Plants of North Africa*. Algonac, Michigan: Reference Publications, 1983.

Boulos, Loutfy, and M. Nabil al-Hadidi. *The Weed Flora of Egypt*. Cairo: American University in Cairo Press, 1984.

Du Ry, Carel J. *Art of Islam*. New York: Harry N. Abrams, 1970.

Egypt: A Country Study. (Area Handbook Series) Washington, D.C.: U.S. Government, 1983.

Carter, B.L. *The Copts in Egyptian Politics, 1918-1952*. Cairo: American University in Cairo Press, 1986.

Ettinghaun, Richard, *Arab Painting*. New York, Skira Rizzoli, 1977.

Geiser, Peter. *The Egyptian Nubian: a Study in Social Symbiosis.* Cairo: American University in Cairo Press, 1986.

Hadidi, M. Nabil al-, and Loutfy Boulos. *Street Trees in Egypt.* Cairo: 1979.

Hayes, John R., ed. *The Genius of Arab Civilization: Source of Renaissance.* 2nd ed. Eurabia Publishing: 1983.

Holt, Peter Malcom. *Egypt and the Fertile Crescent: 1516-1922.* Ithaca, NY: Cornell University Press, 1966.

Hopwood, Derek. *Egypt: Politics and Society: 1945-1984, Second Edition.* Boston: Allen and Unwin, 1985.

Lane, Edward. *The Manners and Customs of the Modern Egyptians.* New York: Dutton, 1908.

McLeave, Hugh. *The Last Pharaoh: Farouk of Egypt.* New York: McCall Publishing, 1969.

Meindrdus, Otto F.A., *Monks and Monasteries of the Egyptian Deserts.* Cairo: American University in Cairo Press, 1989.

Moorehead, Alan. *The White Nile.* New York: Harper and Brothers, 1960.

———. *The Blue Nile.* New York: Harper and Brothers, 1962.

Osborn, Dale J., and Ibrahem Helmy. *Contemporary Land Mammals of Egypt.* Chicago: Field Museum of Natural History, 1980.

Rice, David Talbot. *Islamic Art.* Revised ed. London: Thames and Hudson, 1975.

Rugh, Andrea B. *Family in Contemporary Egypt.* New York: Syracuse University Press, 1984.

———. *Reveal and Conceal: Dress in Contemporary Egypt.* Cairo: American University in Cairo Press, 1986.

Said, Rushdi, ed. *The Geology of Egypt.* Rotterdam/Brookfield, VT: A.A. Balkema, 1990.

———. *The Geological Evolution of the River Nile.* New York: Springer-Verlag, 1981.

al-Sayyid, Marsot, and Afaf Lutfi. *A Short History of Modern Egypt.* New York: Cambridge University Press, 1985.

Schacht, Joseph, ed. *The Legacy of Islam.* 2nd ed. Oxford: Clarendon Press, 1974.

GUIDES TO EGYPT

Amin, Naguib. *Cairo A-Z.* Cairo: Palm Press, 1988. A book of sections of maps for all of Cairo; indispensable for those who want to find their way into the back alleys and obscure settlements. Otherwise, the maps in *Cairo, Practical Guide* (by the same company) are more than enough for most visitors.

Banes, Joh, and Jaromir, Malek. *Atlas of Ancient Egypt.* New York: Facts on File, 1980.

Behrens-Abouseif, Doris. *The Minarets of Cairo.* Cairo: American University in Cairo Press, 1985.

Cairo Today. *Leisure Guide.* Cairo: Cairo Today Magazine, 1992. Updated periodically, this guide, intended for expatriates, often contains the most up-to-date information available.

Cairo Today. *Restaurant Guide.* Cairo: Cairo Today Magazine, 1992.

Congressional Quarterly, *The Middle East (7th Ed.) including a Persian Gulf Supplement.* Washington D.C.: Congressional Quarterly, 1991.

Cowley, Deborah, and Aleya Serour; Cassandra Vivian, ed. *Cairo: A Practical Guide, Sixth Edition.* Cairo: American University in Cairo Press, 1988. The definitive guide to Cairo; if you'll be spending any time in the city, pick up a copy.

Donadoni, Sergio. *Egyptian Museum, Cairo.* New York: Newsweek, 1969.

Forster, E.M. *Alexandria: A History and Guide.* London: Michael Haag, 1982. A reprint of Forster's guide first published in 1922, it remains remarkably up to date.

Freeman-Grenville, G.S.P. *The Beauty of Cairo.* London: East-West Publications, 1981.

Hanauer, Eric, *The Egyptian Red Sea—A Diver's Guide.* Watersport, 1988.

Hewison, R. Neil. *The Fayoum: A Practical Guide.* Cairo: American University in Cairo Press, 1984.

Jobbins, Jenny, *The Red Sea Coasts of Egypt: Sinai and the Mainland.* Cairo: American University in Cairo Press, 1989.

Kamil, Jill, *Coptic Egypt: History and Guide.* Cairo: American University in Cairo Press, 1987.

————. *Luxor, A Guide to Ancient Thebes.* London: Longman, 1983.

————. *The Monastery of Saint Catherine in Sinai: History & Guide.* Cairo: American University in Cairo Press, 1991.

————. *Upper Egypt: Historical Outline and Descriptive Guide.* London: Longman, 1983.

————. *Sakkara: a Guide to the Necropolis and the site of Memphis.* London: Longman, 1978.

Khalil, Father Marcus Aziz. *The Principal Ancient Coptic Churches of Old Cairo.* Cairo: Anba Reuiss Press, 1985. A glimpse into the symbolism of the churches as well as a short tour led by an insider.

Lane, Mary Ellen. *Guide to the Antiquities of the Fayyum.* Cairo: American University in Cairo Press, 1985.

Luxor Museum of Ancient Egyptian Art. Cairo: Egyptian Antiquities Organization, 1978.

Megalli, Mary. *Motoring Guide to Egypt.* Cairo: American University in Cairo Press.

Murnane, William J. *The Penguin Guide to Ancient Egypt.* New York: Penguin Books, 1983. The best guide to the meaning of the ancient monuments, with extensive maps and plans. It has enough travel information to help locate the monuments, but you'll still need a general travel guide.

Papaioannou, Evangelos. *The Monastery of St. Catherine.* Cairo: St. Catherine's Monastery, 1980.

Parker, Richard B., Robin Sabin, and Caroline Williams. *Islamic Monuments in Cairo, A Practical Guide.* Cairo: American University in Cairo Press, 1985.

Riad, Henri. *Alexandria: An Archaeological Guide to the City and the Greco-Roman Museum.* Alexandria: Regional Committee for the Development of Tourism. Although slightly dated, this little guide overflows with quality background information.

Saleh, Mohamed. *The Egyptian Museum Cairo: Official Catalogue.* Cairo: Egyptian Antiquities Organization, 1987. An excellent work laid out as a self-guided tour of the museum.

Vine, Peter, *Red Sea Safety: Guide to Dangerous Marine Animals.* London: Immel, 1986.

GLOSSARY

abacus—rectangular block on top of column supporting architrave

ablaq—alternating courses of colored masonry

adyton—the innermost or secret shrine in ancient places of worship

agora—market or meeting-place.

ahlaq—decorative screens inserted into the necks of pottery drinking jars to filter out bugs and debris

ambon—large pulpit raised on pillars

ambulatory—roofed colonnade around a small temple

Amduat—the book *What is in the Netherworld (see also* Duat)

amir—administrative title in early Islamic times, but after the 10th century the title was adopted by feudal overlords

amulet—a charm to protect the wearer from evil; wrapped with mummies to ensure their successful journey through the Duat and resurrection

ankh—hieroglyphic sign meaning life, this looped cross symbolized divine, eternal existence. Gods hand it to kings to ensure their continued life after death, and the early Coptic Christians adopted it as their *crux ansata.*

apse—the semicircular projecting area at one end (usually eastern) of a church

arabesque—an elaborate design of intertwined flowers, foliage, and geometrical patterns used extensively in Islamic art

architrave—the beam that rests on the columns and their capitals and supports the roof

ba—part of the complex soul envisioned by the ancient Egyptians.

bab—gate or door

baldachin—a canopy supported by columns over a throne, altar, or tomb

baksheesh—money in the form of alms, tips, or bribes frequently demanded by Egyptians

barque—the royal or holy barge used by the ancient Egyptians to transport statues of gods or mummies

barque shrine—niche in the temple containing the god's barque

barrages—the controlling dams installed on the Nile in the modern era

basilica—form of church popular with the Copts; the three aisles are bounded by a transverse narthex at the entrance and a nave at the apse

bas-relief—carving projecting slightly from background

bayt—an Islamic house

benben—*see* obelisk

bennu—the sacred bird of Heliopolis (probably a heron) which symbolized resurrection; the ancient Egyptians' phoenix

bey—a Turkish title conferred by the sultan on governors, high-ranking army officers, or civilians of equal power

birket—lake

broken pediment—a pediment that omits the apex of the triangle

burg—tower

buttress—a side support for an arch or wall that, in contrast to a column or pier, does not itself carry direct weight

calishe—a horse-drawn carriage

canopic jars—a set of four jars for the mummified viscera of the dead

capital—the uppermost part of a column

caravansary—a caravan resthouse built of storage rooms for trade goods around a courtyard for the animals and including bedrooms on the upper floors for the merchants

cartonnage—linen or papyrus held together by glue and molded into coffins and funerary masks

cartouche—an oval ring enclosing the nomen and prenomen of the pharaoh

cavetto cornice—concave projecting corbel running around the summits of walls or gates

cenotaph—a monument or tomb honoring the dead, but one that doesn't hold the body

clerestory—upper part of a hall that is taller than the surrounding ceilings and, by its windows, illuminates the building

coffer—the ornamental recessed panel in a ceiling, vault, or dome

colonnade—a series of columns set at regular intervals

colossus—gigantic figure of king, god, or occasionally private individual that usually stood in a temple

column—a free-standing support, usually round, consisting of a base, shaft, and capital

Coptic—the last form of Egyptian but written in Greek letters rather than with hieroglyphs

Copts—Egyptian Christians who trace their ancestry back to the pharaonic peoples

corbel—a projecting peace of stone, masonry, wood, or metal designed as a support

corbelled arch—an arch or roof designed by corbelling or setting successive supports slightly inward until they meet at the ridgeline

cornice—projecting support running around a building

cornishe—the main street that runs along the Nile or waterfront

cruciform—in the shape of a cross

crux ansata—the "handled" cross adopted by the early Coptic Christians from the yet earlier *ankh,* ancient Egyptian symbol of divine and everlasting life

dar—Islamic house or mansion

darih—tomb

decans—stars or constellations that rose at 10-day intervals and by which the ancient Egyptians told time

deir—walled monastery

demotic—a late form of Egyptian and the cursive hand with which it was written

dentil—a row of small blocks often decorating a cornice

dikkah—platform in a mosque from which the Koran is chanted

dhikr—Sufi litany or prayer service

divan hall—a council chamber

djed **pillar**—an enigmatic hieroglyph and amulet linked to Osiris' backbone and resurrection

Duat—the netherworld to which ancient Egyptians believed the souls of the dead journeyed

electrum—an alloy of gold and silver

encaustic—a method of applying pigment bound in wax by heating

faience—a glaze used to mold small figures and amulets; in Egypt blue or blue- green

fallahin—an Egyptian peasant farmer

false door—a blind door set into a pharaonic tomb to allow the spirit of the deceased to come and go

Feddan—1.038 acres

flail—a whip (or rattle) held by the pharaoh, along with the crook, as a symbol of royal power

fresco—traditionally, pigment applied to a

wet wall, but in Egypt a term often used to refer to the ancient tempera painting

frieze—a band of sculpture or ornament, especially on a wall

galabayya—the long robe worn by Egyptian men

ghaffir—guard at a temple or tomb

Hadith—(The Traditions) sayings of the Prophet Muhammad encoded in the Middle Ages and used to support and expand Islamic law

hajj (hagg)—the pilgrimage all Muslims should make to Mecca once during their lives. One who completes the pilgrimage earns the title *hajji*.

hammam—Islamic bath, public or private

haramlik—(the forbidden) the women's quarters

haykal—the sanctuary of a Coptic church

heb sed—a jubilee celebrated by the ancient Egyptians to commemorate 30 years of their king's reign, and held at various intervals thereafter

hieratic—a script form of hieroglyphs

hieroglyphs—the picture alphabet used for writing Egyptian

hypostyle hall—columned chamber, usually the first and largest room in the temple, which raises its flat roof on rows of columns and generally contains a central clerestory

iconostasis—in a Coptic church, a screen supporting icons and separating the sanctuary from the nave

imam—religious community leader

Isnik—a type of Islamic tile

ithyphallic—a figure (in Egypt usually Min or occasionally Osiris) depicted with an erect phallus

jinn—spirits who, according to legend, were created 2,000 years before Adam. Both good

and evil, they can assume various guises: animal, insect, or human, for example. Solomon controlled them with his magic ring.

joggled—interlocking intricate blocks often found in Islamic arches

ka—a person's double, that part of an ancient Egyptian's soul which was thrown by Khnum on his wheel

Kabah—sacred shrine of Islam at Mecca containing the holy black stone

kaftan—long Oriental tunic tied at the waist

keep—a relatively modern word for the central stronghold or inner tower of a castle

keystone—the central double-tapered voussoir or block that binds an entire arch

khalif—spiritual and political leader of the Muslims. In the 10th century, he became a political figurehead, but the khalifate of Baghdad lasted until the Mongol invasion in 1258. Other khalifs (the Ummayads of Cordoba and the Fatimids of North Africa) splintered off the Islamic Empire as early as the 10th century.

khamsin—(fifty) the hot winds that blow from the southwest every spring for fifty days

khan—Islamic hostel for merchants

khanqah—religious hostel for Sufis not unlike a Christian monastery

khedive—viceroy of Egypt

kheker **frieze**—stylized plants found at the top of ancient Egyptian walls

kiosk—a small open temple, pavilion, or summer house supported by pillars

kubri—bridge

kursi—dais for holding the Koran (literally, chair).

kuttab—Koranic elementary school for boys (often orphans) frequently attached to a mosque or built above a fountain (*see also sabil-kuttab*)

kufic—a square Islamic script often used for monumental decoration

lantern—a cupola or tower containing windows

liwan—Originally a sitting-room with a raised floor and opening onto a courtyard, it also describes the vaulted spaces surrounding the *sahn* of a cruciform *madrasa*.

loggia—a roofed arcade attached to or forming a part of a building often found on the north side of ancient Egyptian houses

lusterware—a type of glass and pottery decoration developed by Islamic craftsmen involving multiple firings

madrasa—a school, usually theological, for orthodox Sunni

malqaf—a wind scoop or vent. Known from predynastic times, they always face north in Egypt to catch the prevailing winds.

mamissi—a small chapel near a Ptolemaic temple for the birthplace of the god, and by extension, the king

Mamluks—Caucasian and Turkish slaves imported by the Islamic rulers to form loyal armies. Eventually in Egypt they took over the government and ran the country until massacred by Muhammad Ali.

maristan—a hospital attached to a medieval mosque; in modern Arabic it refers to a mental hospital only

masgid—mosque

mashhad—a tomb-sanctuary

mashribiyya—a wooden lattice covering windows

mastaba—Arabic bench (like those outside village houses) but also applied to the rectangular tombs of the ancient Egyptians

Melkites—Roman Christians who were pitted against the Copts

menat—a necklace of several rows of beads gathered into a counterpoise (counterweight) at the back of the neck. Worn by the goddess Hathor, it symbolized divine powers of healing.

midan—an open, central space or square

mihrab—the niche in the *qiblah* wall that indicates the direction of Mecca. It may derive from the apse of early Christian churches taken over by the Muslims.

minaret—the tower from which the *muezzin* gives the call to prayer. It may have links to the towers of Roman battlements first used for this purpose in Ummayad times.

minbar—a stepped pulpit from which the address or sermon at Friday prayers is given

monolith—a single large block of stone

Monophysites—Christians, including the Copts, who believed Christ was of one essence and were thrown into controversy with the orthodox Christians of Rome

mosaic—designs created by inlaying small, colored pieces of glass, stone, tiles, etc. (called tessera), which often decorated walls or floors

muezzin—a man who calls the prayer-times from the minaret

mulid—a birthday of a saint or a religious fair

mustashfa—hospital

naos—sanctuary where the divine statues of gods were kept

narthex—the entrance of ancient temples; in later times the porch or transverse vestibule of a church

naskhi—Arabic cursive script, which forms the basis of modern Arabic printing.

nastaliq—an elegantly cursive script that represents the cumulation of Islamic calligraphy

natron—the carbonate salts (especially those from Wadi Natrun) used for desiccating mummies

nave—the main body of a church, usually flanked by side aisles and in a basilican church extending from the entrance to the choir

niello—a type of engraving in which the chased designs are filled with a black alloy, producing a black figure on gold, silver, or brass background (or reversed)

nilometer—a station that registered the height of the Nile

nome—pharaonic administrative divisions of Egypt governed by a nomarch

obelisk—a monolithic tapered shaft, the original *(benben)* symbolized the primordial mound upon which the rays of the sun first shone. The tip, the pyramidion, was probably gilded. Solar symbols, they stood in pairs before temples and tombs.

orans **position**—in Coptic art, the pose of a figure facing front with the weight on one foot and the hands raised in adoration

ostraca—smooth, flat fragments of limestone or pottery used by the ancient Egyptians to draw and write on. Not only did students use them for practice, but daily records were often kept on ostraca.

palace facade—a decorative motif occurring early in Egyptian art that imitated the alternating bays and buttresses of early mud-brick palaces

parapet—a low wall along the edge of a terrace or roof. On fortifications they're high enough to protect defenders.

pectoral—a large piece of jewelry worn on the chest

pediment—a triangular unit used as decoration as over a doorway or window; in classical Greek architecture, the space between the entablature and roof

pendentive—a curved triangular support used to raise a dome above a square base *(see also* squinch) that puts the weight on the corners of the base, braced with multiple smaller domes and half domes

peristyle—an open court with a roofed arcade around the inner walls

portico—colonnaded porch approached by a flight of steps

pronaos—chamber preceding the sanctuary

propylon—gate standing in front of the pylon

pylon—massive entrance, consisting of two units joined by a gate

pyramidion—capstone of pyramid or obelisk

qa'a—main reception hall in an Egyptian house; the sunken central section (the *durqa'a)* is set off with a high roof

qasr—palace, fortress, or mansion

qibba—a dome or domed tomb

qiblah—the direction of Mecca. The wall in the mosque that faces Mecca is therefore called the *qiblah* wall and here the main *mihrab* appears in the covered prayer hall.

rab—an apartment building or tenement

Ramadan—the Islamic month of fasting

repoussé—relief designs produced by hammering out the pattern from the back of a thin sheet of metal

riwaq—an arcade surrounding the *sahn*

rondel—a round decoration, often found in Coptic textiles and on Mamluk buildings

sa—often carried by Taweret and Bes, this depiction of a herdsman's rolled up shelter of papyrus stands for protection

sabil—a public drinking fountain

sabil-kuttab—a combination fountain with a Koranic school above

sahn—an interior court (usually in a mosque)

salamlik—the greeting area of the public or men's apartments

saqiya—a waterwheel

senet—a board game favored by the ancient Egyptians. It's often depicted on tomb walls and several boards and markers were included in Tutankhamun's tomb.

Septuagint—a version of the Bible translated into Greek in Alexandria by 70 authors who, without comparing their work (so tradition maintains) produced 70 identical versions; the basis for most modern translations

Serapeum—a temple to Serapis, the one in Alexandria contains a branch of the famous library; the burial place of the Apis bulls in Saqqara

serdab—a hidden room in an ancient tomb from which a statue of the deceased could view the rituals of his cult

serekh—an early emblem of ancient Egyptian kings in the shape of a palace

shabti—a small figure included in ancient Egyptian tombs to do the work of the owner in the afterworld

shaduf—a pole with a bucket on one end and a counterweight on the other introduced by the Hyksos and still used to lift water

shah—a Persian king

sheikh—the Muslim leader of a community or a religious saint

Shi'i—a movement in Islam supported by the followers of Ali who believe that only a member of the Prophet's family could become his successor. The Fatimids of North Africa and Egypt were a branch of this movement, as are the modern Iranians.

shiisha—a waterpipe; also called a hookah

sistrum—a rattle associated with Hathor and used in her rituals

spandrel—the area just inside or outside an arch

sphinx—a human-headed lion. In Egypt it was male, but in Classical times it became female and was often equipped with wings.

squinch—a device for raising a dome over a square base (*see* also pendentive) in which an octagonal drum spans and relieves the corners of the base

stalactite decorations—honeycomb projections carved out of the niches and arches cut into squinches, in domes, or under cornices

stela—a block covered with pharaonic reliefs or paintings

Sufi—Muslim ascetic, mystic, or dervish

sultan—originally the main rulers of the Muslim world, but a title later adopted by innumerable petty princes of local dynasties

sunk relief—carvings in which the figures are outlined with heavy incised lines but the bodies then carved as if in bas-relief

Sunni—Muslims who believe that the successor to the Prophet should be elected and accept the Sunna or Way of the Traditions (Hadith). In Egypt, this branch of Islam is the most popular.

suqs—markets, either temporary (but usually regular) set up in the open air, or small shops or collections of vendors along specific streets or *midans.*

tabut—a wooden grave marker or a cenotaph

tarboushe—a brimless, usually red, felt cap with a dark, silk tassel. Associated with the Turks, it's no longer fashionable in Egypt, but a few are still made for the tourist market. Also called a fez.

temenos—sacred enclosure

tempera—paint in which the pigments have been mixed with an organic binder or medium like animal fats or egg

tiraz—a band of inscription on textiles (which gave the name to the Egyptian mills and weavers who made them) or around the walls of a mosque

torus molding—convex molding, especially around false doors, with a pattern of crossing cords symbolizing the rope that once held the bundled reeds used to strengthen the mud-brick walls

transept—in a cruciform church, the part that crosses at right angles to the nave

tribune—in a Coptic church, the raised platform at the end of apse upon which is set the bishop's throne

triforium—a gallery above the side aisles of a church which looks down into the nave

trilobe apse—an apse composed of three chapels usually with domes or half-domes

truss—a rigid framework used to support a roof (or bridge)

ushabti—see *shabti*

vault—an arched roof. The earliest known are of mud-brick and date from Ramesside times (at the Ramesseum).

vizier—a high state official or minister, sometimes given the authority of a viceroy. In ancient times, the pharaoh left the administration of the country to his vizier, or often split it (Upper and Lower Egypt) between two; the trend continued under Muslim rulers.

voussoirs—wedge-shaped stones used to build arches

wadi—a dry gully

Wafd—an early nationalistic party led by Sa'ad Zaghlul

waqf—a religious endowment; an assignment of revenues for an educational or charitable purpose which cannot be shifted; similar in concept to the cult foundations of the ancient Egyptians

was-**scepter**—a fetish the ancient Egyptians believed contained the life-giving power of the dog or fox-like protective spirit. Forked at the bottom and terminating in a canid head it became a symbol of well being and happiness.

wedjat-**eye**—the lunar eye of Re which Seth stole. After it was returned Thoth healed it and it became associated with him and called the whole one. It was also used as an amulet; a pair of such eyes on coffins or in tombs protected against the evil eye—a tradition continued in modern Egypt.

wikala—hostel for merchants similar to a khan or caravansary

Yaru, Fields of—the ancient Egyptian fields of the blessed afterlife

zawiya—a small establishment built for a Sufi sheikh to receive his brotherhood

ziyada—the outer court of a mosque

ARABIC VOCABULARY

This vocabulary follows the guide developed by Farouk al-Baz for Dover Publications' *Say it in Arabic (Egyptian Dialect)*. If you like their approach in this limited sample, or you want to expand your conversations, be sure to pick up a copy of their inexpensive, handy guide (available in the U.S. or in Egypt).

Speaking in Arabic entails frequent and complex gender changes, which are indicated as follows: "(m)" = a male speaking to anyone; "(f)" = a female speaking to anyone; "(to m)" = anyone speaking to a male; "(to f)" = anyone speaking to a female; and "(to g)" = anyone speaking to a group.

Pronunciation Marks

An apostrophe (') represents the glottal stop, the gulp-like sound formed in the back of the throat, heard for example in place of the omitted *tt* in the Cockney pronunciation of "better" or the colloquial New York pronunciation of "bottle."

A $\bar{u}$ indicates the vowel sound as in "pull"; an $\bar{\imath}$ indicates the vowel sound as in "rice." An $\bar{h}$ indicates the harsh, guttural sound formed at the back of the mouth, produced by whispering the *h* loudly. An $\bar{r}$ indicates the guttural sound similar to that produced by gargling.

For more notes on pronunciation, see p. 117.

GREETINGS

Hello—sah-EE-dah
Good morning—sah-BAH al-KHAY-re
Greetings (hello and/or goodbye)—mas-sa-LA-mah
How are you? (to m)—iz-ZĪ-yak?
  (to f)—iz-ZĪ-yik?
  (to g)—iz-zi-YOH-kūm?
Very well (m)—KWI-yis
  (f)—kwi-YI-sah
Thanks be to God—al-HAHM-doo lil-LA
Please (to m)—min-FADH-luk
  (to f)—min-FADH-lik
  (to g)—min-fadh-LOH-kūm
Thank you—SHŪK-run

very much—alf SHŪK-re
You're welcome—AF-wan/af

PRONOUNS

I—A-nah
you (m)—EN-tah
you (f)—EN-tee
you (plural)—EN-too
he—HOO-wah
she—HEE-yah
we—EH-nah
they—HOHM-Mah

PEOPLE

man—RAH-gill
lady—sitt
boy—WA-lad
girl—bent
friend (m)—SAH-bee
  (f)—sah-BI-tee
my husband—GOH-zee
my wife—me-RAH-tee
my son—IB-ne
my daughter—BEN-tee
my mother—wal-DI-te
my father—WAL-dee
my brother—ah-KHOO-ya
my sister—ŪKH-tee

COMMON EXPRESSIONS

Yes—Ī-wah
No—la'
Maybe—YIM-kin
Is it possible?—YIM-kin?
God willing—en-SHAH-allah
Come in—et-FAHD-dull
  (f)—et-fahd-DUL-lee
Just a moment—dee-EE-a WAH-da
Excuse me (to m)—es-MAH-lee
  (to f)—es-mah-HEE-lee

(to g)—es-mah-H̄OO-lee
I am sorry (m)—A-nah A-sif
  (f)—A-nah AS-fah
Never mind/it doesn't matter—mah-LESH
There is—fee
There isn't—ma-FEESH
I need (want) (m)—AH-wiz
  (f)—OW-zah
What?—ay?
When?—EM-tah?
Where?—fayn?
Here—HE-nah
There—he-NAK
Who [is it]?—meen?
How long?—ad-dee-AY?
Why?—lay?
Why not?—lay la?
How?—iz-ZI?
How many?—Kam?
How much?—bee-KAM?
What do you want (to m)—AH-wiz ay?
  (to f)—OW-zah ay?
  (to g)—ow-ZEEN ay?

COMMUNICATING

Do you speak English? (to m)—EN-tah be-tit-kal-lim en-gel-LEE-zee?
  (to f)—EN-tee be-tit-kal-LI-mee en-ge-LEE-zee?
Do you understand me? (to m)—fe-hem-TI-nee?
  (to f)—fe-hem-TEE-nee?
  (to g)—fe-hem-TOO-nee?
I understand—fe-HEMT
I don't understand—mahf-HEM-tish
I know (m)—A-nah AH-rif
  (f)—A-nah AHR-fah
I don't know (m)—A-nah mish AH-rif
  (f)—A-nah mish AHR-fah
How do you say ___ in Arabic?—YAH-nee ay ___ bil-AH-rah-bee?
What is the matter?—ay al-h̄e KA-ya?
Look out (to m)—H̄A-sib
  (to f)—H̄AS-bee
  (to g)—H̄AS-boo
Show me (the way)—wah-REE-nee (is-SIK-ka)
good—KWĪ-yis
bad—mish KWĪ-yis

Where is the bathroom (washroom)?—fayn DOH-ret al-MI-yah?
May I smoke?—AH'-dahr ah-DAKH-ahn?

GETTING AROUND

Take me to ___—wahd-DEE-nee ___
Where is ___?—fayn?
Street—SHAR-yah
near—oh-RI-yib
far—bay-EED
turn right—yi-MEEN
left—shi-MAL
north—shi-MAL
south—ga-NOOB
east—shar'
west—r̄ahrb
straight ahead—AH-lah tool
When does ___ open?—Em-tah ___ YIF-tah?
  close?—YE'-fill?
How far is it?—bay-EED ad-dee-AY?
entrance—id-doh-KHOOL
exit—al-khoh-ROOG
airplane—tay-YA-ra
airport—al-mah-TAHR
office—MAK-tab
station—may-H̄AH-tet
train station—may-H̄AH-tet is-SIK-ka al-ha-DEED
platform—ir-rah-SEEF
arrival—woo-SOOL
departure—ee-YAM
taxi—taxi
driver—sow-WA'
Please call me a taxi—min-FAHD-luk na-DEE-lee TAK-si
bus stop—may-HAH-tet al-oh-toh-BEES
bus—al-oh-toh-BEES
ticket—tahz-KAH-rah
roundtrip—rah-yeh̄-GĪ
Please tell me where to get off—min-FAHD-luk UL-lee AN-zill fayn
Stop—bash/KWI-yis
reserved seat—KŪR-see mah̄-GOOZ
reservation—HA-giz
timetable—da-LEEL
first class—DAH-rah-gah OO-lah
second class—DAH rah-gah TAN-ya
bicycle—AH-gah-lah
boat—MAR-kib

CARS

car—ah-rah-BEE-ya
gas station—may-H̄AH-tet ban-ZEEN
gas—ban-ZEEN
Fill it up—im-LA-h̄a
oil—zayt
brakes—fah-RAH-mil
horn—ka-LAKS
map—kha-REE-tah
air—HAW-wa
battery—bat-tah-REE-yah
mechanic—me-ka-NEE-kee
jack—af-REE-ta
tire—AH-gah-lah

SERVICES

telephone—te-le-FOHN
number—NIM-rah
post office—BOSH-tah
letter—gah-WAB
police—boh-LEES
He is not here—mish mow-GOOD

TIME

hour—SA-'a
minute(s)—dee-EE-a (dee-AA-yi)
What time is it?—is SA-a' kam?
(eight) o'clock—saa-'a (ta-MAN-ya)
___A.M.—___is-SOB-h̄e
___P.M.—___bahd id-DOH-re
Half past three—ta-LA-ta wi nos
Quarter past three—ta-LA-ta wi rob'
Quarter to four—ahr-BAH-ah IL-la rob'
In the morning—is-SOB-h̄e
In the afternoon—bahd id-DOH-re
In the evening—al-AHS-re
At noon—id-DOH-re
night—al-LAYL
day—in-nah-HAHR
today—in-nay-HAHR-dah
tonight—al-lay-LA-dee
yesterday—em-BA-reh̄
tomorrow—BOK-rah

ACCOMMODATIONS

hotel—loh-KHAN-dah
I have a reservation [for tonight]—A-nah H̄A-giz [al-lay-LA-dee]
a room—OH-dah
with bath—bee h̄ahm-MAM
with a shower—bee dūsh
key—mohf-TAH̄
The door doesn't lock—al-bab ma-bee-YE'-filsh
double—OH-dah lit-NAYN
fan—mar-WA'-h̄a
with air conditioning—OH-dah moo-ki-YA-fa
bed—si-REER
pillow—may-KHUD-da
blanket—but-tah-NEE-ya
sheet—mee-LA-ya
towel—FOO-tah
soap—sah-BOON
toilet paper—WA-ra' toh-wah-LET
hot water—MĪ-yah SOKH-na
cold water—MĪ-yah bard

DINING

restaurant—mat-AHM
breakfast—foh-TAHR
supper—AH-sha
dinner—R̄A-da (in early afternoon)
menu—LIS-ta
knife—kik-KEE-na
fork—SHOH-ka
spoon—mah-LA-a'
napkin—FOO-tah
plate—TAH-bah'
glass—kūb-BA-ya
sugar—SŪK-kar
salt—MAL-h̄e
pepper—FILL-fill
butter—ZIB-da
bread—aysh
ice—TAL-lag
sandwich—san-da-WITSH
European coffee—Nescafe
with cream—bil-LA-bun
Turkish coffee—AH-wah
Turkish coffee (black)—AH-wah SA-da
with a little sugar—AH-wah REE-ha

with medium sugar—AH-wah muz-BOOT
with heavy sugar—AH-wah zee-YA-da
mineral water—MĪ-yah mah-da-NEE-ya
drinking water—MĪ-yet shurb
beer—BEE-ra
juice—ah-SEER
the bill—ħe-SAB
waiter—gahr-SOHN
a table—tah-tah-BEE-zah

NUMBERS

Egyptian numbers build logically off the names of those from one to 10, but be aware that the ending for 30, 40, 50, etc., is TEEN so Egyptians will often confuse 30, for example, with 13; you may easily do the same.

zero—SIF-re
one—WAH-ħed
two—et-NAYN
three—ta-LA-ta
four—ahr-BAH-ah
five—KHAM-sa
six—SIT-ta
seven—SAB-ah
eight—ta-MAN-ya
nine—TES-ah
ten—AH-shah-rah
eleven—ħe-DAH-sher
twelve—et-NAH-sher
thirteen—tah-laht-TAH-sher
fourteen—ahr-bah-TAH-sher
fifteen—khah-mahs-TAH-sher

sixteen—sit-TAH-sher
seventeen—sah-bah-TAH-sher
eighteen—tahm-mahn-TAH-sher
nineteen—tes-sah-TAH-sher
twenty—ish-REEN

The following numbers are made up of the one's digit followed by wi (and) and the tens digit.

twenty-one—WAH-hed wi ish-REEN
twenty-two—et-NAYN wi ish-REEN
thirty—ta-la-TEEN
forty—ar-bay-EEN
fifty—kham-SEEN
sixty—sit-TEEN
seventy—sab-EEN
eighty—ta-ma-NEEN
ninety—tes-EEN
one hundred—MAY-ya
one thousand—alf

DAYS OF THE WEEK

In Arabic, weekdays are named with derivations from the numbers.

Sunday—al-ĦUD
Monday—lit-ÑAYN
Tuesday—it-tl-lat
Wednesday—LAHR-bah
Thursday—al-kha-MEES
Friday—ig-GOHM-ah
Saturday—is-SABT

CHRONOLOGY OF EGYPT

PREHISTORIC PERIOD

c. 6500 B.C.—Late Paleolithic
c. 5000 B.C.—First farming settlements
develop in the Nile Valley
c. 4500 B.C.—Badarian culture emerges
c. 4000 B.C.—Naqada I culture emerges
c. 3500 B.C.—Naqada II culture emerges

ARCHAIC PERIOD (c. 3150-2686 B.C.)

c. 3100 B.C.—Upper and Lower Egypt united;
capital at Memphis, near Cairo
  King Scorpion
  Horus Narmer

c. 3050-2890 B.C.—Dynasty 1
These kings founded Memphis as the new
capital of Egypt and began building royal
tombs at Abydos and Saqqara:
  Horus Aha
  Horus Djer
  Horus Djet
  Horus Den

c. 2890-2686 B.C.—Dynasty 2
Possible period of civil war that may have
given rise to the myths of the contendings of
Horus and Seth.
  Horus Hotepsekhemwy
  Seth Peribsen
  Horus-and-Seth Khasekhemwy

OLD KINGDOM (c. 2686-2181 B.C.)
Both the alpha and omega of Egyptian
culture, this period started with great
innovations and ended with stagnation. To
the Egyptians, however, the Old Kingdom
remained the perfect period of their
civilization—a model to emulate.

c. 2686-2613 B.C.—Dynasty 3
  Nebka (c. 2686-2668)
  Djoser (c. 2668-2649)

Introduces use of stone in
Step Pyramid at Saqqara
  Horus Sekhemkhet (c. 2649-2643)
  Horus Khaba (c. 2643-2637)
  Huni (c. 2637-2613)

c. 2613-2500 B.C.—Dynasty 4
This pyramid age marks the height of the Old
Kingdom culture, the era the Egyptians
themselves considered golden.
  Snefru (c. 2613-2589)
    Inaugurated the Pyramid Age
    Completed pyramid at Meidum
  Khufu (c. 2589-2566)
    Built Great Pyramid at Giza
  Djedefre (c. 2566-2558)
  Khafre (c. 2558-2532)
    Built second pyramid at Giza
    Carved Sphinx at Giza
  Menkaure (c. 2532-2504)
    Built third pyramid at Giza
  Shepseskaf (c. 2504-2500)
    Built Mastabat Faraun at Saqqara

c. 2500-2345 B.C.—Dynasty 5
Re dominates royal religion, and these
pharaohs built the sun pyramids at Abusir:
  Userkaf (2498-2491)
  Sahure (2491-2477)
  Neferirkare-Kakai (2477-2467)
  Neferefre (c. 2460-2453)
  Niuserre (c. 2453-2422)
  Djedkare-Isesi (c. 2414-2375)
  Unis (c. 2375-2345)

c. 2345-2181 B.C.—Dynasty 6
The first cracks in the invincibility of the
pharaoh occur, and by the end of the period,
Middle Egyptian overlords have enough
power to plunge Egypt into the First
Intermediate Period.
  Titi (c. 2345-2333)
  Pepi I (c. 2332-2283)
  Mernere (c. 2283-2278)
  Pepi II (c. 2278-2181)

FIRST INTERMEDIATE PERIOD
(c. 2181-2040 B.C.)

c. 2181-2160 B.C.—Dynasties 7 and 8
Weak rulers of Memphis governed Egypt in name only.

c. 2160-2040 B.C.—Dynasties 9 and 10
Kings ruling from Herakleopolis (near Beni Suef) forced most nomarchs to recognize them.

2133-2060 B.C.—Dynasty 11/a
Theban princes begin conquest of Herakleopolian collation, making gains in Middle Egypt.
Horus Wahankh Antef II (2117-2069)

MIDDLE KINGDOM
(c. 2040-1782 B.C.)

2060-1991 B.C.—Dynasty 11/b
This dynasty finished conquering Lower Egypt, reuniting the country. Middle Kingdom kings dismembered much of the feudal system and rebuilt the national government, conquered Nubia, and reestablished large-scale foreign trade.
Nebhepetre Mentuhotep I (2060-2010)
Sankhkare Mentuhotep II (2010-1998)
Nebtowyre Mentuhotep III (1997-1991)

1991-1782 B.C.—Dynasty 12
The most prosperous period of the Middle Kingdom, this dynasty moved the capital south to Karnak-Thebes and promoted a resurgence in art and literature, but it was plagued by nomarchs' continual quests for power.
Amenemhet I (1991-1962)
Built pyramid at Lisht
Senwosret I (1971-1928)
Reconquered Nubia
Amenemhet II (1929-1895)
Irrigation projects in Fayyum
Senwosret II (1897-1878)
Built pyramid at al-Lahun
Senwosret III (1878-1841)
Suppressed nomarchs and
reorganized government

Amenemhet III (1842-1797)
Built pyramid and labyrinth
at Hawara
Amenemhet IV (1798-1786)
Queen Sobeknofru (1785-1782)

SECOND INTERMEDIATE PERIOD
(1782-1570 B.C.)

This turbulent era produced a series of ephemeral rulers of fragmented princedoms who were often in conflict, simultaneously claiming title.

1782-1650 B.C.—Dynasty 13
These weak kings ruled in name, but with little power.

Dynasty 14
Multiple separatist movements in the delta

c. 1663-1555 B.C.—Dynasty 15
The Hyksos established their capital at Avaris in the Delta and allied themselves with the Nubians against the Thebans.

Dynasty 16
Artificial dynasty of Hyksos princes

c. 1663-1570 B.C.—Dynasty 17
Once more, Theban princes moved to reunite Egypt.
Sankhenre Mentuhotep VI (c. 1633)
Sekenenre Tao II (c. 1574)
Kamose (c. 1573-1570)
Led armies deep into the delta
against Hyksos.

NEW KINGDOM
(c. 1570-1070 B.C.)

With their finely honed army, the Egyptians swept east and then north, establishing an empire that at its farthest points reached nearly to Turkey. Increased contact with the rest of the Middle East converted Egypt into an international power, and Asian influences worked their way into her culture.

1570-1293 B.C.—Dynasty 18

The kings of this period established the empire and their strong rule supported far-flung vassal states and trade. Treasure poured into the country, creating the foundation for extensive building and art, the most beautiful examples from Tut's tomb.

Ahmose I (c. 1570-1546)
　Took Avaris and reunited Egypt
Amenhotep I (c. 1551-1524)
Thutmose I (c. 1524-1518)
　Conquered Upper Nubia
　Built the first tomb in the
　　Valley of the Kings
Thutmose II (c. 1518-1504)
Thutmose III (1504-1450)
　Conquered Syria, creating the
　　Egyptian Empire from Napata
　　to the Euphrates
　Built jubilee hall at Karnak
Hatshepsut (c. 1498-1483)
　Sent trading expedition to Punt
　Built mortuary temple at
　　Deir al-Bahri, Luxor
Amenhotep II (c. 1453-1419)
Thutmose IV (c. 1419-1386)
Amenhotep III (c. 1386-1349)
　Married Tiyi
　Built mortuary temple—only
　　colossi of Memnon remain
Amenhotep IV/Akhenaten (c. 1350-1334)
　Married Nefertiti
　Moved capital to al-Amarna
　Forbade worship of any god
　　but Aton
　Allowed empire to deteriorate
Smenkhare (c. 1330-1334)
　Return to old order
Tutankhamun (c. 1334-1325)
　Moved capital back to Thebes
Ay (c. 1325-1321)
Horemheb (c. 1321-1293)
　Reestablished the pharaohs'
　　traditional power

c. 1293-1185 B.C.—Dynasty 19

Under the great warrior kings of this dynasty, Egypt recovered much of her former territory and status as an empire. They moved the capital north to Tanis, and Memphis revived. The end of the dynasty was marked by short reigns, anarchy, and decline.

Ramesses I (c. 1293-1291)
Seti I (c. 1291-1278)
　Expanded the empire to nearly
　　its old borders
　Built mortuary temple at Abydos
Ramesses II (1279-1212)
c. 1275 Battle of Kadesh
c. 1259 Peace treaty with Hittites
　Built temple at Abu Simbel and
　　the Ramesseum
Merneptah (c. 1212-1202)
c. 1207 Campaigns against Libyans and
　　Peoples of the Sea
Amenmesse (c. 1202-1199)
Seti II (c. 1199-1193)
Siptah (c. 1193-1187)
Twosret (c. 1187-1185)

c. 1185-1070 B.C.—Dynasty 20

Although Ramesses III repelled several invasions, persistent economic difficulties plagued the country, unrest and marauding bands of Libyans made the countryside unsafe, and the Theban high priests of Amun took advantage to build a power base in Upper Egypt, eventually splitting the country once more.

Sethnakht (c. 1185-1182)
　Reestablished central power
Ramesses III (c. 1182-1151)
　Consolidated rule
　Repelled invasions of Libyans
　　and Sea Peoples
　Built temple at Medinat Habu
Ramesses IV (c. 1151-1145)
Ramesses V (c. 1145-1141)
Ramesses VI (c. 1141-1133)
Ramesses IX (c. 1126-1108)
　Tomb robberies in Upper Egypt
Ramesses XI (c. 1098-1070)
　Tomb robberies in Upper Egypt
At Thebes: Herihor (c. 1080-1072)
　Ruled first as high priest of Amun,
　　later as king
　Detached Nubia from northern
　　kings' influence

THIRD INTERMEDIATE PERIOD
(c. 1069-664 B.C.)

c. 1069-945 B.C.—Dynasty 21, the Tanites
During this chaotic period, Nubia recovered its independence, and Egypt lost her influence in Palestine.
Smendes (c. 1069-1063)
Psusennes I (c. 1059-1033)
Amenemope (c. 1033-981)
At Thebes: Pinedjem I (1070-1026)

c. 945-712 B.C.—Dynasty 22, the Libyan
Descendants of the Libyan tribes who had served as mercenaries for the pharaohs, these kings transferred the capital to Bubastis. Thebes steadily declined.
Shoshenq I (c. 947-942)
Overthrew Tanites
Plundered the Temple of
Solomon in Jerusalem
Osorkon I (c. 924-889)
Shoshenq II (c. 890-875)
Osorkon II (c. 874-850)
Takelot II (c. 850-825)
Shoshenq III (c. 825-773)
At Thebes: Harsiese (c. 870-860)

c. 818-712 B.C.—Dynasties 23 and 24
Period of Libyan anarchy and multiple princelings

c. 772-664 B.C.—Dynasty 25, the Kushites
These Nubian kings, long steeped in Egyptian culture, initiated a resurgence of traditional art and beliefs in Upper Egypt. Although they threatened to take Lower Egypt, they never succeeded and were finally defeated after a series of wars by the Assyrians.
Piankhy/Piyi (c. 753-713)
Shabaka (713-698)
Taharqa (690-664)

LATE PERIOD (664-332 B.C.)

664-525 B.C.—Dynasty 26, the Saites
The last native dynasty, the Saites brought Egypt a short period of prosperity in which extensive trading supported a cultural revival

Psamtik I (664-610)
Necho (610-595)
Victorious at the battle of Megiddo
Defeated at Carchemish by
Nebuchadnezzar of Babylon
Worked on Red Sea canal
Psamtik II (595-589)
Apries (589-570)
Dethroned by military rebellion
Ahmose II (570-526)
Gave the city of Naucratis
to Greek colonists
Psamtik III (526-525)
Defeated at Pelusium by Cambyses
Egypt becomes a Persian province

525-404 B.C.—Dynasty 27, first Persian Period
Cambyses (525-522)
Darius I (521-486)
Completed canal to Red Sea
Built temple to Amun at al-Kharga 487
Egyptians rebelled and expelled Persians
Xerxes (485-465)
Quelled insurrection
Artaxerxes I (465-425)
c. 449 Herodotus visits Egypt
Darius II (423-405)

404-399 B.C.—Dynasty 28

399-380 B.C.—Dynasty 29
Hakoris (393-380)

380-342 B.C.—Dynasty 30
Nectanebo I (380-362)
Teos (362-360)
Nectanebo II (360-342)

342-332 B.C.—Dynasty 31
Second Persian Period

PTOLEMAIC PERIOD (332-30 B.C.)

Alexander the Great (332-323)
Philip Arrhidaeus and Alexander II (323-305)

305 B.C.-A.D. 30—Ptolemaic Dynasty

Ptolemy I Soter (323-282)
Ptolemy II Philadelphus (285-246)
Ptolemy III Euergetes (246-221)
Ptolemy IV Philopator (221-205)
Ptolemy V Epiphanes (205-180)
Ptolemy VI Philometer (180-164,
   163-145)
Ptolemy VIII Euergetes II
   (163, 145-116)
Cleopatra II and Ptolemy IX Soter II (116-
   110, 109-107, 88-80)
Ptolemy X Alexander (110-109, 107-88)
Cleopatra Bernice III (57-55)
Ptolemy XII Neos Dionysus (80-67, 55-51)
Cleopatra VII (51-30)

THE COPTIC TRANSITION
(30 B.C.-A.D. 658)

30 B.C-A.D. 323—Roman Emperors

Augustus (30 B.C.-A.D. 14)
   Strabo travels in Egypt
Tiberius (A.D. 14-37)
   Christ crucified
Caligula (37-41)
   Quarrels between Hellenes and
      Jews in Alexandria
Claudius (41-54)
   Began *pronaos* of temple at Isna
   Began temple at Philae
Nero (54-68)
   Egypt transshipping between
      India and Rome
64 St. Paul beheaded in Rome
Vespasian (69-79)
Titus (79-81)
Domitian (81-96)
Nerva (96-98)
Trajan (98-117)
   Reopened the canal between
      the Nile and Red Sea
Hadrian (117-138)
   Founded city of Antinoupolis in
      memory of Antinous
Antoninuspius (138-161)
c. 150 Ptolemy, the astronomer working
   at Alexandria
Marcus Aurelius (161-180)
Commodus (180-192)

c. 190 School of Catechists in
   Alexandria (Clement, Origen)
Septimius Severus (193-211)
204 Edict against Christianity
Caracalla (209-217)
   Massacre at Alexandria
Valerian (253-260)
   Christian persecutions
Gallienus (260-268)
   Religious tolerance to Christians
   Plague in Egypt
268 Lower Egypt occupied by
   Queen Zenobia of Palmyra
   Upper Egypt occupied by
   Blemmyes of Nubia
Aurelian (270-275)
270 Probus reconquers Egypt
   Diocletian (284-305)
292 Rebellion in Upper Egypt
294 Insurrection in Alexandria
295 Diocletian takes Alexandria
303 Persecution of Christians

A.D. 323-642—Byzantine Period

Constantine (306-337)
313 Edict of Milan recognizes
   Christianity
c. 320 Pachomius founds convent
325 Council of Nicea
328 Athanasius, archbishop of
   Alexandria
330 Moves capital to Byzantium
c. 330 Beginning of anchorite
   communities in deserts
c. 350 Coptic translations of the Bible
Theodosius (379-395)
   Declared Christianity religion
      of Empire
   Persecutions of Arians and pagans
   Destruction of Serapeum
383 Shenute (founder of Coptic
   church) head of White Monastery
395 Partition of Roman Empire
Theodosius II (408-450)
412 Cyril becomes archbishop and
   persecutes Copts
415 Hypatia, pagan
   philosopher stoned to death
   at Alexandria
451 Council of Chalcedon; the Copts
   declared heretics

Justinian I (525-565)
  Closes pagan temples, the last
    at Philae
Heraclius (610-641)
619 Persians take Alexandria
622 Muhammad settles at Medina
    beginning of Islamic calendar
626 Persians expelled from Egypt
632 Death of Muhammad; Abu Bekr
    becomes first khalif
634 Beginning of conquest of Syria;
    Umar, second khalif
636 Fall of Damascus
637 End of Sassanian empire
638 Fall of Jerusalem
641 Muslim armies conquer Egypt and
    found new capital at al-Fustat,
    next to Roman fortress at Babylon
    Islam becomes official religion

EARLY KHALIFS (658-969)

658-720—The Ummayads
Rule from Damascus
661 Succession quarrels split Islam
    into Sunni and Shi'i branches
715 8 Nilometer built on Rhoda Island,
    Cairo
744-750 Marwan II
        Fled to Egypt and was executed
        by the Abbasids

750-868—The Abbasids
Move capital to Baghdad
Builds a new palace city, al-Askar,
  northeast of al-Fustat

868-905—The Tulunids
Ahmad Ibn Tulun (868-884)
  Sent by the Abbasids to govern Egypt
  Assumes absolute power and
    governs Egypt as an
    independent state
  Founds the palace-city, al-Qatal,
    north of al-Askar
878 Ahmad Ibn Tulun mosque
    completed
905-935 Egypt once again
    controlled by Abbasids
925 Attack by Fatimids of West Africa
    repelled

935-969—The Ikhshidids
Muhammad al-Ikhshid (935-946)
  Seized control and ruled
    independently
Kafur (966-968)
  Ruled for sons of Muhammad,
    then took power in his own right
969 Gawhar conquers Egypt for
    Fatimid khalifs

EGYPT UNDER INDEPENDENT RULERS (969-1517)

969-1171—The Fatimids
al-Mu'izz (969-975)
  Founds new palace-city
    of al-Qahira (Cairo)
971 Mosque and *madrasa* of
    al-Azhar founded
al-Aziz (975-996)
  Tolerant and well-loved ruler
  Science flourished
  Prosperous rule
al-Hakim (996-1021)
  Declares himself incarnation of Ali
  al-Darazi founds Durzi sect
1010 al-Hakim mosque completed
al-Mastansir (1036-1094)
1065 Nile fails, creating famine and
    unrest
  Palace and library plundered
1074 Vizier Badr al-Gamali restores order
1099 European armies of First Crusade
    capture Jerusalem from Muslims
al-Adid (1160-1171)
  Last Fatimid khalif
1168 al-Fustat razed by fire to prevent
    occupation by armies of
    Second Crusade
1171 Fatimid dynasty dies out
    Salah al-Din, a Kurdish soldier
    defending Egypt from Crusaders,
    Sunni Islam restored

1171-1250 B.C. The Ayubbids
Salah al-Din (Saladin) (1171-1200)
  The most brilliant period in
    medieval Cairo.
  Fatimid Shi'i doctrines abolished
1175 City fortifications extended and

Citadel construction begins
al-Adil (1200-1218)
- 1211 Sultana al-Shamsa builds mausoleum of Imam al-Shafi

al-Kamil (1218-1238)
- 1218 Damietta captured by army of Fifth Crusade
- 1221 Damietta surrendered to Muslims
- 1229 Treaty between al-Kamil and Emperor Frederick II surrenders Jerusalem and coastal towns to the Christians

al-Salih Ayyub (1240-1250)
- 1250 Louis IX of France, leader of Sixth Crusade, captured at Mansuria. Throne seized by Shagarit al-Durr

1250-1382—The Bahri Mamluks

Aybak (1250-1257)
Baybars I (1260-1277)
- 1258 Mongols take Baghdad; Abbasid khalif moved to Cairo
- 1260 Mamluks halt Mongols in Palestine

Qalawun (1279-1290)
- Mamluk architecture in Cairo flourishes

Ashraf Khalil (1290-1293)
- 1291 Captures Acre, last Christian stronghold

Muhammad al-Nasir (1293-1340)
- 1297-9 Lagin usurps the throne
- 1303 Large earthquake destroys much of Cairo

Hasan (1347-1361)

1382-1517—The Burgi Mamluks

Barquq (1382-1399) successfully stopped the Mongols under Timur (Tamerlane)
Farag (1399-1412) staved off Mongols, but capitulated to his own amirs at Damascus
al Muayyad (1412-1421)
al-Ashraf Barsbey (1422-1438)
Qaytbey (1468-1496)
al-Ghuri (1501-1516)
- 1508 Egyptian fleet defeated Portuguese near Bombay, but in 1509 were compelled to withdraw to Arabian Peninsula

- 1517 Tuman Bey dethroned by Ottoman sultan Salim and Egypt became a Turkish protectorate

MODERN EGYPT (1517-Present)

1517-1914—Turkish Period

Egypt was nominally under the rule of the Ottoman sultan of Turkey, but in practice was controlled by local rulers in an uneasy truce with various Western nations

1798-1801—French Occupation

- 1798 Napoleon Bonaparte arrives in Alexandria and takes Egypt British destroy French fleet at Abuqir
- 1799 Napoleon returns to France leaving Kleber in charge
- 1800 Kleber assassinated in Cairo
- 1801 British force French army to evacuate Egypt

1805-1914—Muhammad Ali and His Successors

Muhammad Ali (1805-1849)
- 1807 British fleet withdraws after British defeat at hand of Mamluks under the leadership of Muhammad Ali
- 1811 Muhammad Ali invites the beys to a feast and murders them
- 1819 Takes Arabia, then Nubia
- 1824-27 Home army of *fallahin* helps Turkish sultan against Greeks in their war of independence until the combined French, British, and Russian fleet defeat the Turkish-Egyptian one at Navarino
- 1827-33 Muhammad Ali encourages agricultural improvements and introduces industry
- 1833 Muhammad Ali's armies invade and take Syria, but the Egyptians are forced by the Europeans to concede to the Turkish government
- 1841 Attacked by Turkey, the sultan is forced by the European powers

once more to concede to Turkey, but he secures the sultanate of Egypt for his family

Ibrahim (1848-1849) ruled in his ailing father's name, but died just before him

Abbas I (1849-1854)

Sa'ad (1854-1863) completed railway from Alexandria to Cairo and Suez, and started construction on the Suez Canal

Ismail (1863-1879) French-educated, he maintained strong ties with Europe and introduced many innovations, improving Egypt's economy, though ultimately, by appropriating and squandering much of the revenue, he bankrupted his country

1867 Ismail raised to rank of *khedive* (viceroy)

1869 Suez Canal opened

1878 Forced by European powers to resign private and family estates to the state, but unworkable situation ended in the *khedive's* resignation in favor of his son

Tawfiq (1879-1892)

1882 General Arabi leads revolt, resulting in British intervention

1883 Sir Evelyn Baring (later Earl of Cromer) becomes British consul-general and oversees writing the first constitution

1885 Rebellion in Sudan under the Mahadi takes Khartoum: Wadi Halfa becomes the southern limits of Egypt

1887 Convention between the British and French establishes the neutrality of the Suez Canal

1898 General Herbert Kitchener retakes Sudan

Abbas II, Helmi (1898-1914)

1902 Nile Dam at Aswan opened

1907 Eldon Gorst becomes British diplomatic agent

1911 Succeeded by Kitchener

1914-1936—British Period

Hussein Kamil (1914-1916)

1914 Egypt declares war on Turkey and Germany; England makes Egypt protectorate; Khedive Abbas II

deposed and Henry MacMahon appointed high commissioner for Egypt

1915 Turkish attacks on Suez Canal repulsed

1917 British, under Edmund Allenby, advance into Palestine

Ahmad Fuad (1918-1936)

1918 Armistice with Turkey

1919 Increased national unrest culminates with deportation of Sa'ad Zaghlul; Allenby appointed special high commissioner

1922 British abolish protectorate and declare Egypt a sovereign state; Ahmad Fuad becomes king

1923 Egyptian constitution proclaims a constitutional monarchy, and the Wafd party of Zaghlul wins the elections for parliament

1924 General Lee Stack (British governor-general of Sudan) assassinated in Cairo; Egypt forced to withdraw from Sudan

1936-1952—Royal Egyptian Rule

1936 Anglo-Egyptian Treaty ends British occupation; national elections return the Wafd to power

Faruq (1936-1952)

1937 Egypt joins the League of Nations

1939 Second World War breaks out

1940 Italy invades Libya

1942 June British troops withdraw from Siwa; Italians fill the void
Sept. Rommel visits Siwa; reaches al-Alamein only to be defeated by Montgomery in October

1945 League of Arab States created

1947 Evacuation of British troops from Alexandria and the Canal zone

1948 Israel created; Egypt and other Arab League countries attack

1949 Israel attacks Egyptian frontier; Egyptian-Israeli armistice gives Egypt Gaza, Beersheba to Israel

1950 Wafd wins first elections in 10 years

1952 Riot over increased British pressure due to Egypt's designs on Sudan; Cairo burned on Black Sunday

REPUBLICAN EGYPT

1952-1970—Gamal Abdul Nasser

1952 Revolution of the Free Officers

1953 Egypt declared republic, Muhammad Nagib president

1954 Nagib removed; Nasser becomes president

1956 Last British soldiers leave Egypt; U.S. and Britain refuse to finance High Dam, so to pay for it, Nasser nationalizes Suez Canal; Israeli forces invade Sinai (British and French troops involved)

1957 Canal, blocked by war, reopened

1962 Declaration of National Charter

1965 U.S. terminates aid to Egypt; Nasser embraces Soviet offers

1967 May Egypt demands removal of UN troops from Sinai and closes Strait of Tiran to Israeli shipping June Israel defeats Egypt, Jordan,and Syria in Six Day war; UN ceasefire

1968 Egypt accepts UN Resolution 242 and thereby implicitly recognizes Israel but also gained a UN commitment to restore the Sinai

1970 Nasser arranges truce between Jordan and the Palestine Liberation Organization and the following day dies of a heart attack

1970-1981—Anwar al-Sadat

1971 High Dam commissioned, and permanent constitution implemented for the Arab Republic of Egypt

1972 Sadat orders Soviet military advisers to leave Egypt

1973 6 Oct. Egypt and Syria attack Israel 22 Oct. UN Security Council calls for ceasefire

1974 Egypt and Israel sign disengagement agreement

1975 Suez Canal reopened for the first time since the 1967 War

1976 Soviet-Egyptian Treaty of Friendship abrogated

1977 Food riots, Sadat visits Israel, and Arab states form Steadfastness and Confrontation Front to oppose Sadat's peace moves

1979 Israeli shipping allowed through the Suez Canal, and the deposed shah of Iran offered asylum in Egypt

1980 Referendum approved making Sadat president indefinitely and Islamic religious code the source of legislation

1981 Sadat assassinated

1981-Present—Husni Mubarak

1982 Sinai returned to Egypt

1986 Riots in Giza and several other Egyptian towns

1988 Cairo Metro opens

1989 Taba returned to Egyptian control Egypt rejoins Arab League

1990 Iraq, under Saddam Hussein, invades Kuwait. Egypt commits troops and equipment

1991 Gulf war frees Kuwait

1992 Earthquake destroys buildings in Cairo and vicinity. Increasing attacks by fundamentalists

NAMES OF KINGS

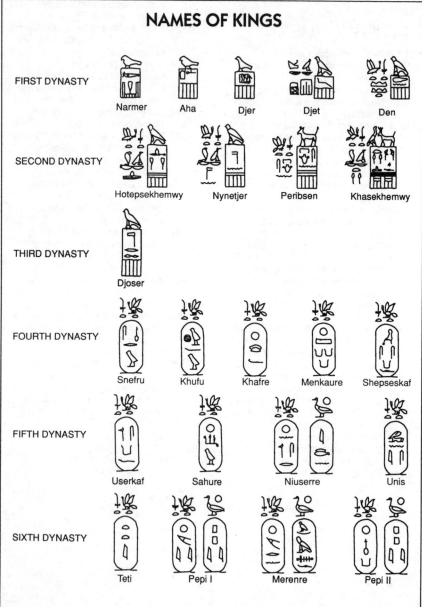

FIRST DYNASTY	Narmer	Aha	Djer	Djet	Den
SECOND DYNASTY	Hotepsekhemwy	Nynetjer	Peribsen	Khasekhemwy
THIRD DYNASTY	Djoser			
FOURTH DYNASTY	Snefru	Khufu	Khafre	Menkaure	Shepseskaf
FIFTH DYNASTY	Userkaf	Sahure	Niuserre	Unis
SIXTH DYNASTY	Teti	Pepi I	Merenre	Pepi II

BOB RACE / 2

NAMES OF KINGS (CONT.)

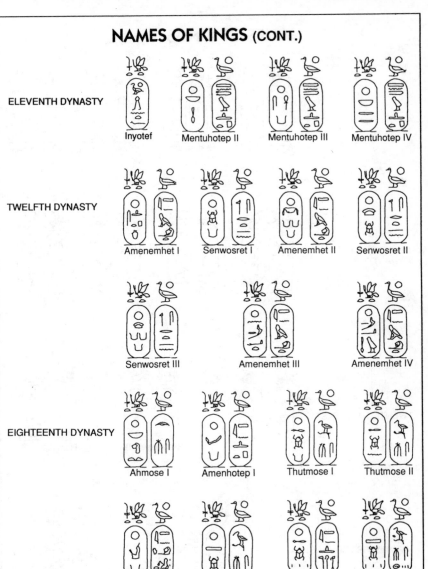

ELEVENTH DYNASTY
Inyotef   Mentuhotep II   Mentuhotep III   Mentuhotep IV

TWELFTH DYNASTY
Amenemhet I   Senwosret I   Amenemhet II   Senwosret II

Senwosret III   Amenemhet III   Amenemhet IV

EIGHTEENTH DYNASTY
Ahmose I   Amenhotep I   Thutmose I   Thutmose II

Hatshepsut   Thutmose III   Amenhotep II   Thutmose IV

NAMES OF KINGS (CONT.)

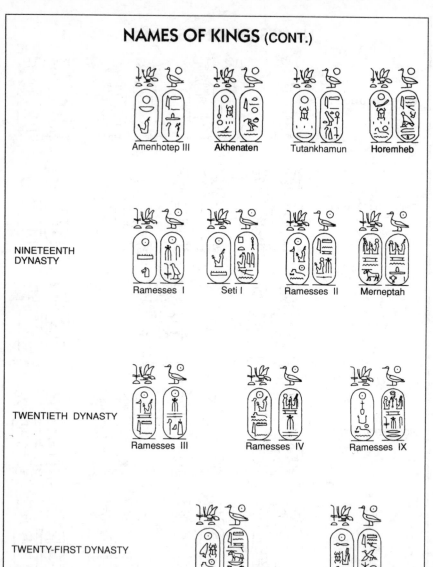

NINETEENTH DYNASTY

TWENTIETH DYNASTY

TWENTY-FIRST DYNASTY

Amenhotep III • Akhenaten • Tutankhamun • Horemheb

Ramesses I • Seti I • Ramesses II • Merneptah

Ramesses III • Ramesses IV • Ramesses IX

Smendes • Psusennes I

NAMES OF KINGS (CONT.)

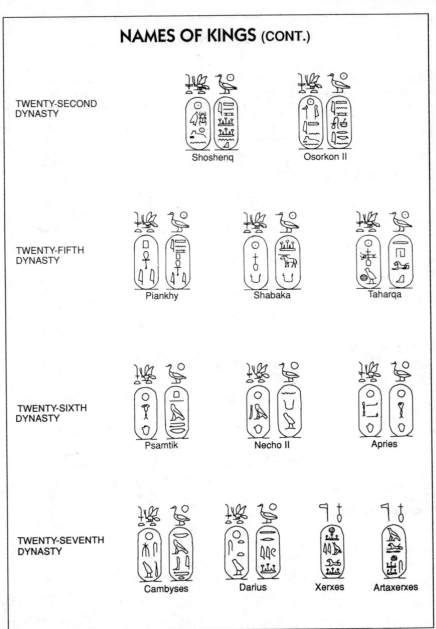

TWENTY-SECOND DYNASTY

Shoshenq

Osorkon II

TWENTY-FIFTH DYNASTY

Piankhy

Shabaka

Taharqa

TWENTY-SIXTH DYNASTY

Psamtik

Necho II

Apries

TWENTY-SEVENTH DYNASTY

Cambyses

Darius

Xerxes

Artaxerxes

NAMES OF KINGS (CONT.)

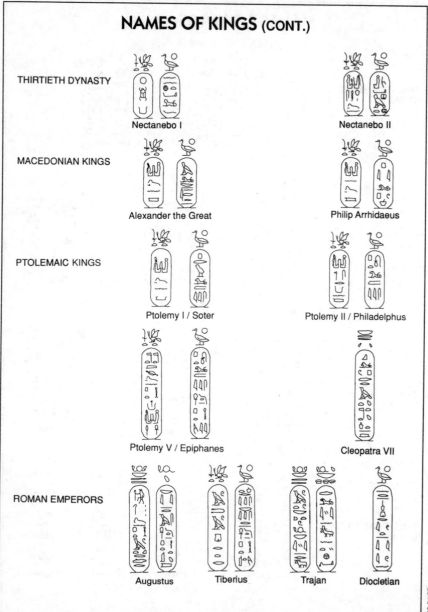

THIRTIETH DYNASTY

Nectanebo I

Nectanebo II

MACEDONIAN KINGS

Alexander the Great

Philip Arrhidaeus

PTOLEMAIC KINGS

Ptolemy I / Soter

Ptolemy II / Philadelphus

Ptolemy V / Epiphanes

Cleopatra VII

ROMAN EMPERORS

Augustus

Tiberius

Trajan

Diocletian

BOB RACE

INDEX

Page numbers in **boldface** indicate a primary reference; *italicized* page numbers indicate
material in charts, callouts, captions, illustrations, or maps.

ABOUT THE AUTHOR

For Kathy Hansen, Egypt is "a place of many kinds of beginnings. So many of Western civilization's roots began in Egypt that almost any avocation—art, architecture, woodworking, sailing, riding—can be traced there."

Kathy traces the beginning of her own interest in the country to an impulsive luncheon with a friend who was moving to Egypt and asked Kathy to visit her there. Kathy stayed six weeks on that trip, and she was hooked. On her third visit, she lived in Egypt for six months and began to gather material for her guidebook.

When Hansen isn't writing books and articles or riding horses, her interest in restoring artifacts has involved her with several museums in Northern California where she has worked on early American pieces. She has numerous articles and a textbook to her credit. A native Californian, she currently lives in Redding with her husband Allan.

THE METRIC SYSTEM

1 inch = 2.54 centimeters (cm)
1 foot = .304 meters (m)
1 mile = 1.6093 kilometers (km)
1 km = .6124 miles
1 fathom = 1.8288 m
1 chain = 20.1168 m
1 furlong = 201.168 m
1 acre = .4047 hectares
1 sq km = 100 hectares
1 sq mile = 2.59 square km
1 ounce = 28.35 grams
1 pound = .4536 kilograms
1 short ton = .90718 metric ton
1 short ton = 2000 pounds
1 long ton = 1.016 metric tons
1 long ton = 2240 pounds
1 metric ton = 1000 kilograms
1 quart = .94635 liters
1 US gallon = 3.7854 liters
1 Imperial gallon = 4.5459 liters
1 nautical mile = 1.852 km

To compute centigrade temperatures, subtract 32 from Fahrenheit and divide by 1.8. To go the other way, multiply centigrade by 1.8 and add 32.

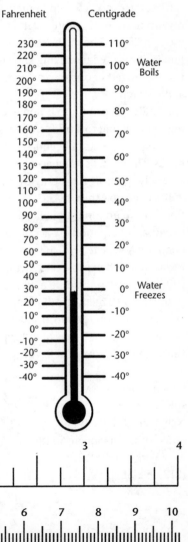

THE AMERICAN RESEARCH CENTER IN EGYPT

The professional organization of American scholars of ancient and modern Egypt is open to all people interested in the study of Egypt, past and present.

The American Research Center in Egypt (ARCE), now 40 years old, is the only organization in the United States that specializes in the the study of ancient and modern Egypt. The membership, drawn from universities, museums, and the lay public, is devoted to making known Egypt's contributions to world civilization. It comes together once a year at an annual conference to share new discoveries and research.

ARCE's office in Cairo is home to American archaeological expeditions working in Egypt and to a fresh crop of Fellows who each year spend up to 12 months working on aspects of Egyptian culture. The Library contains over 15,000 rare books. The center's "Archaeological Club" holds lecture series and seminars, and annually sponsors four study trips to Egypt's most famous archaeological sites.

Basic membership in ARCE is only US$40 per year. Privileges include subscriptions to two important publications: the annual *Journal of the American Research Center,* an internationally acclaimed journal devoted to Egyptian studies, and the quarterly *Newsletter,* which publishes reports of current academic and archaeological research expeditions. Membership also provides access to the research facilities in Cairo (including mail), to the S.S. *Fostat,* an old Nile steamer that can house up to 10 members (if rooms are not reserved by current field expeditions), and discounts on roundtrip air fares on EgyptAir and all ARCE publications.

Join now, in the States or in Egypt, and enjoy the benefits of being a part of the ongoing discovery of Egypt.

IN THE UNITED STATES
ARCE
New Your University
50 Washington Square South
New York, NY 10012
(212) 998-8890

IN EGYPT
ARCE
2 Midan Qasr al~Doubara
Garden City, Cairo
Egypt, 354-8239

MOON HANDBOOKS—THE IDEAL TRAVELING COMPANIONS

Open a Moon Handbook and you're opening your eyes and heart to the world. Thoughtful, sensitive, and provocative, Moon Handbooks encourage an intimate understanding of a region, from its culture and history to essential practicalities. Fun to read and packed with valuable information on accommodations, dining, recreation, plus indispensable travel tips, detailed maps, charts, illustrations, photos, glossaries, and indexes, Moon Handbooks are ideal traveling companions: informative, entertaining, and highly practical.

To locate the bookstore nearest you that carries Moon Travel Handbooks or to order directly from Moon Publications, call: (800) 345-5473, Monday-Friday, 9 a.m.-5 p.m. PST.

THE PACIFIC/ASIA SERIES

BALI HANDBOOK   by Bill Dalton
Detailed travel information on the most famous island in the world. 428 pages.   **$12.95**

BANGKOK HANDBOOK   by Michael Buckley
Your tour guide through this exotic and dynamic city reveals the affordable and accessible possibilities. Thai phrasebook. 214 pages.   **$10.95**

BLUEPRINT FOR PARADISE: How to Live on a Tropic Island   by Ross Norgrove
This one-of-a-kind guide has everything you need to know about moving to and living comfortably on a tropical island. 212 pages.   **$14.95**

FIJI ISLANDS HANDBOOK   by David Stanley
The first and still the best source of information on travel around this 322-island archipelago. Fijian glossary. 198 pages.   **$11.95**

INDONESIA HANDBOOK   by Bill Dalton
This one-volume encyclopedia explores island by island the many facets of this sprawling, kaleidoscopic island nation. Extensive Indonesian vocabulary. 1,000 pages.   **$19.95**

MICRONESIA HANDBOOK: Guide to the Caroline, Gilbert, Mariana, and Marshall Islands
by David Stanley
Micronesia Handbook guides you on a real Pacific adventure all your own. 345 pages.   **$11.95**

NEW ZEALAND HANDBOOK   by Jane King
Introduces you to the people, places, history, and culture of this extraordinary land. 571 pages.
$18.95

OUTBACK AUSTRALIA HANDBOOK   by Marael Johnson
Australia is an endlessly fascinating, vast land, and *Outback Australia Handbook* explores the cities and towns, sheep stations, and wilderness areas of the Northern Territory, Western Australia, and South Australia. Full of travel tips and cultural information for adventuring, relaxing, or just getting away from it all. 355 pages.   **$15.95**

PHILIPPINES HANDBOOK   by Peter Harper and Evelyn Peplow
Crammed with detailed information, *Philippines Handbook* equips the escapist, hedonist, or business traveler with thorough coverage of the Philippines's colorful history, landscapes, and culture. 587 pages.   **$12.95**

SOUTHEAST ASIA HANDBOOK   by Carl Parkes
Helps the enlightened traveler discover the real Southeast Asia. 873 pages.   **$16.95**

SOUTH KOREA HANDBOOK   by Robert Nilsen
Whether you're visiting on business or searching for adventure, *South Korea Handbook* is an invaluable companion. Korean glossary with useful notes on speaking and reading the language. 548 pages.   **$14.95**

SOUTH PACIFIC HANDBOOK   by David Stanley
The original comprehensive guide to the 16 territories in the South Pacific. 740 pages.   **$19.95**

TAHITI-POLYNESIA HANDBOOK   by David Stanley
All five French-Polynesian archipelagoes are covered in this comprehensive guide by Oceania's best-known travel writer. 235 pages.   **$11.95**

THAILAND HANDBOOK   by Carl Parkes
Presents the richest source of information on travel in Thailand. 568 pages.   **$16.95**

THE HAWAIIAN SERIES

BIG ISLAND OF HAWAII HANDBOOK   by J.D. Bisignani
An entertaining yet informative text packed with insider tips on accommodations, dining, sports and outdoor activities, natural attractions, and must-see sights. 347 pages.   **$11.95**

HAWAII HANDBOOK   by J.D. Bisignani
Winner of the 1989 Hawaii Visitors Bureau's Best Guide Award and the Grand Award for Excellence in Travel Journalism, this guide takes you beyond the glitz and high-priced hype and leads you to a genuine Hawaiian experience. Covers all 8 Hawaiian Islands. 879 pages.   **$15.95**

KAUAI HANDBOOK   by J.D. Bisignani
Kauai Handbook is the perfect antidote to the workaday world. Hawaiian and pidgin glossaries. 236 pages.   **$9.95**

MAUI HANDBOOK   by J.D. Bisignani .
"No fool-'round" advice on accommodations, eateries, and recreation, plus a comprehensive introduction to island ways, geography, and history. Hawaiian and pidgin glossaries. 350 pages. **$11.95**

OAHU HANDBOOK   by J.D. Bisignani
A handy guide to Honolulu, renowned surfing beaches, and Oahu's countless other diversions. Hawaiian and pidgin glossaries. 354 pages.   **$11.95**

THE AMERICAS SERIES

ALASKA-YUKON HANDBOOK   by Deke Castleman and Don Pitcher
Get the inside story, with plenty of well-seasoned advice to help you cover more miles on less money. 384 pages.   **$13.95**

ARIZONA TRAVELER'S HANDBOOK   by Bill Weir
This meticulously researched guide contains everything necessary to make Arizona accessible and enjoyable. 505 pages.   **$14.95**

BAJA HANDBOOK   by Joe Cummings
A comprehensive guide with all the travel information and background on the land, history, and culture of this untamed thousand-mile-long peninsula. 356 pages.   **$13.95**

BELIZE HANDBOOK   by Chicki Mallan
Complete with detailed maps, practical information, and an overview of the area's flamboyant history, culture, and geographical features, *Belize Handbook* is the only comprehensive guide of its kind to this spectacular region. 212 pages.   **$13.95**

BRITISH COLUMBIA HANDBOOK   by Jane King
With an emphasis on outdoor adventures, this guide covers mainland British Columbia, Vancouver Island, the Queen Charlotte Islands, and the Canadian Rockies. 381 pages.
$13.95

CANCUN HANDBOOK   by Chicki Mallan
Covers the city's luxury scene as well as more modest attractions, plus many side trips to unspoiled beaches and Mayan ruins. Spanish glossary. 257 pages.   **$12.95**

CATALINA ISLAND HANDBOOK: A Guide to California's Channel Islands
by Chicki Mallan
A complete guide to these remarkable islands, from the windy solitude of the Channel Islands National Marine Sanctuary to bustling Avalon. 245 pages.   **$10.95**

COLORADO HANDBOOK   by Stephen Metzger
Essential details to the all-season possibilities in Colorado fill this guide. Practical travel tips combine with recreation—skiing, nightlife, and wilderness exploration—plus entertaining essays. 422 pages.   **$15.95**

IDAHO HANDBOOK   by Bill Loftus
A year-round guide to everything in this outdoor wonderland, from whitewater adventures to rural hideaways. 275 pages.   **$12.95**

JAMAICA HANDBOOK   by Karl Luntta
From the sun and surf of Montego Bay and Ocho Rios to the cool slopes of the Blue Mountains, author Karl Luntta offers island-seekers a perceptive, personal view of Jamaica. 213 pages.
$12.95

MONTANA HANDBOOK   by W.C. McRae and Judy Jewell
The wild West is yours with this extensive guide to the Treasure State, complete with travel practicalities, history, and lively essays on Montana life. 393 pages.   **$13.95**

NEVADA HANDBOOK   by Deke Castleman
Nevada Handbook puts the Silver State into perspective and makes it manageable and affordable. 400 pages.   **$14.95**

NEW MEXICO HANDBOOK   by Stephen Metzger
A close-up and complete look at every aspect of this wondrous state. 375 pages.   **$13.95**

NORTHERN CALIFORNIA HANDBOOK   by Kim Weir
An outstanding companion for imaginative travel in the territory north of the Tehachapis. 759 pages.   **$16.95**

OREGON HANDBOOK   by Stuart Warren and Ted Long Ishikawa
Brimming with travel practicalities and insider views on Oregon's history, culture, arts, and activities. 422 pages.   **$12.95**

TEXAS HANDBOOK   by Joe Cummings
Seasoned travel writer Joe Cummings brings an insider's perspective to his home state. 483 pages.   **$13.95**

UTAH HANDBOOK   by Bill Weir
Weir gives you all the carefully researched facts and background to make your visit a success. 445 pages.   **$14.95**

WASHINGTON HANDBOOK   by Dianne J. Boulerice Lyons and Archie Satterfield
Covers sights, shopping, services, transportation, and outdoor recreation, with complete listings for restaurants and accommodations. 433 pages.   **$13.95**

WYOMING HANDBOOK   by Don Pitcher
All you need to know to open the doors to this wide and wild state. 427 pages.   **$14.95**

YUCATAN HANDBOOK   by Chicki Mallan
All the information you'll need to guide you into every corner of this exotic land. Mayan and Spanish glossaries. 391 pages.   **$14.95**

THE INTERNATIONAL SERIES

EGYPT HANDBOOK   by Kathy Hansen
An invaluable resource for intelligent travel in Egypt. Arabic glossary. 510 pages.   **$18.95**

MOSCOW-ST. PETERSBURG HANDBOOK   by Masha Nordbye
Provides the visitor with an extensive introduction to the history, culture, and people of these two great cities, as well as practical information on where to stay, eat, and shop. 205 pages.
$13.95

NEPAL HANDBOOK   by Kerry Moran
Whether you're planning a week in Kathmandu or months out on the trail, *Nepal Handbook* will take you into the heart of this Himalayan jewel. 378 pages.   **$12.95**

NEPALI AAMA   by Broughton Coburn
A delightful photo-journey into the life of a Gurung tribeswoman of Central Nepal. Having lived with Aama (translated, "mother") for two years, first as an outsider and later as an adopted member of the family, Coburn presents an intimate glimpse into a culture alive with humor, folklore, religion, and ancient rituals. 165 pages.   **$13.95**

PAKISTAN HANDBOOK   by Isobel Shaw
For armchair travelers and trekkers alike, the most detailed and authoritative guide to Pakistan ever published. Urdu glossary. 478 pages.   **$15.95**

STAYING HEALTHY IN ASIA, AFRICA, AND LATIN AMERICA
by Dirk G. Schroeder, Sc D, MPH
Don't leave home without it! Besides providing a complete overview of the health problems that exist in these areas, this book will help you determine which immunizations you'll need beforehand, what medications to take with you, and how to recognize and treat infections and diseases. Includes extensively illustrated first-aid information and precautions for heat, cold, and high altitude. 200 pages.   **$10.95**

New travel handbooks may be available that are not on this list.
To find out more about current or upcoming titles,
call us toll-free at (800) 345-5473.

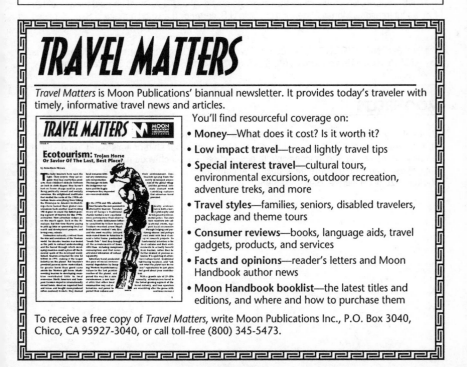

TRAVEL MATTERS

Travel Matters is Moon Publications' biannual newsletter. It provides today's traveler with timely, informative travel news and articles.

You'll find resourceful coverage on:

- **Money**—What does it cost? Is it worth it?
- **Low impact travel**—tread lightly travel tips
- **Special interest travel**—cultural tours, environmental excursions, outdoor recreation, adventure treks, and more
- **Travel styles**—families, seniors, disabled travelers, package and theme tours
- **Consumer reviews**—books, language aids, travel gadgets, products, and services
- **Facts and opinions**—reader's letters and Moon Handbook author news
- **Moon Handbook booklist**—the latest titles and editions, and where and how to purchase them

To receive a free copy of *Travel Matters*, write Moon Publications Inc., P.O. Box 3040, Chico, CA 95927-3040, or call toll-free (800) 345-5473.

IMPORTANT ORDERING INFORMATION

FOR FASTER SERVICE: Call to locate the bookstore nearest you that carries Moon Travel Handbooks or order directly from Moon Publications:

(800) 345-5473 • **Monday-Friday** • **9 a.m.-5 p.m. PST** • **fax (916) 345-6751**

PRICES: All prices are subject to change. We always ship the most current edition. We will let you know if there is a price increase on the book you ordered.

SHIPPING & HANDLING OPTIONS: 1) Domestic UPS or USPS first class (allow 10 working days for delivery): $3.50 for the first item, 50 cents for each additional item.

Exceptions:
- **Moonbelt** shipping is $1.50 for one, 50 cents for each additional belt.
- Add $2.00 for same-day handling.
- UPS 2nd Day Air or Printed Airmail requires a special quote.
- International Surface Bookrate (8-12 weeks delivery):
  $3.00 for the first item, $1.00 for each additional item. Note: Moon Publications cannot guarantee international surface bookrate shipping.

FOREIGN ORDERS: All orders that originate outside the U.S.A. must be paid for with either an International Money Order or a check in U.S. currency drawn on a major U.S. bank based in the U.S.A.

TELEPHONE ORDERS: We accept Visa or MasterCard payments. Minimum order is US$15.00. Call in your order: (800) 345-5473, 9 a.m.-5 p.m. Pacific Standard Time.

MOONBELTS

Made of heavy-duty Cordura nylon, the Moonbelt offers maximum protection for your money and important papers. This all-weather pouch slips under your shirt or waistband, rendering it virtually undetectable and inaccessible to pickpockets. One-inch-wide nylon webbing, heavy-duty zipper, one-inch quick-release buckle. Accommodates traveler's checks, passport, cash, photos. Size 5 x 9 inches. Black.   **$8.95**

ORDER FORM

Be sure to call (800) 345-5473 for current prices and editions or for the name of the bookstore
nearest you that carries Moon Travel Handbooks • 9 a.m.–5 p.m. PST
(See important ordering information on preceding page)

Name: _____ Date: _____

Street: _____

City: _____ Daytime Phone: _____

State or Country: _____ Zip Code: _____

QUANTITY	TITLE	PRICE

Taxable Total_____

Sales Tax (7.25%) for California Residents_____

Shipping & Handling_____

TOTAL_____

Ship: ☐ UPS (no PO Boxes) ☐ 1st class ☐ International surface mail

Ship to: ☐ address above ☐ other _____

Make checks payable to: **MOON PUBLICATIONS, INC.** P.O. Box 3040, Chico, CA 95927-3040
U.S.A. We accept Visa and MasterCard. **To Order**: Call in your Visa or MasterCard number, or send
a written order with your Visa or MasterCard number and expiration date clearly written.

Card Number: ☐ **Visa** ☐ **MasterCard**

☐ ☐ ☐ ☐ ☐ ☐ ☐ ☐ ☐ ☐ ☐ ☐ ☐ ☐ ☐ ☐

Exact Name on Card: _____

expiration date:_____

signature_____

SP/93

WHERE TO BUY THIS BOOK

BOOKSTORES AND LIBRARIES:
Moon Publications Handbooks are sold worldwide. Please write our sales manager for a list of wholesalers and distributors in your area that stock our travel handbooks.

TRAVELERS:
We would like to have Moon Publications Handbooks available throughout the world. Please ask your bookstore to write or call us for ordering information. If your bookstore will not order our guides for you, please write or call for a free catalog.

MOON PUBLICATIONS, INC.
P.O. BOX 3040
CHICO, CA 95927-3040 U.S.A.
TEL: (800) 345-5473
FAX: (916) 345-6751